The Concept of Proportionality in Public Law

The Concept of Proportionality in Public Law

CHUNG Wai Man, Franco

香港城市大學出版社
City University of Hong Kong Press

ISBN: 978-962-937-378-8

Published by
City University of Hong Kong Press
Tat Chee Avenue
Kowloon, Hong Kong
Website: www.cityu.edu.hk/upress
E-mail: upress@cityu.edu.hk

Printed in Hong Kong

Table of Contents

Preface and Acknowledgements

This book is my revised doctoral thesis submitted to the City University of Hong Kong in September 2016. It has been substantially revised and updated to include information regarding recent legal developments in both the United Kingdom (UK) and Hong Kong. In addition to the cases, other sources include scholarly commentaries and news coverage up to the time of publication. My collective research examines the extent to which the concept of proportionality has been integrated into the UK and Hong Kong, as well as what difficulties, either legal or political, the British and Hong Kong courts have encountered during this integration. This book also explores the possibility of the principle's full adoption as a free-standing ground for judicial review litigation in these jurisdictions and its implementation as a basis for cases concerning socio-economic rights as enshrined in the International Covenant on Economic, Social, and Cultural Rights (ICESCR).

Proportionality was originally developed in Germany and has been made more prominent through European Union (EU) law and various international and regional human rights treaties, including the International Covenant on Civil and Political Rights (ICCPR), the ICESCR, and the European Convention on Human Rights (ECHR). My argument in this book is that ongoing developments in EU law and human rights law, as recognised by the Court of Justice of the European Union (CJEU) and the European Court of Human Rights (ECtHR), as well as developments in other common law jurisdictions (such as the United States, Canada, South Africa, and India), offer British and Hong Kong courts various opportunities to reassess their approaches to the integration of domestic standards. Debates concerning the constitutional role of the courts and the continuing institutional demands of EU law and human rights law have also raised questions about the potential benefits of such deeper integration. Although the viability of legal integration is often contested, I argue that full adoption of the proportionality principle would result in a more open approach to domestic adaptation.

In writing this book, I have incurred many debts, and would like to express my thanks, to various people. My research was supervised by Dr Mark Kielsgard, and I want to thank him for his advice and comment on my work. Moreover, Dr Kielsgard did not only provide me with the encouragement, support, and guidance necessary to complete this research, but has also shown his patience to read and comment on my last-minute submission, particularly as I was pursuing my doctoral degree on a part-time basis. I am indebted to his efforts and contributions. I would also like to thank the *Viva Voce* Examination Board Members, namely Professor Zhu Guobin, the Honourable Mr Justice Kemal Bokhary, GBM (Non-Permanent Judge of the Court of Final Appeal in the Hong Kong SAR and the Honorary Professor of the Faculty of Law, Chinese University of Hong Kong), and Dr Surya Deva (Associate Professor), for providing valuable comments to me when finalising the content of my thesis and this book. Furthermore, I would like to express my gratitude to my mother who has supported me throughout my research. I would also like to thank the editorial and design staff at City University of Hong Kong Press, who have helped me through the publishing process. Finally, this book is dedicated to the memory of my father, grandmother, uncle and aunt, my cousin Ms Ho Chui Ching, and my best friend Mr Chan Kwok Wai.

List of Abbreviations

Basic Law	Basic Law of the Hong Kong Special Administrative Region
BORO	Bill of Rights Ordinance, Cap 383
BVerfG	German Federal Constitutional Court
CAP	Common Agricultural Policy
CEDAW	Convention on the Elimination of all Forms of Discrimination Against Women
CSSA	Comprehensive Social Security Assistance
CFA	Court of Final Appeal, Hong Kong SAR
CJEU	Court of Justice of European Union
EC	European Community
ECA 1972	European Communities Act 1972
ECSC	European Coal and Steel Community Treaty
ECHR	European Convention on Human Rights
ECtHR	European Court of Human Rights
EEC	European Economic Community
EHR Commission	European Human Rights Commission
EOC	Equal Opportunities Commission
ESC	European Social Charter 1961 (Revised in 1996)
EU	European Union
EUA 2011	European Union Act 2011
EUCFR	EU Charter of Fundamental Rights 1966
EUW Bill	European Union (Withdrawal) Bill
HRA 1998	Human Rights Act 1998
ICCPR	International Covenant on Civil and Political Rights 1966
ICESCR	International Covenant on Economic, Social and Cultural Rights 1966

IRA	Irish Republic Army
LegCo	Legislative Council in Hong Kong
NDPBs	Non-Departmental Public Bodies
RAF	Royal Air Force
NPCSC	Standing Committee of the National People's Congress, People's Republic of China
TEU	Treaty of European Union
TFEU	Treaty on the Functioning of the European Union
UK	United Kingdom
UN	United Nations
UN Charter	United Nations Charter
UNESCR Committee	United Nations Economic, Social and Cultural Committee
UDHR 1948	Universal Declaration on Human Rights 1948
WTO	World Trade Organisation

List of Cases

Australia

Channel Seven Adelaide Pty Ltd v Manock [2007] 241 ALR 468.

Minister of State for Immigration and Ethnic Affairs v Rah Hin Teoh [1994–1995] 183 CLR 273.

R v Quach [2010] VSCA 106.

Canada

Alberta (Information and Privacy Commissioner) v Alberta Teachers' Association [2011] 2 SCR 654.

Alberta v Hutterian Brethren of Wilson Colony [2009] 2 SCR 567.

Baker v Canada (Minister of Citizenship and Immigration) [1999] 2 SCR 817, (1999) 174 DLR (4th) 193 (SCC).

Canadian Association of Industrial, Mechanical and Allied Workers, Local 14 v Paccar of Canada [1989] 2 SCR 983.

Eldridge v British Columbia (Attorney-General) (1997) 151 DLR (4th) 577 (SCC), [1997] 3 SCR, [1997] 2 SCR 624.

Montreal (City) v Montreal Port Authority [2010] SCC 14, [2010] 1 SCR 427.

R v Askov [1990] 2 SCR 1199.

R v Boulanger [2006] 2 SCR 49.

R v Oakes [1986] 1 SCR 103.

RJR-McDonald Inc v Attorney-General of Canada [1995] 3 SCR 199.

Slaight Communications Inc v Davidson [1989] 1 SCR 1038.

Thomson Newspapers Co v Canada (Attorney General) [1998] 1 SCR 877.

Villeneuve v Montreal (City of), 2016 QCCS 2888.

WIC Radio v Simpson [2008] 2 SCR 420.

Court of Justice of European Union

Adoui and Cornuaille v Belgium (Cases 115 and 116/81) [1982] ECR 1665.

Agrarproduktion Staebelow GmbH v Landrat des Landkreises Bad Doberan (Case C-504/04) [2006] ECR I-679.

Albany International BV v Stichting Bedrijfspensioenfonds Textielindustrie (Case C67-96) [1999] ECR I-5751.

Alpine Investments BV v Minister van Financiën (Case C-384/93) [1995] ECR I-1141.

Alrosa Co Ltd v Commission (Case T-170/06) [2007] ECR II-2601.

Arnold André GmbH & Co. KG v Landrat des Kreises Herford (Case C-434/02) [2004] ECR I-11825.

Atalanta Amsterdam BV v Produktschap voor Vee en Vlees (Case 240/78) [1979] ECR 2137.

Balkan Import-Export v Hauptzollamt Berlin-Packhof (Case 5/73) [1973] ECR 1091.

Bela-Mühle Josef Bergmann KG v Grows-Farm GmbH & Co KG (Case 114/76) [1977] ECR 1211 (the *Skimmed-milk* case).

Bickel and Franz (Case C-274/96) [1998] ECR I-7637.

Bilka-Kaufhaus GmbH v Karin Weber von Hartz (Case 170/84) [1986] ECR 1607.

Biovilac NV v EEC (Case 59/83) [1984] ECR 4057.

Bocchi Food Trade International GmbH v Commission (Case T-30/99) [2001] ECR II-943.

Brentjens' Handelsonderneming BV v Stichting Bedrijfspensioenfonds voor de Handel in Bouwmaterialen (Joined Cases C-115/97, C-116/97 and C-117/97) [1999] ECR I-6025.

Brunnhofer v Bank der österreichischen *Postsparkasse AG* (Case C-381/99) [2001] ECR I-4961.

Buitoni SA v Fonds d'Orientation et de Régularisation des Marchés Agricoles (Case 122/78) [1979] ECR 677.

Campus Oil v Minister for Industry and Energy (Case 72/83) [1984] ECR 2727.

CMC Melkunie (Case 97/83) [1984] ECR 2367, [1986] 2 CMLR 318.

Coenen v Social Economische Raad (Case 39/75) [1975] ECR 1547, [1976] 1 CMLR 30.

Commission v Germany (Case 28/84) [1985] ECR 3097.

Commission v Germany (Case C-24/97) [1998] ECR I-2133.

Commission v Germany (Re Beer Purity Law) (Case 178/84) [1987] ECR 1227 (*Re Beer Purity Law* case).

Commission v Greece (Case C-120/94) [1996] ECR 1513.

Commission v Greece (Case C-140/03) [2005] ECR I-3177.

Commission v Netherlands (Case C-299/02) [2004] ECR I-9761.

Conegate Ltd v HM Customs and Excise (Case 121/85) [1986] ECR 1007.

Costa v ENEL Costa v ENEL Nazionale per l'Energia Elettrica (Enel) (Case 6/64) [1964] ECR 585.

Cowan v Trésor Public (Case 186/87) [1989] ECR 195.

Crispoltoni v Fattoria Autonoma Tabacchi di Citta id Castello (Case C-133, 300 and 362/93) [1994] ECR I-4863.

Decker v Caisse de Maladie des Employés Privés (Case C-120/95) [1998] ECR I-1871.

Denka International BV v Commission (Case 334/07) [2009] ECR II-4205.

Duphar v Netherlands (Case 238/82) [1984] ECR 523.

Elliniki Radiophonia Tileorassi AE v Dimotiki Etairia Pliroforissis and Sotirios Kouvelas (Case C-260/89) [1991] ECR I-2925.

Fédération Charbonnière de Belgique v High Authority of the European Coal and Steel Community (Case 8/55) [1954–1956] ECR 245.

Franz Grad v Finanzamt Traustein (Case 9/70) [1970] ECR 825.

Freistaat Bayern v Eurim-Pharm GmbH (Case C-347/89) [1991] ECR 1747.

Fromançais SA v FORMA (Case 66/82) [1983] ECR 395'

Germany v Council (Bananas), Case C-280/93, [1994] ECR I-4973 (the *Bananas* case).

Gowan Comércio Internacional e Serviços Lda v Ministero della Salute (Case C-77/09) [2010] ECR I-13533, (2011) 48(4) CMLR 1329.

Hauer v Land Rheinland-Pfalz (Case 44/79) [1979] ECR 3727.

Internationale Handelsgesellschaft v Einfuhr-und Vorratsstelle (Case 11/70) [1970] ECR 1125 (the *Solange I* case).

Johnston v Chief Constable of the Royal Ulster Constabulary (Case 222/84) [1986] ECR 1651.

Kadi and Al Barakaat International Foundation (Case C-402 and 415/05) [2008] ECR 1-6351.

Kohll v Union des Caisses de Maladie (Case C-158/96) [1998] ECR I-1935.

Kreil v Bundesrepublik Deutschland (Case C-285/98) [2000] ECR 1-69.

Kremzow v Austria (Case C-299/95) [1997] ECR I-2629.

Ligur Carni (Joined Cases C-277, C-318, and C-319/91) [1993] ECR I-6621.

Maas & Co NV v Bundesanstalt für landwirtschaftliche Marktordnung (Case 21/85) [1986] ECR 3537.

Maatschappij Drijvende Bokken BV v Stichting Pensioenfonds voor de Vervoer-en Havenbedrijven (Case C-219/97) [1999] ECR I-6121.

Musik Metronome GmbH v Music Point Hokamp GmbH (Case C-200/96) [1998] ECR 1-1953.

Netherlands v Commission (Case C-452/00) [2005] ECR I-6645.

Northern Ireland Fish Producers' Organisation Ltd (NIFPO) and Northern Ireland Fishermen's Federation v Department of Agriculture for Northern Ireland (Case C-4/96) [1998] ECR I-681.

Officier van Justitie v Sandoz BV (Case 174/82) [1983] ECR 2445, [1984] 3 CMLR 43.

Omega Spielhallen- und Automatenaufstellungs GmbH v Oberbürgermeisterin der Bundesstadt Bonn (Case C-36/02) [2004] ECR I-9609.

Opinion 2/94 on Accession by the Community to the ECHR [1996] ECR I-1759.

R v Bouchereau (Case 30/77) [1977] ECR 1999, [1977] 2 CMLR 800.

R v Henn and Darby (Case 34/79) [1979] ECR 3795.

R v Intervention Board for Agricultural Produce, ex parte E D & F Man (Sugar) Ltd (Case 181/84) [1985] ECR 2889, [1985] 2 All ER 115, [1985] 3 CMLR 739.

R v Ministry of Agriculture, Fisheries and Food, ex parte Fedesa (Case C-331/88) [1990] ECR I-4023.

R v Royal Pharmaceutical Society of Great Britain, ex parte Association of Pharmaceutical Importers (Joined Cases 266 and 267/87) [1989] ECR 1295.

R v Secretary of State for Health, ex parte British American Tobacco (Investments) Ltd and Imperial Tobacco Ltd (Case C-491/01) [2002] ECR I-11453.

R v Secretary of State for the Environment and Ministry of Agriculture, Fisheries and Food, ex parte Standley (Case C-293/97) [1999] ECR 1-2603.

R v Secretary of State for Transport, ex parte Factortame Ltd (Case C-213/89) (1990) ECR I-2433.

R v Secretary of State for Transport, ex parte Factortame Ltd (Case C-221/89) (1990) ECR I-3905.

Reisebüro Broede v Gerd Sandker (Case C-3/95) [1996] ECR I-6511.

Rewe Zentrale v Bundesmonopolverwaltung für Branntwein (Case 120/78) [1979] ECR 649, [1979] 3 CMLR 494 (the *Cassis de Dijon* case).

Richardt (Case C-367/89) [1991] ECR I-4621.

Rinner-Kühn v FWW Spezial-Gebäudereinigung GmbH & Co KG (Case 171/88) [1989] ECR 2743.

Rutili v Ministre de l'Intérieur (Case 36/75) [1975] ECR 1219, [1976] 1 CMLR 140.

Schräder HS Kraftfutter GmbH & Co KG v Hauptzollamt Gronau (Case 265/87) [1989] ECR 2237.

Schumacher v Hauptzollamt Frankfurt am Main-Ost (Case 215/87) [1989] ECR 617.

Society for the Protection of Unborn Children (Ireland) Ltd v Grogan (Case C-159/90) [1991] ECR I-4865.

SpA Ferriera Valsabbia v Commission (Joined Cases 154, 205, 206, 226–28, 263, and 264/78, 39, 31, 83, and 85/79) [1980] ECR 907.

Stölting v Hauptzollamt Hamburg-Jonas (Case 138/78) [1979] ECR 713.

Van Binsgergen v Bestuur van de Bedrijfsvereniging Metaalnijverheid (Case 33/74) [1974] ECR 1299, [1975] 1 CMLR 298.

Van Duyn v Home Office (Case 41/74) [1974] ECR 1337.

Van Gend en Loos v Nederlandse Administratie der Belastingen (Case 26/62) [1963] ECR 1.

Van Gerven AG in Society for the Protection of Unborn Children Ireland Ltd v Stephen Grogan (Case C-159/90) [1991] ECR I-4685.

Viamex Agrar Handels GmbH and Zuchtvieh-Kontor GmbH (ZVK) v Hauptzollamt Hamburg-Jonas (Cases C-37 and 58/06) [2008] ECR I-69.

Wachauf v Bundesmat Für Ernährung und Forstwirtschaft (Case 5/88) [1989] ECR 2609.

Watson and Belmann (Case 118/75) [1976] ECR 1185.

European Court of Human Rights

A P v Austria (1995) 20 EHRR CD 63.

A v UK (1999) 27 EHRR 611.

A v UK (2002) 36 EHRR 917.

A v UK (2009) 49 EHRR 29.

Airey v Ireland (1979) 2 EHRR 305.

Albert and Le Compte v Belgium (1983) 5 EHRR 533.

Altun v Germany (1983) 36 DR 209.

Anderson and Kullman v Sweden (1986) 46 DR 251.

Artico v Italy (1981) 3 EHRR 1.

Asmundsson v Iceland (App. No. 60669/00) ECHR 12 October 2004.

Aydin v Turkey (1997) 25 EHRR 251.

B v France (1993) 16 EHRR 1.

Barthold v Germany (1985) 7 EHRR 383.

Belgian Linguistic's case (No. 2) (1968) 1 EHRR 252.

Bladet Tromsø and Stensaas v Norway (2000) 29 EHRR 125.

Botta v Italy (1998) 26 EHRR 241.

Bowman v UK (1998) 26 EHRR 1.

Bronda v Italy (1998) 33 EHRR 81.

Bryan v UK (1995) 21 EHRR 342.

Buchholz v Germany (1981) 3 EHRR 597.

Buckley v UK (1997) 23 EHRR 101.

Budina v Russia (App No 45603/05) ECHR 18 June 2009.

Burton v UK (1996) 22 EHRR CD 134.

Casado v Spain (1994) 18 EHRR 1.

Chahal v UK (1996) 23 EHRR 413.

Chapman v UK (2001) 33 EHRR 18.

Chorherr v Austria (1993) 17 EHRR 358.

Cossey v UK (1991) 13 EHRR 622.

Costello-Roberts v UK (1993) 19 EHRR 112.

D v UK (1997) 24 EHRR 425 (the *HIV Deportation* case).

Da Silva Mouta v Portugal (2001) 31 EHRR 4.

Denimark Ltd v UK (2000) 30 ECHR CD 144.

Dudgeon v UK (1981) 4 EHRR 149.

East African Asians v UK (1981) 3 EHRR 76.

EB v France (2008) 47 EHRR 21.

Engel v Netherlands (1976) 1 EHRR 647.

F v Switzerland (1988) 10 EHRR 411.

Fox, Campbell and Hartley v UK (1991) 13 EHRR 157.

Gaskin v UK (1989) 12 EHRR 36.

Golder v UK (1975) 1 EHRR 524.

Goodwin v UK (1996) 22 EHRR 123.

Greece v UK, No 176/56 (1958–1959) 2 Ybk 174 (the *Cyprus* case).

Guerra v Italy (1998) 26 EHRR 357.

Gul v Switzerland (1996) 22 EHRR 93.

Hadjianastassiou v Greece (1992) 16 EHRR 219.

Handyside v UK (1976) 1 EHRR 737.

Hatton v UK (2003) 37 EHRR 611.

Hirst v UK (No. 2) (2006) 42 EHRR 849.

Hokkanen v Finland (1994) 19 EHRR 137.

Hoogendijk v Netherlands (2005) 40 EHRR SE 22.

Hussain v UK (1996) 22 EHRR 1.

Ireland v UK (1978) 2 EHRR 25.

JA Pye (Oxford) Ltd v UK (2008) 46 EHRR 45.

James v UK (1986) 8 EHRR 123.

Jersild v Denmark (1994) 19 EHRR 1.

Johansen v Norway (1997) 23 EHRR 33.

Karner v Austria (2003) 38 EHRR 528.

Karner v Austria (2004) 38 EHRR 24.

Kelly v UK (2001) ECHR 328.

Kjeldsen, Busk Madsen and Pedersen v Denmark (1976) 1 EHRR 711 (the *Danish Sex Education* case).

Kokkinakis v Greece (1994) 17 EHRR 397.

Kozak v Poland (2010) 51 EHRR 16.

L & V Austria [2003] ECHR 20.

La Parola v Italy (App No 39712/98) ECHR 30 November 200

Larioshina v Russia (App. No. 56869/00) ECHR 23 April 2002.

Lawless v Ireland (1961) 1 EHRR 15.

LCB v UK (1998) 27 EHRR 212.

Lingens v Austria (1986) 8 EHRR 407.

Loizidou v Turkey (1996) 21 EHRR 188.

López Ostra v Spain (1995) 20 EHRR 277.

Lustig-Prean and Beckett v UK (2000) 29 EHRR 548.

Malone v UK (1984) 7 EHRR 14.

Marckx v Belgium (1979) 2 EHRR 330, ECtHR (Plenary) 31.

Marzari v Italy (1999) EHRR CD 175.

Mata Estevez v Spain [2001] ECHR 896.

McCann v UK (1996) 21 EHRR 97.

McGinley and Egan v UK (1998) 27 EHRR 1.

Swedish Engine Drivers' Union v Sweden (1979–1980) 1 EHRR 617.

Thlimmenos v Greece (2000) 31 EHRR 15.

TP and KM v UK (2001) 34 EHRR 42.

Tyrer v UK (1978) 2 EHRR 1.

Vgt Verein gegen Tierfabriken v Switzerland (2002) 34 EHRR 4.

Vogt v Germany (1996) 21 EHRR 205.

W v UK (1988) 10 EHRR 29.

Wemhoff v Germany (1979–1980) 1 EHRR 55.

Winer v UK (1986) 48 DR 154.

Wingrove v UK (1996) 24 EHRR 1.

X and Y v Netherlands (1985) 8 EHRR 235.

X v UK (1978) 14 DR 31.

X v UK (1981) 4 EHRR 188.

X, Y and Z v UK (1997) 24 EHRR 143.

Yaker v France, Communication No. 2747/2016, 17 July 2018, UN Doc. CCPR/C/123/D/2807/2016 with ECtHR.

Young, James and Webster v UK (1981) 4 EHRR 38.

Z v UK (2001) 34 EHRR 97.

Germany

B v M, BVerfG, 1/98.

B v R BVerfG, 2074/05.

B v R, BVerfG, 304/07.

Falconry case, *BVerfGE* 55, 159.

Kreutzberg decision of June 14, 1882, *PrOVG* 9, 353.

Land Election case, *BVerfGE* 3, 383.

Lebach case, *BVerfGE* 35, 202.

Pharmacy case, *BVerfGE* 7, 377.

Volkszählung case, *BVerfGE* 65, 1.

Hong Kong

A Solicitor v Law Society of Hong Kong (Secretary for Justice, intervener) (2003) 6 HKCFAR 570, [2004] 1 HKLRD 214.

Akai Holdings Ltd v Ernst & Young (2009) 12 HKCFAR 649.

American International Group Inc v Huaxia Life Insurance Co Ltd (2017) 20 HKCFAR 503.

Andrew Brine v Liquor Licensing Board, HCAL 33/2012.

Attorney-General of Hong Kong v Lee Kwong Kut (1993) 3 HKPLR 72, AC 951 (PC).

Attorney-General v Ming Pao Newspapers Ltd (1994) 4 HKPLR 621 (Mag); (1995) 5 HKPLR 13 (CA); (1996) 6 HKPLR 103 (PC).

Au Yeung Kwok Hing v Attorney-General (unreported, Civil Appeal No 205 of 1994).

Catholic Diocese of Hong Kong v Secretary for Justice [2007] 4 HKLRD 483.

Chan Hau Man Christina v Commissioner of Police [2009] 6 HKC 44, [2009] 4 HKLRD 797 (*The Olympic Torch Relay* Case).

Chan Hei Ling Helen v Medical Council of Hong Kong [2009] 4 HKLRD 174.

Chan Kam Nga v Director of Immigration (1999) 2 HKCFAR 82 (CFA).

Chan Kin Sum v Secretary for Justice [2008] 6 HKC 486, [2009] 2 HKLRD 166 (CFI) (the *Prisoner's Voting Right* case).

Chan Mei Yee v Director of Immigration (unreported, HCAL77/1999 (13 July 2000) (CFI)).

Chan Shu Ying v Chief Executive of the HKSAR [2001] 1 HKLRD 641.

Chan To Foon v Director of Immigration, [2001] 3 HKLRD 109.

Chan Yeuk Ming v Hong Kong Housing Authority (unreported, 7 September 2012, HCAL 25/2012) (CFI).

Chee Fee Ming v Director of Food and Environmental Hygiene (No. 2) [2018] 4 HKLRD 517.

Cheng v Tse Wai Chun (2000) 3 HKCFA 339.

Cheung Tak Wing v Director of Administration (unreported, HCAL 136/2014), [2018] HKCFI 2557 (unreported, CACV 577/2018), [2020] HKCA 124.

Chim Sui Ping v Hong Kong Housing Authority (unreported, HCAL 139/2009, 17 September 2012) (the *Public Housing Eviction* case).

Chow Kwok Leong v Secretary for the Civil Service [2011] HKEC 942.

Chow Mario v Municipal Services Appeal Board [2010] HKCU 2649 (unreported, HCAL 31/2010)

Chu Hoi Dick v Secretary for Home Affairs [2007] HKCU 1370 (unreported, HCAL 87/2007, 10 August 2007).

Chu Ping Tak v Commissioner of Police [2002] 3 HKLRD 679 (CFI).

Clean Air Foundation Ltd v Government of the HKSAR [2007] HKEC 1356 (CFI).

Commissioner of Inland Revenue v Lee Lai Ping (1993) 3 HKLPR 141.

Deacon Chiu v Attorney-General [1992] 2 HKLR 84.

Democratic Party v Secretary for Justice (unreported, HCAL 84/2006 (CFI) (28 December 2007)), [2007] 2 HKLRD 804 (CFI).

Democratic Republic of the Congo v FG Hemisphere Associates LLC (2011) 14 HKCFAR 395.

Director of Immigration v Chong Fung Yuen (2001) 4 HKCFAR 211 (CFA).

Director of Immigration v Lau Fong (2004) 7 HKCFAR 56 (CFA).

Dr Lau Yuk Kong v Medical Council of Hong Kong [2011] 5 HKC 218.

Equal Opportunities Commission v Director of Education [2001] 2 HKLRD 690 (CFI) (the *Gender Discrimination* case).

Fok Chun Wa v Hospital Authority (unreported, 17 December 2008, HCAL 94/2007), [2008] HKEC 2161 (CFI); (unreported, CACV 30/2009), [2010] HKEC 713, (2010) 15 HKPLR 628, [2011] 1 HKLRD A1 (CA); [2012] 2 HKC 413 (CFA), (2012) 15 HKCFAR 409 (the *Obstetric Services* case).

Gurung Kesh Bahadur v Director of Immigration (2002) 5 HKCFAR 480 (CFA).

Gutierrez v Commissioner for Registration [2011] 6 HKC 561.

Harvest Good Development Ltd v Secretary for Justice [2007] 4 HKC 1 (CFI).

HKSAR v Cheung Kwai Choi [2018] HKCFI 2243.

HKSAR v Fong Kwok Shan, Christine (2017) 20 HKCFAR 425.

HKSAR v Hui Kai Ki, Mak Tsz Hei and Sit Tat Wing, DCCC710/2016, [2017] HKDC 377.

HKSAR v Hung Chan Wa (unreported, CACC 411/2003, 61/2004, 26 January 2006) (CA), (2006) 9 HKCFAR 614 (CFA).

HKSAR v Lam Kwong Wai (2006) 9 HKCFAR 574 (CFA).

HKSAR v Leung Tin Kei, Lo Kin Man and Wong Ka Kui [2020] HKCA 275.

HKSAR v Ng Kung Siu [1999] 1 HKLRD 783, (1999) 2 HKCFAR 442, [2000] HKC 117. (the *Flag Desecration* case).

HKSAR v Pun Ganga Chandra [2001] 2 HKLRD 151 (CA).

HKSAR v Tai Yiu Ting, Chan Kin Man, Chu Tiu Ming [2019] HKDC 450.

HKSAR v Wong Hin Wai [2013] HKCFA 102, (2013) 16 HKCFAR 837, [2014] 1 HKC 241.

Ho Choi Wan v HKSAR (2005) 8 HKCFAR 628 (CFA) (the *Affordable Rental Housing* case).

Ho Po Sang v Director of Public Works [1959] HKLR 632.

Hong Kong Cable Television Ltd v The Telecommunications Authority [2004] HKCU (unreported, HCAL 62/2003).

Hong Kong Housing Society v Wong Nai Chung (t/a Sun Chung Flower Shop) (unreported, HCMP 880/2009, 22 September 2010).

Hong Kong Television Network Ltd v Chief Executive [2015] 2 HKLRD 1035.

Hysan Development Co Ltd v Town Planning Board [2012] 5 HKC 432 (CFI), [2015] 1 HKLRD 865 (CA), (2016) 19 HKCFAR 372 (CFA).

Incorporated Owners of Po Hang Building v Sam Woo Marine Works Ltd (2017) 20 HKCFAR 240.

K, Y, and W v the Secretary for Justice [2000] HKC 796.

Kao Lee & Yip v Koo Hoi Yan (2009) 12 HKCFAR 830.

Kong Yunming v Director of Social Welfare [2009] 4 HKLRD 382 (CFI), [2012] 4 HKC 180 (CA), (2013) 16 HKCFAR 950, [2014] 1 HKC 518 (CFA) (the *Comprehensive Social Security Assistance* Case).

Koo Sze Yiu v CE of the HKSAR (2006) 9 HKCFAR 441 (CFA).

Koon Wing Yee v Insider Dealing Tribunal [2007] HKCU 905, [2008] 3 HKLRD 372 (CFA).

Kwok Cheuk Kin v Secretary of Constitutional and Mainland Affairs (2017) HKCFAR 353.

Kwok Wing Hang v Chief Executive in Council; Leung Kwok Hung v Secretary for Justice [2020] HKCA 192 (the *Prohibition of Face Covering Regulation* Case).

Lai Tak Shing v Secretary for Home Affairs [2008] HKEC 553.

Lam Siu Po v Commissioner of Police (2009) 12 HKCFAR 237 (CFA).

Lam Wo Lun v Director of Social Welfare (unreported, HCAL 133/2010, 14 May 2012), [2012] HKEC 670, [2012] HKCU 1006.

Lau Cheong v HKSAR (2002) 5 HKCFAR 415 (CFA).

Lau Kwok Fai Bernard v Secretary for Justice (2005) 8 HKCFAR 304.

Lau Wong Fat v Attorney-General (1996) 7 HKPLR 148.

Lee Miu Ling v Attorney-General [1995] 5 HKPLR 585, [1996] 1 HKC 124.

Lee Yee Shing Jacky v Board of Review (Inland Revenue Ordinance) [2011] 6 HKC 307 (CFI), [2012] 2 HKLRD 981 (CA).

Leung Chun Kwong v Secretary for the Civil Service and Commissioner of Inland Revenue (unreported, FACV No. 8 of 2018), [2019] HKCFA 19, [2018] 3 HKLRD 84 (the *Homosexual Civil Servant's Entitlement to Spouse Medical and Tax Benefits* Case)

Leung Kwok Hung (Long Hair) v Commissioner of Correctional Services [2018] 2 HKLRD 933 (CA).

Leung Kwok Hung v HKSAR [2004] 3 HKLRD 729 (CA), (2005) 8 HKCFAR 229, [2005] HKCU 887, [2005] HKCFA 41, [2005] 3 HKLRD 164 (the *Public Order Ordinance* case).

Leung Kwok Hung v President of the Legislative Council of the HKSAR [2007] 1 HKLRD 387 (CFI), [2008] 2 HKLRD 18 (CA).

Leung Kwok Hung v Secretary for Justice [2019] HKCFI 2820, [2019] HKCFI 2884, [2020] HKCA 192, [2020] HKEC 533 (CA) (the *Prohibition of Face Covering Regulation* case).

Leung T C William Roy v Secretary for Justice [2005] 3 HKC 77 (CFI), [2005] 3 HKLRD 657, [2006] 4 HKLRD 211 (CA) (the *Sexual Orientation Discrimination* Case).

Lo Siu Lan v Hong Kong Housing Authority (2004) 7 HKCFAR 631 (CFA).

Lubiano Almorin v Director of Immigration [2018] 1 HKLRD 1141.

Ma Bik Yung v Ko Chuen [2002] 2 HKLRD 1 (the *Disability Discrimination* case).

MA v Director of Immigration [2011] 2 HKLRD F6 (CFI), [2012] HKEC 1624 (CA), [2014] 3 HKC 11 (CFA).

Mo Yuk Ping v HKSAR (2007) 10 HKCFAR 386.

Mok Charles Peter v Tam Wai Ho (Secretary for Justice, intervener) (2010) 13 HKCFAR 762.

Mok Chi Hung v Director of Immigration [2001] 2 HKLRD 125.

Ng Ka Ling v Director of Immigration (1999) 2 HKCFAR 4 (CFA), [1999] 1 HKLRD 315.

Ng King Luen v Rita Fan [1997] 1 HKLRD 757.

Ng Ngau Chai v The Town Planning Board [2007] HKEC 1207.

Ng Siu Tung v Director of Immigration (2002) 5 HKCFAR 1 (CFA).

Ng Yat Chi v Max Share Ltd (2005) 8 HKCFAR 1.

Official Receiver v Zhi Charles (2015) 18 HKCFAR 467.

PCCW-HKT Telephone Ltd v The Telecommunications Authority, HCAL 152/2002.

Prem Singh v Director of Immigration (2003) 6 HKCFAR 26 (CFA).

Pun Tai Sung v Immigration Tribunal [2006] HKCU 1818 (unreported, HCAL 51/2005).

QT v Director of Immigration (2018) 21 HKCFAR 324.

R v Chan Chak Fan [1994] 3 HKC 145.

R v Chan Kwong-yim (unreported, CACC 968/1983).

R v Director of Immigration, ex parte Hai Ho Tak (1994) 4 HKLPR 324.

R v Director of Immigration, ex parte Wong King Lung (1993) 3 HKLPR 253.

R v Lum Wai Ming (1992) 2 HKPLR 182, [1992] 2 HKCLR 221.

R v Sin Yau Ming (1991) 1 HKPLR 88 (CA), [1992] 1 HKCLR 127.

R v Town Planning Board, ex parte Kwan Kong Company Ltd (1995) 5 HKLPR 261.

R v Yu Yem Kin (1994) 4 HKPLR 75.

Re Lam Kin Chung (1991) HCt, MP No 216 of 1991.

Rediffusion (HK) v Attorney-General of Hong Kong [1970] AC 1136.

Secretary for Justice v Chan Wah (2000) 3 HKCFAR 459, (2000) 9 HKPLR 610 (the *Non-Indigenous Villager's Voting Right* case).

Secretary for Justice v Cheung Chun Chi [2002] 2 HKLRD 233.

Secretary for Justice v Latker [2009] 2 HKC 100 (CA).

Secretary for Justice v Wong Chi Fung (2018) 21 HKCFAR 34.

Secretary for Justice v Wong Chi Fung, Law Kwun Chung and Chow Yong Kang Alex [2018] HKCFA 4.

Secretary for Justice v Yau Yuk Lung [2006] 4 HKLRD 196 (CA), (2007) 10 HKCFAR 335, [2007] 3 HKLRD 903 (CFA) (the *Sexual Orientation Discrimination* Case).

Secretary for Security v Sakthevel Prabakar [2005] 1 HKLRD 289 (CFA).

Shiu Wing Steel Limited v Director of Environmental Protection (2006) 9 HKCFAR 478.

Shum Kwok Sher v HKSAR (2002) 5 HKCFAR 381, [2002] 2 HKLRD 793 (CFA).

Sin Kam Wah v HKSAR (2005) 8 HKCFAR 192.

So Wai Lun v HKSAR (2006) 9 HKCFAR 530.

Society for the Protection of Victoria Harbour Ltd v CE in Council (No. 2) [2004] 2 HKLRD 902, [2004] 2 HKLRD 95 (CFA), (2004) 7 HKCFAR 1 (CFA), [2004] 1 HKLRD 396 (the *Protection of Victoria Harbour* Case).

Sun News Publishers Ltd v Commissioner for Television and Entertainment Licensing Authority [2006] HKCU 1729 (unreported, HCAL 50/2006).

Swire Properties Ltd v Secretary for Justice (2003) 6 HKCFAR 236.

Tam Hing Yee v Wu Tai Wai (1991) 1 HKLPR 261.

The Queen v Phong Ung-cau (unreported, CACC 630/1994).

Town Planning Board v Society for the Protection of the Harbour Ltd [2003] 2 HKLRD 787 (HCAL 19/2003), [2003] 3 HKLRD 960 (CFI), (2004) 7 HKCFAR 1, [2004] 1 HKLRD 396 (CFA).

Ubamaka v Secretary for Security (2012) 15 HKCFAR 743.

W v Registrar of Marriages [2013] 3 HKC 375 (CFA), (2013) 16 HKCFAR 112.

Wong Chung Ki v CE (Chief Executive) (Application for leave to appeal in Court of Appeal) [2000] HKEC 701.

Wong Hin Wai v Secretary for Justice [2012] 4 HKLRD 70 (CFI).

Wong Kam Wah v Fisherman Claims Appeal Board [2012] HKCU 990 (unreported, HCAL 96/2011).

Wong Wai Hing Christopher v Director of Lands (unreported, 24 September 2010, HCAL 95, 97, 98, 99/2010) (CFI).

Wong Wai Tak v Secretary for Civil Service (unrep) HCAL 2335 of 2000, [2002] 3 HKC 1.

Yao Man Fai George v Director of Social Welfare [2010] HKEC 968, [2012] HKCA 79 (CA), [2012] 4 HKC 180 (the *Comprehensive Social Security Assistance* Case).

Yeung Cheong Fat v An Investigation Committee appointed pursuant to section 6 of the Public Service (Discipline) Regulation and section 10 of the Public Service (Administration) Order 1997 [2005] HKCU 62 (unreported, HCAL 93/2003, 13 April 2004).

Yeung May Wan v HKSAR (2005) 8 HKCFAR 137 (CFA), [2005] 2 HKLRD 212 (CFA) (the *Falun Gong* case).

India

A P State Pollution Control Board v *M V Nayudu*, AIR [1999] SC 812.

B R Kapoor v Union of India (1989) 3 SCC 387.

Rakseh Chandra v State of Bihar, AIR 1989 SC 348.

Subhash Kumar v State of Bihar, AIR 1991 SC 420.

Israel

Ganor v Attorney-General HCJ 935/89 [1990] IsrSC 44(2) 485.

Malaysia

Rama Chandran, R v The Industrial Court of Malaysia [1997] 1 AMR 6:433, [1997] 1 MLJ 145 (FC).

Singapore

Oei Hon Leong v Ban Song Long David [2005] 3 SLR 608.

South Africa

Bato Star Fishing (Pty) Ltd v The Chief Director: Marine and Coastal Management, Department of Environmental Affairs and Tourism (CCT 27/03) [2004] ZACC 15; 2004(4) SA 490 (CC); 2004 (7) BCLR 687 (CC).

Ex parte Chairperson of the Constitutional Assembly: In re Certification of the Constitution of the Republic of South Africa 1996, 1996 (10) BCLR 1253 (CC).

Government of Republic of South Africa v Sunday Times Newspapers [1995] 1 LRC 168.

Government of the Republic of South Africa v Irene Grootboom [2000] ZACC 19, 2001 (1) SA 46(CC), 2000 (11) BCLR 1169(CC).

Khosa v Minister of Social Development (2004) 6 SA 505.

Minister of Health v Treatment Action Campaign (2005) 5 SA 721 (CC).

Nyambirai v National Social Security Authority [1996] 1 LRC 64.

S v Manamela (Director-General of Justice Intervening) (CCT25/99) 2000 ZACC 5, 2000 (3) SA 1, 2000 (5) BCLR 491.

Soobramooney v Minister of Health Kwa Zulu Natal (1998) 1 SA 765 (CC).

State v Makwanyane 1995 (3) SA 391 [1995] 1 LCR 269.

United Kingdom

A v Secretary of State for the Home Department [2004] UKHL 56, [2005] 2 WLR 87, [2005] 2 AC 68 (the *Belmarsh Detainees* case).

Ali v Lord Grey School [2006] UKHL 14.

Allied Dunbar (Franck Weisinger) Ltd v Frank Weisinger [1988] 17 IRIR 60.

Anisminic v Foreign Compensation Commission [1969] 2 AC 147, 2 WLR 163.

Anufrijeva v Southwark London Borough Council [2004] QB 1124.

Associated Provincial Picture Houses Ltd v Wednesbury Corporation [1947] 2 All ER, [1948] 1 KB 223 (CA).

Aston Cantlow and Wilmcote with Billesley Parochial Church Council v Wallbank [2003] UKHL 37, [2004] 1 AC 546.

Attorney-General v Guardian Newspapers (No. 2) [1990] 1 AC 109.

AXA General Insurance Ltd v Lord Advocate [2011] UKSC 46, [2012] 1 AC 868.

Bank Mellat v Her Majesty's Treasury (No. 2) [2013] UKSC 39, [2014] AC 700.

Barrett v Enfield London Borough Council [1998] 3 WLR 79 (HL).

Begum v Tower Hamlets London Borough Council [2002] EWCA Civ 239, [2002] 1 WLR 2491, [2003] UKHL 5, [2006] 2 WLR 719, [2007] 1 AC 100.

Belfast City Council v Miss Behavin' Ltd [2007] 1 WLR 1420, [2007] UKHL 19, [2008] LGR 27.

Bellinger v Bellinger [2003] UKHL 21, [2003] 2 WLR 1174.

Boddington v British Transport Police [1998] 2 WLR 639.

British Oxygen Co Ltd v Board of Trade [1971] AC 610.

Brown v Stott (Procurator Fiscal, Dunfermline) [2001] 2 WLR 817, [2003] 1 AC 681 (PC).

Buckoke v Greater London Council [1971] Ch 655.

Bugdaycay v Secretary of State for the Home Department [1987] AC 514.

Campbell v Mirror Group Newspapers Ltd [2004] UKHL 22.

Champion v Chief Constable of the Gwent Constabulary [1990] 1 WLR 116.

Chandler v Director of Public Prosecution [1964] AC 763.

Chief Constable of the North Wales Police v Evans [1982] 1 WLR 1155.

ClientEarth (No. 2) v Secretary of State for the Environment Food and Rural Affairs [2016] EWHC 2740 (Admin).

Commissioners of Customs and Excise v Newbury [2003] EWHC 702, [2003] 2 All ER 964 (DC).

Congreve v Home Office [1976] QB 629.

Council of Civil Service Unions v Minister for the Civil Service [1983] UKHL 9, [1985] 1 AC 374.

Dad v General Dental Council [2000] 1 WLR 1538 (PC).

Docherty v Birmingham City Council [2008] UKHL 57.

Donoghue v Stevenson [1932] AC 562 (HL) (the *Ginger beer* case).

Douglas v Hello! Ltd [2001] 2 WLR 992.

Dr Bonham's case (1610) 8 Co Rep 114 (Court of Common Pleas, England).

Duke v GEC Reliance Ltd [1988] AC 618.

E v Inland Revenue Commissioners, ex parte MFK Underwriting Agencies Ltd [1990] 1 WLR 1545.

Entick v Carrington [1765] 19 St Tr 1029.

Fitzpatrick v Sterling Housing Association Ltd [2001] 1 AC 27.

Garland v British Rail Engineering Ltd [1983] 2 AC 751.

Ghaidan v Godin-Mendoza [2002] EWCA Civ 1533, [2004] UKHL 30, [2004] 2 AC 557.

Gouriet v Union of Post Office Workers [1977] QB 729.

H and L v A City Council [2011] EWCA Civ 403, [2011] LGR 590.

Hall and Company Ltd v Shoreham-by-Sea Urban District Council [1964] 1 WLR 240.

Hayes v Willoughby [2013] UKSC 17.

Huang v Secretary of State for the Home Department. [2007] UKHL 11, [2007] 2 AC 167, [2007] 2 WLR 581.

In Re Recovery of Medical Costs for Asbestos Doseases (Wales) Bill [2015] AC 1016.

Inhabitants of Eastbourne (1803) 4 East 103.

International Transport Roth GmbH v Secretary of State for the Home Department [2002] EWCA Civ 158, [2002] 3 WLR 344, [2003] QB 728.

Jones v First Tier Tribunal [2013] 2 AC 48.

Kay v Lambeth London Borough Council [2006] 2 AC 465.

Kennedy v Charity Commission [2014] UKSC 20, [2014] 2 WLR 808.

Laker Airways Ltd v Department of Trade [1977] QB 643.

Leeds City Council v Price [2006] UKHL 10.

Lindsay v Commissioners of Customs and Excise [2002] EWCA Civ 267, [2002] 1 WLR 1766.

Litster v Forth Dry Dock Co Ltd [1990] 1 AC 546.

Liversidge v Anderson [1942] AC 206.

Lonrho Plc v Tebbit [1991] 4 All ER 973 (CA).

Lord Saville of Newdigate, ex parte B (No. 2) [2000] 1 WLR 1855 (CA).

MaCarthys v Smith [1979] 3 All ER 325.

Malone v Metropolitan Police Commissioner [1979] 1 Ch 344.

Marcic v Thames Water Utilities Ltd [2004] UKHL 66.

Matthews v Ministry of Defence [2003] UKHL 4.

Mayor of Westminster v London and North Western Railway Co [1905] AC 426.

McEldowney v Forde [1971] AC 632.

McWhirter v Attorney-General [1972] CMLR 882.

Michalak v Wandsworth London Borough Council [2002] HLR 721.

Napier v Scottish Ministers Outer House [2001] ScotCS 162, (2005) UKHRR 268.

Napp Pharmaceutical Holdings Ltd v Director General of Fair Trading [2002] EWCA Civ 796.

Neale v Hereford & Worcester County Council [1986] ICR 471.

Oppenheimer v Cattermole [1976] AC 249.

Padfield v Minister of Agriculture, Fisheries and Food [1968] 1 All ER 694.

Perilly v Tower Hamlets Borough Council [1972] EWCA Civ J0621-1, [1973] QB 9.

Pham v Secretary of State for the Home Department [2015] UKSC 19, [2015] 1 WLR 1591, [2015] 3 All ER 1015.

Pickstone v Freemans [1989] AC 66.

Poplar Housing and Regeneration Community Association Ltd v Donoghue [2001] EWCA Civ 595, [2001] 3 WLR 183, [2001] 4 All ER 605, [2002] QB 8.

Porter v Magill [2002] 2 AC 357.

Porter v South Bucks District Council [2002] 1 All ER 425.

Puhlhofer v Hillingdon London Borough Council [1986] AC 484.

R(Jackson) v Attorney-General [2005] UKHL 56, [2006] 1 AC 262.

R (on the application of Aguilar Quila) v Secretary of State for the Home Department [2012] 1 AC 621.

R (on the application of British Civilian Internees — Far East Region) v Secretary for Defence [2003] EWCA Civ 473, [2003] QB 1397 (the *Wartime detainees* case).

R (on the application of Cart) v Upper Tribunal [2012] 1 AC 663.

R (on the application of Farrakhan) v Secretary of State for the Home Department [2002] EWCA Civ 606, [2002] QB 1391.

R (on the application of HS2 Action Alliance Ltd) v Secretary of State for Transport [2014] UKSC 3.

R (on the application of JL (A Child)) v Islington London Borough Council [2009] EWHC 458 (Admin).

R (on the application of Jones) v Mansfield District Council [2003] EWCA Civ 1408, [2004] 2 P & Cr 14.

R (on the application of Alconbury Developments Ltd) v Secretary of State for the Environment, Transport and the Regions [2001] UKHL 23, [2001] 2 WLR 1389, [2001] 2 All ER 929, [2002] Env LR 12, [2003] 2 AC 295.

R (on the application of Anderson) v Secretary of State for the Home Department [2002] UKHL 46, [2003] 1 AC 837.

R (on the application of Assisted Reproduction and Gynaecology Centre) v Human Fertisiliation and Embryology Authority [2003] 1 FCR 266.

R (on the application of Begum) v Headteacher and Governors of Denbigh High School [2006] UKHL 15, [2006] 2 WLR 719, [2007] 1 AC 100.

R (on the application of Bernard) v Enfield London Borough Council [2002] EWHC 2282.

R (on the application of Camgaign Against Arms Trade) v Secretary of State for International Trade [2019] EWCA Civ 1020 (CA).

R (on the application of Campaign to End All Animal Experiments) v Secretary of State for the Home Department [2008] EWCA Civ 417.

R (on the application of ClientEarth) v Secretary of State for the Environment Food and Rural Affairs [2011] EWHC 3623 (Admin), [2015] UKSC 28, [2015] 4 All ER 724 (SC).

R (on the application of D) v Secretary of State for Health [2002] EWHC 2085 (Admin).

R (on the application of Daly) v Secretary of State for the Home Department [2001] UKHL 26, [2001] 1 AC 532, [2001] 2 WLR 1622.

R (on the application of Evans) v Attorney-General [2015] UKSC 21.

R (on the application of Flash) v Southwark London Borough Council [2004] EWHC 717 (Admin).

R (on the application of Gallaher Group Ltd) v The Competition and Markets Authority [2018] UKSC 25.

R (on the application of Gangera) v Hounslow London Borough Council [2003] EWHC 794.

R (on the application of H) v Mental Health Review Tribunal, North and East London Region [2001] EWCA Civ 415, [2002] QB 1 (CA).

R (on the application of Hooper) v Secretary of State for Work and Pensions [2003] 1 WLR 2623, [2005] UKHL 29.

R (on the application of Hoverspeed) Ltd v Commissioners of Customs and Excise [2002] EWHC 1630, [2002] 3 WLR 1219 (DC).

R (on the application of Keyu) v Secretary of State for Foreign and Commonwealth Affairs [2015] UKSC 69, [2015] 3 WLR 1665, [2016] AC1355.

R (on the application of Limbuela) v Secretary of State for the Home Department [2005] UKHL 66, [2006] 1 AC 396 (HL).

R (on the application of Lord Carlile of Berriew) v Secretary of State for the Home Department [2015] AC 945 (SC).

R (on the application of Lumsdon) v Legal Service Board [2016] AC 697.

R (on the application of Mahmood) v Secretary of State for the Home Department [2001] 1 WLR 840 (CA).

R (on the application of Middleton) v West Somerset Coroner and Secretary of State for the Home Department [2004] 2 AC 182.

R (on the application of Miller) v Secretary of State for Exiting the European Union [2017] UKSC 5, [2017] 2 W.L.R. 583.

R (on the application of Miranda) v Secretary of State for the Home Department [2014] EWHC 255, [2014] 1 WLR 3140.

R (on the application of Morris) v Westminster City Council [2005] EWCA Civ 1184.

R (on the application of Munjaz) v Ashworth Hospital Authority [2005] UKHL 58, [2006] 2 AC 148.

R (on the application of N) v Secretary of State for Health, R (on the application of M) v Secretary of State for Health [2003] EWCA Civ 1406, [2003] EWHC 1094 (Admin), [2003] UKHRR 746.

R (on the application of P and Q) v Secretary of State for the Home Department [2001] EWCA Civ 1151, [2001] 1 WLR 202.

R (on the application of P, C and T) v Alperton [2001] EWHC Admin 229.

R (on the application of Pretty) v Director of Public Prosecution [2001] UKHL 61, [2001] 3 WLR 1598, [2002] 1 AC 800.

R (on the application of Q) v Secretary of State for the Home Department [2003] EWHC 195 (Adm).

R (on the application of Razgar) v Secretary of State for the Home Department [2004] UKHL 27, [2004] 2 AC 368.

R (on the application of Reprotech Ltd) v East Sussex County Council [2002] UKHL 8.

R (on the application of Rogers) v Swindon NHS Primary Care Trust [2006] EWCA Civ 392, [2006] 1 WLR 2649.

R (on the application of Rotherham Metropolitan Borough Council) v Secretary of State for Business, Innovation and Skills [2015] 3 All ER 1.

R (on the application of S) v Secretary of State for the Home Department [2006] EWHC Admin 111, [2006] EWCA Civ 1157, [2006] INLR 575.

R (on the application of Samaroo) v Secretary of State for the Home Department [2001] EWCA Civ 1139, [2001] UKHRR 1150.

R (on the application of Prolife Alliance) v BBC [2003] UKHL 23, [2004] 1 AC 185.

R (on the application of SB) v Headteacher and Governors of Denbigh High School [2005] EWCA Civ 199, [2005] 2 All ER 396.

R (on the application of Youssef) v Secretary of State for Foreign and Commonwealth Affairs [2016] UKSC 3.

R (on the application of Saadi) v Secretary of State for the Home Department [2001] 4 All ER 961.

R v A (No. 2) [2001] UKHL 25, [2002] 1 AC 45.

R v Barnet and Camden Rent Tribunal ex parte Frey Investments Ltd [1972] 2 QB 342.

R v Barnsley Metropolitan Borough Council, ex parte Hook [1976] 1 WLR 1052.

R v Brent London Borough Council, ex parte Assegai (1987) 151 LG Rev 891.

R v Cambridge Health Authority, ex parte B [1995] EWCA Civ 49, [1995] 2 All ER 129, [1995] 1 WLR 898.

R v Chaytor [2010] UKSC 52.

R v Chief Constable of Sussex, ex parte International Trader's Ferry Ltd [1998] 3 WLR 1260 (HL), [1999] 2 AC 418 (HL).

R v Civil Service Appeal Board, ex parte Cunningham [1991] 4 All ER 310.

R v Criminal Cases Review Commission, ex parte Pearson [1999] 3 All ER 498.

R v Department of Education, ex parte Begbie [1999] EWCA Civ 2100, [2000] 1 WLR 1115.

R v Deputy Industrial Injuries Commissioner, ex parte Moore [1965] 1 QB 456.

R v Director of Public Prosecution, ex parte Kebilene, [2000] 2 AC 326.

R v East Sussex County Council, ex parte Tandy, [1998] AC 714 (HL), [1998] 2 All ER 769.

R v Fernhill Manor School, ex parte Brown [1993] 5 Admin LR 159.

R v Gloucestershire County Council, ex parte Barry [1997] AC 584 (HL), [1997] 2 All ER 1.

R v Goldstein [1983] 1 All ER 434.

R v Governor of Brixton Prison, ex parte Armah [1968] AC 192.

R v Governor of HMP Franland, ex parte Russell and Wharrie [2000] EWHC Admin 365, [2000] 1 WLR 2027.

R v Highbury Corner Magistrates' Court, ex parte Uchendu (1994) 158 JP 409.

R v Horncastle [2009] UKSC 14.

R v Human Fertilisation and Embryology Authority, ex parte Blood [1997] 2 All ER 687, [1999] Fam 151 (the *Diane blood* case).

R v Inland Revenue Commissioners, ex parte National Federation of Small Businesses Ltd [1982] AC 617.

R v International Stock Exchange, ex parte Else [1992] BCC 11, [1993] QB 534.

R v Jones (Margaret) [2006] UKHL 16, [2006] 2 WLR 772, [2007] 1 AC 136.

R v Lambert [2002] 2 AC 545.

R v Lancashire County Council, ex parte Huddleston [1986] 2 All ER 941.

R v Legal Aid Board, ex parte Parsons [1999] 3 All ER 347.

R v Liverpool Corporations, ex parte Liverpool Taxi Fleet Operator's Association [1972] 2 QB 299.

R v Lord Chancellor, ex parte Witham [1997] 1 WLR 104, [1998] QB 575.

R v Lum Wai Ming (1992) 2 HKPLR 182, [1992] 2 HKCLR 221.

R v Manchester Crown Court, ex parte McDonald [1999] 1 WLR 841.

R v McLoughlin and Newell [2014] EWCA Crim 188.

R v Minister of Agriculture, Fisheries and Food, ex parte Bell Lines [1984] 2 CMLR 502.

R v Minister of Defence, ex parte Walker [2000] 1 WLR 806.

R v Ministry of Agriculture, Fisheries and Food, ex parte First City Trading [1997] 1 CMLR 250.

R v Ministry of Defence, ex parte Smith and Grady [1996] QB 517 (CA).

R v Monopolies and Mergers Commission, ex parte Argyll Group Plc [1986] 2 All ER 257.

R v Monopolies and Mergers Commission, ex parte South Yorkshire Transport [1993] 1 WLR 23, [1993] 1 All ER 289.

R v Newham London Borough Council, ex parte X [1995] ELR 303.

R v North and East Devon Health Authority, ex parte Coughlan [2001] QB 213, [2000] 2 WLR 622, [2000] 3 All ER 850.

R v Offen [2001] 1 WLR 254.

R v Parliamentary Commissioner for Administration, ex parte Balchin [1998] 1 PLR 1.

R v Parole Board, ex parte Watson [1996] 1 WLR 906.

R v Ponting [1985] Crim LR 318.

R v Radio Authority, ex parte Bull [1997] 2 All ER 561.

R v Secretary for the Home Department, ex parte Handscomb (1987) 86 Cr App R 59.

R v Secretary of Agriculture, Fisheries and Food, ex parte Astonquest Ltd [2000] Eu LR 371.

R v Secretary of State for Employment, ex parte Equal Opportunities Commission [1994] 1 WLR 409, [1994] 1 All ER 910.

R v Secretary of State for Environment, ex parte Spath Holme Ltd [2001] 2 AC 349.

R v Secretary of State for Health, ex parte Eastside Cheese Co [1999] 3 CMLR 123.

R v Secretary of State for Home Department, ex parte Benson [1989] COD 329.

R v Secretary of State for Social Security, ex parte Joint Council for the Welfare of Immigrants [1997] 1 WLR 275.

R v Secretary of State for the Environment, ex parte Fielder Estates (Canvey Ltd) (1989) 57 P & CR 424.

R v Secretary of State for the Environment, ex parte Hammersmith and Fulham London Borough Council [1991] 1 AC 521.

R v Secretary of State for the Environment, ex parte NALGO [1993] Admin LR 785.

R v Secretary of State for the Environment, ex parte Nottinghamshire County Council [1986] AC 240.

R v Secretary of State for the Environment, Transport and the Regions, ex parte Spath Homes Ltd [2001] 2 AC 349 (HL).

R v Secretary of State for the Home Department, ex parte Adams [1995] All ER (EC) 177.

R v Secretary of State for the Home Department, ex parte Anderson [1984] 1 QB 778.

R v Secretary of State for the Home Department, ex parte Benwell [1984] ICR 723 (QBD).

R v Secretary of State for the Home Department, ex parte Brind [1991] 696 (HL), [1991] 2 WLR 588, [1991] UKHL 4, [1991] 1 All ER 720.

R v Secretary of State for the Home Department, ex parte Doody [1994] 1 AC 531.

R v Secretary of State for the Home Department, ex parte Fire Brigades Union Fire Brigades Union [1995] 2 WLR 464.

R v Secretary of State for the Home Department, ex parte Hargreaves [1997] 1 All ER 397.

R v Secretary of State for the Home Department, ex parte Hosenball, [1977] 1 WLR 766.

R v Secretary of State for the Home Department, ex parte Leech (No. 2) [1994] QB 198.

R v Secretary of State for the Home Department, ex parte McQuillan [1995] 4 All ER 400.

R v Secretary of State for the Home Department, ex parte Pierson [1998] AC 539.

R v Secretary of State for the Home Department, ex parte Simms and O'Brien [1999] 3 All ER 400, [2000] 2 AC 115.

R v Secretary of State for Trade and Industry, ex parte Lonrho Plc [1989] 1 WLR 525.

R v Secretary of State for Transport, ex parte Factortame Ltd (No. 2) [1991] 1 AC 603.

R v Secretary of State for Transport, ex parte Factortame Ltd (No. 5) [1998] 3 CMLR 192 (CA), [1999] 4 All ER 906 (HL).

R v Secretary of State for Transport, ex parte Factortame Ltd [1990] 2 AC 85.

R v Secretary of State for Transport, ex parte Factortame Ltd [1995] 1 AC 1.

R v Secretary of State for Work and Pensions, ex parte Carson and Reynolds [2003] EWCA Civ 797, [2003] 3 All ER 577, [2005] 4 All ER 545, [2005] UKHL 37, [2006] 1 AC 173.

R v Shayler [2002] UKHL 11, [2003] 1 AC 247.

R v Somerset County Council, ex parte Fewings [1995] 1 WLR 1037.

R v Stratford Justices, ex parte Imbert [1999] 2 Cr App R 276.

R v Tamworth Justices, ex parte Walsh [1994] COD 227.

Raymond v Honey [1983] AC1.

Re G (Adoption: Unmarried Couple) [2009] 1 AC 173.

Re HK (An Infant) [1967] 2 QB 617.

Re Northern Ireland Human Rights Commission's Application for Judicial Review [2018] UKSC 27.

Reyes v R [2002] 11 UKPC, [2002] 2 AC 235.

Roberts v Hopwood [1925] AC 578.

Roy v Kensington and Chelsea Family Practitioner Committee [1992] 2 WLR 239 (HL).

Royal Borough of Kensington and Chelsea v O'Sullivian [2003] EWCA 371.

Salomon v Commissioners of Customs and Excise [1967] 2 QB 116.

Secretary of State for Education and Science v Tameside Metropolitan Borough Council [1977] AC 1014.

Secretary of State for Social Security, ex parte Joint Council for the Welfare of Immigrants [1997] 1 WLR 275.

Secretary of State for the Home Department, ex parte Rehman [2001] UKHL 47, [2003] 1 AC 153.

Shields v E Coomes (Holdings) Ltd [1979] 1 All ER 456.

Short v Poole Corporation [1926] Ch 66.

Somerville v Scottish Ministers [2007] UKHL 44, [2007] 1 WLR 2734.

South Buckinghamshire District Court v Porter [2003] UKHL 265, [2003] 2 WLR 1547.

South Bucks District Council v Porter [2001] EWCA Civ 1549, [2003] UKHL 26.

Southwark London Borough Council v Tanner [2001] 1 AC 1.

Stoke-on-Trent City Council v B & Q [1984] AC 754.

Stubbing v Webb [1993] AC 498.

Sugar v Associated Newspapers Ltd (unreported, 6 February 2001 QBD).

TD v Minister for Education [2001] 4 IR 256.

Tesco Stores Ltd v Secretary of State for the Environment [1995] 1 WLR 759.

Thoburn v Sunderland City Council [2001] EWHC Admin 934, [2002] EWHC 195, [2002] Eu LR 253, [2003] QB 151 (the *Metric Martyrs* case).

Thomas v Adjudication Officer [1991] 2 QB 164 (CA).

Torfaen Borough Council v B & Q [1990] 3 CMLR 455.

Venables and Thompson v News Group Newspapers [2001] 2 WLR 1038.

Webb v EMO [1993] 1 WLR 49.

Weinberger v Inglis [1919] AC 606.

Wells v Parole Board [2007] EWHC 1835.

Wheeler v Leicester City Council [1985] AC 1054.

Wilkinson v Inland Revenue Commissioner [2002] EWHC 182 (Admin), (2002) STC 347.

Wilson v First County Trust Ltd [2003] UKHL 40, [2004] 1 AC 816.

X (on the application of Minors) v Bedfordshire County Council [1995] 2 AC 633 (HL).

X Ltd v Morgan-Gampian (Publishers) Ltd [1990] 2 All ER 1, [1990] 1 All ER 616, [1991] 1 AC 1 (CA).

YL v Birmingham City Council [2007] UKHL 27, [2008] 1 AC 95.

Privy Council of the United Kingdom

De Freitas v Permanent Secretary of Ministry of Agriculture, Fisheries, Lands and Housing [1998] UKPC 30, [1998] 3 WLR 675, [1998] 1 AC 69.

Panday v Gordon [2005] UKPC 36.

UN International Courts of Justice

Germany v Netherlands [1969] ICJ Rep 3, (1969) 41 ILR (1969) ICJ Rep; 41 ILR (the *North Sea Continental Shelf* case).

United States

Browder v Gayle, 142 F Supp 707 (1956).

Chevron v Natural Resources Defense Council, 467 US 837 (1984).

Marbury v Madison, 5 US (1 Cranch) 137.

Tennessee v Garner, 471 US 1 (1985).

Texas v Johnson, 491 U.S. 397 (1989).

United States v Mead, 533 US 218 (2001).

US v Eichman, 496 U.S. 310 (1990).

Willard Mikesell, 243 NW 2d 86, 101 (1976) (Michigan Supreme Court).

Zimbabwe

Retrofit v Post and Telecommunications Authority [1996] 4 LRC 489.

List of Legislation

Canada

Canadian Charter of Rights and Freedoms, Constitution Act 1982

France

French Declaration of Rights of Man and of the Citizen 1789

Germany

German Basic Law (*Grundgesetz*)

Hong Kong (including delegated and secondary legislation)

Air Pollution Control Ordinance, Cap 311

Basic Law

Bill of Rights Ordinance, Cap 383

Court of Final Appeal Ordinance, Cap 484

Crimes Ordinance, Cap 200

Dangerous Drugs (Amendment) (No. 2) Ordinance, Cap 134

Dangerous Drugs Ordinance, Cap 134

Disability Discrimination Ordinance, Cap 487

Emergency Regulations Ordinance, Cap 241

Hospital Authority Ordinance, Cap 113

Housing Ordinance, Cap 283

Legislative Council (Powers and Privileges) Ordinance, Cap 382

Legislative Council Ordinance, Cap 542

National Flag and National Emblem Ordinance, Cap 2401

Prevention of Bribery Ordinance, Cap 201

Prevention of Child Pornography Ordinance, Cap 579

Prohibition on Face Covering Regulation, Cap 241K

Protection of the Harbour Ordinance, Cap 531

Public Order Ordinance, Cap 245

Regional Flag and Regional Emblem Ordinance, Cap 2602

Road Traffic Ordinance, Cap 374

Sex Discrimination Ordinance, Cap 480

Village Representative Election Ordinance, Cap 576

Voting by Imprisoned Persons Ordinance

India

Constitution of India

International Treaties

Community Charter of Fundamental Social Rights of Workers 1989

Convention on the Elimination of All Forms of Discrimination Against Women

European Union Charter of Fundamental Rights 1966

European Atomic Energy Community (Euratom) Treaty 1957

European Coal and Steel Community Treaty 1957

European Convention on Human Rights

European Economic Community (EEC) Treaty 1957

European Social Charter 1961

European Union Charter of Fundamental Rights European Social Charter 1961 (Revised in 1996)

Geneva Conventions of 1949 (Geneva Protocol I 1977)

Hague Convention 1907

International Covenant on Civil and Political Rights

International Covenant on Economic, Social and Cultural Rights 1966

Rome Statute of the International Criminal Court

Sino-British Joint Declaration 1984

Treaty of European Union

Treaty on the Functioning of the European Union

Universal Declaration of Human Rights 1948

Vienna Convention on the Law of Treaties

Ireland

Offences Against the State Act 1939

Prussia

Prussian General Law of 1794 (*Allgemeines Landrecht für die Preußischen Staaten* (ALR))

Netherlands

Dutch General Administrative Law Act 1994 (*Algemene wet bestuursrecht*)

South Africa

Constitution of the Republic of South Africa 1996

Uruguay

Pietraroia v Uruguay, Communication No. 44/1979; U.N. Doc. CCPR/C/12/D/44/1979

United Kingdom (including delegated or secondary legislation)

Act of Settlement 1701

Act of Union 1707

Anti-Terrorism, Crime and Security Act 2001

Bill of Rights 1689

Broadcasting Act 1981

Chronically Sick and Disabled Persons Act 1970

Claim of Rights Act 1689 (Scotland)

Commonwealth Immigrants Act 1968

Constitutional Reform Act 2005

Consumer Protection Act 1987

Contempt of Court Act 1981

Criminal Law Amendment Act 1885

Deregulation and Contracting Out Act 1994

Disabled Persons Act 1970

Education Act 1993

Employment Protection (Consolidation) Act 1978

European Communities Act 1972

European Union (Withdrawal Agreement) Act 2020

European Union (Withdrawal) Act 2018

European Union Act 2011

European Union Referendum Act 2015

Government of Wales Act 2006 (replacing Government of Wales Act 1998)

Health and Social Care Act 2008

Human Rights Act 1998 (Designated Derogation) Order 2001

Human Rights Act 1998

Limitation Act 1980

Local Government Act 1985

Magna Carta 1215

Merchant Shipping Act 1984

Merchant Shipping Act 1988

Misuse of Drugs Act 1971

National Assistance Act 1948

Northern Ireland Act 1998

Official Secrets Act 1911

Official Secrets Act 1989

Petition of Right 1628

Prison Act 1952

Race Relation Act 1976

Reforms Acts 1829–1867

Rent Act 1977

Representation of the People Act 1983

Road Traffic Act 1988

Scotland Act 1998

Sunday Entertainments Act 1932

Terrorism Act 2000

Town and Country Planning Act 1990

Unfair Terms in Consumer Contracts Regulations 1994

Units of Measurement Regulations 1994

Weights and Measures Act 1985 (Metrication) (Amendment) Order 1994

Weights and Measures Act 1985

Youth Justice and Criminal Evidence Act 1999

Introduction

Proportionality (*Verhältnismäßigkeit*)[1] is a continental public law concept that originated in Germany and has been adopted both by the Court of Justice of the European Union (CJEU) and the European Court of Human Rights (ECtHR). It concerns the relationship between the ends of public action and the means, be they administrative or legislative, used to attain them and thereby informs and controls the implementation of public policy by administrative authorities. The proportionality principle specifies that measures adopted by public authorities should not exceed the limits of what is appropriate and necessary in order to achieve legitimate objectives in the public interest. When there is a choice between several appropriate measures, recourse should be made in accordance with the least onerous, and the disadvantages caused to individual citizens should not be disproportionate to the aims pursued. Simply put, administrative measures must not be more drastic than necessary for achieving the desired result. Therefore, the principle ensures substantive fairness in the exercise of any discretionary power. Its rationale is based on the idea of basic rights and individual freedoms so that if individual rights are to be taken seriously, then the state may only impose restrictions that are justified by a legitimate purpose and are absolutely necessary.[2]

Owing to the growth of administrative power over the last century, implementing proportionality has become a major challenge for the legal

1. Literal translation: relativity.

2. Nigel Foster and Satish Sule, *German Legal System and Laws* (4th edn, OUP 2010) 184–185.

systems of most economically (and politically) developed countries and regions, including the United Kingdom (UK) and Hong Kong. The modern administrative state undertakes tasks and manages programmes on an unprecedented scale to satisfy the needs of the complex societies in which we live. As the range of tasks they perform has increased, these administrations must adopt effective means of policy implementation to achieve their objectives since the justification for the very existence of public administration is to realise collective goals through programmes of state action.

To achieve these goals, executives have a number of different tools at their disposal, including the use of coercive and discretionary powers to collect and distribute wealth and limited resources for promoting the public good. In doing so, however, there is the potential for arbitrary or unfair action against individual citizens. This is largely because it is impossible for the administration, be it democratically elected or not, to fulfil social needs without interfering with individual interests owing to the commonly agreed principle that individual interests have to be subordinate to the collective good.

Although furthering public interest is the overriding aim of most administrations, public power, in particular discretionary power, should be reasonably exercised in the interest of the public as a whole and not in the interest of any individual or group of individuals alone. Following this principle will prevent private concerns from obstructing the overall mission. However, men, as James Madison once put it, may not always behave like angels,[3] and thus, unfettered discretion, even in the hands of the most compassionate administrator, tempts tyranny.[4] As Lord Acton put to Bishop Mandell Creighton in 1887, 'power tends to corrupt; absolute power corrupts absolutely'.[5] Even when administrators perform legitimate social functions without intending unjust enrichment for themselves or prejudice to others, they may still exercise power that may adversely affect the interests of individual citizens. These effects occur because an individual's behaviour is largely controlled by their role and situation,

3. Rabinder Singh, 'The Place of the Human Rights Act in a Democratic Society' in Jeffrey Jowell and Jonathan Cooper (eds), *Understanding Human Rights Principles* (Hart Publishing 2001) 199.

4. Jeffrey Jowell, 'Administrative Law' in Vernon Bogdanor (ed), *The British Constitution in the Twentieth Century* (OUP 2003) 373.

5. John Acton, *Essays on Freedom and Power* (The Beacon Press 1949) 364.

rather than their personal characteristics and traits. This phenomenon as well as their subordinates' obedience to follow orders, whether right or wrong, are reflected in the Stanford Prison Experiment and the Milgram Experiment, two psychological trials performed in the early 1960s and 1970s (see Chapter One).

Human nature being what it is, there is always a risk that a government may exceed the limits of its powers, betray the trust of people, or be incompetent. Therefore, it is necessary for people to be able to hold governments accountable. Although the supervision of the executive was traditionally under the hands of the legislature — Parliament in the UK and the Legislative Council (LegCo) in Hong Kong — this task has become more complicated than ever before because of the exposure of individuals to the growing governmental regulations that affect them. In parliamentary systems like that in the UK, although the legislature is supposed to hold the executive accountable, there has long been concern that this legislative supervision is ineffective because of the political bond between the government and the majority in Parliament. Moreover, Parliament in the UK has also been increasingly dominated by organised political parties, whereas the LegCo in Hong Kong is largely controlled by pro-Beijing government members. These attributes have significantly undermined the government's legislative capacity to provide adequate checks and balances on the executive.

Against this background, there have been indications that courts have taken on a compensatory role by acting as a substitute for this legislative oversight. That is, the courts have sought to check the executive branch via judicial review, by requiring the executive authorities to exercise their power fairly, reasonably, and consistently with a scheme that the UK Parliament or Hong Kong LegCo has prescribed in the enabling legislations. As most constitutional and human rights norms, be they civil and political rights or socio-economic rights, are not absolute and are subject to limitation, balancing, and regulation, the courts have, for the purpose of carrying out these obligations, developed principles to scrutinise the exercise of legislative and executive powers. Some of the typical tests or standards that have been developed include those that ask whether the powers have been exercised in a way that is reasonable, rational, and proportionate.

This book explores how proportionality can offer a more structured and intensive approach to scrutinise administrative decisions compared to the traditional approaches currently in force in the UK and Hong Kong — namely, *Wednesbury* unreasonableness (i.e., a decision is unreasonable only when it contains something so absurd that no sensible person could ever dream that it lay within the powers of the authority)[6] and *GCHQ* irrationality (i.e., a decision is irrational when it is so outrageous in its defiance of logic or of accepted moral standards that no sensible person who has applied his mind to the question to be decided could have arrived at it; based on a decision involving Government Communication Headquarters (GCHQ).[7] Compared to the proportionality principle, these two approaches have long been criticised to be too deferential to the administrative authorities because they hold that a court should not interfere with an executive decision unless the decision is so unreasonable or outrageous in its defiance of logic or accepted moral standards that no sensible person or reasonable authority would have come to it.[8]

Moreover, proportionality has also been adopted under European Union (EU) law via the European Communities Act 1972 (ECA 1972) (as at 31 January 2020, the day of Brexit)[9] and the European Convention on Human Rights (ECHR) and implemented in the UK through the enactment of the Human Rights Act 1998 (HRA 1998). It is also incorporated in the International Covenant on Civil and Political Rights (ICCPR) through the Bill of Rights Ordinance (BORO) and in the constitutional or legislative review adjudications in Hong Kong, thanks to the judges' consideration of jurisprudence from other common law jurisdictions as stipulated in the Basic Law.[10] Therefore, in view of the rise of the administrative state and its resulting growth in state activities and discretionary powers, there has been a growing appeal for proportionality to be fully recognised and adopted as a new ground of judicial review in both the UK and Hong Kong. It is believed that this principle could serve as a check-

6. *Associated Provincial Picture Houses Ltd v Wednesbury Corporation* [1947] 2 All ER, [1948] 1 KB 223, 229 (CA) (Lord Greene MR).
7. *Council of Civil Service Unions v Minister for the Civil Service* [1983] UKHL 9, [1985] 1 AC 374, 410E (Lord Diplock).
8. Ibid., 410E. See also the *Wednesbury* case (N6) [1948] 1 KB 223, 229 (CA) (Lord Greene MR).
9. That said, I argue, in Chapter Seven of this book, that EU law and its institutional forces are still, and will, be able to exert some degree of influence on the UK's decision-making and its jurisprudence.
10. Basic Law, Art 84.

and-balance mechanism to save individual citizens or minorities from being exploited by the majoritarian government.

In common law jurisdictions, such as the UK and Hong Kong, the proportionality principle has not been well received in the context of judicial review applications challenging domestic laws and policies, particularly those challenging policy formulations (and their implementation) related to polycentric socio-economic rights issues. This is largely because many believe that the use of proportionality marks an undesirable shift in the constitutional role of courts and that judges are 'constitutionally un-qualified' and 'institutionally ill-equipped' owing to their lack of democratic mandate [11] and their lack of expertise, experience, etc.[12] to adjudicate on matters of social or economic policy traditionally decided by the executive branch. However, this principle is enshrined in the ECA 1972, in the ECHR (via the HRA 1998 in the UK), and in the ICCPR (via the BORO in Hong Kong), and is, coupled with other socio-economic rights as stated in the International Covenant on Economic, Social, and Cultural Rights (ICESCR), further entrenched in Hong Kong by the Basic Law.

As consistency of law is one of the elements under the rule of law that is, if being fulfilled, capable of guiding human behaviour,[13] there is no justification why all judicial review cases should not be assessed consistently. In the UK, there have been arguments that if the courts are to insist upon the strict division of legal tests between challenges based on EU law and human rights law, on one hand, and those based on domestic law, on the other, then an apparent difference in the legal protection of individuals is created, which is difficult to justify.[14] Similar arguments have been made in Hong Kong.[15] To provide consistent legal protection for individuals, EU law and human rights law have,

11. See, for example, *R v Secretary of State for the Home Department, ex p Brind* [1991] 696 (HL) 766–767.

12. Ibid.

13. Peter Wesley-Smith, *Constitutional and Administrative Law in Hong Kong* (Longman Asia 1995) 15.

14. *R v Secretary of State for the Home Department, ex p McQuillan* [1995] 4 All ER 400, 422h (Sedley J); Gordon Slynn, *European Law and the National Judge* in Butterworths Lectures 1991–1992 (Butterworths 1993) 27–28; Robert Thomas, 'Continental Principles in English Public Law' in Andrew Harding and Esin Örücü (eds), *Comparative Law in the 21st Century* (Kluwer 2002) 131.

15. Johannes Chan, 'Administrative Law' in Simon Young and Yash Ghai, *Hong Kong's Court of Final Appeal: The Development of the Law in China's Hong Kong* (CUP 2014) 438.

in reality, acted as a pressure on judges in the UK to develop proportionality as a general principle and thereby close the gap between domestic law and EU law and international human rights standards. The same argument also applies in Hong Kong, insofar as judges are authorised to consider the precedents of other common law jurisdictions.[16]

There have been various scholarly enquiries concerning proportionality in UK law, EU law, and the ECHR. There has also been much discussion about whether the proportionality principle should be recognised as an independent ground for judicial review in common law jurisdictions, such as the UK, or whether the terrain of substantive review should continue to be divided between the *Wednesbury* unreasonableness test, the *GCHQ* irrationality formula, and the proportionality principle, with the latter confined to rights-based cases and those concerning EU law.[17] Thus, this is not the first in-depth comparison of the case law of UK courts with that of the CJEU and the ECtHR, but it is the first to compare the case law of these entities with that of Hong Kong. Moreover, the aim of this book is to contribute to and further the debate concerning these topics. This book also aims to increase the awareness of administrative decision-makers of their legally bound obligations authorised by the legislature when discharging their public duties as a way to enhance their effectiveness and efficiency in policy making as well as its implementation. The topics addressed will ultimately help these policy-makers pay due respect to (and thereby protect the interests of) individuals and minorities.

16. Basic Law, Art 84.

17. Mark Elliott, 'The Human Rights Act 1998 and the Standard of Substantive Review' (2001) 60 *CLJ* 301; Michael Taggart, 'Reinventing Administrative Law' in Nicholas Bamforth and Peter Leyland (eds), *Public Law in a Multi-Layered Constitution* (Hart Publishing 2003) Ch. 12; Philip Joseph, *Constitutional and Administrative Law in New Zealand* (3rd edn, Brookers 2007) [21.7.5]; Michael Taggart, 'Proportionality, Defence, *Wednesbury*' (2008) *NZLR* 423; Murray Hunt, 'Against Bifurcation' in David Dyzenhaus, Murray Hunt, and Grant Huscroft (eds), *A Simple Common Lawyer — Essays in Honour of Michael Taggart* (Hart Publishing 2009) Ch. 6; Tom Hickman, *Public Law after the Human Rights Act* (Hart Publishing 2010) Ch. 9; Paul Craig, 'Proportionality, Rationality and Review' (2010) *NZLR* 265; Tom Hickman, 'Problems for Proportionality' (2010) *NZLR* 303; Jeff King, 'Proportionality: A Halfway House' (2010) *NZLR* 327; Dean Knight, 'Calibrating the Rainbow of Judicial Review: Recognizing Variable Intensity' (2010) *NZLR* 393; David Mullan, 'Proportionality — A Proportionate Response to an Emerging Crisis in Canadian Judicial Review Law?' (2010) *NZLR* 233; Paul Craig, *Administrative Law* (7th edn, Sweet & Maxwell 2012) 664–675.

Insofar as the judiciary is concerned, there has been a tendency for many judges in common law jurisdictions to refer to the government as being somehow removed from the courts, without acknowledging that the judiciary is in fact as much a part of government as the executive and legislature. This tendency has led to an 'exaggerated level of judicial respect' [18] towards the executive and legislature. If the courts continue in this manner, in the name of upholding the separation of powers, they will undermine the foundational rationale for the separation of powers, which prevents the over-accumulation of power in one governing body. As the concept of governance — a broader notion than government, whose principal elements include the constitution, the legislature, the executive, and the judiciary — involves the 'interaction between these formal institutions and those of civil society' [19] and corresponds to some traditional political theories, such as social contract theory, an idea of constitutional dialogue has emerged. This dialogue, as well as concomitant dialogic judicial review, the purpose of which is to encourage co-operative engagement amongst the different branches of government, including the judiciary, and people from different roles in civil society, needs to be assessed in the context of rights protection. In this regard, this book also contributes to these debates by recommending approaches the UK and Hong Kong courts should adopt if they are to fully recognise and adopt the proportionality principle in their jurisdictions. This book also attempts to show the importance of adopting a robust approach to enforce socio-economic rights and highlights how these rights, if properly interpreted and understood, will support collaboration between various branches of the government and the international community as they address the most fundamental interests of individuals.

Throughout this book, a functional comparative approach has been adopted to evaluate the extent to which proportionality has been integrated into UK and Hong Kong laws. This assessment is conducted by comparing the case laws of the CJEU and the ECtHR with those of the UK and Hong Kong courts. As the CJEU and the ECtHR introduced the proportionality principle at almost

18. Hugh Corder, 'Comparing Administrative Justice Across the Commonwealth: A First Scan' in Hugh Corder (ed), *Comparing Administrative Justice Across the Commonwealth* (JUTA 2008) 6.

19. Gavin Drewry, 'The Executive: Towards Accountable Government and Effective Governance?' in Jeffrey Jowell and Dawn Oliver (eds), *The Changing Constitution* (6th edn, OUP 2007) 189–190.

the same time as the UK and Hong Kong courts,[20] the jurisprudence of the former is used for the purpose of comparison. Further reasons for using the jurisprudence of the CJEU and the ECtHR arise from the duty on the UK courts to apply this principle when they are enforcing EU law as well as the ECHR and from their persuasive effect in Hong Kong courts. In this environment, it is necessary to examine whether the application of the proportionality principle as a matter of EU law and the ECHR has had any influence on domestic law, in both the UK and Hong Kong.

In **Chapter One**, I first examine how the growth of administrative power over the last century has resulted in the augmentation of state activities and of discretionary powers and how the simultaneously emerging civil society has responded to the increasing scale and complexity of modern government. Similar to Madison, I propose that human beings may not always behave like angels, and thus uncontrolled discretionary powers, even in the hands of the most compassionate administrator, tempt tyranny. In this chapter, I also highlight the need to regulate the growth of the executive authority and indicate that this need is indeed the underlying premise of a participatory democracy, particularly one that emphasises accountability and justification — from a 'culture of authority' to a 'culture of justification', as advocated by the late Etienne Mureinik. To achieve this, I believe the courts need to take on a compensatory role by acting as an alternative for this failing legislative oversight to, via judicial review, hold the executive accountable.

In **Chapter Two**, I examine the conceptual nature of proportionality, explore its application in different jurisdictions (both international and regional), trace its origin, and ascertain its methodologies. Parallel to the proportionality principle is the doctrine of margin of appreciation (which the CJEU and the ECtHR must grant to their Member States when judicially reviewing their decisions) and deference, discretionary area of judgment, etc. (which the domestic courts of the Member States must grant to administrative decision-makers and the

20. In this regard, Aharon Barak has provided a chart showing the migration of proportionality to different jurisdictions; see Aharon Barak, *Proportionality: Constitutional Rights and their Limitations* (CUP 2012) 181–183. However, Barak is wrong to state that the principle of proportionality migrated to Hong Kong in 1999. In fact, it migrated in 1991; see *R v Sin Yau Ming* (1991) 1 HKPLR 88 (CA), [1992] 1 HKCLR 127, 162–164.

legislature when judicially reviewing their policies and choices). Thus, these doctrines are discussed at length in this chapter.

In **Chapter Three**, I examine the basis of the *Wednesbury* formula (and its near-synonymous companion, *GCHQ* irrationality), as well as the rationale behind its development, the extent to which it has been fused with the proportionality principle, and its influence in Hong Kong. A comparative analysis between the pros and cons of the *Wednesbury* test and the proportionality analysis was conducted to determine whether the UK and Hong Kong have provided rubric for judicial review of irrationality in their administrative law. There have long been allegations that the full recognition of the proportionality principle would be incompatible with the distinction between appeal and review and that the courts are unelected and lack the expertise, experience, etc. required (i.e., they are constitutionally unqualified and institutionally ill-equipped) to adjudicate on matters concerning politically and economically sensitive disputes. This is especially true for polycentric socio-economic rights disputes, which involve prioritising and allocating scarce resources. As these issues affect the application of proportionality, their discussion in this chapter is essential to fully understand this principle.

In **Chapter Four**, I focus on the development of international and regional human rights in recent decades. This chapter includes a discussion of the evolution of socio-economic rights adjudication and the rejection of non-justiciability of socio-economic rights as well as the new tripartite theory of obligations — duties to avoid, protect, and aid — of the state and our evolving understanding of the separation of powers. I argue that these theories, when taken together, make the courts constitutionally and institutionally competent to deal with socio-economic rights issues.

In **Chapter Five** and **Chapter Six**, I examine the application of the proportionality principle by the CJEU and the ECtHR, respectively, to demonstrate how the principle has contributed to constructively controlling and guiding the EU (and its Member States) as well as signatories of the ECHR in the implementation of EU law and the ECHR, respectively. The case law survey presented here also provides an indication of what factors the CJEU and the ECtHR consider relevant when determining how strictly they should examine the challenged measures, what degree of justification should be required of state authorities (be they legislative, administrative, or judicial), and when they should defer to the discretion of primary decision-makers. Recently, socio-economic rights have been treated as essential corollaries of civil and political rights (i.e., an integrated approach) and are protected through the expansive application of equality or non-discrimination provisions.[21] Thus, Chapter Six also examines compatibility of the ECtHR's jurisprudence with this trend.

In **Chapter Seven** and **Chapter Eight**, I examine the extent to which the principle of proportionality has been integrated into and re-formulated in the UK and Hong Kong, respectively. As proportionality has been applied in respect of directly effective EU law (via the ECA 1972) and of the ECHR (via the HRA 1998) in the UK and in respect of the ICCPR (via the BORO) and of the constitutional or legislative review adjudications as empowered by the Basic Law (effective from 1 July 1997) in Hong Kong, particular attention will be paid to these regimes. As European jurisprudence prefers to treat socio-economic rights as essential corollaries of civil and political rights and protect them with an integrated approach and through the expansive application of equality or non-discrimination provisions by imposing positive duties on state authorities, these two chapters also analyse how the principle has contributed to such realisation and explore the possible application of the principle in cases other than the above regimes. In Chapter Eight, particular attention is given to poverty and the level of social welfare provided, as well as the enforcement of socio-economic rights, in Hong Kong after the change of sovereignty in 1997. Unlike Britain, Hong Kong has been experiencing growth in 'legal mobilisation', in which its citizens, especially minorities and political dissidents, have started invoking their legal rights. They largely do this via litigations to defend or develop their rights against the government. Since 1997, this legal mobilisation has gained more traction, particularly in response to the lack of democratic development, resulting in civil disobedience movements as well as anti-government protests in 2014, 2016, and 2019.

In **Chapter Nine**, I provide a broader conclusion for my arguments. This chapter also includes a global assessment of how the UK and Hong Kong

21. Ida Koch, 'The Justiciability of Indivisible Human Rights' (2003) 2 *NJIL* 3, 25; Paul O'Connell, *Vindicating Socio-Economic Rights: International Standards and Comparative Experiences* (Routledge 2012) 179.

courts have judged, as well as how they could integrate, the principle more effectively in future.

Overall, I argue that through its full adoption, proportionality would secure better governance via enhanced transparency (and thereby accountability) in administrative decision-making as well as judicial adjudications, particularly those in the sphere of polycentric socio-economic rights issues which involve the prioritisation of conflicting interests and allocation of scarce resources. When applying the principle of proportionality, courts 'will test the solution arrived at [by the authority], and pass it only if substantial factual considerations are put forward in its justification: considerations which are relevant, reasonable and proportionate to the aim in view'.[22] As the basic orientation underpinning the common law has long been accused of failing to respond constructively to the growth in scale and complexity of state activity,[23] law (including the proportionality principle) has come to be seen as a means of preventing 'the powerful engines of authority ... from running amok'.[24] The full adoption of this principle would also improve the quality of the decision-making process by encouraging officials to focus on alternative courses of action. Thus, this book provides a strong justification for adopting and implementing proportionality in full in judicial decisions in both the UK and Hong Kong.

22. *R v Secretary of State for the Home Department, ex p McQuillan* (N14) 428 (Laws J).

23. This assertion is concurred on by an English judge who expressed his concern well before, in 1956, that the common law had 'no longer ... [possessed] ... the strength to provide any satisfactory solution to the problem of keeping the executive ... under proper control'; see Patrick Devlin, 'The Common Law, Public Policy and the Executive' (1956) 9(1) *CLP* 1, 14–15. In Hong Kong, Kemal Bokhary, now the Non-Permanent Judge, after his retirement as a Permanent Judge, of the Hong Kong Court of Final Appeal, has said that the real danger to the common law was judicial inactivism; see Kemal Bokhary, 'Justice and the Law: The Evolving Role of the Lawyer' (2004) 34(1) *HKLJ* 133, 136.

24. H.W.R. Wade and Christopher Forsyth, *Administrative Law* (10th edn, Clarendon Press 2009) 4.

1

From a 'Culture of Authorisation' to a 'Culture of Justification'

1.1 Introduction

The principle of proportionality requires that there be a reasonable relationship between a particular objective to be achieved and the means used to achieve that objective. It should, thereby, be used to inform and control the implementation of public policies administered by executive authorities. The principle specifies that an executive body has to adopt only those measures that are strictly necessary for the performance of its functions and that if the executive body has a choice between several appropriate measures, then the mildest and least restrictive course of action should be taken. Thus, proportionality is a key tool of modern administrative law that was developed by the courts to control and prevent the abuse of power, to protect statutorily socio-economic rights in welfare states,[1] and to ensure the purposive rationality of public action.

Notably, proportionality has been incorporated into the decisions of various court cases. For example, in *R v Barnsley Metropolitan Borough Council, ex parte Hook*,[2] the Court of Appeal quashed the council's decision to deprive a market stallholder of his livelihood by withdrawing his licence because of a minor breach of market discipline when he obeyed 'an urgent call of nature' in an open area that resulted in an abusive altercation between Harry Hook and the council's staff. Although the Court held that Hook's suspension was unlawful

1. Jeff King, 'United Kingdom: Asserting Social Rights in a Multi-Layered System' in Malcolm Langford (ed), *Social Rights Jurisprudence* (CUP 2009) 276.
2. [1976] 1 WLR 1052.

owing to the lack of a fair hearing,[3] Lord Denning, Master of Rolls (MR), struck down the decision on the basis that 'the punishment had been altogether excessive and out of proportion to the occasion', adding that disciplinary action would have been sufficient.[4] As Lord Diplock once put it, 'you must not use a steam hammer to crack a nut, if a nutcracker would do'.[5] This decision, and others like it, corresponds with long-established principles of justice that 'for a trivial offence, a free man will be fined only in proportion to the degree of his offence, and for a serious offence correspondingly, but not so heavily as to deprive him of his livelihood, as explicitly stated in Article 20 of [the] Magna Carta', and that penalties should not be excessive, as acknowledged in the Bill of Rights 1689, which forbids 'excessive baile … excessive fines and cruell and unusuall punishments'.[6] While this example highlights the support of proportionality by administrators and legislation, it is important to note that the application of proportionality is largely influenced by the role of the administrative state.

The emergence of an administrative state over the last century has resulted in the augmentation of various state activities and discretionary powers. Furthermore, the simultaneously emerging civil society has also had to respond to the increasing scale and complexity of the modern government. The discretionary powers, authorised by the legislature to public personnel to exercise their power, are expected to be exercised in a reasonable manner to further the interests of the public. However, unfettered discretionary power, even in the hands of the most compassionate administrator, tempts tyranny, and the growth of executive authority, therefore, needs to be regulated. This need is indeed the underlying premise of a participatory democracy that emphasises accountability and justification. Thus, as the administrative state expands, the courts need to take on a compensatory role by acting as a substitute for this failing legislative oversight to, via judicial review, hold the executives

3. Ibid., 1061–1062 (Lord Scarman).

4. Ibid., 1057H (Lord Denning MR) and 1063 (Sir John Pennycuick).

5. *R v Goldstein* [1983] 1 All ER 434, 436e.

6. Jeffrey Jowell and Anthony Lester, 'Proportionality: Neither Novel nor Dangerous' in Jeffrey Jowell and Dawn Oliver (eds), *New Directions in Judicial Review* (Stevens & Sons 1988) 51, 60, citing the English Bill of Rights, 1 Wm. and Mary, Sess. 2, Ch. 2 (December 1689). Spelling in the original is retained.

accountable. Such a change would reflect a shift from a 'culture of authority' to a 'culture of justification', as advocated by the late Etienne Mureinik.

1.2 The Rise of the Administrative State

The growth of administrative power over the last century has presented a major challenge for the legal systems of most economically (and politically) developed countries and regions, including the United Kingdom (UK)[7] and Hong Kong.[8] The modern administrative state undertakes tasks and manages programmes on an unprecedented scale in order to satisfy the needs of the complex societies in which we live. It assumes responsibility not only for providing order and security but also for managing and promoting economic and social development and for maintaining the welfare of its citizens. This ever-increasing role has resulted in the government becoming a large and sophisticated administrative apparatus.

Such growth can be traced back to the late nineteenth century. In fact, from 1865 to 1900, there was an outburst of regulatory legislation, and more power was entrusted to the state.[9] A.V. Dicey opined that this era was 'the period of collectivism'.[10] This is supported by Dennis Davis, who further observed that during the second period of modern legal thought, commencing around 1900 and continuing until at least 1968, group and social rights replaced individual rights as the dominant legal focus, leading to a greater emphasis on social welfare generally as opposed to individual rights.[11] This period involved a combination of urbanisation, industrialisation, and global market expansions that, in turn, promoted interdependence. According to Duncan Kennedy, this

7. H.W.R. Wade and Christopher Forsyth, *Administrative Law* (10th edn, Clarendon Press 2009) Chs. 1 and 5; Jack Beatson, Martin Matthews, and Mark Elliott, *Administrative Law* (3rd edn, OUP 2005) Ch. 1.

8. David Clark and Gerard McCoy, *Hong Kong Administrative Law* (2nd edn, Butterworths 1993) Ch. 1; Peter Wesley-Smith, *Constitutional and Administrative Law in Hong Kong* (Longman Asia 1995) 226; Swati Jhaveri, Michael Ramsden, and Anne Scully-Hill, *Administrative Law in Hong Kong* (2nd edn, LexisNexis 2013) 8–25.

9. Wade and Forsyth (N7) 3.

10. A.V. Dicey, *Lectures on the Relationship Between Law and Public Opinion in England during the Nineteenth Century* (Macmillan 1905) 64.

11. Dennis Davis, 'To Defer and then When? Administrative Law and Constitutional Democracy' in Hugh Corder (ed), *Comparing Administrative Justice Across the Commonwealth* (JUTA 2008) 24.

was also a period of social legislation, or so-called positive law, which included the birth of modern labour laws, social insurance, and anti-trust legislation as well as the establishment of institutions to police these legislations.[12] He claimed that 'social legislation meant expanding the regulatory functions of the state, carving out and redefining as public law vast areas that had fallen safely within the domain of rights, will and fault'.[13] These fundamental changes began to shape the law, particularly administrative law. At the same time, a progressive programme of social reform based on a regulated mixed economy was developing. This programme emphasised social entitlements paid for by taxes,[14] which were increased thanks to the Labour government's commitment in 1945 to major social reform based on Keynesian economic policies.[15] As Frederic Maitland predicted in 1888, 'we are becoming a much governed nation, governed by all manners of councils and boards and officers, central and local, high and low, exercising the powers which have been committed to them by modern statutes'.[16]

Such augmentation of administrative power has also been driven by, *inter alia*, the increasing complexity and interconnectedness of modern life as well as by people's changing expectations of government. Nowadays, when citizens want something to be done, whether it is reducing childhood obesity, improving public transport to reduce carbon emissions, increasing food safety, etc., they often turn to the executive to make and implement related policies. When major catastrophes or public health scares occur, the government is expected to respond. For example, the public looked to the government to instil remedial policy in response during the outbreak of bovine spongiform encephalopathy (i.e., Mad Cow disease) in the national cattle herd in the UK in 1995, the Severe Acute Respiratory Syndrome (SARS) epidemic in Hong Kong in 2003, and the coronavirus (COVID-19) pandemic which originated in Wuhan, China, in late 2019, as well as during the global financial crises in recent

12. Duncan Kennedy, 'Two Globalisations of Law and Legal Thought 1850–1968' (2003) 36 *SULR* 631.

13. Ibid., 654.

14. Davis (N11) 24–25.

15. John Keynes, *The General Theory of Employment, Interest and Money* (Prometheus 1997).

16. Wade and Forsyth (N7) 3, citing the original source Frederic Maitland, *Constitutional History of England* (CUP 1955) 501.

decades.[17] As the complexity of modern societies has increased, so too has state intervention. Thus, whether we like it or not, the modern administrative state, or the so-called 'regulatory state',[18] ultimately governs us all. This state is comprised of an executive and government ministers, who act as our political leaders, as well as civil servants, who implement and administer the established policies.

As the government gains additional and expanded functions, the size of the civil service will extend beyond the grasp of day-to-day ministerial control. Indeed, many senior civil servants (who are not directly answerable to Parliament; not subject, as ministers are, to periodic re-election; and operate largely out of the public eye) have acquired a great deal of power. Moreover, a functionally specialised class of administrators has also grown in number in order to achieve various social changes. This increase has, in turn, resulted in an explosion of positive law development, largely in response to the demands placed upon the government. Such laws are highly specific, differentiated, and variable.

One consequence of such institutional specification and differentiation in government is that many tasks are now being privatised and contracted out [19] to non-governmental regulatory agencies [20] or non-departmental public bodies (NDPBs).[21] There are various reasons to support this change. For one, it is desirable to remove these industries from the public sector for financial reasons. It also creates a regulatory structure that minimises or removes short-term political interference [22] or turbulence.[23] Cosmo Graham argues that '[t]hese two ideas go together because, if there is one thing private investors require before investing in an industry, it is reassurance that there will not be short-term political interference in the operation of the industries'.[24] Additionally,

17. John Foster and Harry Magdoff, *The Great Financial Crisis* (Monthly Review Press 2009).

18. Giandomenico Majone, 'The Rise of the Regulatory State in Europe' (1994) 17 *WEP* 77; Michael Moran, *The British Regulatory State* (OUP 2004).

19. See, for example, Deregulation and Contracting Out Act 1994.

20. Colin Scott, 'Regulatory Governance and the Challenge of Constitutionalism' in Dawn Oliver, Tony Prosser, and Richard Rawlings (eds), *The Regulatory State* (OUP 2010) 20.

21. Paul Craig, *Administrative Law* (7th edn, Sweet & Maxwell 2012) [4.004].

22. Cosmo Graham, 'Socio-Economic Rights and Essential Services: A New Challenge for the Regulatory State' in Oliver, Prosser, and Rawlings (N20) 159.

23. *Secretary of State for Education and Science v Tameside MBC* [1977] AC 1014.

24. Graham (N22) 159.

the easier it is for the central government to get rid of these personnel or public bodies, the more obedient they would be, which according to Rodney Austin,[25] further supports privatisation of these government tasks.

Constitutional, and thus governmental, power in the UK traditionally springs from the top of the pyramid to its base — from the Crown directly exercising its prerogative (i.e., executive) powers and from the Crown in Parliament — whereby the executive can, having a majority vote in Parliament, exercise their legislative powers (i.e., the fused government). This authoritarian structure was, for most of this century, made tolerable by a political culture in which the government of the day sought to achieve consensus between the major political and economic power centres within the country. During the 1980s, however, the Tory government (1979–1997) changed the rules of the game, seizing greater power by diminishing that of other authorities, such as the local government, and limiting the influence of other public institutions or bodies, such as universities, trade unions, professional bodies, and pressure groups. For example, the central government abolished metropolitan counties and the Greater London Council by enacting the Local Government Act in 1985 primarily because the latter had opposed and obstructed its policies. The Tory government has also used its immense financial power and resources to control public authorities by limiting public expenditure, reducing or removing various grants, etc.[26]

As Austin rightly pointed out, when the Tories were in office and governmental tasks were contracted out, the nature of the central UK government was transformed. The administration ceased to work by consensus and instead sought to impose their policies and their will on all other public authorities by every means available to them. They have also effectively extinguished and rendered impotent all potential opposition to their policies. In doing so, they have created an even more centralised and authoritarian state in which power flows down from the top. In this political climate, the Cabinet, in particular the Prime Minister, became even more powerful, to the point where the UK

25. Rodney Austin, 'Administrative Law's Reaction to the Changing Concepts of Public Service' in Peter Leyland and Terry Woods, *Administrative Law Facing the Future* (Blackstone 1997) 9.

26. Ibid., 9–10.

was moving much closer to a presidential style of government, while retaining the trappings of the parliamentary system.[27] These practices prompted the development and rule of the New Labour government from 1997 to 2010.

It is also important to note that the efficiency, effectiveness, and accountability arising from privatisation of specific tasks have also played a key role in motivating fundamental reforms in the UK government. As the major component of the Tory and New Labour governments' ideology over the past 41 years (1979–1997, 1997–2010, and 2010–present, respectively) was the public choice theory (i.e., the translation of free market consumer choice from the private sector into the public sector [28]), the overriding consideration for the government has been to reduce public expenditure. However, these NDPBs are operating at a considerable distance from the main institutions of democratic legitimation. As Austin warned:

> If the delivery of public services and the implementation of policy are no longer the responsibility of central government departments led or at least headed by elected government ministers but have been 'farmed out' in one form or another, by one method or another, to non-elected, appointed bodies, there will be little or nothing for political responsibility or accountability to bite on.[29]

Worse yet, contracting out governmental tasks has also created legal consequences for the recipients of these public services (i.e., the taxpayer). Owing to the doctrine of privity of contract, the consumer has no legal remedy against the contractor (i.e., the service provider) for failure to perform the contracted public service. Since the contract is an agreement freely arrived at between the governmental department or public authority and the contractor, its terms fall outside the scope of judicial review.[30] Thus, taxpayers, while being the primary consumers, have no legal means of challenging the contract or of holding the contractor accountable. They must solely rely on political

27. Ibid., 11.

28. Norman Lewis, *Choice and the Legal Order* (Butterworths 1996).

29. Austin (N25) 5.

30. *Roy v Kensington and Chelsea Family Practitioner Committee* [1992] 2 WLR 239 (HL). See also Mark Freedland, 'Government by Contract and Private Law' (1994) Spring *PL* 86.

accountability, which is a poor substitute for the legally enforceable remedy implied by the notion of a contract.

In this environment, the traditional operational arrangement utilised by the minister-headed central government departments has been eroded, being replaced by more differentiated arrangements consisting of service networks in which a great number of public regulatory bodies operate at some distance from the electorally authorised sources of authority. For example, decisions made by independent central banks, energy sector regulators, various inspectorates (such as schools, pension, and prisons), and a variety of miscellaneous bodies (such as the National Health Service) have greatly impacted public policy formulation, often more so than those of ministers and other elected politicians. Fuelled by the strong market ideology of the time [31] and the then New Public Management initiative (and its resulting Next Steps re-organisation [32] with the functional values of economy, efficiency, and effectiveness), a fundamental re-ordering of the role and functions of the state occurred, one that would find strong echoes in other European Union (EU) countries [33] as well as globally.[34] As Richard Rawlings once said, although it might be going too far to characterise the UK as 'a regulatory laboratory', there has been experimentation with various institutional designs and modalities shaped by 'exploiting, and sometimes recasting, constitutional understanding and practice over the last three decades'.[35] This experimentation is largely thanks to the long administrative years of the Tory and New Labour parties (whose ideology was changed in 1995 in order to be electable).

As there has been a firm principle that all civil servants and administrators of the executive agencies or public bodies are politically neutral, they only give loyal service to the government of the day, regardless of party. These administrators, particularly senior ones, are required to refrain from active

31. Cento Veljanovski, *Selling the State: Privatisation in Britain* (Weidenfeld & Nicolsom 1987).

32. *Improving Management in Government: The Next Steps* (Cabinet Office 1988). See also Peter Leyland, *The Constitution of the United Kingdom* (Hart Publishing 2012) 178–179; Peter Cane, *Controlling Administrative Power* (CUP 2016) 439–446.

33. Michael Moran and Tony Prosser (eds), *Privatisation and Regulatory Change in Europe* (OUP 1994).

34. Leyland (N32) 178.

35. Richard Rawlings, 'Introduction' in Oliver, Prosser, and Rawlings (N20) 4.

involvement in party politics, including campaigning or standing as candidates for elected offices. In the UK, civil servants are, in theory, Crown servants, and technically speaking, they hold office at the pleasure of, and could be dismissible at will by, the Crown. However, in exercising their various statutory and prerogative powers, ministers and senior civil servants can, in reality, choose to implement administrative rules, official guidelines, and other types of informal quasi-legislation of varying degrees of enforceability. In many cases, this power is exercised without any parliamentary scrutiny or control.[36] Numerous civil service codes and guidelines [37] make it abundantly clear that the civil servant's primary duty is to the minister, who holds, by constitutional convention, the power of the Crown. Criminal law also makes it clear that civil servants cannot claim to be acting in the interest of the public to excuse or justify conduct contrary to the civil servant's duty to the minister.[38] All of these attributes, however, make them unaccountable to the public. Ultimately, these administrative changes have serious implications for the political accountability of the civil service. As Edward Rubin argued, the three-branch metaphor underpinning the traditional doctrine of separation of powers is now an outdated model of limited government and provides a poor conceptual framework for understanding contemporary governmental processes. The growth of the administrative apparatus now outstrips the ability of the tripartite scheme of legislature, executive, and judiciary to capture the complex dynamics of contemporary government.[39]

1.3 The Emergence of Civil Society

Parallel to the increasing scale and complexity of modern government is the augmentation of people's expectations of the government, which has resulted

36. Austin (N25) 7.

37. *Civil Service Code*, Hansard HL Deb, 30 October 1995, coll. 146–148, [2]; *Osmotherly Rules on the Conduct of Civil Servants appearing before Select Committees*, Departmental Evidence and Response to Select Committees (Cabinet Office 1994) [38]–[41].

38. Official Secrets Act 1911, s. 2. See also *Chandler v DPP* [1964] AC 763; *R v Ponting* [1985] Crim LR 318.

39. Edward Rubin, *Beyond Camelot: Rethinking Politics and Law for the Modern State* (PUP 2005) 73. See also Gavin Drewry, 'The Executive: Towards Accountable Government and Effective Governance?' in Jeffrey Jowell and Dawn Oliver (eds), *The Changing Constitution* (6th edn, OUP 2007) Ch. 8.

in the emergence of civil society.[40] The term 'civil society' has a number of, albeit sometimes confusing, definitions. Historically, the term is bound to the notion of rules to protect citizens and their civil rights. It may have been used in ancient Rome (*societas civilis*), but appears to have been particularly applied during the Enlightenment to express opposition to the idea that a ruler could treat his subjects as he pleased.[41] In this regard, civil society can refer to a voluntary association that is based on a hypothetical social contract outlining the rights and obligations of citizens.[42]

Although the relationship between society and the government shapes the way that the state is conceived, the rise of civil society does not lead to the decline of government. Since the workings of market stemming from individual actions possess the power to create and destroy, such operations stand in need of regulation by the government.[43] For a government to realise these responsibilities, an extensive administrative apparatus is needed. Thus, the modern state becomes an administrative state or a regulatory state. Colin Scott has argued that such a shift in power towards regulatory governance, coupled with the creation of independent agencies and greater deployment of legal rules, risks creating a high-handed state apparatus with broad discretion and concentrated power.[44] This shift, in turn, has led to a greater need for oversight of the executive and good governance by the people.

1.4 The Notion of Good Governance

Although the desirability of good governance, or administration, is beyond dispute, it is difficult to define what it actually is and how it can be achieved. In fact, there is no definitive or universal set of standards of good governance or administration upon which everyone agrees. There are, however, some core principles that are widely accepted as comprising good governance or administration even though their precise meanings vary and change over time.

40. Martin Loughlin, *Foundations of Public Law* (OUP 2010) 435.

41. Michael Goodhart, *Human Rights* (2nd edn, OUP 2013) 145.

42. Adam Seligman, *The Idea of Civil Society* (Free Press 1992).

43. Loughlin (N40) 435.

44. Scott (N20) 15.

Academically, Mark Elliott and Robert Thomas have argued that the notion of good governance is inseparable from that of democracy. At a basic level, the notion of democracy is straightforward and is based on the idea that people should be allowed to have a say in how they are governed. Thus, good governance can ultimately be reduced to the idea that the government, and its businesses, operate in ways that are acceptable to the majority of people.[45] It follows that the principle of good governance derives from values that are widely held within society,[46] and these values do, as Paul Daly has suggested, provide 'the motor for administrative law'.[47] This is supported by the definition advocated in the United Nations Development Programme, whereby:

> Good governance is, among other things, participatory, transparent and accountable. It is also effective and equitable. And it promotes the rule of law and equal justice under the law. Good governance ensures that political, social and economical priorities are based on a broad consensus in society and that the voices of the poorest and most vulnerable are heard in decision-making over the allocation of development resources.[48]

This definition is also reflected judicially. In *R v Monopolies and Mergers Commission, ex parte Argyll Group Plc*,[49] for example, Donaldson MR noted that '[g]ood public administration' has a number of concerns: 'substance rather than form; the speed of decision; a proper consideration of the public interest; a proper consideration of the legitimate interests of individual's citizens; and decisiveness and finality'.[50] Furthermore, Daly has suggested that the principles of good administration can be grouped under the category of 'effectiveness', saying that official decisions should be rational, in the sense that they should attain the objectives to which they are directed; policies should be consistent but open to change if required; and both policies and decisions should be

45. Mark Elliott and Robert Thomas, *Public Law* (OUP 2011) 342.

46. Ibid.

47. Paul Daly, 'Administrative Law: A Values-Based Approach' in John Bell, Mark Elliott, Jason N.E. Varuhas, and Philip Murray, *Public Law Adjudication in Common Law Systems* (Hart Publishing 2016) 26.

48. United Nations Development Program, 'Governance for Sustainable Human Development: A UN Policy Document' (United Nations Development Program 1997) 3.

49. [1986] 2 All ER 257.

50. Ibid., 266.

transparent and capable of being complied with. Therefore, the value of good administration is that of effective policy-making and implementation.[51]

Moreover, Gavin Drewry suggests that it has become increasingly fashionable to try to break free of traditional constitutional and institutional categories by considering more flexible and wide-ranging definitions of public institutions. Therefore, the traditional notion of government has given way to the broader and more flexible concept of governance. The working definition of 'governance' can be broken into three points:

(a) Governance refers to the process whereby elements in society wield power, authority, and influence to enact policies and decisions concerning public life, the economy, and social development.
(b) It is a broader notion than government, whose principal elements include the constitution, legislature, executive, and judiciary. Governance involves interaction between these formal institutions as well as the people of civil society.
(c) It has no automatic normative connotation.

However, the typical criteria for assessing governance in a particular context might include the degree of legitimacy, representativeness, popular accountability, and efficiency with which public affairs are conducted.[52]

Executive functions have, as previously indicated, been complicated by the emergence of modern (i.e., politically and economically developed) administrative states. These, coupled with increased bureaucratic size and complexity as well as the executive functions of presidents, prime ministers, and cabinets being shared with salaried administrators, have expanded and blurred the boundaries of executive power. One by-product of this is the endless

51. Daly (N47) 27–28.

52. Drewry (N39) 189–190. See also R.A.W. Rhodes, *Understanding Governance: Policy Networks, Governance, Reflexivity and Accountability* (OUP 1997); Jody Freeman, 'The Private Role in Public Governance' (2000) 75 *NYULR* 543.

debate in public administration about the policy-and-administration dichotomy and about the division of responsibility for policy and operational matters.[53]

In view of the above, the need to regulate the substantial growth in executive authority is increasingly supported because the state has intervened tremendously in the private sphere. Such need can also be interpreted as a requirement for a 'participatory democracy' that emphasises accountability and justification.[54] Further, Sandra Fredman has argued for 'deliberative democracy',[55] which moves from interest bargaining to value-oriented decision-making based on the persuasiveness of the reasons given.[56] This has become a prominent ideal of good governance over the past several decades, leading to a focus on administrative justice rather than administrative law.[57]

Another objective, which Jeffrey Jowell describes as the promotion of 'good public administration',[58] has also asserted itself. This notion has shifted the perspective of administrative law in the direction of the consumers (i.e., those persons affected by official decisions).[59] In this light, public service is no longer regarded as the service of the public as a collective, but rather the service of the individual consumer of specific and limited public services.[60] This is supported by Dawn Oliver, who stated (first in John Major's *Citizen's Charter* and later in *Service First* as well as other manifestations) that in the last decades of the twentieth century the government has 'consumerised' the concept of a citizen in their development of consumers' rights in relation to public services.[61] The consumers of services, individually rather than collectively, have some oversight of these services in that they are entitled to information about their operation, can expect a certain standard level of service, and can complain if

53. Ibid., Drewry, 191.

54. Etienne Mureinik, 'Reconsidering Review: Participation and Accountability' (1993) *Acta Juridica* 35.

55. Sandra Fredman, 'New Horizons: Incorporating Socio-Economic Rights in a British Bill of Rights' (2010) Spring *PL* 297.

56. Jurgen Habermas, *Between Facts and Norms* (MITP 1996).

57. Hugh Corder, 'Comparing Administrative Justice Across the Commonwealth' in Corder (N11) 2.

58. Jeffrey Jowell, 'The Democratic Necessity of Administrative Justice' in Corder (N11) 13.

59. Ibid.

60. Austin (N25) 23.

61. Dawn Oliver, 'Regulation, Democracy, and Democratic Oversight in the UK' in Oliver, Prosser, and Rawlings (N20) 245. See also Anne Barron and Colin Scott, 'The Citizen's Charter Programme' (1992) 55 *MLR* 526.

that standard is not met. However, Oliver criticises that such consumer-oriented concepts of the relationship between the individual and these public service providers (i.e., the regulatory or public bodies) by-pass the political representative process, as previously mentioned. These observations all beg the question: is such a rights-based, consumerist approach democratic?[62] As Oliver noted:

> [On one hand, to] the extent that democracy entails recognition of the rights and interests of individuals in their autonomy, dignity, and respect, then giving consumers of public (and other) services special consideration is surely not inconsistent with democracy. But [, on the other hand,] to the extent that 'citizenship' and democracy are linked, and that 'citizenship' implies that individuals' demands and grievances should be made to and responded to by elected bodies, then the focus on consumer rights is not an aspect of citizenship.[63]

1.5 Administrative Discretion

As society becomes more complex and the level of state intervention increases, the role of the executive will continue to become more pronounced, thereby having greater control over the decisions by which society is governed. The executive and related authoritative bodies have a number of tools at their disposal to achieve this, including the use of coercive power and of discretionary power to collect and distribute wealth and limited resources for promoting the public good.[64]

As L'Heureux Dube J commented in *Baker v Canada (Minister of Citizenship and Immigration)*,[65] the concept of administrative discretion 'refers to decisions where the law does not dictate a specific outcome, or where the decision-maker is given a choice of options within the statutorily imposed set of boundaries'.[66] Therefore, central to the exercise of discretionary power is a degree of autonomy,

62. Ibid., Oliver.

63. Ibid.

64. Elliott and Thomas (N45) 107.

65. [1999] 2 SCR 817, (1999) 174 DLR (4th) 193 (SCC).

66. Ibid., 223.

within a defined context, vested in decision-makers acting on behalf of the public. In this regard, D.J. Galligan made the following observation:

> A noticeable feature of modern legal systems is the extent to which officials, whether they be judicial or administrative, make decisions in the absence of previously fixed, relatively clear, and binding legal standards. Frequently it appears that decisions are made and so power exercised according to considerations which vary from one area of state activity to another, from one type of institution to another, and even from one set of circumstances to another, in the absence of that pattern of normative standards and principles which [are] generally thought to be so central to the very notion of legal order. ... The vagaries of language, the diversity of circumstances, and the indeterminacy of official purposes are, as H.L.A. Hart reminded us, considerations which guarantee discretion some continuing place of the legal order and make its elimination an impossible dream.[67]

According to its etymological origins, discretion refers to judgment, in particular good judgment. Having good judgment, or making correct decisions, is an essential principle of a good administration. It involves collecting information relevant to the task being judged and then applying the legal rules or standards to produce a decision that not only corresponds with the facts but is also well reasoned and robust.[68] There are several reasons why governments should have good judgment and make correct decisions.[69] First, as public officials exercise considerable public power over people's lives, any error or inefficiency in the handling or outcome of such decisions will be potentially distressing for the individuals concerned. A single administrative decision or action may not seem that important to the government, but it may be significant to the persons affected. Poor decisions also create unnecessary anxiety for individual citizens, who may feel they have no choice but to challenge it via judicial review. Second, poor judgment generates unnecessary costs, thus wasting taxpayers' money and generating unnecessary delays when it is impugned via the judicial process. Ordinarily, decision-makers reach appropriate outcomes

67. D.J. Galligan, *Discretionary Powers: A Legal Study of Official Discretion* (Clarendon Press 1990) 1.

68. Robert Thomas, 'Administrative Justice, Better Decisions, and Organisational Learning' (2015) January *PL* 111, 112.

69. Ibid., 112–113.

more quickly and efficiently than the courts, but remitting a matter for further decision by the courts, particularly in cases where the outcome is obvious, would undermine good administration.[70] Third, decision-making is an essential part of implementing policy. If the government is to accomplish its policy goals, for such things as collecting taxes, administrating benefits, etc., as approved by the legislature, then good decisions are required. Finally, good judgment enhances the legitimacy of government agencies and their decision-making processes. On the contrary, poor judgment, or poor decision-making, carries a reputational risk for those public agencies and can undermine public confidence in, and the legitimacy of, the government as a whole. Such problems are exacerbated if the government repeats the same mistakes rather than learning from them.

In its modern legal usage, discretion has come to connote autonomy in judgment and decision.[71] To have discretion is to have a sphere of autonomy within which one's decisions are, to some degree, a matter of personal judgment and assessment. Within such an area of autonomy, decision-makers make choices according to whatever reasons they see fit or, indeed, without reason, provided that the decision is within the circumference of their power.[72] Interestingly, there has been a recent trend emerging where primary statutes enacted by the legislature leave a wide opportunity for officials (or those whose power is delegated by the former) to establish rules as they see fit without stating the objects for which the powers may be exercised.[73] Within these boundaries, administrative decision-makers are free to choose between competing statutory interpretations. In the UK, this situation has been made worse by the implicit constitutional role of the courts in giving effect to the will of Parliament.[74] This means that when the courts are interpreting legislation, the presumption of liberty under common law only comes into play on the condition that it was not compatible with the presumed intention of Parliament in passing the statute in

70. *Alberta (Information and Privacy Commissioner) v Alberta Teachers' Association* [2011] 2 SCR 654, [55] (Rothstein J).

71. Galligan (N67) 8.

72. Ibid., 6.

73. Helen Mountfield, 'The Concept of a Lawful Interference with Fundamental Rights' in Jeffery Jowell and Jonathan Cooper (eds), *Understanding Human Rights Principles* (Hart Publishing 2001) 23.

74. Similar rationale also prevails in the United States; see *Chevron v Natural Resources Defense Council*, 467 U.S. 837 (1984), 842–843; *United States v Mead*, 533 U.S. 218 (2001), 227.

question.[75] Thus, in cases such as *Liversidge v Anderson,*[76] *Malone v Metropolitan Police Commissioner,*[77] and *R v Secretary of State for the Home Department, ex parte Hosenball,*[78] the enabling legislations were interpreted as conferring wide discretionary powers to the executive to interfere with individual rights in a manner that was exempt from any meaningful judicial scrutiny.[79]

1.6 Reasoned Exercise of Discretionary Power

The 'discretionary' aspect of a public official's discretionary power refers to their freedom to choose among multiple courses of action. However, this simplified definition does not take into account that discretion not only involves the authority's freedom to choose among different actions but also needs to be reasoned and justified. Mureinik advocates for discretionary authority to be used in a manner that is reasoned and justified, saying that in South Africa,

> the apartheid order rested on the doctrine of Parliamentary sovereignty, ... what [the South African] Parliament says is law, without the need to offer justification to the courts ... [or to] those governed by the law. ... The effect of [this culture] ... was to foster an ethic of obedience. The leadership of the ruling party commanded Parliament, Parliament commanded its bureaucracy, the bureaucrats commanded the people.
>
> This culture of authority was an indispensable nursery for the feature of apartheid that most people consider its defining characteristic: the reduction to law of racial discrimination — differentiation on the ground of race that is not justified. Without a culture of authority it is difficult to imagine how its gardeners could have cultivated the forest of apartheid statutes whose most distinctive feature was their want of justification.

75. Colm O'Cinneide, 'Human Rights and the UK Constitution' in Jeffrey Jowell, Dawn Oliver, and Colm O'Cinneide (eds), *The Changing Constitution* (8th edn, OUP 2015) 72–73.

76. [1942] AC 206.

77. [1979] 1 Ch 344. In contrast to the subsequent judgment of the ECtHR in *Malone v UK* (1984) 7 EHRR 14.

78. [1977] 1 WLR 766.

79. O'Cinneide (N75) 73.

> If the new Constitution is a bridge away from a culture of authority, it is clear what it must be a bridge to. It must lead to a culture of justification — a culture in which every exercise of power is expected to be justified; in which the leadership given by government rests on the cogency of the case offered in defence of its decisions, not the fear inspired by the force at its command. The new order must be a community built on persuasion, no coercion'.[80]

Therefore, any decision made must satisfy the requirement of reasonableness or rationality as doing so will ultimately lead to more accurate decision-making 'by ensuring that issues and reasoning are well articulated and therefore more carefully thought out'.[81] The concept of reasonableness also innately refers to that which lies within the limits of reason and allows for a legitimate diversity of views. Hence, a reasonable decision is one that is supported by reason and evidence, rationally connected to a purpose, and objectively capable of furthering that purpose. A reasonable decision also undoubtedly reveals proportionality between the ends and means, between benefits and detriments.[82]

In the decision-making process, the concept of reasonableness or rationality is deeply ingrained in the human psyche.[83] It has been alluded to by various scholars, including social contract theorists and modern positivists. Assessing the significance of the word 'reason', John Locke, a social contract theorist, observed:

> The word reason in the English language has different significations: sometimes it is taken for true, and clear principles; sometimes for clear, and fair deductions from those principles; and sometimes for the cause, and particularly the final cause. But the consideration I shall have of it here, is in a signification different from all these; and that is, as it stands for a faculty in man, that faculty, whereby man is supposed to be distinguished from beasts, and wherein it is evident he much surpasses them.[84]

80. Etienne Mureinik, 'A Bridge to Where? Introducing the Interim Bill of Rights' (1994) 10 *SAJHR* 31, 32.
81. *Baker v Canada (Minister of Citizenship and Immigration)* (N65) [1999] 2 SCR 817, [39] (L'Heureux Dube J); *R v Secretary of State for the Home Department, ex p Doody* [1994] 1 AC 531, 563.
82. Cora Hoexter, 'The Future of Judicial Review in South African Administrative Law' (2000) 117 *SALJ* 484, 509–513.
83. Shivaji Felix, 'Engaging Unreasonableness and Proportionality as Standards of Review in England, India and Sri Lanka' in Corder (N11) 96.
84. John Locke, *An Essay concerning Human Understanding* (Kitchener 1996) 312–313.

Joseph Raz, a modern positivist, on the other hand, made the following observation concerning the human capacity to understand and respond:

> Our capacities to perceive and understand how things are, and what response is appropriate to them, and our ability to respond appropriately, make us into persons — creatures with the ability to direct their own life in accordance with their appreciation of themselves and their environment, and of the reasons which, given how they are, the world presents them.[85]

In short, human beings are unique amongst animals: we alone have reason and, therefore, we alone are able, and thus required, to act rationally. Only a rationale creature capable of using reason to determine what to do and what not to do can be regarded as being truly free. Animals who live according to their instincts are not free in the same way that we are because they are unable to use reason to freely choose their actions. Thus, while animals blindly follow their instincts, human beings, as rational creatures, are by their very nature free because their rationality allows them to contemplate alternative courses of action and to freely choose that which they will undertake. Lord Wrenbury, in *Roberts v Hopwood*,[86] said the following concerning this aspect of rationality:

> A person in whom is vested a discretion must exercise his discretion upon reasonable grounds. A discretion does not empower a man to do what he likes merely because he is minded to do so — he must in the exercise of his discretion do not what he likes but what he ought to do. In other words, he must, by the use of his reason, ascertain and follow the course which reason directs. He must act reasonably.[87]

These views are supported by Frank Michelman, who summarised 'reasonableness' as a standard that is uncontroversially justiciable in traditional areas of law like the tort of negligence,[88] as well as Sir John Laws, who extra-judicially wrote that 'ultimate sovereignty rests, in every civilised constitution, not with those who wield governmental power, but in the conditions under

85. Joseph Raz, *Engaging Reason* (OUP 1999) 67.

86. [1925] AC 578.

87. Ibid., 613.

88. Frank Michelman, 'The Constitution, Social Rights, and Liberal Political Justification' (2003) 13 *IJCL* 13–14.

which they are permitted to do so. The constitution not Parliament is in this sense sovereign'.[89] In *R (on the application of Daly) v Secretary of State for the Home Department*,[90] one of the first full judgments by the then Appellate Committee of the House of Lords under the new Human Rights Act 1998 (HRA 1998) regime in late 2001 that used the proportionality formula, Murray Hunt mentioned that the case was 'a major landmark on the road to a true culture of justification' [91] implicit in all human rights adjudication. According to Ellie Palmer, such justification has come to be seen as a central aspect of constitutional adjudication in mature democracies, the purpose of which is to allow for an appropriate interchange between primary decision-makers and the courts within the boundaries of their relative institutional competencies.[92]

Viewed this way, a culture of justification promotes the idea that citizens are entitled to participate in decisions that affect them and determine their rights. Decisions made by different organs of the government must, therefore, be justified by the decision-makers within public discourse, which is infused with foundational values such as human dignity, equality, freedom, and democracy, so that transparency, respect for others in society, and state accountability will be promoted.[93] In short, although public authorities have wide discretionary power to promote the public good, a law that confers a discretionary power must give an adequate indication of the scope of this power.

1.7 Personal Prejudices Affect Human Behaviour

People exercising public power may be 'haunted' by existential envy, which may compel them to act in an irrational manner owing to a range of personal prejudices. As Aristotle once said, 'for those who sit in judgement, love, hate, or personal interest is often involved, so that they are no longer capable of

89. John Laws, 'Law and Democracy' (1995) Spring *PL* 72, 92.

90. [2001] UKHL 26.

91. Murray Hunt, 'Sovereignty's Blight: Why Contemporary Public Law Needs the Concept of "Due Deference"' in Nicholas Bamforth and Peter Leyland (eds), *Public Law in a Multi-Layered Constitution* (Hart Publishing 2003) 342.

92. Ellie Palmer, *Judicial Review, Socio-Economic Rights and the Human Rights Act* (Hart Publishing 2007) 191.

93. Davis (N11) 30.

discerning the truth adequately, their judgement being obscured by their own pleasure or pain'.[94] Thus, reasonableness demands that supportable decisions are made for rational reasons based on our limited understanding of the world. Galligan specifically noted the rationale underpinning the quest for rationality in public law:

> Power [is] conferred in order to serve and achieve certain ends and goals, and no matter how difficult they may be to discern, or no matter how vaguely they may be stated, officials must seek them out and direct their actions towards them in ways which are rational and reasonable.[95]

He further explained that the conceptual notion of rationality requires responsiveness to moral values or principles,[96] and made the following observation:

> These may be seen as part of the axioms of rational action, or as providing subsidiary goals to be achieved, or simply as constraints on the pursuit of goals. Perhaps the most basic moral principle in this context is that the rights and interests of individuals be treated with understanding and respect; from this more specific principles, including ideas of fairness, both in substance and procedure, and non-discrimination, may be generated. These concepts taken together in their interdependent relationships, constitute the foundations of a political morality which can be developed into more specific principles and priorities; these provide guidance and constrain the exercise of discretion by officials, and they also provide the basis for scrutiny and review of decision-making by legislatures, courts, and other special authorities.[97]

Therefore, the notion of reasonableness or rationality cannot be evaluated in isolation, but it should instead be considered a complex issue that requires objective justification in order to be sustainable in public law. When executive authorities make decisions, they are operating in an atmosphere absent of perfect knowledge. The absence of perfect information prevents perfect choices from being made. Indeed, one of the justifications for market order is that we live

94. Aristotle, *The 'Art' of Rhetoric* (translated by John Freese, HUP 1975) Book 1, 1.7.

95. Galligan (N67) 5.

96. Ibid.

97. Ibid.

in a relative state of ignorance.[98] It would naturally ensue that the minimum expectation from those who exercise public power is that they should act rationally. The absence of reasonableness or rationality in their decision-making would result in individuals being subject to the idiosyncrasies of public officials and sometimes occasioning arbitrariness that is incompatible with the rule of law.[99]

1.8 Majority Interests vs Minority Interests in a Democracy

The growth of administrative power and activities, coupled with the augmentation of administrative discretion empowered by the legislature, influences people from all walks of life. However, despite realising collective goals, administrative authorities have the potential to act arbitrarily against, or unfair to, individual citizens or minorities. Indeed, under democratic principles, minority interests are often subordinate to the majority good.[100] As James Madison once suggested:

> [T]he 'majoritarian' system of law-making offers no protection to society when oppressive or irrational ideas are favoured by a majority of the population. An idea [enjoying] majority support does not necessarily make it conducive to the 'public good': majorities might proceed on the basis of false information, be temporarily persuaded to abandon their better judgement by the seductive rhetoric of charismatic leaders, or simply be prepared to sacrifice their country's long term welfare to gain a short term, sectional advantage.[101]

According to Rabinder Singh, this is especially so in the UK as the dominant strand in British liberalism has been Bentham's utilitarianism. Singh argues that this concept fits with the general *zeitgeist* because, in the economic sphere, it is suited to the creation of free markets in which individuals decide what ought to be produced through consumer demand. In the political sphere, this concept

98. Lewis (N28) 8.

99. John Ely, *Democracy and Distrust* (HUP 1980) 56; Jeffrey Jowell, 'The Rule of Law Today' in Jeffrey Jowell and Dawn Oliver (eds), *The Changing Constitution* (4th edn, OUP 2000) 19; T.R.S. Allan, *Constitutional Justice: A Liberal Theory of the Rule of Law* (OUP 2001) 17.

100. Robert Thomas, *Legitimate Expectations and Proportionality in Administrative Law* (Hart Publishing 2000) 1.

101. Ian Loveland, *Constitutional Law, Administrative Law, and Human Rights* (4th edn, OUP 2006) 8.

is also related to the extension of the franchise, which is the equivalent of the free market in that it allows everyone to have a say, thus allowing majority rule to prevail.[102] After World War I, the Labour party took over from the Liberal Democrats as the main opposition to the Tories, and the utilitarians found their new home. The Fabian socialism practised by this group was not particularly concerned about the rights of the individual but was focused on improving the general welfare of society instead. It used parliamentary power, captured through the democratic franchise, to mediate this improvement. Therefore, the dominant creed, despite being progressive, was neutral at best and at worst, hostile to individual rights.[103] This is largely evident in a statement from Anthony Wright, a Labour Member of Parliament (MP) (1992–2010):

> If British socialism was about using the state to achieve social and economic objectives, then the British constitution seemed to put the state at the disposal of majority parties. The left was instrumental in defining a twentieth-century theory and practice of the constitution that sustained this view, and in defending it against those who hankered after something else. … Dicey may not have liked socialism … but socialists have nevertheless liked Dicey's constitution. Its doctrine of sovereignty, once rooted in an enfranchised people, enabled a parliamentary majority to get its way.[104]

Thus, British democracy fits well with utilitarianism. Those in support of this system largely believe that the correct course to maximise happiness is to do what the majority wants, thus satisfying the greatest number of people. According to this principle, the opinions of other people, especially those of minorities, do not matter, however deeply held they may be, and will inevitably be crushed under this system.[105] Furthermore, although a democracy requires each individual to vote for representatives of their choice, with decisions in society being decided by a majority of these representatives, issues can result when a majority is in power because they can marginalise minorities in such a way that the latter are effectively incapable of expressing their views and

102. Rabinder Singh, 'The Place of the Human Rights Act in a Democratic Society' in Jowell and Cooper (N73) 181–182.

103. Ibid., 182.

104. Anthony Wright, *Citizens and Subjects* (Routledge 1994) 59–60.

105. Singh (N102) 183.

of competing for power on equal-footing. For example, even if minorities retain the ability to vote, a statute preventing those with minority opinions from campaigning politically would, in effect, deprive them of their ability to influence others and so change majority opinion.[106]

Even though it would, at least in theory, be possible for today's minorities to turn the tables and become tomorrow's majority by joining forces with others around a common programme, there is, sometimes, a systematic failure in the democratic process. There may be no conventional political party that has much interest in representing the interests of a particular group, especially those seeking to protect minorities. This is particularly troubling when these minorities have no voting rights. Under such circumstances, the ordinary give-and-take of the democratic process is unlikely to protect the rights of vulnerable or unpopular minorities.[107]

1.9 Parliamentary Sovereignty or Supremacy in the UK

The inevitability of a majority bias is also manifest in the structure of representative democratic institutions in the UK, whereby the perspectives of minorities who possess limited social capital or political power are often neglected in favour of the views of popular majorities or more powerful interest groups who exert greater influence over the electoral process.[108] The doctrine of parliamentary sovereignty or supremacy, as originally revealed in Bentham's work, states that law reflects the preferences of the majority of a society as developed through the medium of the democratically elected legislature.[109] Although the idea of law being reflective of the people through the medium of Parliament has long been related to democracy, the sovereignty of Parliament, in reality, refers to the sovereignty of the executive.[110] Therefore, the political party dominant in the legislature has access to unlimited power. This phenomenon is evident, for example, in the apartheid regime in South

106. David Bilchitz, *Poverty and Fundamental Rights: The Justification and Enforcement of Socio-Economic Rights* (OUP 2007) 104.

107. Singh (N102) 191.

108. O'Cinneide (N75) 72.

109. Davis (N11) 29.

110. Singh (N102) 195.

Africa.[111] As Lord Lester said, the concept of parliamentary sovereignty 'has come to mean, between general elections, the supremacy of the government in Parliament'.[112] This tallies with what Austin noted in 1997:

> The historical continuity of British government without a genuine revolution for nearly a millennium (since the Glorious Revolution of 1688 was merely the transfer of absolute legislative sovereignty from the King to another select group of powerful and wealthy men, already institutionalised as part of the existing constitutional structure, i.e. Parliament) has meant that the UK continues to have a top-down system of government, which the advent of popular democracy in the 19th century did not fundamentally change. Indeed, the creation of mass political parties which resulted from the extension of the franchise under the Reforms Acts 1829–1867, and the control exercised by the modern party leadership over the party MPs via its immense powers of patronage, the whip system and the payroll vote, have strengthened the executive's power over the legislature and transferred effective sovereignty over to the 'elective dictatorship' of the Prime Minister and Cabinet, creating an even more autocratic and politically top-down system.[113]

As the UK has never had a constitutional settlement under which its people delegate their sovereignty to the government to be exercised on behalf of the people and for no other purpose, British citizens are still regarded as 'subjects' of the monarchy, under which the latter grants protection against foreign attack and lawlessness in exchange for the former's loyalty and service.[114] In short, despite the success in wresting power from the Crown and vesting it in the legislature during the Glorious Revolution of 1688 and the subsequent passing of the Bill of Rights in 1689, Britain still operates utilising sovereignty of parliament rather than sovereignty of the people (i.e., a government of the people, by the people, and for the people).[115]

111. Mureinik (N80) 32.

112. Anthony Lester and Kate Beattie, 'Human Rights and the British Constitution' in Jowell and Oliver (N39) 72.

113. Austin (N25) 2.

114. Oliver (N61) 244.

115. Abraham Lincoln, President of the United States of America, The Gettysburg Address (19 November 1863), transcript available at: https://rmc.library.cornell.edu/gettysburg/good_cause/transcript.htm, last accessed 8 August 2019.

Although the concept of 'citizenship' had, in the years following World War II, come to include civil, political, and social rights, which together enabled each individual to take part in community life, the aspect of citizenship that most concerned the government from the 1950s to the 1980s tended to be productivity, whether as owners of, or workers in, industries.[116] During this period, the government itself was a regulator and, politically speaking, was open, and thus vulnerable, to pressures from these producer groups. Keith Middlemas invented the term 'corporate bias' to highlight the influence of powerful trade unions and businesses on the government.[117] This term is illustrated by the social contract entered into by the government, employers' organisations, and trade unions regarding the control of wages and inflation in the late 1970s. However, corporate influence was inconsistent with traditional representative democracy as it is now understood because it allowed the government to bypass Parliament and negotiate policies with businesses and the trade unions, thus prioritising the interests of producers (i.e., employers and employees) over those of other citizens and minorities, such as the disabled, involuntarily unemployed, etc.[118] Jeremy Richardson and A.G. Jordan referred to this as the development of a 'post-parliamentary democracy'.[119]

In 1978, Lord Hailsham wrote a book called *The Dilemma of Democracy*, describing the Westminster system as 'an elective dictatorship' and saying that 'we live under the authority of a rule [of parliamentary supremacy] absolute in theory if tolerable in practice'.[120] He further explained:

> In our lifetime the use of its powers has continuously increased, and the checks and balances have been rendered ineffective by the concentration of their effective operation more and more in the House of Commons, in the government side of the House of Commons, in the Cabinet within the government side, and to some extent in the Prime Minister within the Cabinet. The sovereignty of Parliament, absolute in theory, has become

116. T.H. Marshall and Tom Bottomore, *Citizenship and Social Class* (Pluto Classics 1992).

117. Keith Middlemas, *Politics in Industrial Society* (A Deutsch 1979).

118. Oliver (N61) 245.

119. Jeremy Richardson and A.G. Jordan, *Governing under Pressure: The Policy Process in a Post-Parliamentary Democracy* (Robertson 1979).

120. Quintin Hailsham, *The Dilemma of Democracy* (Collins 1978) 126.

> more and more the sovereignty of the House of Commons, and like all absolute rulers, having more and more to do, and in consequence less and less time within which to do it, is becoming more and more the tool of its professional advisers, more and more intolerant of criticism, and less and less in control of the detail of what is done in its name.[121]

In view of the potential arbitrary or unfair action taken by the administration, Sir John Laws also said the following:

> The dangers of democracy are, first, the possibility of Lord Hailsham's 'elective dictatorship' — the use of a democratic mandate to override minority rights or interests. Secondly, the use of discretionary power by Parliament's delegate may be too exuberant — may forget the constraints of the statute, or of reasonableness, for being too in love with a particular policy. Thirdly, the drive towards a policy end vouched by a democratic mandate may override the dictates of fair procedure.[122]

Furthermore, Allan Rosas also claimed that we all take it for granted that a decision taken by the political majority is absolutely legitimate or correct. However, this is not the case. It is only legitimate or correct if it is in line with the natural rights of a human being, as recognised in the Universal Declaration of Human Rights 1948 (UDHR 1948) and subsequent international instruments and national constitutions.[123] In connection to this, Abdullahi An-Náim challenged the assumption that the implementation of socio-economic and cultural rights should be confined to the realm of social policy and administrative processes of governments merely because these rights do not fit the model of judicial enforcement developed for specific civil and political rights. He claims that to leave these matters to the unfettered discretion of governments, however democratic they may be, without any judicial guidance and supervision,

121. Ibid.

122. John Laws, 'Wednesbury' in Christopher Forsyth and Ivan Hare, *The Golden Metwand and the Crooked Cord* (Clarendon Press 1998) 196.

123. Allan Rosas, 'Social Rights and the European Union' in Peter Van der Auweraert, Tom De Pelsmaeker, Jeremy Sarkin, and Johan Vande Lanotte (eds), *Social, Economic and Cultural Rights* (Maklu 2002) 149.

defeats the whole purpose of recognising socio-economic and cultural rights as international human rights.[124]

Although it is generally recognised that the overriding aim of the administration is to further public interest, and thus public discretionary power should be exercised in the interest of the public as a whole and not in the interest of an individual or group of individuals alone, this is not always the case. As mentioned in the Introduction of this volume, Madison put it best when he said that men may not always behave as angels.[125] Thus, unfettered discretion, even in the hands of the most compassionate administrator, tempts tyranny.[126] Even if administrators perform legitimate social functions without intending to unjustly enrich themselves or prejudice others, they may exercise powers that adversely affect the interests of individual citizens. This is because individual behaviour is largely controlled by role and situation, rather than personal characteristics and traits. This phenomenon has been documented in governments, social situations, and various psychological experiments, such as the Stanford Prison Experiment carried out in 1971.[127]

1.9.1 The Stanford Prison Experiment

The Stanford Prison Experiment is a classic study that shows how social settings influence human behaviour. Co-ordinated by Dr Philip Zimbardo, the test was intended to examine the psychology of prison life. In the study, normal healthy middle-class male college students (24 years old) were randomly divided into two groups (prisoners and prison guards) to act in a simulated prison setting. After just two days in 'jail', the inmates quickly became servile,

---

124. Abdullahi An-Náim, 'To Affirm the Full Human Rights Standing of Economic, Social and Cultural Rights' in Yash Ghai and Jill Cottrell (eds), *Economic, Social and Cultural Rights in Practice: The Role of Judges in Implementing Economic, Social and Cultural Rights* (Interights 2004) 7.

125. Singh (N102) 199.

126. Jeffrey Jowell, 'Administrative Law' in Vernon Bogdanor (ed), *The British Constitution in the Twentieth Century* (OUP 2003) 373.

127. Andrew Crane and Dirk Matten, *Business Ethics: Managing Corporate Citizenship and Sustainability in the Age of Globalisation* (3rd edn, OUP 2010) 174–175. For full account of the Standard Prison Experiment, see Philip Zimbardo, *The Lucifer Effect: Understanding How Good People Turn Evil* (Random House 2007).

dependent, helpless, and depressed, thinking only of their own survival and their hatred of the guards. Each day, the guards tormented the prisoners with more commands, insults, and demeaning tasks. The prisoners also grew restless and defiant. When they staged a disturbance, the guards unmercifully suppressed the rebellion. The guards clamped down with increasing brutality. In a surprisingly short time, the fake convicts acted like real prisoners — dejected, traumatised, and de-humanised. Indeed, after only 36 hours, one prisoner had to be released following fits of rage, uncontrollable crying, and depression, whereas the rest of the inmates were released the following day, suffering from similar symptoms. Although the study was designed to last two weeks, it was abruptly stopped after only six days.

What happened? Apparently, the assigned social roles were so powerful that in just a few days the experiment became reality for those involved. After the experiment, it was difficult for many of the guards to believe their own behaviour. As one recalled: 'I was surprised at myself. I made them call one another names and clean toilets out with their bare hands. I practically considered them prisoners cattle'.[128] The study showed that despite being randomly allocated to their roles, all the participants rapidly adopted the thinking and behaviours associated with their assigned roles, and the arbitrary rules of their new environment were accepted as legitimate. Thus, the experiment supports the theory that individual behaviour is largely controlled by role and situation rather than personal characteristics and traits and that people easily (and quickly) adopt the roles they are assigned. As Dr Zimbardo said of the guards: 'These guys were all peaceniks. They became like Nazis'.[129] This tallies with what Lord Acton suggested, that 'power tends to corrupt; absolute power corrupts absolutely'.[130] Similarly, Baron de Montesquieu warned that 'constant experience shows us that every man invested with power is apt to

128. Dennis Coon and John Mitterer, *Introduction to Psychology: Gateways to Mind and Behavior* (13th edn, Wadsworth 2013) 548.

129. David Buchanan and Andrzej Huczynski, *Organizational Behavior* (Prentice Hall 1997) 380–381.

130. John Acton, *Essays on Freedom and Power* (The Beacon Press 1949) 364, republishing Lord Acton, 'Letter to Bishop Mandell Creighton' (3 April 1887).

abuse it, and to carry his authority as far as it will go'.[131] To prevent this abuse, it is necessary for those in power to be checked.[132] All these assertions are consistent with the long-established belief of Niccolò Machiavelli that the inner life of man is not a sphere of repose, harmony, or self-control but one of continual motion. Thus, man is ruled not by reason but by appetite and ambition, and these characteristics, which provide the source of action, lead to competition and conflict.[133] Machiavelli also argued that 'since the scarcity of objects is the result of the nature of appetite and passion, and not the other way around, competition and conflict between men are natural and inevitable'.[134] Indeed, politics is concerned with the pursuit of power and rejects the classical view that it should be understood simply as maintaining the good community.[135] Taken together, these beliefs suggest that man is a political animal precisely because people are required to engage with one another as a means to obtain their own satisfaction. Because people strive not only to achieve material success but also to attain fame and glory — qualities which require some degree of public acknowledgement — politics must be conceived to be a natural condition.[136]

1.9.2 The Milgram Experiment

The fact that individual behaviour of those in power is likely controlled by role and situation, rather than personal characteristics and traits, is made worse because of their subordinates' obedience to authority, as shown in the Milgram Experiment, another psychological experiment carried out in the early 1960s. Such subordinates' obedience, fuelled by their lack of social capital to resist orders (owing to their being dependent upon the remunerations given by

131. Baron de Montesquieu, *The Spirit of the Law* (Hafner 1949) 150; Jamie Grierson, 'Hundreds of police in England and Wales accused of sexual abuse' *The Guardian* (8 December 2016), available at: www.theguardian.com/uk-news/2016/dec/08/hundreds-police-officers-accused-sex-abuse-inquiry-finds, last accessed 27 December 2016.

132. Ibid., Montesquieu.

133. Martin Fleisher, 'A Passion for Politics: The Vital Core of the World of Machiavelli' in Martin Fleisher (ed), *Machiavelli and the Nature of Political Thought* (Atheneum 1972) 114.

134. Ibid.

135. Ibid., 130.

136. Martin Loughlin, 'Constitutional Law: The Third Order of the Political' in Bamforth and Leyland (N91) 36.

the authorities or by the incentive of getting promoted if loyal, or simply to curry favour with their bosses), has tremendous adverse effects on the rule of law, as manifested locally in the disproportionate responses of the Hong Kong police towards some of the unarmed protesters during events in early June 2019 and continuing now.

The Milgram experiment was a social psychology experiment conducted by Yale University psychologist Stanley Milgram. It measured the willingness of study participants from different walks of life to obey an authority figure who instructed them to perform acts conflicting with their personal conscience. The experiment assumed that the essence of obedience to authority is that the person comes to view themselves as the instrument of carrying out another's wishes and, therefore, no longer regards themselves as being responsible for their actions. The experiment began in July 1961, three months after the start of the trial of the German Nazi war criminal Adolf Eichmann in Jerusalem. Milgram devised his psychological study to answer popular questions at that time: Could it be that Eichmann and his million accomplices in the Holocaust were just following orders? Or are they fully accountable for their own actions?

In this experiment, participants were told that the trial was being conducted to study the effects of punishment on learning ability. Although the participants thought that they had an equal chance of playing the role of a student or of a teacher, the process was rigged — all of them ended up playing the role of teacher. The student was, in fact, an actor working as an associate of the experimenter. Being the teacher, each participant was asked to administer increasingly severe electric shocks to the student when the latter gave a wrong answer. Shock levels ranged from 15 to 450 volts, but in reality, no shocks were given. In response to the supposed jolts, the actor playing the student would pretend to grumble at 75 volts, complain at 120 volts, ask to be released at 150 volts, and let out agonised screams at 285 volts. Eventually, the student would, in pretend desperation, yell loudly and complain of heart pains.

If, at any point, the teacher hesitated to inflict the shocks, the experimenter would pressure them to proceed. Such demands would take the form of increasingly severe commands, ranging from 'The experiment requires that you continue' to 'You have no other choice, you must go on'. Despite this urging from the experimenter, some teachers refused to continue with the shocks. This is the response Milgram expected would be the norm. However, Milgram was surprised to find that only a minority of participants challenged the commands given by the authority figure and that 65 percent of participants were willing to progress to the maximum voltage level.

During the experiment, the participants demonstrated a range of negative emotions about continuing. Some requested and then pleaded with the student to answer questions carefully, while others started laughing and acting strangely. Some participants even appeared cold, hopeless, sombre, or arrogant. Some thought that they had killed the student without mercy. Regardless of their behaviour and, for some, their obvious discomfort, the majority of the participants continued to obey the commands and discharged the full shock to the student.

Milgram summarised the experiment by saying that ordinary people, simply doing their job and without any particular hostility on their part, can become agents in a terrible or destructive process. Moreover, even when the destructive effects of their work become patently clear and they are asked to carry out actions incompatible with their fundamental standards of morality, relatively few people have the resources needed to resist authority. In this climate, obedience to authority, despite being long praised as a virtue, now takes on a new aspect when it serves a malevolent cause. Far from appearing as a virtue, it is transformed into a heinous sin.[137]

1.10 The Need to Control Administrative Discretion

Human nature being what it is, there is always a risk that government may exceed the limits of its powers, betray the trust of the people, or be incompetent.[138] Those in authority may exercise their power in arbitrary, abusive, unwise, or corrupt ways. It is, therefore, necessary for the people to be able to hold the government and its officials accountable as it arbitrates governmental responsiveness to

137. See, generally, Stanley Milgram, *Obedience to Authority: An Experimental View* (Perennial Classics 2004).

138. Elliott and Thomas (N45) 38.

what the people want. Public-mediated accountability also ensures that the government is efficient and effective in addition to preventing abuses of power and incompetence. Therefore, an effective system of accountability is an essential adjunct of a healthy democracy.

The need to control the administrative state is premised on a classic libertarian mistrust of government.[139] Global experience has repeatedly shown that threats to individuals mostly come from states.[140] The most authoritative statement on this point was made by Madison in *The Federalist Papers*:

> Ambition must be made to counteract ambition. The interest of the man must be connected with the constitutional rights of the place. It may be a reflection on human nature that such devices should be necessary to control the abuses of government. But what is government itself but the greatest of all reflections on human nature. If men were angels, no government would be necessary. If angels were to govern men, neither would be necessary. In framing a government which is to be administered by men over men, the greatest difficulty lies in this: you must first enable the government to control the governed; and in the next place oblige it to control itself.[141]

The result of this thinking is that constitutional order presupposes that officials may abuse their power and thus provides stipulations to prevent them from doing so for very long before sufficient checks are conducted.[142] The practical reason why abuses by officials are likely to be more dangerous than private individuals is premised on the fact that power, especially coercive power, of a public person is frequently greater. As Algernon Sidney once put it, 'the fury of an unlimited prince would drive whole nations into ruin'.[143]

139. David Hume, *Essays: Moral, Political and Literary (1752)* (Liberty Classics 1987) 38; James Mill, *Essay on Government (1820)* (Library of Liberal Arts 1955) 54; Clinton Rossitor (ed), *The Federalist Papers* (Mentor Books 1961) 37.

140. Andrew Le Sueur, Maurice Sunkin, and Jo Eric Khushal Murkens, *Public Law* (OUP 2010) 194. In recent decades, however, threats to individuals mostly come from corporations; see Steven Ratner, 'Corporation and Human Rights: A Theory of Legal Responsibility' (2001) 111 *YLJ* 443, available at: https://digitalcommons.law.yale.edu/ylj/vol111/iss3/1/, last accessed 13 March 2020.

141. Rossitor (N139) 37.

142. Clark and McCoy (N8) 21, citing Henry Bolingbroke, *A Dissertation on Parties (1735) in Works Vol. 2* (Frank Cass 1967).

143. Algernon Sidney, *Discourses Concerning Government (1698)* (Liberty Classics 1990) 390.

As states have demonstrated that they cannot be trusted to respect and protect human dignity of those under their jurisdiction, the United Nations has established a set of universal standards.[144] According to the Preamble of the UDHR 1948, these standards establish a common standard for all peoples and nations. To adhere to these standards, Andrew Le Sueur, Maurice Sunkin, and Jo Eric Khushal Murkens suggest that a system has to be devised that would prevent states from infringing rights and give individuals and groups ways of challenging their treatment.[145]

1.11 The Red Light (or Conservative Normativist) Theory

The presumption that officials may abuse their power agrees with the rationale of both the Red Light theory, advocated by Carol Harlow and Rawlings,[146] and Conservative Normativist Theory, backed by Martin Loughlin.[147] In general, red light theorists are motivated by their 'overt suspicion of the "vast empires of executive power", coupled with the expectation that government will "run amok"'.[148] There is also a concern that executives are capable of arbitrary infringements of an individual's rights. In view of these suspicions, emphasis has been placed on the need to control executive power. Notably, this control has to be external to the executive to be effective and is typically exerted by the court system and legislature in a balanced government. As Harlow and Rawlings observed, 'central to red light theory ... is the idea of the rule of law. Closely linked is the view that law courts are the primary weapon for protection of the citizen and control of the executive'.[149]

144. An-Náim (N124) 8.

145. Le Sueur, Sunkin, and Khushal Murkens (N140) 194.

146. Carol Harlow and Richard Rawlings, *Law and Administration* (3rd edn, CUP 2009) Ch. 1.

147. Nicholas Bamforth illustrates that when Harlow and Rawlings talk of red light, green light, and amber light theories, Loughlin talks of conservative normativist, functionalist, and liberal normativist theories, adding that the two characterisations are essentially the same; see Nicholas Bamforth, 'Courts in a Multi-Layered Constitution' in Bamforth and Leyland (N91) 302.

148. Harlow and Rawlings (N146) 23.

149. Ibid., 25.

Comments from both H.W.R. Wade and Christopher Forsyth highlight that the red light theory has a 'preference for a minimalist state' in which 'the primary function of administrative law should be to control any excess of state power and subject it to legal, and more specifically judicial, control'.[150] In this context, the definition of administrative law is the law relating to the control of government power.[151] Thus, the primary purpose of administrative law is to keep the powers of the government within their legal bounds to protect citizens against abuse. It is important to note that 'abuse' carries no necessary innuendo of malice or bad faith. Government departments may misunderstand their legal position as easily as other people may, and the laws they have to administer are frequently complex and uncertain. Unintentional abuse is therefore inevitable, and it is necessary for the law to provide a means to check it.[152] This is supported by a statement from Lord Denning:

> No one can suppose that the executive will never be guilty of the sins that are common to all of us. ... But if and when wrongs are thereby suffered by any of us what is the remedy? Our procedure for securing our personal freedom is efficient, our procedure for preventing the abuse of power is not. Just as the pick and shovel is no longer suitable for the winning of coal, so also the procedure of *mandamus*, *certiorari*, and actions on the case are not suitable for the winning of freedom in the new age. They must be replaced by up to date machinery. ... Of all the great tasks [for courts] that lie ahead this is the greatest. Properly exercised the new powers of the executive lead to the welfare state; but abused they lead to a totalitarian state.[153]

In addition to power, there is also duty. Indeed, administrative law is also concerned with compelling public authorities to perform their duties even following a fault. The law provides compulsory remedies for such situations, thus dealing with the negative as well as the positive side

150. Wade and Forsyth (N7) 5.

151. Ibid., 5–6.

152. Ibid., 5.

153. Alfred Denning, *Freedom under the Law* (Stevens & Sons 1949) 126.

of maladministration.[154] Adam Tomkins, a conservative normativist, has characterised red-light theorists as believing:

> (1) that law is autonomous to and superior over politics; (2) that the administrative state is something which needs to be kept in check by the law; (3) that the preferred way of doing this is through rule-based adjudication in courts; and (4) that the goal of this project should be to enhance individual liberty ... and [the] idea of liberty which is best realized by having [a] small government.[155]

1.12 'Fused' and 'Quasi-Fused' Governments

Supervision of the executive has traditionally been in the hands of the legislature — Parliament in the UK and the Legislative Council (LegCo) in Hong Kong — and has become increasingly complicated as individuals are more exposed to the growing governmental regulations affecting them.[156] In the UK's Westminster parliamentary system, there has long been concern that this legislative supervision is ineffective owing to the political bond between the government of the day and the majority in Parliament [157] (considered a fused government). Moreover, the conduct of some MPs in Britain was called into question during the 1990s and, again, in 2009.[158] Parliament in the UK has also become increasingly dominated by organised political parties,[159] whereas the LegCo in Hong Kong is largely controlled by pro-Beijing members,[160] the vast majority of which are returned by functional

154. Wade and Forsyth (N7) 5.

155. Adam Tomkins, 'In Defence of the Political Constitution' (2002) 22 *OJLS* 157, 158.

156. Mark Elliott, *The Constitutional Foundations of Judicial Review* (Hart Publishing 2001) 1.

157. Matthew Flinders, *Politics of Accountability in the Modern State* (Ashgate 2001) 54–71.

158. *R v Chaytor* [2010] UKSC 52. See also Leyland (N32) 122–126.

159. Elliott (N156) 1.

160. Tony Cheung, 'LegCo chair monopoly: Hong Kong's pro-establishment camp snaps up key posts on Legislative Council committees' *South China Morning Post* (10 October 2015), available at: www.scmp.com/news/hong-kong/politics/article/1865946/hong-kongs-pro-establishment-camp-snaps-key-posts, last accessed 17 October 2015.

constituencies [161] (considered a quasi-fused government). More damagingly, under the spilt vote system, any bills, amendments, or motion debates sponsored by individual members can only be passed by a majority of each of the two constituencies in the LegCo as opposed to a simple majority of the whole house for government-sponsored bills. This further diminishes the influence of the members directly elected from geographical constituencies.[162] As Johannes Chan commented, 'Hong Kong has a strange political system. Those who are in power have no popular mandate, and those who have popular mandate have no power'.[163] All of these attributes have significantly undermined their capacity to provide an adequate check-and-balance on the executive. As Ho Hei-wah, the Director of the Society for Community Organisation, said, 'after July 1997, they found it more difficult to advance their causes in the political arena. The legislature was weakened and failed to effectively check and balance the government'.[164] In *R v Secretary of State for the Home Department, ex parte Fire Brigades Union Fire Brigades Union,*[165] Lord Mustill expressed the following concern:

> [The accountability of government by Parliament has] on occasion been perceived as falling short, and sometimes well short, of what was needed to bring the performance of the executive into line with the law, and with

161. Functional constituency is a unique feature in Hong Kong, under which a member of the functional constituency is entitled to vote for the return of a member to the LegCo. It creates an elitist group whose members enjoy a vote in addition to the vote in a geographical constituency. This system has long been criticised for being discriminatory. The Human Rights Committee has concluded in its Concluding Observations on the Fourth Periodic Report of the United Kingdom on Hong Kong that functional constituency elections were incompatible with Art. 25 of the ICCPR: 'The Committee considers that the electoral system in Hong Kong does not meet the requirements of Art 25, as well as Arts 2, 3 and 26 of the Covenant. It underscores in particular that only 20 of 60 seats in the LegCo are subject to direct popular election and that the concept of functional constituencies, which gives undue weight to the views of the business community, discriminates among voters on the basis of property and functions. This clearly constitutes a violation of Art 2, para 1, 25(b) and 26'; see Johannes Chan, 'Administrative Law, Politics and Governance: The Hong Kong Experience' in Tom Ginsburg and Albert Chen (eds), *Administrative Law and Governance in Asia* (Routledge 2009) 159, 173.

162. Johannes Chan, 'Hong Kong's Umbrella Movement' (2014) 103(6) *The Round Table: The Commonwealth J of Int'l Aff.* 571, 572, available at: www.tandfonline.com/eprint/VuA9DJBgi6TNPWXcX3QF/full, last accessed 20 July 2016.

163. Ibid.

164. Ho was interviewed by Tam Wai Keung on 16 September 2008, and this interview was subsequently cited by Wai Keung Tam, *Legal Mobilization under Authoritarianism: The Case of Post-Colonial Hong Kong* (CUP 2013) 153.

165. [1995] 2 WLR 464.

> the minimum standards of fairness. [As a way] to avoid a vacuum in which the citizen would be left without protection against a misuse of excessive powers the courts have had no option but to occupy the dead ground [left by Parliament] in a manner, and in areas of public life, which could not have been foreseen 30 years ago.[166]

Even Lord Irvine, who is highly sceptical of how far judicial review may legitimately be used as a democratising medium, also valued the growth of domestic judicial review:

> Let me begin with a recognition that the consequence of the 'democratic deficit', the want of parliamentary control of the executive in recent years, have been, to an important degree, mitigated by the rigours of judicial review. I pay tribute to the high quality of judicial review in this country. It has so often rightly held the executive to account and improved the quality of administrative decision-making.[167]

This sentiment was supported by Li CJ (as he then was) in the Ceremonial Openings of the Legal Year in 2007 when he said:

> The availability and use of judicial review has had a significant impact on the conduct of the business of government and has exercised a considerable influence on public debate on many issues. It would not be right for judicial review to be viewed negatively as a hindrance to government. On the contrary, it would be seen as providing an essential foundation for good governance under the rule of law.[168]

Sir John Laws once described Parliament as 'too weak to vindicate to the just satisfaction of the citizen its historic power to control the Executive in the name of the people',[169] a statement echoed by Sir Stephen Sedley who said

166. Ibid., 488B–C.

167. Derry Irvine, 'Judges and Decision-Makers: The Theory and Practice of *Wednesbury* Review' (1996) *PL* 59.

168. Andrew Kwok-nang Li, Chief Justice of the Hong Kong Court of Final Appeal, 'Speech at Ceremonial Opening of the Legal Year 2007' (8 January 2007), available at: www.info.gov.hk/gia/general/200701/08/P200701080120.htm, last accessed 9 October 2016.

169. John Laws, 'Judicial Remedies and the Constitution' (1994) 57 *MLR* 223.

that 'Parliament has no way and no hope of supervising, through ministerial accountability, the myriad activities which in increasing volume it delegates to the executive'.[170] Thus, the need for judicial review, particularly in fused and quasi-fused governments, is essential.

1.13 A Compensatory Role for the Judiciary to Correct Legislative Oversight

There have been indications that the courts do take on a compensatory role by acting as an alternative for failing legislative oversight.[171] It is the courts that have sought to remedy the deficit in accountability by requiring, via judicial review, that the administrative authorities exercise their power fairly, reasonably, and consistently with the scheme prescribed by Parliament in the enabling legislations. Indeed, the courts have articulated the grounds of administrative law, highlighting the importance of legality, fairness (be it substantial or procedural), reasonableness, and rationality.[172] Recently, it has become evident that the circumstances in which the courts will review the exercise of administrative functions have significantly increased.[173] In the UK, the number of judicial review applications, both civil (including immigration and asylum) and criminal, has dramatically increased from 4,238 cases in 2000 to 15,594 cases in 2013.[174] In Hong Kong, this number has increased steadily from 137 cases (including right of abode claims) in 2003 to 182 cases in 2013.[175]

170. Stephen Sedley, 'Governments, Constitutions and Judges' in Genevra Richardson and Hazel Genn (eds), *Administrative Law and Government Action* (Clarendon Press 1994) 42.

171. Flinders (N157) 54–71.

172. Jowell (N58) 13.

173. Hilary Delany, *Judicial Review of Administrative Action* (2nd edn, Thomson Reuters 2009) 1.

174. The Ministry of Justice of the UK, 'Civil Justice Statistics Quarterly, England and Wales (Incorporating Privacy Injunction Statistics January to June 2015)' (3 September 2015) 15–16, available at: www.gov.uk/government/uploads/system/uploads/attachment_data/file/457979/civil-justice-statistics-april-june-2015.pdf, last accessed 21 July 2016.

175. The Secretary for Justice, *Press Releases* (a written reply by the Secretary for Justice in the Legislative Council concerning 'Statistics provided by the Judiciary on applications for leave to apply for judicial review for the period from 1997 to 2013', as set out in Annex A), available at: www.info.gov.hk/gia/general/201404/09/P201404080747.htm, last accessed 9 August 2019. The statistics that are referenced in the press release are available at: http://gia.info.gov.hk/general/201404/09/P201404080747_0747_126907.pdf, last accessed 21 July 2016.

During the past three decades, there have been increasing challenges lodged by individuals and groups impugning the extent to which governments and public authorities can be held accountable by the judicial branch for delay or failure to provide access to welfare services, such as health treatment, education, and housing.[176] There have also been discussions about the potential for the courts to make effective and constitutionally appropriate contributions to the resolution of such disputes,[177] as judicially agreed by Lord Bridge, who advocated the concept of dual, or divided, sovereignty (i.e., Parliament and the judiciary) in both *R (on the application of Jackson) v Attorney-General* [178] and *X Ltd v Morgan-Gampian (Publishers) Ltd.*[179] In the latter, he stated:

> [T]he maintenance of the rule of law is in every way as important in a free society as the democratic franchise. In our society the rule of law rests upon twin foundations: the sovereignty of the Queen in Parliament in making the law and the sovereignty of the Queen's courts in interpreting and applying the law.[180]

Sir Stephen Sedley concurred with this view and wrote of 'a new and still emerging constitutional paradigm, ... of a bi-polar sovereignty of the Crown in Parliament and the Crown in its courts, to each of which the Crown's ministers are answerable — politically to Parliament, legally to the courts'.[181] Such assertions also agrees with the *ratio decidendi*, as held by Lord Coke CJ in *Dr Bonham*'s case [182] in 1610:

> [I]n many cases the Common Law will control Acts of Parliament and sometimes adjudge them to be utterly void: for when an Act of Parliament

176. Fons Coomans (ed), *Justiciability of Socio-Economic Rights* (Intersentia 2006); Palmer (N92) Ch. 2.

177. David Beatty, 'The Last Generation: When Rights Lose their Meaning' in David Beatty (ed), *Human Rights and Judicial Review* (Kluwer 1994) 321–361; Asbjørn Eide, 'Economic Social and Cultural Rights as Human Rights' in Asbjørn Eide, Catarina Krause, and Allan Rosas (eds), *Economic Social and Cultural Rights* (2nd edn, Kluwer 2001) 9–28.

178. [2005] UKHL 56; [2006] 1 AC 262, [102].

179. [1990] 2 All ER 1, [1990] 1 All ER 616, [1991] 1 AC 1 (CA).

180. Ibid., 48E.

181. Stephen Sedley, 'Human Rights: A Twenty-First Century Agenda' (1995) *PL* 386, 389.

182. (1610) 8 Co Rep 114 (Court of Common Pleas, England), cited by Wen-Chen Chang, Li-ann Thio, Kevin Y.L. Tan, and Jiunn-rong Yeh, *Constitutionalism in Asia* (Hart Publishing 2014) 311.

> is against common right and reason, or repugnant, or impossible to be performed, the Common Law will control it and adjudge such Act to be void.[183]

F.A. Mann also felt that he had been compelled to concede with this position, citing Blackstone's comment, with examples:

> Acts of Parliament that are impossible to be performed are of no validity; and if there arise out of them collaterally any absurd consequences, manifestly contradictory to common reason, they are, with regard to those collateral consequences, void ... Suppose Parliament enacts a statute depriving Jews of their British nationality, [prohibiting] marriages between Christians and non-Christians, [and] marriages between blacks and whites or vesting the property of all red haired women in the state. Is it really suggested that English judges would have to apply such a law? ... Would the hypothetical question really have to be answered in the affirmative, while a similar German statute was condemned by four Law Lords as constituting 'so grave an infringement of human rights that the courts of this country ought to refuse to recognise it as a law at all?'.[184]

As Lord Steyn argued, while parliamentary sovereignty may well continue to be the 'general principle of our [British] constitution', unchecked executive power does not hold such sway.[185] His Lordship further asserted that the constitution is not uncontrolled, as a Diceyan reading of parliamentary supremacy might claim, and that sovereign power is now effectively divided among the Westminster Parliament, the devolved administration,[186] and the courts.[187] As Lady Hale, President of the Supreme Court (as she then was), noted: 'The [UK] has become a federal state with a Constitution regulating the relationship between the federal

183. Ibid.

184. Harry Woolf, 'Droit Public — English Style' in Christopher Campell-Holt (ed), *The Pursuit of Justice* (OUP 2008) 82–83, citing F.A. Mann, *3rd Blackstone Lecture* (1978) 91, citing *Oppenheimer v Cattermole* [1976] AC 249, 278.

185. Johan Steyn, 'The Weakest and Least Dangerous Department of Government' (1997) *PL* 84, 87.

186. Northern Ireland Act 1998, Government of Wales Act 2006 (replacing Government of Wales Act 1998) and Scotland Act 1998. See also Brice Dickson, 'Devolution' and Ian Leigh, 'The Changing Nature of the Local State' both in Jowell, Oliver, and O'Cinneide (N75) Chs. 9 and 10; Robert Hazell and Richard Rawlings (eds), *Devolution, Law Making and the Constitution* (Academic Imprint 2005).

187. *R (Jackson) v AG* (N178) [102].

centre and the component parts'.[188] Consequently, any attempt by Parliament to render specific exercises of governmental power non-justiciable [189] may be rejected by the judges as follows:

> In exceptional circumstances involving an attempt to abolish judicial review or the ordinary role of the courts, the Appellate Committee of the House of Lords or a new Supreme Court may have to consider whether this is a constitutional fundamental which even a sovereign Parliament acting at the behest of a complaisant House of Commons cannot abolish.[190]

Moreover, Lady Hale further speculates that the courts' jurisdiction may be expressly limited where human rights are at stake. Although she recognises that 'in general ... the constraints upon what Parliament can do are political and diplomatic rather than constitutional', she also notes that 'the courts will treat with particular suspicion (and might even reject) any attempt to subvert the rule of law by removing governmental action affecting the rights of the individual from judicial scrutiny'.[191] As Jowell observed in 2004:

> [I]t is no longer self-evident, therefore, that our courts would inevitably concede parliament's right to ride roughshod over fundamental rights and ... constitutional principles. And the issue that is most likely to provoke the courts finally to question parliament's paramount rule if an attack on the courts' own constitutional duty [is] to hear out people claiming injustice.[192]

As a result, the courts have been much more confident and have demonstrated their willingness to scrutinise executive action in the absence of effective legislative oversight.[193] Since World War II, the courts have introduced more rigorous standards to review administrative action. As most constitutional and

188. Ibid.

189. The same applies to Hong Kong. See, for example, *A Solicitor v Law Society of Hong Kong (Secretary for Justice, intervener)* (2003) 6 HKCFAR 570 (CFA), [2004] 1 HKLRD 214.

190. *R (Jackson) v AG* (N178) [102].

191. Ibid., [159].

192. Jeffrey Jowell, 'Immigration Wars' *The Guardian* (2 March 2004), available at: www.theguardian.com/world/2004/mar/02/law.immigration, last accessed 9 August 2019.

193. Tom Zwart, 'Overseeing the Executive: Is the Legislature Reclaiming Lost Territory from the Courts?' in Susan Rose-Ackerman and Peter Lindseth (eds), *Comparative Administrative Law* (Edward Elgar 2010) 149.

human rights norms, be they civil and political rights or socio-economic rights, are not absolute and are subject to limitation, balancing, or regulation, the courts have, for the purpose of carrying out these obligations, developed principles to scrutinise the exercise of legislative and executive powers. Some of the typical tests or standards that have been developed include those that ask whether the powers are exercised in a way that is reasonable, rational, and proportionate.

The deferential tests traditionally applied by the courts to review the lawfulness of discretionary acts, as exemplified by *Wednesbury* unreasonableness [194] and *GCHQ* irrationality,[195] have gradually been replaced by grounds that subject administrative acts to a more probing review. The proportionality principle is one of them.[196] Proportionality has been described as a defining principle of limited government and a key requirement of good governance [197] because it requires that a fair balance be found between individual and collective interests.[198] It also underlies the familiar evaluative mechanisms with which the courts adjudicate claims that a state actor has exceeded its power. When the courts require that a coercive or intrusive state action be narrowly tailored to serve a compelling state interest, they enforce this principle to ensure that state power is proportional to the interests that justify its power.[199]

Proportionality is a more structured and intensive approach to scrutinise administrative decisions and their implementations than the traditional *Wednesbury* or *GCHQ* formula currently in force in Britain and in Hong Kong. It has also been applied in respect to EU law via the European Communities Act 1972 (ECA 1972) (as at 31 January 2020, the day of Brexit) as well as the European Convention on Human Rights (ECHR) via the HRA 1998. Further, proportionality has also been applied in the International Covenant on Civil and Political Rights (ICCPR) via the Bill of Rights Ordinance (BORO), coupled with some provisions of the International Covenant on Economic, Social, and

194. *Associated Provincial Picture Houses Ltd v Wednesbury Corporation* [1947] 2 All ER, [1948] 1 KB 223 (CA).

195. *Council of Civil Service Unions v Minister for the Civil Service* [1983] UKHL 9, [1985] 1 AC 374.

196. Zwart (N193) 151.

197. Alice Ristroph, 'Proportionality as a Principle of Limited Government' (2005) 55 *DLJ* 263, 287–288; Linda Senden, *Soft Law in European Community Law* (Hart Publishing 2006) 86.

198. Mark Janis, Richard Kay, and Anthony Bradley, *European Human Rights Law* (3rd edn, OUP 2008) 520.

199. Ristroph (N197) 293.

Cultural Rights (ICESCR). It has also been applied via constitutional review adjudications empowered by the Basic Law in Hong Kong.

As consistency of law is one of the elements under the rule of law that is, if being fulfilled, capable of guiding human behaviour,[200] there is no justification that it should not be applied to other types of judicial review cases under a presumption that the legislature, be it Parliament in Britain or the LegCo in Hong Kong, confers power to the executive on the basis that the exercise of it should not exceed what is necessary for the achievement of the statutory objectives.[201] The more important the statutory objectives are, the graver the restrictions on the exercise of discretionary power should be.[202] In the UK, it has been argued that if the courts insist upon the strict division of legal tests between challenges based on EU law and human rights law as well as those based on domestic law, then an apparent difference in the legal protection for the individual is created, which is difficult to justify.[203] Thus, in response to the rise of the administrative state, as well as the resulting increase in administrative activities and discretionary powers, proportionality should be fully recognised as a new ground of judicial review in both the UK and Hong Kong. The principle could serve as a check-and-balance rule to save individual citizens or minorities from being exploited by the majoritarian government.

1.14 Concluding Remarks

In view of the growth of administrative activities and discretionary power, traditional political control of governmental power proves to be unsatisfactory, and the courts have had to take on a compensatory role by acting as a substitute for this failing legislative oversight to, via judicial review, hold the executive accountable. Against this background, many regard the control of executive

200. Wesley-Smith (N8) 15.

201. Tom Bingham, *The Rule of Law* (Penguin 2010) 60–65.

202. Ibid., 65.

203. *R v Secretary of State for the Home Department, ex p McQuillan* [1995] 4 All ER 400, 422h (Sedley J); Gordon Slynn, 'European Law and the National Judge' in *Butterworths Lectures 1991–1992* (Butterworths 1993) 27–28; Robert Thomas, 'Continental Principles in English Public Law' in Andrew Harding and Esin Örücü (eds), *Comparative Law in the 21st Century* (Kluwer 2002) 131.

discretionary power by the courts as an example of a participatory democracy that emphasises accountability and justification.

As accountability for the way public power is exercised is fundamental to the notion of representative democracy, it is only by knowing what the government is doing, and on what basis, that the electorate can seek to influence the development and application of policy and, when an election comes, be in a position to make an informed judgment as to its performance. Accountability is also an essential element of safeguarding against the abuse and misuse of power since administrative autonomy and executive taciturnity provide fertile conditions for the growth of arbitrary and unconstrained government. The more transparent the decision-making process and the greater the opportunity to hold the executive answerable for their actions, the easier it is to ensure that they are performing their duties with propriety and in the public interest.[204] Thus, it is high time for those in executive positions to change their mind-set from the 'culture of authority' to the 'culture of justification'.

204. Mike Radford, 'Mitigating the Democratic Deficit? Judicial Review and Ministerial Accountability' in Leyland and Woods (N25) 35–36.

2

Proportionality and Margin of Appreciation

2.1 Introduction

The principle of proportionality concerns the relationship between the ends of public action and the means used to attain them. According to Bernhard Schlink, if you pursue an end, you must use a means that is helpful, necessary, and appropriate. A means that does not help reach the end is not a real means, and thus to use it would be out of proportion. It is also out of proportion to use a means that does more than necessary — for instance, a means that is more expensive than necessary. Equally, it is out of proportion to use a means that is inappropriate because, despite it being necessary, by using it, you do more harm than the end is worth.[1] Thus, enough is enough, and more is too much. More than enough is out of proportion, more than necessary is out of proportion, and more than appropriate is out of proportion. So 'don't do more', argues Schlink.[2]

With this understanding, the proportionality principle demands that laws, actions, and measures of public bodies should not go beyond those that are strictly required to achieve their legal purposes. Its rationale is based on the concept of basic rights and individual freedoms so that if individual rights are to be taken seriously, then the state may only impose restrictions that are justified by a legitimate purpose and are necessary.[3]

1. Bernhard Schlink, 'Proportionality in Constitutional Law: Why Everywhere But Here?' (2012) 22 *DJCIL* 292.

2. Ibid.

3. Nigel Foster and Satish Sule, *German Legal System and Laws* (4th edn, OUP 2010) 184–185.

The notion of proportionality has been applied at the international, regional, and national levels. To understand this application, it is necessary to be versed in the present day concept itself as well as its origin and methodologies. Parallel to the proportionality principle are the margin of appreciation doctrine granted to Member States by the ECtHR and CJEU when judicially reviewing their decisions and the notions of deference and discretionary area of judgment that domestic courts of the Member States must give to administrative decision-makers and the legislature when judicially reviewing their policies and choices.

2.2 The Concept of Proportionality

At its most basic level, proportionality requires a subjective weighing of two fixed values.[4] The Oxford English Dictionary echoes the way in which fixed standards are part of proportionality by defining proportion as the 'relation between one thing and another in terms of size, quantity, number, or the like; comparative relation, ratio.' It also frames 'proportion' in a more useful, though subjective, manner: the appropriate, fitting, or pleasing relation (of size, etc.) between things or parts of a thing; the due relation of one part to another; balance, symmetry, and harmony. In the sphere of law, as highlighted in *Black's Law Dictionary*, the term 'proportionate' means 'adjusted to something else according to a certain rate of comparative relation'. In short, proportionality requires that a decision-maker reach two or more evaluative judgments and assess those judgments against each other.

The definitions above, particularly the last, indicate that proportionality is not an alien concept in the legal field. It is found in most legal systems at both the international [5] and local levels.[6] It has been received into the constitutional doctrine of the courts in, *inter alia*, Continental Europe, Canada, New Zealand, Israel, and South Africa as well as the jurisprudence of multiple human rights treaties, such as the European Convention on Human Rights (ECHR), the International Covenant on Civil and Political Rights (ICCPR), and the American

4. Michael Newton and Larry May, *Proportionality in International Law* (OUP 2014) 16.
5. Jost Delbrück, 'Proportionality' in Rudolf Bernhardt, *Encyclopedia of Public International Law* (North-Holland 1984) Vol. 7, 396.
6. Jeffrey Jowell and Anthony Lester, 'Beyond *Wednesbury*: Substantive Principles of Administrative Laws' (1987) *PL* 368; Sophie Boyron, 'Proportionality in English Administrative Law: A Faulty Translation?' (1992) 12 *OJLS* 237.

Convention on Human Rights. There is also consensus that the proportionality test plays an indispensable role in constitutional rights reasoning.[7] The same term also occurs in criminal sentencing decisions and other law enforcement scenarios, election disputes, regulation of international financial markets, and in decisions to wage war and how to do so lawfully.[8]

2.2.1 International Level

2.2.1.1 Military (Armed) Conflicts

At the international level, proportionality, coupled with distinction, necessity, and humanity, has been used to govern armed conflict decisions for hundreds of years.[9] It features prominently in the relations between states,[10] particularly in the assessment of reprisals, retaliatory measures, and non-performance of a treaty.[11] It is a key component of the traditional 'just war' theory, which stipulates that force may be used only after all viable peaceful alternatives have been tried and exhausted.[12] The 'just war' theory also requires that the anticipated benefits of waging a war must be proportionate to its expected evils or harms.[13] Therefore, proportionality in war or armed conflict often means that whatever the advantages of waging war are, they must not involve even greater burdens, especially on innocent parties.

Traditionally, the main burden to be weighed against military advantage is the loss of civilian life or property. The principle has also been expanded to include the aberrant effects of the death or disability of service members.[14] In both traditional and contemporary variations of war or armed conflicts, proportionality requires weighing what could be gained by military force in

7. Mattias Klatt and Moritz Meister, *The Constitutional Structure of Proportionality* (OUP 2012).

8. Newton and May (N4) 2.

9. Ibid., 1.

10. Judith Gardam, *Proportionality, Necessity and Force in International Law* (CUP 2004).

11. Jürgen Schwarze, *European Administrative Law* (Revised 1st edn, Sweet & Maxwell 2006) 703.

12. Michael Walzer, *Just and Unjust Wars* (Basic Books 1977); Nicholas Remgger, 'On the Just War Tradition in the Twenty-First Century' (2002) 78 *IA* 353.

13. Christopher Michaelsen, 'The Proportionality Principle, Counter-Terrorism Laws and Human Rights: A German-Australian Comparison' (2010) 2 *City U HK L Rev* 19, 26.

14. Newton and May (N4) Ch. 6.

advance of initiating war to ensure that it is greater than what could be lost. According to the Rome Statute of the International Criminal Court, which establishes four core international crimes (i.e., genocide, crimes against humanity, war crimes, and the crime of aggression), the war crime of a disproportionate strike is committed by

> intentionally launching an attack in the knowledge that such attack will cause incidental loss of life or injury to civilians or damage to civilian object or widespread, long-term and severe damage to the natural environment which would be clearly excessive in relation to the concrete and direct overall military advantage anticipated.[15]

In relation to this, Michael Newton and Larry May have suggested that the framework of proportionality for an armed force be divided into five categories:

(a) for war or armed conflict;
(b) for the special case of self-defence during war and in other contexts;
(c) for emergency situations, such as terrorist attacks, and for other hostile acts committed by non-state actors against states;
(d) for the pre-emption of hostilities and the accompanying erosion of human rights and safety; and
(e) for areas where states exercise a very high degree of control over their population, such as during occupation or relief operations in the wake of natural disasters.[16]

2.2.1.2 Self-Defence

Among the categories listed above, proportionality is a key requirement of lawful self-defence in contemporary international law.[17] When a state takes defensive measures against intrusions, particularly those that fall short of

15. Rome Statute of the International Criminal Court, Art 8(2)(iv), 1 July 2002, 2187 UNTS 90.
16. Newton and May (N4) 5.
17. Ibid., 2.

armed attack (such as border incidents or the penetration of aircraft into another state's sovereign territory), military measures should be based solely on the proportionality principle.[18] Indeed, self-defence proportionality implies that any measures taken in response to an attack must be neither retaliatory nor punitive in nature, but must be aimed to stop and repel an attack.[19] In the well-known *Caroline Affair* of 1837, the then United States Secretary of State, Daniel Webster, emphasised that a state invoking use of force must show the 'necessity of self-defence, instant, overwhelming, leaving no choice of means and no moment for deliberation', and that the act of self-defence itself must be 'limited by that necessity, and kept clearly within it'.[20] Moreover, the use of force for self-defence, which is allowed under Article 51 of the United Nations (UN) Charter and under customary international law, must also comply with the proportionality principle so that a reasonable balance between the measures and the severity of an initial or incumbent attack is found.[21]

2.2.1.3 Humanitarian Intervention

The proportionality principle also plays an important role in the emerging doctrine of humanitarian intervention,[22] or the 'responsibility to protect', as well as in international humanitarian law (*jus in bello*) (i.e., the rules and laws of conducting war after it has been initiated).[23] Contemporary international humanitarian law stipulates that an attack cannot be launched if the incidental civilian injuries would be excessive in relation to the anticipated military advantage.[24] In fact, the civilian precautionary principle clearly states that 'whenever civilian lives are greatly risked incidental to a tactic, very clear and

18. W. Kewenig, 'Gewaltverbot und noch zulässige Machteinwirkung und Interventions-mittel' in Schaumann, *Völkerrechtliches gewaltverbot und friedenssicherung* (Nomos 1971), cited by Schwarze (N11) 703–704.
19. Stanimir Alexandrov, *Self-Defence Against the Use of Force in International Law* (Kluwer 1996).
20. R.Y. Jennings, 'The *Caroline* and *McLeod* Cases' (1938) 32 *AJIL* 82, cited by Yutaka Arai-Takahashi, *The Margin of Appreciation Doctrine and the Principle of Proportionality in the Jurisprudence of the ECHR* (Intersentia 2002) 191.
21. Ian Brownlie, *International Law and the Use of Force by States* (Clarendon Press 1963) 261–264.
22. Sean Murphy, *Humanitarian Intervention: The United Nations in an Evolving World Order* (University of Pennsylvania 1996) 311–312.
23. Newton and May (N4) 2.
24. Michaelsen (N13) 26–27.

weighty military objectives have to be enunciated for the tactic to be *prima facie* proportionate'.[25] Proportionality also limits the use of severe lethal force, ensuring that it is only used in a way that is commensurate with the goal to be achieved.[26] Furthermore, this principle has also been incorporated into treaties codifying humanitarian law, such as the 1907 Hague Convention [27] and 1977 Geneva Protocol I addition to the Geneva Conventions of 1949.[28] Taken together, war and armed conflict must be initiated and conducted, as well as ended, proportionately.

2.2.1.4 State Responsibilities under Public International Law

Proportionality is also regarded as a crucial part of public international law, including state responsibility laws. It is one of the few established legal constraints used by customary international law on non-forcible counter-measures.[29] In the *North Sea Continental Shelf* case,[30] the UN International Court of Justice invoked the principle of proportionality in evaluating whether an equitable solution was reached in the delimitation of continental shelves, stating that:

> the element of a reasonable degree of proportionality, which a delimitation carried out in accordance with equitable principles ought to bring about between the extent of the continental shelf area appertaining to the coastal State and the length of its coast measured in the general direction of the coastline, account being taken for this purpose of the effects, actual or prospective, of any other continental shelf delimitations between adjacent States in the same region.[31]

25. Newton and May (N4) 11.
26. Ibid., 2.
27. Art 23(e) (prohibition of unnecessary suffering).
28. Art 35(2) (prohibition of weapons causing superfluous injury or unnecessary suffering) and Art 51(4)(c) (protection of civilian populations).
29. Art 49 of the Draft Articles on State Responsibility, Report of the International Law Commission (48th session), Doc A/51/10.
30. *Germany v Netherlands* [1969] ICJ Rep 3, (1969) 41 ILR (1969) ICJ Rep; 41 ILR.
31. Ibid., [98].

2.2.1.5 International Human Rights System

According to Grant Huscroft, Bradley Miller, and Grégoire Webber, 'to speak of human rights is to speak of proportionality. It is no exaggeration to claim that proportionality has overtaken rights as the orienting idea in contemporary human rights law and scholarship'.[32] In the international human rights system, the proportionality principle plays a key role in the application of international instruments, such as the ECHR and the ICCPR. In *R v Shayler*,[33] in which a former intelligence officer was prosecuted under the broad disclosure provisions of the United Kingdom (UK) Official Secrets Act of 1989, Lord Hope observed that there was 'a general international understanding as to the matters that should be considered where a question is raised as to whether an interference with a fundamental right is proportionate'.[34]

There are numerous provisions that invoke proportionality. Examples include rights to respect private and family life; rights to freedom of thought, conscience, and religion; and rights to freedom of expression, assembly, and association. Although these rights are not absolute or qualified, any interference with them may only be such as is necessary in a democratic society for the protection of public order, health, morals, or the rights of others.[35] Moreover, both the ECHR and the ICCPR also stipulate that in emergencies certain specified rights may be derogated only 'to the extent strictly required by the exigencies of the situation'.[36] There is also a reference to the proportionality principle by the UN Human Rights Committee, which specifies that it is 'the most important limitation on permissible derogation measures'.[37] As Manfred Nowak noted:

> The degree of interference and the scope of the measure (both territorially and temporally) must stand in reasonable relation to what is actually necessary

32. Grant Huscroft, Bradley Miller, and Grégoire Webber (eds), *Proportionality and the Rule of Law: Rights, Justification, Reasoning* (CUP 2014) 1.
33. [2002] UKHL 11.
34. Ibid., [60].
35. Paul Craig, 'Unreasonableness and Proportionality in UK Law' in Evelyn Ellis (ed), *The Principle of Proportionality in the Laws of Europe* (Hart Publishing 1999) 85–106; Marc-André Eissen, 'The Principle of Proportionality in the Case-Law of the European Court of Human Rights' in Ronald Macdonald, Franz Matscher, and Herbert Petzold (eds), *The European System for the Protection of Human Rights* (Dordrecht 1993) 125.
36. ECHR, Art 15(1); ICCPR, Art 4(1).
37. Manfred Nowak, *UN Covenant on Civil and Political Rights* (NP Engel 1993) 84.

> to combat an emergency threatening the life of the nation. The principle of proportionality requires that the necessity of derogation measures be reviewed at regular intervals by independent national organs, in particular, by the legislative and judicial branches.[38]

For this reason, the duty to review derogating emergency measures contained in human rights instruments, such as the ECHR and the ICCPR, is significant because it adds another dimension to the proportionality principle. To remain proportionate, extraordinary measures introduced to combat an emergency must be reviewed by the government itself, regardless of any review undertaken by the courts in the context of a judicial challenge. This means that a procedural aspect is added to the proportionality principle that examines the legitimacy of a public policy measure beyond its inherent nature and content.[39]

2.2.2 Regional Level: The European Union

The proportionality principle has also migrated to international and regional treaty-based regimes, such as the World Trade Organisation (WTO)[40] and the European Union (EU). In the latter, proportionality is enshrined in law through Article 5(4) of the Treaty of the EU, which stipulates that '[u]nder the principle of proportionality, the content and form of Union action shall not exceed what is necessary to achieve the objectives of the Treaties'. In this context, the proportionality principle ensures that no action shall be taken against an individual that goes further than is necessary to achieve the goals of the action, and this applies to actions of both the collective EU and individual Member States.[41]

The European Commission has also adopted this principle in its White Paper on European Governance, in which the term 'European governance'

38. Ibid.
39. Michaelsen (N13) 29.
40. Alec Stone Sweet and Jud Mathews, 'Proportionality, Balancing and Global Constitutionalism' (2008) 47 *CJTL* 74.
41. E. Erling, R. Kugan, and J. Schnaider, 'The Principle of Proportionality: A Comparison between Canada and the European Law' (Paper presented at the Faculty of Law, University of Lund on 24 February 2006) 4–13, cited by Michaelsen (N13) 28.

refers to the rules, processes, and behaviour that affect the way in which powers are exercised by the EU, particularly regarding openness, participation, accountability, effectiveness, and coherence.[42] These five principles of good governance reinforce those of subsidiarity and proportionality, and 'underpin democracy and the rule of law in the Member States, but they apply to all levels of government — global, European, national, regional, and local'.[43]

2.2.3 Proportionality as a Prerequisite for Promoting Good Governance

The liberal state, which has advanced steadily since the end of the nineteenth century, holds the notion that it should restrict itself to the achievement of objectives that are limited or capable of limitation.[44] This interpretation of the proportionality principle, which is not directly concerned with the notion of justice, is based on the premise that the law must serve a useful purpose (i.e., be geared to the objective it seeks to achieve) and must, consequently, form part of a quantifiable causal relationship between means and ends aimed at achieving a desired result.[45] Seen in this light, proportionality is a fundamental element of regulatory policy and public administration. It has been described as a defining principle of limited governments and is a key requirement of good governance.[46] Thus, the proportionality principle is used as an analytical and evaluative tool for regulating policy and concerns the ends of public action and the means used to attain them. Robert Thomas stated that:

> Proportionality concerns the relationship between the ends of public action and the means used to attain them. To achieve its objectives the administration must adopt effective means of policy implementation since the justification for the very existence of public administration is to realise collective goals through programmes of state action ... However, it may be argued that the extent of the interference was unnecessary since the public goal could

42. Commission of the European Communities, European Governance — A White Paper (25 July 2001) 428, available at: http://europa.eu/legislation_summaries/institutional_affairs/decisionmaking_process/l10109_en.htm, last accessed 7 November 2014.

43. Ibid.

44. Schwarze (N11) 679.

45. Ibid.

46. Alice Ristroph, 'Proportionality as a Principle of Limited Government' (2005) 55 *DLJ* 263, 287–288; Linda Senden, *Soft Law in European Community Law* (Hart Publishing 2006) 86.

> have been achieved through different means. The role of the administrative court in applying proportionality is to examine the effectiveness of such alternative courses of action in light of the administration's objective. If there are alternative means, less restrictive of the individual's interests but equally effective for the realisation of the public objective, then the interference is unnecessary and disproportionate.[47]

What is more, Newton and May have also suggested that proportionality is an umbrella concept that captures two seemingly incompatible, but equally important, aspects. On one hand, it limits the exercise of governmental power by insisting that such power be tailored to certain acceptable goals. On the other hand, it legitimises power itself by authorising its exercise provided that it meets the requirements of this principle. Proportionality is, therefore, both power limiting and power enhancing.[48] In practice, it serves as an external principle of limited government that defines the optimal relationship between states and citizens independent of specific situational applications.[49]

2.2.4 The Origins of Proportionality

Proportionality is not a common law concept and is thus unknown to many English-speaking countries,[50] with the exception of the United States,[51] New Zealand, and South Africa.[52] Its unfamiliarity in common law [53] was previously commented on by Lady Arden, now the Justice of the Supreme Court of the UK, who stated:

> Proportionality is not a common law concept ... However, one can say that proportionality is a very ancient concept. Precisely how ancient is a matter

47. Robert Thomas, *Legitimate Expectations and Proportionality in Administrative Law* (Hart Publishing 2000) 77.
48. Newton and May (N4) 33.
49. Ristroph (N46) 263.
50. J.F. Garner, 'The Principle of Proportionality' in *UK National Reports Submitted to the 10th International Congress on Comparative Law* (Budapest 1978) section IVD2/1.
51. Newton and May (N4) 41–43.
52. Aharon Barak, *Proportionality: Constitutional Rights and their Limitations* (CUP 2012) 181–183.
53. Mahendra Singh, *German Administrative Law in Common Law Perspective* (Springer-Verlag 2001) 160.

of debate as academics have for years disputed its precise origin. It may be as old as Hammurabi.[54]

In fact, the concept of proportionality has been in existence in different forms in different cultures from the earliest civilisations. Traces of it have been found in ancient times — from the images of balancing in Egyptian tomb paintings (whereby a deceased person that has committed a heavy wrong will be denied access to the realm of the dead) to the Talion principle (which requires punishment identical to the offence or 'an eye for an eye' as described in the Hammurabi and the Old Testament).[55] Moreover, different versions of the proportionality principle also emerge in Section 20 of the Magna Carta (1215), which limits arbitrary use of governmental power, as well as Article 8 of the French Declaration of Rights of Man and Citizen (1789), which prohibits disproportional punishment.[56]

2.2.4.1 Ancient Greece

Aristotle is credited as the first person to advocate proportionality as a form of social justice in ancient Greece.[57] Indeed, in *Nicomachean Ethics*, he states that: '[w]e allow only reason, not a human being, to be ruler, otherwise, we have tyranny',[58] thus suggesting that proportionality should be used to find the right relationship between the citizen and the state. As the principle was later understood in the Middle Ages, particularly by Thomas Aquinas, this formulation refers to a belief in an objective order that threads across centuries and societies and a kind of *jus universum* (all right) derived from common sense.[59] Therefore, proportionality both warrants and limits positive law

54. Lady Justice Arden, 'Proportionality: The Way Ahead?' (2013) *PL* 498, 499.

55. Exodus 21:23–25.

56. Gerhard Robbers, in *Bonner Kommentar zum Grundgesetz Loseblattsammlung* Band 5 (C F Müller Verlag 2012) Art 20 Abs 1 Rn 1890, cited by Moshe Cohen-Eliya and Iddo Porat, *Proportionality and Constitutional Culture* (CUP 2013) 24.

57. Eric Engle, 'History of the General Principle of Proportionality: An Overview' (2012) 10 *DLJ* 1.

58. Aristotle, *The Nicomachean Ethics*, Bk 5 (2nd end, translated by Terrence Irwin, Hackett Publishing 1999) Ch. 6, 1134a35, 77, cited by Newton and May (N4) 34.

59. Thomas Aquinas, *The Summa Theological: Second Part of the Second Part (QQ. 1–189)* Question 64, cited by Barak (N52) 176.

proclamations from legislatures, kings, and public referendums.[60] In short, proportionality, as far back as ancient Greece, was seen as a limit on what a government can do to its people.

Viewed in this Aristotelian way, justice is determined by the establishment and maintenance of a proper ratio of power exercised upon people in relation to the natural rights they possess. For Aristotle, this meant that 'the just is the proportional, the unjust is what violates the proportion'.[61] When society distributes honour, money, or other goods to reward merits, Aristotelian proportionality demands that the goods be in proportion to the merits. When transactions occur, what one side gives and gets should be in proportion to what the other side gets and gives. When one person robs and hurts another person, there are involuntary transactions. Therefore, the damage and the compensation or punishment must be in proportion. Taken together, Aristotle argues: 'Evil for evil ... good for good'.[62]

Franz Wieacker points to three factors that facilitated the development of proportionality in ancient Greek and Roman traditions.[63] First, there was the need to restrict private revenge and punishment. The rationale behind this Talion principle is not to satisfy the private need for revenge, but to ensure public order by allowing only moderate and proportional punishment for offences. Second, the notion of justice in Greek and Roman philosophies suggests that proportionality was required between wrongs and compensations as well as rights and burdens. Third, Greek and Roman philosophers believed that proportionality is an essential mechanism for achieving efficiency.

Although the concept of proportionality goes back to ancient times, the spirit of it was encapsulated in the Greek dictum *'pan metron ariston'* (all good

60. Newton and May (N4) 34.

61. Aristotle, *The Nicomachean Ethics*, Bk 5 (N58) 1131b15 in Jonathan Barnes (ed), *The Complete Works of Aristotle* (PUP 1995) Vol. 2, 1786.

62. Ibid., 1788.

63. Franz Wieacker, 'Geschichtliche Wurzeln des Prinzips der verhältnismäßigen Rechtsanwendung' in *Festschrift für Fischer* (de Gruyter Verlag, Berlin 1979) 874–80, cited by Cohen-Eliya and Porat (N56) 24.

things in moderation),[64] which has inspired thinkers in various generations.[65] Furthermore, the classical Greek notions of retributive, or corrective, justice (*justitia vindicativa*) and distributive justice (*justitia distributiva*) have also contributed to the development of proportionality as a rational concept.[66] Aristotle identified retributive or corrective justice as 'that which plays a rectifying part in transactions between man and man' and compared it to distributive justice 'which is manifested in distributions of honour or money or other things that fall to be divided among those who have a share in the constitution'.[67] Many theorists also believe that the courts are best suited to achieving retributive or corrective justice between two parties to a dispute and that distributive justice among citizens should be left to the legislature.[68]

2.2.4.2 Ancient China

Insofar as punitive law, or restorative justice, is concerned, proportionality as a governing principle was also a normative goal in ancient China.[69] A Confucian philosopher and early legalist, Xun Zi, is credited with the third-century BCE imperial Chinese axiom: 'Let the punishment fit the crime'.[70]

In this regard, being proportionate is based on a common-sense approach. Even children would be able to recognise the injustice of a parental or school punishment that is too harsh for a minor offence. This is because harsh parenting or schooling is often motivated by anger, shame, or peer pressure rather than sound correction and teaching measures. What is true for our families and schools is also true for society, as reflected in the excessive and violent responses

64. Takis Tridimas, *The General Principles of EC Law* (OUP 1999) 89.

65. For a discussion of proportionality in Christianity, see Garth Hallet, *Greater Good: The Case for Proportionalism* (GUP 1995).

66. Ernest Weinrib, 'Corrective Justice' (1992) 77 *ILR* 403; Izhak England, *Corrective and Distributive Justice: From Aristotle to Modern Times* (OUP 2009).

67. Aristotle, *The Nicomachean Ethics*, Bk 5 (N58) Chs. 2–4, cited by Kent Roach, 'The Challenges of Crafting Remedies for Violations of Socio-Economic Rights' in Malcolm Langford (ed), *Social Rights Jurisprudence* (CUP 2008) 47.

68. Ernest Weinrib, *The Idea of Private Law* (HUP 1995).

69. Newton and May (N4) 40.

70. John Haley, 'Introduction – Beyond Retribution: An Integrated Approach to Restorative Justice' (2011) 36 *WUJLP* 1, 9.

by the Hong Kong police towards unarmed protesters and innocent passers-by in early June 2019, and again in subsequent months. Live news coverage documented the use of abusive language (e.g., degrading the protesters as 'cockroaches') and disproportionate force, in combination with arrogance and a seemingly blind belief that what they were doing was legally legitimate and correct for the purpose of maintaining law and order. This response functioned to dehumanise the 'opposition', a strategy not unlike that used in Nazi Germany in their 'elimination' of 'rats' (i.e., the Jews). Reasonable viewers of these events can see that these responses are principally motivated by anger, shame, and peer pressure rather than simply a desire to maintain law and order.[71] Thus, a proper ratio between the wrong committed and the expected penalty is a foundational principle of justice and human decency that span cultures.[72]

2.2.4.3 Prussian Origin

A discussion about the origin of proportionality is incomplete without mentioning its role in Prussian administrative law in the late eighteenth century. The concept of proportionality in German legal terms is prominent in the work of multiple jurists, including Carl Gottlieb Svarez and Günther Heinrich von Berg, and according to Alec Stone Sweet and Jud Matthews, states were bound to respect natural rights to liberty.[73] Their assessment corresponds to Kant's Maxim Two of the Categorical Imperative that as a citizen you should '[a]ct so that you treat humanity, whether in your own person or in that of another,

71. See Chapter Eight of this book for further discussion of these events in Hong Kong. Similar events arising from anger, shame, peer pressure, or even revenge as fuelled by racism have also persistently occurred in the United States, most recently in response to the death of George Flyod on 25 May 2020 at the hands of Minneapolis police officer Derek Chauvin, who spent almost nine minutes kneeling on his neck. The event, which was widely viewed on social media, has led to nation-wide protests against police brutality, abuse of power, and systemic racism. At the time of writing, the officer has been charged with murder. A media report indicates that both Floyd and Chauvin have worked together at one time in a club called El Nuevo Rodeo, implying that revenge or previous grievences may have been a factor; Austin Horn, 'George Floyd and Derek Chauvin were once co-workers, ex-club owner tells TV station', *The Guardian*, 29 May 2020, available at: www.npr.org/2020/05/29/865803157/george-floyd-and-derek-chauvin-were-co-workers-says-former-club-owner, last accessed 2 June 2020.

72. Newton and May (N4) 40.

73. Stone Sweet and Mathews (N40) 98–103.

always as an end and never as a means only'.[74] Kant also believed that humans deserve respect as autonomous, rational actors and that this human dignity should never be ignored.[75] Therefore, even though we all use people as a means as soon as we employ them or pay them to provide us with a good or service, this does not mean we should only treat them as a means to achieve what we want and forget about their needs, goals, expectations, or choices.[76] Anticipating the modern approach to necessity and minimal impairment, von Berg further contended that:

> The first law ... is this: the police power may go no farther than its own goals require. The police law may abridge the natural freedom of the subject, but only insofar as a lawful goal requires as much. This is its second law.[77]

Svarez promoted a similar idea in the Prussian General Law of 1794 (*Allgemeines Landrecht für die Preußischen Staaten*, ALR), which states that '[t]he office of the police is to take the necessary measures for the maintenance of public peace, security, and order'.[78] This provides the textual linkage for the judicial development of the proportionality principle by the Prussian Supreme Administrative Court. During the 1880s, the Prussian Court began using 'necessary measures' in the above provision as a principle of limitation in reviewing police action and measures.[79] In *Kreutzberg*,[80] the Prussian Supreme Administrative Court developed a principle that required the state to obtain special permission before interfering with a citizen's civil liberties. In this particular case, the police sought to rely on a specific provision of the law that allowed them to adopt such measures 'as are necessary for the maintenance of public order'. The Court held that to test this reliance, it had to examine whether the police measures exceeded in intensity what was required by the

74. Andrew Crane and Dirk Matten, *Business Ethics: Managing Corporate Citizenship and Sustainability in the Age of Globalisation* (3rd edn, OUP 2010) 104.

75. Ibid.

76. Ibid., 104–105.

77. Stone Sweet and Mathews (N40) 99.

78. Ch. 2, Title 17, §10 ALR, cited ibid., 100.

79. Stone Sweet and Mathews (N40) 101.

80. Decision of 14 June 1882, *PrOVG* 9, 353.

pursued objective. The Court subsequently concluded that the police were not permitted to take into account considerations of an aesthetic nature without being given additional authority.

In an 1895 treatise surveying the Prussian Court's cases, Otto Mayer popularised the term 'proportionality' and, like von Berg and Svarez, connected it to natural rights and liberties, stating that 'natural rights demand that the use of police powers by the government be proportionate'.[81] Originally, judges regarded proportionality in terms of necessity or minimal impairment (as in the case just mentioned) and did not articulate the multi-step approach we are familiar with today. By the end of the nineteenth century, administrative courts in other German states were following Prussia's example, and proportionality subsequently became a general principle of the administrative law in the whole country.[82] In fact, the proportionality principle has been a fundamental principle of German constitutional law since the adoption of German Basic Law (*Grundgesetz*), the constitution of the Federal Republic of Germany, in 1949. Although it has not been specifically mentioned in any provision of the German constitution, proportionality is regarded as an unwritten constitutional principle, and the German Federal Constitutional Court (*BVerfG*) has regularly applied the proportionality test in the context of alleged infringements of basic rights that are protected by the first 20 Articles of the German Basic Law.[83] The Court also regards the principle as inherent in the nature of the basic rights themselves.[84] In the *Land Election* case [85] of 1954, which upheld an election law of Nordrhein-Westfalen against a constitutional challenge, the Court observed that:

(a) The law served a constitutionally permissible end;

(b) It included means that were suitable for achieving the end; and

(c) It did not 'exceed the limits drawn by the principle of proportionality between ends and means'.[86]

81. Stone Sweet and Mathews (N40) 101.

82. Ibid.

83. *BVerfG*, 2 February 1999, *2 B v M* 1/98; *BVerfG*, 10 May 2007, *2 B v R* 304/07; *BVerfG*, 11 March 2008, 1 *B v R* 2074/05, cited by Michaelsen (N13) 26.

84. Arden (N54) 500.

85. *BVerfGE* 3, 383, cited by Stone Sweet and Mathews (N40) 107.

86. Ibid., 399.

Moreover, Stone Sweet and Mathews further stated that the first case to recognise balancing as a distinct step is the *Pharmacy* case [87] of 1958, in which the Court said:

> The individual's claim to freedom will have a stronger effect ... the more his right to free choice of a profession is put into question; the protection of the public will become more urgent, the greater the disadvantages that arise from the free practicing of professions. When one seeks to maximize both ... demands in the most effective way, then the solution can only lie in a careful balancing of the meaning of the two opposed and perhaps conflicting interests.[88]

In short, the proportionality assessment, in its German form, first requires that the public interest being protected is important enough to justify an encroachment on the basic right involved. Second, the measure must be appropriate for attaining the objective. Third, the measure must be necessary for the purpose, which would not be achievable by less severe means. Finally, the measure must not be excessive, and it must be strictly reasonable.[89]

Based on these requirements, the Court once held that police cannot enforce an absolute ban and must allow exceptions from measures when it is not necessary to have a blanket rule.[90] This principle, which reflects the proportionality principle, constitutes one of the general rules governing all actions by the state, including both the law-making process and application of the law, and ensures that the state is ruled by law.[91] Thus, when the legislator fails to observe the proportionality principle in enacting a statute, the illegality of such a statute should be queried, unless it precisely expresses a rule that is contrary to, equally valid as, or higher than the proportionality principle.[92]

As the Court has applied the proportionality principle as a generalised head of review for administrative action, German public bodies are prevented from

87. *BVerfGE* 7, 377, cited by Stone Sweet and Mathews (N40) 107–108.

88. Ibid., 405.

89. David Currie, *The Constitution of the Federal Republic of Germany* (CUP 1994) 19–20.

90. Arden (N54) 500.

91. *BVerfG* 19, 348; 23, 133; 43, 106; 61, 134, cited by Schwarze (N11) 688.

92. Ibid., 689.

acting in a disproportionate or excessive manner against individual rights and interests.[93] However, the German courts did not generate their proportionality principle based on the need to prevent unreasonable exercise of legislative powers. Instead, they found its basis in the fundamental principle of means and ends and in common cause-and-effect relationships.[94]

In the context of German private law, which has been influenced by fundamental rights through the general provisions of the Constitution, the proportionality principle is applied to private individuals. In the *Lebach* decision,[95] the German Constitutional Court required that the proportionality principle be observed 'in court decisions concerning conflicting provisions of private law'.[96]

2.2.5 The Methodologies of Proportionality

2.2.5.1 The German Three-Stage Test

The principle of proportionality (*Grundsatz der Verhältnismäßigkeit*) was initially applied in the context of policing as a ground for challenging measures on the basis that they were excessive or unnecessary in relation to the objective being pursued. However, in its modern formulation within Germany, the consensus is that proportionality involves the evaluation of three factors — suitability, necessity, and proportionality — as advocated by Nigel Foster and Satish Sule.[97] Kai Möller also stated that there is an additional stage — the legitimate goal stage, whereby any legitimate goal will be accepted — which should occur prior to the other three stages.[98]

To justify their assertion, Foster and Sule provide the following fictional example to explain this structure. A young boy steals an apple in the market and is just about to leave. A police officer, having observed the theft, reacts by

93. Raymond Youngs, *Sourcebook on German Law* (2nd edn, Cavendish Press 2002) 108.

94. Lothar Hirschberg, *Der Grundsatz der Verhältnismäßigkeit* (Schwartz 1981) 43f., cited by Singh (N53) 160.

95. *BVerfGE* 35, 202.

96. Ibid., (221), cited by Singh (N53) 160.

97. Foster and Sule (N3) 185.

98. Kai Möller, 'Constructing the Proportionality Test: An Emerging Global Conversation' in Liora Lazarus, Christopher McCrudden, and Nigel Bowles, *Reasoning Rights: Comparative Judicial Engagement* (Hart Publishing 2014) 34.

drawing their pistol and shooting the boy. The purpose to be achieved here is the prevention of the theft, but is the police officer's action proportionate? They break down the example into the following three stages:

(a) Suitability (*Geeignetheit*): Shooting the boy is a suitable measure to prevent the completion of the theft.

(b) Necessity (*Erforderlichkeit*): However, the measure is not necessary. A less restrictive measure could have been used (for example, arresting the boy). Therefore, the measure fails the proportionality test already in this stage and is, therefore, considered disproportionate.

(c) Proportionality (*Angemessenheit*): For the sake of argument, the example can be slightly altered. In the new scenario, the police officer instead tried to grab the boy in order to arrest him but slips and falls. When the officer gets up, the boy is too far away to be caught, and the only way to stop him would be to shoot him. In this altered example, the measure would be suitable and necessary because no other, more conservative, measure could be taken to prevent the theft. At this point, the proportionality test works as a safety net to balance the boy's interests (i.e., his right to life) and the public's interests (i.e., preventing the theft of an apple). A rational police officer will place the apple second and let the boy go.[99]

The above example, according to Aharon Barak, illustrates the nature of the proportionality test, its potentially moral content, and its importance:

> Assume a law that allows the police to shoot a person (even if this shooting would lead to that person's death) if it is the only way to prevent that person from harming another's property. This law is designed to protect private property, and therefore its purpose is proper. The means chosen by the legislator are rational, since it advances the proper purpose. Therefore, the law meets the necessity test as well. However, the provision is still unconstitutional because the protection of private property cannot justify the taking of human life.[100]

99. Foster and Sule (N3) 185.

100. Barak (N52) 342–343.

In practice, the German Constitutional Court has applied the proportionality test in a number of cases, especially when dealing with the protection of basic rights. The *Falconry* case [101] is a good example of how a provision can already fail the first stage of the proportionality test. In this case, a hunting law provision [102] required falconers to prove their knowledge of firearms in order to get a falconry licence. This was challenged as a disproportionate restriction of the falconer's basic right to freedom of action.[103] Applying the proportionality test, the Court looked at the purpose of the provision — to make sure that falcons would be treated properly — and held that, while this was a legitimate purpose, the required knowledge of firearms was not a suitable measure to serve this purpose. The provision was, thus, disproportionate and declared unconstitutional.

Failure of the second stage of the proportionality test can be seen in the heavily disputed census law of 1982. In *Volkszählung*,[104] within the census framework, the highest federal authorities got wide access to personal data 'in order to fulfil their tasks'. These data were not truly anonymous as birthdays and addresses were still connected to them, and thus, the authorities could easily link the data to each person and potentially pass it to other, lower authorities. As this collection of data was challenging data protection and privacy rights, its proportionality was questioned. Ultimately, the German Constitutional Court held that it was not necessary for the authorities to have such general access to personal data to fulfil their tasks. It would have been less restrictive to name only the few authorities in the statute that needed access and only to relevant data.

An instructive case for the third stage of the proportionality test is the *Lebach* case,[105] which shows how the German Constitutional Court balances two interests against each other. It focuses on law related to freedom of expression, information, press, broadcasting, and film.[106] In this case, the Court deliberated whether a television station could broadcast a documentary exposing private

101. *BVerfGE* 55, 159 — *Falknerjagdschein* (Falconer hunting license), cited by Foster and Sule (N3) 185–186.

102. § 15 VII 1 BjagdG a. F., cited ibid., 186.

103. German Basic Law (*Grundgesetz*), Art 2(1).

104. *BVerfGE* 65, 1, cited by Foster and Sule (N3), 186.

105. *Lebach* decision (N95), 202, cited ibid., 255–256.

106. German Basic Law (*Grundgesetz*), Art 5(1).

information about a prisoner on the eve of his release. In 1969, a raid on an armed forces base in the village of Lebach took place during which four soldiers were killed and their arms and ammunition were stolen. The criminals were apprehended and convicted. One of them, being an accessory to the crime, was only sentenced to six years of imprisonment. Shortly before his release, the broadcasting channel ZDF was planning to show a documentary about the incident that named all the persons involved. In its decision, the Court weighed the extent to which the broadcast would harm the prisoner's right to privacy, and thus, his right to personality and human dignity, against the extent of harm to free speech that would ensue from banning the programme. The prisoner obtained a civil court injunction against the broadcasting station to protect his right to personality. The channel appealed, claiming freedom of broadcasting as enshrined under German Basic Law.

As the Court noted, this case required balancing the freedom of broadcasting, on one hand, and a general right to personality, as enshrined under the German Basic Law, on the other. It held that freedom of broadcasting would be less harmed than the right to personality. The main reason for this decision is that the person affected was to be released soon, and his re-integration into society would be severely hampered if his involvement in the crime was exhibited in the documentary. This would amount to an intolerable violation of his right to dignity and personality.[107] In short, what this German three-part test requires is that the disputed measure be appropriate and necessary to attain the objective legitimately pursued by the legislation in question, that where there exists a choice between different means of achieving that objective, the least interventive recourse should be taken, and the disadvantages caused must not be disproportionate to the aims pursued.[108]

According to Möller, one remarkable characteristic of the German three-stage test is that it tends to push most of the important issues into the last stage (i.e., the

107. It is noteworthy that in 1996, another channel (SAT 1) attempted to broadcast a new documentary on the same subject. Again, the person affected obtained injunctions. This time, however, the constitutional complaints of the broadcasting channel were successful. It was held by the German Constitutional Court that re-integration was no longer endangered, especially as the names were altered and that under these circumstances, the right to personality had to stand back in favour of German Basic Law (*Grundgesetz*) Art 5(1); Decision of 25 November 1999. *BVerfGE* (N95).

108. Schwarze (N11) 687.

balancing stage).[109] When establishing the existence of a legitimate goal at the suitability stage, even a marginal contribution to the attainment of the goal will suffice (i.e., any legitimate goal will be accepted). At the necessity stage, it is very rare for a policy to fail because less restrictive alternatives normally come with some disadvantages and cannot, therefore, be considered equally effective. Thus, the balancing stage dominates the legal analysis and is usually determinative of the outcome.[110]

2.2.5.2 Other Approaches Developed by Courts, Practitioners, and Academics

2.2.5.2.1 *The Court of Justice of the European Union*

Despite the German three-stage test approach, there has long been no consensus on the specific methodology of proportionality. Rather, there are many formulations of the proportionality test.[111] For example, Francis Jacobs questioned whether proportionality should only be confined to three constituents.[112] The case law of the Court of Justice of the European Union (CJEU) is a typical example. On one hand, the CJEU identified only two aspects to their proportionality analysis — namely, whether the means employed by the legislature to achieve the objective in question corresponds to the importance of that objective and whether the means is 'necessary' for the achievement of that objective — in 1983 and 1991, respectively.[113] On the other hand, it also formulated the three-stage test (i.e., suitability, necessity, and proportionality in a narrow sense) in *R v Ministry of Agriculture, Fisheries and Food, ex parte Fedesa*,[114] in 1990.

Associated with this lack of clear methodology is the uncertainty over its precise scope since the proportionality principle has been so widely

109. Möller (N98) 34.

110. Ibid.

111. Tom Hickman, 'Proportionality: Comparative Law Lessons' (2007) 12(1) *JR* 31.

112. Francis Jacobs, 'Recent Developments in the Principle of Proportionality in European Community Law' in Ellis (N35) 1.

113. *Fromançais SA v FORMA* (Case 66/82) [1983] ECR 395, [8]; Van Gerven AG in *Society for the Protection of Unborn Children Ireland Ltd v Stephen Grogan* (Case C-159/90) [1991] ECR I-4685, [27] of the Opinion.

114. (Case C-331/88) [1990] ECR I-4023.

applied. In *ex parte Fedesa*,[115] the CJEU stated that the impugned measure will be disproportionate only if it is 'manifestly inappropriate' in light of its objectives,[116] whereas in other cases, the CJEU will scrutinise the content of the measure 'closely' with a less deferential formula — namely, the 'excessive disproportionate' test, as applied in the '*Skimmed-milk*' case.[117] For this reason, the principle appears to operate as a sliding scale of review, in that the concept of legality required by the CJEU will vary depending upon the context of the particular policy objective, the nature of the competing interests involved, the competence of the CJEU to make certain evaluative findings regarding the implementation of policy objectives, and so on. As Advocate-General Capotorti intimated, an infringement of proportionality will not be held to have occurred 'without careful reflection on the scope of that principle and on the importance which the facts given assume in its light'.[118]

2.2.5.2.2 *The European Court of Human Rights*

The case law of the European Court of Human Rights (ECtHR) is also unable to provide full guidance as to the precise scope and application of the proportionality test. In fact, there is considerable variation between cases, with the ECtHR taking an extremely hands-off approach in some [119] but exacting scrutiny, and even applying a more exacting standard, in others.[120]

In this regard, the ECtHR has been criticised for not giving any apparent reason for its variation in approach.[121] On one hand, the standard varies with the subject matter. On the other hand, however, the ECtHR's approach to the proportionality principle derives from its status as an international court

115. Ibid.

116. Ibid., [14].

117. *Bela-Mühle Josef Bergmann KG v Grows-Farm GmbH & Co KG* (Case 114/76) [1977] ECR 1211.

118. *SpA Ferriera Valsabbia v Commission* (Joint Cases 154, 205, 206,.226–228, 263 and 264/78, 39, 31, 83, and 85/79) [1980] ECR 9007, 1055 (col 2) of the Advocate-General's opinion.

119. *Müller v Switzerland* (1991) 13 EHRR 212; *Otto-Preminger-Institut v Austria* (1994) 19 EHRR 34.

120. Jack Beatson, Stephen Grosz, Tom Hickman, and Rabinder Singh, *Human Rights: Judicial Protection in the United Kingdom* (Sweet & Maxwell 2008) [3–40].

121. Michael Fordham and Thomas de la Mare, 'Identifying the Principles of Proportionality' in Jeffrey Jowell and Jonathan Cooper (eds), *Understanding Human Rights Principles* (Hart Publishing 2001) 27.

that is considerably detached from, and may have little or no experience with, the various national authorities whose conduct it is called upon to scrutinise.[122] Indeed, Lord Hope, in *Shayler*,[123] remarked that the ECtHR had not identified 'a consistent or uniform set of principles' when considering the doctrine of proportionality.[124]

2.2.5.2.3 *Other Courts*

Unlike Germany, the Supreme Court of Canada has formulated the last question of their proportionality test as a comparison of the deleterious effects on a right against the importance of the objective, rather than against the beneficial effects of the limitation, as shown in *R v Oakes*.[125] According to the *Oakes* test, the objective must be 'of sufficient importance to warrant overriding a constitutionally protected right or freedom', there must be a rational connection between measure and objective, the means must 'impair "as little as possible" the right or freedom in question', and, finally, 'there must be a proportionality between the effects of the measures which are responsible for limiting the Canadian Charter right or freedom and the objective which has been identified as of "sufficient importance"'.[126]

When compared with the German test, Möller argued that under the *Oakes* test, more issues are addressed in the earlier stages. Instead of accepting any legitimate goal, the *Oakes* test requires a goal 'of sufficient importance to warrant overriding a constitutionally protected right or freedom'. This 'minimal impairment test' is also different from the German 'necessity test' both in the way it is formulated (as there is no requirement that the less restrictive measure be equally effective) and in the way it is applied (as the Canadian Supreme Court tends to resolve cases at that stage and not, as the German Federal Constitutional Court does, at the balancing stage).[127]

122. Beatson, Grosz, Hickman, and Singh (N120) [3–40].

123. *Shayler* (N33).

124. Ibid., [60].

125. [1986] 1 SCR 103, [71] (Dickson CJ).

126. Ibid., [69]–[70] (Dickson CJ).

127. Möller (N98) 34.

However, Dieter Grimm, after contrasting and comparing the German and Canadian approaches, defends the German one.[128] He contends that the purpose of the second and third stages (i.e., suitability and necessity) is 'confined to a strict means-end examination'. As such, they differ from the analysis at the final stage, which compares the fundamental right losses with the gains of the public good in accordance with the law. Grimm further objects to the Canadian practice of handling what should, in his view, be carried out at the balancing stage in the legitimate goal stage and the necessity stage — the so-called 'minimal impairment' stage. For Grimm, the perceived attraction of such a view may be the desire to avoid, as far as possible, balancing the perceived political, rather than legal, aspects. However, this would be a fallacy primarily because balancing is unavoidable, and all that the Canadian approach does is shift what properly belongs to the final stage of the test into the earlier one.[129]

Tennessee v Garner,[130] as a U.S.-based example, tested a Tennessee statute put in force in 1985, which stated that a police officer 'may use all the necessary means to effect the arrest' after they have given notice of their intent to arrest a criminal suspect if the latter flees or forcibly resists. In this case, a Memphis police officer had shot and killed a young man who, after being told to stop, fled over the fence of a house he was suspected of burgling. The officer used deadly force despite being reasonably sure the suspect was unarmed. Thus, one of the questions tabled before the U.S. Supreme Court was 'would a law be proportionate which allows the police to shoot a perpetrator to death if this is the only means of protecting private property?'

As Grimm argued, a proper proportionality analysis should be conducted as follows. To satisfactorily resolve the case, there is no way to avoid balancing. The legitimate goal is the protection of property, thus shooting and killing the perpetrator is suitable and, when no alternatives are available to protect the property, such shooting is also necessary. It is only when comparing the relative importance of life and property in the specific circumstances of the case that the disproportionate nature of the shooting is determined. Therefore,

128. Dieter Grimm, 'Proportionality in Canadian and German Constitutional Jurisprudence' (2007) 57 *UTLJ* 383, cited by Möller (N98) 34.

129. Ibid., 34–35.

130. 471 U.S. 1 (1985).

balancing is required, and given that it is required, it is preferable to conduct it openly in the early stage.[131] After conducting such an analysis in *Garner*, the U.S. Supreme Court held that the Tennessee statute violated the Fourth Amendment and was

> unconstitutional insofar as it authorizes the use of deadly force against, as in this case, an apparently unarmed, non-dangerous fleeing suspect; such force may not be used unless necessary to prevent the escape and the officer has probable cause to believe that the suspect poses a significant threat of death or serious physical injury to the officer or others.[132]

In the UK, however, the Judicial Committee of the Privy Council has largely employed the proportionality framework without explicit reference to the final question. This is indicated in *De Freitas v Permanent Secretary of Ministry of Agriculture, Fisheries, Lands, and Housing*,[133] the formula of which was subsequently adopted by the House of Lords in *R (on the application of Daly) v Secretary of State for the Home Department* [134] and *Huang v Secretary of State for the Home Department*.[135] Moreover, the ECtHR and the House of Lords have also, on several occasions, insisted that the question of fair balance is 'inherent in the whole' of the ECHR, which on its best reading, is concerned both with 'the demands of the general interest of the community and the requirements of the protection of the individual's human rights'.[136] Overall, although some courts insist on a systematic review of each of the questions of proportionality, others, such as the Constitutional Court of South Africa, maintain that the role of the judge is to 'arrive at a global judgment on proportionality and not [to] adhere mechanically to a sequential check-list'.[137] Other courts — for instance, the Supreme Court of Canada — also commit themselves to the formality

131. Grimm (N128).

132. *Garner* (N130) 2.

133. [1991] 1 AC 69 (PC).

134. [2001] UKHL 26.

135. [2007] UKHL 11.

136. *Soering v UK* (1989) 11 EHRR 439, [89]; *Wilson v First County Trust Ltd* [2003] UKHL 40, [2004] 1 AC 816, [181] (Lord Roger).

137. *S v Manamela (Director-General of Justice Intervening)* (CCT25/99) [2000] ZACC 5, 2000 (3) SA 1, [32], 2000 (5) BCLR 491 (14 April 2000).

of proportionality's framework only to entertain arguments relevant to one question in their answers to another.[138]

2.2.5.2.4 *Practitioners and Academics*

There was also a four-stage test, as advocated by Huscroft, Miller, and Webber,[139] developed to evaluate whether the limitation of a right is justifiable using the following questions:

(a) Does the legislation (or other government action) establishing the right's limitation pursue a legitimate objective of sufficient importance to warrant limiting a right (legitimacy)?

(b) Are the means in service of the objective rationally connected (suitable) to the objective (suitability)?

(c) Are the means in service of the objective necessary (i.e., minimal impairment of the limited right) taking into account alternative means of achieving the same objective (necessity)?

(d) Do the beneficial effects of the limitation on the right outweigh the deleterious effects of the limitation? In short, is there a fair balance between the public interest and the private right (means-end fit)?

What is more, Michael Fordham and Thomas de la Mare further developed ten suggested principles as follows:[140]

(P1) The four-question template:

- (Q1) *Legitimacy*: Is the measure adopted to pursue a legitimate aim?
- (Q2) *Suitability*: Can it serve to further that aim?
- (Q3) *Necessity*: Is it the least restrictive way of doing so?
- (Q4) *Means-Ends fit*: Viewed overall, do the ends justify the means?

138. *Eldridge v British Columbia (AG)* (1997) 151 DLR (4th) 577 (SCC), [1997] 3 SCR, [1997] 2 SCR 624, 93.

139. Huscroft, Miller, and Webber (N32) 2.

140. Fordham and de la Mare (N121) 28–29.

(P2) The starting point is always to identify and respect the *legislative mandate*: any supreme instrument stating: (1) what measures are permissible; (2) what objectives are legitimate; or (3) how wide the authority's margin is.

(P3) Q1–Q4: (1) operate together and not in mutual isolation; (2) may not each appear to be in play (if obvious satisfied); and (3) can each involve its own margin.

(P4) Alongside them is a concept of *pressing need*, both in a *threshold* sense (a problem whose resolution satisfies Q1) and *overall* sense (informing Q2–Q4).

(P5) Q1 and Q4 involve a *value-judgment inquiry*: (1) identifying the competing *interests* (rights and objectives); (2) *weighting* their relative importance; (3) asking whether, in principle and in the circumstances, any can properly take *precedence*.

(P6) Q2–Q3 involve protecting individuals from ineffective and unnecessary regulation.

(P7) The four-question template (and value-judgment inquiry) should be used by public authorities because: (1) good public administration requires a disciplined and focused reasoning process; which (2) will protect the public authority from judicial interference.

(P8) The Court is entitled to scrutinise, with reference to the four-question template and value-judgment inquiry: (1) the public authority's *reasoning process* (questions it asked); and (2) its *substantive conclusions* (answers it arrived at).

(P9) Scrutiny of substantive conclusions involves setting the appropriate *margin* (and so *intensity of review*), which depends on the nature of: (1) *the right infringed* (how fundamental?); (2) *the objective pursued* (how compelling?); (3) *the measure and decision-maker* (what status?); (4) *the context of the dispute* (how sensitive?).

(P10) The *onus* is on the public authority to demonstrate an appropriate reasoning process and justified conclusions. The Court should insist on: (1) *evidence* (operative rationale); not (2) *submission* (subsequent rationalisation).

Moreover, there have also been other formulations proposed. For instance, Mark Elliott advocates the following five-question approach:[141]

(a) Does the measure impinge upon a highly regarded interest (e.g., a human right)?

(b) Does the measure pursue a legitimate objective?

(c) Is the measure capable of securing that objective?

(d) Is the adoption of the measure necessary in order to secure that objective?

(e) Are the losses inflicted by the measure (e.g., in terms of the restriction of human rights) justified, or outweighed, by the gains which it purchases (e.g., in terms of benefits which flow from securing the legitimate objective)?

2.2.5.2.5 Methodology Adopted in Hong Kong

Insofar as Hong Kong is concerned, although there has been no universal methodology, the Court of Final Appeal (CFA), in the *Public Order Ordinance* case,[142] held that if the 'legitimate purposes' had been set out in the constitutional provision, the list was considered exhaustive. The CFA explained that if the test had been formulated in this way, an additional requirement to ascertain that the legitimate purpose is sufficiently important to justify limiting a fundamental right, as required in the *De Freitas* case,[143] was not needed:

> In *De Freitas* ... the Privy Council adopted a three stage test which has been extensively cited in many jurisdictions: ... whether: (i) the *legislative objective* is sufficiently important to justify a limiting fundamental right; ... Compared to

141. Mark Elliott, 'Proportionality and Deference: The Importance of a Structured Approach' in Christopher Forsyth, Mark Elliott, Swati Jhaveri, Michael Ramsden, and Anne Scully-Hill, *Effective Judicial Review: A Cornerstone of Good Governance* (OUP 2010) 265.

142. *Leung Kwok Hung v HKSAR* [2005] 3 HKLRD 164.

143. *De Freitas* (N133).

> the proportionality test formulated above for Hong Kong, the *De Freitas* ... test has incorporated an extra requirement, namely whether the legislative objective is sufficiently important to justify limiting a fundamental right. The Privy Council considered this extra requirement appropriate ... as the relevant constitutional instrument prescribed only the general formula of what is reasonably justifiable in a democratic society without specifying the permissible purposes for which a restriction could be imposed. In contrast, in the Hong Kong context, in relation to the right of peaceful assembly, the legitimate purposes for which a restriction may be imposed on the right are constitutionally set out in a comprehensive manner. That being so, the extra requirement, whatever its relevance may be in other situations, is unnecessary in the present context.[144] [emphasis added]

In agreement with this, Johannes Chan also opined that as the importance of the legitimate purpose was already embodied in the proportionality formula, to ascertain it via the same analysis is of little importance primarily because, if the legitimate objective is not important, it could hardly justify the restriction of a fundamental right, and thus form one of the criteria under the proportionality analysis.[145]

Nevertheless, I disagree, with my greatest respect. In common law jurisdictions (especially the British whose constitution is unwritten), since there has been no constitutional requirement for legislations to specify the purposes for which it was adopted, whether such law-making refers to the reason for which it is adopted, or the objective it is designed to achieve, tends to depend on specific requirements in legislations or established practices. Such reluctance to detail the purposes pursued by the legislation is reflected in the Merchant Shipping Act 1988 (MSA 1988). In *R v Secretary of State for Transport, ex parte Factortame Ltd (No 5)*,[146] the House of Lords found that there had been a variety of objectives pursued under the MSA 1988. The discovery of additional documents also revealed that some ministers had different views towards the objectives pursued by the legislation.[147] It is surely a matter of concern if the legitimate

144. The *Public Order Ordinance* case (N142) 84–85.

145. Johannes Chan, 'Basic Law and Constitutional Review: The First Decade' (2007) 37(Pt 2) *HKLJ* 407, 424.

146. [1999] 4 All ER 906 (HL).

147. Thomas (N47) 103.

purposes for which a restriction may be imposed on the right, even if they are constitutionally set out in a comprehensive manner, are not ascertained and are, thus, not interpreted correctly by the courts during the process of adjudication or aired correctly to the general public. Notably, the final interpretation of the Basic Law in the Hong Kong Special Administrative Region (SAR) is vested in the Standing Committee of the National People's Congress (NPCSC).[148] As Chan argued, the implication of the NPCSC's interpretative power is that the scope of the Basic Law will be determined by a political organ as authorised under the Constitution of the People's Republic of China (PRC), so the NPCSC can

> without any request from Hong Kong, without an imminent crisis, without any prior warning, without any consultation or debate, without any meaningful participation from the people of Hong Kong, without any transparency in the process, and on its own motion and for political reasons, determine the scope and meaning of any provision of the Basic Law. The meaning of the law rests on the will of the Sovereign. Is this not precisely the evil that will undermine the rule of law that distinguishes the two systems?[149]

A typical example of this occurred during the oath taking ceremony for a Legislative Council (LegCo) election held in September 2016. Several newly elected legislators, who were suspected by Mainland Chinese authorities to have been advocating Hong Kong's independence, were accused of failing to take their oaths of office properly. In response, the NPCSC adopted an interpretation of Article 104 of the Basic Law, resulting in removing their status as legislative councillors.[150] In short, the clearer the legitimate purpose is ascertained — and thus interpreted correctly — and made known to the public during the proceedings, the more likely that lesser arbitrary interpretation will ensue.

Overall, regardless of methodology, the proportionality principle does promise a common analytical framework, the significance of which is not in its

148. Basic Law of the HKSAR, Art 158.

149. Johannes Chan and Lison Harris (eds), 'Preface: Back to Basics' II in *Hong Kong's Constitutional Debates* (HKLJ Ltd 2008) 48–49.

150. *South China Morning Post*, 'Topic: Legislative Council oath-taking saga', multiple publication dates, available at: www.scmp.com/topics/legislative-council-oath-taking-saga, last accessed 6 February 2017.

ubiquity but in how its structure influences, or controls, the court's decisions in moral and political controversies confronting communities.

2.3 Margin of Appreciation

Parallel to the application of the proportionality principle in the CJEU and the ECtHR is the margin of appreciation doctrine, or in the Member States' courts, the 'discretionary area of judgment', 'margin of deference', or 'deference that a court must allow to a decision-maker when judicially reviewing decisions', according to Swati Jhaveri, Michael Ramsden, and Anne Scully-Hill.[151] This margin of appreciation doctrine was developed by the ECtHR, accepted by the CJEU, and from there has migrated to inter-American human rights law and the UN Human Rights Commission and Committee.[152] However, the doctrine is not limited to the sphere of international human rights law. Academic discourse surrounding the standard of review applied by the General Agreement on Tariffs and Trade as well as various WTO panels also bears some resemblance to arguments based on the margin of appreciation and judicial self-restraint.[153]

In general, the margin of appreciation doctrine refers to the degree of latitude or deference afforded to Member States in their observance of the ECHR.[154] It concerns the leeway that a government enjoys in evaluating factual situations and in applying the provisions enumerated in international rights treaties.[155] Its relationship with the proportionality principle is clearly reflected in *Bato Star Fishing (Pty) Ltd v The Chief Director: Marine and Coastal Management, Department of Environmental Affairs and Tourism*,[156] where the Constitutional Court in South Africa grappled with the application of this doctrine in the allocation of fishing quotas. In this case, Justice O'Regan introduced the notion that in order to meet specified standards, a decision 'requires an equilibrium to be struck between

151. Swati Jhaveri, Michael Ramsden, and Anne Scully-Hill, *Administrative Law in Hong Kong* (2nd edn, LexisNexis 2013) 257–588.

152. Barak (N52) 418.

153. Steven Croley and John Jackson, 'WTO disputes Procedures, Standard of Review, and Deference to National Governments' (1996) 90 *AJIL* 193.

154. Arai-Takahashi (N20) 2.

155. Ibid.

156. (CCT 27/03) [2004] ZACC 15; 2004 (4) SA 490 (CC); 2004 (7) BCLR 687 (CC) (12 March 2004).

a range of competing interests or considerations and [a decision] which is taken by a person or institution with specific expertise in that area must be shown respect by the courts'.[157]

To the ECtHR, the doctrine indicates that 'the contracting state is allowed a certain measure of discretion, subject to European supervision, when it takes legislature, administrative or judicial action in the area of a Convention right'.[158] Its primary purposes are (1) to delineate the ECtHR's respective areas of competence as an international court as well as those of national authorities, including national courts, in securing ECHR rights; (2) to balance these institutions against competing rights and interests; and (3) to put in place a remedial system for breaches or potential breaches of those rights.[159] In short, the concept of margin, or latitude, has three main features:

(a) It recognises that national authorities will have some *freedom of choice or appraisal* when answering the questions posed by the proportionality template.
(b) It serves as a reminder that intensive review by the Court is *still intensive review*: the judge is asking 'is the measure justified?', not 'would I have adopted it?'.
(c) It introduces the idea of *variability*, whereby margins can differ in their width, depending on the nature of the power and subject matter.[160]

The legal basis of the doctrine is found in the jurisprudence of not only the martial law doctrine,[161] but also the French *Conseil d'Etat*, which used the term '*margé d'appréciation*'.[162] However, Yutaka Arai-Takahashi argues that

157. Ibid., [49].

158. David Harris, Michael O'Boyle, and Colin Warbrick, *Law of the European Convention on Human Rights* (Butterworths 1995) 12.

159. Beatson, Grosz, Hickman, and Singh (N120) [2–133].

160. Fordham and de la Mare (N121) 28.

161. Howard Yourow, *The Margin of Appreciation Doctrine in the Dynamics of European Human Rights Jurisprudence* (Kluwer 1996) 14.

162. Francis Jacobs, *The European Convention on Human Rights* (Clarendon Press 1980) 201–202.

its legal basis is indeed found in the system of administrative law within every civil law jurisdiction.[163]

2.3.1 Application by the European Court of Human Rights

At the international law level, the first recourse to the margin of appreciation doctrine occurred in the jurisprudence of the ECtHR. The ECHR was adopted in 1950, being endorsed as a unified and minimum standard by the Member States of the Council of Europe, all of which (more or less) shared similar traditions of democracy and fundamental rights. Therefore, the ECHR was envisaged as the lowest common denominator in the face of the diverse cultural and legal traditions embraced by each Member State and was expected to act as a uniform European standard of human rights.[164]

Since the issue of deference to the sovereignty of each Member State was, and has continued to be, raised and the enforcement of the margin of appreciation by the ECtHR has ultimately depended on the good faith and continuing co-operation of the Member States, the doctrine is, therefore, an attempt to strike a balance between national views of human rights and the uniform application of ECHR values.[165] As Ronald Macdonald observed, the process of realising a European-wide system of human rights protection and uniform standard of human rights must be gradual because

> the entire legal framework rests on the fragile foundations of the consent of the Contracting States. The margin of appreciation gives the flexibility needed to avoid damaging confrontations between the Court and Contracting States over their respective spheres of authority and enables the Court to balance the sovereignty of Contracting Parties with their obligations under the [ECHR].[166]

163. Arai-Takahashi (N20) 2–3.

164. Ibid., 3.

165. Ibid.

166. Ronald Macdonald, 'The Margin of Appreciation' in Macdonald, Matscher, and Petzold (N35) 123.

Moreover, it is also inherent in the original understanding of the doctrine that the ECHR should serve as a complementary, but subsidiary, system to the national systems.[167] In other words, the primary responsibility for protecting human rights lies with the Member States, and the roles of the ECHR and ECtHR are subsidiary to those of the national systems. As Paul Mahoney noted, the ECtHR's responsibility for reviewing the implementation of ECHR standards by the Member States is based on the recognition that:

> An area of discretionary choice of action as to both initial policy and then implementation in individual cases is available to the national authorities in certain contexts when they are regulating the exercise of [an ECHR stipulation]. The result of this principle of interpretation, whenever it enters into play, is that the Strasbourg Court will exercise a degree of judicial self-restraint when reviewing decisions taken by national authorities, in particular rulings by national courts, the degree of restraint varying according to the context.[168]

In short, the doctrine acts as a sphere of deference to the Member States when they take measures that affect the implementation of the ECHR. It is the natural product of the distribution of power between national authorities and the ECtHR.

Furthermore, the margin of appreciation doctrine is also a means through which the ECtHR has sought to reconcile the protection of fundamental rights standards with the concerns and demands of the Member States. The doctrine was first relied on in the context of the derogation clause under the ECHR. It was born into the ECHR jurisprudence in the European Human Rights Commission's Report via the *Cyprus* case.[169] In relation to an emergency arising on the island of Cyprus, two applications were lodged with the European Human Rights Commission (EHR Commission) alleging multiple violations of the ECHR by the UK. The UK pleaded Article 15 of the ECHR, which allows Member States to derogate from the ECHR when a public emergency threatens the life of the

167. Arai-Takahashi (N20) 3.

168. Paul Mahoney, 'The Relationship between the Strasbourg Court and the National Courts' (2014) 130 *LQR* 568, 586.

169. *Greece v UK*, No. 176/56 (1958–1959) 2 Ybk 174.

nation. The EHR Commission noted that the UK authorities 'should be able to exercise a certain measure of discretion in assessing the extent strictly required by the exigencies of the situation' [170] and endorsed the national margin of appreciation in evaluating whether a measure was in strict proportion to an unquestioned situation of emergency.

Lawless v Ireland [171] was the first detailed exposition of the margin of appreciation doctrine as applied to the EHR Commission's presentations to the ECtHR. The EHR Commission allowed the respondent State 'a certain discretion — a certain margin of appreciation ... in determining whether there exists a public emergency which threatens the life of the nation and which must be dealt with by exceptional measures derogating from its normal obligations under the Convention'.[172] In this case, the applicant — an Irish citizen and a member of the Irish Republican Army (IRA) — was detained without trial for five months under the Irish Offences Against the State Act 1939. Extraordinary detention powers were invoked by the Irish authorities as a reaction to IRA activities. The applicant claimed breaches of Articles 5 to 7 (i.e., the right to liberty and security, the right to a fair trial, and no punishment without law) of the ECHR. However, the Irish authorities pleaded the existence of emergency conditions under Article 15 (i.e., a public emergency threatening the life of the nation) and applied detention only to the extent strictly required by the exigencies of the situation.[173] The ECtHR upheld the Irish government's discretion in taking action as the detention in question was executed to quell civil strife and IRA activities in Ireland and Northern Ireland even though these actions might otherwise have violated rights and freedoms guaranteed under the ECHR.

The margin of appreciation doctrine has been operating most obviously in relation to qualified rights, such as those contained in Articles 8 to 11 of the ECHR (i.e., the right to respect for private and family life; freedom of thought, conscience, and religion; freedom of expression; and freedom of association).[174]

170. Ibid., 176.

171. (1961) 1 EHRR 15.

172. Ibid., [82].

173. Ibid., [1]–[30].

174. Yourow (N161).

2.3.1.1 Issues Involving Political, Social, and Economic Aspects

Although the ECHR is premised upon the need to guarantee a minimum standard of fundamental rights protection, the ECtHR equally recognises that Member States are sometimes better placed to determine whether certain individual rights should be limited. This is because they have particular knowledge of the political, social, and economic circumstances in which opinions in a democratic society may widely differ.[175] When considering such decisions, particularly those concerning social and economic policies, the ECtHR

> will respect the legislature's judgment as to what is 'in particular interest' unless that judgment be manifestly without reasonable foundation. In other words, although the court cannot substitute its own assessment for that of national authorities, it is bound to review the contested measures ... and, in so doing, to make an inquiry into the facts with reference to which the national authorities acted.[176]

However, there are two conflicting points in the statement above. On one hand, in the social and political decisions of national authorities that impact the allocation of public funds, the ECtHR will hesitate to intervene, and the proportionality test may be reduced to one of 'manifest unreasonableness'. In *Hatton v UK*,[177] for example, the ECtHR mentioned that

> the court reiterates the fundamentally subsidiary nature of the Convention. The national authorities have direct democratic legitimation and are, as the court has held on many occasions, in principle better placed than an international court to evaluate local needs and conditions. In matters of general policy, on which opinions within a democratic society may reasonably differ widely, the role of the domestic policy maker should be given a special weight.[178]

Moreover, the ECtHR also recognises that national authorities, particularly national courts, may have the benefit of direct contact with the parties and

175. *James v UK* (1986) 8 EHRR 123, [43].

176. *JA Pye (Oxford) Ltd v UK* (2008) 46 EHRR 45, [75].

177. (2003) 37 EHRR 611.

178. Ibid., [97].

witnesses, thus allowing them to assess their demeanours when giving evidence and placing them in a better position to balance the interests of those involved.[179] In such cases, the ECtHR is reluctant to substitute its own view for that of the domestic courts.[180]

On the other hand, despite a wide margin of appreciation being afforded for social policy decisions,[181] the political nature of the decision itself will not be deferred completely to the judgment of national authorities. Thus, although the extent to which national authorities make public funds available to mediate an individual's ECHR right is a political, rather than judicial, decision,[182] the determination of whether the ECHR standards themselves have been breached is a matter for the ECtHR.[183]

2.3.1.2 The Protection of Morality

As there is currently no consensus concerning morality at the European level, a certain weight should be accorded to the opinions of the state organs. In *Handyside v UK*,[184] the English court convicted Handyside for publishing obscene materials containing the British version of *The Little Red Schoolbook*, a handbook that recommends an alternative lifestyle to school children and contains information about sex, *inter alia*. It was widely distributed in Europe free of charge but was considered obscene in the UK. Handyside argued that its freedom of expression [185] had been violated.

In applying the margin of appreciation doctrine, the ECtHR adopted a two-stage test. First, the Court asked whether the actual interference had been relevant and sufficient. Second, it asked whether the interference had been

179. Beatson, Grosz, Hickman, and Singh (N120) [2–133].

180. *Hokkanen v Finland* (1994) 19 EHRR 137, [55]; *Johansen v Norway* (1997) 23 EHRR 33, [64]; *Bronda v Italy* (1998) 33 EHRR 81, [59]; *TP and KM v UK* (2001) 34 EHRR 42, [70].

181. *Penticova v Moldova* (2005) 40 EHRR SE23; *Marzari v Italy* (1999) EHRR CD 175.

182. *Chapman v UK* (2001) 33 EHRR 18, [99].

183. *Bladet Tromsø and Stensaas v Norway* (2000) 29 EHRR 125, [79]; *Vgt Verein gegen Tierfabriken v Switzerland* (2002) 34 EHRR 4, [67].

184. (1976) 1 EHRR 737.

185. ECHR, Art 10.

necessary. Based on the doctrine, an action is considered necessary unless the applicant can prove otherwise. The first stage of this test required the ECtHR to consider not only whether the UK authorities thought they had sufficient reason for their derogation but also whether they had been justified in their belief. The Court found that the reaction of the public to the published material rendered relevant and sufficient moral grounds for action against the publisher.

Once the ECtHR decided that the grounds for interference were relevant and sufficient, it needed to ascertain whether the interference was necessary. The UK government argued that their alleged violation of the publisher's freedom of expression was within an exception mentioned in paragraph 2, Article 10 of the ECHR (i.e., the protection of morality). This is because the seizure and confiscation of the publication in question was necessary in a democratic society to protect the morals of the public. In deciding whether the seizure and confiscation of the publication were necessary, the ECtHR determined that the adjective 'necessary' was equated with 'pressing social need'. The Court then examined whether the English legislation was an expression of a 'pressing social need' that justified limiting the freedom of expression of the publisher. The Court held that

> [i]t is not possible to find in the domestic law of the various Contracting States a uniform European conception of morals. The view taken by their respective laws of the requirements of morals varies from time to time and from place to place, especially in our era which is characterized by a rapid and far-reaching evolution of opinions on the subject. By reason of their direct and continuous contact with the vital forces of their countries, State authorities are in principle in a better position than the international judge to give an opinion on the exact content of these requirements as well as on the 'necessity' of a 'restriction' or 'penalty' intended to meet them ... It is for the national authorities to make the initial assessment of the reality of the pressing social need implied by the notion of 'necessity' in this context. Consequently, Article 10 para. 2 leaves to the Contracting States a margin of appreciation. This margin is given both to the domestic legislator ('prescribed by law') and to the bodies, judicial among others, that are called upon to interpret and apply the laws in force.[186]

186. *Handyside* (N184) [48].

Based on this assessment, the ECtHR ruled that there had been no violation of Article 10(1), saying that to ensure national institutions are given the opportunity to determine whether seizure is necessary, while at the same time maintaining ECtHR supervision, they are provided a margin of appreciation. The Court further explained that only if they stepped outside this margin would they be in violation of the ECHR. Therefore, the ECtHR held that the UK was entitled to form its own view on moral issues and to enforce these views during a pressing social need.

Similarly, in *Belfast City Council v Miss Behavin' Ltd*,[187] the House of Lords rejected an ECHR challenge regarding the refusal to license a sex shop on the grounds that

> the proximity of certain public buildings and shops of particular attraction to children, and of places of worship, appears to ... represent a rational ground for making and adhering to a nil determination: indeed it is just the sort of assessment that a local authority is best able to judge.[188]

In this case, the specific right invoked — the right to free expression under Article 10 (in the form of the right to vend pornography) — is of low significance, and the lower the significance, the broader the margin of discretion is likely to be. Lord Hoffmann noted that

> [i]f Article 10 [freedom of expression] and Article 1 of the First Protocol [protection of property] are engaged at all, they operate at a very low level. The right to vend pornography is not the most important right of free expression in a democratic society and the licensing system does not prohibit anyone from exercising it. It only prevents him from using unlicensed premises for that purposes. ... This is an area of social control in which the Strasbourg court has always accorded a wide margin of appreciation to member states, which in terms of the domestic constitution translates into the broad power of judgment entrusted to local authorities by the legislature.[189]

187. [2007] 1 WLR 1420, [2007] UKHL 19, [2008] LGR 27.
188. Ibid., [2008] LGR 27, 155 (Lord Neuberger).
189. Ibid., [2007] 1 WLR 1420, [16].

Although the core assumption underpinning the margin of appreciation is the need to observe the respective spheres of influence of different institutional forces, the ECtHR's deference to a Member State will vary according to the nature of the right in question. In *S and Marper v UK*,[190] the ECtHR summarised its approach as follows:

> A margin of appreciation must be left to the competent national authorities ... The breadth of this margin varies and depends on a number of factors including the nature of the [ECHR provision] in issue, its importance for the individual, the nature of the interference and the object pursued by the interference. The margin will tend to be narrower where the right at stake is crucial to the individual's effective enjoyment of intimate or key rights ... Where a particularly important fact of an individual's existence or identity is at stake, the margin allowed to the State will be restricted ... Where, however, there is no consensus within the Member State of the Council of Europe, either as to the relative importance of the interest at stake or as to how best to protect it, the margin will be wider.[191]

2.3.2 Application by the Court of Justice of the European Union

When supervising the development and implementation of human rights' jurisprudence in EU law, the CJEU is accustomed to applying the margin of appreciation doctrine in a number of contexts. For example, in economic decisions, such as the administration of the Common Agricultural Policy, a wide margin of appreciation is allowed by the CJEU to EU institutions upon which the decision-making power has been conferred.[192] To illustrate the concept of the margin of appreciation under the EU regime, Gráinne de Búrca [193] has coined the term 'federalism dimension' to describe

> the extent to which the aim of a particular measure is one which lies primarily within the competence of the Member State, rather than the competence

190. (2009) 48 EHRR 50, 1169, ECtHR (GC).

191. Ibid., [108]–[111].

192. *ex p Fedesa* (N114).

193. Gráinne de Búrca, 'The Principle of Proportionality and its Application in EC Law' (1993) 13 *YEL* 105, 112.

> of the Community institutions. Where the measure is seen to be primarily within the competence of the State, the Court is likely to be reluctant, unless a very important Community interest is adversely affected, to examine the proportionality of the national measure too closely.[194]

Moreover, de Búrca also believes that there may be different interests at play when the CJEU considers a challenge on the ground of proportionality to an EU measure rather than to a state measure. As a result, the 'federalist tensions' over the proper sphere of State versus EU competence are less likely to arise when it is EU acts being challenged.[195]

2.4 Margin of Appreciation vs Deference

With regard to the extent to which an international court can exercise its jurisdiction over sovereign states, domestic courts cannot deploy the margin of appreciation doctrine when considering ECHR issues arising within their own countries.[196] In *R v Director of Public Prosecutions, ex parte Kebilene*,[197] Lord Hope said:

> The doctrine of 'margin of appreciation' is a familiar part of the jurisprudence of the ECHR ... This doctrine is an integral part of the supervisory jurisdiction which is exercised over state conduct by the international court ... This technique is not available to the national courts when they are considering [ECHR] issues arising in their own countries. But in the hands of national courts ... the [ECHR] should be seen as an expression of fundamental principles rather than as a set of mere rules. The questions which courts will have to decide in the application of these principles will involve questions of balance between competing interests and issues of proportionality ... In this area difficult choices may have to be made by the executive or the legislature between the rights of the individual and the needs of society. In some circumstances, it will be appropriate for courts to recognise

194. Ibid.

195. Ibid.

196. *Porter v South Bucks DC* [2002] 1 All ER 425, 438–439 (Brown LJ); *AXA General Insurance Ltd v Lord Advocate* [2011] UKSC 46, [2012] 1 AC 868, [32] (Lord Hope DPSC) and [131] (Lord Reed).

197. [2000] 2 AC 326.

> that there is an area of judgment within which the judiciary will defer, on democratic grounds, to the considered opinion of the elected body or person whose act or decision is said to be incompatible with the [ECHR] ... It will be easier for such an area of judgment to be recognised where the [ECHR] itself requires a balance to be struck, much less so where the right is stated in terms which are unqualified. It will be easier for it to be recognised where the issues involve questions of social or economic policy, much less so where the rights are of high constitutional importance or are of a kind where courts are especially well placed to assess the need for protection. But even where the right is stated in terms which are unqualified, courts will need to bear in mind the jurisprudence of the European Court which recognises that due account should be taken of the special nature of terrorist crime and the threat which it poses to a democratic society.[198]

For this reason, the doctrine has no application in English law.[199] As stated in *Handyside*,[200] 'state authorities are in principle in a better position than the international judge to give an opinion of restrictions on ECHR rights',[201] and to assess their necessity, as well as the subsidiary role of the ECtHR, in protecting human rights. Thus, a transposition of the margin of appreciation doctrine to the domestic context would be wholly inappropriate.[202]

Julian Rivers concurred with these views, saying that the international and domestic margins of appreciation cannot be identical, so judges and academic writers in Britain have avoided using the term 'margin of appreciation' and use 'discretionary area of judgment', 'area of discretion', 'margin of discretion', or 'judicial deference' instead.[203] The difference between the margin of appreciation and deference is, according to Rivers, that as an international tribunal, the ECtHR supervises complete domestic legal systems with legislative, executive,

198. Ibid., 379.

199. Ibid., 380; *R (Begum) v Headteacher and Governors of Denbigh High School* [2006] UKHL 15, [2006] 2 WLR 719, [2007] 1 AC 100; *Re G (Adoption: Unmarried Couple)* [2009] 1 AC 173, 187–188 (Lord Hoffmann) and 214–215 (Baroness Hale); *A v UK* (2009) 49 EHRR 29, 184.

200. *Handyside* (N184).

201. Ibid., 753–754.

202. Stephen Grosz, Jack Beatson, and Peter Duffy, *Human Rights: The 1998 Act and the European Convention* (Sweet & Maxwell 2000) 19.

203. Julian Rivers, 'Proportionality and Variable Intensity of Review' (2006) 65 *CLJ* 174, 175.

and judicial branches. In contrast, the domestic equivalent is to address the relationship of the judiciary with other branches of government (i.e., the executive and the legislature) and to require that regard be had to their assessments of proportionality.[204] Moreover, Mahoney further argues that the ECtHR, being an international court, is also facing, and so needs to take account of, the cultural diversity of human rights conceptions among different nations in a way that would be inappropriate for the domestic courts of a single political community.[205] In short, Cora Hoexter provides a useful definition for deference:

> [The judiciary must display] a willingness to appreciate the legitimate and constitutionally-ordained province of administrative agencies; to admit the expertise of those agencies in policy-laden or polycentric issues; to accord their interpretations of fact and law due respect and to be sensitive in general to the interests legitimately pursued by administrative bodies and the practical and financial constraints under which they operate.[206]

Although national courts conducting a review or exercising their supervisory jurisdiction will act with restraint in assessing the actions of public bodies, particularly in connection with certain policy issues (e.g., complex economic matters, national security, and the conduct of diplomatic relations), the national court does not, and should not, determine the 'margin' allowed to a public body using the same process as the ECtHR. This point has been recognised by the UK Divisional Court in *R v Stratford Justices, ex parte Imbert*.[207] During this case, Buxton LJ stated that

> the application of the doctrine of the margin of appreciation would appear to be solely a matter for the Strasbourg Court ... the English judge cannot therefore himself apply or have recourse to the doctrine of the margin of appreciation as implemented by the Strasbourg Court. He must, however, recognise the impact of that doctrine upon the Strasbourg Court's analysis of the meaning and implications of the broad terms of the [ECHR] provisions.[208]

204. Ibid.

205. Paul Mahoney, 'Marvellous Richness of Diversity or Invidious Cultural Relativism' (1998) 19 *HRLJ* 1.

206. Cora Hoexter, 'The Future of Judicial Review in South African Administrative Law' (2000) 117 *SALJ* 484, 501.

207. [1999] 2 Cr App R 276.

208. Ibid., 394. See also *ex p Kebilene* (N197) 379 (Lord Hope).

The earliest decisions under the Human Rights Act 1998 (HRA 1998) indicate that domestic courts in Britain would not, and indeed should not, apply the margin of appreciation doctrine 'undiluted' to rights adjudication in the domestic context.[209] To do so would, as Roger Masterman argues, result in a less-than-rigorous standard of review at the domestic level and allow the margins of appreciation designed for other Member States to 'creep into' domestic law.[210] Although the respondents (i.e., the government or public authorities) did, in several cases, argue for its transposition into domestic law, they were all rejected by the courts.[211]

However, there are contrary views. For example, in *ex parte Kebilene*,[212] although Lord Hope mentioned that it should not be open to national courts to afford the margin of appreciation in the domestic context, the Court also noted that 'the extent to which domestic courts have sought to disentangle the margin of appreciation from Strasbourg decisions when giving effect to them in the domestic context is open to questions'.[213] In this regard, Helen Fenwick and Gavin Phillipson have given a strong argument that

> in numerous appellate decisions under the HRA, the courts have paid lip service to the notion that the margin of appreciation has no role to play in domestic decision-making. *In nearly every case* ... the courts have then gone on to apply Strasbourg case law heavily determined by that doctrine, thus precisely applying the margin of appreciation.[214] [emphasis added]

Whatever the outcome of the debate may be, reliance on the concept was, in *R (on the application of Prolife Alliance) v BBC*,[215] held to be 'confusing and therefore inapposite'.[216]

209. Roger Masterman, *The Separation of Powers in the Contemporary Constitution: Judicial Competence and Independence in the United Kingdom* (CUP 2011) 117; Helen Fenwick and Gavin Phillipson, 'Direct Action, Convention Values and the Human Rights Act' (2001) 21 *LS* 535, 553–554.

210. Ibid., Masterman, 117–118; Fenwick and Phillipson, 553–554.

211. Margit Cohn, 'Legal Transplant Chronicles: The Evolution of Unreasonableness and Proportionality Review of the Administration in the United Kingdom' (2010) 58 *AJCL* 583, 623.

212. *ex p Kebilene* (N197).

213. Ibid., 380–381.

214. Helen Fenwick and Gavin Phillipson, *Media Freedom under the Human Rights Act* (OUP 2006) 146.

215. [2003] UKHL 23, [2004] 1 AC 185.

216. Ibid., 254 (Lord Bridge).

Despite the above-mentioned view, the margin of appreciation doctrine is not a new idea in Britain. Prior to the enforcement of the HRA 1998, the courts showed a relatively high degree of 'deference', 'margin of discretion', or 'discretionary areas of judgment' towards certain primary decision-makers regarding particular kinds of issues and applied a less intense standard of review to those decisions accordingly.[217] Although there is no accepted legal definition of the term 'deference',[218] Paul Horwitz has suggested that in the context of applying proportionality during constitutional rights limitations, 'deference' can be defined as 'a situation where a judge adopts an opinion expressed by another branch of government (either the legislative or executive) regarding the components of proportionality when, without this expression, the judge would not have adopted that opinion'.[219]

As with that of their European counterparts, the area where the highest level of discretionary judgment, or high degree of deference, is given to primary decision-makers in the UK is that where decisions involve matters of economic and social policy, managerial questions, or issues involving the allocation of scarce resources.[220] These matters are best not decided by judges because they admit to not having objective criteria for their decisions.[221] They are not suitable for making political decisions because these verdicts often involve utilitarian cost and benefit calculations.[222] In *ex parte Kebilene*,[223] Lord Hope famously stated:

> There will be times during [ECHR] adjudication, when a court will need to recognise that difficult choices may have to be made by the executive or the legislature between the rights of the individual and the needs of society. In some circumstances it will be appropriate for the courts to recognise that there is an area of judgment within which the judiciary will defer on

217. David Feldman and Andrew Burrows (eds), *English Public Law* (2nd edn, OUP 2009) 373.

218. T.R.S. Allan, 'Common Law Reason and the Limits of Judicial Deference' in David Dyzenhaus (ed), *The Unity of Public Law* (Hart Publishing 2004) 291.

219. Paul Horwitz, 'Three Faces of Deference' (2008) 83 *NDLR* 1061, 1072.

220. *ex p Kebilene* (N197) 381; *R (Hooper) v Secretary of State for Work and Pensions* [2003] 1 WLR 2623, [2005] UKHL 29, [36]; *Marcic v Thames Water Utilities Ltd* [2004] UKHL 66, [68] and [71].

221. *R v Secretary of State for the Environment, ex p Hammersmith and Fulham London Borough Council* [1991] 1 AC 521, 596–597 (Lord Bridge).

222. *R v Cambridge Health Authority, ex p B* [1995] 2 All ER 129 (CA), [1995] 1 WLR 898.

223. *ex p Kebilene* (N197).

> democratic grounds to the considered opinion of the elected body ... where the issues involve questions of social or economic policy, much less where the rights are of high constitutional importance or are of a kind where the courts are especially well placed to assess the need for protection.[224]

Even after enactment of the HRA 1998, the notion of deference has been increasingly relied upon as one of the reasons, if not the sole reason, to deny ECHR claims in diverse areas of executive power,[225] including national security,[226] immigration,[227] public order,[228] and the allocation of public resources.[229] Notably, most judges subscribe to the following summary given by Laws LJ in *International Transport Roth GmbH v Secretary of State for the Home Department*:[230]

> (1) First, greater deference is to be paid to an Act of Parliament than to a decision of the executive or a subordinate measure ... where the decision-maker is not Parliament but a minister or other public or governmental authority exercising power conferred by Parliament. A degree of deference will be due on democratic grounds because 'the decision-maker is Parliament's delegate';[231]
>
> (2) Second, 'there is more scope for deference where the [ECHR] itself requires a balance to be struck, much less so where the right is stated in terms which are unqualified. Hence, where the qualified rights of the [ECHR] are at issue, the courts should be mindful of the legitimacy of the decision-maker's assessment of what action is deemed to be necessary in a democratic society';[232]

224. Ibid., 381.

225. John Wadham and Helen Mountfield, *Blackstone's Guide to the Human Rights Act 1998* (3rd edn, OUP 2003) 82–86.

226. *Secretary of State for the Home Department, ex p Rehman* [2001] UKHL 47, [2003] 1 AC 153.

227. *R (Farrakhan) v Secretary of State for the Home Department* [2002] EWCA Civ 606, [2002] QB 1391.

228. Ibid.

229. *R (Alconbury Developments Ltd) v Secretary of State for the Environment, Transport and the Regions* [2001] UKHL 23; *R v Secretary of State for the Environment, Transport and the Regions, ex p Spath Homes Ltd* [2001] 2 AC 349 (HL); *Poplar Housing and Regeneration Community Association Ltd v Donoghue* [2001] EWCA Civ 595, [2001] 3 WLR 183, [2001] 4 All ER 605; *R v Secretary of State for Work and Pensions, ex p Carson and Reynolds* [2003] EWCA Civ 797, [2003] 3 All ER 577, [2005] 4 All ER 545, [2005] UKHL 37, [2006] 1 AC 173.

230. [2002] 3 WLR 344, [2003] QB 728.

231. Ibid., [2003] QB 728, [83].

232. Ibid., [84].

(3) Third, 'greater deference will be due to the democratic powers where the subject matter in hand is peculiarly within their constitutional responsibility, and less when it lies more particularly within the constitutional responsibility of the courts. The first duty of government is the defence of the realm. It is well settled that executive decisions dealing directly with matters of defence, while not immune from judicial review (that would be repugnant to the rule of law), cannot sensibly be scrutinised by the courts on grounds relating to their factual merits ... The first duty of the courts is the maintenance of the rule of law. That is exemplified in many ways, not least by the extremely restrictive construction always placed on no-*certiorari* clauses';[233]

(4) Finally, 'greater or less deference will be due according to whether the subject matter lies more readily within the actual or potential expertise of the democratic powers or the courts. Thus, quite aside from deference, government decisions in the area of macro-economic policy will be relatively remote from judicial control'.[234]

Overall, the concept of a discretionary area of judgment, within which the judiciary will defer, clearly indicates that there is an area of decision-making in which the primary decision-maker is immune from any interference by the courts. Therefore, the primary decision-maker must be immune from any review by the courts within that area as there is no point in conducting a review if there can be no interference at the end of it.[235] In other words, it is a justiciability issue, being premised on the idea that certain issues are simply not amenable to judicial determination. Examples of this include areas of judgment where the rights at stake are qualified rights, where the ECHR itself requires a balance to be struck, or where the issues involve questions of social or economic policy.[236]

However, Geneviève Cartier has a different view. She claims that the justification for judicial restraint is not based on judicial deference or the

233. Ibid., [85].

234. Ibid., [87].

235. Murray Hunt, 'Sovereignty's Blight: Why Contemporary Public Law Needs the Concept of "Due Deference"' in Nicholas Bamforth and Peter Leyland (eds), *Public Law in a Multi-Layered Constitution* (Hart Publishing 2003) 345.

236. Ibid., 345–346.

recognition of a legitimate role for the executive in law. Rather, such justification is premised on the idea of judicial abstinence, or the necessity to keep the judiciary away from decisions that are viewed as being outside the realm of law. Such a hands-off approach to discretion by the courts is, as Cartier argues, primarily dictated by the necessity to keep the judiciary in a position that is compatible with a 'formal view of the separation of powers'.[237] As discretion requires choices to be based on political or policy considerations, applying discretion to substantive legal scrutiny is seen as subjecting the courts to the 'slippery ground of politics'.[238] Cartier further states that judicial review based on *Wednesbury* unreasonableness or *GCHQ* irrationality by the courts is a way for them to show their faith in 'the rationale for deference or abstinence'.[239] Overall, whatever the rationale for it, such judicial deference has gained widespread acceptance.[240]

2.5 Similar Approaches in Hong Kong Courts

In Hong Kong, the approach taken by the CFA does tally with that of its British counterparts. In the *Obstetric Services* case, [241] the CFA noted that the discretionary area of judgment of the executive and the legislature reflects the different constitutional roles of the courts, on one hand, and of the executive and the legislature, on the other. The courts are responsible for applying the law but matters of state policy — socio-economic policy, for instance — are predominantly handled by the executive and the legislature. Where public funds are involved, the courts do recognise that lines have to be drawn by both the executive and the legislature. However, exceptions are made when a line is drawn in contravention of fundamental values in relation to personal characteristics (e.g., race, colour, gender, etc.) and when it has been shown to be

237. Geneviève Cartier, 'The *Baker* Effect: A New Interface between the Canadian Charter of Rights and Freedoms and Administrative Law — The Case of Discretion' in Dyzenhaus (N218) 65.

238. Ibid.

239. Cartier (N237) 65.

240. Hunt (N235) 346.

241. *Fok Chun Wa v Hospital Authority* (unrep., 17 December 2008, HCAL 94/2007) [2008] HKEC 2161, [72]–[77] and [96]–[117] (CFI); (unrep., CACV 30/2009) [2010] HKEC 713, [78] and [99], (2010) 15 HKPLR 628, [2011] 1 HKLRD A1 (CA); [2012] 2 HKC 413 (CFA), (2012) 15 HKCFAR 409.

manifestly without reasonable foundation. In view of the above, Cora Chan [242] has, in accordance with other scholars, observed:

> Deference is a form of judicial restraint, invented by courts to uphold the separation of powers. The point of the separation of powers is (1) to enhance efficiency: allocating functions to institutions that are most capable of performing them well (the institutional consideration for deference);[243] and (2) to uphold constitutional values of a particular society (eg respect for majority will; protecting liberties):[244] allocating functions in a way that best achieves these values and is hence most constitutionally legitimate (the constitutional consideration for deference).[245]

In contrast to this, I contest that the argument that the discretionary area of judgment is justified on democratic grounds since the executive and the legislature are constitutionally competent to do so is less convincing in Hong Kong because a fully democratic regime has not been in operation before or after 1997. On the other hand, Cora Chan has claimed that since the Basic Law [246] established constitutional democracy as the central constitutional values that inform the separation of powers, the LegCo, or the majority will, is no longer sovereign in the old sense of the term.[247] Rather, it is now constrained by constitutional instruments that embodied the values of a modern democracy, such as that of fundamental rights.[248] As ruled in *RJR-McDonald Inc v Attorney General of Canada*,[249] no area of policy is free from the 'limiting framework' of our constitution.[250]

242. Cora Chan, 'Focus What's So "Unusual" about *W*? Deference and the Separation of Powers: An Assessment of the Court's Constitutional and Institutional Competences' (2011) 41 *HKLJ* 7, 9.

243. N.W. Barber, 'Preclude to the Separation of Powers' (2001) 60(1) *CLJ* 59, 65.

244. Eric Barendt, 'Separation of Powers and Constitutional Government' (1995) *PL* 599.

245. Hunt (N235) 354.

246. Effective on 1 July 1997, and prior to that, it was established by the ICCPR in the Letters Patent from 1991 to 1997.

247. Chan (N242) 11.

248. Ibid.

249. [1995] 3 SCR 199.

250. Ibid., [136].

As constitutional democracy admits both the value of respect for majority will and the value of constitutionalism, the courts will respect the majority will on the condition that it is constitutional.[251] Therefore, the courts are mandated, and thus legally obliged, to ensure that laws and policies returned by majoritarian will comport with those constitutional values, and to strike them down if they do not.[252] The courts must, when fulfilling this constitutional mandate, scrutinise the executive's policies and make an independent judgment to ascertain whether they are constitutional. If they defer to the government on the 'very question' of whether a certain policy is constitutional, they would leave our constitutional entitlements unpoliced; hence, abdicating their responsibility under a constitutional rights order.[253]

In fact, the Hong Kong courts have changed social values from time to time in order to bring them in line with constitutional rights.[254] In the *Prisoner's Voting Right* case,[255] for instance, the Court of First Instance liberalised the election regime by allowing prisoners to exercise their right to vote. In order to achieve this, there have been situations in which the courts' independent judgment of the constitutional values has differed from those of the majority.[256] In a constitutional democracy, the courts are mandated, and thus obliged, to depart from the majority will if that is necessary to safeguard constitutional values. As Cora Chan has argued, 'the courts have played a role in leading changes in social values'.[257] In *Leung T C William Roy v Secretary for Justice*,[258] both the Court of First Instance and the Court of Appeal struck down buggery law [259] as they discriminated against homosexual men. In this case, Cora Chan opines that the courts are so robust 'not [to] revert value judgments on rights back to the public', saying that if they do so, it would be regarded as evading their duty to ensure that 'the majority does not trample upon constitutional rights'.[260]

251. Chan (N242) 11.

252. Ibid.

253. Ibid., 12.

254. Ibid., 13.

255. *Chan Kin Sum v Secretary for Justice* [2008] 6 HKC 486, [142]–[143], [148]–[149], and [154].

256. Chan (N242) 13.

257. Ibid.

258. [2005] 3 HKC 77 (CFI), [2005] 3 HKLRD 657, [2006] 4 HKLRD 211 (CA).

259. Crimes Ordinance, Cap 200, s 118C.

260. Chan (N242) 13.

In short, we are now living in an era of a vast administrative state, in which a number of government departments and public bodies, as well as their officials, make rules as to how social benefits should be distributed, how and the degree to which rule-breakers should be punished, etc. Therefore, Parliament in the UK and the LegCo in Hong Kong must delegate power to that effect primarily because they cannot possibly fulfil modern citizens' expectations through primary legislation. Experts are employed as agents to achieve legislators' policy goals and to identify legislation with varying degrees of specificity. The courts, in contrast, are said to be 'institutionally incompetent' because they lack similar expertise, have long endured the shortcomings of adversarial decision-making procedures, are removed from the political process, and are generally not delegated significant administrative powers. More importantly, judges are not elected via a democratic process.

At the same time, however, most civil societies also place various limits on governmental action through an independent judiciary. Thus, in spite of the above drawbacks, the courts still retain an important role. The difficulty for administrative law lies in the need to establish the competency of judges, who assess legality, and of expert decision-makers, who choose the wisest policies and adopt efficient and effective means to implement them. This proper allocation of decision-making authority between the courts and administrative decision-makers lies at the heart of this book. Although the courts should defer, in appropriate circumstances and to varying degrees, to administrative authorities, a broad and general principle of deference has to be, as Paul Daly argues, developed by answering three questions: why, how, and when should the courts defer?[261]

2.6 Constitutional Legitimacy of Judicial Deference

According to Barak, although there are three common justifications for the notion of deference — namely, the lack of democratic legitimacy for judging; the lack of institutional capacity; and judicial wisdom — he is of the opinion

261. Paul Daly, *A Theory of Deference in Administrative Law* (CUP 2012) 1.

that none of these justifications is proper.[262] First, judicial decisions enjoy full democratic legitimacy because they are derived directly from the constitution, either explicitly or implicitly.[263] Jeffrey Jowell agreed with this when he stated that 'courts have a constitutional duty to exercise their guardianship over a rights-based democracy, irrespective of their non-elected status'.[264] In the *Belmarsh Detainee*'s case,[265] Lord Bingham, concurred by the majority, held that '[t]he Attorney General is fully entitled to insist on the proper limits of judicial authority, but he is wrong to stigmatise judicial decision-making as in some way undemocratic',[266] adding that the fact that the executive or Parliament is accountable through elections to the public is not itself a reason for deference.[267]

Second, the institutional structure allows the courts to receive information concerning different considerations in the same way that it is presented to other branches of government. More importantly, judges do not set social policy. As Barak said, 'this assertion, however, has nothing to do with deference, and everything to do with the principle of separation of powers and the scope of the court's authority within that principle'.[268] Therefore, a court's limited investigative capacity should not automatically exclude judicial interrogation.[269] In *Bato Star*,[270] Justice O'Regan held that having acknowledged due respect for the expertise of the administrative decision-makers, the Court should not 'rubber stamp an unreasonable decision simply because of the complexity of the decision or the identity of the decision-maker'.[271]

Finally, judicial wisdom cannot replace constitutional responsibility, so there is, as Barak argues, 'no room for deference'.[272] Although the courts must

262. Barak (N52) 398.

263. Ibid.

264. Jeffrey Jowell, 'The Democratic Necessity of Administrative Justice' in Hugh Corder (ed), *Comparing Administrative Justice across the Commonwealth* (JUTA 2008) 21.

265. *A v Secretary of State for the Home Department* [2004] UKHL 56.

266. Ibid., [42].

267. Ibid., [97].

268. Barak (N52) 398.

269. Jowell (N264) 21.

270. *Bato Star* (N156).

271. Ibid., [48].

272. Barak (N52) 398; David Beatty, *The Ultimate Rule of Law* (OUP 2004) 156.

recognise the limits of their institutional capacity to decide certain matters, they should also be prepared to assert their constitutional duty to enter upon the review of a matter, irrespective of their ultimate institutional shortcomings.[273] Judges should always be prepared to do what judges do best — to probe the issue as best as they can, to seek as much available evidence as possible to ensure that relevant matters have been considered (and irrelevant matters disregarded), and to confirm a rational relation between the means and the end.[274]

In agreement with this, Murray Hunt said that the introduction of a discretionary area of judgment or margin of discretion, within which primary decision-makers are beyond the reach of judicial interference, is completely at odds with the concept of review for justification. This is because it treats certain areas of decision-making and decision-makers' responsibilities as being beyond the reach of legality and within the realm of pure discretion in which remedies for wrongs are predominantly political.[275] An argument that an issue is within the decision-maker's discretion is the very opposite of the culture of justification. It amounts to telling courts that a matter is none of their business, which is difficult to reconcile with modern conceptions of legality and the political branches' own professed commitment to the rule of law and respect of human rights.[276] Eyal Benvenisti noted that:

> Margin of appreciation, with its principled recognition of moral relativism, is at odds with the concept of the universality of human rights. If applied liberally, this doctrine can undermine seriously the promise of international enforcement of human rights that overcomes national politics. Moreover, its use may compromise the credibility of the applying international organ. Inconsistent applications in seemingly similar cases due to different margins allowed by the court might raise concerns about judicial double standards. Even more importantly, the rhetoric supporting national margin of appreciation and the lack of corresponding emphasis on universal values and standards may lead national institutions to resist external review altogether, claiming that they are the better judges of their particular domestic

273. Jowell (N264) 21.

274. Ibid., 21–22.

275. Hunt (N235) 338–339.

276. Ibid., 351.

constraints and hence the final arbiters of their appropriate margin. Thus, not only would universal standards be undermined, but also the very authority of international human rights bodies to develop such standards in the long run also may be compromised.[277]

Thus, what is at stake when the courts misuse the margin of appreciation is that it would not be conducive to maintaining the universal standards in the protection of human rights. However, there is evidence suggesting that the English courts have begun to accept the deference argument.[278] For one, English courts have long been reluctant to recognise error of fact, or non-jurisdictional error, as a ground justifying judicial intervention.[279] Against this background, the notion of parliamentary democracy is one of the factors attributable to such phenomenon since Parliament has given responsibility for fact-finding to administrative decision-makers, not courts.[280]

2.7 Concluding Remarks

Although there are many methodologies used to apply the proportionality principle internationally, regionally, and locally, what the principle ultimately promises is a common analytical framework, the significance of which is not in its omnipotence, but in how its structure influences how the courts reason many of the great moral and political controversies confronting political communities.

Analysis of the margin of appreciation doctrine also reveals that while international courts, like the ECtHR and the CJEU, will examine the proportionality of any Member State decision, a certain margin is given to the national authorities, be they executive, legislative, or judicial, because of their cultural diversities, direct democratic legitimacy, and familiarity with national and local situations. The purposes of the doctrine are to (1) delineate the respective areas of competence of the ECtHR and the CJEU as international courts and national authorities in securing the ECHR and EU citizen rights, (2) balance them

277. Eyal Benvenisti, 'Margin of Appreciation, Consensus, and Universal Standards' (1999) 31 *ILP* 843.

278. *Jones v First Tier Tribunal* [2013] 2 AC 48.

279. Paul Daly, 'Judicial Review of Factual Error in Ireland' (2008) 30 *DULJ* 187.

280. *R v Governor of Brixton Prison, ex p Armah* [1968] AC 192, 234 (Lord Reid).

against competing rights and interests, and (3) put in place a remedial system for breaches or potential breaches of those rights. There is a sharp difference with the notion of deference, in that deference addresses the relationship of the judiciary with legislative and executive branches of government and requires that regard be given to their assessments of proportionality according to their constitutional and institutional competences in discharging their duties.

Despite there being support for the notion of deference, I concur with Barak's and Hunt's views that none of these justifications is convincing. Acting as supervisory bodies whose powers are enshrined under the doctrine of separation of powers and the constitution, the courts are constitutionally competent to review any decision made by other branches of government. The institutional procedures in place also result in the courts receiving and assessing information regarding different considerations in the same way that it is presented to other government branches. Therefore, it is hardly convincing for the courts, without thinking of their constitutional and institutional roles, to fully adopt the concept of deference solely for the purpose of showing respect to other branches of government.

Taken together, to talk of proportionality, together with the notion of deference, assumes that the administration is entitled, via their discretionary powers, to pursue its own desired objective, assuming that the objective is legitimate and necessary and that the means used are not disproportionate to the aim pursued. Thus, if the means is disproportionate to the objective pursued, then the exercise of discretion should be struck down.

3

Wednesbury Unreasonableness vs Proportionality: A Common Law Debate

3.1 Introduction

In the United Kingdom (UK), proportionality has been applied in respect of directly effective law in the European Union (EU) via the European Communities Act 1972 (ECA 1972) (as at 31 January 2020, the day of Brexit) and of the European Convention on Human Rights (ECHR) via the Human Rights Act 1998 (HRA 1998), whereas in Hong Kong it has been applied in respect of the International Covenant on Civil and Political Rights (ICCPR) via the Hong Kong Bill of Rights Ordinance (BORO) and of the constitutional or legislative review litigation as empowered by the Basic Law of the Hong Kong Special Administrative Region (SAR) with effect from 1997. Apart from these regimes, however, the principle of proportionality is not, or at least not formally recognised as, an independent ground of judicial review in Britain [1] and Hong Kong. Rather, '*Wednesbury* unreasonableness', and its partner '*GCHQ* irrationality', as termed by Lord Diplock in the *GCHQ* case,[2] has long been dominating the sphere of judicial review litigation in Britain and Hong Kong to test reasonableness and rationality, and thereby the legality, of decision-makers in reaching their decisions.

1. *R v Secretary of State for the Environment, ex p NALGO* [1993] Admin LR 785; *Tesco Stores Ltd v Secretary of State for the Environment* [1995] 1 WLR 759; *R v Secretary of State for the Home Department, ex p Hargreaves* [1997] 1 All ER 397; *R v Radio Authority, ex p Bull* [1997] 2 All ER 561; *R (British Civilian Internees—Far East Region) v Secretary for Defence* [2003] EWCA Civ 473, [2003] QB 1397; *R (Jones) v Mansfield DC* [2003] EWCA Civ 1408, [2004] 2 P & CR 14; *Kennedy v Charity Commission* [2014] UKSC 20, [2014] 2 WLR 808.
2. *Council of Civil Service Unions v Minister for the Civil Service* [1983] UKHL 9, [1985] 1 AC 374, 410E.

Under the *Wednesbury* formula, the question asked by the courts is not whether the decision-maker strayed outside the purposes as defined by the governing statute (i.e., the test of illegality), nor whether the decision is procedurally unfair (i.e., the test of procedural impropriety).[3] The question here is whether the power under which the decision-maker acts — a power normally conferring a broad discretion — has been improperly exercised.

This chapter examines what the *Wednesbury* formula is all about: the rationale behind its development, the extent to which it has been fused with the proportionality principle, and its influence in Hong Kong. It then provides a comparative analysis between the pros and cons of the *Wednesbury* test and of the proportionality formula to see whether they have provided a rubric for the judicial review of irrationality in administrative law in Britain and Hong Kong. Finally, the chapter addresses the allegations that full recognition of the proportionality principle is incompatible with the distinction between appeal and review and that unelected members of the judiciary lack the expertise, experience, etc. (i.e., are 'constitutionally un-qualified' and 'institutionally ill-equipped', as some critics claim) to adjudicate on matters of politically and economically sensitive disputes, in particular, polycentric socio-economic rights issues which involve the prioritisation and allocation of scarce resources.

3.2 *Wednesbury* Unreasonableness

Wednesbury unreasonableness has been dominating the sphere of judicial review litigations in Britain and Hong Kong for several decades. However, what is 'unreasonableness'? What are its components? There is no consensus on these matters,[4] and the notion of 'unreasonableness' has many context-dependent definitions.[5] According to Aharon Barak, the conventional wisdom is that unreasonableness is decided on a case-by-case basis, in accordance with each case's

3. Ibid., 411 (Lord Diplock).

4. Aharon Barak, *The Judge in a Democracy* (PUP 2006) 248; Wojciech Sadurski, '"Reasonableness" and Value Pluralism in Law and Politics' in Giorgio Bongiovanni, Giovanni Sartor, and Chiara Valentini (eds), *Reasonableness and Law* (Springer 2009) 129.

5. Tom Hickman, 'The Reasonableness Principle: Reassessing its Place in the Public Sphere' (2004) 63 *CLJ* 166.

special circumstances.[6] In *Ganor v Attorney-General,* he states that 'reasonableness is not personal; it is substantive. It is not the decision-maker's reasonableness that renders the decision reasonable. Rather, the decision's reasonableness turns its maker into a reasonable person'.[7]

In Britain, the courts have developed and modified the *Wednesbury* formula to help define the proper boundaries of reasonableness within administrative law. However, these decisions portray the judiciary as being hesitant to intervene in the decisions made by administrative bodies unless the unreasonableness of their decision or action was extreme (i.e., 'something so absurd that no sensible person could ever dream that it lay within the powers of the authority' [8] or 'so outrageous in its defiance of logic or accepted moral standards that no sensible person who had applied his mind to the question to be decided could have arrived at it' [9]). As Jeffrey Jowell has pointed out, in the interests of integrity and accountability, the standard of unreasonableness should, where possible, be clarified by more precise categories, criteria, and principles to guide and govern all official decisions.[10]

In the *Wednesbury* case,[11] the plaintiff, Associated Provincial Picture Houses, was running cinemas in the Wednesbury area in the Midlands. The company wanted to open the cinema on Sundays. However, opening on Sundays was controversial at that time because many Christians believed that the Sabbath should be given over to prayer and contemplation as opposed to entertainment. Empowered by Section 1(1) of the Sunday Entertainments Act 1932 to allow cinemas to open on Sundays 'subject to such conditions as the authority thinks fit to impose', the defendant corporation, being a public body, permitted the plaintiff to open its cinema on the condition that no children under 15 were admitted to Sunday performances under any circumstances for the purpose of

6. Aharon Barak, *Proportionality: Constitutional Rights and their Limitations* (CUP 2012) 373.

7. [1990] IsrSC 44(2) 485 (Barak J).

8. *Associated Provincial Picture Houses Ltd v Wednesbury Corporation* [1948] 1 KB 223 (CA), 229 (Lord Greene MR).

9. *GCHQ* case (N2) 410E (Lord Diplock).

10. Jeffrey Jowell, 'Proportionality and Unreasonableness: Neither Merger nor Takeover' in Hanna Wilberg and Mark Elliott (eds), *The Scope and Intensity of Substantive Review: Traversing Taggart's Rainbow* (Hart Publishing 2015) 42.

11. *Wednesbury* case (N8).

protecting the moral welfare of children in the area. This meant that children under 15 could not be admitted to the cinemas even if they were accompanied by an adult. The plaintiff feared that the condition would prevent families from going to the cinema on Sundays, making it uneconomical to open on that day and so undermining the value of the licence.

The plaintiff then challenged the legality of the condition by using two arguments. First, they argued that the discretion of the local authority to impose conditions was not unfettered. In particular, such discretion had to be used to further the purposes contemplated by the legislation by which it had been conferred. That legislation concerned licensing, and it did not concern the protection of the moral welfare of children. The defendant therefore used its power for reasons that were irrelevant in order to achieve purposes that had been improper in the context of the legislation. Second, they argued that even if the authority could use its discretion to protect the welfare of children, the actual condition imposed was unlawful because it had been unreasonably wide. The moral welfare of children, argued the plaintiff, could have been protected without a total exclusion of children from cinemas on Sundays. A narrower condition, such as one that required children to be accompanied by a parent or guardian, would have been just as effective and less damaging to the plaintiff.

Nevertheless, the plaintiff lost their case. The Court of Appeal held that the local authority could take the moral welfare and spiritual well-being of children into account when exercising its discretion as to whether to permit a cinema to be open on Sunday. Regarding the second argument, the Court said that it would have intervened had the condition been so unreasonable or absurd that no reasonable authority could have imposed it. However, this was not the case here.

Holding that the condition imposed for protecting the moral welfare of children in its area was lawful and thus was not unreasonable, Lord Greene MR explained that the Court might have a different opinion from the defendant as to whether children under 15 should be admitted to a cinema on Sunday, and that, in fact, 'all over the country I have no doubt on a thing of that sort honest and sincere people have different views'.[12] His Lordship further explained

12. *Wednesbury* case (N8) 228.

that it was not for the courts to impose their view on the public authority, and providing that the authority acted lawfully, the courts would not intervene to change a decision that was legally taken.

Ruling that the condition imposed for protecting the moral welfare of children was not unreasonable, Lord Greene MR used the term 'unreasonable' in two senses. The first was a general description of things that must not be done by public bodies exercising discretionary powers, and could, as Paul Craig has suggested,[13] be called 'umbrella sense' as follows:

> The exercise of ... a discretion must be a real exercise of discretion. If, in the statute conferring the discretion, there is to be found expressly or by implication matters which the authority ... ought to have regard to, then in exercising the discretion it must have regard to those matters. Conversely, if the nature of the subject-matter and the general interpretation of the Act make it clear that certain matters would not be germane to the matter in question, the authority must disregard those irrelevant ... matters.[14]

This 'umbrella sense' of unreasonableness is used to describe actions based on illegality, irrelevancy, and the like.[15] Thus, if a person is entrusted with a discretion by the legislature (i.e., the one acting as an executive), they must direct themselves properly in administering the law. They must call their attention to the matters which they are bound to consider. On the contrary, they must exclude from their consideration matters which are irrelevant to what they have to consider. If they do not obey these rules, then they may truly be said to be acting 'unreasonably', and the courts would invalidate their decision.[16]

In *Padfield v Minister of Agriculture, Fisheries and Food*,[17] the Minister was held to have acted *ultra vires* when he used his statutory discretion for self-serving political motives in refusing to refer a complaint by certain milk producers to a Milk Marketing Board Committee. Lord Reid held that the purpose of the

13. Paul Craig, *Administrative Law* (7th edn, Sweet & Maxwell 2012) 562.
14. *Wednesbury* case (N8) 228–231.
15. Craig (N13) 646.
16. *Wednesbury* case (N8) 228–231.
17. [1968] 1 All ER 694.

Minister's discretion under the relevant statute was to enable him to consider whether a particular complaint was likely to be resolved via the statutory machinery, and it was not to enable him to avoid political embarrassment.[18] Lord Upjohn also said that error of law in the exercise of discretion means 'taking into account some wholly irrelevant or extraneous consideration, or ... wholly omitting to take into account a [mandatory] relevant consideration'.[19] Lord Pearce further stated that if all the known facts pointed to the conclusion that a discretionary power would be exercised in a certain way and the decision-maker takes the contrary course, the Court may infer that he had no good reason for doing so and conclude that he is exceeding his powers.[20] This case established the principle that there are no unfettered discretions in public law and that statutory powers must be used to promote the policy and objects of the statute, to be determined by the courts as a matter of law.

The second meaning of unreasonableness, which could be called 'substantive' meaning in its own right, says Craig,[21] is that 'something so absurd that no sensible person could ever dream that it lay within the powers of the authority',[22] or, says Lord Denning, something 'so wrong that no reasonable person could sensibly take that view'.[23] Even if an exercise of discretion survives the hurdles of propriety of purpose and relevancy, it may be invalidated if it is so unreasonable that none can reasonably reach such a decision.[24]

In *Short v Poole Corporation*,[25] Warrington LJ provided a good example as to what unreasonableness, or absurdity, is. In this case, although the local authority was empowered by a statute to employ teachers on such terms as it deems fit, a refusal to employ, or a dismissal of, a red-haired teacher merely because she had had red hair was held to be unreasonable or irrational. The

18. Ibid., 701C.

19. Ibid., 717F.

20. Ibid., 1053–1054.

21. Craig (N13) 562.

22. *Wednesbury* case (N8) 228–231 (Lord Greene MR).

23. *Secretary of State for Education and Science v Tameside MBC* [1977] AC 1014, 1026.

24. Craig (N13) 646.

25. [1926] Ch 66.

Court mentioned that it is unreasonable in one sense, and that in another sense, it is taking extraneous matters into consideration.[26] Referred to in the *Wednesbury* case, the decision in *Short v Poole Corporation* was regarded as so unreasonable that it might almost be described as being done in bad faith, and, in fact, all these things run into one another.[27] In this regard, Craig has observed that if the considerations relevant to refusal to employ, or dismissal of, the teacher are broadly defined as 'any physical characteristic' of the teacher, then of course dismissal on the above ground is relevant. However, common sense dictates that this is not the way that we would approach the matter. The question would be posed more specifically, and it should have distinguished between the types of physical characteristics that were felt to be relevant to teaching and those, such as hair colour, which were not.[28]

Unreasonableness can also be used to denote particularly extreme behaviour (such as acting for an improper motive or purpose, or making a 'perverse' or 'absurd' decision), which implies that the decision-maker has 'taken leave of his senses'.[29] There had been abundant law reports suggesting that the courts struck down discretionary decisions where administrative bodies had used their statutory power for an improper purpose.[30] In *Congreve v Home Office*,[31] the Home Secretary's decision to withdraw television licences from those who had failed to pay a higher fee (but were nevertheless within their rights so to do) was held to be unlawful because it imposed a punishment which related to no wrong (where people had bought a new licence early in order to avoid a price increase).

Sometimes, the expressions 'arbitrary and capricious' or an 'abuse of discretion' are also used as a synonyms for 'unreasonable'.[32] In *R v Barnet and*

26. Ibid., 90–91 (Warrington LJ).

27. *Wednesbury* case (N8) 228–231 (Lord Greene MR).

28. Craig (N13) 646–647.

29. *R v Secretary of State for the Environment, ex p Nottinghamshire CC* [1986] AC 240, 247–248 (Lord Scarman).

30. *Mayor of Westminster v London and North Western Railway Co* [1905] AC 426; *Porter v Magill* [2002] 2 AC 357.

31. [1976] QB 629.

32. *Weinberger v Inglis* [1919] AC 606.

Camden Rent Tribunal ex parte Frey Investments Ltd,[33] 'unreasonableness' has also been translated as 'frivolous or vexatious' and 'capricious and vexatious'. All in all, as both H.W.R. Wade and Christopher Forsyth have observed, the meaning of all such expressions is necessarily the same since the true question must always be whether the statutory power has been abused.[34]

3.3 Rationale behind the *Wednesbury* Formula

In general, *Wednesbury* unreasonableness reflects the traditional demarcation of powers between the administrative branches (i.e., the legislature and the executive) and the judicial branch, as heavily influenced by the doctrine of separation of powers,[35] or the so-called 'constitutional division of labour between the three branches of government'.[36] Under the doctrine of separation of powers, the legislative function includes the making of general application rules for the governance and order of society. The executive function includes the administration of the state and conducting foreign affairs, as well as the design of domestic policy subject to parliamentary approval prior to its implementation. The judicial function includes the independent determination of civil and criminal cases, along with the interpretation and application of statutory and common law. There is a clear boundary of administrative discretion beyond which judicial supervision should not cross. As M.J.C. Vile stated:

> It is essential for the establishment and maintenance of political liberty that the government be divided into three branches or departments, the legislature, the executive, and the judiciary. To each of these branches, there is a corresponding feature of government, legislative, executive or judicial. Each branch of government must be confined to the exercise of its

33. [1972] 2 QB 342.

34. H.W.R. Wade and Christopher Forsyth, *Administrative Law* (10th edn, OUP 2009) 296.

35. As Montesquieu famously put it: 'When the legislative and executive powers are united in the same person, or in the same body of magistracies, there can be no liberty; because apprehensions may arise, lest the same monarch or senate should enact tyrannical laws to execute them in a tyrannical manner'; see Montesquieu, *The Spirit of the Law* (Hafner 1949) 151–152.

36. Aileen Kavanagh, *Constitutional Review under the UK Human Rights Act* (CUP 2009) 8–9.

> own function and not allowed to encroach upon the functions of the other branches. Furthermore, the persons who compose these three agencies of government must be kept separate and distinct, no individual being allowed to be at the same time a member of more than one branch. In this way each of the branches will be a check on the others and no single group of people will be able to control the machinery of the State.[37]

Against this background, the courts do not, and should not, substitute their choice as to how discretion ought to be exercised for that of the administrative authority. They do not, and should not, intervene or re-assess the matters afresh and decide that funds ought to be allocated in one way rather than the other. Decisions as to political and social choice are made by the legislature, or by a person assigned the task by the legislature.[38] The courts accept that it is not their task to substitute judgment.[39] Thus, in *Chief Constable of the North Wales Police v Evans*,[40] Lord Brightman cautioned:

> [J]udicial review is concerned, not with the decision, but with the decision-making process. ... Judicial review, as the words imply, is not an appeal from a decision, but a review of the manner in which the decision was made. ... Unless that restriction on the power of the court is observed, the court will ... under the guise of preventing the abuse of power, be itself guilty of usurping power.[41]

In this environment, decisions as to political and social choice, such as socio-economic rights and polycentric issues which involve the prioritisation of conflicting interests and allocation of scarce resources, are, and should be, made by the legislature, or by a person assigned the task by the legislature (i.e., the one acting as an executive). This is especially the case if the decision under review is concerned with national economic policy. In *ex parte Nottinghamshire*

37. M.J.C. Vile, *Constitutionalism and the Separation of Powers* (2nd edn, Clarendon 1967) 14.

38. *R v Ministry of Agriculture, Fisheries and Food, ex p First City Trading Ltd* [1997] 1 CMLR 250, 278 (Lord Bridge).

39. *R v Cambridge Health Authority, ex p B* [1995] EWCA Civ 49, [1995] 2 All ER 129, [1995] 1 WLR 898.

40. [1982] 1 WLR 1155.

41. Ibid., 1173F–1174G.

County Council,[42] the House of Lords had to consider the exercise of the Secretary of State's statutory power to 'rate-cap' local authorities. In their decision, Lord Scarman said:

> We are in the field of public financial administration and we are being asked to review the exercise by the Secretary of State of an administrative discretion which inevitably requires a political judgment on his part and which cannot lead to action by him unless that action is first approved by the House of Commons ... I cannot accept that it is constitutionally appropriate, save in very exceptional circumstances, for courts to intervene on the ground of 'unreasonableness' to quash guidance framed by the Secretary of State and by necessary implication approved by the House of Commons, the guidance being concerned with the limits of public expenditure by local authorities and the incidence of the tax burden as between taxpayers and ratepayers ... For myself, I refuse in this case to examine the detail of the guidance or its consequences ... Such an examination by a court would be justified only if a *prima facie* case were to be shown for holding that the Secretary of State had acted in bad faith, or for an improper motive, or that the consequences of his guidance were so absurd that he must have taken leave of his senses.[43]

His Lordship further explained:

> If, as in this case, effect cannot be given to the Secretary of State's determination without the consent of the House of Commons and the House of Commons has consented, it is not open to courts to intervene unless the minister and the House have misconstrued the statute or the minister has — to put it bluntly — deceived the House.[44]

In view of the above, judicial review is, it is claimed, studiously designed to maintain a distinction between appeal and review,[45] a

42. *ex p Nottinghamshire* (N29).

43. Ibid., 247C–H.

44. Ibid., 250E.

45. Roger Masterman, *The Separation of Powers in the Contemporary Constitution: Judicial Competence and Independence in the United Kingdom* (CUP 2011) 62.

concept which was most famously noted by Lord Greene MR in the *Wednesbury* case. He stated:

> The power of the court to interfere in each [judicial review] case is not as an appellate authority to override a decision of the local authority, but as a judicial authority which is concerned, and concerned only, to see whether the local authority has contravened the law by acting in excess of the powers which Parliament has confined in them.[46]

Such deferential attitude has been attributable to Dicey's influence, which exemplifies a deep distrust for any supervisory role of the courts over the administration.[47] For Dicey, all exercise of public power is to be channelled through Parliament. Executive action should be subject to oversight by the House of Commons. Parliament reflects the will of the people and is, therefore, the appropriate mechanism within a democratic state to exercise such an oversight role. In short, Parliament is sovereign, and the rule of law requires all individuals and public authorities to be subject to the ordinary law of the land.

In this climate, *Wednesbury* review is, by definition, a standard that incorporates orthodox understandings of the courts as the implementers of Parliament's intentions.[48] The core assumption of *Wednesbury* unreasonableness is that the courts control exercises of administrative discretion of power delegated to the executive by Parliament.[49] As such, the notion of control within the standard does not allow the courts to examine the merits of a decision as judicial review is concerned not with the questions of substance but only with questions of legality.[50] Therefore, the *Wednesbury* formula is inextricably linked to an institutional understanding that where Parliament has delegated discretionary powers to a subordinate body, it is for that body, not the courts, to exercise the power received.[51] In the *Wednesbury* case, Lord Greene MR said

46. *Wednesbury* case (N8) 234.

47. A.V. Dicey, *Lectures Introductory to the Study of the Law of the Constitution* (J.W.F. Allison ed, OUP 2013).

48. Gordon Anthony, *UK Public Law and European Law* (Hart Publishing 2002) 105.

49. Ibid.

50. *Evans* (N40) 154 (Lord Brightman); *Tesco Stores* (N1) 771ff (Lord Hoffmann).

51. Anthony (N48) 105.

that the courts perform only a limited role relative to the review of powers delegated to other subordinate bodies by the sovereign Parliament.[52] Even several decades later, Lord Irvine has maintained that:

> Public authorities receive their powers from Parliament ... [and] Parliament ... entrusts that authority with decision-making power ... it follows that the courts are, in relative terms, ill-equipped to take decisions in place of the designated authority ... What this reduces to is a doctrine of judicial self-restraint in deference to the sovereignty to Parliament.[53]

3.4 From *Wednesbury* Unreasonableness to *GCHQ* Irrationality

In the *Wednesbury* case, Lord Greene MR defined 'unreasonableness' as a ground for judicial review of administrative discretion by referencing the council's decision in *Roberts v Hopwood*.[54] He stated that

> the decision was 'unreasonable' ... in the sense ... that in fixing the [wage level] they had fixed it by reference to something which they ought not to have entertained and to the exclusion of those elements which they ought to have taken into consideration.[55]

In this regard, 'unreasonableness' as thus understood is plainly a type of 'illegality' in terms of Lord Diplock's *GCHQ* classification, showing that the decision-maker has failed to 'understand correctly the law that regulates his decision-making power and [to] give effect to it'.[56]

What is more, in the *Wednesbury* case, Lord Greene MR furthered that 'there is no authority to support the proposition that the court has got some sort of

52. *Wednesbury* case (N8) 230.
53. Derry Irvine, 'Judges and Decision-Makers: The Theory and Practice of *Wednesbury* Review' (1996) *PL* 59, 60–61.
54. [1925] All ER Rep 24, [1925] AC 578.
55. *Wednesbury* case (N8) 684C.
56. *GCHQ* case (N2) 951.

overriding power to decide what is reasonable and what is unreasonable'.[57] However, if the purpose is correctly seen as masking what is, in reality, a process whereby judges rather than Parliament set the bounds of administrative discretion, there may be virtue in acknowledging this reality. In the *GCHQ* case,[58] Lord Diplock seems to have done so when he said that '*Wednesbury* unreasonableness' can stand upon its own feet as an accepted ground on which a decision may be attacked by judicial review (preferring to use the term 'irrational'). He also included moral criteria in his consideration:

> By 'irrationality' I mean what can now succinctly be referred to as '*Wednesbury* unreasonableness' ... It applies to a decision which is so outrageous in its defiance of logic or of accepted moral standards that no sensible person who had applied his mind to the question to be decided could have arrived at it. Whether a decision falls within this category is a question that judges by their training and experience should be well-equipped to answer, or else there would be something badly wrong with our judicial system.[59]

In this case, the House of Lords held that although the Prime Minister, acting as Minister for the Civil Service, had to adduce evidence that the decision to ban national unions at Government Communication Headquarters (GCHQ) was based on considerations of national security, the question of whether such considerations outweighed the *prima facie* duty of fairness was for the Minister herself to decide, so the banning decision was held to be rational.[60] According to Jowell, this definition is more specific than the traditional *Wednesbury* formula because it directs attention to two particular aspects of unreasonableness: 'defiance of logic' and 'accepted moral standards'.[61]

R v Secretary of State for the Environment, ex parte Fielder Estates (Canvey Ltd) [62] also illustrates behaviour of a kind that was deemed irrational. After a planning

57. *Wednesbury* case (N8) 684C.

58. *GCHQ* case (N2).

59. Ibid., 410E–H.

60. Ibid., 402–403, 406–407, 412–413, and 420–421; unless it seems the minister's decision was one which no reasonable minister could make, 406.

61. Jowell (N10) 46.

62. [1989] 57 P & CR 424.

application to build houses close to Canvey Island was refused, a public inquiry was set up which was expected to last for three days. During the inquiry, one of the objectors, the Canvey Ratepayers Association, was to present its evidence on the second day. When it turned up to do so, the Association found that the inquiry had already been closed by the inspector. After a complaint had been made to the Secretary of State, another inquiry was set up. However, this time, the other parties who had been present at the first inquiry, including Fielder Estates, were not notified about the second inquiry. It was held that the conduct of the Secretary of State was so unreasonable as to verge on irrationality and even absurdity. It also amounted to a failure to act with procedural fairness.

According to Paul Walker, irrationality underlies the crucial feature that the courts are not concerned with what they regard as reasonable, but rather with the quite different test of whether no sensible person entrusted with such a discretion could have regarded the conclusion under review as a reasonable one.[63] The test is stringent. Reasonable people may differ about moral standards and about the rigour with which logic must be applied. An assertion that a decision is illogical or fails to meet moral imperatives must be weighed against the needs of good administration, having regard to the fact that decision-makers will sometimes find themselves confronted with difficult or seemingly impossible tasks and must not shirk from applying common sense solutions. Only if the solution strays so far from logic or morally acceptable standards that no reasonable decision-maker could have thought it right will it be condemned as irrational. This involves a value judgment by the courts, but it is a judgment of a very limited kind.[64] The precise limits will depend on the circumstances of each case, and the intensity of the court's review may vary according to the nature of the case. For one thing, it has been said that interference with human rights should be subject to close scrutiny,[65] and that when the result of a flawed decision may endanger life or liberty, a special responsibility lies

63. Paul Walker, 'Irrationality and Proportionality' in Michael Supperstone and James Goudie, *Judicial Review* (Butterworths 1997) 121, as affirmed in *R v Secretary of State for Trade and Industry, ex p Lonrho Plc* [1989] 1 WLR 525, 535.

64. Ibid.

65. *R v Secretary of State for the Home Department, ex p Brind* [1991] 1 AC 696 (HL), 757 (Lord Ackner), [1991] 2 WLR 588.

on the courts.[66] By contrast, when considering the allocation of scarce housing resources among applicants who are homeless, the House of Lords, in *Puhlhofer v Hillingdon London Borough Council*,[67] urged judicial restraint.[68] Christopher Forsyth has a different view, arguing that 'irrationality' and 'unreasonableness' have different definitions, with the former meaning 'devoid of reason' and the latter meaning 'devoid of satisfactory reason'.[69] Taken together, although *GCHQ* irrationality is a well-established ground of judicial review in UK public law, its definition is still far from clear. Yossi Nehushtan lists [70] the following six context-dependent definitions:

> (1) Rationality as indistinguishable from reasonableness. It is quite common in UK public law to use the terms 'reasonableness review' (or *Wednesbury* unreasonableness) and 'rationality review' (or *Wednesbury* rationality) indistinguishably, yet without always explaining the exact meaning of these grounds of review. It was probably the influential view of Lord Diplock's in the *GCHQ* case ... that made the most significant contribution to enshrining the conceptual mistake of seeing reasonableness and rationality as indistinguishable. This was done by classifying the grounds of judicial review to three main categories, 'illegality', 'irrationality' and 'procedural impropriety'; and by clarifying that 'irrationality' is in fact identical to '*Wednesbury* unreasonableness'.
>
> (2) Rationality as a distinct ground of review that, compared to reasonableness, sets a lower hurdle for the administrative body. This approach, albeit within a specific context, was taken by the Supreme Court's in its decision in *Evans* ... according to which a demand to base a decision on 'reasonable grounds' sets a higher hurdle than 'mere rationality'.[71]

66. *Bugdaycay v Secretary of State for the Home Department* [1987] AC 514, 537 (Lord Bridge).

67. [1986] AC 484.

68. Ibid., 518 (Buxton LJ).

69. Wade and Forsyth (N34) 296.

70. Yossi Nehushtan, 'The Unreasonable Perception of Rationality and Reasonableness in UK Public Law', *UK Constitutional Law Blog*, 1 July 2019, available at: https://ukconstitutionallaw.org/2019/07/01/yossi-nehushtan-the-unreasonable-perception-of-rationality-and-reasonableness-in-uk-public-law/, last accessed 2 July 2019.

71. *R (Evans) v AG* [2015] UKSC 21, [91] and [129], cited ibid.

(3) Rationality as a ground of review that focuses on the decision-maker's 'mental process' as opposed to reasonableness review that focuses on the outcome — i.e. the decision-maker's decision. See for example Lord Sumption's view in *Hayes* ... that 'reasonableness is an external, objective standard applied to the outcome of a person's thoughts or intentions ... A test of rationality, by comparison, applies a minimum objective standard to the relevant person's mental processes'.[72]

(4) Rationality as a mega ground of judicial review that covers more specific grounds of review such as acting in bad faith, acting capriciously or arbitrarily etc. For this view see also in *Hayes*, where Lord Sumption held that 'a test of rationality ... imports a requirement of good faith, a requirement that there should be some logical connection between the evidence and the ostensible reasons for the decision, and (which will usually amount to the same thing) an absence of arbitrariness, of capriciousness or of reasoning so outrageous in its defiance of logic as to be perverse'.[73]

(5) Rationality as fairness, consistency or equality. This approach was taken in *Gallaher* ... especially by Lords Carnwath and Sumption who asserted that it is irrational to treat like cases differently — if there is no 'objective justification' for the different treatment.[74]

(6) 'Instrumental rationality' that requires logical or causal relation between means and end. Instrumental rationality is in fact part of the principle of proportionality. It is common to refer to the principle of proportionality as a four-stage test which includes legitimate aim; suitability (or rational connection); necessity (or applying the least intrusive measure); and proportionality in the narrow sense (proportionality *stricto sensu*). When we apply the second stage that sets the suitability or rationality test we are asking whether the means (interfering with a protected right or interest) can achieve the legitimate aim of the law or of the administrative decision. If there is no rational connection of any kind between the means and the end,

72. *Hayes v Willoughby* [2013] UKSC 17, [14], cited ibid.

73. Ibid.

74. *R (Gallaher Group Ltd) v The Competition and Markets Authority* [2018] UKSC 25, [27], [43], [44], and [55], cited by Nehushtan (N70).

that is, if the means cannot or does not achieve the end, then this is a decision that no rational person could have made.

Worse still, in *R (on the application of Camgaign Against Arms Trade) v Secretary of State for International Trade*,[75] the *GCHQ* irrationality review has been applied in a rather confusing way. In this case, the Court of Appeal invalidated the decision made by the Secretary to grant licences for the selling of military equipment to Saudi Arabia for their possible use in the conflict with Yemen. Although the question of whether there was a historic pattern of breaches of international humanitarian law on the part of the coalition led by Saudi Arabia had been central to the estimation of the risk of future violations, the Court found that such a 'historic pattern issue' was not addressed by the Secretary. Thus, it held that the decision-making process was irrational and therefore illegal as the UK government had violated Article 2.2 of the EU Common Council Position 2008/944/CGSP, as adopted in the Secretary of State's 2014 Guidance, in that Article 2.2 compels Member States to reject a licence for the selling of military equipment to other countries if there is a real risk that this equipment might be used in the commission of serious violations of international humanitarian law.

On reaching the decision, the Court, on one hand, equated rationality with the duty to take into account all relevant considerations, and, on the other, equated with reasonableness, by holding that it was irrational for the Secretary not to consider the historic pattern of breaches of international humanitarian law on the part of the coalition led by the Saudi Arabia while making the decision in question.[76] Based on the proposition that a public body has a duty to carry out a sufficient enquiry before making a decision, as held in *Tameside*,[77] the Court emphasised that 'the only legal error which is alleged to have been committed is founded on the public law doctrine of irrationality', saying that rationality refers to the decision-making process and the duty to take into account all relevant considerations.[78]

75. [2019] EWCA Civ 1020 (CA).

76. Ibid., [35], [37–59], [62], [139], [144], [145], and [153].

77. *Tameside* (N23).

78. *Camgaign Against Arms Trade* (N75) [57].

Nevertheless, Nehushtan argues that since not taking into account all relevant considerations is not a distinct, well-established ground of judicial review, equating this ground of review with *GCHQ* irrationality adds nothing to 'our understanding of that ground of review', so *GCHQ* irrationality review has, in effect, 'no distinct meaning in UK public law'.[79] Referring to the Court's assertion that *Camgaign Against Arms Trade* shows that the process which was adopted by the Secretary was one which was not reasonably open to him,[80] Nehushtan claims that the Court has associated irrationality with unreasonableness, thus 'equating both with the duty to take into account all relevant consideration'.[81] He explains:

> [A]rguing that it is unreasonable or irrational to not take all relevant considerations into account is conceptually confusing and in fact misguided. It is not more helpful than arguing that it is unreasonable or irrational to take irrelevant considerations into account, act in bad faith, be in a state of conflict of interests, act for an improper purpose etc. describing distinct grounds of review by attaching the concepts 'unreasonable' or 'irrational' to them adds nothing to our understanding of these distinct grounds of review — and makes reasonableness and rationality mega-grounds of review with no distinct meaning.[82]

Unreasonableness as a distinct ground of review can only be conceived as a weighing and balancing test — 'one that refers to the content of the administrative decision rather than to the decision-making process'.[83] As Nehushtan has intimated, 'an unreasonable decision is one that results from according distorted weight to relevant considerations', and 'for reasonableness to have any distinct meaning, it must only refer to the weight that was accorded to the relevant considerations — and not the relevancy of these considerations'. Thus, in *Camgaign Against Arms Trade*, if the Court labels the UK government's failure to take into account a relevant consideration as irrational or unreasonable,

79. Nehushtan (N70).

80. *Camgaign Against Arms Trade* (N75) [57].

81. Nehushtan (N70).

82. Ibid.

83. Ibid.

then it is 'unnecessary, confusing and in fact misguided'.[84] This is because the decision to grant licences could have been unreasonable only if the Secretary took into account all relevant considerations, but accorded them distorted weight.[85] As Nehushtan has argued:

> Rationality as a distinct ground of review can only be understood as 'instrumental rationality'. This is perhaps the most common perception of rationality. It is often applied in the legal world and especially in public law — as part of the proportionality test. It describes rationality as deploying the appropriate means in order to achieve certain ends ... Perceiving rationality as [a] ground of review that focuses on the relation between means and end is the most helpful and accurate way to understand the distinctiveness of this ground of review. This perception of rationality is sufficiently specific — but not too narrow. It avoids vagueness and uncertainties.[86]

All in all, the test in all these cases remains the same: has the decision-maker gone beyond what a reasonable person could have regarded as justifiable? However, there has been criticism that what Lord Diplock said in the *GCHQ* case is just a re-phrasing of unreasonableness into irrationality, and that it was 'not intended to be creative', but was a mere summary of the *Wednesbury* formula.[87]

3.5 Anxious or Heightened Scrutiny Test or Sliding Scale of Intensity Test

Prior to the introduction of the HRA 1998, there had been attempts by judges to widen the scope of the traditional *Wednesbury* review by introducing an 'anxious scrutiny' formula,[88] a 'heightened scrutiny' test, or a 'sliding scale of intensity of scrutiny' review.[89] They require that interferences with human

84. Ibid.

85. Ibid.

86. Ibid.

87. Jowell (N10) 47.

88. *Bugdaycay* (N66) 531 (Lord Bridge).

89. *R (Mahmood) v Secretary of State for the Home Department* [2001] 1 WLR 840 (CA), [19] (Laws LJ); *R v Ministry of Defence, ex p Smith and Grady* [1996] QB 517 (CA), 554 (Lord Bingham).

rights be justified by the decision-maker by a strong competing public interest.[90] In *Bugdaycay v Secretary of State for the Home Department*,[91] Lord Bridge, when adopting the anxious scrutiny formula, stated that within limits the courts were entitled

> to subject an administrative decision to the more rigorous examination, to ensure that it is in no way flawed, according to the gravity of the issue which the decision [is determined]. The most fundamental of all human rights is the individual's right to life and when an administrative decision under challenge is said to be one which may put the applicant's life at risk, the basis of the decision must surely call for the most anxious scrutiny.[92]

In this connection, Conor Gearty has argued that the 'anxious scrutiny' formula is similar to the proportionality enquiry.[93] Johannes Chan concurred, saying that 'the difference between the heightened scrutiny test and the proportionality test is a matter of degree'.[94]

Moreover, when considering whether a decision-maker has acted irrationally, the courts would also use the 'sliding scale intensity of review' ranging from managerial decisions where there is a high degree of deference to the decision-maker, such as decisions involving the allocation of resources or policy matters, to administrative decisions where there is a low deference to the decision-maker, such as decisions affecting fundamental rights.[95] In *R v Ministry of Defence, ex parte Smith and Grady*,[96] the ban on homosexuals in the armed forces was considered by the Court of Appeal. Sir Thomas Bingham MR laid down the foundation of the 'sliding scale of intensity of scrutiny' test as follows:

> The court may not interfere with the exercise of an administrative discretion on substantive grounds save where the court is satisfied that the decision is

90. *Bugdaycay* (N66) 531 (Lord Bridge), 537–538 (Lord Templeman).

91. Ibid.

92. Ibid., 531.

93. Conor Gearty, 'Reconciling Parliamentary Democracy and Human Rights' (2002) 118 *LQR* 248, 336–353.

94. Johannes Chan, 'A Sliding Scale of Reasonableness in Judicial Review' in Hugh Corder (ed), *Comparing Administrative Justice Across the Commonwealth* (JUTA 2008) 238.

95. *ex p Nottinghamshire* (N29); *R v Secretary of State for the Environment, ex p Hammersmith and Fulham LBC* [1991] AC 521.

96. *ex p Smith and Grady* (N89), 554 (Lord Bingham).

> unreasonable in the sense that it is beyond the range of responses open to a reasonable decision-maker. But in judging whether the decision-maker has exceeded this margin of appreciation the human rights context is important. The more substantial the interference with human rights, the more the court will require by way of justification before it is satisfied that the discretion is reasonable in the sense outlined above.[97]

This concept is also found in the judgment of Laws LJ in *R (on the application of Mahmood) v Secretary of State for the Home Department*, when he states:[98]

> in a case involving human rights the second approach ... as to the intensity of review is generally to be followed, leaving aside incorporation of the [ECHR]; but that approach and the basic *Wednesbury* rule are by no means hermetically sealed one from the other. There is, rather, what may be called a sliding scale of review; the graver the impact of the decision in question upon the individual affected by it, the more substantial the justification that will be required. It is in the nature of the human condition that cases where, objectively, the individual is most gravely affected will be those where we have come to call his fundamental rights are or are said to be put in jeopardy.[99]

In this case, it concerned a challenge of a decision to remove an illegal immigrant who was married to a British citizen. Laws and May LJJ adopted an opinion that since the fundamental right to family life under Article 8 of the ECHR is involved, the Court should insist that this fact be respected by the decision-maker, who was accordingly required to demonstrate either that his proposed action did not in reality interfere with the right or, that if it did, that considerations existed which might reasonably be accepted as amounting to a substantial and objective justification for the interference.[100] Despite it being a more general statement of a sliding scale of review, the case was eventually decided on the basis that although a fundamental human right was at stake in this case, the Court has 'not taken the matter beyond the situation where

97. Ibid., 554E.
98. *Mahmood* (N89).
99. Ibid., [19].
100. Ibid., [27].

neither a constitutional nor a fundamental human right is involved'.[101] In view of the above, the UK now has a distinction between what is called 'super-*Wednesbury*' [102] and just plain ordinary unreasonableness or irrationality, the so-called mini-*Wednesbury*. Super-*Wednesbury* involves a low intensity of review and a great deference given to the decision-maker, and the courts will only intervene in extreme circumstances if the decision-maker's 'stairs don't reach his attic'.[103] Mini-*Wednesbury* involves a higher intensity of review and thus a lower margin of deference for the decision-maker.

In this regard, Chan has been of the opinion that depending on the nature of the subject matter, the sliding scale of intensity of review may provide 'a more encompassing concept recognizing that the degree of intensity could vary from the traditional *Wednesbury* test to the intermediate heightened degree of scrutiny to the more stringent test of proportionality'.[104] Therefore, the notion of proportionality simply means that the standard of review must be commensurate with the importance of the subject matter.[105] This argument is justified by legislative intent, in that if Parliament has attached such weight to certain factors, the courts should ensure that such weight has been duly given by the administrative authorities in the decision-making process. It follows that in cases concerning human rights issues, it can be presumed that Parliament will not restrict a fundamental right, save on the most compelling circumstances.[106] Seen in this light, the heightened degree of scrutiny is merely an aspect of the proportionality analysis, so there is, in effect, no difference in substance between the proportionality test and the sliding scale of intensity of scrutiny.[107] As Lord Steyn pointed out, 'in law, context is everything',[108] adding that:

> The differences in approach between the traditional grounds of review and the proportionality approach may therefore sometimes yield different

101. Ibid.

102. *ex p Nottinghamshire* (N29) 250 (Lord Scarman); *ex p Hammersmith and Fulham LBC* (N95) 596 (Lord Bridge).

103. Words used in a book review by Sir John Laws (1996) *JR* 49, 50, cited by Jeffrey Jowell, 'Is Proportionality an Alien Concept?' (1996) 2(3) *EPL* 401, 405.

104. Chan (N94) 238.

105. Ibid.

106. Ibid., 255.

107. Ibid., 238.

108. *R (Daly) v Secretary of State for the Home Department* [2001] UKHL 26, [2001] 1 AC 532.

> results. It is therefore important that cases involving [the ECHR] must be analysed in the correct way. This does not mean that there has been a shift to merit review. On the contrary, ... the respective roles of judges and administrators are fundamentally distinct and will remain so ... [and] 'the intensity of review in a public law case will depend on the subject matter in hand'. That is so even in cases involving [the ECHR].[109]

However, despite its heightened scrutiny test, the European Court of Human Rights (ECtHR), in *Smith and Grady v UK*,[110] upheld the challenge to the government's ban on homosexuals serving in the armed forces which had been litigated unsuccessfully before the English national courts. The ECtHR contrasted the traditional, albeit heightened, *Wednesbury* approach of the English Administrative Court and of the Court of Appeal with that of proportionality adopted by the ECtHR, stating that:

> The threshold at which the High Court and the Court of Appeal could find the Ministry of Defence policy irrational was placed so high that it effectively excluded any consideration by the domestic courts of the question of whether the interference with the applicants' rights answered a pressing social need or was proportionate to the national security and public order aims pursued, principles which lie at the heart of the Court's analysis of complaints under Article 8 [i.e., the right to family life] of the [ECHR].[111]

Overall, Lord Carnwath (quoting Andrew le Sueur) states that the concept of sliding scale is not satisfactory, claiming that 'sliding scales only work if one has measurable standards to which they can be applied; otherwise it is a matter less of sliding scales than of "slithering about in grey areas"'.[112]

In Hong Kong, when deciding the intensity of review to be applied in cases that involve human rights, the courts have kept pace with their UK counterparts and applied the British administrative law cases that were determined at a time when the ECHR had not been incorporated in Britain via the HRA 1998.

109. Ibid., [2001] 1 AC 532, 548.

110. (1999) 29 EHRR 493.

111. Ibid., [138].

112. Robert Carnwath, 'From Judicial Outrage to Sliding Scales', *ALBA Annual Lecture 2013*.

Lord Ackner, as manifested in *ex parte Brind*,[113] noted that '[i]n a field which concerns a fundamental human right — namely, that of free speech — close scrutiny must be given to the reasons provided as justification for interfering with that right'.[114] This approach has, for example, been applied in Hong Kong in relation to environmental conservation.[115]

Moreover, in *MA v Director of Immigration*,[116] Hong Kong courts have also applied the sliding scale of unreasonableness review. This case concerned a blanket policy of not allowing mandated refugees or screened-in torture claimants to work in Hong Kong pending settlement. However, the Court of First Instance has, as endorsed by the Court of Appeal, determined that the policy in question is not irrational because the Director was not bound to devise the policy based on relevant human rights which had not been directly enforceable owing to treaty reservations.[117] When the case was tabled before the Court of Final Appeal (CFA), the applicant failed again as the CFA clarified that Article 39 of the Basic Law does not have the direct effect of domestically incorporating the International Covenant on Economic, Social, and Cultural Rights (ICESCR), and that as Hong Kong adopts dualism, non-self-executing treaties are not part of local law unless they are incorporated via local legislation.[118]

3.6 Principle of Legality with the Use of Proportionality for Protecting Human Rights Prior to the Human Rights Act 1998

There have been various pre-HRA 1998 prison law cases identifying the principle of legality with the use of the proportionality formula [119] as a common law

113. *ex p Brind* (N65).

114. Ibid., [1991] 696 (HL), 757.

115. See the *Protection of Victoria Harbour* saga in Chapter Eight of this book.

116. [2011] 2 HKLRD F6 (CFI), [2012] HKEC 1624 (CA), [2014] 3 HKC 11 (CFA).

117. Ibid., [2011] 2 HKLRD F6 (CFI), 104; [2012] HKEC 1624 (CA), 151–152.

118. Ibid., [2014] 3 HKC 11 (CFA), [58].

119. Tim Owen, 'Fair Trial Rights, Due Deference and the Wider Impact of the Human Rights Act in Administrative Law' in Jeffrey Jowell and Jonathan Cooper (eds), *Delivering Rights: How the Human Rights Act is Working* (Hart Publishing 2003) 66–67.

basis for protecting fundamental rights.[120] In *R v Secretary of State for the Home Department, ex parte Leech (No 2)*,[121] the UK Court of Appeal scrutinised the UK Prison Act 1952 (PA 1952), which it found lacked express authority for any interference with the rights of access to court and to legal advice. However, the prison authorities interpreted the rule making power under Section 47(2) of PA 1952 to authorise, by necessary implication, a measure of interference with the right to legal professional privilege.

In determining whether a particular measure is authorised by necessary implication, the UK Court of Appeal held that it was insufficient to simply establish that a pressing need existed for some interference. Rather, one must establish that a pressing need existed for that *degree* of interference. Such a need could only be established if the legitimate object could not be met by a less intrusive measure. In this regard, Steyn LJ has articulated a 'common law proportionality' in the sphere of basic or constitutional rights, such as those of access to courts and to legal advice. The Court applied this approach to test the *vires* of a blanket rule authorising the routine reading of all mail passing between prisoners and their legal advisers.

Learning that a rule of such breadth had created a considerable disincentive to a prisoner exercising his basic rights of access to court and to legal advice, the Court held that the legitimate need to establish that privileged legal correspondence was *bona fide* and could be met by a far less intrusive measure. No pressing need for the blanket rule was established. The legitimate aim only authorised a rule that permitted correspondence to be read in exceptional circumstances where the prison authorities had reasonable grounds to believe that the privilege was being abused and then only to the extent necessary to decide the *bona fides* of the communication.

120. *Raymond v Honey* [1983] AC1; *R v Secretary of State for the Home Department, ex p Anderson* [1984] 1 QB 778; *R v Secretary of State for the Home Department, ex p Leech (No 2)* [1994] QB 198; *R v Secretary of State for the Home Department, ex p Pierson* [1998] AC 539; *R v Secretary of State for the Home Department, ex p Simms and O'Brien* [1999] 3 All ER 400, [2000] 2 AC 115.

121. Ibid., *ex p Leech (No 2)*.

In *R v Secretary of State for the Home Department, ex parte Simms and O'Brien*,[122] the UK House of Lords adopted the *Leech (No 2)* approach, finding that the Secretary of State had not established a pressing need for the policy of preventing journalists from visiting prisoners in relation to alleged miscarriages of justice. The Court, despite not invoking the language of 'minimum interference', held that the policy was unlawful because no pressing need for the degree of interference had been established. In other words, the pressing need of maintaining order and discipline could have been met by a less intrusive measure. More importantly, Lord Hobhouse held that the administrative policy was unjustifiable in part because it was disproportionate.[123] Thus, while the Court enquired whether interference was authorised according to the principle of legality, the 'common law proportionality', whose requirements mirror its European counterpart, was already being recognised prior to the enactment of the HRA 1998. In this connection, Gearty asserts that the test adopted in *ex parte Simms and O'Brien* is the most obvious overlap between 'anxious scrutiny' and proportionality.[124]

3.7 An Attempt to Recognise Proportionality in the Early 1990s

In the *GCHQ* case,[125] although Lord Diplock said that 'the reasons for the decision-maker taking one course rather than another do not normally involve questions to which, if disputed, the judicial process is adapted to provide the right answer',[126] his Lordship, after identifying the domestic grounds of judicial review (i.e., illegality, irrationality, and procedural impropriety), proceeded to state that the grounds should not be seen as exhaustive. Rather, he explained, they might come to be joined by the European proportionality principle:

> That is not to say that further development on a case-by-case basis may not in the course of time add further groups. I have in mind particularly the possible adoption in the future of the principle of 'proportionality' which

122. Ibid., *ex p Simms and O'Brien*.

123. Ibid., 422.

124. Gearty (N93) 336–353.

125. *GCHQ* case (N2).

126. Ibid., [1985] 1 AC 374, 410–411.

is recognised in the administrative law of several of our fellow members of the European Economic Community.[127]

However, in *ex parte Brind*,[128] the House of Lords, Lords Lowry and Ackner in particular, emphatically rejected the proportionality principle as a ground of judicial review. This case concerned an application for judicial review made by several journalists who wished to challenge the validity of the UK Home Secretary's decision to ban the British Broadcasting Corporation (BBC) from directly broadcasting statements made by representatives of certain groups and political parties, in particular Sinn Féin and the Irish Republic Army (IRA). The UK Home Secretary made his decision pursuant to discretion belonging to him under Section 29(3) of the UK Broadcasting Act 1981. The applicants challenged the decision on several grounds, one of which was that the decision had been disproportionate to the end to be achieved. The applicants also argued that the UK Home Secretary's decision was contrary to Article 10 (i.e., the right to freedom of expression) of the ECHR.

Nevertheless, the House of Lords unanimously dismissed the application, rejecting the argument that the proportionality principle had any role to play in the instant case on various grounds. Lord Lowry aligned himself to more orthodox understandings of the institutional role of the courts, holding that the adoption of the proportionality principle as a ground of review would move the courts unacceptably away from the standards of the *Wednesbury* review.[129] Lord Roskill, by contrast, delivered a judgment reflective of Lord Diplock's expectation in the *GCHQ* case, indicating that the facts of the instant case were not the appropriate ones on which to develop the law in the manner proposed.[130] Lord Ackner's judgment fell somewhere in the middle, holding that the incorporation of the ECHR might provide the most appropriate legal basis for the importation of the principle in question.[131]

127. Ibid.

128. *ex p Brind* (N65).

129. Ibid., [1991] 2 WLR 588, 606–610.

130. Ibid., 593–594.

131. Ibid., 595–606.

In short, the courts continue to use the *Wednesbury* formula. Even a decade later, the Court of Appeal, in the *British Civilian Internees* case,[132] held that proportionality had not replaced *Wednesbury* unreasonableness, or irrationality, for judicial review claims which raise no EU law or human rights law dimensions.[133] The Court maintained that despite having strong reservations about the justification for retaining the *Wednesbury* test, it had not been their role to perform its burial rites, and that only the House of Lords could hammer the final nail into the *Wednesbury* coffin.[134] A similar conclusion was also reached in a judicial challenge to the Scottish government about policies on segregating prisoners, in that it would not be appropriate for the Lordships to reach a decision on whether 'want of proportionality' was a relevant complaint of unlawfulness in common law.[135]

So far, neither the then Judicial Committee of the House of Lords [136] nor the newly established Supreme Court has performed its burial rites.[137] Writing extra-judicially, Sir Philips Sales has commented that the adoption of proportionality as a general standard of review would represent a significant change in the law, involving a shift in the balance of power between the judiciary and the political branches of government.[138] In his opinion, if such a substantial change is to be made, it ought to be due to a decision made by Parliament, as has been the case in the contexts of EU law and the ECHR, rather than by the Supreme Court.[139]

3.8 British Influence in Hong Kong

In Hong Kong, the judicial attitudes mirror those of the British. The *Wednesbury* formula has, for decades, represented the dominant position in judicial review litigations owing to the 'entrenched belief' that the proper role of the judiciary

132. *British Civilian Internees* (N1).

133. Ibid., [32]–[37]; *Kennedy* (N1) [2014] 2 WLR 808, [54] (Lord Mance).

134. *British Civilian Internees* (N1) [34] and [35] (Dyson LJ).

135. *Somerville v Scottish Ministers* [2007] UKHL 44, [2007] 1 WLR 2734.

136. *Docherty v Birmingham CC* [2008] UKHL 57, [134]–[135] (Lord Mance).

137. Andrew Le Sueur, Maurice Sunkin, and Jo Eric Khushal Murkens, *Public Law* (OUP 2010) 762.

138. Cited by Neil Parpworth, *Constitutional and Administrative Law* (8th edn, OUP 2014) 304.

139. Ibid.

is to ensure the legality of administrative decisions, not to substitute them with its own.[140] Thus, the courts, in reviewing a particular administrative decision, only evaluate the legality, rationality, and fairness of the decision-making process rather than the merits of a decision. Although Liu J, in *Re Lam Kin Chung*,[141] once considered proportionality during the early 1990s, he found no justification for applying it in the circumstances of that case. This situation remains the status quo,[142] save a few human rights cases [143] and specific constitutional or legislative review cases.[144] These judgments have tallied with a landmark case, *Attorney-General of Hong Kong v Lee Kwong Kut*,[145] decided by the Privy Council before the handover. In this case, the Privy Council used the proportionality principle to deny stepping into the domain of the legislature when Lord Woolf suggested:

> While the Hong Kong judiciary should be zealous in upholding an individual's rights under the Hong Kong [BORO], it is also necessary to ensure that disputes as to the effect of the [BORO] are not allowed to get out of hand. The issues involving the Hong Kong [BORO] should be approached with realism and good sense, and kept in proportion. If this is not done the [BORO] will become a source of injustice rather than justice and it will be debased in the eyes of the public. In order to maintain the balance between the individual and the society as a whole, rigid and inflexible standards should not be imposed on the legislature's attempt ... It must be remembered that questions of policy remain primarily the responsibility of the legislature.[146]

140. Johannes Chan, 'Administrative Law' in Simon Young and Yash Ghai (eds), *Hong Kong's Court of Final Appeal: The Development of the Law in China's Hong Kong* (CUP 2014) 435.

141. (1991) HCt, MP No. 216 of 1991.

142. *Hong Kong Cable Television Ltd v The Telecommunications Authority* [2004] HKCU (unreported, HCAL 62/2003); *PCCW-HKT Telephone Ltd v The Telecommunications Authority*, HCAL 152/2002; *Secretary for Security v Sakthevel Prabakar* [2005] 1 HKLRD 289 (CFA); *Pun Tai Sung v Immigration Tribunal* [2006] HKCU 1818 (unreported, HCAL 51/2005); *Sun News Publishers Ltd v Commissioner for Television and Entertainment Licensing Authority* [2006] HKCU 1729 (unreported, HCAL 50/2006); *Chow Mario v Municipal Services Appeal Board* [2010] HKCU 2649 (unreported, HCAL 31/2010); *Gutierrez v Commissioner for Registration* [2011] 6 HKC 561; *Dr Lau Yuk Kong v Medical Council of Hong Kong* [2011] 5 HKC 218; *Wong Kam Wah v Fisherman Claims Appeal Board* [2012] HKCU 990 (unreported, HCAL 96/2011).

143. See, for example, *R v Sin Yau Ming* (1991) 1 HKPLR 88 (CA), [1992] 1 HKCLR 127.

144. See, for example, *A Solicitor v Law Society of Hong Kong (Secretary for Justice, intervener)* (2003) 6 HKCFAR 570 (CFA), [2004] 1 HKLRD 214; *Leung Kwok Hung v HKSAR* [2005] 3 HKLRD 164 (CFA).

145. (1993) 3 HKPLR 72, [1993] AC 951 (PC).

146. Ibid., 975.

Moreover, the Court, in *Yeung Cheong Fat*,[147] further stated that in an application for judicial review, it is not so much concerned with the wisdom of a decision, but with the propriety of the decision-making process. Concurring, Lam J in *Chu Hoi Dick v Secretary for Home Affairs*,[148] said:

> In judicial review, the court is concerned with the legality of administrative decisions. The court can examine whether an administrative decision has been made in accordance with the relevant legislative provisions and other common law principles securing the procedural and substantive fairness of the process. However, the court cannot substitute its own view as regards what decision should be made. Provided that the administrative decision is one a minister or an executive body can lawfully make, the court cannot interfere.[149]

Worst of all, though acknowledging the inadequacy of the *Wednesbury* formula and thus following its British counterpart to adopt the 'anxious or heightened scrutiny' test as developed by Lords Bridge and Bingham in *Bugdaycay* [150] and *ex parte Smith and Grady* [151] respectively, or the 'sliding scale of intensity of scrutiny' test as advocated by Laws LJ in the *Mahmood*,[152] Hong Kong courts have used them only in human rights and constitutional or legislative review cases.[153]

Insofar as penalties are concerned, what is more worrying is that despite the decision in *R v Barnsley Metropolitan Borough Council, ex parte Hook* [154] that 'the court can interfere by *certiorari* if a punishment is altogether excessive and out

147. *Yeung Cheong Fat v An Investigation Committee appointed pursuant to Section 6 of the Public Service (Discipline) Regulation and Section 10 of the Public Service (Administration) Order 1997* [2005] HKCU 62 (unreported, HCAL 93/2003, 13 April 2004).

148. [2007] HKCU 1370 (unreported, HCAL 87/2007, 10 August 2007).

149. Ibid., [1].

150. *Bugdaycay* (N66).

151. *ex p Smith and Grady* (N89).

152. *Mahmood* (N89).

153. *Town Planning Board v Society for the Protection of the Harbour Ltd* (2004) 7 HKCFAR 1 (CFA), [2004] 1 HKLRD 396; *Fok Chun Wa v Hospital Authority* (unreported, HCAL 94/2007, 17 December 2008) (CFI), (2010) 15 HKPLR 628 (CA), [2012] 2 HKC 413 (CFA).

154. [1976] 1 WLR 1052.

of proportion to the occasion',[155] followed by various similar UK judgments,[156] Hong Kong has generally not followed this approach. Instead of using the proportionality analysis, Hong Kong courts have preferred to use irrationality to review such decisions regarding the assessment of penalties.

In *Chu Ping Tak v Commissioner of Police*,[157] the applicant was a police officer who had accumulated debt and subsequently filed for bankruptcy. He was formally charged for 'conduct calculated to bring the public service into disrepute' owing to his 'serious pecuniary embarrassment', and was thus dismissed summarily. He sought to argue, *inter alia*, that the decisions to charge, and thus dismiss, him were disproportionate to the disciplinary offence. However, Cheung DJ, despite citing *ex parte Hook*, was not convinced, saying that the issue was one of irrationality:

> It is not really essential to determine whether the doctrine of proportionality exists as an independent ground under English and Hong Kong law on judicial review or it should be subsumed under the traditional headings ... In either case, the same judicial restraint must be exercised. As I said, the court essentially plays a supervisory role over the decision of the tribunal below. It does not exercise an appellate role as such. This is true in relation to a decision on liability as well as a decision on punishment or sentencing. Unless the sentence or punishment is so out of proportion to the offence in question, as to be perverse or unduly oppressive. I see no ground for intervention ... In the circumstances of the present case, although it could be reasonably argued that the punishment meted out to the applicant, i.e. immediate [dismissal] without compensation or payment, was extremely severe and even on the high side, bearing in mind the various levels and forms of punishment open to the Commissioner to impose as set out in the Schedule to the Police (Discipline) Regulations, I do not take the view that the eventual award made was one so disproportionate to the offence in

155. Ibid., 1057 (Lord Denning).

156. *R v Secretary of State for the Home Department, ex p Benwell* [1984] ICR 723 (QBD); *R v Brent LBC ex p Assegai* (1987) 151 LG Rev 891; *R v Tamworth Justices, ex p Walsh* [1994] COD 227; *R v Newham LBC, ex p X* [1995] ELR 303; *R v Secretary of State for Health, ex p Eastside Cheese Co* [1999] 3 CMLR 123; *Dad v General Dental Council* [2000] 1 WLR 1538 (PC).

157. [2002] 3 HKLRD 679 (CFI).

> question as to be perverse, or put another way, was so unduly oppressive as to be unreasonable. I do not consider the award as 'altogether excessive and out of proportion to the occasion' (per Lord Denning MR in *Hook*) [even though] I have borne in mind the various factors urged upon me by counsel for the applicant during submission ... As I said, if I were sitting as the first instance tribunal, I might have [been] inclined to come to a less severe or more lenient sentence. But that is neither here nor there. I do not consider that the sentence reached below can be interfered with. I therefore reject this ground of judicial review as well.[158]

In this climate, a penalty imposed by a public body in Hong Kong will only be scrutinised on an irrationality basis, rather than on a proportionality basis, unless the decision 'is severe beyond all rational relationship to the seriousness of the offence and the situation of the offender'.[159] This judicial attitude has recently been reiterated by Reyes J, who stated:

> Government bodies may reasonably disagree on what are relevant circumstances to take into account and so come to opposing conclusions ... The possibility of disagreement over relevant factors and the possibility of different assessments of particular factors would not by themselves render a decision irrational.[160]

In view of the above, Hong Kong courts are arguably more conservative than those of the British, and thus more deferential to administrative authorities, even though Hong Kong has suffered from a 'democratic deficit' pre- and post-1997.

3.9 Criticisms of *Wednesbury* Unreasonableness and Irrationality

Although the *Wednesbury* formula has been evolving in response to ever-changing circumstances, there are various criticisms against it, one of which

158. Ibid., 696.

159. *Wong Wai Tak v Secretary for Civil Service* (unreported) HCAL 2335 of 2000, 14–15, [2002] 3 HKC 1, 16R–17D (Hartmann J); *Au Yeung Kwok Hing v AG* (unreported) Civil Appeal No. 205 of 1994, 14 (Bokhary JA) and 22 (Nazareth VP).

160. *Andrew Brine v Liquor Licensing Board*, HCAL 33/2012, 62.

is that the test is so imprecise when being applied. When *Wednesbury* review is used to assess the reasoning process, it requires that a public authority ask itself the right questions and take into account relevant considerations.[161] Nevertheless, it does not tend to prescribe any particular logical sequence, or template, of relevant questions. In *R v Parliamentary Commissioner for Administration, ex parte Balchin*,[162] Sedley J complained that *Wednesbury* unreasonableness was apt to mean 'an error of reasoning which robs the decision of logic'.[163] This is truly reflected in what D.J. Galligan has opined: that within such an area of administrative autonomy, the decision-maker may decide according to whatever reasons they see fit, or indeed without reasons, on the condition that the decision remains within the circumference of their power.[164] Furthermore, Sir John Law has also argued that the 'monolithic' standard of irrationality is 'an imperfect and inappropriate mechanism for the development of differential standards of judicial review'.[165]

3.9.1 Being Circular and Tautologous

Academically, one of the criticisms of unreasonableness as a basis of review, according to le Sueur, is well-known and frequently repeated as follows:

> It is a circular definition; it is an uncertain guide as to the extent of the 'margin of discretion' to be permitted to a public authority in any given situation or (the flip side of the coin) the intensity of review to be conducted by the court; it is a cloak which may tempt lawyers and courts to deal with the merits of grievances rather than questions of legality. These conceptual weaknesses have led to proposals for the common law to recognise a number of substantive principles in place of unreasonableness (e.g. equality) or for the replacement of the reasonableness test with one of proportionality.[166]

161. *Wednesbury* case (N8) 229 (Lord Greene MR).

162. [1998] I PLR I.

163. Ibid., [13E]–[13F].

164. D.J. Galligan, *Discretionary Powers: A Legal Study of Official Discretion* (Clarendon Press 1990) 6.

165. John Laws, 'Is the High Court the Guardian of Fundamental Constitutional Rights?' (1993) *PL* 59, 69.

166. Andrew le Sueur, 'The Rise and Ruin of Unreasonableness' (2005) *JR* 32.

Alongside its circularity, Jowell and Lord Lester have also criticised the traditional *Wednesbury* test for being inadequate, unrealistic, and tautologous, adding that 'its pragmatic approach should be replaced by principles which would satisfy the need in a fast growing area of law for clarity and coherence'.[167] They have also suggested that there be more specific categories and principles to articulate why a decision was unreasonable. These were decisions that (1) were irrational in the accepted sense (i.e., lacking logic or that were simply arbitrary); (2) violated standards of administrative probity (namely, fraudulent decisions or those taken in bad faith); (3) were contrary to standards of good administration; and (4) violated human rights.[168]

Judicially, Lord Cooke, in *R v Chief Constable of Sussex, ex parte International Trader's Ferry Ltd*,[169] regarded the *Wednesbury* formula as tautologous and exaggerated. His Lordship stated that it was not necessary to have such an extreme formulation in order to ensure that the courts remained within their proper bounds as required by the separation of powers. He further advocated a simpler and less extreme test that asks *was the decision one that a reasonable authority could have reached?* [170]

3.9.2 A Vague and Confused Formula

Although *Wednesbury* unreasonableness or irrationality is able to make the courts employ both logic and accepted moral standards as criteria by which to assess official decisions, critics argue that it does not explain any more specific categories of legally unacceptable substantive decisions.[171] Other questions that might well be posed: *when judges use the terms 'unreasonableness' or 'irrationality', what exactly do they mean? Is it simply that there is a general*

167. Jeffrey Jowell and Anthony Lester, 'Beyond *Wednesbury*: Substantial Principles of Administrative Law' (1987) *PL* 368, 371–372.

168. Jowell (N10) 46.

169. [1999] 2 AC 418.

170. Ibid., 452.

171. Stanley de Smith, Harry Woolf, and Jeffrey Jowell, *Judicial Review of Administrative Action* (Sweet & Maxwell 1995) 550.

duty for a public body to act reasonably, or is unreasonableness used to describe manifestly outrageous behaviour? [172]

Furthermore, the term irrationality has the drawback of casting doubt on the mental capacity of the decision-maker because many decisions which fall foul of this head might have been coldly rational. In *Lord Saville of Newdigate, ex parte B (No 2)*,[173] Lord Woolf MR held that to label a decision as irrational would often not do justice to the decision-makers and not make them accountable because they could, on the face of it, be the most rational persons.[174] Furthermore, that a decision is illegal does not necessarily mean that it is irrational. A decision-maker might, after the most careful and sensible consideration of a particular course of action, proceed on the basis of misunderstanding of their legal powers.[175] This is exacerbated by the fact that those holding powers to regulate society (e.g., the police are empowered to maintain law and order), like everyone, have a limited understanding of the world. In many such cases, the true explanation for the decision being flawed is that although such perversity was not established, the decision-maker did misdirect themselves in the law. That may be unlawful, but it is a mistake that could be made by the most prudent persons.

Moreover, in *R v North and East Devon Health Authority, ex parte Coughlan*,[176] the UK Court held that rationality covered not only decisions that defied comprehension but also included those made by 'flawed logic'.[177] Even though attempts have been made to simplify the ground as saying that 'whether the decision in question was one which a reasonable authority could reach',[178] or to re-formulate it as denoting 'a decision so unreasonable that no person acting reasonably could have come to it',[179] or a decision which elicits the exclamation: 'My goodness, that is certainly wrong!',[180] which may perhaps help give an

172. Peter Leyland and Gordon Anthony, *Administrative Law* (7th edn, OUP 2013) 315.
173. [2000] 1 WLR 1855 (CA).
174. Ibid., [33].
175. *Roberts* (N54).
176. [2001] QB 213, [2000] 2 WLR 622, [2000] 3 All ER 850.
177. Ibid., [65].
178. *ex p International Trader's Ferry* (N169) 452 (Lord Cooke).
179. *Champion v Chief Constable of the Gwent Constabulary* [1990] 1 WLR 116 (Lord Lowry).
180. *Neale v Hereford & Worcester CC* [1986] ICR 471, 483 (May LJ).

indication of the flavour of the conduct which qualifies as being within the concept of unreasonableness, they are no more helpful as guides to its precise parameters.[181] As Fiona Donson has observed, the *Wednesbury* test is seen as a concept open to 'development and manipulation', and that its 'vague and circular' definition means that it could be difficult to argue successfully in many cases.[182]

3.9.3 The Threshold Being Too High and Too Deferential to the Administrative Authorities

What is more, the standard required under the *Wednesbury* formula is extremely high. In general, decisions which are extravagant or capricious cannot be legitimate. However, if the decision is within the confines of reasonableness, it is not part of the court's function to look further into its merits. As Warrington LJ mentioned in *Short v Poole Corporation*, 'with the question whether a particular policy is wise or foolish the court is not concerned: it can only interfere if to pursue it is beyond the powers of the authority'.[183]

Viewed in this way, such a standard is too deferential to the administrative authorities, and therefore provides for considerably less judicial scrutiny than the proportionality formula which has emerged as a veritable Esperanto of, and as an emergent global 'best practice' standard in, constitutional rights adjudication. Under the *Wednesbury* formula, the courts can only interfere if a decision is so unreasonable or absurd that no reasonable authority could ever have come to it. In other words, it is not enough for the decision to be unreasonable. Rather, it has to be so unreasonable that it is not possible for the authority to conceivably come to such a conclusion if they are of sound mind. Since the *Wednesbury* decision, there have been cases to support and re-state the threshold at which substantive unreasonableness would permit judicial intervention. The most famous one of these re-formulations is from Lord Diplock's *dicta* that the courts would be able to intervene on the grounds

181. de Smith, Woolf, and Jowell (N171) 550.

182. Fiona Donson, 'Civil Liberties and Judicial Review: Can the Common Law Really Protect Rights?' in Peter Leyland and Terry Woods (eds), *Administrative Law Facing the Future: Old Constraints and New Horizons* (Blackstone 1997) 350.

183. *Short v Poole Corporation* (N25).

of unreasonableness when the decision taken was 'so outrageous in its defiance of logic or of accepted moral standards that no sensible person who had applied his mind to the question to be decided could have arrived at it'.[184] However, it would still be necessary to ask why the decision defied logic or accepted moral standards because

> rationality requires that decisions be made for reasons which are rational in terms of our understanding of the world. But of course rationality is an extremely complex notion; decisions can be more or less rational from different points of view, and indeed what constitutes a rational decision may itself depend upon the objects to be achieved and the means available.[185]

Although the courts can interfere if a decision on a competent matter is so unreasonable that no reasonable authority could ever have come to it, satisfying this burden of proof would be very difficult, in spite of the above modifications. Under such circumstances, the courts can only strike down an administrative decision in extreme cases, such as one in which a decision-maker said 'we made this rule because on the date of its issuance Mars was in the seventh house of Jupiter and in conjunction with the moon'.[186] Another extreme example relates to *Willard Mikesell*,[187] an American court case in which the judge agreed to reduce the bail bond required of the defendant from US$10,000 to US$500 on the condition that the defendant had 'his hair cut in a fashion similar' to that of the judge. In this connection, Jowell and Lord Lester have opined that:

> [i]f courts are only to interfere with decisions verging on the insane, a zone of immunity would be drawn around many oppressive or improper decisions that are in reality vulnerable to judicial review. And public authorities which had taken leave of their senses could use the language of rationality to circumvent judicial review.[188]

184. *GCHQ* case (N2) 410E.

185. Galligan (N164) 5.

186. Martin Shapiro, 'Two Transformations in Administrative Law: American and European?' in Karl-Heinz Ladeur (ed), *The Europeanisation of Administrative Law: Transforming National Decision-Making Procedures* (Ashgate 2002) 16.

187. 243 NW 2d 86, 101 (1976) (Michigan Supreme Court).

188. Jowell and Lester (N167) 372.

In *Daly*,[189] Lord Cooke also stated:

> I think the day will come when it will be more widely recognised that [*Wednesbury* unreasonableness] was an unfortunately retrogressive decision in English administrative law, insofar as it suggested that there are degrees of unreasonableness and that only a very extreme degree can bring an administrative decision within the legitimate scope of judicial invalidation. The depth of judicial review and the deference due to administrative discretion vary with the subject matter. It may well be, however, that the law can never be satisfied in any administrative field merely by a finding that the decision under review is not capricious or absurd.[190]

Moreover, the definition of unreasonableness (i.e., a decision so absurd that no sensible person could ever dream that it lay within the powers of the authority) is not structured. It is not founded on consecutive analytical steps. It does not distinguish between the lack of a rational connection, necessity, and balancing.[191] As Dickson CJ of the Canadian Supreme Court once said, when comparing the notions of reasonableness according to the *Wednesbury* test and proportionality formula, 'unreasonableness rests to a large extent on unarticulated and undeveloped values and lacks the same degree of structure and sophistication of analysis'.[192]

Furthermore, Michael Fordham and Thomas de la Mare have also argued that the *Wednesbury* formula is normally associated with 'abuses of power' as it has been driven by the concept of wide margin or latitude.[193] Aside from certain matters which the courts identify, usually from the statute, as relevant or irrelevant as a matter of legal duty, the executive authority is given freedom to decide for itself if '[t]here is, in short, a margin of appreciation [to be precise, discretion] within which the decision-maker may decide just what considerations

189. *Daly* (N108) [2001] 2 AC 532, 548.

190. Ibid., [2001] 3 All ER 433, 447.

191. Barak (N6) 375.

192. *Slaight Communications Inc v Davidson* [1989] 1 SCR 1038, 1074.

193. Michael Fordham and Thomas de la Mare, 'Identifying the Principles of Proportionality' in Jeffrey Jowell and Jonathan Cooper (eds), *Understanding Human Rights Principles* (Hart Publishing 2001) 31.

should play a part in his reasoning process'.[194] Some judges have begun to speak of this as a 'margin of appreciation', or, to be precise, 'deference' or 'discretionary area of judgment',[195] though some case law uses different phrases such as 'the range of reasonable decisions open to a decision-maker',[196] the 'field of judgment',[197] the 'sphere',[198] and the 'area of judgment'.[199] Similarly, the weight to be attributed to a relevant consideration is also a matter for the authority, subject only to unreasonableness. In this connection, Lord Keith stated that 'it is entirely for the decision-maker to attribute to the relevant considerations such weight as he thinks fit, and courts will not interfere unless he has acted unreasonably in the *Wednesbury* sense'.[200]

3.9.4 Lack of Transparency

Parallel to this drawback is the methodological critique that the *Wednesbury* test, when being applied by the courts, lacks transparency, and thereby accountability. This is because a finding of unreasonableness risks creating the impression of judicial decision-making by intuition since such a conclusion may not be accompanied by any structured explanation of the judicial reasoning process which yielded it.[201] In this regard, what criteria do the courts employ in order to determine the degree of unreasonableness?

If the 'unreasonable' decision is defined simply in terms of that which no reasonable decision-maker would reach, then little scope exists for the elaboration of a structured and transparent judicial-making process. Seen in this way, this test naturally encourages an intuitive adjudicative method. Ultimately, it would run the risk of allowing judges to 'obscure their social and economic preferences more easily' under the vagueness of the *Wednesbury*

194. *R v Somerset CC, ex p Fewings* [1995] 1 WLR 1037, 1050A (Simon Brown LJ).
195. As discussed in Chapter Two of this book.
196. *Boddington v British Transport Police* [1998] 2 WLR 639, 666B.
197. *R v Manchester Crown Court, ex p McDonald* [1999] 1 WLR 841, 851A.
198. *R v Legal Aid Board, ex p Parsons* [1999] 3 All ER 347, 354A.
199. *R v Criminal Cases Review Commission, ex p Pearson* [1999] 3 All ER 498, 523.
200. *Tesco Stores* (N1) 764H.
201. Jack Beatson, Martin Matthews, and Mark Elliott, *Administrative Law* (3rd edn, OUP 2005) 257.

test than if their reasoning for intervention had to be 'guided by established legal principles'.[202] In the briefly reasoned judgment in *Wheeler v Leicester City Council*,[203] the House of Lords held that the decision was 'unreasonable' but did not articulate the basis for such a decision. In this case, the defendant authority invited a rugby club to condemn the participation of some of its players in a tour of South Africa during the apartheid era. The club refused to do so, saying that they condemned apartheid, but considered that there were differences of opinion as to how best to break it down. The club further said that its players had individual choice as to where to play. Purporting to act under discretionary powers to regulate the use of its own land and pursuant to its general statutory duty under the UK Race Relation Act 1976 to promote good race relations, the council passed a resolution to ban the rugby club from using its recreation ground for 12 months.

The House of Lords held that it was unreasonable for the local council to prevent the rugby club from using the city's sports grounds on account of differences in political opinions about South Africa. The Court added that the council could not use its statutory powers of management or any other statutory powers for the purpose of punishing the rugby club when it had done no wrong. Although it was conceded that the council could claim to be properly motivated by a desire to promote harmonious race relations in the city, this reasonable objective could not justify the pursuit of a policy that was, in itself, unreasonably punitive. In this connection, the defendant authority adopted the 'he-who-is-not-with-me-is-against-me' attitude to punish the club. Similarly, in *ex parte Hook*,[204] the council's decision to withdraw Hook's licence was not because of his minor breach of urinating in the street, but because he used abusive language with, and thus disrespected, the council's staff. In Hong Kong, the disproportionate use of force by the police when dealing with unarmed protesters and innocent passers-by from early June 2019 onwards has similarly been viewed as a response to, among other things, feeling disrespected by the foul language used against them while performing their duties.

202. Jeffrey Jowell, 'Of Vires and Vacuums: The Constitutional Context of Judicial Review' (1999) *PL* 461, 454–455.

203. [1985] AC 1054.

204. *ex p Hook* (N154).

In the administrative field, the possible consequences resulting from the lack of transparency would be that in the absence of reasons, executives are in danger of acting arbitrarily, as shown in *Wheeler* and *ex parte Hook* above. Their reluctance to articulate a reasoned justification for their decision-making naturally encourages suspicion that prejudices the persons affected. In this connection, policy considerations may be hiding underneath the *Wednesbury*'s ample cloak.[205] Lord Keith, in *R v Secretary of State for Trade and Industry, ex parte Lonrho Plc,*[206] observed that reasonableness does not require reasons to be stated.[207] However, in the absence of reasons, the administration is in danger of being held to have acted arbitrarily. Jowell and Lord Lester, concurring with this view, argue:

> The *Wednesbury* test is confusing, because it is tautologous. It allows the courts to interfere with decisions that are unreasonable, and then defines an unreasonable decision as one which no reasonable authority would take. (Imagine a law allowing the demolition of unfit houses, and then defining 'unfit' not in the normal sense of that word but in the sense that no fit house could so be!) One can understand that Lord Greene's definition of unreasonableness sought to make the judges think twice about interfering with the merits of official decisions, but a test which requires the official action not to be ordinarily reasonable, but only, in effect, extremely unreasonable, is unhelpful as a practical guide.[208]

In view of the above, the test of *Wednesbury* unreasonableness has come to be perceived as an inadequate form of substantive review. Its anti-rationalist test (indicative of the common law tradition of artificial reasoning by judges) has been criticised as unrealistic and for not providing any constructive guidance as to how the executive should pursue their goals.[209] In face of such problems, some judges have increasingly come to recognise that if they consider there to be something wrong in the substantive legality of an administrative measure,

205. Jowell and Lester (N167) 371–372.

206. *ex p Lonrho Plc* (N63).

207. Ibid., 539.

208. Jowell and Lester (N167) 371–372.

209. Robert Thomas, 'Continental Principles in English Public Law' in Andrew Harding and Esin Örücü (eds), *Comparative Law in the 21st Century* (Kluwer 2002) 129–130.

then proportionality can provide a more legitimate basis of intervention than the traditional *Wednesbury* formula.

3.9.5 Limited Protection of Human Rights

Finally, the traditional *Wednesbury* formula also stands accused of providing limited protection for human rights. For human rights to receive adequate protection, the courts need to apply the proportionality test rather than require applicants to surmount the high threshold of *Wednesbury* unreasonableness or irrationality.[210] In *ex parte Smith and Grady*,[211] the Court of Appeal was confronted with a legal challenge to the policy of the UK Ministry of Defence to prohibit homosexuals from serving in the armed forces. The Court stated that although the case raised human rights concerns, the applicants still had to demonstrate that the policy was irrational. While the Court would require more by way of justification before it was satisfied that a decision was reasonable, it also had to exercise caution when reviewing matters with a high policy content. Applying this test, the Court felt bound to conclude that the policy was not unreasonable.

In contrast, when the same policy was challenged before the ECtHR, it was struck down on the premise that it constituted a disproportionate infringement of the right to private life.[212] The Court found that instead of operating a blanket policy that discriminated against homosexuals, the UK Ministry of Defence should have adopted a conduct-based code in order to meet concerns relating to the operational effectiveness of the armed services. The British government had not shown that a conduct-based code could not adequately deal with the behavioural issues arising from the presence of homosexuals in the armed services, and therefore the blanket policy was struck down as disproportionate. Following the judgment of the ECtHR, the UK government responded by withdrawing the blanket policy and introducing a new code of conduct.

210. Ibid., 130.

211. *ex p Smith and Grady* (N89).

212. *Smith and Grady v UK* (N110).

In addition, the ECtHR also noted that the threshold of review adopted by the English judges was placed so high that it effectively excluded any consideration of the question of whether the interference with the applicants' rights was proportionate. This failure of the English courts to examine the legality of the policy beyond the limits of the *Wednesbury* formula constituted a violation of the right to an effective remedy for the protection of ECHR freedoms. Following the establishment of the HRA 1998, the courts must now recognise that *Wednesbury* review is inapplicable in their new jurisdiction to examine whether or not administrative action infringes the ECHR.

Over the past few decades, the question of substantive review has been one of the most heated debates in the field of public law in the UK and Hong Kong. Although there have been many contributions from the courts and academics, Britain and Hong Kong are still left uncertain as to its nature, scope, and structure.

> It is over 60 years since *Wednesbury*, and over 250 years since the advent of some form of rationality review in the UK. The bottom line remains that we cannot produce a modern definition of rationality review which is legally authoritative and where the mode of application coheres with the legal test.[213]

Thus, *Wednesbury* review is a standard which, by its nature, seeks to minimise courts' involvement in the process of administrative decision-making. In Britain, the lack of a general power to strike down Acts of Parliament has allowed the supremacy of Parliament, at its most absolute in the contemporary constitution, to endure.[214] In connection to this, J.A.G. Griffith has been of the opinion that the fundamental pillar of parliamentary sovereignty or supremacy seems to ensure the ultimate dominance of the political over the legal in the constitution.[215] As a result, parliamentary legislation remains substantially immune from judicial review. In Hong Kong, this premise is more complicated. Although *Wednesbury* unreasonableness has gone largely unused since mid-1991 (i.e., the period in which

213. Jake Rylatt and Joseph Tomlinson, 'Neuberger's Novelties: Keyu and the Substantive Review Debate', *UK Constitutional Law Blog*, 17 February 2016, available at: https://ukconstitutionallaw.org/2016/02/17/jake-w-rylatt-and-joseph-tomlinson-neubergers-novelties-keyu-and-the-substantive-review-debate/, last accessed 17 February 2016.

214. Masterman (N45) 105.

215. J.A.G. Griffith, 'The Political Constitution' (1979) 42 *MLR* 1.

the BORO was enacted), the attitude of judges in Hong Kong is more conservative than their UK counterparts, especially post-handover. This shift can be attributed to their fear of provoking the Chinese Communist Party ('Big Brother' in Orwellian language) or the Standing Committee of the National People's Congress (NPCSC), which has the power of final interpretation of the Basic Law. Topics related to the complex situation in Hong Kong are discussed in Chapter Eight of this book.

3.10 The Principle of Proportionality

There have been arguments that the duty placed on English courts to apply the proportionality principle in the field of EU law via the ECA 1972 prompts them to reconsider whether they should restrict themselves to the *Wednesbury* formula when being confronted with a challenge on purely domestic law.[216] Sir John Laws has further recognised that while *Wednesbury* unreasonableness and the proportionality principle are both models of the 'same concept', the former is somewhat looser than the latter regarding the imposition of legal standards on decision-makers necessary to secure the repudiation of arbitrary power.[217] Listed below are arguments that justify this assertion.

3.10.1 A More Structured and Reasoned Analysis

Rather than being confused and tautologous, proportionality is said to be able to provide a more structured analysis of the kind which is often lacking under the *Wednesbury* formula. According to Craig, '[i]ts more structured analysis has a beneficial effect in that it requires the administration to justify its policy choice more specifically than under the traditional *Wednesbury* approach'.[218] Craig furthers explains that proportionality is beneficial to the courts, saying that 'courts, when striking down a decision, do so on grounds which are more readily identifiable and ascertainable than is often the case under the *Wednesbury* test'.[219]

216. Thomas (N209) 131.

217. *ex p First City Trading* (N38) 279.

218. Paul Craig, 'Unreasonableness and Proportionality in UK Law' in Evelyn Ellis (ed), *The Principle of Proportionality in the Laws of Europe* (Hart Publishing 1999) 99–100.

219. Ibid., 100.

What is more, another advantage of providing a more systematic structure to the analysis is that it makes the various stages of enquiry more transparent and explicit,[220] thereby constraining the elected branches of government and the courts in the factors they can take into account in assessing the feasibility, and thus legality, of their decisions. As has been argued by Jowell and Lord Lester, 'intellectual honesty' requires the courts to move beyond the vague language of orthodoxy and to embrace instead the more transparent and structured method of the proportionality principle.[221]

Jowell has also suggested that proportionality review has two advantages over traditional *Wednesbury* or irrationality review.[222] First, it enables a greater understanding of the exercise that a court undertakes because it requires the court to articulate more precisely why a particular decision is unlawful.[223] Its adoption is able to enhance the intelligibility of English law. By being explicit about why a decision is unreasonable, public understanding of the law will be increased, and the law's legitimacy and certainty will also be enhanced.[224] Although proportionality does not itself offer a perfectly precise and measurable standard, it specifies sufficiently one feature of good public administration so as to provide a guidepost to primary decision-makers and the public that is more visible than the *Wednesbury* formula.

Second, proportionality review also promotes improved decision-making by public authorities by encouraging them to consider alternatives and focus on the relationship between the aims that they are trying to achieve and the means that they are using to attain those aims.[225] This is because the principle requires consideration to be given to alternatives which are less onerous or oppressive than others. In Britain, the system of public decision-making has relatively little that requires officials to consider alternative courses of action to those initially conceived. A principle which requires attention to

220. Gráinne de Búrca, 'The Principle of Proportionality and its Application in EC Law' (1993) 13 *YEL* 105, 146.

221. Jeffrey Jowell and Anthony Lester, 'Proportionality: Neither Novel nor Dangerous' in Jeffrey Jowell and Dawn Oliver (eds), *New Directions in Judicial Review* (Stevens & Sons 1988) 51.

222. Jeffrey Jowell, 'In the Shadow of *Wednesbury*' (1997) *JR* 75, 80.

223. Ibid.

224. Jowell (N103) 410.

225. Jowell (N221) 80.

different options would have a marked effect on the quality of the British public administration.[226] Thus, proportionality would be able to improve the quality of the decision-making process.

Although there have been debates about how proportionality may provide judges with a strong weapon to interfere with public officials, little has been done to examine the primary aim and intent of proportionality, which is to act as a standard of good public administration — a standard which requires means to have a reasonable relation to ends.[227] Therefore, the principle of proportionality is capable of enhancing the sensitivity of decision-makers to the impact of their actions. It will heighten their awareness of balance and proportion. All in all, public administration is talking about means and ends, so is democracy, whereas one of the hallmarks of tyranny has been the priority of ends over means.[228]

Concurring, Fordham and de la Mare have said that proportionality provides a systematic approach to judicial review of a measure (normally a decision or rule) adopted by a public authority which restricts a basic right.[229] It is a concept with three important, general features:

(a) It identifies a logical template of questions to be addressed;

(b) It provides for an intensive review by the courts as to the way in which those questions are to be asked and answered; and

(c) It involves placing upon the public authority an important onus of satisfying itself and the courts that there are proper answers.[230]

David Dyzenhaus, Murray Hunt, and the late Michael Taggart have also been of the view that 'the catechetic doctrine of proportionality, with its sequenced series of questions requiring reasoned answers from decision-makers, underscores

226. Jowell (N103) 411.

227. Ibid., 410.

228. Ibid.

229. Fordham and de la Mare (N193) 27.

230. Ibid.

the need for justification. Vague assertions of deference or of non-justiciability under the cloak of *Wednesbury* unreasonableness will no longer do'.[231]

In *Daly*,[232] Lord Steyn observed that proportionality is a 'more precise and more sophisticated' test which allows for a 'somewhat greater' intensity of review than its predecessor.[233] First, it 'may require the reviewing court to assess the balance which the decision-maker struck, not merely whether it is within the range of rational or reasonable decisions'. Second, proportionality 'may go further than the traditional grounds of review as it may require attention to be directed to the relative weight to be accorded to interests and considerations'. The third difference concerns the process of reasoning. To take Article 8 of the ECHR (i.e., the right to respect private and family life) as an example, proportionality requires the courts to engage with 'the twin requirements that the limitation of the right was necessary in a democratic society, in the sense of meeting a pressing social need, and the question whether the interference was really proportionate to the legitimate aim being pursued', rather than the threshold question for 'anxious scrutiny'.[234] Although the courts may use either approach, and the outcomes are often the same, sometimes a different conclusion would follow a proportionality enquiry,[235] so it is 'important that cases involving [the ECHR] ... be analysed in the correct way'.[236] His Lordship has further criticised that even the heightened scrutiny test, as developed in *ex parte Smith and Grady*,[237] is not necessarily appropriate to the protection of human rights.[238]

Lord Mance agreed with this line of thinking in *Kennedy v Charity Commission*,[239] when he said that 'the advantage of the terminology of

231. David Dyzenhaus, Murray Hunt, and Michael Taggart, 'The Principle of Legality in Administrative Law: Internationalisation as Constitutionalisation' (2001) 1 *OUCLJ* 5, 20.

232. *Daly* (N108) [2001] 2 AC 532.

233. Ibid., 548.

234. *ex p Smith and Grady* (N89).

235. *R (P and Q) v Secretary of State for the Home Department* [2001] EWCA Civ 1151, [2001] 1 WLR 202; *R v Shayler* [2002] UKHL 11, [2003] 1 AC 247; *South Buckinghamshire DC v Porter* [2003] UKHL 265, [2003] 2 WLR 1547; *A v Secretary of State for the Home Department* [2004] UKHL 56, [2005] 2 WLR 87, [2005] 2 AC 68; *R (SB) v Headteacher and Governors of Denbigh High School* [2005] EWCA Civ 199, [2005] 2 All ER 396.

236. *Daly* (N108) [2001] 2 AC 532, 548.

237. *ex p Smith and Grady* (N89).

238. *Smith and Grady v UK* (N110) [138].

239. *Kennedy* (N1).

proportionality is that it introduces an element of structure into the exercise, by directing attention to factors such as suitability or appropriateness, necessity and the balance or imbalance of benefits and disadvantages'.[240] Therefore, proportionality, in its structured sense, introduces a more explicit justification than mere 'unreasonableness' allows. In *R (on the application of Lord Carlile of Berriew) v Secretary of State for the Home Department*,[241] Lady Hale, the President of the UK Supreme Court (as she then was), called the proportionality approach 'an orderly process of decision-making', advocating that this approach should be preferred over the relatively amorphous standard of reasonableness.[242]

The UK Treasury and Civil Service Committee agreed that judicial review had 'improved the quality of decision-making by making it more structured and consistent' and contributed 'to upholding the values of fairness, reasonableness and objectivity in the conduct of public business'.[243] Such a clearer articulation of standards derived from proportionality analysis also promotes what the late Etienne Mureinik has called a 'culture of justification' in place of a 'culture of authority'.[244] Overall, the intensity of review under proportionality may well be greater than that under *Wednesbury* test, and the amount of discretion enjoyed by the decision-maker will be correspondingly smaller.

3.10.2 Proportionality as a Facet of *Wednesbury* Unreasonableness

It sometimes happens that the legal principles developed to impose the rule of law on the substance of administrative discretion often overlap with each other, and they are, by their nature, difficult to define precisely. In the *Wednesbury* case,[245] for example, the plaintiff argued that the condition that no children under the age of 15 should be admitted to Sunday performances under any circumstances was an unreasonable exercise of discretion and therefore *ultra vires* or illegal. In this regard, Lord Greene MR made it clear that lawfulness

240. Ibid., [54].

241. [2015] AC 945.

242. Ibid., [89].

243. Treasury and Civil Service Committee, *Role of the Civil Service*, HC 27 (HMSO, London 1993) [136].

244. For further discussion, see Chapter One of this book.

245. *Wednesbury* case (N8).

was linked to reasonableness, and that in order to act lawfully, the authority had to act reasonably. Therefore, it is clear from the *Wednesbury* judgment that the judicial review grounds of illegality and unreasonableness or irrationality overlap with each other, and the exercise of power may be challenged on more than one ground of review. His Lordship also used *Short v Poole Corporation*,[246] which concerned a teacher who had been dismissed merely because she had red hair, as an example. In one sense, the decision in this case is invalid on the ground that we now call illegality because the decision-maker had taken into account an irrelevant consideration, but it is also an unreasonable decision because it is so unreasonable to dismiss a teacher because she has red hair that no reasonable person could make such a decision. This case also provides the evidence that the grounds of illegality and irrationality are blurred.

Into this mixture of different forms of unreasonableness, the concept of proportionality is introduced. In *ex parte Brind*,[247] Lord Lowry said *Wednesbury* unreasonableness was held to include the proportionality principle when the former was applied to a decision 'which suffers a total lack of proportionality'.[248] As Lord Woolf put it in *R v Brent LBC ex parte Assegai*,[249] where the response is out of proportion with the cause, this provides a clear indication of unreasonableness in the *Wednesbury* sense. Against this background, the principles of *Wednesbury* unreasonableness and proportionality seem to cover a great deal of common ground. In *ex parte Hook*,[250] where the revocation of a market trader's licence was quashed as being an unreasonably severe penalty for a small offence, the decision could have been based on disproportionality as easily as on unreasonableness. Concurred on by Lord Steyn in *Daly*,[251] he stated that 'the starting point is that there is an overlap between the traditional grounds of review and the approach of proportionality. Most cases would be decided in the same way whichever approach is adopted'.[252]

246. *Short v Poole Corporation* (N25).
247. *ex p Brind* (N65) [1991] 1 AC 696 (HL).
248. Ibid., 762D.
249. *ex p Assegai* (N156).
250. *ex p Hook* (N154).
251. *Daly* (N108) [2001] 2 AC 532.
252. Ibid., 547.

A similar rationale is also used at the European level in that a decision will be overturned only if it is 'manifestly inappropriate or disproportionate' to the objective which the institution is seeking to pursue.[253] Therefore, when proportionality is given this meaning, there will be little difference between this review and one using *Wednesbury* unreasonableness.[254] As Craig has observed:

> It is readily apparent that if the [CJEU] wishes to adopt a less intensive standard of review in a particular area then this will carry across to proportionality, as well as to other grounds of illegality. A decision will only be overturned if it is 'manifestly inappropriate' to the objective being pursued. When proportionality is given this meaning then there will be little difference between it and *Wednesbury* unreasonableness.[255]

Although Lord Diplock did suggest in 1985 that proportionality might be adopted as a free-standing ground for judicial review, the courts have continued to regard it as simply an aspect of *Wednesbury* irrationality.[256] However, the courts have, sometimes, approached the issues as if they were considering a proportionality test, holding that a decision was *Wednesbury* irrational if:

(a) the decision-maker has failed to balance the relevant considerations;[257]

(b) the impact of a decision has been oppressive in the sense that it subjects complainants to excessive hardship;[258]

(c) disproportionate penalties have been imposed;[259]

(d) the decision-maker has failed to take the least harmful means when there were more than one available means of achieving an objective.[260]

253. *R v Ministry of Agriculture, Fisheries and Food, ex p Fedesa* (Case C-331/88) [1990] ECR I-4023.

254. Paul Craig, 'The Impact of Community Law on Domestic Public Law' in Leyland and Woods (N182) 280.

255. Paul Craig, *Administrative Law* (5th edn, Sweet & Maxwell 2003) 627.

256. *ex p Hook* (N154) 1062; *ex p Assegai* (N156).

257. *R v Secretary of State for Home Department, ex p Benson* [1989] COD 329; *Tesco Stores* (N1).

258. *R v Secretary for the Home Department, ex p Handscomb* (1987) 86 Cr App R 59; *ex p Leech (No 2)* (N120).

259. *ex p Assegai* (N156); *R v Highbury Corner Magistrates' Court, ex p Uchendu* (1994) 158 JP 409.

260. *Hall and Company Ltd v Shoreham-by-Sea UDC* [1964] 1 WLR 240.

In *ex parte International Trader's Ferry*,[261] the House of Lords was called upon to apply both the principles in their respective contexts. In this case, shipments of livestock to Europe were violently obstructed at the port by protesting animal rights groups and required so much police protection that the police could not adequately cover the rest of their area. When the Chief Constable reduced police cover at the port to two days a week, traders who had been unable to make shipments sought judicial review of his decision. What the traders alleged was that it was unreasonable, on one hand, and that it was disproportionate, on the other, for enforcing the EU Treaty which prohibits quantitative restrictions on exports and measures having equivalent effect, subject to an exception for, *inter alia*, public policy.

The challenge failed on both counts. The House of Lords, with regard to the domestic law argument for unreasonableness, held that it was for the Chief Constable to decide how to use his limited resources, and that such a decision was not *Wednesbury* unreasonable. The EU law claim was that the Chief Constable's decision constituted an export ban, which was prohibited by Article 35 of the Treaty on the Functioning of the European Union (TFEU). The Court accepted that if there had been a breach of Article 35 of the TFEU, proportionality would be relevant in deciding on the application of Article 36 of the TFEU, which allows a defence for limitations on the free movement of goods for reasons of, *inter alia*, public security or public health, providing that the limitation is not disproportionate. However, the Chief Constable's decision was held to be a proportionate response — suitable, necessary, and well within the margin of discretion. In particular, Lord Slynn stated that the difference between *Wednesbury* unreasonableness and proportionality was in practice much less than suggested, and that whichever test was adopted, the result will be the same.[262]

3.10.3 Constitutional Rights as 'Optimisation Requirements'

If we accept Robert Alexy's understanding of constitutional rights as 'optimisation requirements' — as they are imperfectly realised ideals, the full realisation of

261. *ex p International Trader's Ferry* (N169).

262. Ibid., 439.

which can only ever be approximate in light of factual constraints and competing values and principles [263] — it can be argued that proportionality is the ideally suited form of analysis for constitutional rights adjudication.[264] Moreover, in the context of any such proportionality analysis, it is essential that the question of resources be addressed. As Sandra Liebenberg has noted:

> Allowing the state to rely simply on its own budgetary allocations would defeat the purpose of socio-economic rights by allowing the state to determine the extent of its own obligations. Thus courts should examine the resources available in the national budget as a whole as opposed to focusing exclusively on existing allocations. To enable the courts to conduct this assessment, it is imperative that the state be required to place the necessary budgetary and policy information before the court in support of its justificatory arguments.[265]

Concurring with this, Alec Stone Sweet and Jud Mathews went on to say that:

> Over the past fifty years, proportionality analysis ... has widely diffused. It is today an overarching principle of constitutional adjudication, the preferred procedure for managing disputes involving an alleged conflict between rights, or between rights provisions and a legitimate state or public interest ... Although other modes of rights adjudication [are] available ... [proportionality] has emerged as a multi-purpose, best practice, standard ... By the end of the 1990s, virtually every effective system of constitutional justice in the world ... had embraced the main tenets of [proportionality analysis]'.[266]

In addition, David Beatty is also of the opinion that proportionality is the only approach which can adequately resolve the tension between popular sovereignty and the exercise of judicial power in a system of constitutional

263. Robert Alexy, *A Theory of Constitutional Rights* (translated by Julian Rivers, OUP 2002) 47–49.

264. Robert Alexy, 'The Construction of Constitutional Rights' (2010) 4 *LEHR* 19, 24.

265. Sandra Liebenberg, 'Socio-Economic Rights: Revisiting the Reasonableness Review/Minimum Core Debate' in Stu Woolman and Michael Bishop (eds), *Constitutional Conversations* (PUP 2008) 327.

266. Alec Stone Sweet and Jud Mathews, 'Proportionality, Balancing and Global Constitutionalism' (2008) 47 *CJTL* 72, 73–74.

supremacy. This is because such an approach provides an objective and impartial method for resolving conflicts between competing constitutional values.[267]

To sum up, adopting a form of 'positive proportionality', as termed by Paul O'Connell,[268] allows the courts to more rigorously scrutinise state policies which impact socio-economic rights, to decide whether, given the importance of such rights, the state's policies are likely to be realised and are moving as expeditiously as possible in this respect.

3.10.4 Reinvigoration of Judicial Review

Some commentators and judges also see proportionality as a way of reinvigorating judicial review.[269] Among them, Jowell and Lord Lester have mentioned that proportionality provides not only a more structured way of negotiating the issue of substantive review than the traditional *Wednesbury* formula, but it, being infused with moral colour, has the potential to ensure that the relationship between government and individual citizens is effectively policed by the courts.[270] In this regard, Beatty has contended that proportionality accounts for 'virtually every case in which courts have responded politically to protect people's welfare and well being',[271] adding that the principle provides 'the only conceptual apparatus judges have, and all that they need, to harmonize the autonomy of each person with the general will of the community'.[272] Furthermore, Thomas Poole observed:

> Whereas *Wednesbury* required nothing more than a Delphic utterance of 'unreasonable' or 'not unreasonable', proportionality at least requires judges to show their 'workings out'. By requiring courts to specify whether or

267. David Beatty, *The Ultimate Rule of Law* (OUP 2014).
268. Paul O'Connell, *Vindicating Socio-Economic Rights: International Standards and Comparative Experiences* (Routledge 2012) 190.
269. Thomas Poole, 'Between the Devil and the Deep Blue Sea: Administrative Law in an Age of Rights' in Linda Pearson, Carol Harlow, and Michael Taggart (eds), *Administrative Law in a Changing State* (Hart Publishing 2008) 35.
270. Jowell and Lester (N167).
271. Beatty (N267) 144.
272. Ibid., 116.

not there was a 'sufficient' connection between the measures adopted and a (legitimate) aim, the test seems to demand more from judges by way of articulation and elaboration.[273]

Against this background, there have been arguments for proportionality review to be fully adopted as a new ground for judicial review in the UK[274] and other common law jurisdictions, including Hong Kong.[275] As a result of dissatisfaction with the limits placed on judicial review by the traditional model in Britain, T.R.S. Allan has argued that a more rational model of judicial review premised upon liberal constitutionalism should be sought.[276] Within this liberal approach, law can be viewed as deriving from principles, not rules. Judges articulate points of principle but not policy.[277] Francis Jacobs has also noted that proportionality is a 'rational and well-structured test'[278] in which the courts 'decide whether a particular exercise of power ... [is] the most appropriate way of achieving a particular policy goal'.[279]

Moreover, Jowell has also argued that proportionality will improve the coherence of English judicial review, claiming that in Britain, public law is now in the uncomfortable position of having two different standards: those of 'pure' English law, and those of EU law and human rights law.[280] The convergence of the two may take time, 'but insofar as convergence could be accommodated without any obvious strain, the interests of a coherent and comprehensive system of public law so demand'.[281] As consistency of law is one of the elements under the rule of law that is, if being fulfilled, capable of

273. Thomas Poole, 'Tilting at Windmills? Truth and Illusion in "the Political Constitution"' (2007) 70 *MLR* 250, 268.

274. Jowell and Lester (N221) 51–72; T.R.S. Allan, *Law, Liberty, and Justice: The Foundations of British Constitutionalism* (Clarendon Press 1993); Craig (N218) 85–106.

275. Johannes Chan, 'Administrative Law, Politics and Governance: The Hong Kong Experience' in Tom Ginsburg and Albert Chen (eds), *Administrative Law and Governance in Asia* (Routledge 2009) 159.

276. Allan (N274).

277. Ronald Dworkin, *Taking Rights Seriously* (Duckworth 1977); *Law's Empire* (Fontana 1986).

278. Francis Jacobs, 'Public Law — The Impact of Europe' (1999) *PL* 232, 239.

279. Francis Jacobs, 'Recent Developments in the Principle of Proportionality in European Community Law' in Ellis (N218) 20.

280. Jowell (N103) 410.

281. Ibid.

guiding human behaviour, there is no justification that it should not be applied to other judicial review cases other than those involving EU law and human rights law. In *R (on the application of Alconbury Developments Ltd) v Secretary of State for the Environment, Transport and the Regions,*[282] Lord Slynn concurred on Lord Diplock's view, stating that proportionality should be recognised as a general head of review within domestic law as follows:

> I consider that even without reference to the [HRA 1998] the time has come to recognise that this principle [of proportionality] is part of English administrative law, not only when judges are dealing with Community acts but also when they are dealing with acts subject to domestic law. Trying to keep the *Wednesbury* principle and proportionality in separate compartments seems to me to be unnecessary and confusing. Reference to the [HRA 1998] however makes it necessary that the court should ask whether what is done is compatible with [the ECHR]. That will often require that the question should be asked whether the principle of proportionality has been satisfied.[283]

All in all, it is not an exaggeration to say that proportionality has attracted widespread support as a legal test primarily because it can be used with equal force by those wishing to maintain the tradition of deference to the executive and legislative branches, and by advocates of more intensive review.[284] As I have intimated, the recognition of proportionality would greatly strengthen the coherence and clarity of administrative law. This is because implicit in the proportionality formula is the fact that the courts must ask not only whether human rights considerations have been taken into account but also *how* they have been taken into account. Therefore, proportionality is able to provide a more structured and robust approach to scrutinise administrative decisions and their implementation than the *Wednesbury* formula.

282. [2001] 2 All ER 929, [2003] 2 AC 295.

283. Ibid., [2003] 2 AC 295, 321.

284. Ian Leigh, 'The Standard of Judicial Review after the Human Rights Act' in Helen Fenwick, Gavin Phillipson, and Roger Masterman (eds), *Judicial Reasoning under the Human Rights Act* (CUP 2007) 182.

3.11 Opposition to Proportionality

As Britain has been a Member State both of the EU and the ECHR, its membership requires application of the proportionality principle in the fields of EU law and fundamental rights law, respectively. Moreover, as membership has also created an impetus to adopt proportionality fully in Britain, some scholars question whether the common law needs to recognise this new principle.[285] However, Lord Wilberforce has opposed this, saying that the CJEU only operates in a narrow field and is 'not a court which develops doctrines or jurisprudential theories which have any impact on English law'.[286] The main arguments in support of this assertion are that the application of the proportionality principle would (1) be incompatible with the distinction between appeal and review; (2) be incompatible with the doctrine of separation of powers; and (3) lower the threshold of unreasonableness, leading to more judicial review litigations.

3.11.1 Incompatibility with the Distinction between Appeal and Review

Although proportionality has been 'partially' adopted in cases involving EU law and human rights law in Britain, its scope for rigorous scrutiny of justifications for measures which infringe human rights or other sufficiently regarded interests leads some judges to argue strongly against its full adoption in English law.[287] The principal argument is that its application would be incompatible with received perceptions of the distinction between appeal and review, or the so-called 'forbidden appellate approach' as advocated by Lord Lowry in *ex parte Brind*.[288] This is because it would involve the courts considering the merits and facts of administrative decisions,[289] thus trespassing the invisible line as constitutionally set by the doctrine of separation of powers. As Lord Donaldson noted:

> [I]t must never be forgotten that [judicial review] is a supervisory and not an appellate jurisdiction … Acceptance of 'proportionality' as a separate

285. Thomas (N209) 131.

286. Lord Wilberforce, interviewed in Garry Sturgess and Philip Chubb (eds), *Judging the World: Law and Politics in the World's Leading Courts* (Butterworths 1988) 271, 276.

287. *ex p Brind* (N65) [1991] 1 AC 696 (HL).

288. Ibid., 767.

289. Ibid., 762, 766–767 (Lords Lowry and Ackner).

> ground for seeking judicial review ... could easily and speedily lead to courts forgetting the supervisory nature of their jurisdiction and substituting their view of what was appropriate for that of the authority whose duty it was to reach that decision.[290]

In this regard, Lord Lowry has also observed that judges were not well equipped by training or experience to 'decide the answer to an administrative problem where the scales are evenly balanced',[291] adding:

> There can be very little room for judges to operate an independent judicial review [of the] proportionality doctrine in the space which is left between the conventional judicial review doctrine and the admittedly forbidden appellate approach [i.e., review on the merits].[292]

Lord Ackner has also indicated that the use of the proportionality test would inevitably require the courts to make 'an inquiry into and a decision upon the merits [of the matter that] cannot be avoided', in the sense that the courts would have to balance the pros and cons of the impugned decision.[293] As such, it would ultimately amount to a 'wrongful usurpation of power'.[294]

Furthermore, judicial review, it is said, involves an assessment of the manner in which a decision has been made, so it is not an appeal and the jurisdiction exercised by the judiciary is supervisory in nature.[295] This assertion is evidenced in Lawton LJ's comment, in *Laker Airways Ltd v Department of Trade*,[296] that 'I regard myself as a referee. I can blow my judicial whistle when the ball goes out of play; but when the game restarts I must neither take part in it nor tell the players how to play'.[297] As Jowell has correctly

290. Ibid., 722.

291. Ibid., 735.

292. Ibid.

293. Ibid., 762.

294. Ibid.

295. Hilary Delany, *Judicial Review of Administrative Action* (2nd edn, Round Hall 2009) 5.

296. [1977] QB 643.

297. Ibid., 724.

pointed out, the most obvious reason courts may be reluctant to admit to substantive review is because

> it is too often conflated with the notion of 'correctness review', where judges second-guess the primary decision-maker on the merits of the case, in the way of appeal rather than review (such as when courts may disagree with a planning authority about whether a proposal is out of character with the area by impeding an historic view).[298]

Affirming the need to observe the 'constitutional imperative of judicial self-restraint',[299] as exemplified in the *Wednesbury* principle, Lord Irvine has further argued that proportionality 'invites review of [the] merits of public decisions ... and would involve the court in a process of policy evaluation which goes far beyond its allotted constitutional role'.[300] Millett J, in a non-public-law case concerning a test of validity of a restraint of trade covenant, has also opined that proportionality is viewed as a 'novel and dangerous' principle which the courts should refuse to entertain.[301] Academically, Hunt provides the following explanation:

> The principal reason for the reluctance of most English judges to countenance proportionality as a ground of review in its own right is that, in their view, it would inevitably collapse the crucial distinction between a supervisory and an appellate jurisdiction, on which the legitimacy of judicial review is presumed to depend. This fear of judicial usurpation of executive or administrative functions was very much in evidence in the judicial responses to the attempt to rely on proportionality as a separate ground of challenge in [*ex parte*] *Brind*.[302]

298. Jowell (N10) 49.
299. Irvine (N53) 60.
300. Ibid., 74.
301. *Allied Dunbar (Franck Weisinger) Ltd v Frank Weisinger* [1988] 17 IRIR 60, 65.
302. Murray Hunt, *Using Human Rights Law in English Courts* (Hart Publishing 1997) 212, referring to *ex p Brind* (N65).

All in all, to invite judges to assess administrative decisions on a proportionality basis would, it is alleged, invite them to cross 'the constitutional Rubicon into merits review'.[303]

3.11.2 Constitutional and Institutional Incompetence and Incompatibility with the Doctrine of Separation of Powers

There are also critics that believe the use of proportionality marks an undesirable shift in the constitutional role of courts. This is because, on its mirror image vis-à-vis the above appeal-and-review argument, judges have for so long been said to be 'constitutionally un-qualified' and 'institutionally ill-equipped' owing to their lack of democratic mandate, and their lack of expertise, experience, etc., to adjudicate on matters of social or economic policy traditionally decided by the political branches.

Regarding the 'constitutional incompetence' argument, Lord Lowry has, in *ex parte Brind*,[304] stated the following:

> There is no authority for saying that proportionality ... is part of the English common law and a great deal of authority the other way. This, so far as I am concerned, is not a cause for regret for several reasons. First, the decision-makers, very often elected, are those to whom Parliament has entrusted the discretion and to interfere with that discretion beyond the limits as hitherto defined would itself be an abuse of judges' supervisory jurisdiction.[305]

This is especially the case when the courts are confronted with politically or economically sensitive disputes, and in particular, socio-economic rights and multi-centred or polycentric issues (i.e., problems that have complex interacting centres of tension). Choosing any solution will inevitably have consequences for other reasons and priorities. In consequence, a broad focus is required, and not

303. Ian Leigh and Roger Masterman, *Making Rights Real: The Human Rights Act in its First Decade* (Hart Publishing 2008) 295.

304. *ex p Brind* (N65) [1991] 1 AC 696 (HL).

305. Ibid., 766–767.

only on the rights and wrongs as they appear to emerge from two competing parties' positions in opposed litigation.[306] These matters are poorly suited to judicial solution. They should be, and only be, left to the discretion of the political authorities which are elected representatives or those to whom powers and duties have been delegated by such representatives. With their access to empirical evidence and sensitivity to competing demands, the executive and the legislature are said to be better suited to polycentric decision-making, which entails the ability to make broad judgments about the best solutions to complex problems. In particular, polycentric decision-making needs the careful allocation of scarce resources.[307] As the courts are said to be best suited to achieve retributive or corrective justice between two parties to a dispute whereas distributive justice among citizens should be left to the legislature,[308] polycentric decision-making for the purpose of distributive justice should not be subject to review by, or interference of, the judicial branch which is unelected and unaccountable to the general public.

Although Yash Ghai and Jill Cottrell have agreed that the courts can perform various important tasks in adjudicating on socio-economic rights (such as elaborating the contents of rights, indicating the responsibilities of the state, identifying the ways in which the rights have been violated by the state, and suggesting the framework within which policy has to be made by highlighting the priority of human rights), they claim there is always a risk that the courts may cross the line between indicating failures of policy and priorities and indicating what those priorities ought to be. If that is the case, they are actually making policy.[309] In short, decision-makers, very often elected, are those to whom Parliament has entrusted the discretion to allocate these priorities, and to interfere with that discretion beyond limits hitherto defined would itself be an abuse of the judges' supervisory jurisdiction.

306. Edwin Cameron, 'A South Africa Perspective on the Judicial Development of Socio-Economic Rights' in Liora Lazarus, Chirstopher McCrudden, and Nigel Bowles, *Reasoning Rights: Comparative Judicial Engagement* (Hart Publishing 2014) 320.

307. Ibid.

308. Ernest Weinrib, *The Idea of Private Law* (HUP 1995).

309. Yash Ghai and Jill Cottrell, 'The Role of the Courts in the Protection of Economic, Social and Cultural Rights' in Yash Ghai and Jill Cottrell (eds), *Economic, Social and Cultural Rights in Practice: The Role of Judges in Implementing Economic, Social and Cultural Rights* (Interights 2004) 86.

Insofar as the 'institutional incompetence' argument is concerned, it is said that the courts also do not have the requisite expertise (e.g., administrative and managerial knowledge, advice and experience, etc.) to evaluate an administrative problem where the interests of each party are balanced, and in particular, to make decisions on how limited resources are allocated (e.g., for particular treatments within the health care system). Expanding on this, Lord Lowry, again, in *ex parte Brind*,[310] explains that

> judges are not, generally speaking, equipped by training or experience, or furnished with the requisite knowledge and advice, to decide the answer to an administrative problem where the scales are evenly balanced, but they have a much better chance of reaching the right answer where the question is put in a *Wednesbury* form.[311]

Agreeing with this, Lord Bridge has pointed out that the formulation and implementation of economic policy are essentially matters of political judgment, and will not be susceptible to challenge except on the extremes of bad faith, improper purpose, or manifest absurdity.[312] In *Southwark London Borough Council v Tanner*,[313] Lord Millett succinctly stated: 'These cases raise issues of priority in the allocation of resources. Such issues must be resolved by the democratic process, national and local. The judges are not equipped to resolve them'.[314] Moreover, the courts have also exhibited reluctance to interfere with the conclusions of 'a separate tribunal',[315] stressing that 'it is not the function of the court to enter the scientific debate'.[316] Further, Lord Lester and Colm

310. *ex p Brind* (N65) [1991] 1 AC 696 (HL).

311. Ibid., 766–767.

312. *ex p Hammersmith and Fulham LBC* (N95) 597F–H.

313. [2001] 1 AC 1.

314. Ibid., 26.

315. *R v Parole Board, ex p Watson* [1996] 1 WLR 906, 917; *Napp Pharmaceutical Holdings Ltd v Director General of Fair Trading* [2002] EWCA Civ 796.

316. *R (Assisted Reproduction and Gynaecology Centre) v Human Fertisiliation and Embryology Authority* [2003] 1 FCR 266, [15]; *R (Campaign to End All Animal Experiments) v Secretary of State for the Home Department* [2008] EWCA Civ 417.

O'Cinneide have noted that there are 'limits to what can be achieved by the judicial process in implementing fundamental rights'.[317]

In this climate, decisions about the allocation of public resources (e.g., health care, social housing, disability benefits, etc.) are best made by the legislature or the executive primarily because they have an overview of the entire area and access to expert opinion about the advantages and disadvantages of certain priorities within the allocation. They can also assess the consequences of different distributive decisions and make a decision in light of overall budgetary concerns.

3.11.3 Lowering the Threshold of Unreasonableness Leads to Increased Judicial Review Litigations

Another argument against the principle of proportionality is that stability would be jeopardised. This is because, according to Lord Lowry, 'there is nearly always something to be said against any administrative decision',[318] and parties who felt aggrieved would be even more likely than at present to try their luck with a judicial review application both at first instance and on appeal.

To lower the thresholds of unreasonableness, and thus of judicial intervention, would inevitably lead to increasing applications for judicial review of administrative action, and this would in turn result in the expenditure of time and money by litigants and the taking up of court time which could have otherwise been devoted to other matters.[319] The losers in this respect will be members of the public, for whom the courts provide a service. All in all, as proportionality requires the courts to engage in assessments of policy and administration questions, it is, as Sir Thomas Bingham said, 'perhaps beginning to enter the administrator's mind rather than simply reviewing the process by which the decision was reached'.[320]

317. Anthony Lester and Colm O'Cinneide, 'The Effective Protection of Socio-Economic Rights' in Ghai and Cottrell (N309) 19.

318. *ex p Brind* (N65) [1991] 1 AC 696 (HL), 767.

319. Ibid., 767.

320. Thomas Bingham, '"There is a World Elsewhere": Changing Perspectives on English Law' (1992) 41 *ICLQ* 513, 524.

3.11.4 The Same Deferential Attitude in Hong Kong

Similar deferential attitude also prevails in Hong Kong. At the Ceremonial Opening of the Legal Year 2006, Li CJ (as he then was) repeated a similar call:

> On judicial review, the courts do not assume the role of the maker of the challenged decision. The courts are concerned and only concerned with the legality of the decision in question, [adjudge] in accordance with common law principles and the relevant statutory and constitutional provisions. It follows that the courts' judgment can only establish the limits of legality. The courts could not possibly provide an answer to, let alone a panacea for, any of the various political, social and economic problems which confront society in modern times.[321]

At the same ceremony in 2010, he also made very clear that

> the court's role on judicial review is only to define the limits of legality. And that the solution to political, social and economic problems cannot be found through the legal process and can only be found through the political process.[322]

Ma CJ, at the Ceremonial Opening of the Legal Year 2014, concurred with his predecessor's comments, stating:

> Public law cases — many of them in judicial review proceedings — involve not only topics of immense public importance and interest, but may sometimes also involve testing the demarcation lines between the legislature, the executive and the judiciary. For me, the constitutional line drawn for the Judiciary is a clear one: courts and judges only deal with the legal issues arising in the disputes that come before them and we determine only these legal issues. Although disputes between parties may have political, economic or social consequences, such as those cases involving matters of government policy, at all times the courts look only to the legal issues that

321. 'Chief Justice's speech at Ceremonial Opening of the Legal Year 2006', 9 January 2006, available at: www.info.gov.hk/gia/general/200601/09/P200601090137.htm, last accessed 4 August 2015.

322. 'CJ's speech at Ceremonial Opening of the Legal Year 2010', 11 January 2010, available at: www.info.gov.hk/gia/general/201001/11/P201001110174.htm, last accessed 4 August 2015.

> divide the parties. As I have said on numerous occasions, it is not part of the courts' role to decide on any aspect other than the legal issues which arise. The Basic Law sets out clearly the principle of the separation of powers between the legislature, the executive and the judiciary, and in quite specific terms, the different roles of the three institutions. So far as the Judiciary is concerned, the ambit of its constitutional role is the exercise of judicial power, that is, the adjudication of disputes that come before the courts in accordance with the law.[323]

Adopting the principle of deference as developed by Lord Hope in *R v Director of Public Prosecution, ex parte Kebilene*[324] and by Lord Steyn in *Brown v Stott (Procurator Fiscal, Dunfermline)*[325] — namely, that the courts will accord a discretionary area of judgment in relation to policy decisions which the legislature and the executive are better placed than the judiciary to decide — Hartmann J was the first judge to observe that when applying the proportionality test (with a burden on the government to justify using convincing and weighty reasons), a restriction of a fundamental right did not empower the court to re-decide the issue. This is because

> [s]uch an assumption of jurisdiction would be 'profoundly undemocratic' ... nevertheless, while full deference is given to the legislature and to the makers of administrative policies, it is for the court to reach its own judgment on whether there has been a breach of fundamental rights. Where those rights are of special importance ... a high degree of protection is appropriate and the court will give less deference than otherwise would be the case to the primary decision-maker.[326]

Moreover, the Court of Appeal and the CFA also endorsed the English view that the courts should give due weight to the views of the legislature on

323. 'CJ's speech at Ceremonial Opening of the Legal Year 2014', available at: www.info.gov.hk/gia/general/201401/13/P201401130352.htm, last accessed 4 August 2015. See also Allen Au-yueng and Julie Chu, 'Hong Kong's legal system "misused" and "drowning in irrelevance", says former top judge', *South China Morning Post*, 3 December 2015, available at: www.scmp.com/news/hong-kong/law-crime/article/1886359/hong-kongs-legal-system-misused-and-drowning-irrelevance, last accessed 12 May 2020.

324. [2000] 2 AC 326, 381A–E.

325. [2003] 1 AC 681 (PC) 703C–D.

326. *Equal Opportunities Commission v Director of Education* [2001] 2 HKLRD 690 (CFI) 733G–J.

issues of policy when considering international human rights instruments in a series of cases dealing with the consistency of the mandatory sentence of life imprisonment for murder under the Basic Law.[327]

So far, Hong Kong courts have, according to Lo Pui Yin, applied the proportionality formula only after 'giving due weight' to the views of the executive authorities and the legislature to justify restrictions of fundamental rights when:[328]

(a) convicting a male for unlawful sexual intercourse with a female under the age of sixteen on the basis of absolute liability;[329]

(b) imposing a persuasive burden in reversed onus provisions towards the proof of criminal offences;[330]

(c) criminalising homosexual buggery with a man under the age of 21;[331]

(d) establishing the statutory scheme for adverse possession;[332]

(e) disqualifying imprisoned persons from voting in elections;[333]

(f) requiring the registered owner of a motor vehicle to disclose the identity of the driver in specified situations;[334]

(g) empowering the clearance of occupiers of unleased government land following resumption;[335] and

(h) disqualifying persons with an unserved period of imprisonment from standing in LegCo elections.[336]

327. *Lau Cheong v HKSAR* (2002) 5 HKCFAR 415 (CFA); *HKSAR v Pun Ganga Chandra* [2001] 2 HKLRD 151 (CA).

328. Lo Pui Yin, *The Judicial Construction of Hong Kong's Basic Law: Courts, Politics and Society after 1997* (HKUP 2014) 295–296.

329. *So Wai Lun v HKSAR* (2006) 9 HKCFAR 530.

330. *HKSAR v Lam Kwong Wai* (unreported, 6 January 2005, CACC 213/2003) (CA), (2006) 9 HKCFAR 574 (CFA).

331. *Leung TC William Roy v Secretary for Justice* [2005] 3 HKC 77 (CFI), [2006] 4 HKLRD 211 (CA).

332. *Harvest Good Development Ltd v Secretary for Justice* [2007] 4 HKC 1 (CFI).

333. *Chan Kin Sum v Secretary for Justice* [2008] 6 HKC 486, [2009] 2 HKLRD 166 (CFI).

334. *Secretary for Justice v Latker* [2009] 2 HKC 100 (CA).

335. *Wong Wai Hing Christopher v Director of Lands* (unreported, 24 September 2010, HCAL 95, 97, 98, 99/2010) (CFI).

336. *Wong Hin Wai v Secretary for Justice* [2012] 4 HKLRD 70 (CFI).

Such deference is also reflected in some public interest litigations in Hong Kong. Public interest litigation is a type of legal action in which the claimants concerned have no private interests in the subject matter of the case. Rather, they are bringing the claim in question on behalf of the community at large or a sector of the community against the government or public authorities on a matter that has a wide impact on society.[337] The success of public interest litigation requires a liberal court and activist judges who are eager to loosen traditional adversarial procedural rules in litigation and to allow non-governmental organisations and individuals to bring public interest issues to the court even though such issues are often highly political.[338]

Despite having a surge of judicial review cases concerning matters of wider public interest in recent years, there has been reluctance from Hong Kong courts to adjudicate on disputes that are intertwined with politics in these cases, the prime reason being that they fear judges may take over the roles of the legislature and the administration.[339] As Jowell has noted, political matters are 'non-justiciable' (i.e., not amendable to decision in the context of an adversarial setting),[340] so they should be left for the democratic process. This deferential attitude is well reflected in Reyes J's judgment in a public interest litigation concerning environmental issues in which he stated:

> I fully sympathise with ... concerns about the deteriorating quality of the environment ... But the court can only apply law. The Judiciary cannot manage the environment. That is the role of the Executive. There is a limit to what can be done through the Court by way of judicial review.[341]

In short, even though public interest litigation is seen to be an important tool for social transformation in many developed and developing countries,[342]

337. Carol Harlow, 'Public Interest Litigation in England: The State of the Art' in Jeremy Cooper and Rajeev Dhavan (eds), *Public Interest Law* (Basil Blackwell 1986) 90.

338. Karen Kong, 'Public Interest Litigation in Hong Kong: A New Hope for Social Transformation?' (2009) 28(3) *CJQ* 327, 328.

339. Ibid.

340. Jeffrey Jowell, 'What Decisions Should Judges Not Take?' in Mads Andenas and Duncan Fairgrieve (eds), *Tom Bingham and the Transformation of the Law* (OUP 2009) 129.

341. *Ng Ngau Chai v The Town Planning Board* [2007] HKEC 1207, [28].

342. Sangeeta Ahuja, *Law and Justice: Casebook on Public Interest Litigation* (Orient Longman 1997).

the blanket refusal by judges to adjudicate on some public interest matters on such grounds is an 'over-zealous adherence to the doctrine [of the separation of powers] in its pure form'.[343]

Sophie Boyron concurs and argues that the adoption of proportionality could give rise to problems of an institutional and conceptual nature, and in particular, its adoption would, as far as the UK is concerned, be unduly restricted by the supremacy of Parliament.[344] In view of the above, the courts have long been accused of lacking both the constitutional legitimacy and institutional confidence to perform the exercise demanded of them.[345] It ultimately makes some judges feel unable to undertake a proportionality review regarding the implementation of political or economic policy because they lack the necessary training of public administrators and understanding of governmental processes.

To sum up the position of most critics, as proportionality analyses require the courts to carry out merit-based review of administrative decisions, it trespasses the received perceptions of the distinction between appeal and review and of the doctrine of separation of powers. Its application would inevitably entail a reallocation of power from the legislature and executive to the courts.[346]

3.12 Political, Economic, and Social Policy, and Socio-Economic Rights

The 'constitutional incompetence' and 'institutional incompetence' arguments are further intensified when the courts are confronted with sensitive issues (such as disputes involving socio-economic rights, the prioritisation of conflicting interests, or the allocation of scarce resources). Under such circumstances, E.W. Vierdag has commented that social rights are not imbued with legal content

343. Kong (N338) 329.

344. Sophie Boyron, 'Proportionality in English Administrative Law: A Faulty Translation?' (1992) 12(2) *OJLS* 237, 264.

345. Martin Loughlin, *Legality and Locality: The Role of Law in Central-Local Government Relations* (Clarendon Press 1996) 320.

346. Paul Craig, 'Fundamental Principles of Administrative Law in Relation to Basic Principles of Constitutional Law' in David Feldman and Andrew Burrows (eds), *English Public Law* (2nd edn, OUP 2009) 608.

because they are not inherently justiciable on the basis that 'implementation of these provisions [in the ICESCR] is a political matter, not a matter of law' since a court must engage in prioritisation of resources by 'putting a person either in or out of a job, a house or school'.[347] Given that issues concerning resource allocation are frequently accompanied by an electoral mandate, the courts should, it is claimed, remain sensitive to issues of accountability and legitimacy when making decisions in the social policy sphere. As Lord Woolf noted in the *Poplar Housing and Regeneration Community Association Ltd v Donoghue* [348] decision:

> The economic and other implications of any policy in this area are extremely complex and far-reaching. This is an area where, in our judgment, courts must treat the decisions of Parliament as to what is in the public interest with particular deference.[349]

An example involving judicial reluctance to step into the shoes of the executive to consider resource allocation issues is *R v Cambridge Health Authority, ex parte B*,[350] which concerned the allocation of medical resources. There the father of a ten-year-old girl who was on the brink of death owing to her suffering from leukaemia applied for judicial review, challenging a decision by Cambridge Health Authority not to fund treatment because of its view that further treatment would not be in his child's best interests. The treatment in question would have cost £75,000, and was estimated by some expert medical professionals to have as much as a 10 to 20 percent chance of success.

Having heard the case in the High Court, Laws J held that the health authority's decision interfered with the child's fundamental right to life, adding that it was incumbent upon the health authority to provide a sufficient public interest justification for its decision. Although the health authority argued that the heavy expenses of the proposed treatment had to be balanced against the interests of other patients, particularly in light of the child's marginal

347. E.W. Vierdag, 'The Legal Nature of the Rights Granted by the International Covenant on Economic, Social and Cultural Rights'(1978) IX *NYIL* 69–105, 103.

348. [2001] EWCA Civ 595, [2001] 3 WLR 183, [2001] 4 All ER 605, [2002] QB 48.

349. Ibid., [2002] QB 48, 71.

350. *ex p B* (N39). See also R. James and D. Longley, 'Judicial Review and Tragic Choices: *Ex p B*' (1995) *PL* 367.

chances of recovery, Laws J was unimpressed, saying that 'where the question is whether the life of a girl aged 10 might be saved by however slim a chance, the responsible authority has to do more than toll the bell of tight resources' and that 'they must explain the priorities that have led them to decline to fund the treatment'.[351] He found that they had not adequately done so here. Accordingly, a *certiorari* was granted which required the health authority to reconsider its decision.

However, Laws J's ruling was subsequently overturned by the Court of Appeal.[352] At the outset, the Court considered that Laws J had gone too far in requiring the health authority to justify its use of resources. Finding that it would be 'totally unrealistic' to expect health authorities to come 'to court with its accounts', it held that judicial intervention of the kind preferred by Laws J would prevent the health authorities from discharging their obligations properly.[353] On the question of the relevance of budgetary considerations, Lord Bingham MR stated:

> It is common knowledge that health authorities of all kinds are constantly pressed to make ends meet ... Difficult and agonising judgments have to be made as to how a limited budget is best allocated to the maximum advantage of the maximum number of patients. That is not a judgement which the court can make. In my judgment, it is not something that a health authority such as this authority can be fairly criticised for not advancing before the court.[354]

His Lordship also restated the orthodox understanding that the courts, in a judicial review case, are only concerned with the legality of a decision and not its merits. Though recognising the tragic nature of the child's situation, Lord Bingham MR stressed that the courts were not the arbiters of the merits in such cases. It was not for the courts to express any opinion as to the likely success or failure of the relevant medical treatment.[355] The courts should confine

351. Ibid., *ex p B* [1995] EWCA Civ 49, 16–17.
352. Ibid., [1995] 2 All ER 129.
353. Ibid., 137 (Sir Lord Bingham MR).
354. Ibid., 137e–f.
355. *ex p B* (N39) [1995] 1 WLR 898, 905–906.

themselves to the lawfulness of the decision under scrutiny. The basic rationale for the heath authority's refusal to press further with treatment for the child was scarcity of resources. He added that the court's role in this respect was perforce limited, stating:

> I have no doubt that in a perfect world any treatment which a patient ... sought would be provided if doctors were willing to give it, no matter how much it costs, particularly when a life was potentially at stake. It would however, in my view, be shutting one's eyes to the real world if the court were to proceed on the basis that we do live in such a world. It is common knowledge that health authorities of all kinds are constantly pressed to make ends meet. They cannot pay their nurses as much as they would like; they cannot provide all the treatments they would like; they cannot purchase all the extremely expensive medical equipment they would like; they cannot carry out the research they would like; they cannot build all the hospitals and specialist units they would like. Difficult and agonising judgments have to be made as to how a limited budget is best allocated to the maximum advantage of the maximum number of patients. That is not a judgment which the court can make. In my judgment, it is not something that a health authority such as this authority can be fairly criticised for not advancing before the court.[356]

Overall, the influence of *ex parte B* has remained visible. This is because, ironically, Laws LJ, the one who had robustly been willing to get himself involved in the case in determining the resource allocation issues, subsequently 'confirmed' in *Wells v Parole Board*[357] that the courts were ill-suited to determine competing claims to public funds, claiming that 'it is well-settled that courts are generally in no position to make judgments upon competing claims for the allocation of scarce resources, and will decline to do so'.[358] In *R v Department of Education, ex parte Begbie*,[359] Laws LJ even said that 'the greater the policy element in the decision, the lower the degree of scrutiny of the decision is required'.[360]

356. Ibid., 906.
357. [2007] EWHC 1835.
358. Ibid., [39].
359. [1999] EWCA Civ 2100, [2000] 1 WLR 1115.
360. Ibid., 1130.

3.12.1 Issues Involving Environment, Economic, and Social Policies

There have also been cases showing that the courts are unwilling to step into the executive's domain by substituting their decisions in areas concerning economic and social policies. In *R (on the application of Jones) v Mansfield District Council*,[361] Dyson LJ held that a planning authority's conclusion as to whether a proposed development was likely to significantly affect the environment involved 'an exercise of judgement or opinion', and was therefore subject only to *Wednesbury* review.[362]

In *ex parte Hammersmith and Fulham London Borough Council*,[363] the House of Lords reviewed 'charge capping', an economic policy developed by the UK Secretary of State. In this case, the charge capping which the applicant local authorities claimed was in breach of the relevant statute. Lord Bridge held that while the court could intervene if the Secretary of State had acted illegally (i.e., for improper purposes or on irrelevant considerations), it should, in the sphere of national economic policy, be wary of irrationality review unless there was some manifest absurdity, improper motive, or bad faith.

Similarly, in *R v Secretary of State for Environment, ex parte Spath Holme Ltd*,[364] the House of Lords was unwilling to go beyond the *Wednesbury* test in reviewing a social policy issue. In this case, an administrative order regulating the rent which could be charged in respect of regulated tenancies was tested on a *Wednesbury*-unreasonableness basis even though the order in question was alleged to be in breach of the right to property under Article 1 of Protocol 1 to the ECHR. The Court held that striking an economically fair balance between landlords and tenants was a question of social policy for UK Ministers to answer, and could be set aside only if found to be perverse.[365] As Lord Bingham noted, 'the allocation of public resources is a matter of ministers, not courts'.[366]

361. [2003] EWCA Civ 1408, [2004] 2 P & CR 14.

362. Ibid., [17].

363. *ex p Hammersmith and Fulham LBC* (N95).

364. [2001] 2 AC 349.

365. Ibid., 395–396 (Lord Bingham).

366. Ibid., 395.

3.12.2 Issues Involving Allocation of Scarce Resources

A similar assertion is also found in *R (on the application of Flash) v Southwark London Borough Council*,[367] which concerned the allocation of scarce resources. It was held that a relaxed *Wednesbury* standard was appropriate in reviewing whether a local authority had legitimately concluded that accommodation offered to the claimant in discharge of its statutory duty was 'suitable'.[368]

The scarce-resource-allocation issue also arose in *R v Gloucestershire County Council, ex parte Barry*.[369] The legal issue in this case concerned whether the availability of resources could be taken into account under Section 2(1) of the UK Chronically Sick and Disabled Persons Act 1970. The law in question provided that if a local authority was satisfied that it was necessary to make arrangements in order to meet the needs of a chronically sick or disabled person, then it was the duty of that authority to make those arrangements. The applicant had been provided with home help twice a week, meals-on-wheel four times a week, and cleaning and laundry services pursuant to this provision since 1992. Then, in 1994, the local authority withdrew these services due to cuts in funding from the central government, claiming that it would no longer be able to meet his 'full needs as assessed'.[370] The House of Lords held that as a matter of construction, the needs of such a person for services could not sensibly be assessed without having some regard for the costs of providing them.

However, in what circumstances will it be lawful for an authority to take into account the scarcity of its resources when it exercises statutory discretions? In the absence of any express statutory provision on the matter, when will the courts infer that it falls within the ambit of the statutory purpose for the authority to shape its exercise of statutory powers by reference to the size of its budget? The courts have made it clear that when Parliament confers discretionary powers on public authorities, they are fully aware that budgets are finite. Decisions as to whether (and if so, how) to exercise such powers necessarily involve hard financial choices. Hence, it is for the authority, not the courts, to match limited

367. [2004] EWHC 717 (Admin).

368. Ibid., [19].

369. [1997] AC 584 (HL), [1997] 2 All ER 1.

370. Ibid., 3g.

resources to competing needs on the understanding that many highly deserving calls will have to be rejected.[371]

A perception is also spreading that in contrast with civil and political rights, socio-economic rights, be they enshrined in international or domestic instruments, are 'ideological aspirations' or 'programmatic goals'. They are highly dependent on sufficient resources for their fulfilment, and therefore inherently unsuited to the mechanisms and techniques developed by the courts for the protection of fundamental human rights.[372] Thus, whether controversy centres on the efficacy of legal measures for their implementation and enforcement, there is an inextricable link between socio-economic rights and the allocation of scarce resources.[373]

3.12.3 Socio-Economic Rights vs Separation of Powers: A Zero-Sum Separation-of-Powers Thesis?

According to O'Connell, the fundamental problem with the prevailing discourse on socio-economic rights and the separation of powers is the combative language that is used and the way in which they are presented with false binaries, the so-called the 'zero-sum separation-of-powers' thesis.[374] This approach has been exemplified in the Irish Court by Hardiman J, who has argued that judicial enforcement of socio-economic rights will lead to the growth of judicial power at the expense of the elected branches of government. He goes on to say:

> If the courts (or either of the other organs of government) expand their powers beyond their constitutional remit, this expansion will necessarily be at the expense of the other organs of government. It will also be progressive. If citizens are taught to look to the courts for remedies for matters within the legislative or executive remit, they will progressively seek further

371. Carl Emery, *Administrative Law: Legal Challenges to Official Action* (Sweet & Maxwell 1999) 94.

372. Asbjørn Eide, 'Economic Social and Cultural Rights as Human Rights' in Asbjørn Eide, Catarina Krause, and Allan Rosas (eds), *Economic Social and Cultural Rights* (2nd edn, Kluwer 2001) 22ff.

373. Philip Alston, 'Economic and Social Rights' in Henry Steiner and Philip Alston, *International Human Rights in Context Law, Politics, Morals* (OUP 2000) 237–249.

374. O'Connell (N268) 182.

> remedies there, and progressively cease to look to the political arms of government. Such a development would certainly downgrade the political arms of government.[375]

For this reason, it is not uncommon for the unaccountable and inexpert nature of the courts to be used as excuses to support an argument that their involvement in adjudicating on sensitive polycentric policy issues which concern prioritising conflicting interests and allocating scarce resources (or on positive duties arising from socio-economic rights issues) is anti-democratic.[376] In this regard, Jeremy Waldron has opined that 'there is no reason why a decision by a majority of nine judges should be given more weight than a decision by a majority of the electorate'.[377] Insofar as the inexpert nature is concerned, Cass Sunstein has succinctly said that 'judges have limited wisdom and limited tools. Their role is therefore catalytic rather than preclusive'.[378]

3.13 Concluding Remarks

This chapter has examined the elements of *Wednesbury* unreasonableness, its rationale, its development, the extent to which it has been fused with the proportionality principle, and its influence in Hong Kong. The pros and cons of these dual concepts have also been analysed. The proportionality formula has emerged as a veritable Esperanto of, and as a global 'best-practice' standard in, constitutional rights adjudication. One of the advantages of proportionality review is that it is qualitatively different from *Wednesbury* unreasonableness review, in that it imposes a more structured, rigorous, and transparent standard of review on governmental and judicial decision-makings. This, in turn, reduces the extent of administrative and judicial subjectivity. Although it cannot be guaranteed that adopting the proportionality test over *Wednesbury* unreasonableness could completely remove elements of administrative and judicial subjectivity, it arguably makes the process of administrative and judicial reasoning more structured and transparent.

375. *TD v Minister for Education* [2001] 4 IR 256, 361–362.

376. Sandra Fredman, *Human Rights Transformed: Positive Rights and Positive Duties* (OUP 2008) 32.

377. Jeremy Waldron, *Law and Disagreement* (OUP 1999) 15.

378. Cass Sunstein, *Designing Democracy: What Constitutions Do* (OUP 2001) 11.

This chapter has also explored a variety of views advocating against the full adoption of the proportionality principle in the UK and Hong Kong. These critics allege that the application of the proportionality principle would be incompatible with the distinction between appeal and review if the courts are going to fully recognise it as an independent ground of judicial review. They also claim that the courts are constitutionally and institutionally incompetent to adjudicate on matters concerning politically or economically sensitive disputes, in particular socio-economic rights issues which involve the prioritisation of conflicting interests and allocation of scarce resources. Such beliefs have further been bolstered by the view that in contrast with civil and political rights, socio-economic rights are aspirational in nature and highly dependent on sufficient resources for their realisation. In consequence, all of these attributes, when taken together, make us inclined to believe that these rights are inherently unsuited to the mechanisms and techniques developed by the courts for such protection.

4

Civil and Political Rights vs Socio-Economic Rights: An Outdated Bifurcation

4.1 Introduction

The decades since the Universal Declaration on Human Rights 1948 (UDHR 1948) have witnessed what one writer calls 'the rise and rise of human rights'.[1] While human rights have traditionally been understood as providing protection for individual freedom against an intrusive state (i.e., 'negative' duties on states to prevent governments from interfering with individuals), these rights are now more expansively interpreted as imposing positive duties on states, as well.[2] According to Kemal Bokhary:

> Human rights in today's world represent the minimum which people everywhere are entitled to demand for themselves and must accord to others so that we may all live and let live as human beings enjoying the maximum personal autonomy consistent with life in organized society. These entitlements — unified by principles of justice — involve civil liberties, personal security, security of property however modest, self-expression, public participation, respect for otherness, education, healthcare, and at least a tolerable standard of living. They enable each and every one of us to be ourselves and to live and let live with human dignity: in how we treat others and are treated by them.[3]

---

1. Kirsten Sellars, *The Rise and Rise of Human Rights* (Sutton 2002).
2. Sandra Fredman, *Human Rights Transformed: Positive Rights and Positive Duties* (OUP 2008) 1.
3. Kemal Bokhary, *Human Rights* (Sweet & Maxwell 2015) 1.

However, there has been another school of thought that claims such positive duties are a question of politics not legal rights. Where positive obligations are acknowledged, they are associated with socio-economic rights. For this reason, socio-economic rights are generally regarded as being merely 'aspirational', and their status as human rights is in doubt.[4]

This chapter examines the development of human rights in recent decades at national and international levels, and discusses issues ranging from the evolution of socio-economic rights adjudication and the rejection of non-justiciability of socio-economic rights to a new tripartite theory of obligations by the state. It also considers our evolving understanding of the doctrine of separation of powers, which makes the courts constitutionally and institutionally competent to adjudicate cases that involve socio-economic rights-related issues.

4.2 Civil and Political Rights vs Socio-Economic Rights

The view that matters concerning social policy and socio-economic rights issues should be left to the hands of the executive has long haunted the British judiciary, and perhaps elsewhere in the common law world.[5] This stems from the 'entrenched belief' that human rights are of two types: civil and political rights, on one hand, and socio-economic and cultural rights, on the other. The former have been understood to refer to rights which protect individuals against intrusion by the state (i.e., negative duties), whereas the latter concern rights to be protected by the state against want or need (i.e., positive duties).[6] This divide is reflected in the structure of international human rights instruments, with civil and political rights being protected by the International Covenant on Civil and Political Rights (ICCPR) and socio-economic rights being protected by the International Covenant on Economic, Social, and Cultural Rights (ICESCR). A similar pattern is also evident at the European level where the European

4. Fredman (N2) 1.

5. The *GCHQ* principle was adopted *in toto* in Malaysia in the case of *Rama Chandran, R v The Industrial Court of Malaysia* [1997] 1 AMR 6:433, [1997] 1 MLJ 145 (FC).

6. Sandra Fredman and Murray Wesson, 'Social, Economic and Cultural Rights' in David Feldman and Andrew Burrows (eds), *English Public Law* (2nd edn, OUP 2009) 453.

Convention on Human Rights (ECHR) covers a separate set of rights from that of the European Social Charter 1961 (ESC).

The constructs of civil and political rights and socio-economic rights are, indeed, products of different political philosophies,[7] with correspondingly different ideas of the relationship between individual and state and the role of the individual as a citizen in society.[8] In this regard, civil and political rights are the creatures of political philosophies that conceive of the state as a potential threat to individual liberty,[9] whereas socio-economic rights are associated with moral and political theories of citizenship in which positive state action is essential to the achievement of liberty.[10]

Although there have been proclamations that all rights are equal and indivisible, interdependent and interrelated, and that they should be treated in an equal manner with the same emphasis,[11] socio-economic rights are generally accorded lesser status than civil and political rights. Many do not regard them as rights at all, but 'aspirations' or 'programmatic goals' instead. For this reason, socio-economic rights are often referred to as 'second-generation rights' owing to these rights being drafted later in time.[12] However, Allan Rosas has suggested that interests for social rights date back to the eighteenth and nineteenth centuries, and that with the creation of the International Labour Organisation in 1919, the international promotion of some social rights, such as workers' rights, started well before the international work on civil and political rights.[13]

---

7. Friedrich Hayek, *The Constitution of Liberty* (CUP 1960); Robert Nozick, *Anarchy State and Utopia* (Basic Books 1974); Charles Fried, *Right and Wrong* (HUP 1994); Asbjørn Eide, 'Economic Social and Cultural Rights as Human Rights' in Asbjørn Eide, Catarina Krause, and Allan Rosas (eds), *Economic Social and Cultural Rights* (2nd edn, Kluwer 2001) 3; Ellie Palmer, *Judicial Review, Socio-Economic Rights and the Human Rights Act* (Hart Publishing 2007) 14.
8. Ibid., Palmer, 15.
9. Hayek; Nozick; and Fried (N7).
10. T.H. Marshall, *Citizenship and Social Class* (Routledge 1959).
11. UN General Assembly, Vienna Declaration and Programme of Action, A/CONF157/23 (12 July 1993) [5].
12. Karel Vasak, 'Human Rights, A Thirty-Years Struggle' (Nov 1977) UNESCO Courier, 2–32.
13. Allan Rosas, 'Social Rights and the European Union' in Peter Van der Auweraert, Tom De Pelsmaeker, Jeremy Sarkin, and Johan Vande Lanotte (eds), *Social, Economic and Cultural Rights: An Appraisal of Current European and International Developments* (Maklu 2002) 150.

There are many views that favour the lesser-status argument.[14] The first is the differentiation between civil and political rights and socio-economic rights as being negative and positive duties, respectively. Second, the former are said to be capable of being immediately enforceable, but the latter require the state to take steps towards its realisation. Third, the former are regarded as cost-free, whereas the latter require the state to provide resources. Finally, the civil and political rights are said to be determinate, while socio-economic rights are inherently open-ended standards. This negative-and-positive-rights divide has been reflected and reinforced in the UK. Under the UK Human Rights Act 1998 (HRA 1998), it was assumed without question that 'Bringing Rights Home' [15] entailed incorporation only of the ECHR. Incorporation of socio-economic rights was never considered, even though Britain is also a signatory to the ICESCR and ESC.

4.3 The Negative-and-Positive Rights Argument

However, characterising socio-economic rights as lower-status rights is clearly inconsistent with the concept of social democracy that has been prevailing in Europe and in many new democracies since the end of the Second World War. In fact, governments in these regions have become accustomed to accepting international and domestic obligations to safeguard traditional democratic freedoms while, at the same time, protecting the well-being of citizens by ensuring varying levels of economic and social rights.[16] Throughout the latter half of the twentieth century, social democratic theorists argued that affirmative state duties to protect citizens (for instance, against poverty and homelessness) are implicit in the traditional liberal values that are founded on equal respect for the dignity of persons and enshrined in the UDHR 1948.[17] Against this background, socio-economic rights must be seen as equal in status to civil and political rights, or in some cases, superior — without access to food, shelter,

14. Fredman and Wesson (N6) 454.

15. Jack Straw and Paul Boateng, 'Bringing Rights Home: Labour's Plan to Incorporate the European Convention of Human Rights into UK Law' (1997) 1 *EHRLR* 71–80.

16. Palmer (N7) 16.

17. Jeremy Waldron, 'Liberal Rights: Two Sides of the Coin' in Jeremy Waldron, *Liberal Rights* (CUP 1993) 31.

education, and health, rights such as freedom of speech or the right to trade freely become meaningless.

Experience has also shown that it is too simplistic to view civil and political rights as distinct from socio-economic rights. In fact, some rights are difficult to classify under the traditional dichotomy of civil and political rights or socio-economic rights. Trade union rights, for example, are difficult to label under this dichotomy as freedom of association is a civil and political right, but trade union rights as such are covered by the ICESCR. Family rights are protected under both the ICCPR and the ICESCR. Minority rights and the right of indigenous people involve a web of participatory rights, linguistic rights, property rights, and so on.[18] Thus, there is no point in trying to force such rights into the straight-jacket of being labelled as either civil and political or socio-economic rights.

Furthermore, civil and political rights, like their socio-economic counterparts, also have resource implications. Conversely, not all socio-economic rights are resource intensive. Instead, both sets of rights give rise to both positive and negative duties. This assertion is based on theoretical perspectives that human rights are universal and indivisible, as officially mentioned as 'indivisibility and interdependence and interrelatedness' in the UN Vienna Declaration and Programme of Action on Human Rights as adopted by the World Conference on Human Rights, and that there are important interactions between these two sets of rights.

This position was restated by the UN General Assembly in its 2006 Resolution creating the Human Rights Council. Without basic socio-economic entitlements, civil and political rights cannot be fully exercised. Freedoms of speech or assembly, for example, are of little use to a starving or homeless person. Conversely, a right to education is not meaningful unless a person also has the freedom to create knowledge and exchange information. Moreover, those without resources will find it hard to access the legal system to redress breaches of their rights. This means that even the most fundamental rights, such as the right not to be detained without trial or the right not to be subjected

18. Martin Scheinin, 'The Right to Enjoy a Distinct Culture: Indigenous and Competing Uses of Land' in Theodore Orlin, Allan Rosas, and Martin Scheinin (eds), *The Jurisprudence of Human Rights Law: A Comparative Interpretive Approach* (Turku 2000) 159–222.

to torture, may be less available to those without socio-economic means than others. Concurring, Sir John Laws also mentioned that the reach of 'compulsory negative rights' is not fixed, that there are circumstances in which negative rights can be 'overridden by the claims of positive rights', and that 'the enjoyment of negative rights very often depends on achievement or standards in the field of positive rights'.[19] Sometimes, strict distinction of the positive-and-negative-right divide is blurred. As Lord Irvine noted:

> Some may see the right to a good education as a positive right; others may claim that it is an essential component of, say, the right to freedom of speech, since without education, we are disabled from communicating our opinions to others effectively.[20]

Moreover, the view that socio-economic rights generally require greater resources to achieve than some resource-focused civil and political rights has tremendously affected the full development and realisation of some socio-economic rights over the years, especially in developing countries.[21] However, Article 25 of the UDHR 1948 proclaims that

> everyone has the right to a standard of living adequate for the health and well-being of himself and of his family, including food, clothing, housing and medical care and necessary social services, and the right to security in the event of unemployment, sickness, disability, widowhood, old age or other lack of livelihood in circumstances beyond his control' as well as 'the right to education', 'the right to social security', and 'the right to work'.

Subsequently, the UDHR 1948 was updated and extended, which created the rights to treaty form (i.e., the ICCPR and ICESCR) in 1966.

In 1968, the International Conference on Human Rights, held in Teheran, called upon 'all Governments to focus ... on developing and perfecting legal

19. John Laws, 'The Constitution: Morals and Rights' (1996) *PL* 622.

20. Derry Irvine, 'The Philosophical Case for a Bill of Rights: A Response to Sir John Law 1996' in Derry Irvine, *Human Rights, Constitutional Law and the Development of the English Legal System* (Hart Publishing 2003) 5.

21. Matthew Craven, *The International Covenant on Economic, Social and Cultural Rights: A Perspective on its Development* (OUP 1995) 15.

procedures for [the] prevention of violations and defence of economic, social and cultural rights'.[22] In response, the UN Secretary-General undertook a detailed 'preliminary study of issues relating to the realization of economic and social rights'.[23] The study noted the desirability of both constitutional and legislative measures at the national level to promote respect for social rights. It added that Article 8 of the UDHR 1948, which recognised 'the right to an effective remedy by the competent national tribunals for acts violating the fundamental rights granted him by the constitution or by law', applies 'to economic, social and cultural rights'.[24] The study also noted that many of these rights were capable of being protected at the national level 'by the ordinary courts', and that in many respects, this was already the situation in various countries.[25]

Moreover, the UN Committee on Economic, Social, and Cultural Rights (UNESCR Committee) has further indicated that the resource-implication argument must not be seen as watering down the obligations of states under the ICESCR. The UNESCR Committee has stated that while the ICESCR 'provides for progressive realization and acknowledges the constraints due to the limits of available resources, it also imposes various obligations which are of immediate effect'.[26] For instance, the obligation to ensure the right of everyone to form and join a trade union under Article 8 of the ICESCR is of immediate effect.

4.4 Philosophical Basis and Evolution of Socio-Economic Rights Adjudication

The philosophical basis of socio-economic rights adjudication is that apart from the augmentation of the traditional trade union movement, which focused on labour rights, these new socio-economic rights movements, especially in Latin America, are, as Javier Couso has argued, the result of the political left

22. *Final Act of the International Conference on Human Rights* (United Nations Publication, Sales No. E68 SIV2) resolution XVI, [6].

23. Preliminary Study on Issues Relating to the Realisation of Economic and Social Rights contained in the Universal Declaration of Human Rights and the International Covenant on Economic, Social and Cultural Rights, E/CN 4/988 (20 January 1969).

24. Ibid., [157].

25. Ibid., [159].

26. UNESCR Committee, General Comment No. 3, [1].

accepting the 'stark reality of failed socialist states' and moving towards more reformist rights-based models, which see law as a vehicle for social change.[27]

Within the provisions of the ICESCR, socio-economic rights comprise, among other things, the right to social security and social insurance,[28] the right of family to protection and assistance,[29] the right to an adequate standard of living,[30] the right to the highest attainable standard of physical and mental health,[31] the right to education,[32] and so on. This group of rights, as J.K. Mapulanga-Hulston has argued, is considered to be essentially humanitarian, aiming to provide human beings with a right to those basic subsistence needs that make life liveable in dignity.[33] In this regard, no dignity can be said to be inherent in a jobless, hungry, sick, homeless, illiterate, or impoverished human being. Thus, by their intrinsic nature, socio-economic rights 'imply a commitment to social integration, solidarity and equality, and include tackling the issue of income distribution ... [which] ... are indispensable for an individual's dignity and the free development of their personality'.[34] In agreement with this, Henry Shue views socio-economic rights, coupled with cultural rights, as important basic rights, and that no one can fully, if at all, enjoy any right that is supposedly protected by society if they lack the essentials for a reasonably healthy life.[35]

4.5 Socio-Economic Rights Are No Longer Non-Justiciable

The view that socio-economic rights, unlike their civil and political counterparts, are not 'real' human rights but are merely aspirational 'societal goals' to be

27. Javier Couso, 'Case Studies: Social Rights as Middle-Class Entitlements in Hungary: The Role of the Constitutional Court' in Robert Gargarella, Pilar Domingo, and Theunis Roux (eds), *Courts and Social Transformation in New Democracies: An Institutional Voice for the Poor?* (Aldershot 2006) 255.

28. ICESCR, Art 9.

29. Ibid., Art 10.

30. Ibid., Art 11.

31. Ibid., Art 12.

32. Ibid., Arts 13 and 14.

33. J.K. Mapulanga-Hulston, 'Examining the Justiciability of Economic, Social and Cultural Rights' (2002) 6(4) *IJHR* 29–48.

34. Ibid., 34.

35. Henry Shue, *Basic Rights: Subsistence, Affluence and US Foreign Policy* (2nd edn, PUP 1996) 24–25.

determined by social policy,[36] and that they are vague and non-justiciable, and thus cannot be claimed against a state in the same manner as civil and political rights,[37] is inapt. Since 1989, the UNESCR Committee has provided considerable conceptual clarity and elaboration regarding the nature and scope of many socio-economic rights contained in the ICESCR, especially through the publication of General Comments. Among them, the UNESCR Committee noted that believing the ICESCR to be merely 'aspirational' is based on a mistaken belief of legal obligations arising from the ICESCR.[38]

Of more significance is the question of 'non-justiciability' which seems to have been the most impeding factor against the development and judicial enforceability of socio-economic rights. The term 'justiciability' refers to the ability to claim a remedy before an independent and impartial body when a right has been violated or is likely to be violated. Justiciable rights grant right-holders a legal course of action to enforce them. The existence of legal remedy, be it substantial or procedural, is one of the defining features of a full-fledged right.[39] Such legal remedy is important when the matter at stake is a violation of human rights, which are inherent to a human being's condition and identity.[40]

One rationale of this non-justiciability argument is that the courts and quasi-judicial institutions cannot adjudicate on socio-economic rights because they involve policy decisions that fall within the purview of the legislature and of the executive rather than that of the judiciary, and that the courts cannot take over policy making from governments concerning socio-economic rights.[41] Since policy is political, it should be addressed by the more directly accountable branches of government and by those representatives who could be easily

36. David Harris, *Cases and Materials on International Law* (6th edn, Sweet & Maxwell 2004) 655.

37. E.W. Vierdag, 'The Legal Nature of the Rights Granted by the International Covenant on Economic, Social and Cultural Rights' (1978) 9 *NYIL* 99.

38. Concluding Observations of the Committee on Economic, Social and Cultural Rights (Hong Kong) China, E/C 12/1/Add58 (05/21/2001), [16].

39. International Commission of Jurists, *Courts and the Legal Enforcement of Economic, Social and Cultural Rights: Comparative Experiences of Justiciability* (ICJ 2008) 6, available at: www.icj.org/wp-content/uploads/2009/07/Courts-legal-enforcement-ESCR-Human-Rights-Rule-of-Law-series-2009-eng.pdf, last accessed 20 June 2020.

40. Ibid., 7.

41. Ralph Beddard and Dilys Hill (eds), *Economic, Social and Cultural Rights: Progress and Achievement* (Macmillan 1992).

removed by popular vote, not by 'unelected courts'. Thus, socio-economic rights adjudication by the courts is said to be anti-democratic, or counter-majoritarian, in nature, because the role of nationally elected representatives is usurped by the courts which pass judgment on matters of social policy and resource allocation.[42] Nevertheless, this view has been challenged, as mentioned in the Coalition for an Optional Protocol to the ICESCR's Fact Sheet under 'The Question of Justiciability', as follows:

> Adjudicating economic, social and cultural rights claims does not require courts to take over policy making from governments. Courts have neither the inclination nor the institutional capacity to do so. Rather, just as in civil and political rights cases, courts and other bodies adjudicating economic, social and cultural rights review governmental decision-making, to ensure consistency with fundamental human rights. Holding governments accountable to human rights [whether civil and political or socio-economic and cultural rights] enhances democracy. It does not undermine it.[43]

Concurring with this, Dennis Davis is of the view that 'the role of the judiciary and hence judicial review is to foster a culture of democracy rather than create rule by "juristocracy"'.[44] Furthermore, the UNESCR Committee General Comment No. 3 (namely The Nature of States Parties' Obligations),[45] which was adopted in 1990, separated the key state obligations into a duty to take steps to progressively realise the socio-economic and cultural rights, and a minimum core obligation to ensure the satisfaction of, at the very least, minimum essential levels of each right. Regarding the latter, the UNESCR Committee also asserted that

> a State party in which any significant number of individuals is deprived of essential foodstuffs, of essential primary health care, of basic shelter and

42. Malcolm Langford, 'The Justiciability of Social Rights: From Practice to Theory' in Malcolm Langford (ed), *Social Rights Jurisprudence: Emerging Trends in International and Comparative Law* (CUP 2008) 31.
43. Coalition for an Optional Protocol to the ICESCR's Fact Sheet No. 7, 'The Question of Justiciability', [3].
44. Dennis Davis, 'To Defer and then When? Administrative Law and Constitutional Democracy' in Hugh Corder (ed), *Comparing Administrative Justice Across the Commonwealth* (JUTA 2008) 30.
45. UN Doc E/1991/23 (1991) Annex III at [86], reprinted in Compilation of General Comments and General Recommendations Adopted by Human Rights Treaty Bodies, UN Doc HRI/GEN/1/Rev6 (2003) [14].

> housing, or of the most basic forms of education is, *prima facie*, failing to discharge its obligations under the [ICESCR].[46]

This statement justifies the position that 'if the [ICESCR] were to be read in such a way as not to establish such a minimum core obligation, it would be largely deprived of its *raison d'être*'.[47] Therefore, the all-important resources dimension was addressed as follows:

> The Committee is of the view that a minimum core obligation to ensure the satisfaction of, at the very least, minimum essential levels of each of the rights is incumbent upon every State Party. ... In order for a State party to be able to attribute its failure to meet at least its minimum core obligations to a lack of available resources, it must demonstrate that every effort has been made to use all resources that are at its disposition in an effort to satisfy, as a matter of priority, those minimum obligations.[48]

Similarly, the UNESCR Committee has also observed that the classification of socio-economic rights as non-justiciable rights is arbitrary and 'would drastically curtail the capacity of courts to protect the rights of the most vulnerable and disadvantaged groups in society'.[49] In South Africa, the Constitutional Court specifically rejected a similar non-justiciability argument in *Government of the Republic of South Africa v Irene Grootboom*.[50] This case concerned a group of extremely poor people (i.e., the respondents) who felt compelled by the desperation of their living conditions in the informal settlement in Wallacedene to move onto vacant land. However, this land was privately owned and earmarked for formal low-cost housing. Eviction proceedings were successfully instituted against these people, and the resulting court order was implemented in a manner 'reminiscent of apartheid-style evictions',[51] with the eviction destroying their

46. Ibid., [10].
47. Ibid.
48. Ibid.
49. UNESCR Committee, General Comment No. 9: The domestic application of the Covenant, 3 December 1998, E/C.12/1998/24, [10].
50. [2000] ZACC 19, 2001 (1) SA 46 (CC), 2000 (11) BCLR 1169 (CC).
51. Ibid., [10].

possessions and materials in the process.[52] Ultimately, the respondents landed up on the Wallacedene sports field, with nothing other than plastic sheeting to protect them against the elements. They complained against the government, demanding that the municipality fulfil its constitutional obligations towards them, which they claimed would involve the provision of at least basic shelter. In reaching the decision, the Court emphasised that 'socio-economic rights are expressly included in the [South African] Bill of Rights' and the 'question is therefore not whether socio-economic rights are justiciable under [the South African] Constitution, but how to enforce them in a given case'.[53] All in all, as Geraldine Van Bueren has contended, *Grootboom* 'hammered the final nail into the coffin of non-justiciability'.[54] Thus, rights without adjudication and enforcement are no rights at all.

In Canada, the Supreme Court, in *Eldridge v British Columbia (AG)*,[55] rejected the British Columbian provincial government's plea that the right to equality did not require governments to allocate resources in a healthcare centre in order to address the pre-existing disadvantage of particular groups, concluding that the said right included a duty to provide sign language interpretation in hospitals for patients with hearing impairment.[56] The Court noted that the estimated cost of providing sign language interpretation for the whole of British Columbia was only $150,000 or approximately 0.0025 percent of the provincial healthcare budget at the time.[57] In reaching the conclusion against the provincial government, the Court emphasised that discrimination can 'accrue from a failure to take positive steps to ensure that disadvantaged groups benefit equally from services

52. Similar uncivilised events also happened in Hong Kong, resulting in some police officers being suspended because of their alleged assault of a homeless man and the destruction of his belongings with a hammer; see Danny Mok, 'Hong Kong police suspend officer accused of assaulting homeless man and smashing his belongings with hammer', *South China Morning Post,* 5 March 2020, available at: www.scmp.com/news/hong-kong/law-and-crime/article/3065079/hong-kong-police-suspend-officer-after-alleged-assault, last accessed 19 May 2020; Danny Mok, 'Arrest follows suspension for Hong Kong police officer accused of smashing homeless man's possessions in Sham Shui Po park', *South China Morning Post*, 7 March 2020, available at: www.scmp.com/news/hong-kong/law-and-crime/article/3074039/arrest-follows-suspension-hong-kong-police-officer, last accessed 19 May 2020.

53. *Grootboom* (N50) [41].

54. Geraldine Van Bueren, 'Including the Excluded: The Case for an Economic, Social and Cultural Human Rights Act' (2002) Autumn *PL* 456, 461.

55. [1997] 3 SCR 624.

56. Ibid., [87].

57. Ibid., [96].

offered to the general public'.[58] Indeed, failure to recognise such an obligation would reflect 'a thin and impoverished vision of Section 15(1) [equality rights]'.[59] In this regard, Murray Wesson has commented that the boundaries between civil and political rights review and socio-economic rights review are rapidly crumbling in many parts of the world.[60]

Moreover, the enforcement of rights within the traditional cannon of civil and political rights (for example, the right to a fair trial) may also require substantial government expenditure.[61] In *R v Askov*,[62] the Canadian Supreme Court found that a government failed to try individuals within a reasonable time — a delay of 34 months from the defendant's first court appearance to the dismissal of the case — and thus violated the guarantee of trial within a reasonable time in the Canadian Charter,[63] and was legally obliged to expend resources to reduce trial delay. As a result, about 50,000 criminal charges in Ontario were set aside, and the provincial government had to spend over 28 million dollars on improving court resources and recruiting more legal personnel to reduce delays in the criminal process. Against this background, Colm O'Cinneide has argued that 'the orthodox assumption that courts should not become involved in enforcing social rights is increasingly being called into question' and that 'the distinction it draws between "enforceable" civil/political rights and "non-enforceable" social rights is difficult to reconcile with the intertwined and interdependent nature of both sets of rights'.[64]

In 1998, the UNESCR Committee also issued General Comment No. 9,[65] stating that cases involving financial implications were not necessarily off-limits to the courts. In relation to this, Malcolm Langford has opined that despite

58. Ibid., [78].

59. Ibid., [73].

60. Murray Wesson, 'The Emergence and Enforcement of Socio-Economic Rights' in Liora Lazarus, Christopher McCrudden, and Nigel Bowles, *Reasoning Rights: Comparative Judicial Engagement* (Hart Publishing 2014) 283.

61. Stephen Sunstein and Cass Holmes, *The Cost of Rights: Why Liberty Depends on Taxes* (Norton 1999) 48.

62. [1990] 2 SCR 1199.

63. Canadian Charter of Rights and Freedoms, Constitution Act 1982, as amended, Part I, s 11(b).

64. Colm O'Cinneide, 'The Problematic of Social Rights — Uniformity and Diversity in the Development of Social Rights Review' in Lazarus, McCrudden, and Bowles (N60) 299.

65. UNESCR Committee, General Comment No. 9: The domestic application of the Covenant, 3 December 1998, E/C.12/1998/24, [10].

acknowledging the doctrine of separation of powers of the various branches of government, the courts are already 'involved in a considerable range of matters which have important resource implications'.[66] All in all, the argument of non-justiciability of socio-economic rights can no longer be legitimately sustained.

4.6 A New Classification Adopted by the United Nations

Rather than labelling civil and political rights as the negative duties and socio-economic rights as positive duties, the United Nations (UN) Committee of the Convention on the Elimination of Discrimination Against Women (CEDAW), has adopted a new approach on the basis that both sets of rights give rise to a cluster of both obligations, be they negative or positive, on the state (i.e., 'duty to avoid', 'duty to protect', and 'duty to aid'),[67] as advocated by Shue.[68] As Shue noted in 1979 (well before the UNESCR Committee adopted this approach):

> There is considerable danger that all the difficulties that haunt the dichotomy of positive rights and negative rights will simply move across the rights/duties line and continue to rattle around in the more spacious trichotomy of forbearance duties, protection duties, and assistance duties. One might suspect that forbearance duties are largely 'negative', assistance duties are largely 'positive', and protection duties are intermediate, and one might wonder whether the 'new' conceptualization, even if marginally more adequate, [was] not fairly superficial.[69]

A similar classification is also elaborated on in the work of Asbjørn Eide, which is expressed in his UN reports on the right to food under the ICESCR.[70]

66. Langford (N42) xii.

67. UN Committee of the CEDAW, General Recommendation No. 24: on Art 12 of the CEDAW, on Women and Health), 1999, A/54/38/Rev.1, Ch. I, [14]–[17]; UN Committee of the CEDAW, General Recommendation No. 25: on Art 4, para 1, of the CEDAW, on Temporary Special Measures, 2004, Part II; and the Constitution of the Republic of South Africa, s 7(2).

68. Shue (N35).

69. Henry Shue, 'Rights in Light of Duties' in Peter Brown and Douglas Maclean (eds), *Human Rights and US Foreign Policy* (Lexington Books 1979) 65, 76.

70. Asbjørn Eide, The Right to Food (Final Report), UN Doc E/CN 4/ Sub 2/1887/23 (1987), [66]–[69]. See also Asbjørn Eide, 'State Obligations Revisited' in Wenche Eide and Uwe Kracht (eds), *Food and Human Rights in Development, Vol II: Evolving Issues and Emerging Applications* (Antwerp 2007) 137–160.

The UNESCR Committee introduced a typology of obligations known as respect, protect, and fulfil in General Comment No. 12, namely the Right to Adequate Food (Article 11 of the ICESCR), and has continued to use it in all subsequent general comments as follows:

> The obligation to respect existing access to adequate food requires State parties not to take any measures that result in preventing such access. The obligation to protect requires measures by the State to ensure that enterprises or individuals do not deprive individuals of their access to adequate food. The obligation to *fulfil (facilitate)* means the State must pro-actively engage in activities intended to strengthen people's access to and utilization of resources and means to ensure their livelihood, including food security. Finally, whenever an individual or group is unable, for reasons beyond their control, to enjoy the right to adequate food by the means at their disposal, States have the obligation to fulfil (facilitate) that right directly.[71]

Insofar as the right to social security is concerned, paragraphs 43 to 51 of General Comment No. 19, namely the Right to Social Security (Article 9 of the ICESCR), also adopt the obligations to 'respect, protect and fulfill'.[72] Therefore, member states are now obliged to respect the right to social security by refraining from interference with the enjoyment of it, to protect the same by preventing third parties from interfering with the enjoyment of it, and to fulfil it by adopting the measures necessary for its full realisation. This obligation to fulfil includes facilitating access to such measures, promoting awareness of them, and providing the social security under them by seeing to it that they reach everyone entitled to the same.[73]

In this regard, Shue has argued that on one hand, there are no one-to-one pairings between kinds of duties and kinds of rights, and that 'the complete fulfilment of each kind of right involves the performance of multiple kinds of

71. UNESCR Committee, General Comment No. 12: Right to adequate food (12th session), E/C 12/1999/5 (1999), [15].

72. UNESCR Committee, General Comment No. 19: The right to social security (Art 9) (39th session), E/C 12/GC/19 (2008).

73. Bokhary (N3) 284–285.

duties'.[74] On the other hand, breaches, or threatened breaches, of all human rights give rise to a series of concomitant obligations — a primary obligation 'to respect' (i.e., 'duty to avoid'), a secondary obligation 'to protect' (i.e., 'duty to protect'), and a tertiary obligation 'to promote' (i.e., 'duty to aid')[75] — adding that all of them must be performed if the basic right is to be fully honoured.[76] In his work, Shue postulates that the primary 'duty to avoid' obligation demands the state to refrain from violating human rights, whereas the secondary 'duty to protect' obligation requires it to protect these rights against interference by others.[77] Moreover, the tertiary 'duty to aid', which is further sub-divided into the 'duty to facilitate' and the 'duty to promote', requires the state to aid people's access to resources and facilitate their effective use in achieving independent satisfaction of the right.[78] For example, the basic right of security would impose on the State the duty to avoid eliminating a person's security, the duty to protect people against deprivation of security by other people, and the duty to aid by providing for the security of those unable to provide for themselves.[79] Shue later refined these rights as the primary duty to refrain from infringing rights, the secondary duty to protect rights against invasion by others, and the tertiary obligation to 'transfer resources directly to those who cannot provide their own survival'.[80]

Although Shue has accepted that civil and political rights are generally framed in terms of negative duties, he points out that most of them frequently give rise to primary obligations which are immediate and perfunctory. He has also recognised that socio-economic rights may be cast in terms of negative rights, which also give rise to primary obligations.[81] For instance, under the South African Constitution 1996, the right to home has been expressed in terms of a primary obligation on the state not to carry out forced evictions.[82] This approach is also endorsed in the UN 1997 Maastricht Guidelines on Violations

74. Shue (N35) 24–25.

75. Ibid.

76. Henry Shue, *Basic Rights* (PUP 1980) 51.

77. Shue (N35) 24–25.

78. Ibid.

79. Shue (N76) 51.

80. Shue (N35) 56.

81. Ibid., 24–25.

82. Constitution of the Republic of South Africa 1996, s 26(3).

of Economic, Social, and Cultural Rights, which states: 'Like civil and political rights, economic, social and cultural rights impose three different types of obligations on States: the obligations to respect, protect and fulfill'.

Shue's tripartite theory of obligations not only provides an explanation for what has been dismissed as narrow anomalies in the adjudication of civil and political rights but also offers constitution drafters, human rights theorists, and judges a working model to identify different levels of state responsibility in accordance with the seriousness of threats to rights. In human rights disputes where issues of resource allocation are raised, this theory also provides a basis for moderating the standard of judicial scrutiny, not in accordance with the classification of rights as either civil and political or socio-economic, but in accordance with the tripartite duties inherent in all human rights and the extent to which resources are implicated in their satisfaction.[83]

Furthermore, this tripartite theory of obligations is also manifested in the growing social law jurisdiction of the EU. In fact, the EU Charter of Fundamental Rights has not only made it clear that the document should include civil and political rights, but it also stresses that social and economic rights be included as well. It has also consciously eschewed the division between civil and political rights and socio-economic rights, and included both types of rights within the same document. Other jurisdictions have similarly recognised the indivisibility of human rights. In South Africa, for instance, the Constitution includes both civil and political as well as socio-economic rights, and provides that the state must 'respect, protect, promote and fulfill the rights in the Bill of Rights'.[84] Moreover, the South African Constitutional Court has also adopted Shue's tripartite structuring of state obligations in seeking to maintain an appropriate constitutional balance,[85] together with the creative use of strategically tailored remedial orders, in its efforts to stay outside the vexed arena of budgetary

83. Palmer (N7) 23–24.

84. Constitution of the Republic of South Africa 1996, s 7(2).

85. Danie Brand, 'Introduction to Socio-Economic Rights in the South African Constitution' in Danie Brand and Christof Heyns (eds), *Socio-Economic Rights in South Africa* (PU Law Press 2005) 1.

allocation while reinforcing the Constitution's commitment to the protection of social justice in several landmark cases.[86]

Based on the criteria of equality which require that progressive realisation must be sure to prioritise the needs of the most disadvantaged and marginalised, the South African Constitutional Court, in *Grootboom*,[87] also held that although the Constitution did not create a right to shelter or housing immediately upon demand (i.e., the right to housing), the duty to progressively realise the right to housing (i.e., the right of access to housing) was breached because the authorities concerned did not pay sufficient attention to the rights of the most disadvantaged and marginalised. The Court also issued a declaration, requiring the State to make reasonable provisions within its available resources for people in the Cape Metropolitan area with no access to land, no roof over their heads, and who were living in intolerable conditions or crisis situations. The effect of the declaration resulted in the State having to devise and implement a coherent, co-ordinated programme designated to meet its obligations.[88]

4.7 The 'Incompatibility with Appeal-and-Review Distinction' Argument

In response to the allegation that proportionality enquiry would involve the courts considering the merits and facts of administrative decisions and that it would thus trespass the invisible line as constitutionally set by the doctrine of separation of powers,[89] Paul Craig has opined that what is not in dispute is that it is not for the courts to substitute their judgment on the merits of the case for that of the primary decision-maker. This is accepted by all, even those who are in favour of the full recognition of proportionality as a free-standing ground of review in its own right.[90]

86. *Soobramooney v Minister of Health Kwa Zulu Natal* (1998) 1 SA 765 (CC); *Grootboom* (N50); *Khosa v Minister of Social Development* (2004) 6 SA 505; *Minister of Health v Treatment Action Campaign* (2005) 5 SA 721 (CC).

87. Ibid., *Grootboom*.

88. Edwin Cameron, 'What You Can Do with Rights' (2012) 2 *EHRLR* 148–161.

89. As mentioned in Chapter Three of this book.

90. Paul Craig, 'Unreasonableness and Proportionality in UK Law' in Evelyn Ellis (ed), *The Principle of Proportionality in the Law of Europe* (Hart Publishing 1999) 85.

Similarly, Richard Clayton and Hugh Tomlinson are of the view that proportionality analysis does not compel merit review. This, they have explained, is because 'the defining characteristic of the proportionality test is that it requires a court to undertake a structured analytical exercise'.[91] Adherence to the structural test for proportionality will guard against the courts from reviewing a decision solely on its merits and preserve the separation of powers between the judicial and executive arms of government, requiring courts to adjudicate only on the executive's decision-making processes.[92]

Another school of thought has claimed that since proportionality operates as a sliding scale of review, it does not necessarily involve a substitution of the court's review of the merits for that of the administrator.[93] Nevertheless, this cannot be considered determinative. Claiming that the courts will only strike down measures that are manifestly disproportionate or inappropriate does not elucidate adequately whether this involves an illegitimate interference with the merits, or whether the courts are respecting the limits of its jurisdiction.[94] Thus, Robert Thomas has argued that it may be questioned whether the focus on the issue of review of the merits is appropriate. The distinction between merits and legality can hardly be drawn in advance with any certainty. Rather, it may be more suitable to look into how proportionality contributes to achieving chosen policy objectives.[95] Thus, Thomas suggests that proportionality be used to optimise the interests of individuals to the extent that the achievement of the policy goal remains factually possible.[96] The courts need not examine the expediency of an administrative purpose. Instead, they only consider whether it could have been satisfactorily attained by a better-designed and less-onerous measure.[97] Therefore, the courts are to undertake a comparison of possible solutions to an administrative task. The tests of appropriateness and

91. Richard Clayton and Hugh Tomlinson, *The Law of Human Rights* (2nd edn, OUP 2009) [6.91].

92. Ibid.

93. Gráinne de Búrca, 'The Principle of Proportionality and its Application in EC Law' (1993) 13 *YEL* 105; Robert Thomas, *Legitimate Expectations and Proportionality in Administrative Law* (Hart Publishing 2000) 79.

94. Ibid., Thomas, 84.

95. Ibid.

96. Ibid.

97. John Temple Lang, 'The Constitutional Principles Governing Community Legislation' (1989) 40 *NILQ* 227, 242; Gordon Slynn, 'European Law and the National Judge' in *Butterworths Lectures 1991–1992* (Butterworths 1993) 18, 28.

of suitability decide whether the means chosen are capable of promoting the goal. Insofar as the necessity of a measure is concerned, it is clear that if there is no alternative means of achieving the objective, it will be necessary to interfere with individual interests. When determining a measure as disproportionate, the courts are, in effect, telling the decision-maker that 'we invalidate the decision you have made because we can think of a better decision — one that achieves your goal but at less cost to competing interests'.[98] In this regard, the courts do not examine the expediency of achieving a certain objective, but ask the expediency of the means used to attain that objective. This intricate enquiry of optimising competing values requires the courts to examine assessments of fact and appraise economic considerations.[99]

For this reason, Thomas has contended that proportionality review of a public measure is best understood within a purposive conception of administrative law.[100] Law is used to advance policy goals and objectives as selected through the processes of political decision-making. The courts do not seek to impose their own set of values on what the executive ought to be doing. Rather, the courts, in finding the most effective means of protecting the individuals or minorities, seek to rationalise public action in light of the chosen policy objective. The identification of alternative possible courses of action is precisely the task with which an administrative authority ought to concern itself. Collective goals must be attained and, if possible, through means which entail minimal interference with individual interests.[101]

As Garreth Wong has observed, judges have, in administrative law cases, been prudent of the distinction between review and appeal, so the courts will only pass judgment if the claim is one that goes essentially to the legality of the impugned administrative conduct and not to its merits, the latter being within the lawful discretion of the administration and hence the function of an administrative appeal.[102] For Continental jurists, the rule governing the whole of

98. Thomas (N93) 84.

99. Ibid.

100. Ibid.

101. Ibid.

102. Garreth Wong, 'Towards the Nutcracker Principle: Reconsidering the Objections to Proportionality (2000) Spring *PL* 92–93.

administrative law is the principle of the purpose pursued.[103] The administration acts in the public interest and the law must recognise its purposes. According to Maxime Letourneur, 'administrative law is, by its very nature, an unequal law; for the general interest must be accorded supremacy over private rights'.[104] However, I argue that even though there has long been tension between the democratic right of the majority to exercise political power and the democratic need of individuals and minors to have their rights secured, the ultimate aim of justice is a balance between social considerations of utility and individual concerns of liberty and equality. In this regard, the role of the administrative judge is to reconcile the imperative requirements of the general interest with the legitimate interests of the individual by advising the executive upon their courses of action. The rationale behind the judicial control of the executive is to recognise the different needs of the state and the individual and to balance them accordingly. The purpose of this balancing test is to make sure that when exercising powers, the state does not act arbitrarily towards individuals.[105]

Against this background, Wong has argued that the role of the reviewing court is not to ensure that the right balance was struck between opposing interests. Rather, its role is to decide whether the decision thus made was in fact 'disproportionate'. It is a form of negative control and hence it would be more correct to say that it is a 'test of disproportionality', instead of the test of proportionality.[106] This approach was adopted in the Dutch General Administrative Law Act 1994 (*Algemene wet bestuursrecht*), which prohibits administrative decisions from being disproportionate in connection with the intended goals and the consequences for those interested parties [107] and allows judicial review of administrative conduct breaching this principle. In this regard, the prohibition of disproportionality expresses the principle of administrative restraint — intervention by the administration in social life is inevitable, necessary, and useful, but at the same time, it should not extend

103. Léon Duguit, *Law in thẹ Modern State* (translated by F. Laski and H.J. Laski, George Allen & Unwin 1921) 142–144, cited by Thomas (N93) 13.

104. Maxime Letourneur, 'The Concept of Equity in French Public Law' in Ralph Newman (ed), *Equity in the World's Legal Systems* (Brussels 1973) 261–262.

105. Thomas (N93) 13.

106. Wong (N102) 93.

107. Art 3:4 ss 2.

beyond that which is necessary to serve the general interest in a proper manner. Therefore, in the Hong Kong Court's decision in *Chu Ping Tak v Commissioner of Police*,[108] despite Cheung DJ's reluctance to intervene on the ground that the Court essentially plays a supervisory role over the decision of the tribunal below and thus it does not exercise an appellate role as such, what he did apply, by deciding not to interfere with the administrative decision in question, is in fact the 'principle of disproportionality'. He said:

> Unless the sentence or punishment is so out of proportion to the offence in question, as to be perverse or unduly oppressive, I see no ground for intervention ... In the circumstances of the present case, although it could be reasonably argued that the punishment [i.e., immediate dismissal without compensation or payment] was extremely severe and even on the high side, bearing in mind the various levels and forms of punishment open to the Commissioner [of the Police] ... I do not take the view that the eventual award made was one so disproportionate to the offence in question as to be perverse, or ... was so unduly oppressive as to be unreasonable. I do not consider the award as 'altogether excessive and out of proportion to the occasion' (per Lord Denning MR in *Hook*) [even though] I have borne in mind the various factors urged upon me by counsel ... As I said, if I were sitting as the first instance tribunal, I might have [been] inclined to come to a less severe or more lenient sentence.[109]

Concurring with Wong's assertion, Thomas has opined that in undertaking this balancing exercise, the administrative court does not substitute its own assessment of discretionary choices for that of the executive, but intervenes if a decision incurs abnormally high costs or is unreasonable or badly thought-out.[110] This forces the executive to provide serious and plausible justifications for their decisions to the public and, if necessary, to the administrative judge. A typical example is the *Protection of Victoria Harbour* saga,[111] in which the Court of First Instance of Hong Kong held that the alternative would not be viable if

108. [2002] 3 HKLRD 679 (CFI).

109. Ibid., 696.

110. Thomas (N93) 13.

111. *Society for the Protection of Harbour v Town Planning Board* [2003] 2 HKLRD 787 (HCAL 19/2003), [2003] 3 HKLRD 960 (CFI), (2004) 7 HKCFAR 1, [2004] 1 HKLRD 396 (CFA).

it involved incurring costs or paying a price that would be disproportionate to the harm of carrying out the proposed reclamation. However, there should be no reclamation if the alternative merely involved a more costly method. In this respect, the Court was only concerned with whether the decision-maker had properly considered or attempted other viable alternatives, but it would not 'weigh' the alternatives itself.[112] In *Chan Hei Ling Helen v Medical Council of Hong Kong*,[113] it was held that the proportionality test does not require that the least possible intrusive means of achieving the objective be searched out and adopted as long as it is 'from the range of means which impairs [the right] as little as is reasonably possible'.[114] Moreover, Craig has also suggested that a proper respect for the difference between appeal and review be in favour of introducing a more structured and transparent form of judicial control, rather than relying constantly on the 'blunt tool' of *Wednesbury* unreasonableness.[115]

Canadian scholar Paul Daly has another view, saying that reviewing the unreasonableness of a challenged decision inevitably requires a court to consider the merits or substance of the impugned decision. However, the consideration of matters which go to the merits of a decision, or its substance, is not particularly problematic. This is because a consideration of the merits or substance is inevitable in any review for unreasonableness.[116] Daly used Sopinka J's *dictum* to justify his assertion as follows:

> Any adjudication upon the reasonableness of a decision must involve an evaluation of the merits. Reasonableness is not [a] quality that exists in isolation. When a court says that a decision under review is 'reasonable' or 'patently unreasonable' it is making a statement about the logical relationship between the grounds of the decision and premises thought by the court to be true. Without the reference point of an opinion (if not a conclusion) on the merits, such a relative statement cannot be made.[117]

112. Ibid., [2003] 2 HKLRD 787, [62].
113. [2009] 4 HKLRD 174.
114. Ibid., [52], citing *AG of HK v Lee Kwong Kut* (1993) 3 HKPLR 72, AC 951 (PC), 972D.
115. Paul Craig, 'The Impact of Community Law on Domestic Public Law' in Peter Leyland and Terry Woods, *Administrative Law Facing the Future: Old Constraints and New Horizons* (Blackstone 1997) 283.
116. Paul Daly, *A Theory of Deference in Administrative Law* (CUP 2012) 139.
117. *Canadian Association of Industrial, Mechanical and Allied Workers, Local 14 v Paccar of Canada* [1989] 2 SCR 983, 1018, cited ibid.

Thus, a consideration of the merits is not, as Daly has argued, the same as a decision on the merits.[118]

Daly furthers that this is also true where correctness is the appropriate standard of review. If a standard of review of correctness is appropriate, it will be appropriate because the legislature has delegated the decision to the courts. In most cases, in the absence of a direct delegation of authority to the courts or an appeal to the courts from the original decision, correctness review of discretionary decisions is unlikely.[119] He quoted a comment by LeBel J to justify his argument as follows:

> [Where] a discretion exists, exercising it can lead to the adoption of varying opinions and solutions depending on the application of the relevant legal principles to the facts of the case, and on reviewing a decision of this nature, the court must show deference to the administrative decision-maker.[120]

In any event, even in reviewing a decision to exercise or not to exercise a discretionary power for correctness, the courts would not, argues Daly, have expansive powers. The fact that a reviewing court will be, broadly speaking, limited to affirming or quashing a delegated decision-maker's discretionary decision is important. Consequently, it will not stand in the domain of the delegated decision-maker.[121]

Looking from a different angle, Jeffrey Jowell has contended for principles of substantive review short of correctness or merits review,[122] summarising them into three categories:

(1) Review of the quality of the decision itself. Under this category, the courts assess the decision itself, asking 'whether it passes

---

118. Ibid., Daly, 140.

119. Ibid.

120. *Montreal (City) v Montreal Port Authority* [2010] SCC 14, [2010] 1 SCR 427, 446, cited ibid.

121. Ibid., Daly, 140.

122. Jeffrey Jowell, 'Proportionality and Unreasonableness: Neither Merger nor Takeover' in Hanna Wilberg and Mark Elliott (eds), *The Scope and Intensity of Substantive Review: Traversing Taggart's Rainbow* (Hart Publishing 2015) 49–50.

muster'.[123] They also invalidate decisions which are uncertain,[124] incomprehensible, or inconsistent, or where the decision is fettered by such a rule, contract or policy.[125]

(2) Review of the justification of the decision.[126]

(3) Review of the impact of the decision.[127]

With the prevalence of parliamentary sovereignty in Britain, however, Sophie Boyron has, when objecting to an introduction of proportionality, argued that English courts hold an 'inferior rank' to Parliament, which is supreme in that it can make and unmake any law.[128] It is evident in their constant reference during statutory interpretation to the legislative intent, and is regarded as an expression of the subordination of the courts to Parliament and the 'desire of the judiciary to disavow a large creative role in the interpretation of statutes.[129] For this reason, having the proportionality principle fully incorporated would, without express Parliamentary approval, result in judicial legislation 'through the back door'.[130] It would be contrary to the constitutional doctrine which gives Parliament a monopoly on legislative capacity. Consequently, to allow wide powers of policy-making to unelected judges raises the 'the spectre in common law jurisdictions of "government by judges"'.[131]

123. Ibid., 50.

124. *McEldowney v Forde* [1971] AC 632.

125. *British Oxygen Co Ltd v Board of Trade* [1971] AC 610.

126. *R v Deputy Industrial Injuries Commissioner, ex p Moore* [1965] 1 QB 456; *Puhlhofer v Hillingdon LBC* [1986] AC 484; *R v Civil Service Appeal Board, ex p Cunningham* [1991] 4 All ER 310; *R v Parliamentary Commissioner for Administration, ex p Balchin* [1998] 1 PLR 1; *R v Minister of Defence, ex p Walker* [2000] 1 WLR 806.

127. *R v Liverpool Corporations, ex p Liverpool Taxi Fleet Operator's Association* [1972] 2 QB 299; *E v Inland Revenue Commissioners, ex p MFK Underwriting Agencies Ltd* [1990] 1 WLR 1545; *R v Secretary of State for the Home Department, ex p Pierson* [1998] AC 539; *R v Chief Constable of Sussex, ex p International Trader's Ferry Ltd* [1999] 2 AC 418; *R (Reprotech Ltd) v East Sussex CC* [2002] UKHL 8.

128. Sophie Boyron, 'Proportionality in English Administrative Law: A Faulty Translation?' (1992) 12 *OJLS* 237, 257.

129. Ibid.

130. Ibid.

131. Carol Harlow, 'Proceduralism in English Administrative Law' in Karl-Heinz Ladeur (ed), *The Europeanisation of Administrative Law: Transforming National Decision-Making Procedures* (Ashgate 2002) 65.

Refuting Boyron's claim, Wong has stated that many current grounds of review are judicially developed notions, without Parliament's seal of approval.[132] For one thing, *Wednesbury* unreasonableness has not been voted or developed by Parliament.[133] The rules of natural justice are another example of current judicial review that were not developed or approved by Parliament.[134] Instead, all of these principles are given life and nurtured by the courts, and there has been nothing to suggest that they are less legitimate owing to their lack of explicit legislative approval.

This assertion is compatible with Craig's 'modified theory of *ultra vires*',[135] in that there is an indirect relationship between judicial principles of good administration and Parliamentary intention.[136] This modified theory contends that in the absence of contrary evidence, it is assumed that Parliament intends to legislate in conformity with the rule of law, so any exercise of governmental power should be just and principled as follows:

> [Parliament] is therefore taken to withhold from decision-makers the power to act unfairly and unreasonably, while recognising that the detailed requirements of fairness and rationality can most appropriately be determined incrementally by the courts through the forensic process. Hence, Parliament grants to the judges a margin of freedom ... to set the precise limits of administrative power.[137]

According to Wong, this view of the relationship between Parliament and the courts gives itself far more readily to a judicial incorporation of the proportionality principle, with no accusations of judicial legislation. Such incorporation makes the administration exercise its power in a fair, reasoned, and balanced manner with due regard to all individuals whose interests are

132. Wong (N102) 98.

133. John Laws, '*Wednesbury*' in Christopher Forsyth and Ivan Hare, *The Golden Metwand and the Crooked Cord: Essays on Public Law in Honour of Sir H W R Wade QC* (Clarendon Press 1998) 193.

134. Wong (N102) 98.

135. Paul Craig, 'Competing Models of Judicial Review' (1999) *PL* 428, 429.

136. Christopher Forsyth, 'Of Figs Leaves and Fairy Tales: The *Ultra Vires* Doctrine, the Sovereignty of Parliament and Judicial Review' (1996) 55(1) *CLJ* 122; Mark Elliott, 'The *Ultra Vires* Doctrine in a Constitutional Setting: Still the Central Principle of Administrative Law' (1999) 58(1) *CLJ* 129.

137. Ibid., Elliott, 143.

adversely affected. It would also fulfil the duty authorised to the courts by Parliament to ensure that proper respect for the law and for the rule of law are attained with the precise delineation of administrative discretion.[138]

Overall, modern administration is simply too complex to suppose that the administrator will always take sufficient care in implementing policies.[139] The role of the administrative courts is to recognise what the executive wants to attain and seek to accommodate individual interests as far as possible. To label proportionality review as 'the most potent weapon in the arsenal of the public law judge' is mistaken.[140] In fact, the role played by proportionality is to promote the achievement of policy objectives. As Francis Jacobs once said, proportionality is a 'rational and well-structured test',[141] in which the courts 'decide whether a particular exercise of power ... [was] ... the most appropriate way of achieving a particular policy goal'.[142] Proportionality may be a far-reaching and intensive ground of review and may permit engagement with the substances of a government decision, but it should not be equated with review on the basis of those merits alone because the role of the courts is to further the chosen policy goal that it avoids substitution of opinion.

4.8 The 'Incompatibility with the Separation of Powers' or 'Constitutional and Institutional Incompetence' Arguments

Another important set of objections to the judicial enforceability of socio-economic rights,[143] concerns the constitutional and institutional incompetence arguments, or their mirror image — the incompatibility with the separation-

138. Wong (N102) 100.

139. Haley Yu, 'Letter: Typhoon Mangkhut transport chaos could have been avoided, if Carrie Lam had been proactive', *South China Morning Post*, 18 September 2018, available at: www.scmp.com/comment/letters/article/2164681/typhoon-mangkhut-transport-chaos-could-have-been-avoided-if-carrie, last accessed 16 September 2019.

140. Takis Tridimas, 'Proportionality in Community Law: Searching for the Appropriate Standard of Scrutiny' in Ellis (N90) 65, 69.

141. Francis Jacobs, 'Public Law — The Impact of Europe' (1999) *PL* 232, 239.

142. Francis Jacobs, 'Recent Developments in the Principle of Proportionality in European Community Law' in Ellis (N90) 20.

143. Also discussed in Chapter Three of this book.

of-powers argument — in that since the fulfilment of these rights should be left to the discretion of the political authorities (i.e., the executive and the legislative branches of the government), judges lack democratic legitimacy, technical expertise, experience, etc. to implement and enforce socio-economic rights. Thus, decisions regarding socio-economic rights (such as decisions to prioritise assistance to certain groups, to allocate budgetary resources, or to design adequate measures to implement these rights) should be left to the executive and the legislature, and exempt from judicial review.

4.8.1 Law vs Politics

The rationale behind this school of thought is that socio-economic rights are said to belong more in the 'political' sphere, whereas civil and political rights have a stronger 'legal' foundation, making them better suited for judicial adjudication.[144] However, the implication of this distinction between the 'political' and 'legal' spheres ignores the fact that these spheres are not mutually exclusive. Laws are the outcome of political choices and reflect a choice of certain political values such as democracy, the rule of law, and respect for human rights. These are political choices aimed at preventing the practices of an autocratic regime or the unfettered exercise of power by political authorities.[145]

Conversely, politics employs law as one of the means for its realisation, as manifested in the rise of the administrative state, as well as the resulting increase in state activities and discretionary powers, so political decisions often take the form of legal rules or norms. In this broad sense, law is often a means through which political values are conveyed, and political ideas are often expressed through legislation. When judges apply law in judgments, they issue decisions that implement and execute the policies, and, broadly understood, the political choices enshrined in law.[146] Therefore, the key question in the debate over the protection of socio-economic rights is the appropriate relationship between the courts and the elected branches of government, or what role the courts should

144. International Commission of Jurists (N39) 73.

145. Ibid., 74.

146. Ibid.

play in supervising the implementation of these policies, in accordance with constitutional and international human rights standards.

During the last several decades in common law jurisdictions, commentators and practitioners have increasingly embraced the idea of 'a shared public law discourse' that is concerned with the identification of fundamental values in constitutional, public, and international human rights law — a discourse that seeks to prevent vulnerable, marginalised, and dispossessed individuals from being placed beyond the protection of the rule of law.[147] As David Dyzenhaus has argued, a 'common public law' is emerging, which rejects the artificial divide between legal and political spheres of decision-making, with its tendency to cordon off certain types of sensitive policy decisions from a standard of judicial scrutiny apposite to the fundamental rights at issue.[148] This 'common system' is 'reminiscent of the common law's traditional understanding of positive law, as serving a kind of evidentiary function for the enduring values of the common law articulated by judges from time immemorial'.[149]

4.8.2 Incompatibility with the Separation of Powers Argument

Even though it has long been complained that the concept of separation of powers is 'infected with so much imprecision and inconsistency that it may be counted little more than a jumbled portmanteau of arguments for policies which ought to be supported or rejected on other grounds',[150] it can, under its modern concept, be understood as follows. First of all, there is the distinction between the three branches of government — namely, the legislative branch, the executive branch, and the judicial branch. Each branch has its own function. The main function of the legislative branch is making law; the main function of the executive branch is executing law; and the main function of the judicial branch is judging. The relationship between each branch and its main function

147. *Baker v Canada (Minister of Citizenship and Immigration)* [1999] 2 SCR 817, (1999) 174 DLR (4th) 193 (SCC). See also David Dyzenhaus, '*Baker*: The Unity of Public Law?' in David Dyzenhaus (ed), *The Unity of Public Law* (Hart Publishing 2004) 1.

148. Ibid., Dyzenhaus, 2.

149. Ibid.

150. Geoffrey Marshall, *Constitutional Theory* (Clarendon Press 1971) 124.

are determined, either explicitly or by implication, by the constitution, be it written or unwritten.[151] Second, in line with the constitutional framework, each branch fulfils its main function according to its own approach, exercising discretion without the intervention of the other branches.[152]

However, the concept of separation of powers is not a static one. It has been evolving over time and takes disparate forms in different countries and in different legal orders.[153] As the South African Constitutional Court has held:

> There is, however, no universal model of separation of powers, and in democratic systems of government in which checks and balances result in the imposition of restraints by one branch of government upon another, there is no separation that is absolute ... Moreover, because of the different systems of checks and balances that exist in [different] countries, the relationship between the different branches of government and the power or influence that one branch of government has over the other, differ from one country to another. The principle of separation of powers, on the one hand, recognises the functional independence of branches of government. On the other hand, the principle of checks and balances focuses on the desirability of ensuring that the constitutional order, as a totality, prevents the branches of government from usurping power from one another. No constitutional scheme can reflect a complete separation of powers.[154]

Nevertheless, the doctrine of separation of powers could, for convenience sake, also be substantively divided into a spectrum of more or less rigid separation between the various branches of government.[155] Historically, the rationale behind the doctrine has been concerned less with formal separation of distinct functions (i.e., the division of labour) and more with the ultimate

151. Aharon Barak, *Proportionality: Constitutional Rights and their Limitations* (CUP 2012) 385.

152. Ibid., 385–387.

153. Bruce Ackerman, 'The New Separation of Powers' (2000) 113 *HLR* 633.

154. *Ex p Chairperson of the Constitutional Assembly: In re Certification of the Constitution of the Republic of South Africa 1996*, 1996 (10) BCLR 1253 (CC), 108–109.

155. M.J.C. Vile, *Constitutionalism and the Separation of Powers* (2nd edn, Liberty Fund 1998) 14–20.

aim of avoiding the concentration of power and the concomitant threat of tyranny.[156] As Montesquieu once put it,

> [w]hen the legislative and executive powers are united in the same person, or in the same body of magistracies, there can be no liberty; because apprehensions may arise, lest the same monarch or senate should enact tyrannical laws to execute them in a tyrannical manner.[157]

In this regard, Eric Barendt has recommended that a strict, rigid, or 'pure' theory of the doctrine be eschewed. Instead, a more nuanced 'partial separation of powers' is favoured. As Barendt has said, 'the separation of powers is not in essence concerned with the allocation of functions as such. Its primary purpose ... is the prevention of the arbitrary government, or tyranny, which may arise from the concentration of power'.[158] The notion that power should not be concentrated in one branch of government can also be interpreted as the desirability of 'multiple mutually reinforcing forms and criteria of accountability'.[159] In short, the concept of separation of powers incarnates the idea of checks and balances that, as Cass Sunstein has noted, 'foxes should not guard henhouses'.[160]

Against this background, Barendt furthers that

> the separation of powers should not be explained in terms of a strict distribution of functions between three branches of government, but in terms of a network of rules and principles which ensure that power is not concentrated in the hands of one branch ... In practice the danger now is that the executive have too much power.[161]

156. Ibid, 15.

157. Montesquieu, *The Spirit of the Law* (Hafner 1949) 151–152.

158. Eric Barendt, 'Separation of Powers and Constitutional Government' (1995) *PL* 599, 606.

159. Peter Cane, 'Theory and Values in Public Law' in Paul Craig and Richard Rawlings (eds), *Law and Administration in Europe: Essays for Carol Harlow* (OUP 2003) 15.

160. Cass Sunstein, *After the Rights Revolution: Re-Conceiving the Regulatory State* (HUP 1990) 143.

161. Barendt (N158) 608–609.

Although, historically, the fear of tyranny borne of concentrated power was the driving force behind the separation of powers, the focus has now been shifting to the global rise of the administrative state and the resulting growth of state activities and discretionary power.[162]

4.8.3 Constitutional Incompetence Argument

There are two justifications that judges are constitutionally competent to have powers of review. One has been termed the 'democracy-supporting' justification,[163] which Aharon Barak has explained as follows:

> [O]nce a society has made a decision — explicitly or implicitly — to adopt judicial review, its exercise by the courts is a reflection of the people's will, and thus in effect not only embraces basic notion of democracy but actually entrenches them. The same 'we the people' who adopted the constitution also adopted the institution of judicial review.[164]

In this regard, considerations of 'lack of sufficient democratic foundation', or 'counter-majoritarian difficulty',[165] should not affect the actual exercise of judicial review.[166] Rather, judicial review should be conducted in a way that would allow judges the full ability to look into whether the other branches which limited a constitutionally protected human right have properly followed the requirements of proportionality as prescribed by the constitution's 'we the people'.[167] This assertion also tallies with Craig's 'modified theory of *ultra vires*' in that there is an indirect relationship between judicial principles of good administration and Parliamentary intention. Therefore, in the absence of contrary evidence, it is legally presumed that Parliament intends to legislate in

162. Paul Craig and Adam Tomkins, *The Executive and Public Law* (OUP 2006) 1; Cass Sunstein, 'Beyond *Marbury*: The Executive's Power to Say What the Law Is' (2006) 115 *YLJ* 2580.

163. David Bilchitz, *Poverty and Fundamental Rights: The Justification and Enforcement of Socio-Economic Rights* (OUP 2007) 104–105.

164. Barak (N151) 382–383.

165. Alexander Bickel, *The Least Dangerous Branch: The Supreme Court at the Bar of Politics* (YUP 1986) 16–23.

166. Barak (N151) 383.

167. Ibid.

conformity with the rule of law, so any exercise of governmental power should be just and principled, and that 'the detailed requirements of fairness and rationality can most appropriately be determined incrementally by the courts through the forensic process. Hence, Parliament grants to the judges a margin of freedom ... to set the precise limits of administrative power'.[168] Furthermore, Jowell has also argued that when confronting substantive review, the courts may pronounce on 'a matter of principle but not policy',[169] the latter involving the utilitarian calculation of the public good that is the constitutional function of the executive and the legislature.

The second justification is 'rights-based' and involves the belief that there are fundamental rights that must be safeguarded to all individuals in any just society, irrespective of whether the majority agree to recognise these rights.[170] Unlike the democracy-supporting justification described above, the rights-based justification recognises that at a certain level, there may be a conflict of values associated with the institution of judicial review. It provides reasons for thinking that the moral benefits of the institution, such as the greater protection offered for fundamental rights, outweigh the moral costs thereof and removes certain decisions from the final control of the citizenry and allowing the will of the majority to be overridden.[171] To achieve this, certain institutional features of the courts, such as its structural independence, impartiality, etc., render them able to provide adequate protection for such rights as opposed to representative institutions, such as legislatures. It is desirable to assign the power to protect fundamental rights to judges, who are justified in, and thus capable of, overruling decisions of majoritarian institutions where the decisions themselves conflict with fundamental rights.[172]

However, as Hugh Corder observed, there has long been a tendency of many judges in the common law world to refer to the 'government' as somehow removed from the courts, without acknowledging that the judiciary is

168. Elliott (N136) 143.

169. Jowell (N122) 43–44.

170. Bilchitz (N163) 105.

171. Ibid.

172. Ibid.

naturally as much part of government as Parliament and the Cabinet.[173] Worst of all, for those countries whose constitutional order has been founded in the parliamentary sovereignty or supremacy, such as Britain, there has historically been an 'exaggerated level of judicial respect' paid to the legislature and the executive.[174] If the courts, despite acting in the name of upholding the separation of powers, continue to defer to the elected branches of government, vis-à-vis the growth of modern political parties dominating the executive of the day and its resulting executive-dominated legislature, they are in fact undermining the very foundational rationale for the separation of powers (i.e., preventing the over-accumulation of power in one body). As Jeanne Woods has noted:

> Separation of powers as a normative principle is not an end in itself — it is a means of keeping the government in check in order to ensure the protection of preferred rights. In the case of social rights, judicial review serves the function of checking the political branches to ensure they are responsive to the constitutional rights of the least privileged in society, and that policymakers do not lose sight of their suffering in the inevitable political games of compromise and horse-trading.[175]

The traditional notion of 'government' has given way to the broader and more flexible concept of 'governance'. It is a broader notion than government, whose principal elements include the constitution, the legislature, the executive, and the judiciary, while governance involves 'interaction between these formal institutions and those of civil society'.[176] This assertion is compatible with Barendt's understanding of the evolved concept of the separation of powers in that it should be explained in terms of a network of rules and principles which ensure that power is not concentrated in one branch.

173. Hugh Corder, 'Comparing Administrative Justice Across the Commonwealth: A First Scan' in Corder (N44) 6.

174. Ibid.

175. Jeanne Woods, 'Justiciable Social Rights as a Critique of the Liberal Paradigm' (2003) 38 *TILJ* 763, 773.

176. Gavin Drewry, 'The Executive: Towards Accountable Government and Effective Governance?' in Jeffrey Jowell and Dawn Oliver (eds), *The Changing Constitution* (6th edn, OUP 2007) 189–190.

To achieve this, an 'idea of constitutional dialogue' and the concomitant method of 'dialogic' judicial review,[177] or 'catalytic' mode of review,[178] are emerging.[179] According to Paul O'Connell, the rationale behind this model of review is to encourage co-operative engagement among the different branches of government in the context of rights protection.[180] For Mark Tushnet, the key advantages of the dialogic model, from the perspective of democratic constitutionalism, are that

> [dialogic] review capitalizes on the institutional advantages courts have in constitutional attentiveness by allowing the courts to bring constitutional values, in connection with specific problems, into focus in the legislative forum. This advances the constitutionalist value of limitations on democratic self-governance. With the issues brought to the legislature's attention, we can then advance the value of democratic self-governance by leaving the final decision to the legislature.[181]

For this reason, central to the idea of 'dialogic review' is the encouragement of interactions among different branches of government about which of the competing reasonable interpretations of constitutional provisions is correct.[182] A model dialogue might take the following form:

> The legislature enacts a statute, and the court finds the statute unconstitutional because it violates the court's understanding of the meaning of the constitution's protection of freedom of expression. The legislature then responds. It might say that the court helpfully has directed its attention to a constitutional concern that the legislature had ignored or undervalued earlier. It might then find, with its attention focused on the constitutional question, that it agrees with the court's interpretation, and

177. Peter Hogg, 'Charter Dialogue Revisited — or "Much Ado About Metaphors"' (2007) 45 *OHLJ* 1; Mark Tushnet, 'Dialogic Judicial Review' (2008) 61 *ALR* 205, 213.

178. O'Cinneide (N64) 307.

179. Tushnet (N177) 206; Paul O'Connell, *Vindicating Socio-Economic Rights: International Standards and Comparative Experiences* (Routledge 2012) 174–175.

180. Ibid., O'Connell, 174.

181. Tushnet (N177) 212.

182. Ibid., 209.

> the legislature would then modify the statute to make it consistent with its and the court's interpretation, or, alternatively, abandon the legislation because [it] would not be a good policy.[183]

This tallies with some traditional political theories, namely the evolutionary theory and the social contract theory, as advocated by Edmund Burke and Jean Jacques Rousseau, respectively. According to Burke:

> [A] state is a partnership in all science, a partner in all art; a partnership in every virtue, and in all perfection. As the ends of such a relationship cannot be obtained in many generations, it becomes a partnership not only between those who are living, but between those who are dead, and those who are to be born.[184]

As Burke has rightly pointed out, 'a state is a partnership in all virtue'. This means that a state is a unit bound by co-operation among the members in all aspects. Political partnership among the citizens is a natural phenomenon as there are common interests shared by all. As Aristotle once said, individuals need co-operation because an individual is not self-sufficing.[185] Therefore, various problems and tasks facing society may require joint efforts of different people from different walks of life, be they government officials (either administrative, legislative, or judicial) or individual citizens in civil society.

Insofar as the social contract theory is concerned, Rousseau has mentioned that the origin of state is the theory which stresses the artificial and deliberative nature of the formation of state. The essence of this theory is that people feel the need to group together and enter into a contract specifying the creation of a state, as well as obligations of, and the rights from, joining the state. Therefore, the origin of a state is an artificial creation rather than a natural phenomenon.[186] The theory stresses that people are active and rational when creating a state. People are conscious of the reason why they have to form a state. They will gather together to discuss the possibilities and the arrangement of the new political

183. Ibid.

184. Edmund Burke, *Reflections on the Evolution in France* (Gateway 1962) 139.

185. Cited by Jermain Lam, *Politics and Government* (Writers' and Publishers' Cooperative 1994) 58.

186. Ibid., 59–60.

organisation. The structure of the political unit is subject to approval, and the agreement to join is voluntary.[187] In theory, people agree with the rights and obligations of joining the new state, and they also consent to the structure and to the ruler of the state. The existence of the state and the position of the ruler are legitimate since people join and agree with the contract voluntarily. Therefore, the social contract theory is characterised by three general features. The first feature is the assumption that men are rational in resolving problems by forming a state. The second feature is the vision that people play an active part in designing the form and the structure of a state. The third feature is popular sovereignty, so the authority and power of the ruler come from the people who give their consent to the position of the ruler.[188]

Against this background, Rousseau has suggested that the state of nature is peaceful and free. This is because every person enjoys equal rights and liberty. Nevertheless, the state of nature is disrupted by civilisation and natural incidents, which stimulate the production of agricultural tools and weapons. New developments continue to change the living environment. People, in turn, adapt to the new situation, which gradually leaves the original state of nature. Property is created and inequality results. Conflict and chaos arise and increase as the environment grows more and more distant from the state of nature. Thus, people try to end this situation by co-operating together, thus entering into a social contract based on general will, which is the expression of their common interests. A state and a government are therefore created to help people survive.[189] Rousseau's social contract theory seems compatible with John Rawls' theory that '[i]n justice as fairness the members of society are conceived in the first instance as moral persons who can cooperate together for mutual advantage, and not simply as rational individuals who have aims and desire they seek to satisfy'.[190] However, moral persons do not simply have the capacity to co-operate, but doing so is one of their highest-order interests. As Rawls' has said, citizens have 'the regulative desire to cooperate on fair terms with others for reciprocal advantage over a complete life'.[191] In view of

187. Ibid., 59.

188. Ibid., 59–60.

189. Ibid., 60.

190. John Rawls, *A Theory of Justice* (Belknap Press of HUP 1999) 385.

191. Ibid., 386.

the above, various problems and tasks facing society may require joint efforts of different government officials, including judges, and individual citizens in civil society to deal with them.

As David Feldman has rightly pointed out, under the civic republican tradition, citizens are expected or permitted to represent public interests and to participate in political decision-making. Public interest litigation, for example, is one means of doing so. Although it has been said that a claim to sufficient interest by a group cannot be better than that of the individuals who make up its membership, based on the fact that 'an aggregate of individuals, each of whom has no interest, cannot of itself have an interest',[192] it is generally recognised that a group of people who join together to make an application may gain 'enhanced authority to speak on a subject on behalf of a section of the public'.[193] Indeed, it is relatively clear that pressure groups and non-governmental organisations (e.g., Help the Aged, the Child Poverty Action Group, etc. in the UK) are increasingly playing an important part in judicial review proceedings. They often have much greater awareness of the existence and potential of judicial review than ordinary citizen, and many of them are more familiar with the procedural requirements than average lawyers.

Their contribution is more than simply tactical. Pressure groups can make an application on behalf of those who are not in a position to do so themselves owing to their circumstances. They can also step in when there is no obvious individual to do so. Moreover, they can also bring a degree of expertise and informed argument to the matter in dispute.[194] Hence, in Britain, the courts now countenance groups who represent the interests of third parties, groups who seek to represent the interests of their members, and groups who seek to further their own objectives.[195] In short, so long as judges do not act as surrogate legislature, but take merely a secondary role to oversee the reasoning of the

192. *R v Inland Revenue Commissioners, ex p National Federation of Small Businesses Ltd* [1982] AC 617, 663 (Lord Wilberforce).

193. Stanley de Smith, Harry Woolf, and Jeffrey Jowell, *Judicial Review of Administrative Action* (5th edn, Sweet & Maxwell 1995) [1-025].

194. Mike Radford, 'Mitigating the Democratic Deficit? Judicial Review and Ministerial Accountability' in Leyland and Woods (N115) 52–53.

195. Ibid., 53.

primary decision-makers, public interest litigation could actually help promote participatory democracy and public scrutiny of the public authorities.[196]

In this connection, Christine Bateup has opined that the key point about the dialogic theory is that this approach does 'not privilege the contributions of judges' at the expense of the elected branches of government.[197] The key value of this dialogic model is that within it, 'concerns that judicial review necessarily sets judges against the electorally accountable branches are greatly attenuated', because the courts and elected branches are understood to be equal partners in a co-operative enterprise to protect constitutional rights.[198]

Such 'equal partnership' has been accepted in the UK, with support from both Lord Bridge, who advocated the concept of 'dual sovereignty' or 'divided sovereignty' [199] (i.e., Parliament and the judiciary), and Sir Stephen Sedley, who said that 'a new and still emerging constitutional paradigm ... of a bi-polar sovereignty of the Crown in Parliament and the Crown in its courts, to each of which the Crown's ministers are answerable — politically to Parliament, legally to the courts'.[200] Well before its acceptance, in 1986, Lord Donaldson MR stressed the need for '[a] new relationship between the courts and those who derive their authority from the public law, one of partnership based on a common aim, namely the maintenance of the highest standards of public administration'.[201]

In this context, then, the courts do not, argues Bateup, act as 'Delphic oracles' dispensing constitutional justice from on high, but rather as 'facilitators' that are 'fostering society-wide constitutional discussion and debate'.[202] In this regard, the Indian courts are arguably one of the most robust judicial institutions in the world in dispensing constitutional justice by acting as 'facilitators' to safeguard

196. David Feldman, 'Public Interest Litigation and Constitutional Theory in Comparative Perspective' (1992) 55 *MLR* 44.

197. Christine Bateup, 'The Dialogic Promise: Assessing the Normative Potential of Theories of Constitutional Dialogue' (2006) 71 *BLR* 1109, 1112.

198. Ibid., 1118.

199. *R (Jackson) v AG* [2005] UKHL 56, [102].

200. Stephen Sedley, 'Human Rights: A Twenty-First Century Agenda' (1995) *PL* 386, 389.

201. *R v Lancashire CC, ex p Huddleston* [1986] 2 All ER 941, 945.

202. Bateup (N197) 1174.

socio-economic rights. In *Rakseh Chandra v State of Bihar*,[203] for instance, the Court addressed the right to health 'request' arising from the mismanagement of a mental hospital which had led to untold misery for patients. Two citizens, without initiating a judicial claim, wrote a letter addressed to the Chief Justice of India, exposing the miserable conditions of the mental hospital. The Indian Supreme Court, in response, deputed the Chief Judicial Magistrate to visit the hospital and submit a report. The report revealed a disturbing picture. The hospital was under-staffed. There was an inadequate supply of water. Toilets were not in working condition. Lights and fans needed repairing. There was no supply of sheets or pillows. Physicians rarely visited the hospital and the medicine was not fully stocked. Based on the report, the Court appointed a committee of management to improve the functioning of the hospital. Thus, the role of the judiciary in fundamental rights adjudication and in maintaining the rule of law should not be one of deference to Parliament, but one of equal partnership in promoting democratic values for the well-being of citizens.[204] In short, the idea of constitutional or institutional dialogue between the courts and the elected branches of government is, as T.R.S. Allan argues, not simply a desirable option, but is indeed imperative in a modern, constitutional, and democratic state.[205]

Furthermore, the above suggestion is also compatible with the concept of 'consociational democracy', or sometimes called 'power-sharing', as advocated by Arendt Lipjhart in the late 1970s.[206] Lipjhart identifies four classic elements in a 'consociational (political power-sharing) government':

(a) Grand coalitions are established to ensure that elites come together to rule so that minorities are not permanently excluded from political power.

(b) Proportionality is introduced at every level, with electoral systems using proportional representation and the allocation of resources.

203. AIR 1989 SC 348.

204. Shivaji Felix, 'Engaging Unreasonableness and Proportionality as Standards of Review in England, India and Sri Lanka' in Corder (N44) 116.

205. T.R.S. Allan, 'Constitutional Dialogue and the Justification of Judicial Review' (2003) 23 *OJLS* 563, 565.

206. Arendt Lipjhart, *Democracy in Plural Societies* (YUP 1977).

(c) Segmental group autonomy is apparent (e.g., through territorial division)

(d) Minority or mutual veto is available, thus giving each group 'a guarantee that it will not be outvoted by the majority when its vital interests are at stake'.[207]

Christine Bell has stated that the UK is moving towards a form of 'consociational constitutional settlement'. Indeed, 'consociationalism' already exists within the British constitution in two places, one being the Northern Ireland's devolution framework and the other being the Westminster's arrangement of partial consociationalism in respect to the inclusion of different sub-state 'national' interests.[208]

The 'assumption that governmental functions must be compartmentalised' no longer holds sway.[209] Instead, the focus has shifted to acknowledging that effective protection and implementation of socio-economic rights 'can be carried out only where the proper roles and limits of each branch of government [are] fully understood' and that 'to secure the protection of socio-economic rights across all three branches of [the] constitutional system remains the task of all three branches'.[210]

The correct approach of the doctrine of the separation of powers should not pit one branch of the government against the other, but rather see them as engaged in a co-operative enterprise to ensure the protection of fundamental rights, be they civil and political or socio-economic. Rosalind Dixon argues that this dialogic model of judicial review 'allows courts both to define rights in relatively broad terms and to adopt strong remedies, provided they defer to legislative sequels that evidence clear and considered disagreement with their rulings'.[211] As she

207. Ibid., 118.

208. Christine Bell, 'A Model Proposal: Power-Sharing for the UK', *UK Constitutional Law Blog*, 13 November 2015, available at: https://ukconstitutionallaw.org/2015/11/13/christine-bell-a-modest-proposal-power-sharing-for-the-uk/, last accessed 14 November 2015.

209. Craig Scott and Patrick Macklem, 'Constitutional Ropes of Sand or Justiciable Guarantees? Social Rights in a New African Constitution' (1992) 141 *UPLR* 1.

210. Anthony Lester and Colm O'Cinneide, 'The Effective Protection of Socio-Economic Rights' in Yash Ghai and Jill Cottrell (eds), *Economic, Social and Cultural Rights in Practice: The Role of Judges in Implementing Economic, Social and Cultural Rights* (Interights 2004) 22.

211. Rosalind Dixon, 'Creating Dialogue about Socio-Economic Rights: Strong-Form Versus Weak-Form Judicial Review Revisited' (2007) 5 *IJCL* 391, 393.

has noted, this approach is desirable because it allows the courts to 'counter failures of inclusiveness and responsiveness in the political process', or what she refers to as 'blind spots' or 'burdens of inertia', without usurping the role of the elected branches of government in the formulation of social policy.[212]

Lord Steyn agrees and argues that although the enforcement of all rights, whether civil and political or socio-economic, 'involves matters of policy', this alone does not mean that 'these are issues which constitutional principle withdraws from decision by the courts'.[213] Adjudication always has a political dimension. Judicial enforcement of any rights will entail some degree of overlap with the activities of the elected branches of government.[214] As Alec Stone Sweet and Jud Mathews have observed, 'a political commitment to rights requires massive delegation to judges; and, if the judges do their job properly, they will at times impinge upon policy processes and outcomes'.[215] Agreeing with this, Edward Rubin and Malcolm Feeley have opined that 'policy making inheres in the basic structure of a modern judiciary. For the foreseeable future, therefore, any discussion of litigation against the government must incorporate the fact that such litigation will regularly induce the judiciary to make public policy'.[216] It follows that although friction between the different branches of government is inevitable in any system of separation of powers, the dialogic approach at least goes some way towards structuring and mitigating such tensions.[217] Furthermore, as Helen Hershkoff has noted, in a regime which values and respects socio-economic rights, the constitution

> not only [retains] the government's exercise of power, but also compels its exercise, constraining the government to use its assigned authority to carry out a specified constitutional purpose. Judicial review in such a regime must serve to ensure that the government is doing its job and moving policy closer to the constitutionally prescribed end. The enforcement of positive rights

212. Ibid., 394.

213. Johan Steyn, 'Deference: A Tangled Story' (2005) *PL* 346, 355.

214. Jutta Limbach, 'The Concept of the Supremacy of the Constitution' (2001) 64 *MLR* 1, 8.

215. Alec Stone Sweet and Jud Mathews, 'Proportionality, Balancing and Global Constitutionalism' (2008) 47 *CJTL* 72, 93.

216. Edward Rubin and Malcolm Feeley, 'Judicial Policy Making and Litigation Against the Government' (2003) 5 *UPJCL* 617, 618; Ida Koch, 'The Justiciability of Indivisible Human Rights' (2003) 2 *NJIL* 3, 35.

217. O'Connell (N179) 185.

> thus requires [courts] to share explicitly in public governance, engaging in principled dialogue [to resolve social and economic issues].[218]

Hershkoff further contends that even though there would be overlap between the courts and the elected branches of government, it would not be a case of one exercising power at the expense of another, or usurping the role of the other. Rather, it would be a 'synergistic relationship'.[219] She states:

> When a ... constitution commits the state to particular public policies, the role of the ... court is to ensure that government uses its assigned power to achieve, or at least move closer to achieving, the specified goals. Although the legislature retains discretion over how to implement the state constitutional requirements, its discretion over the various 'manners' and 'means' is constrained by the constitutional mandate. In exercising review, the court would not itself construct welfare policy, but rather would impose a burden on the legislature to show that the chosen 'manner' and 'means' are likely to carry forward the specified constitutional aim.[220]

Therefore, giving the courts the power to tell the executive authorities to do 'X' does not entail giving the former the power to tell the latter *how* to do 'X'. For the government to be under a duty to do 'X' does not imply that the government is under the duty to do 'X' in a certain way.[221] For one thing, if the constitution specifies that one has a right to a reasonable standard of housing, given the level of economic development and competing expenditures and given what other needy people require, the courts will have to determine whether the income of the government allows for that level of provision, and whether the government is right to spend certain amount of money on certain things. However, if judges find that the government can afford to provide people with housing, they can simply tell the government that housing provision must be raised by a certain date.

218. Helen Hershkoff, 'Positive Rights and State Constitution: The Limits of Federal Rationality Review' (1999) 112 *HLR* 1131, 1138.

219. Ibid., 1145.

220. Ibid.

221. Cécile Fabre, *Social Rights Under the Constitution* (OUP 2000) 149.

There may be even stronger reasons to grant the judiciary a primary role, at least in the enforcement of a basic level of socio-economic rights. The primary function of socio-economic rights is to ensure the basic conditions of livelihood for the most vulnerable sections of the society. If part of the justification for an active role for the courts is the protection of the rights of those vulnerable minorities in society against abuse from the majority, it should be particularly important to promote, and not to deny, the participation of judges in the adjudication of socio-economic rights. Denying, or limiting access to, socio-economic rights affects democratic participation. Therefore, judicial supervision of their application is able to promote effective access to democratic values.[222] In short, if a society adopts or accepts a prior commitment to the protection of socio-economic rights, it is possible to conceive of a more nuanced conception of the separation of powers which sees both the courts and the elected branches of government working co-operatively towards the realisation of such rights. Within this system, the role of the courts could entail, among the others, once founding breaches of a right, remitting the matter back to the elected branches of government to re-formulate a proportionate response.[223] Such an approach would thus allow the courts to ensure that fundamental socio-economic rights are protected, while at the same time, leaving to the elected branches of government the decisions about the best way to realise such rights.

As far as the constitutional justification of substantive review by the courts is concerned, Jowell has suggested that the constitutional principle — namely the rule of law — be referred to.[224] Despite it being a contested concept and unduly vague, Lord Bingham has suggested six principal ingredients:

(1) Legality: that power be authorised and not exercised in an arbitrary fashion (so, the rule of law is the antithesis of arbitrary power).

(2) Legal certainty: that fair warning be given of changes in the law, that law not be retrospectively applied, and that law be comprehensible and accessible.

222. International Commission of Jurists (N39) 83.

223. O'Connell (N179) 186.

224. Jowell (N122) 55–56.

(3) Equality: that the law be equally applied to the rich and the poor, the powerful and the marginalised.

(4) Access to justice: it includes the opportunity to impugn decisions made about one's rights or interests.

(5) Fair trial: that, when a challenge is made, the decision is made in a fair manner.

(6) Impartial courts: that such trial be held before an independent and unbiased court or tribunal.[225]

According to Jowell, many of the principles of substantive review short of correctness or merits review, as discussed above, do fall under the above rule of law's requirements.[226] As the rule of law is the antithesis of arbitrary power, it can be relied upon or provide reference to any rational justification. Moreover, the strictures of the rule of law against arbitrariness and in favour of legal certainty also capture the prohibition on decisions that are unduly vague, irrational, or lacking an adequate evidentiary base.[227] As upholding a legitimate expectation has judicially been referred to as an example of the application of the rule of law in its substantive sense,[228] inconsistent decisions do inevitably offend the rule of law's core requirement of equal application.[229] Moreover, the rule of law as a constitutional principle has also been invoked to read down discretion in order to forbid the curtailing of access to the courts.[230] Overall, the rule of law gives judges direct licence to reshape judicial review, and they thus become part of the policy design team.[231] As Lord Phillips has acknowledged, the role of judges is to improve upon the statutes as follows:

> The administration of justice and upholding of the rule of law involves a partnership between Parliament and the judges. Parliament has to provide

225. Tom Bingham, *The Rule of Law* (Penguin 2010).

226. Jowell (N122) 56.

227. Ibid.

228. *ex p Pierson* (N127) 591 (Lord Steyn).

229. Jowell (N122) 56.

230. *R v Lord Chancellor, ex p Witham* [1997] 1 WLR 104, [1998] QB 575.

231. Mark Aronson, 'The Growth of Substantive Review: The Changes, Their Causes and Their Consequences' in John Bell, Mark Elliott, Jason NE Varuhas, and Philip Murray, *Public Law Adjudication in Common Law Systems* (Hart Publishing 2016) 126.

> the resources needed for the administration of justice. The size and the jurisdiction of the judiciary is determined by statute. Parliament has not sought to oust or fetter the common law powers of judicial review of the judges ... It should be for the judges to decide whether the statutory provisions for the administration of justice adequately protect the rule of law and, by judicial review, to supplement these should it be necessary.[232]

Finally, although proportionality is seen as European in origin, it has 'an impeccable origin by way of [the] Magna Carta'.[233] This is also one of the constitutional justifications for the prohibition of a disproportionate decision. When 'structured proportionality' is engaged, proportionality is simply a tool to restrain the unnecessary violation of a fundamental norm or right, and the role of the courts is one of assessing the legality, rather than the reasonableness, of the administrative decision by ascertaining whether the decision-maker has sufficiently demonstrated that the departure from the norm or right was in proportion to its legitimate aim, which is a stipulated exception to the norm or right in question.[234] When proportionality is applied in the sense of 'fair balance', such as to constrain unduly oppressive decisions, it supports and interacts with another traditional English constitutional principle — namely, the presumption of liberty.[235] Even though the executive may interfere with liberty when being authorised to do so, such authorisation must be clear and cannot permit licence to impose onerous and unnecessary burdens to the persons affected.[236]

All in all, there is no doubt that the courts are constitutionally competent and thus have authority to deal with those polycentric socio-economic rights disputes which involve the prioritisation of conflicting interests and allocation of scare resources, despite the fact that they may sometimes defer on the ground that the primary decision-maker is institutionally better informed and thus well-equipped to make the decision.

232. *R (Cart) v Upper Tribunal* [2012] 1 AC 663, 698.

233. Jowell (N122) 56.

234. Ibid., 55–56.

235. Ibid., 56–57.

236. *Entick v Carrington* [1765] 19 St Tr 1029.

4.8.4 Institutional Incompetence Argument

There have also been arguments against the judicial enforceability of socio-economic rights because the courts are ill-equipped, and thus ill-suited, to identify and enforce breaches of these rights. The concerns include the inadequacy of the judicial hearing as a forum for deciding conflicts that involve policy-making in polycentric socio-economic rights issues, as well as the professional capacity of judges and the institutional capacity of the courts to confront and solve conflicts around, and thus enforce decisions concerning, these issues.[237]

First and foremost, these allegations are based on a misunderstanding. They pre-suppose that every socio-economic rights case is complex, involving large numbers of actors, intricate or expensive evidentiary issues, important financial impacts, or potential conflicts between different branches of the state or government departments.[238] These assumptions are incorrect. In fact, many socio-economic rights cases are not so complex. A report compiled by the International Commission of Jurist in 2008 [239] shows that in many jurisdictions an important percentage of socio-economic rights cases determined by the courts are individual claims which have involved both positive and negative obligations. Most of the allegations concerning the institutional incapacity of the judiciary to tackle socio-economic rights are not applicable — decisions regarding labour, health, housing, education, and social security do not differ considerably from decisions regarding any other state activity which may affect individuals.[240]

When presiding over cases concerning socio-economic rights disputes, judges are not designing policies in these areas on the basis of their own initiative, but, as in any other area, they determine cases on the basis of existing rules — rules which are enshrined in constitutions, human rights treaties, statutes, or regulations. If it is possible to decide the contents of the duties that originate from socio-economic rights obligations, then the role of judges, when adjudicating these cases, would not differ from their role in any other case (i.e., determining whether a duty has been complied with by a duty-

237. International Commission of Jurists (N39) 89.

238. Ibid.

239. Ibid.

240. Ibid.

bearer).[241] Judges are able to do this in many other areas that are often technically complex, such as telecommunication law, anti-trust law, and environmental law, to name just a few. Therefore, there is no reason to grant judges the power to adjudicate in these fields and not in other areas that implicate socio-economic rights issues.

Furthermore, judges hear cases in a regulated framework that limits their discretion. In the common law tradition, judicial creativity is restrained by respect for precedent and the role of Parliament, and limited mostly to incremental change based primarily on legal principle. Within this framework of trials or hearings, judges cannot just assess public policy at their will. Initially, someone with *locus standi* (i.e., standing) needs to bring a claim. Judgments on complicated technical issues can be resolved with the help of expert testimony, as in any other area.[242] For instance, the Indian courts have devised a number of procedural mechanisms so as to overcome possible shortcomings, such as appointing expert committees before taking a decision that may involve technical complexities and securing the effectiveness of judicial orders by guaranteeing that the courts remain seized of a case when there is evidence of failure to comply with any remedies ordered.[243] For example, in *B R Kapoor v Union of India*,[244] the Court appointed an expert committee of eminent psychiatrists to visit a mental hospital run by the Delhi Administration and submit a report to the Court about the allegations made in a public interest litigation. The committee's report made 35 suggestions for the better functioning of the hospital, and the Court gave several directions to the government to implement the recommendations of the committee. Overall, having experts in the process of adjudication allows judges to intervene confidently and in a way which the administrative authorities would respect. In connection with this, John Allison has also advocated that the courts, when handling public law cases, should use inquisitorial rather than adversarial procedures. This is because, with adversarial procedures, the courts are only informed by the representations of the parties to the immediate dispute, and it makes them unable to investigate

241. Ibid., 90.

242. Ibid.

243. Ibid., 96.

244. (1989) 3 SCC 387.

the consequences of a ruling one way or another. Given the range of interests involved in public law disputes, if the courts are inadequately informed, they cannot intervene confidently in a case.[245]

Moreover, procedural rules, such as the imposition of burden of proof, are also safeguards against allegations of unsound or frivolous claims.[246] Moreover, the loser party is able to lodge an appeal against a judicial decision. When matters reach the final court of appeal, all the disputed issues will be fully aired and can be appropriately framed. Hence, the above safeguards, taken together, can have the effect that eliminates the risk of unbounded policy-making by judges in areas that go beyond their knowledge. Therefore, these make the courts institutionally competent in tackling socio-economic rights issues.

It is evident that the courts do, in some cases, adjudicate on disputes concerning public policies by using various common law principles of judicial review. The justification of these judicial review cases lies in the wider principles of fairness and good administration. A decision which is unfair can also be regarded as amounting to abuse of power and is thus illegal.[247] An executive body has a duty to act fairly to the person whose right is adversely affected by its decision, otherwise it is acting outside of its powers.[248] Fairness is interpreted as, among other things, the right to be heard and consulted in the decision-making process.[249] It also embraces the principle of equality in participation.[250] The legitimation of executive decisions demands that decisions be fair. The courts can provide a channel for the under-represented parties in the political process to voice their concerns in the court room and to have their rights upheld.

The notion of judicial independence as enshrined in the constitution, be it implicit or explicit, does form the legitimacy of the courts and thus render

245. John Allison, *A Continental Distinction in the Common Law* (Clarendon Press 1996) 131.

246. International Commission of Jurists (N39) 90.

247. *R v North and East Devon Health Authority, ex p Coughlan* [2001] QB 213, [2000] 2 WLR 622, [2000] 3 All ER 850.

248. *Re HK (An Infant)* [1967] 2 QB 617, 630.

249. Ronald MacDonald, 'Judicial Review and Procedural Fairness in Administrative Law' (1980) 25 *MLJ* 520.

250. Genevra Richardson, 'The Legal Regulation of Process' in Genevra Richardson and Hazel Genn (eds), *Administrative Law and Government Action* (Clarendon Press 1994) 124–218.

them institutionally competent to act as an objective adjudicator to deal with socio-economic rights issues. As Feldman has pointed out:

> The legitimacy of the judiciary arises from three ... different sources: first, the obligation to justify its decisions by means of rational arguments; secondly, the requirement that the reasons be formulated with reference to objective, publicly accessible standards with legal authority derived from a source other than the opinions of an individual judge; and thirdly, the independence of the judiciary from the political arms of government, guaranteeing an unbiased and objective assessment of the legality of the acts and decisions of the executive. This independence of political processes is a positive, not negative, characteristic, because of the distinctive role of judges.[251]

Considering the above, the severity of the 'institutional incompetence' argument may be exaggerated. If one takes the Court of Justice of the European Union (CJEU) as an example, it becomes obvious that over half of the past and present judges have been pure academics or members of national courts without any extensive political or administrative experience.[252] Those appointments to the CJEU are restricted to 'persons ... who possess the qualifications required for appointment to the highest judicial offices in their respective countries or who are jurisconsults of recognised competence'.[253] There is nothing in this section indicating that extensive administrative experience is a must for such appointment. Neither does it preclude the CJEU from developing a detailed principle of proportionality, nor does its composition deter the Court from such application.[254]

Wong has also argued that in the UK, as the application of proportionality is currently recognised under the European Communities Act 1972 (ECA 1972) (as at 31 January 2020, the day of Brexit) and under the HRA 1998 as empowered by Parliament, it is logical to conclude that Parliament considers the courts

251. David Feldman, 'Human Rights, Terrorism and Risk: The Roles of Judges and Politicians' (2006) *PL* 364, 374–375.

252. Wong (N102) 105.

253. Consolidated EC Treaty, Art 223 (previously Art 167).

254. Wong (N102) 105.

to be institutionally capable of exercising such control. Therefore, it is less convincing to say that the courts are competent to apply proportionality to cases involving the ECA 1972 and the HRA 1998, but are incompetent in relation to cases outside of these regimes.[255]

Moreover, shortcomings in administrative expertise are also a concern, so courts must be in a position to rectify malpractice, be it conscious or subconscious, committed by the executive and the legislature. To use Daly's words, 'despite the foregoing paean to expertise, the limitations of expertise — and experts — ought to be appreciated',[256] and thus the application of expertise by administrative experts is unable to resolve all issues.[257] Administrative experts, 'however adroit, are merely human [and] bear the burden of human limitations'.[258] They have the same foibles as the rest of us, sometimes an even greater number owing to their arrogance and self-interest.[259]

With regard to their arrogance, it is said that administrative experts are apt to be over-confident in their decision-making. They fail to look beyond the factors that their training and experience pre-dispose them to consider, and they tend to not thoroughly test their assumptions. As Jeffrey Rachlinkski and Cynthia Farina have noted, 'experts are right more often than lay persons, but not as often as they think'.[260] Additional factors which also afflict administrative experts just as much as they afflict other individuals include:

(a) Bounded rationality: humans are limited in their decision-making by cognitive and physical limitations, personal values which may diverge from those of the organisation and the absence of full knowledge and information.[261]

255. Ibid., 106.

256. Daly (N116) 82.

257. Martin Shapiro, *Who Guards the Guardians? Judicial Control of Administration* (UGP 1988) 140–144.

258. Clayton Gillette and James Krier, 'Risk, Courts and Agencies' (1990) 138 *UPLR* 1027, 1090.

259. Anthony Downs, *Inside Bureaucracy* (Little Brown 1967) 18–20; Feldman (N251) 379.

260. Jeffrey Rachlinkski and Cynthia Farina, 'Cognitive Psychology and Optimal Government Design' (2002) 87 *CLR* 549, 579.

261. Herbert Simon, *Administrative Behaviour: A Study of Decision-Making Processes in Administrative Organisation* (4th edn, Free Press 1997) 93–97.

(b) Cognitive defects (such as information and reputational cascades): humans follow the decisions of others rather than trusting the (sometimes limited) information that is immediately available.[262]

(c) The availability heuristic: humans estimate the likelihood of future events based on the salience of past events rather than the probability of the events recurring.[263]

(d) Hindsight-choice bias: once events have occurred, humans tend to think that the events were more *ex ante* than was actually the case.[264]

Insofar as bounded rationality and cognitive defects are concerned, Harold Laski has argued that the administrative expert who 'sacrifices the insight of common sense to intensity of experience',[265] 'dislikes the appearance of novel views',[266] and 'too often ... fails to see his results in their proper perspective',[267] has a 'caste-spirit'.[268] He goes on to say that 'there is ... no expert group which does not tend to deny that truth may possibly be found outside the boundary of its private Pyrenees' and that 'simply by reason of his immersion in a routine tends to lack flexibility of mind once he approaches the margins of his special theme'.[269] In consequence, the administrative expert

> is incapable of rapid adaptation to novel situations. He unduly discounts experience which does not tally with his own. He is hostile to views which are not set out in terms he has been accustomed to handle ... Specialism seems to breed a horror of unwonted experiment, a weakness in achieving adaptability, both of which make the expert of dubious value when he is in supreme command of a situation.[270]

262. Sushil Bikhchandani, David Hirshleifer, and Ivo Welch, 'Learning from the Behaviour of Others: Conformity, Fads, and Informational Cascades' (1998) 12(3) *JEP* 151.

263. Amos Tversky and Daniel Kahneman, 'Availability: A Heuristic for Judging Frequency and Probability' (1973) 5 *Cognitive Psychology* 207.

264. Kip Viscusi and Richard Zeckhauser, 'Recollection Bias and the Combat of Terrorism' (2005) 34 *JLS* 27.

265. Harold Laski, 'The Limitations of the Expert' (1931) 162 *HMM* 101, 4; Martin Shapiro, 'Administrative Law Unbounded: Reflections on Government and Governance' (2001) 8 *IJGLS* 369, 373–374.

266. Ibid., Laski, 5.

267. Ibid., 6.

268. Ibid.

269. Ibid.

270. Ibid, 6–7.

Furthermore, I also contend that administrative decision-makers, whose powers are delegated by the legislature because of their expertise in particular fields, are also subject to the following:

(1) The dangers of agency capture: a phenomenon whereby government entities come to favour the interests of entities in a regulated industry, often for the innocent reason that their success is equated with ensuring success in the regulated industry.[271]

(2) Groupthink: a mode of thinking that people engage in when they are deeply involved in a cohesive in-group, when the members' strivings for unanimity override their motivation to realistically appraise alternative courses of action.[272]

(3) Regulatory "arteriosclerosis": when the evil which gives rise to a reform has been partially alleviated, the initial dynamism of the delegated decision-maker may be dispersed.[273]

(4) Group polarisation: a phenomenon whereby group judgments become more extreme than the judgment of individuals in a group if the individuals' initial judgments all tilt in a similar direction.[274]

(5) A variety of structural defects.[275]

The above-mentioned correspond to what Lord Hailsham has described in *The Dilemma of Democracy*:

> In our lifetime the use of [executive] powers has continuously increased, and the checks and balances have been rendered ineffective by the concentration of their effective operation more and more in the House of Commons, in the government side of the House of Commons, in the Cabinet within the government side, and to some extent in the Prime Minister within the

271. Marver Bernstein, *Regulating Business by Independent Commission* (PUP 1955) 157–160.

272. Irving Janis, *Groupthink: Psychological Studies of policy Decisions and Fiascos* (2nd edn, Houghton Mifflin 1982) 9.

273. Louis Jaffe, *Judicial Control of Administrative Action* (Little Brown 1965) 12.

274. Serge Moscovici and Marisa Zavalloni, 'The Group as a Polariser of Attitudes' (1969) 12(2) *JPSP* 125; Cass Sunstein, 'Group Judgments, Statistical Means, Deliberation and Information Markets' (2005) 80 *NYULJ* 962.

275. Downs (N259).

> Cabinet. The sovereignty of Parliament, absolute in theory, has become more and more the sovereignty of the House of Commons, and like all absolute rulers, having more and more to do, and in consequence less and less time within which to do it, is becoming more and more the tool of its professional advisers, more and more intolerant of criticism, and less and less in control of the detail of what is done in its name.[276]

In addition, Laski has further argued that the administrative expert 'rarely understands the plain man', and only 'remains expert upon the condition that he does not seek to coordinate his specialism with the total sum of human knowledge'.[277] I argue further that administrative expertise is unable to solve all problems owing to their limited understanding of the world. It follows that having administrative expertise as the sole rationale for the delegation of power would give rise to 'administrative hegemony'.

Although, in a democratic state, the limitations of the judicial role must be taken seriously and judicial deference must respect the democratic legitimacy of the elected bodies and the expertise of legislative and administrative officials, it must also recognise that the most effective campaigns for wider access to socio-economic rights combine litigation, and the threat of litigation, with civil society mobilisation and engagement or dialogue [278] with government authorities inside and outside the courts.[279] The 'technology' of judicial review has evolved in recent decades, in particular with the development of new forms of remedial order, the greater involvement of third-party interveners in court proceedings, and the emergence of 'catalytic' or 'dialogical' modes of review whereby the courts act as 'prods' and enter into a dialogical relationship with different constitutional stakeholders to address violations of constitutional

276. Quintin Hailsham, *The Dilemma of Democracy: Diagnosis and Prescription* (Collins 1978) 126.

277. Laski (N265) 7–8.

278. Kent Roach, 'Dialogue Judicial Review and its Critics' (2004) 23 *SCLR* 49; Kent Roach, *The Supreme Court on Trial: Judicial Activism or Democratic Dialogue* (Irwin Law 2009); Dennis Davis, 'Adjudicating the Socio-Economic Rights in the South African Constitution: Towards "Deference Lite"' (2006) 22 *SAHR* 301, 320, 323–324; Dixon (N211) 393.

279. Marc Galanter and Jayanth Krishnan, '"Bread for the Poor": Access to Justice and the Rights of the Needy in India' (2004) 55 *HLJ* 789, 796; Mark Heywood, 'South Africa's Treatment Action Campaign: Combining Law and Social Mobilization to Realize the Right to Health' (2009) 1 *JHRP* 14.

rights.[280] As judicial review evolves, the assumption that the legal process lacks the capacity to tackle complex issues of resource allocation that involve the interests of multiple stakeholders is being increasingly questioned.

Judging from the above, litigation could act as a catalyst for dialogue, and judges may facilitate continued engagement between interested parties through creative remedies.[281] When judges are called upon to settle rights-based disputes, be they civil and political or socio-economic, they must do so in a manner that encourages further dialogue. Therefore, the extent to which it is appropriate for the courts to intervene is central to effective rights implementation.

4.9 Positive Duties Implicit in Civil and Political Rights

In general, there have been four different paradigms through which socio-economic rights can be protected in international and domestic levels, namely:

(a) through direct constitutional entrenchment of socio-economic rights;[282]

(b) protection in the form of non-justiciable 'directive principles' of state policy;[283]

(c) protection of socio-economic rights as essential corollaries of civil and political rights, the so-called 'integrated approach' (i.e., protecting socio-economic rights as integral aspects of explicitly protected civil and political rights);[284] and

(d) protection of socio-economic rights through the expansive application of equality or non-discrimination provisions.[285]

280. Katherine Young, 'A Typology of Economics and Social Rights Adjudication: Exploring the Catalytic Function of Judicial Review' (2010) 8 *IJCL* 385.

281. O'Connell (N179) 191–198.

282. Scott and Macklem (N209) 39.

283. Cass Sunstein, *Designing Democracy: What Constitutions Do* (OUP 2001) 224; Scott and Macklem (N209) 38–39.

284. Koch (N216) 25; Ida Koch, 'Economic, Social and Cultural Rights as Components in Civil and Political Rights: A Hermeneutic Perspective' (2006) 10 *IJHR* 405, 408.

285. Jeanne Woods, 'Emerging Paradigms of Protection for "Second-Generation" Human Rights' (2005) 6 *LJPIL* 103; Matthew Craven, 'Assessment of Progress on Adjudication of Economic, Social and Cultural Rights' in John Squires, Malcolm Langford, and Bret Thiele (eds), *The Road to a Remedy: Current Issues in the Litigation of Economic, Social and Cultural Rights* (UNSW Sydney 2005) 37.

Among them, (c) the 'integrated approach' and (d) protection of socio-economic rights through the expansive application of equality or non-discrimination provisions, despite not being the ideal mechanisms for the protection to socio-economic rights,[286] have been adopted. Starting from late 1970s, the European Court of Human Rights (ECtHR) has cautiously opened the door to the integrated approach that an interpretation of the ECHR may extend into the sphere of socio-economic and cultural rights,[287] and held that certain positive obligations are implicit in the ECHR.[288] In *Airey v Ireland*,[289] the ECtHR held that there is no 'watertight division' between civil and political rights and socio-economic rights as follows:

> Whilst the Convention sets forth what are essentially civil and political rights, many of them have implications of a social or economic nature. The Court therefore considers ... that the mere fact that an interpretation of the [ECHR] may extend into the sphere of social and economic rights should not be a decisive factor against such interpretation; there is no watertight division separating that sphere from the field covered by the [ECHR].[290]

> Although the object of Article 8 is essentially that of protecting the individual against arbitrary interference by the public authorities, it does not merely compel the State to abstain from such interference; in addition to this primarily negative undertaking, there may be positive obligations inherent in an effective respect for private or family life.[291]

Moreover, both the CJEU and the ECtHR have also, through the expansive application of equality or non-discrimination provisions, protected socio-economic rights. Such positive obligations can also be substantive or procedural in nature. In *Marckx v Belgium*,[292] the ECtHR stated that in the context of the right to respect for family life in Article 8, 'it does not merely compel the

286. O'Connell (N179) 179; Koch (N216) 25.

287. Langford (N42) 6.

288. *Marckx v Belgium* (1979) 2 EHRR 330, ECtHR (Plenary) 31.

289. (1979) 2 EHRR 305.

290. Ibid., [26], reiterated in *Budina v Russia* (App No. 45603/05) ECHR 18 June 2009.

291. Ibid., [32].

292. *Marckx* (N288).

state to abstain from such interferences: in addition to this primary negative undertaking, there may be positive obligations inherent in an "effective respect" for family life'.[293] In this case, Marckx, who was unmarried, gave birth to a daughter. Under Belgian law, no legal bond between an unmarried mother and her child results from the mere fact of birth. To create the bond, the mother had either to recognise maternity in specific proceedings or to adopt the child. In both cases, the child's inheritance rights remained less than those a child born in marriage received automatically. The state's obligation in this case was to grant the legal status, rights, or privileges as necessary to ensure that ECHR provisions were secured for the individual. The Court then ruled that a positive obligation had been infringed because Belgian family law did not recognise a child born out of wedlock as a member of the mother's family, and thus did not allow the mother and child 'to lead a normal family life'.[294]

Moreover, there has been growing ECtHR jurisprudence which attaches positive duties to the apparently civil and political rights in the ECHR.[295] Among other things, the ECtHR has determined that the civil right to respect for family life obliges governments to guarantee protection from industrial pollution,[296] from prohibitively expensive divorce proceedings (as ruled in *Airey*[297]), and, in certain cases, from homelessness.[298] So far, the Court has mainly done so under Article 3 (prohibition of torture and degrading treatment), Article 6 (right to a fair trial), Article 8 (right to respect for private and family life), and in combination of these rights with Article 14 (prohibition of discrimination) and Article 1 of the Protocol No. 1 (right to, and peaceful enjoyment of, property).

4.10 Concluding Remarks

This chapter has in large part examined the development of human rights within the national and international legal spheres in recent decades. Such

293. Ibid., [31].

294. Ibid.

295. Fredman and Wesson (N6) 455, [10.08].

296. *López Ostra v Spain* (1995) 20 EHHR 277.

297. *Airey* (N289).

298. *Botta v Italy* (1998) 26 EHRR 241.

an assessment has naturally touched on issues ranging from the evolution of socio-economic rights adjudication and the rejection of non-justiciability of socio-economic rights to a new tripartite theory of obligations by the state. Our understanding of the doctrine of separation of powers is undoubtedly evolving, and by examining each of these points in turn, it has become clear that courts are indeed constitutionally and institutionally competent to hear cases that involve socio-economic rights issues.

Where programmatic duties and resources collide, the greatest challenge for the courts is to carve out a constitutionally defensible role, without simply throwing up their hands and denying that there is any duty at all. This must also be done while considering the fact that socio-economic rights are implicit in, and should be treated as essential corollaries of, civil and political rights. As global experience has repeatedly shown, threats to individual rights (whether civil and political or socio-economic) mostly come from states. It follows that states cannot be trusted to respect and protect the inherent human dignity of those who are subject to their jurisdictions, so there not only needs to be a set of universal standards of human rights, regardless of national boundaries, but also an impartial, independent, and constitutionally entrenched judicial system (either international or domestic) to act as a guardian to safeguard inherent human rights for all.

This obligation corresponds with some traditional political theories, such as the social contract theory, in that as people feel the need to gather together, they enter into a contract specifying the creation and obligations of a state, as well as the rights secured for joining the state. It ensures that people have a right to determine how they are, and should be, governed. With this emerges the concept of 'governance' which involves 'interaction between these formal institutions and those of civil society'.[299] This interaction is compatible with an 'idea of constitutional dialogue' and the concomitant method of dialogic judicial review that encourage co-operative engagement among the different branches of government and the people within its jurisdictions in the context of rights protection. Viewed in this way, the courts can be said to have been engaging in an exercise 'to impose upon all decision-makers standards that

299. Drewry (N176) 189–190.

are inherent in a democracy',[300] an undertaking which gives 'no weight to the politicians' arts of point-scoring, partisanship, presentation and spin'.[301]

Thus, the real challenges for English and Hong Kong public laws arise, not when a socio-economic right is subject to adjudication, but when a right, of whatever sort, gives rise to positive duties. These challenges can arise in respect of both sets of rights, and have already been confronted in adjudications under the ECA 1972 and the HRA 1998 in the UK,[302] and under the Bill of Rights Ordinance (BORO) and the Basic Law in Hong Kong.

300. de Smith, Woolf, and Jowell (N193) [1-026].

301. Radford (N194) 54.

302. Fredman and Wesson (N6) 455.

5

Application of Proportionality in the European Union

5.1 Introduction

The principle of proportionality applies to ascertaining the relationship between the ends of public action and the means adopted to achieve them. In order to attain its objectives, the executive must adopt effective means of policy implementation because the justification for every administrative action is to realise collective goals via varying state programmes. In so doing, the executive may adversely affect the interests of an individual owing to the fact that it would be an impossible task for them to fulfil social needs without interfering with individual interests by reason of the democratic principle that individual interests have to be subordinate to the collective good.[1] Under the proportionality principle, however, the extent of the interference is unnecessary if the public goal could have been achieved via alternative less restrictive means.

In this regard, Bernhard Schlink gives a good example to illustrate that it would be a difficult, if not impossible, task for the administration to fulfil social needs without interfering with individual interests. Schlink said that on one hand, the police are entitled to do what is necessary to fight dangers to public safety and order. On the other hand, citizens' life, liberty, and property are protected against police intrusion. Put together, the two premises

1. Robert Thomas, *Legitimate Expectations and Proportionality in Administrative Law* (Hart Publishing 2000) 1; Ian Loveland, *Constitutional Law, Administrative Law, and Human Rights* (4th edn, OUP 2006) 8.

create a dilemma. It is impossible to fight dangers without intruding to some extent into citizens' lives. So, how can this paradox be remedied? How can police protect citizens from danger while at the same time protecting them against undue intrusion? The German courts have resolved this dilemma by allowing the police to intrude, but only in a non-arbitrary way, which is by definition the proportionate way.[2]

Against this background, the administrative courts, while applying the proportionality principle, are responsible for examining the effectiveness of such alternative courses of action in view of the administrative objective. Once alternative means that are less restrictive of the individual's interests but equally effective for realising public objective are identified, then the interference is regarded as being unnecessary and disproportionate. To ascertain whether a public action is proportionate, courts are required to formulate judicial opinions in relation to policy implementation. In other words, it undertakes a goal-oriented balancing exercise to establish whether it is factually possible for the executive to use alternative means. Thus, proportionality is a tool of modern administrative law to ensure the purposive rationality of public action.[3]

By examining the application of the proportionality principle by the Court of Justice of the European Union (CJEU), it becomes clear how this principle has contributed to controlling and constructively guiding the European Union (EU) and its Member States, such as the United Kingdom (UK) (as at 31 January 2020, the day of Brexit).[4] The survey of CJEU jurisprudence in this chapter shows what relevant factors the Court considers when determining how strictly it should examine the challenged measures, what degree of justification it should require of the EU institutions or state authorities, and when it should defer to the discretion of the original decision-makers.

2. Bernhard Schlink, 'Proportionality in Constitutional Law: Why Everywhere But Here?' (2012) 22 *DJCIL* 291, 294–295.

3. Thomas (N1) 77.

4. *BBC*, 'Brexit: All you need to know about the UK leaving the EU', 17 February 2020, available at: www.bbc.com/news/uk-politics-32810887, last accessed 23 May 2020.

5.2 Proportionality in the European Union

EU administrative law is a unique hybrid of different legal traditions specifically adapted for the purpose of integrating EU Member States.[5] The CJEU has adopted the proportionality principle when reviewing the legality of both EU measures (legislative and administrative) and national measures. Having adopted the principle from German law, the CJEU applies it across an array of different activities.[6] As Advocate General Jacobs once said, 'there are few areas of Community law … where [the principle] is not relevant'.[7] The principle is also laid down in Article 5 of the Treaty of the European Union (TEU).[8] In fact, proportionality has even been described as 'the most important general legal principle in Common Market law'.[9]

Under the EU regime, it is possible for the European Commission and Member States to issue proceedings in the CJEU if they believe that a Member State is acting contrary to EU law. If a Member State is doing so and subsequently fails to comply with a CJEU judgment, then the Court can impose financial penalties as enshrined by the Treaty on the Functioning of the European Union (TFEU).[10]

It is also possible for national courts, under the TFEU, to refer to the CJEU questions in relation to the interpretation of EU law.[11] Article 267 of the TFEU provides for a mechanism of co-operation between national courts and the CJEU, whereby the former may, and in some cases must, refer certain questions of EU law to the CJEU for a preliminary ruling before the national courts proceed to give judgment. In this regard, a reference is not considered to be a remedy in itself, but a step in the proceedings leading to

5. Carol Harlow, 'European Administrative Law and the Global Challenge' in Paul Craig and Gráinne de Búrca, *The Evolution of EU Law* (Clarendon Press 1999) 261.
6. Gráinne de Búrca, 'The Principle of Proportionality and its Application in EC Law' (1993) 13 *YEL* 105; Jürgen Schwarze, *European Administrative Law* (Revised 1st edn, Sweet & Maxwell 2006) Ch. 5.
7. *Commission v Greece* (Case C-120/94) [1996] ECR I-1513, [70] of the Advocate General's opinion.
8. TEU, Art 5 ('the content and form of Union action shall not exceed what is necessary to achieve the objectives of the Treaties').
9. Schwarze (N6) 677; Paul Craig and Gráinne de Búrca, *EU Law* (4th edn, OUP 2008) 551–554; Nigel Foster, *EU Law* (2nd edn, OUP 2009) 121.
10. TFEU, Arts 258–260.
11. Ibid., Art 267.

the final determination of the case by the national court. The purpose behind this mechanism is to ensure that one supra national body (i.e., the CJEU) has jurisdiction to provide definitive interpretations of EU law. This is designed to ensure the uniform interpretation of EU law in all Member States and to prevent divergences between national courts on matters of EU law.[12]

5.2.1 Development

The principle of proportionality was first developed by the CJEU to counter-balance the effects of market-regulation measures restricting economic freedom adopted under the European Coal and Steel Community (ECSC) Treaty during the early 1950s.[13] At the time there was no mention of human rights in the ECSC Treaty, nor was there any mention in the subsequent European Atomic Energy Community (Euratom) Treaty or the European Economic Community (EEC) Treaty in 1957. Thus, the CJEU was initially reluctant to adjudicate rights-based claims against EU law as there was no legal basis for intervention. However, there have since been institutional and policy developments that have paved the way for the Court to acknowledge human rights as part of the general principles of EU law. This move also subsequently gained political approval, with a series of declarations, non-binding initiatives, and resolutions published to support this trend.[14] Thus, human rights have eventually found their way into various EU Treaties, with the changes being introduced by the Maastricht, Amsterdam, Nice, and Lisbon Treaties (which are all versions of the Treaty Establishing the European Community, or EC Treaty).[15] These have been amended over time. Of particular importance is the EU Charter of Fundamental Rights, approved by the Member States at the Nice European Council Summit in December 2000.[16] Several general principles, including the proportionality principle, are also

12. Clive Lewis, *Judicial Remedies in Public Law* (5th edn, Sweet & Maxwell 2015) [18-001].
13. Takis Tridimas, *The General Principles of EC Law* (OUP 1999) 93.
14. The Joint Declaration of the Parliament, Council, and Commission [1977] OJ C103/1; the Declaration of Fundamental Rights and Freedoms by the European Parliament in 1989; the Community Charter of Fundamental Social Rights of Workers in 1989.
15. TEU, Art 6(1).
16. EU Charter of Fundamental Rights [2000] OJ C364/1.

found in this Charter.[17] Today, these various treaties are held as equals, and the foundation of EU law is based on three consolidated documents: the TEU (which sets out the objectives and principals of the EU), the TFEU (formerly the EC Treaty, which provides organisational and functional details of the EU), and the EU Charter of Fundamental Rights, along with the protocols, declarations, and directives accompanying each.

Initially being a mechanism to counter-balance the effects of market-regulation measures restraining economic freedom, the proportionality principle constitutes one of the 'oldest' general principles of the EU legal order as applied in *Fédération Charbonnière de Belgique v High Authority of the European Coal and Steel Community*.[18] However, it was not until the early 1970s that proportionality was 'explicitly' applied in the *Solange I* case.[19] This case concerned the lodging and forfeiting of deposits for import and export licences. The applicant argued that the forfeiture of his deposit constituted a disproportionate burden in light of the minor delay he had caused. For this reason, the rule in question should, argued the applicant, provide sufficient types of measures, such as forfeiture in part or other enforcement measures. The CJEU was not impressed, holding that the compulsory lodging of a deposit was lawful and noting that the provision in question was the appropriate measure for the purpose of ensuring, in the general interest, the proper functioning of the organisation of the cereals market without imposing an excessive burden on importers or exporters. Since *Solange I*, the proportionality principle has been recognised as being the overriding principle to set limits on EU law measures that impose burdens. As Advocate General Dutheillet de Lamothe has noted, proportionality in public administration requires that 'citizens may only have imposed on them, for the purposes of the public interest, obligations which are strictly necessary for those purposes to be attained'.[20]

17. Ibid., Art 52.

18. (Case 8/55) [1956] ECR 245.

19. *Internationale Handelsgesellschaft v Einfuhr-und Vorratsstelle* (Case 11/70) [1970] ECR 1125.

20. Ibid., 1146 (col 1) of the Advocate General's opinion.

5.2.2 The Three-Stage Formula

In 1990, the CJEU articulated the principle of proportionality in terms of three constituent tests of suitability, necessity, and proportionality in a narrow sense in *R v Ministry of Agriculture, Fisheries and Food, ex parte Fedesa* [21] as follows:

> By virtue of that principle, the lawfulness of the prohibition of an economic activity is subject to the condition that the prohibitory measures are appropriate and necessary in order to achieve the objectives legitimately pursued by the legislation in question; when there is a choice between several appropriate measures recourse must be had to the least onerous, and the disadvantages caused must not be disproportionate to the aims pursued.[22]

The first test of this involves an examination of whether the challenged measure is *appropriate or suitable* in achieving its legitimate objective. Simply put, it focuses on whether it is reasonably effective in attaining its aim. The second test involves an assessment of whether the measure is *necessary* in order to achieve its objective, thus focusing on whether there is an alternative and equally effective means of attaining that aim which interferes less with the applicant's interest. The third test requires an examination of whether the measure is *proportionate* in achieving its aim and involves weighing the adverse effects on the applicant's interest against the importance of the aim to determine whether that adverse effect is justified in the circumstances.[23] This three-test formula adopted by the CJEU is similar to that used by the European Court of Human Rights (ECtHR) as the basis for the proportionality inquiry.[24] The tests provide a broad structure for considering the proportionality of a challenged measure.

Although proportionality is widely applied, there has been uncertainty as to its precise scope.[25] In some cases, the CJEU has stated that the challenged measure is disproportionate only if it has been 'manifestly inappropriate' [26] in

21. (Case C-331/88) [1990] ECR I-4023.

22. Ibid., [13].

23. de Búrca (N6) 117.

24. *Sunday Times v UK* (1979–1980) 2 EHRR 245.

25. Thomas (N1) 79.

26. *Germany v Council (Bananas)* (Case C-280/93) [1994] ECR I-4973.

light of its objective,[27] whereas in other cases, the Court has only scrutinised the contents of the measure by adopting the excessively disproportionate formula.[28] In this regard, Robert Thomas has argued that the proportionality principle operates on a 'sliding-scale-of-review' basis.[29] Therefore, the inquiries undertaken by the CJEU within this structure will differ on a case-by-case basis, depending on the context and circumstances of the measure in question. The above structure of inquiry requires the CJEU to weigh different interests. The degree of the CJEU's scrutiny of a measure will depend on the test's application, how thoroughly it has investigated the existence of less restrictive alternatives, and the degree of weight it gives to the EU's or the Member State's assessment of the importance of the objective allegedly served by the measure.[30] Whatever standard of scrutiny is applied, the scope of the review must reflect the intensity of such factors. Advocate General Capotorti has concurred with this assertion on at least two occasions: one being when he concluded that whether a measure exceeds what is necessary must be appraised in light of the economic and social conditions, considering the means available,[31] and the other being when he stated that an infringement of proportionality will not be held to have occurred 'without careful reflection on the scope of that principle and on the importance which the facts given assume in its light'.[32]

In general, there are four types of cases, albeit inter-connected, which are worth examining, namely the challenged measures that concern:

(a) the choices of EU economic policies;
(b) EU treaty provisions and fundamental rights;
(c) the imposition of charges, penalties, etc.; and
(d) the grounds of public policy, public morality, national security, and public health.

27. *ex p Fedesa* (N21) [14].

28. *Bela-Mühle Josef Bergmann KG v Grows-Farm GmbH & Co KG* (Case 114/76) [1977] ECR 1211.

29. Thomas (N1) 79.

30. de Búrca (N6) 113.

31. *Skimmed-milk* case (N28) 1232.

32. *SpA Ferriera Valsabbia v Commission* (Joined Cases 154, 205, 206, 226–228, 263 and 264/78, 39, 31, 83 and 85/79) [1980] ECR 907, 1055 (col 2) of the Advocate General's opinion.

5.2.3 Challenged Measures Involving Choices of European Union Economic Policies

The EU was established to promote competition and to ensure that the market functions effectively and efficiently so that economic performance, not only for the EU as a whole but also for individual Member States, could be improved. Thus, EU institutions have powers to intervene to correct imbalances and orient economic development in accordance with general EU objectives. Such intervention in the economic sphere is bound to impact individuals and traders. To ensure that the process of economic integration does not undermine the freedom necessary for its success, there must be some checks on the method of policy implementation. The principle of proportionality enables the CJEU to determine whether such intervention is able to achieve its aim and to ensure that it goes no further than is necessary.[33]

Starting from the 1970s, the application of the proportionality principle as a ground of review has gradually expanded beyond administrative discretion to cover policy measures of general application.[34] The most common type of case is where an individual argues that the very policy choice made by the EU administration is disproportionate to the desired aim. However, the CJEU is cautious in this type of case. This is because the EU administrative authorities, being a political arm of the EU, are responsible for making policy choices, and the CJEU should not overturn these decisions merely because they think that a different way of doing things would have been better. The Court should not substitute its judgment for that of the EU administrations.

However, this does not mean that the proportionality principle has no use in such circumstances, but rather that the CJEU is likely to apply the principle less intensively in these categories and will overturn the policy choice only if it is 'manifestly disproportionate or inappropriate'.[35] As stated in *R v Secretary of State for Health, ex parte British American Tobacco (Investments) Ltd and Imperial Tobacco Ltd*,[36] the guiding principle is that this measure of review will be deemed appropriate whenever the EU legislature exercises broad discretion

33. Thomas (N1) 79.

34. Tridimas (N13) 94.

35. *ex p Fedesa* (N21) [14].

36. (C-491/01) [2002] ECR I-11453.

involving political, economic, or social choices requiring it to make complex assessments.[37] With the use of the margin of appreciation doctrine, the CJEU has also developed a substantial body of jurisprudence involving the protection of human rights in EU law.[38]

5.2.3.1 Common Agricultural Policy: From Less Deferential to Highly Deferential

Many of these types of cases arise from the Common Agricultural Policy (CAP), whose aims were originally specified in the EC Treaty and are now set out in a high level of generality in Article 39 of the TFEU. The CAP's objectives are to increase agricultural productivity by promoting (1) technical progress, (2) the rational development of agricultural production, and (3) the optimum utilisation of factors of production. This is to ensure a fair standard of living for the agricultural community, market stability, and the availability of supplies (and that those supplies reach consumers at reasonable prices).[39] However, these aims can clash, resulting in situations in which the European Commission and the European Council will have to make difficult discretionary choices, often under exigencies of time, in order to determine how best to balance and achieve these aims.[40] Against this background, the CJEU has constantly emphasised that EU institutions possess a wider discretionary power in operating the CAP, so a great margin of appreciation is allowed, and review of their decisions will not be intensive.[41]

Originally, the CJEU was not so deferential in its consideration of proportionality and adopted an excessively disproportionate formula to

37. Ibid., [123].

38. Andrew Drzemczewski, 'The Domestic Application of the European Human Rights Convention as European Community Law' (1981) 30 *ICLQ* 118; Koen Lenaerts, 'Fundamental Rights to Be Included in a Community Catalogue' (1991) 16 *ELR* 367.

39. Paul Craig, *EU Administrative Law* (2nd edn, OUP 2012) 593.

40. Ibid.

41. *Schräder HS Kraftfutter GmbH & Co KG v Hauptzollamt Gronau* (Case 265/87) [1989] ECR 2237; *Stölting v Hauptzollamt Hamburg-Jonas* (Case 138/78) [1979] ECR 713.

compare with alternative courses of action.[42] In the *Skimmed-milk* case,[43] the CJEU annulled a Council regulation concerning the compulsory purchase of skimmed-milk powder on this basis. The EU had long been confronted with an increasing surplus of skimmed-milk powder, so it adopted a regulation to reduce this surplus by forcing animal-feed producers to use the skimmed-milk powder (rather than soya) in their products. However, the compulsory purchase of this powder was imposed at a price equal to about three times that of soya, resulting in the producers increasing the price of their product. The applicants, poultry producers who were required to purchase animal feed, claimed to have been seriously affected by the resulting increase in price and thus challenged the regulation on the ground that it infringed the principle of non-discrimination between producers and the proportionality of the measure. The Court ruled in favour of the applicants, saying that the obligation to purchase the excessively expensive skimmed milk imposed a disproportionate burden on the animal feed producers and their consumers.

The CJEU ruled that although the EC Treaty (as it was still called then) allowed for a wide choice of intervening measures in setting out the CAP, it embodied the requirement of proportionality in that proposed measures should achieve its objectives and be limited to the pursuit of such objectives. The Court then held that the obligation to purchase at such a disproportionate price was not only discriminatory but was also unnecessary in order to attain the objective of disposing of surplus skimmed-milk powder. Simply put, even though the measure had pursued a legitimate aim, its excessively severe effect in imposing such a heavy burden on the applicants and others who were not responsible for the surplus went further than necessary to achieve that aim. A less restrictive alternative, such as offering the skimmed-milk powder at a cheaper price, was available. Overall, this case shows that if a measure imposes a particularly onerous burden and its objective could have been achieved through alternative means, it will be invalidated on a disproportionality basis.

While the CJEU ruled on this and similar cases in the 1970s, since the early 1980s, it has become more deferential to EU administrative authorities.

42. Thomas (N1) 80–81.

43. *Skimmed-milk* case (N28).

In *Biovilac NV v EEC*,[44] for example, the applicants argued that a Commission Regulation which had been intended to prevent skimmed-milk powder from being used as feed for piglets, was ineffective to achieve that objective and caused significant loss to the applicants. The CJEU held that it was clear that the Commission had attempted to reconcile the aim of ensuring a fair standard of living for the agricultural community with the aim of stabilising the markets. Accordingly, even if the method chosen to achieve that aim proved later to be partially ineffective, this would not alter the earlier appraisal of the legality of the legislation since it could only be adversely affected if the measure was 'manifestly unsuitable' for achieving the aim pursued.

During the early 1990s, such deference intensified, as manifested in *ex parte Fedesa*,[45] in which the CJEU adopted a 'manifestly disproportionate' test. In this case, a Council Directive provided that it would make a decision as soon as possible on the prohibition of certain hormone substances for administration to animals, but that in the meantime, any arrangements made by the Member States regarding such substances would continue to apply. In 1988, another Council Directive was adopted prohibiting the use of certain of hormonal substances in livestock farming. The earlier directive was thus declared void by the CJEU on the ground of it being an infringement by the Council of an essential procedural requirement. The applicants in the case were manufacturers and distributors of veterinary medicine who challenged the validity of the national legislative measure implementing the new Directive on the ground that it was invalid. They argued that the new Directive lacked proportionality in three respects. First, the outright prohibition on the administration of the five hormones in question was inappropriate in order to achieve the declared objectives as it was impossible to apply in practice and led to the creation of a dangerous black market. Simply put, it would not be effective to achieve its stated aim. Second, the prohibition in question was not necessary because consumer anxieties could have been alleviated simply by the dissemination of information and advice, especially since there were divergent views amongst the Member States as to the safety and quality of the substances in question. In other words, there was a less restrictive and equally effective means of attaining

44. (Case 59/83) [1984] ECR 4057.

45. *ex p Fedesa* (N21).

the objective sought. Finally, the prohibition in question entailed excessive disadvantages, including considerable financial losses on the part of the traders concerned, in relation to the alleged benefits accruing to the general interest. Hence, any advantages brought about by the measure were outweighed by their adverse effects upon the applicants' interests and financial position. Against this background, the competing interests at play could thus be seen — namely, the interest of the Council in protecting public health and in responding to different levels of consumer concern over the safety of particular hormonal substances, on one hand, and the commercial interests of the applicants when there was no conclusive scientific evidence as to the dangerousness of the substances, on the other.

In these circumstances, the CJEU noted that the lawfulness of the prohibition of an economic activity was subject to the condition that the prohibitory measures were appropriate and necessary in order to achieve the objectives legitimately pursued by the legislation in question. If there was a choice between several appropriate measures, then priority must be given to the least onerous, and the disadvantages caused must not be disproportionate to the aims pursued. Since the first part of the proportionality test (i.e., the 'appropriateness' query) relates partly to the effectiveness of the measure, the Court was being asked to examine the applicants' contention that it would be ineffective and would in fact give rise to a dangerous black market in the substances. Nevertheless, the standard which the Court applied in assessing the appropriateness of the measure was not a close examination of the prospects of its issues in eradicating the substance completely from use. Rather, the Court adopted a considerably more relaxed standard, holding that the Council's measure would only fail the first stage of the test if it was 'manifestly inappropriate' to achieve its objective. The Court's reason for adopting a less stringent level of review was that in matters regarding CAP, EU institutions were given discretionary power to promote agriculture under the EC Treaty (now embodied in the TFEU). The Court further explained that its role in reviewing the exercise of such discretion by a politically responsible body was confined to looking for clear ineffectiveness or unsuitability. Consequently, the legality of a measure adopted in that sphere could be affected only if the measure was 'manifestly inappropriate or disproportionate' compared with the objective the competent institution was seeking to pursue. Therefore, while the applicants had tried to show that the measure was manifestly inappropriate, the Court found that they had failed to discharge this burden. The prohibition, even though it caused financial loss to some traders, could not be regarded as manifestly inappropriate.

The *ex parte Fedesa* reasoning has been applied in many other cases. As a result, most applicants have found it difficult to convince the CJEU that a challenged measure is manifestly disproportionate.[46] Apart from measures prohibiting or restricting the use of certain products or substances, as in *ex parte Fedesa,* the 'manifestly inappropriate' test has also been applied to measures seeking to control production [47] as well as measures setting up monetary compensatory amounts.[48]

5.2.3.2 Measures for which EU Institutions Bear 'Political Responsibility'

In other areas involving measures in which EU institutions bear 'political responsibility' during their exercise of discretionary power (e.g., for measures taken to organise the market), the CJEU will also be deferential and adopt the 'manifestly disproportionate' test in its examination of the measure against an interest claimed by an applicant.[49] This is because the Council has to reconcile divergent interests and thus select options 'within the context of the policy choices which are its own responsibility'.[50]

46. *Crispoltoni v Fattoria Autonoma Tabacchi di Citta id Castello* (Cases C-133, 300, and 362/93) [1994] ECR I-4863; *Northern Ireland Fish Producers' Organisation Ltd (NIFPO) and Northern Ireland Fishermen's Federation v Department of Agriculture for Northern Ireland* (Case C-4/96) [1998] ECR I-681; *Bocchi Food Trade International GmbH v Commission* (Case T-30/99) [2001] ECR II-943, [92]; *Arnold André GmbH & Co KG v Landrat des Kreises Herford* (Case C-434/02) [2004] ECR I-11825, [46]–[56]; *Netherlands v Commission* (Case C-452/00) [2005] ECR I-6645, [101]–[102]; *Agrarproduktion Staebelow GmbH v Landrat des Landkreises Bad Doberan* (Case C-504/04) [2006] ECR I-679, [36]; *Alrosa Co Ltd v Commission* (Case T-170/06) [2007] ECR II-2601; *Viamex Agrar Handels GmbH and Zuchtvieh-Kontor GmbH (ZVK) v Hauptzollamt Hamburg-Jonas* (Cases C-37 and 58/06) [2008] ECR I-69, [36]; *Denka International BV v Commission* (Case T-334/07) [2009] ECR II-4205, [139]; *Gowan Comércio Internacional e Serviços Lda v Ministero della Salute* (Case C-77/09) [2010] ECR I-13533, (2011) 48(4) CMLR 1329, [82].

47. *Schräder*; *Stölting* (N41).

48. *Balkan Import-Export v Hauptzollamt Berlin-Packhof* (Case 5/73) [1973] ECR 1091.

49. *Bananas* case (N26).

50. Ibid., [91].

5.2.4 Challenged Measures Infringing European Union Treaty Provisions and Fundamental Rights

A second type of case is where an individual has argued that they were unduly restricted either by the EU's action or the Member State's action. A number of these cases deal with proportionality in the context of rights granted by an EU treaty and a Member State's action to restrict the ambit of those rights. In these cases, the CJEU has tended to engage in vigorous scrutiny to ascertain whether the restriction on the right is necessary or warranted. The rationale of such vigorous scrutiny is that under Common Market law, EU citizens are granted four fundamental freedoms — namely, the free movement of goods, services, workers, and establishments — which give them 'positive economic rights'. These rights have been accorded great importance by the CJEU in terms of how the EU affects the ordinary lives of its citizens, and they are central to the whole enterprise of economic integration.[51] However, these rights are not absolute, and challenges commonly arise when a Member State has argued that a restriction on one of these rights is justified on the grounds of public policy, public health, or one of the other limits recognised in the specific treaty.[52] Even so, the very denomination of certain interests as EU rights means that any interference should be kept to a minimum.

From the late 1970s onwards, the ECtHR has cautiously adopted an 'integrated approach' to treat socio-economic rights as essential corollaries of civil and political rights and has adopted the 'equality' or 'non-discrimination' approach to protect the same.[53] The CJEU has done the same during this period by applying the proportionality principle in relation to those 'positive economic rights'.

5.2.4.1 Measures Affecting Treaties and Fundamental Rights Adopted by the European Union

There have been many complex cases involving EU discretionary policy choice. The applicants normally allege that the discretionary policy has infringed

51. Thomas (N1) 82.

52. Paul Craig and Gráinne de Búrca, *EU Law* (2nd edn, OUP 1998) 355.

53. As discussed in Chapter Four of this book.

their property rights or their right to pursue a profession, trade, or occupation. Although the CJEU has acknowledged such rights within the EU legal order, it makes it clear that they are not absolute and must be viewed in connection with their social function. Therefore, in such cases, the Court will typically consider whether the restrictions imposed by the measure correspond to the aims of general interest pursued by the EU, and whether they constitute a disproportionate and intolerable interference which impairs the very substance of the rights guaranteed.[54]

Hauer v Land Rheinland-Pfalz[55] provides a good example of the way in which the CJEU applies the proportionality principle in this type of case. Here, the applicant sought to challenge a Regulation which placed limitations on the planting of new grape vines for wine manufacturing. The Court found that this did not, in itself, constitute an invalid restriction on property rights. It then proceeded to determine whether the planting restrictions were disproportionate as the measure had been 'impinging upon the very substance of the right to property'.[56] It found that they were not, but in reaching this conclusion, it carefully examined the purpose of the general scheme within which the contested regulation fell. The objects of this scheme were to attain a balanced wine market, to eradicate surpluses, and to improve wine quality. The disputed regulation, which prohibited new plantings, was part of this overall plan. It was not disproportionate in light of the legitimate EU policy. The policy was designed to deal with the immediate problem of surpluses while at the same time laying the foundation for more permanent measures to promote fair prices for consumers and a fair return for producers.

However, the preceding decision contrasts with that in *Kadi (Yassin Abdullah) and Al Barakaat International Foundation v Council and Commission*.[57] In *Kadi*, the applicant sought the annulment of a Regulation freezing his assets, pursuant to a UN Security Council resolution to curb Al-Qaeda. The applicant alleged

54. *Schräder* (N41) [15]; *Bananas* case (N26) [78]; *Musik Metronome GmbH v Music Point Hokamp GmbH* (Case C-200/96) [1998] ECR I-1953, [21]; *R v Secretary of State for the Environment and Ministry of Agriculture, Fisheries and Food, ex p Standley* (Case C-293/97) [1999] ECR I-2603, [54].

55. (Case 44/79) [1979] ECR 3727.

56. Ibid., [23].

57. (Case C-402 and 415/05) [2008] ECR I-6351.

that the Regulation constituted a disproportionate infringement of his property rights. The CJEU noted that property rights were not absolute and thus could be restricted, providing that the restrictions corresponded to the aims of EU public interest and did not constitute a disproportionate and intolerable interference.[58] The Court then concluded that the freezing of funds could not be regarded as disproportionate *per se*, considering the importance of the fight against terrorism.[59] However, the fact that the Regulation provided no means whereby the applicant could contest his inclusion within the list of those liable to sanctions meant that it did indeed constitute a disproportionate infringement of his property rights.[60] Furthermore, the CJEU also assessed the compliance of EU legal measures adopted to give effect to a UN Security Council resolution. Even though the obligation to obey the Security Council's measures is among the most serious obligations in international law, the Court was nevertheless clear that

> the obligations imposed by an international agreement cannot have the effect of prejudicing the constitutional principles of the EC Treaty [now embodied in the TFEU], which include the principle that all Community acts must respect fundamental rights, that respect constituting a condition of their lawfulness which it is for the Court to review in the framework of the complete system of legal remedies established by the Treaty.[61]

5.2.4.2 Measures Affecting Treaties and Fundamental Rights Adopted by Member States

Regarding challenges to Member State actions, the TEFU allows Member States to derogate from its provisions in a limited range of circumstances. Therefore, the proportionality formula is seen as a key technique to review the extent to which such derogations are acceptable. Nevertheless, any limitation on such a right for a specific purpose must not go beyond what is necessary to achieve its objective. Therefore, proportionality is applied with a greater level of scrutiny in this context. The CJEU regards it as a proper part of its legitimate function to

58. Ibid., [355].
59. Ibid., [363]–[366].
60. Ibid., [368]–[371].
61. Ibid., [285].

adjudicate on the boundaries between state action and individual rights, even though where this line can appropriately be drawn is controversial.[62]

5.2.4.2.1 *Measures Affecting the Free Movement of Goods, Services, Establishments, and Workers*

First of all, there are numerous examples of the application of the proportionality principle in cases challenging limitations placed on the free movement of goods. According to Jürgen Schwarze, more than 50 percent of all cases brought before the CJEU concern the free movement of goods.[63] In the famous *Cassis de Dijon* case,[64] the CJEU decided that a German rule which had prescribed the minimum alcohol content for a certain alcoholic beverage could constitute an impediment to the free movement goods. The Court then considered whether the rule was necessary in order to protect consumers from being misled. It rejected the defence on the basis that the interest of consumers could be safeguarded in other less restrictive ways, such as by displaying the alcohol content on the packaging of the drinks. Weighing up the various interests involved, Advocate General Capotorti observed that

> protection of the consumer against frauds may, in fact, be attained by other means which are less harmful to trade; in relation to that objective, the obstacles placed in the way of the free movement of goods are excessive and, therefore, disproportionate.[65]

This approach of applying greater scrutiny when searching for a proper balance between legitimate state action and protection of individual rights is also evident in cases concerning freedom to provide services [66] and free

62. Paul Craig and Gráinne de Búrca, *EU Law* (5th edn, OUP 2011) 529.

63. Schwarze (N6) 773.

64. *Rewe Zentrale AG v Bundesmonopolverwaltung für Branntwein* (Case 120/78) [1979] ECR 649, [1979] 3 CMLR 494.

65. Ibid.

66. *Van Binsgergen v Bestuur van de Bedrijfsvereniging Metaalnijverheid* (Case 33/74) [1974] ECR 1299, [1975] 1 CMLR 298; *Coenen v Social Economische Raad* (Case 39/75) [1975] ECR 1547, [1976] 1 CMLR 30; *Commission v Netherlands* (Case C-299/02) [2004] ECR I-9761.

movement of establishments.[67] Regarding the freedom to provide services, the CJEU, in *Van Binsgergen*,[68] considered a provision of Dutch law requiring those who acted as legal representatives to be established in The Netherlands. The applicant lawyer was a Dutch national but had moved to Belgium. The Court accepted that the nature of the service provided could justify the imposition of special requirements to achieve some common good, such as rules concerning professional ethics, supervision, and liability, particularly if those rules could be evaded if the person providing the service is from another Member State. Therefore, the CJEU found that the Dutch law was not incompatible with the provisions concerning services, where the requirement was objectively justified on the preceding grounds and if the objective could not be secured by less restrictive measures. When applied, however, the objectives could be achieved by less restrictive means — an address for service within the jurisdiction could be demanded, without stipulating that the lawyer should actually reside in The Netherlands. In other words, the residence requirements limiting this freedom might be justified, but only where they were strictly necessary to prevent the evasion by those outside the territory of professional rules which were applicable to the activity in question.

Insofar as the free movement of establishments is concerned, in *Commission v Greece*,[69] the CJEU found that a Greek law that prohibited a qualified optician from operating more than one shop constituted a restriction on the freedom of establishment. Greece contended that the prohibition was to protect public health, to safeguard the personal relationship of trust within the optician's shop, and to ensure the liability of the optician who owned the shop. The Court held that protection of public health could be achieved by less restrictive measures, 'for example by requiring the presence of qualified, salaried opticians or associates in each optician's shop, rules concerning civil liability for the actions of others, and rules requiring professional indemnity insurance'.[70]

The same approach is also at work in cases concerning the free movement of workers and of their families. This freedom represents a crucial element in

67. *Commission v Greece* (Case C-140/03) [2005] ECR I-3177.

68. *Van Binsgergen* (N66).

69. *Commission v Greece* (N67).

70. Ibid., [35].

the 'mobility of factors of production' in that it improves the balance between supply and demand in the labour market and ensures that labour is available where the best economic advantages prevail.[71] Accordingly, the free movement of workers is linked to an economic objective, subject to limitations justified on the grounds of public policy, public security, or public health. Thus, in relation to the entry and residence of aliens, Member States are entitled to apply special provisions which are justified by reason of national *'ordre public'*.[72] Nevertheless, the CJEU has insisted that derogation from the principle of free movement of workers and services can only be sanctioned in cases which pose a genuine and serious threat to public policy, public health, etc., and even then the measures must be the least restrictive possible in the circumstances.[73]

In *Watson and Belmann*,[74] the CJEU ruled that the deportation of a worker from another Member State who failed to register his presence with the local police was too serious and was a disproportionate punishment to the offence committed. The Court added that a fine would have been the proportionate response in such circumstances. Similarly, in *Commission v Germany*,[75] the CJEU held that the German law breached the free movement of workers, establishments, and services provisions by treating nationals of other Member States residing in Germany disproportionately different in terms of the degree of fault and the scale of fines resulting from their failure to present a valid identity document.

5.2.4.2.2 Equality or Non-Discrimination

5.2.4.2.2.1 Sex Discrimination

Proportionality is also relevant in equality or non-discrimination cases. Council Directive 76/207 [76] stipulates that men and women must receive equal treatment

71. Schwarze (N6) 814–815.
72. Ibid., 815.
73. *Rutili v Ministre de l'Intérieur* (Case 36/75) [1975] ECR 1219, [1976] 1 CMLR 140; *R v Bouchereau* (Case 30/77) [1977] ECR 1999, [1977] 2 CMLR 800.
74. (Case 118/75) [1976] ECR 1185.
75. (Case C-24/97) [1998] ECR I-2133.
76. Council Directive 76/207 [1976] OJ L39/40.

in three employment-related areas — namely, access to employment and promotion, vocational training, and working conditions. However, Article 2(2) of the Directive allows a Member State to exclude 'those occupational activities and, where appropriate, the training leading thereto, for which, by reason of their nature or the context in which they are carried out, the sex of the worker constitutes a determining factor'.

In *Johnston v Chief Constable of the Royal Ulster Constabulary*,[77] the Chief Constable in Northern Ireland sought to justify the police force's decision not to employ women as full-time members of the reserve team. The force argued that if women were permitted to carry and use firearms, they would be at greater risk of becoming targets for assassination by the Irish Republic Army (IRA). The CJEU accepted the argument submitted by the UK that the carrying of firearms by policewomen might create additional risks of assassination. However, the Court did not inquire whether women might not be trained to use firearms just as safely and effectively as men. It therefore accepted that the sex of police officers could constitute a 'determining factor' for carrying out certain police activities. The issue of proportionality was thus left to the national court, which should consider whether 'the refusal to renew Mrs Johnston's contract could not have been avoided by allocating to women duties which, without jeopardising the aims pursued, can be performed without firearms'.[78] In view of the political turmoil in the Northern Ireland during the 1980s, a great margin of appreciation has been left to the UK authorities to determine the proportionality of such differential treatment. However, proportionality should be used wisely and consider the facts of each case. For example, if it comes to light that the genuine reason for Mrs Johnston's dismissal was that she did not ingratiate herself with her bosses and peers or condone their obsequious behaviours (such as abusing their power, falsifying records, not fulfilling their duties, or even perverting the course of justice, etc.), then the rationale (i.e., that having female officers carry and use firearms would create a greater risk of their becoming targets for assassination) is simply an excuse to remove her from her post. In such a situation, proportionality may not do justice for Mrs Johnston.

77. (Case 222/84) [1986] ECR 1651.

78. Ibid., [39].

However, in *Kreil v Bundesrepublik Deutschland*,[79] the CJEU adopted a different attitude. The applicant challenged a prohibition under German law that barred women from military posts involving the use of firearms and allowed them access only to the medical and military-music services. The Court found that the Equality Directive was applicable, notwithstanding that the contested sphere of activity was military-related. It ruled that when the scope of any derogation from a fundamental right such as the equal treatment of men and women is in issue, the principle of proportionality must be observed.[80] It acknowledged that Member States have discretion when adopting measures considered necessary to guarantee public security, but affirmed that judicial review could be used to assess whether the measures taken really had that purpose, and whether they were appropriate and necessary to attain that objective.[81] It then ruled that since the Article 2(2) derogation had been intended to apply only to specific activities, the scope of the prohibition exceeded the discretion given to Member States when they were adopting measures that they considered necessary to guarantee public security.[82] The impugned rule that excluded women from all military posts involving the use of firearms was thus held to be disproportionately broad, given the fact that basic training in the use of firearms was already provided to women in the services of the *Bundeswehr* (Federal Defence Forces of Germany) which remained accessible to them.[83]

5.2.4.2.2.2 Equal Pay

As far as equal pay is concerned, a right can be infringed where there is direct or indirect discrimination in the remuneration granted to men and women. Indirect discrimination, once established, is prohibited unless the defendant can show some objective justification. The CJEU did provide guidance on objective justification, and the test formulated is very similar to that of the proportionality analysis used in the case law on the four freedoms.[84]

79. (Case C-285/98) [2000] ECR 1-69.
80. Ibid., [23].
81. Ibid., [24]–[25].
82. Ibid., [40].
83. Ibid., [28]–[29].
84. Craig (N39) 625.

Bilka-Kaufhaus GmbH v Karin Weber von Hartz [85] concerns the eligibility of part-time workers for an occupational pension scheme. Weber was a part-time worker, who had worked for 15 years at Bilka. She was refused pension payments because one of the provisions under the employment contract required her to have worked full-time for 15 years. She claimed this was sex discrimination under Article 119 of the EEC (later Article 157 of the TFEU), alleging that women work part-time more often because of family obligations, which put them at a disadvantage. Bilka argued that it was justified in excluding part-time workers because there were higher administrative costs for giving pensions to them. This exclusion from the occupational pension scheme was intended solely to discourage part-time work since, in general, part-time workers refused to work in the afternoon and on Saturdays. Thus, to ensure an adequate workforce during these periods, it was necessary to make full-time work more attractive than part-time work by making the occupational pension scheme open only to full-time workers. A preliminary ruling to the CJEU indicated that there could be potentially indirect discrimination, but that it was up to the Member State's court to determine the facts. The Court went on to say:

> If the national court finds that the measures chosen by Bilka correspond to a real need on the part of the undertaking, are appropriate with a view to achieving the objectives pursued, and are necessary to that end, the fact that the measures affect a far greater number of women than men is not sufficient to show that they constitute an infringement of [the] article.[86]

The above guidance given to the national court is, arguably, a proportionality inquiry, in that there could be objective justification for indirectly discriminatory measures if the employer showed that the disparate treatment was based on a 'real need' of the business, if the measure was 'appropriate' to attain its aim and if it was 'necessary' to achieve that end.[87]

In short, the CJEU's jurisprudence has so far recognised that even though these rights are not absolute, any restriction must correspond to general EU objectives

85. (Case 170/84) [1986] ECR 1607.

86. Ibid., [36].

87. *Rinner-Kühn v FWW Spezial-Gebäudereinigung GmbH & Co KG* (Case 171/88) [1989] ECR 2743; *Brunnhofer v Bank der österreichischen Postsparkasse AG* (Case C-381/99) [2001] ECR I-4961, [67]–[68].

and not constitute a disproportionate and intolerable interference with the substance of the rights. Thus, in exercising its discretion in the implementation of EU rules, each Member State should go no further than is necessary in interfering with fundamental rights, including an individual's positive economic rights.[88]

5.2.5 Challenged Measures Imposing Penalties and Forfeiture of Deposits

A third type is where the attack has been on the measures imposing charges, sanctions, and penalties, as well as forfeiture of deposits, the typical argument of which is that they are excessive. Under EU law, administrative institutions may impose penalties upon traders or individuals to make sure that what they are doing is EU-law compliant. However, a decision as to whether the penalty imposed is excessive is judicially reviewable, and the CJEU is likely to be intensively critical in this type of case. This is not only because penalties can impinge on personal liberties, but because the Court can strike down a penalty without undermining the relevant administrative policy.[89] In this regard, Thomas has opined that unlike economic policy measures, the competing interests involved are usually specific, in that the individual's interest is in the degree of the penalty while the EU's interest is in ensuring that EU law is effectively applied.[90] In reviewing whether a penalty is disproportionate to the offence committed, the CJEU will try to ensure its effectiveness for attaining its purpose as well as to ensure that the individual trader concerned will not suffer an excessive or disproportionate burden.[91]

5.2.5.1 Penalties Imposed by Member States Pursuant to European Union Measures

Under CAP, penalties may be imposed if the trader fails to fulfil its obligations.[92] The purpose of the deposit system is to enable the EU to have a good

88. *Wachauf v Bundesmat Für Ernährung und Forstwirtschaft* (Case 5/88) [1989] ECR 2609.

89. Craig and de Búrca (N62) 530.

90. Thomas (N1) 82.

91. Ibid.

92. Rene Barents, 'The System of Deposits in Community Agricultural Law: Efficiency v Proportionality' (1985) 10 *ELR* 239.

understanding of trade movements, as this system reflects real trade through the issuing of licences subject to deposits. A deposit will be lost if the goods are not imported or exported according to licence. There has been a regular stream of such cases in which the essence of the proportionality argument is that the penalty imposed was excessive in relation to the aim of the measure in question. On a number of occasions, the CJEU has not been deferential, and has found certain instances of forfeiture to have been too severe.[93] In *Buitoni SA v Fonds d'Orientation et de Régularisation des Marchés Agricoles*,[94] for instance, an importer of tomato purée obtained import certificates for which a deposit had been lodged, but the French intervention agency refused to return the deposit because the importer had failed to submit proof of importation within six months. Although the forfeiture of deposit had been intended to guarantee importation, it was imposed in this case owing to the failure to submit proof of importation. Ruling in favour of the importer, the CJEU held that the

> fixed penalty, which is applied to an infringement which is considerably less serious than that of failure to fulfil the obligation which the security itself is intended to guarantee, which is sanctioned by an essentially proportionate penalty, must therefore be held to be excessively severe in relation to the objectives of administrative efficiency in the context of the system of import and export licences.[95]

5.2.5.2 Deposits or Securities Forfeited by Member States Pursuant to European Union Measures

Similarly, in *R v Intervention Board for Agricultural Produce, ex parte E D & F Man (Sugar) Ltd*,[96] the UK Divisional Court referred a judicial claim challenging a penalty regime for sugar export licences to the CJEU on the basis of proportionality. In this case, a company was required to give a security deposit when seeking a licence to export sugar outside the EU. The company, E D & F

93. *Atalanta Amsterdam BV v Produktschap voor Vee en Vlees* (Case 240/78) [1979] ECR 2137; *Maas & Co NV v Bundesanstalt für landwirtschaftliche Marktordnung* (Case 21/85) [1986] ECR 3537.

94. (Case 122/78) [1979] ECR 677.

95. Ibid., 685.

96. (Case 181/84) [1985] ECR 2889, [1985] 2 All ER 115, [1985] 3 CMLR 739.

Man (Sugar), was late in applying for a licence, but only by four hours. In line with the relevant EU Regulation, however, the company lost its entire deposit of £1,670,317 because of the strict application of forfeiture clause. The CJEU found a violation of the principle of proportionality, holding that the automatic forfeit of the entire deposit in the event of any failure to fulfil the time requirement was too drastic, given the function performed by the system of export licences.[97]

Overall, the CJEU, when adjudicating cases involving penalties and forfeiture of deposits, has not used the 'marginal review' formula, but has drawn a tighter framework of review by reason of the different nature of the decision-making. The penalty is usually of an individual nature regarding one trader, rather than a decision requiring an overall assessment of the economic situation. Deciding on the proportionality of penal measures is a task which is generally accepted as an appropriate one for the judicial process as it does not usually involve a discretionary choice among alternative policy options, but rather an individual decision in a particular set of circumstances.[98] Therefore, the Court takes a more robust approach by intensively reviewing penal measures to ensure that they are proportionate.

5.2.6 Challenged Measures Adopted on Public Policy, Public Morality, National Security, and Public Health Grounds

In the context of concerns regarding national public policy and public morality, the CJEU is reluctant to intervene.[99] This is because different Member States will have different views as to what should be regulated or banned, and as to what will threaten its particular concept of public morality. Its choice as to the nature of the measures a Member State wishes to adopt ought not to be interfered with merely because there is another measure which a different Member State or a different court might choose instead. Like the cases concerning CAP, the doctrine of margin of appreciation is also applicable here, thus giving Member

97. Ibid., (Case 181/84) [1985] ECR 2889, [29].

98. de Búrca (N6) 136.

99. Ibid., 127.

States some discretion, subject to CJEU's supervision, when they take legislative, administrative, or judicial action in this area of EU law.[100]

However, this does not mean that the CJEU will always show deference to the opinion of a Member State in these types of cases. Despite its reluctance to interfere, the CJEU does not regard 'public morality' as a trump card for reducing the level of its review of proportionality.

5.2.6.1 Public Policy and Public Morality Considerations Affecting the Free Movement of Workers and Goods

In *Van Duyn v Home Office*,[101] which involved the free movement of persons, the CJEU paid due respect to the UK administration as to what was required in the interests of 'public policy'. In this case, the Court accepted that EU nationals could be excluded from the UK by reason of public policy. The specific reason for their exclusion in this case was that they belonged to the Church of Scientology, which was officially considered to be socially harmful, even though no legal restrictions were being enforced on British nationals wishing to become members or employees of that organisation. It accepted that different Member States would have entirely different concepts of public policy and morality, and it may have led the CJEU to be cautious in examining the proportionality of the national measures. Although the measures seemed to go beyond what was required by that admittedly legitimate state aim, they were not disproportionate in that the comparable restrictions were not imposed on the disapproved conduct within the UK. In this regard, de Búrca has opined that this approach is something along the lines of the 'not reasonable' test imposed.[102]

Insofar as the free movement of goods is concerned, one case example is *R v Henn and Darby*,[103] in which the defendants were charged with customs

100. A. Bleckmann, 'Der Beurteilungsspielraum im Europa – und im Völkerrecht' (1979) *EuGRZ* 485, cited by Yutaka Arai-Takahashi, *The Margin of Appreciation Doctrine and the Principle of Proportionality in the Jurisprudence of the ECHR* (Intersentia 2002) 4.

101. (Case 41/74) [1974] ECR 1337.

102. de Búrca (N6) 130.

103. (Case 34/79) [1979] ECR 3795.

offences as they had imported Danish pornographic films into the UK. They argued that UK laws on the prohibition of pornography were in breach of the grounds for derogation, saying that there was arbitrary discrimination between imports and domestic products. They further contended that the laws in different part of the UK varied considerably and that the laws governing importation were actually stricter than the ones governing possession of pornography materials within the UK. When the matters were referred to the CJEU, it held that the requirements of public morality in its own territory were, in principle, 'for each Member State to determine in accordance with its own scale of values and in the form selected by it',[104] so that rules governing the importation of pornography could fall within the scope of the exceptions. The Court also decided that a Member State could have a unitary concept of public morality in relation to imports, without necessarily having to ensure that laws are enforced identically within different parts of the State. Thus, the CJEU was of the opinion that this did not amount to discrimination between imports and domestically produced goods since there was no 'lawful trade' in pornography within the UK.

However, the CJEU did not seem to accept the argument that the import ban was arbitrary, given the variable enforcement of obscenity laws within the UK which were not as strict as the absolute ban on imports.[105] Being put in the language of proportionality, the importer's argument can be seen as an assertion that the absolute ban on importing such pornographic materials was not necessary for the protection of public morality as possession of the same materials would not necessarily be unlawful within the UK. To put it simply, the ban, as Henn and Darby had alleged, went further than the accepted legitimate state interest in restricting obscene articles required since that state interest clearly did not require the possession of pornography *per se* to be criminalised, as evident in the variable enforcement of laws within the UK. Nevertheless, the CJEU did not accept this argument, saying that so long as there was no lawful trade in pornography within the UK, the Member State was entitled to ban imports even if the same standard had not uniformly been applied within the UK. The only conclusion that can be inferred from the Court's analysis

104. Ibid., [15].

105. de Búrca (N6) 129.

is that it did not wish to question the policy of the UK on pornography any further, given the fact that different Member States could take very different approaches to the issue of pornography. As Advocate General Warner had, when applying the proportionality principle, noted, any discrimination inherent in the restriction on imports was 'reasonable' and not disproportionate to its purpose which could include the avoidance by the State of 'any excessive administrative burdens or public expenditure'.[106]

This deference tallies with the ECtHR's case law, as exemplified in *Handyside v UK*,[107] primarily because there has been no agreement at the European level as to the relative social importance of the public interest or of human rights in cases concerning political, social, economic, and moral aspects. In this climate, a certain weight or margin of appreciation should be accorded to the opinion of the state organs.

It was not until the early 1980s that the CJEU's attitude changed. The Court then became more willing to closely examine the necessity of a national measure even though the ground had been one concerning a national concept of public policy and public morality.[108] The joint case of *Adoui and Cornuaille v Belgium* [109] provides a typical example. In this case, the question tabled before the CJEU was whether a measure restricting non-nationals from engaging in certain activities that were deemed to be a threat to national interests could be necessary in the pursuit of a sufficiently pressing public interest if no steps were taken against nationals engaging in the same activities. In *Adoui*, the applicants were refused entry and residence in Belgium because their conduct was alleged to have been contrary to public policy since they were waitresses in a bar which was morally suspect. The Belgian law in question prohibited keeping a brothel, soliciting, and other activities relating to prostitution, but it did not prohibit prostitution itself. Once referenced to the CJEU, the Court was required to determine whether a State could deny access to a national of

106. Ibid., 129.

107. (1976) 1 EHRR 737.

108. Stephen Hall, 'The ECHR and Public Policy Exceptions to the Free Movement of Workers under the EEC Treaty' (1991) 16 *ELR* 466.

109. (Cases 115 and 116/81) [1982] ECR 1665.

another Member State by virtue of activities which, when engaged in by the former State's own nationals, did not give rise to repressive measures.

To put this question within the proportionality framework, the CJEU was tasked with deciding the following. First, could a refusal to admit sex workers from other Member States be justified in the interests of public policy (i.e., presumably the prevention of prostitution) when no repressive action was taken against Belgian nationals who were suspected of being sex workers? Second, could the ban be necessary or appropriate to achieve that objective, if no repressive action was deemed necessary to be taken against nationals engaged in the same activities? The Court noted that a public policy ground for a derogation would have to be very strong, presupposing the existence of a genuine and sufficiently serious threat affecting the fundamental interests of society. The Court held that although different Member States have legitimately different views as to what conduct was contrary to public policy, the public policy ground was not sufficiently serious if it did not also require the adoption of same measures against the State's own nationals in respect of that conduct. Several years later, in *Conegate Ltd v HM Customs and Excise*,[110] the CJEU also moved from its stance in *Henn and Darby*,[111] holding that a prohibition on the importation of obscene materials could not be justified on public morality grounds unless penal or other serious measures were taken in relation to the same goods manufactured or marketed within the Member State.

By comparing these four cases (i.e., *Henn and Darby, Adoui, Cornuaille,* and *Conegate*), de Búrca has argued that the CJEU did not just consider the measures, in terms of their impact on the freedom, as being more than necessary to achieve the stated public policy aim, but that the Court was also querying whether the legitimate objective pleaded by the Member States was the real reason for adopting the challenged measures. For instance, the CJEU might have doubted that a total ban on imports of pornography materials and refusal of entry to non-nationals suspected of prostitution were necessary to attain the States' objectives, or alternatively, it might have doubted whether the eradication of pornography and prostitution were the real objectives of the Member States

110. (Case 121/85) [1986] ECR 1007.

111. *Henn and Darby* (N103).

concerned.[112] Indeed, the genuine objectives of the Member States concerned might actually be to prohibit non-nationals from engaging in prostitution or importing pornography, as opposed to, more broadly, prohibiting prostitution and banning pornography, be it domestic or imported.[113]

Viewed in this way, de Búrca has argued that the Member States concerned in these cases were not acting to protect consumers, but to retain their marketing advantages on domestically produced goods and services or from some other partly protectionist motives. Simply put, they were not pursuing their legitimate objectives under the first part of the proportionality analysis. As previously noted,[114] we all take it for granted that a decision made by an administrative body is absolutely legitimate,[115] but as shown in de Búrca's analysis, this is not always the case.

de Búrca's suspicion also corresponds to what is manifest in *R v Barnsley Metropolitan Borough Council, ex parte Hook*[116] and *Wheeler v Leicester City Council*[117]: that the defendant authorities misused, and thus abused, their statutory powers by taking revenge against the defendants. In the former, the disciplinary action was not imposed against Hook as a result of his minor breach of urinating in the street, but because of his using abusive language and disrespect of the council's staff in the market. In the latter case, the authority punished the rugby club because of its unwillingness to side with the authority to defy the South African apartheid regime, not because of its refusal to condemn its players' participation in a tour of South Africa during the apartheid era. Furthermore, it is surely a matter of concern in Hong Kong if the legitimate purpose is not ascertained during the process of proportionality analysis and aired to the general public in an open court. This is largely related to the power of final interpretation of the Basic Law in Hong Kong being vested in the Standing Committee of the

112. de Búrca (N6) 131.

113. Ibid.

114. In Chapter One of this book.

115. Allan Rosas, 'Social Rights and the European Union' in Peter Van der Auweraert, Tom De Pelsmaeker, Jeremy Sarkin, and Johan Vande Lanotte (eds), *Social, Economic and Cultural Rights: An Appraisal of Current European and International Developments* (Maklu 2002) 149.

116. [1976] 1 WLR 1052. Discussed further in Chapter One of this book.

117. [1985] AC 1054. Discussed further in Chapter Three of this book.

National People's Congress (NPCSC).[118] The clearer the legitimate purpose is ascertained, interpreted correctly, and made known to the general public during the proceedings, the less likely an arbitrary interpretation will ensue.

Finally, the CJEU has also been willing to interpret proportionality in light of the Member State's particular values despite the fact that these values differ from those of other Member States.[119] In the *Omega* case,[120] the Bonn police issued an order forbidding the applicant company from allowing laser games that simulated the killing of opponents because they infringed the right to human dignity in the German Constitution. The CJEU found that the order in question limited the freedom to provide services and then considered the public policy justification. The Court held that the concept of public policy as a derogation from a fundamental freedom had to be interpreted strictly. Although it accepted that public policy might vary from country to country, the national authorities had to be accorded a margin of appreciation within the limits imposed by EU law.

In view of the above, Paul Craig and de Búrca have suggested that there are three variables which appear to affect the intensity of the CJEU's review in these types of cases.[121] First, the CJEU has tended to more intensively review challenges as time goes on.[122] Cases concerning similar principles seem to be more rigorously scrutinised upon subsequent review, with the result that a Member State's action which was regarded as lawful in the earlier case has been held not to be so in a later action.[123] Second, the intensity of the CJEU's review will depend upon how seriously it takes the Member State's argument that measures were really necessary to protect, for instance, public health.[124] If the Court feels that these measures were really a 'front' for a national protective

118. Discussed further in Chapter Two and Chapter Eight of this book.

119. *Alpine Investments BV v Minister van Financiën* (Case C-384/93) [1995] ECR I-1141; *Reisebüro Broede v Gerd Sandker* (Case C-3/95) [1996] ECR I-6511.

120. *Omega Spielhallen und Automatenaufstellungs GmbH v Oberbürgermeisterin der Bundesstadt Bonn* (Case C-36/02) [2004] ECR I-9609.

121. Craig and de Búrca (N62) 532.

122. Ibid.

123. Compare *Van Duyn* (N101) with *Adoui and Cornuaille* (N109), and *Henn and Darby* (N103) with *Conegate* (N110).

124. Craig and de Búrca (N62) 532.

policy designed to insulate its producers from foreign competition, then the Member State's argument will be more closely scrutinised. Finally, the CJEU has also been willing to interpret proportionality in light of the Member State's particular values in spite of the fact that these values differ from those of other Member States.[125]

5.2.6.2 National Security Considerations Affecting the Free Movement of Goods

A second area the CJEU may consider as being of largely national concern is that of national security. In general, the Court is more deferential in its review of national security measures, partly because of the considerable political importance attached to it. In this respect, a judicial body, like the CJEU itself, is not well place (constitutionally or institutionally) to consider available alternatives to the measure chosen. This is especially true under institutional considerations because it is a matter of knowledge and expertise, and a court will often not have all of the necessary information or as much time available to it compared to the decision-maker, nor does it have experience assessing the needs of national security. Much of the information available to the political branches may be confidential, and decisions on national security may have to be made at short notice or involve complex judgments with evenly balanced arguments for and against.[126] Against this background, the CJEU has largely accepted a State's own assessment as to the necessity and appropriateness of the impugned measure, and has given Member States a great margin of appreciation.

While it is rare for the CJEU to hear claims challenging national security measures, several such challenges have been brought against measures that have restricted the free movement of goods. In *Campus Oil v Minister for Industry and Energy*,[127] the CJEU held that an Irish law, which compelled importers of petroleum product to purchase a certain amount of their requirements

125. *Alpine Investments* (N119); *Omega* (N120). See also ibid., 532.

126. de Búrca (N6) 132–133.

127. (Case 72/83) [1984] ECR 2727.

from a refinery in Ireland at prices laid down by the relevant Minister from a domestic firm operating a refinery on Irish territory, was justified by reason of national security. At the time, Ireland possessed only one refinery, whose activity could be sustained only if all importers of refined petroleum products obtained 35 percent of their requirements from this refinery at prices officially laid down by the State. The main proceedings were based on actions brought by six Irish petroleum firms against the legal provisions adopted in this context. The Irish government justified the measures in question on the grounds that the refinery was of critical importance for the national security of the country. Thus, the competing interests in this case were the interests of the EU in free movement of inter-state trade and those of petroleum importers in being capable of buying imported oil without any restriction versus the interest of the Member State in ensuring the survival of the domestic oil refinery. The method by which Ireland had chosen to protect its domestic oil refinery was to impose a specific purchasing obligation on importers, presumably at a higher cost than they would have been able to secure by buying imports only.

The CJEU accepted that the security interest pleaded by the Irish government could be considered a pressing one, stating that an interruption in a country's supplies of petroleum products could have very serious consequences. The Court further noted that the operation of a refinery could indeed be a measure of protection for a State's security in the event of an oil crisis. Therefore, it was of the opinion that the aim of ensuring a minimum supply of petroleum products at all times was more than a purely economic concern and was capable of constituting a national security objective.

This case clearly shows a rather generous interpretation by the CJEU of what constitutes a national security aim because the measure was not only motivated by economic concerns, but national security considerations as well.[128] Isolating the first part of the proportionality analysis (i.e., the legitimate aim of the measure), the CJEU went on to the second stage of inquiry to ascertain whether the restrictive measure was no more than was 'necessary' to achieve that aim. Applying the 'no less restrictive means' test to a national security measure,

128. de Búrca (N6) 134.

the Court assessed what alternative ways the State might have had to ensure a continuation of domestic oil supplies. This could have involved an inquiry that would be beyond the competence of a court with limited factual findings before it and with little or no knowledge of the Member State market in question.[129]

However, the CJEU did not defer to the State's opinion and did conduct a hypothetical inquiry into other possibilities at the national level. The Court laid down certain conditions which, if satisfied, would ensure that the national purchasing requirement was not excessive in terms of its aim of ensuring a continuous supply of domestic oil. These conditions included that it was not possible to market the refinery's products freely and that the quantities required to be purchased by importers should not exceed the minimum supply requirements of Ireland without which the operation of its essential public services and the survival of its inhabitants would be affected.

While the application above is somewhat ambiguous, a clearer application of the proportionality analysis is shown in *Richardt*, where a Member State argued its measure was justified on national security grounds.[130] This case concerned the director of a French company who had contracted with the Soviet central purchasing agency for the supply of certain scientific equipment from the United States to the Soviet Union. The company obtained French authorisation for its export and transport to the Soviet Union. However, owing to the cancellation of a flight from France, it was transported to Luxembourg to fly from there instead. The Luxembourg authorities inspected the goods, determining that the EU transit declarations accompanying the goods were inaccurate and that the transit declarations had been completed only to conceal the real nature of the equipment so as to allow its transit to the Soviet Union. Thus, as this is a breach of Luxembourg law, the goods were then confiscated. When the confiscation order was challenged, the CJEU was asked to consider whether EU law required a Member State to recognise an EU transit document without reservation, or whether the State could require special permission, on grounds of external security for goods considered to be strategic equipment.

129. Ibid.

130. (Case C-367/89) [1991] ECR I-4621.

The CJEU held that in order to verify the nature of goods described as 'strategic material', the Member State could subject the transit of such goods to the grant of a special authorisation. The Court also ruled that the authorisation requirement would not be disproportionate if no other less restrictive means of ascertaining the nature of the goods was available. Considering the impact of the requirement on the EU's interest in the free movement of goods and on the company's interest in un-restricted transit, the CJEU held that it was not excessive in view of the security concern over strategic goods.

Regarding the second part of the national measure, namely the confiscation order, however, the CJEU took a stricter view, holding that confiscation could be disproportionate if the return of the goods to the Member State from which they had come would be sufficient to satisfy the State's interest. The Court stated that the question of whether any particular instance of confiscation went beyond what was necessary, and thus disproportionate, would be for the national court to decide. This, again, as in *Campus Oil*, indicates a recognition of the CJEU that it will not, in many cases, be the appropriate institution to decide the factual question of the proportionality of national measures in specific instances, where the national court has more information about the particular circumstances of the case.

Overall, the CJEU seems, on the face of it, to be more deferential when adjudicating cases involving national security and the institutional competence of the national authorities in terms of specialised knowledge, experience, and the like. However, this does not necessarily mean that the Court will not interfere with the decisions made by political authorities. In *Richardt*, despite the matter being referred back to the national court to decide, the guidance given by the CJEU as to what the national court should consider strongly suggests what the CJEU's conclusion on the matter would be in those circumstances — namely, that an automatic penalty of confiscation for any breach of the authorisation requirement should be deemed disproportionate. This is presumably because such a measure would interfere in a specific and draconian way with the legally recognised interests (i.e., the property) of an individual when a less restrictive measure would suffice to achieve the same aim. In this case, the penal nature of the confiscation, as compared with the requirement of authorisation, caused the CJEU to question the necessity for the measure more closely by applying the proportionality analysis somewhat more rigorously.

The deferential approach, or the 'not manifestly inappropriate' test as termed by de Búrca,[131] adopted by the CJEU when considering national security matters tallies with the approach taken in some cases involving CAP matters owing to the reality that EU institutions are constitutionally competent and are thus given discretionary power that corresponds to their political responsibilities to promote agriculture under EU law. However, the Court is prepared to look more closely and vigorously at penal measure, be it a CAP or national security matter, and so to rule that the forfeiture of an agricultural deposit, as shown in *Buitoni SA*,[132] or the confiscation of suspected military equipment, as in *Richardt*,[133] are disproportionate.

5.2.6.3 Public Health Considerations Affecting the Free Movement of Goods

As shown in *ex parte Fedesa*,[134] when the CJEU considered the proportionality of an EU measure adopted in pursuit of the protection of public health, it showed a great margin of appreciation to the EU institutions' assessment of the necessity for that measure. Certain case law also shows that when the State's derogation is based on a concern that relates partly to the protection of public health and partly to a broader public policy issue, the CJEU will more readily accept the State's assessment of the necessity for the measure. In *R v Royal Pharmaceutical Society of Great Britain, ex parte Association of Pharmaceutical Importers*,[135] the CJEU did not interfere with a measure that sought to preserve the position of the medical profession vis-à-vis the pharmaceutical profession, where the measure's overriding objective was to protect public health. Similarly, the CJEU has taken a hands-off approach when assessing the legitimacy of a national measure that substantially affected the importation of certain medical products, when the decision to enact the measure concerned a choice relating to the organisation and financing of a national health service.[136]

131. de Búrca (N6) 136.

132. *Buitoni SA* (N94).

133. *Richardt* (N130).

134. *ex p Fedesa* (N21).

135. (Joined cases 266 and 267/87) [1989] ECR 1295.

136. *Duphar v Netherlands* (Case 238/82) [1984] ECR 523.

However, it is clear from many cases that despite allowing the Member States to adopt restrictive measures for the protection of public health, the CJEU has consistently required that they do not go beyond what is necessary, such as stating that the Member States must not duplicate or impose excessive inspection requirements, or charge any more for them than their actual cost. Against this background and as suggested earlier in the cases of *Adoui and Cornuaille* [137]and *Conegate*,[138] de Búrca has opined that the CJEU is keen to ensure that national restrictive measures do not have adverse effects beyond what their aim requires, while also ensuring that their aim is not simply protectionist or to preserve an advantage for domestic goods or services.[139]

However, in *Officier van Justitie v Sandoz BV* [140] and *CMC Melkunie*,[141] the CJEU allowed the Member States a wide margin of appreciation in relation to derogations on the grounds of public health. These cases concerned national restrictions on the use of certain vitamins and bacteria at a time when there was scientific uncertainty about their benefits or harmful effects. In this context, the Court held that Member States could, on their own accord, determine the level of protection for public health they wished to ensure.

One possible difference between the public morality and national security grounds of exception and the public health ground of exception is that the margin of appreciation left to the Member States is likely to diminish in the public health context because health standards are becoming increasingly harmonised.[142] In the case of public morality or national security, as the CJEU has acknowledged in *Henn and Darby*,[143] there is likely to be considerable divergence between what is acceptable in different Member States, depending on different historical and cultural traditions. The progress of scientific research and developments in health care, in contrast, are likely to be of uniform concern

137. *Adoui and Cornuaille* (N109).

138. *Conegate* (N110).

139. de Búrca (N6) 138.

140. (Case 174/82) [1983] ECR 2445, [1984] 3 CMLR 43.

141. (Case 97/83) [1984] ECR 2367, [1986] 2 CMLR 318.

142. *Commission v Germany* (Case 28/84) [1985] ECR 3097; *Schumacher v Hauptzollamt Frankfurt am Main-Ost* (Case 215/87) [1989] ECR 617; *Freistaat Bayern v Eurim-Pharm GmbH* (Case C-347/89) [1991] ECR I-1747; *Ligur Carni* (Joined Cases C-277/91, C-318/91, and C-319/91) [1993] ECR I-6621.

143. *Henn and Darby* (N103).

and relevance in all Member States, so that the greater the level of harmonisation, the narrower the area of Member States' discretion.

Last but not least, in the *German Beer* case,[144] the Commission brought an enforcement action against Germany, claiming that its prohibition on the marketing of beer, which was lawfully manufactured and marketed in other Member States, unless that beer complied with the requirement of the German law on beer duty, was in breach of Article 28 of the EC Treaty (now Article 34 of the TFEU). The German law provided that only certain ingredients could be used in the manufacturing of beer, and that only beers manufactured in conformity with the provisions of that law could be marketed under the name 'bier'. Moreover, marketing beer containing additives was absolutely prohibited. Germany argued that these rules were justified under Article 30 of the EC Treaty (now Article 36 of the TFEU) since they were vital in order to safeguard public health as well as being necessary in the interests of consumer protection, a 'mandatory requirement' which had been recognised by the Court in earlier case law.

The interests in this case were the EU's interest in ensuring the free movement of goods between the Member States, on one hand, and Germany's interest in protecting public health and thus consumers, on the other. Germany argued that this was indeed necessary for the protection of consumers since the designation 'bier' was inseparably linked in their minds to the beverage manufactured with the ingredients required by German law. Nevertheless, the CJEU strictly applied the criterion of proportionality, saying that if the Member State has a choice between multiple measures to attain the same objective, it should choose the means which least restricts the free movement of goods. This 'least-restrictive-means' part of the proportionality test is often used by the CJEU in assessing the free movement of goods when a national measure has the effect of completely excluding products lawfully marketed in other Member States from the market of the State in question. Put simply, since the impact on the EU's interest is quite severe, the CJEU requires a stronger justification from the Member State.

144. *Commission v Germany (Re Beer Purity Law Case)* (Case 178/84) [1987] ECR 1227.

In this case, the CJEU seemingly felt that the aim of protecting beer consumers was not one which required a substantial area of discretion to be left to the Member State in making a policy choice. The Court was not satisfied with the identification of an apparently 'legitimate aim' and went further than checking whether the rule was 'not manifestly inappropriate'. In this regard, what had been required was a demonstration that there was no less restrictive way of pursuing that aim. The Court was neither convinced of the genuineness of the aim, nor of the necessity for the German rule even if the aim was a legitimate one.[145] The Court also noted that consumers' conceptions of, for instance, what constituted a good 'bier', were likely to evolve over time within a Member State, and that the establishment of the Common Market was one of the factors which could contribute to that development. In any case, the CJEU indicated that even though it was legitimate to enable consumers to choose their beer based on that beverage's specific qualities compared to others, this objective could be satisfied by the compulsory affixing of suitable labels indicating the nature and composition of the product sold.

Regarding the stronger ground of justification (i.e., the protection of public health), Germany argued that the ban was fully justified and that it did not infringe the proportionality principle. It claimed that given the dangers arising from the use of additives, whose long-term effects were not known, in particular their interaction with other substances, it was necessary to minimise the quantity of additives consumed. They argued that a ban on additives in beer was desirable in view of the large quantities consumed in Germany. However, the CJEU ruled that the Member State's competence to prohibit a specific additive on the ground of public health would not apply once the additive in question was found by international scientific research (in particular, by certain research bodies like the World Health Organisation as approved by the Court) not to present a risk to public health. Therefore, the blanket nature of the German ban (i.e., applying the rule to all additives and not just to those with unknown public health risks), as well as the absence of any procedure by which traders could apply for authorisation for the use of a specific additive, constituted a substantial restriction on the EU's interest in freedom of inter-state

145. de Búrca (N6) 139.

trade. In view of the above, the Court applied a strict proportionality test and inquired thoroughly into the proportionality of the ban and the availability of alternatives. It is plausible that the Court did not believe that the only interest was a public health one in this case, and that it suspected a certain element of protectionism. This is particularly obvious in the following:

> It must be emphasized that mere reference to the fact that beer can be manufactured without additives if it is made from only the raw materials prescribed in the Federal Republic of Germany does not suffice to preclude the possibility that some additives may meet a technological need. Such interpretation of the concept of technological need, which results in favouring national production methods, constitutes a disguised means of restricting trade between Member States.[146]

In connection to this, Craig and de Búrca have indicated that the nature of the subject matter is one of the variables which influences the intensity of the CJEU's review.[147] Where a Member State raises genuine public health concerns and there is scientific uncertainty about the effects of certain foodstuffs, the CJEU has been more willing to accept that limitations on free movement are warranted.[148]

To date, CJEU case law has been heavily criticised because the Court has applied a more stringent proportionality review when assessing Member State actions as compared to those of the EU.[149] However, there is a rationale for the differing levels of review. As mentioned, when the case involves a breach of one of the four freedoms, the Member State in question must then raise a defence based on the relevant treaty provision. As the four freedoms are central to the very idea of market integration that lies at the economic heart of the EU, they also embody non-economic values.[150] Therefore, it is unsurprising that the CJEU has, by using the proportionality principle, closely monitored (and defenced) issues related to free movement.

146. *Re Beer Purity Law Case* (N144) [51].

147. Craig and de Búrca (N52) 356–357.

148. *Sandoz* (N140); *CMC Melkunie* (N141).

149. Craig and de Búrca (N62) 532.

150. Ibid.

5.3 Socio-Economic Rights as Developed by the Court of Justice of the European Union

Apart from pursuing economic goals, the EU has other tasks to do, such as maintaining high levels of employment and social protection, pursuing equality or non-discrimination between men and women, raising the standard of living and quality of life, and facilitating social cohesion and solidarity among Member States.[151] To implement these objectives, the EU must have competencies that go beyond economics. These competencies are, according to Koen Lenaerts and Petra Foubert, 'scattered translations' of socio-economic rights that are meant to give the free market economy a more 'human face'.[152] Since the Treaty of Amsterdam 1997, Article 136 of the EC Treaty (now Article 151 of the TFEU) has explicitly referred to 'fundamental social rights', such as those set out in the European Social Charter 1961 (revised in 1996) (ESC) and the Community Charter of Fundamental Social Rights of Workers 1989. In the same year as the latter, the European Parliament also adopted a Declaration of Fundamental Rights and Freedoms, which covers not only civil and political rights but also socio-economic and cultural rights.[153] Moreover, in 2000, the EU Charter of Fundamental Rights was also proclaimed and included in the founding Treaties, as mentioned earlier, and made binding by the Treaty of Lisbon 2007 and entered into force on 1 December 2009. As a result, the CJEU now has the power to interpret and enforce the socio-economic rights in these Charters as well as the rights inherent in the TEU and TFEU. According to Jeffrey Jowell, the effect of the EU Charter of Fundamental Rights is an example of the progressive articulation of what Immanuel Kant called a 'cosmopolitan right ... of a universal nature'.[154]

Although the achievement of a 'common market' in which goods, workers, services, and capital can move freely is the EU's main concern, the process of

151. Philippa Watson, 'European Court of Justice: Creative Responses in Uncharted Territory' in Malcolm Langford (ed), *Social Rights Jurisprudence: Emerging Trends in International and Comparative Law* (CUP 2008) 453.

152. Koen Lenaerts and Petra Foubert, 'Social Rights in the Case-Law of the European Court of Justice' in Vab der Auweraert, De Pelsmaeker, Sarkin, and Vande Lanotte (N115) 160.

153. Resolution adopting the Declaration of Fundamental Rights and Freedoms (De Gucht report) of 12 April 1989, A2-3/89, OJ C 120 of 16.05.1989. See also *Society for the Protection of Unborn Children (Ireland) Ltd v Grogan* (Case C-159/90) [1991] ECR 4605.

154. Jeffrey Jowell, 'The Democratic Necessity of Administrative Justice' in Hugh Corder (ed), *Comparing Administrative Justice across the Commonwealth* (JUTA 2008) 16.

economic integration would automatically result in social progress.[155] The CJEU has, on many occasions, shown concerns for the Member States' social policies even if they are not entirely in line with the concepts of a common market and the principle of free movement. The Court's main concern is clearly the protection of socio-economic rights.[156]

As a consequence of this focus, all EU Member States are required to provide for their citizens social assistance and social security benefits, including health care.[157] For social security and social assistance schemes to be workable, the competent national authorities must be able to control expenditure in order to balance the budget of the system. These authorities usually reimburse medical expenses incurred in another Member State providing that they give prior authorisation for foreign medical treatment or that the treatment is urgent. Such rules, nevertheless, may deter insured persons from getting medical services or goods in another Member State. As a result, those rules may constitute a barrier to free movement within the EU.[158]

In *Decker v Caisse de Maladie des Employés Privés*,[159] Mr Decker, a Luxembourg national, was denied reimbursement of the cost of a pair of spectacles with corrective lens on a prescription established in Luxembourg, but purchased from an optician established in Belgium. The refusal was based on the fact that Mr Decker had bought the spectacles without prior authorisation of his sickness fund. Similarly, in *Kohll v Union des Caisses de Maladie*,[160] Mr Kohll, also a Luxembourg national, was denied authorisation for his minor daughter to receive treatment from a German orthodontist because the treatment was not urgent and could be provided in Luxembourg. The CJEU stated that the special nature of medical services and goods does not remove them from the ambit

155. Ingwer Ebsen, 'Social Policy in the European Community between Competition, Solidarity and Harmonisation: Still on the Way from a Free Trade Area to a Federal System' (1996) 2 *CJEL* 424 and 426; Manfred Weiss, 'Fundamental Social Rights for the European Union' (1998) *BCLR* 97.

156. Lenaerts and Foubert (N152) 165.

157. Derrick Wyatt, 'Community Competence to Regulate Medical Services' in Eleanor Spaventa and Michael Dougan (eds), *Social Welfare and EU Law* (Hart Publishing 2005) 131–144.

158. Lenaerts and Foubert (N152) 165.

159. (Case C-120/95) [1998] ECR I-1871.

160. (Case C-158/96) [1998] ECR I-1935.

of the fundamental principle of freedom of movement.[161] Although Member States are free to organise their social security systems in the way they wish, they should also respect EU law, including the prohibition of creating barriers to free movement, when exercising those powers.[162]

However, in these cases, the CJEU did note that 'it cannot be excluded that the risk of seriously undermining the financial balance of the social security system may constitute an overriding reason in the general interest capable of justifying a barrier of that kind'.[163] With this qualification, the Court safeguarded the right of social security, holding that the balance tipped in favour of free movement, so the benefits sought (i.e., reimbursement for a pair of spectacles in *Decker* and orthodontic treatment in *Kohll*) were not of the kind to have significant effect on the financing of the national social security systems.[164] As a result, the right to social security benefits was not endangered in either case.

Moreover, the CJEU was further inspired by social-rights-thinking in three Dutch cases in 1999 concerning the compatibility of a compulsory affiliation to a sectoral pension scheme with EU law.[165] Under the Dutch pension system, the compulsory statutory basic pension scheme entitles the whole population to receive a pension of a fixed limited amount. In most cases, supplementary pensions top up this basic pension. Such supplementary pensions are normally managed within the framework of collective schemes covering a certain undertaking or sector of the economy. According to Dutch law, affiliation to such a scheme can be made compulsorily. In this connection, some employers took the view that such compulsory affiliation to a fund was contrary to EU competition rules.

The CJEU agreed that the activities of the EU include a system ensuring that competition in the internal market is not distorted. The Court added, however,

161. *Decker* (N159) [24]; Ibid, [20].

162. Ibid., *Decker* [22]–[23], *Kohll* [18]–[19].

163. Ibid., *Decker* [39], *Kohll* [41].

164. Ibid., *Decker* [40], *Kohll* [42].

165. *Brentjens' Handelsonderneming BV v Stichting Bedrijfspensioenfonds voor de Handel in Bouwmaterialen*, Joined Cases (Joined cases C-115/97, C-116/97, and C-117/97) [1999] ECR I-6025; *Maatschappij Drijvende Bokken BV v Stichting Pensioenfonds voor de Vervoer-en Havenbedrijven* (Case C-219/97) [1999] ECR I-6121; *Albany International BV v Stichting Bedrijfspensioenfonds Textielindustrie* (Case C67-96) [1999] ECR I-5751.

that the EU also seeks the harmonious, balanced, and sustainable development of economic activities, and a high level of employment and social protection through policies in the social sphere.[166] The Court also noted that one of the aims of the EU is to encourage the development of a dialogue and the conclusion of collective agreements between management and labour at the European level.[167] Those observations ultimately led the CJEU to determine that collective agreements concluded in pursuit of social policy objectives, by virtue of their nature and purpose, do not fall within the scope of EU competition rules. As a result, the decision by public authorities to make affiliation to a sectoral pension fund compulsorily at the request of organisations representing employers and employees was considered acceptable. This judgment intended to protect both the right to social security benefits and the right to collective bargaining and action.

Moreover, in *Cowan v Le Trésor Public* [168] and *Bickel and Franz*,[169] the Court also established the principle that recipients of services had to be treated in the same manner as citizens of the country in which the services were provided. Thus, Mr Cowan was entitled to compensation under the French criminal injury compensation for injuries received as a result of an attack outside a Paris metro station even though he was in Paris as a tourist, whereas Bickel and Franz were also held to have the same linguistic rights in relation to court proceedings arising from some criminal offences committed whilst they were recipients of services in the Province of Bolzano in Italy. They have a right to have proceedings conducted in Germany in the same way the German-speaking people of that region had. In short, in multiple cases, the CJEU has held that persons receiving services on the territory of another Member State must be treated in the same way as citizens of the area in which those services are provided even if the rights being claimed were unconnected to the services being provided. Since discrimination on the basis of nationality is prohibited by Article 18 of the TFEU, any person in a situation governed by EU law must be placed on equal footing with nationals of the Member State in which they seek to exercise their EU law rights.

166. Lenaerts and Foubert (N152) 167–168.

167. Ibid., 168.

168. (Case 186/87) [1989] ECR 195.

169. (Case C-274/96) [1998] ECR I-7637.

Overall, it is evident from the above analysis that the CJEU has engaged in proportionality review that has essentially taken the form of a structured weighing of interests. The Court is called upon to examine the proportionality of legislative and administrative measures made not only by the EU institutions but by Member States as well. In either context, the Court has to consider the status of the complainant whose interests have been adversely affected, on one hand, and the interests of the EU or the Member State in adopting the impugned measure, on the other. The case law adjudicated by the CJEU also shows that, irrespective of the context in which the review takes place, a central consideration is the respective importance of the interests and rights at stake in the case, along with the extent to which the promotion of a restricted measure adversely affects the other. When an action is brought against the EU in an area of discretionary policy-making power, a looser form of the proportionality inquiry is generally used. The Court would only ask whether the measure was a 'manifestly inappropriate or disproportionate' way of attaining its objective.[170] However, this does not necessarily mean that the CJEU would automatically be deferential to these broadly discretionary EU measures. Even though the EU administrative authorities have such discretionary powers, the Court is of the view that if the right or interest of the applicant is sufficiently important and is seriously affected, or if the policy in question is enforced by exceptionally harsh means or by a severe penalty, it is more likely that it will question the necessity and proportionality of the measure more closely and find against it.

Insofar as Member State measures having a restrictive effect on EU interests and rights are concerned, the CJEU seems to balance the interest of the State against the interest of the EU which is adversely affected. The degree of rigour with which the proportionality inquiry is pursued will depend largely on the nature and importance of the respective interests. All in all, the more important the EU's interest and the more restrictive the measure, the more likely the CJEU is to look closely for a less restrictive measure. However, this will depend on the nature of the State's aim in adopting the measure.[171]

170. de Búrca (N6) 146.

171. Ibid., 146–147.

5.4 Concluding Remarks

Analysis of the CJEU's proportionality jurisprudence has revealed that, first and foremost, although there have been various methodologies developed, its spirit is essentially to provide a common analytical framework, the significance of which is not in its omnipotence but in how its structure influences or controls how the CJEU reasons to conclusions in many of the great moral and political controversies confronting political communities. In some cases, the Court has stated that the challenged measure would be disproportionate only if it was 'manifestly inappropriate' [172] in light of its objective [173] whereas, in other cases, it only scrutinises the contents of the measure by adopting an excessively disproportionate formula.[174] In this regard, the proportionality principle operates on a sliding-scale-of-review basis.

The CJEU's standard of review or level of scrutiny varies depending on the context of the particular policy objective, the nature of the competing interests involved, the competence of the courts and administrative authorities along with their specialised knowledge, experience, and the like. For one thing, under the margin of appreciation doctrine, a national judge of a Member State is said to be in a better position, and thus better equipped, than an international judge to evaluate the pressing social needs (e.g., public policy, public health, national security, and national morality) that prompted local decision-makers to enact a measure in derogation of EU law. By reason of their direct and continuous contact with the vital forces of their countries, state authorities (including the local legislature, executive, and judiciary) are, in principle, in a better position and thus better equipped than international judges to give an opinion on the exact content of these requirements as well as on the 'necessity' of the measures designed and promulgated to meet them.[175]

When pursuing the EU's economic goals, the CJEU has also started maintaining a high level of social protection and increased equality among different genders, thus raising the quality of life, social cohesion, and solidarity among Member States. To attain these objectives, EU administrations have

172. *Bananas* case (N26).

173. *ex p Fedesa* (N21) [14].

174. *Skimmed-milk* case (N28).

175. *Handyside* (N107) [48].

adopted various measures to safeguard and protect socio-economic rights of EU citizens in order to 'humanise' the free market economy. Therefore, various EU treaty documents must be observed not only by the EU administrations, but by the CJEU as well. The CJEU has also shown concerns for the Member States' social policies aimed at protecting socio-economic rights of the Member States' citizens.

Taken together, there are important, albeit significantly different, points to consider in the debate over the proportionality principle. It is to these differences in reasoning that reference is made to CJEU jurisprudence concerning the development of the proportionality principle, coupled with the margin of appreciation doctrine, to determine to what extent the courts should intervene with the substances of decisions taken by other branches of government (i.e., the executive and the legislature) and how they can balance the demands of judicial supervision and judicial deference.

6

Application of Proportionality in the European Convention on Human Rights

6.1 Introduction

The European Convention for the Protection of Human Rights and Fundamental Freedoms, otherwise known as the European Convention on Human Rights (ECHR),[1] is said to have been very much a by-product of the Second World War, being used as a means to promote unity within Europe and to ensure that human rights will be properly respected and protected thereafter. It recognises various human rights, some of which are accompanied by a specific limitation clause, which determines the criterion according to whose rights may be limited. These criterion require that a limitation of a right be done only to the extent 'necessary in a democratic society'.[2]

As far as the European Court of Human Rights (ECtHR) is concerned, the proportionality principle, though not being explicitly recognised in the ECHR, is a central feature of human rights.[3] Although there have been debates as to when the principle officially appeared in a judgment of the ECtHR, the first decision to

1. ETS No. 005, signed in Rome on 4 November 1950, entered into force on 2 September 1953, Council of Europe; details of the ECHR are available at: www.coe.int/en/web/conventions/full-list/-/conventions/treaty/005, last accessed 25 May 2020.
2. ECHR, Arts 8, 9, 10, and 11.
3. Jeremy McBride, 'Proportionality and the European Convention on Human Rights' in Evelyn Ellis (ed), *The Principle of Proportionality in the Laws of Europe* (Hart Publishing 1999) 23.

include a discussion of proportionality, according to Marc-André Eissen,[4] was in the case of *Handyside v UK*[5] in 1976. In this freedom of expression case, the ECtHR held, *inter alia*, that '[e]very "formality", "condition", "restriction", or penalty imposed in this sphere must be proportionate to the legitimate aim pursued'.[6]

Examining the ECtHR's application of the proportionality principle in greater detail will provide a greater understanding of how this principle has contributed to controlling and guiding the implementation of the ECHR in Member States. By reviewing ECtHR case law, we can assess what factors the Court has deemed to be relevant when scrutinising challenged measures, what level of scrutiny is appropriate in different contexts, what degree of justification is required of the Member States authorities (be they executive, legislative, or judicial), and when it should defer to the discretion of these decision-makers. This chapter also discusses how the ECtHR's approach tracks the modern day trend of treating socio-economic rights as essential corollaries of civil and political rights (i.e., the 'integrated approach') and protects them through the expansive application of equality or non-discrimination provisions.

6.2 Proportionality in the European Convention on Human Rights

In view of the atrocities of the Second World War largely attributed to Nazism and Fascism, the world's leaders started taking steps to prevent similar catastrophes from recurring. Founders of the United Nations (UN) expressed their determination 'to save succeeding generations from the scourge of war' and 'to reaffirm faith in fundamental human rights'.[7] It resulted in the adoption of the Universal Declaration of Human Rights 1948 (UDHR 1948), which

4. Marc-André Eissen, 'The Principle of Proportionality in the Case-Law of the European Court of Human Rights' in Ronald Macdonald, Franz Matscher, and Herbert Petzold (eds), *The European System for the Protection of Human Rights* (Dordrecht 1993) 126.
5. (1976) 1 EHRR 737.
6. Ibid., [47].
7. R.A. Lawson and H.G. Schermers (eds), *Leading Cases of the European Court of Human Rights* (Ars Aequi Libri 1997) xvii.

states that a 'common standard of achievement for all peoples and all nations' is necessary. The UDHR 1948 also contains a wide range of civil, political, economic, social, and cultural rights. In spite of the UN's determination, Member States failed to agree or grant legally binding effect to the UDHR 1948. However, out of the disappointment over the legal weakness of the UDHR 1948, a subsequent European movement, motivated by an alliance of non-governmental organisations favouring European integration, continued to press for legally binding obligations to ensure effective respect for human rights. This ultimately led to the signing of the ECHR.

The ECHR, now comprising 47 Member States,[8] was drafted within the Council of Europe founded in 1949. As an international organisation formed after the Second World War, the purpose of its founding was to promote greater co-operation and understanding between European States and ultimately to unify Europe.[9] ECHR institutions are based in Strasbourg, where the Council has its headquarters. The ECHR is also a part of a network of international human rights treaties of universal or regional application. It is the regional counterpart to the International Covenant on Civil and Political Rights (ICCPR), to which most Member States of the ECHR are also parties.

The ECHR protects predominantly civil and political rights. This was a matter of priorities and tactics. Although it was not disputed that socio-economic and cultural rights required protection too, the immediate need was for a short, non-controversial text which governments could accept at once. Owing to the values dominant within Western Europe, having the ECHR confined to the civil and political rights was 'essential for a democratic way of life'.[10] Socio-economic and cultural rights were said to be too problematic and thus left for separate and later treatment.

8. A list of current Member States is available at: www.coe.int/en/web/about-us/our-member-states, last accessed 2 December 2019.

9. Iain Cemeron, *An Introduction to the European Convention on Human Rights* (4th edn, Iustus Förlag 2002) 26.

10. David Harris, Michael O'Boyle, Ed Bates, and Carla Buckley, *Law of the European Convention on Human Rights* (3rd edn, OUP 2009) 5. They also cited M. Teitgen, CE Consult. Ass, Debates, 1st Session, 408, 19 August 1949 to support this.

6.2.1 Standard of Scrutiny: From 'Minimum Standard' to 'Absolute Standard'

The institutional design of the ECHR is different from that of EU law, not least because the ECHR pursues minimum standards of fundamental rights protection rather than absolute standards that govern social, economic, and political integration in the EU. This means that the ECtHR does not consider it necessary to impose far-reaching substantial and procedural demands on its national counterparts.[11] In this regard, Stephen Grosz, Jack Beatson, and Peter Duffy have commented:

> [T]here is no imperative that parties to the [ECHR] should adopt a uniform approach, only that they should not fall below an irreducible minimum, which will be monitored by the Strasbourg institutions. It is therefore open to national courts to develop a domestic jurisprudence under the [ECHR] which may be more generous to applicants than that dispensed in Strasbourg, while remaining broadly consistent with it.[12]

However, when a national court is attempting to protect rights in line with the ECHR, its capacity to do so will depend upon its ability to replicate, at the domestic level, the standards of scrutiny applied by the ECtHR.[13] Thus, the ECtHR's jurisprudence ultimately enjoys strong indirect influence at the national level, whether that influence is facilitated by EU law or by the terms of any domestic legislation concerning implementation.[14] In view of the above, the legal principles or standards applied both by the Court of Justice of the European Union (CJEU) and the ECtHR are arguably the same.[15]

11. Gordon Anthony, *UK Public Law and European Law* (Hart Publishing 2002) 67.
12. Stephen Grosz, Jack Beatson, and Peter Duffy, *Human Rights: The 1998 Act and the European Convention* (Sweet & Maxwell 2000) 20.
13. Anthony (N11) 67.
14. Human Rights Act 1998 (HRA 1998) s 2.
15. *Elliniki Radiophonia Tileorassi AE v Dimotiki Etairia Pliroforissis and Sotirios Kouvelas* (Case C-260/89) [1991] ECR I-2925, [41]; *Opinion 2/94 on Accession by the Community to the ECHR* [1996] ECR I-1759, [33]; *Kremzow v Austria* (Case C-299/95) [1997] ECR I-2629, [14]. For more discussion of the CJEU, see Chapter Five of this book.

6.2.2 A 'Living Instrument'

Although the ECtHR did not infuse the ECHR with constitutional qualities directly comparable to those which inform EU law, the Court has long regarded it as a 'living instrument' because its provisions were written in an open-textured manner and permitted adaptation to modern conditions.[16] This allows each provision to be interpreted in light of changing political and social values of the Member States.[17] This is apparent in *Tyrer v UK*,[18] which concerned birching inflicted on a teenager as a form of judicial corporal punishment. When finding the exercise of whipping to constitute 'degrading treatment' as proscribed by Article 3 (i.e., prohibition of torture and degrading treatment), the ECtHR held that:

> the [ECHR] is a living instrument which ... must be interpreted in the light of present-day conditions. In the case now before it the Court cannot but be influenced by the developments and commonly accepted standards in the penal policy of the Member States of the Council of Europe in this field.[19]

In this regard, judgments given some years ago, particularly those on moral issues, may no longer be a reliable guide to the approach needed today. Even a decade later, the ECtHR's view in *Tyrer* remains the status quo. This is evident in *Cossey v UK*,[20] in which the ECtHR confirmed that 'the [ECtHR] is not bound by its previous judgments ... the Court [can depart] from an earlier decision ... in order to ensure that the interpretation of the [ECHR] reflects and remains in line with present day conditions'.[21]

In short, drawing on teleological interpretative techniques [22] and related understandings that the provisions of the ECHR enjoy autonomous and

16. *R (Pretty) v DPP* [2001] UKHL 61, [2001] 3 WLR 1598, [56] (Lord Steyn), [2002] 1 AC 800.
17. Anthony (N11) 66.
18. (1978) 2 EHRR 1.
19. Ibid., [31].
20. (1991) 13 EHRR 622.
21. Ibid., 639.
22. *Wemhoff v Germany* (1979–1980) 1 EHRR 55.

independent meaning,[23] the ECtHR can expand the reach of the ECHR's guarantees and emphasise that it represents a constitutional instrument of European public order.[24]

6.2.3 Dual Purpose

The proportionality principle, coupled with the principle of effectiveness, plays an important role in the jurisprudence of the ECHR since it is the test normally used to assess whether there is a violation of ECHR provisions.[25] The Committee of Ministers of the Council of Europe described this as '[a]n appropriate balance ... between the adverse effects which an administrative authority's decision may have on the rights, liberties, or interests of the person concerned and the purpose which the authority is seeking to pursue'.[26] In this regard, the framework of the ECHR has a dual purpose. On one hand, it upholds the principle of democracy, and on the other, it seeks to balance the rights of the individual or minority in society against other public or majority interests. According to Ellie Palmer, the ECHR seeks to ensure that the 'tyranny of the majority' is not allowed to disproportionately interfere with the rights of minorities in the Member States.[27] In *Soering v UK*,[28] the ECtHR also noted that '[i]nherent in the [ECHR] is a search for a fair balance between the demands of the community and the protection of [an individual's] fundamental rights'.[29]

As Paul Walker has argued, the essence of proportionality is that a measure must impose no greater restriction upon a right than is absolutely necessary to achieve its objectives.[30] Moreover, the ECHR also seeks to ensure that limitations on individual rights are imposed only if they are prescribed by law for the purpose of achieving a legitimate objective. Therefore, the notion

23. *Engel v Netherlands* (1976) 1 EHRR 647.
24. *Loizidou v Turkey* (1996) 21 EHRR 188.
25. Richard Clayton and Hugh Tomlinson, *The Law of Human Rights* (2nd edn, OUP 2009) Vol. 1, [6.63].
26. Recommendation No. R (80) 2, 11 March 1980.
27. Ellie Palmer, *Judicial Review, Socio-Economic Rights and the Human Rights Act* (Hart Publishing 2007) 59.
28. (1989) 11 EHRR 439.
29. Ibid., [89].
30. Paul Walker, 'Unreasonableness and Proportionality' in Michael Supperstone and James Goudie (eds), *Judicial Review* (2nd edn, Butterworths 1997) 49.

of proportionality is inherently infused in the ECHR in the requirement that interference is 'necessary in a democratic society'. In practice, this requires restrictions on rights to be justified by 'a legitimate aim' that is 'proportionate to the need at hand' (i.e., a 'pressing social need').[31]

Apart from the general principles for determining the legitimacy of interference in the case of some rights, specific limits have also been implied or expressly provided in the Articles themselves. For example, Article 8 (the right to respect for private and family life), paragraph two states:

> There shall be no interference by a public authority with the exercise of this right except such as is in accordance with the law and necessary in a democratic society, in the interests of national security, public safety or the economic well-being of the country, for the prevention of disorder or crime, for the protection of health or morals, for the protection of the rights and freedoms of others.

Against this background, proportionality is used by the ECtHR when deciding whether a Member State has fallen below the required standard of fundamental rights protection, despite the fact that the Court does not expressly oblige national courts to give effect to the principles when they are adjudicating cases raising ECHR-related issues.[32]

6.2.4 Different Methodologies of Proportionality

Proportionality, together with the principle of legality, seeks to limit the circumstances under which a Member State may impose restrictions upon an individual's rights. Both principles find support in the text of the ECHR and seek to ensure that any derogation from ECHR guarantees is regulated by law and implemented in a manner that accounts for the competing demands of the public interest and an individual's interests.[33]

31. *Handyside* (N5) [48].
32. Anthony (N11) 67.
33. Ibid., 68.

Under the ECHR regime, the rights contained therein are sub-divided into absolute and qualified rights. Absolute rights (e.g., Article 3, prohibition of torture and degrading treatment) cannot be subject to any limitations, whereas qualified rights (e.g., Article 8, the right to respect for private and family life; Article 10, the right to freedom of expression; and Article 11, the right to freedom of association and assembly) can be subject to such constraints as are 'prescribed by law' (i.e., the issue of legality) and 'necessary in a democratic society' (i.e., the issue of proportionality).

Against this background, the proportionality principle seeks to ascertain that public authorities which impose limitations on an individual's rights do so only insofar as necessary to achieve a particular objective, such as national safety, public health, or the like.[34] Thus, according to Jason Coppel, 'the restrictive effects of a measure are strictly in proportion to its legitimate aims and objectives'.[35] There is an array of tests which the ECtHR applies when gauging the proportionality of a measure.[36] These tests include:

(a) the 'balancing' test, whereby 'a measure is disproportionate if it imposes restrictions which are not justified in light of the objectives which it seeks to achieve';[37]

(b) the 'relevant and sufficient reasons' test, whereby 'a measure will be held disproportionate if it is not supported by relevant and sufficient reasons';[38]

(c) the test of 'careful design', whereby 'a restriction will be disproportionate if it is "over-broad" and covers a wider range of situations than is justifiable';[39]

34. ECHR, Arts 8(2), 9(2), 10(2), and 11(2).

35. Jason Coppel, *The Human Rights Act 1998: Enforcing the European Convention in the Domestic Courts* (Wiley 1999) 160.

36. Ibid., 160, 161–164.

37. *Young, James and Webster v UK* (1981) 4 EHRR 38; *Dudgeon v UK* (1981) 4 EHRR 149; *Nasri v France* (1996) 21 EHRR 458.

38. *Goodwin v UK* (1996) 22 EHRR 123; *Vogt v Germany* (1996) 21 EHRR 205.

39. *Open Door Counselling and Dublin Well Woman v Ireland* (1993) 15 EHRR 244.

(d) the 'essence of the right' test, whereby 'a restriction "will always be disproportionate where it impairs the very essence of the right"';[40] and

(e) the 'evidential' test, whereby 'the State is required "to produce satisfactory evidence of the pressing social need which its restriction seeks to address"'.[41]

In this regard, Richard Clayton has expressed concern that the ECtHR does not identify a consistent or uniform set of principles for applying the proportionality formula.[42] Sometimes, the Court has confined itself to asking whether an interference is justifiable in principle and proportionate (i.e., the 'balancing' test)[43] and whether there is a reasonable relationship between the interference and the legitimate aim pursue (i.e., the 'relevant and sufficient reasons' test).[44] More frequently, however, a more rigorous approach (i.e., the 'essence of the right' test) has been applied, particularly in the context of freedom of expression.[45] In *Sunday Times v UK*,[46] for example, the ECtHR propounded a three-fold test: first, whether the interference complained of corresponded to a 'pressing social need'; second, whether it was 'proportionate to the legitimate aim pursued'; and, finally, whether the reasons given by the national authority to justify it were 'relevant and sufficient'.[47] In view of this, Clayton has opined that this stricter formulation is appropriate where fundamental rights are at issue, such as freedom of expression or prisoner aspects of private life. However, where less important rights, such as property rights, are at stake, the Court may use the looser formulation of a reasonable relationship between the means and the objective sought to be achieved (i.e., the 'relevant and sufficient

40. *F v Switzerland* (1988) 10 EHRR 411.

41. *Kokkinakis v Greece* (1994) 17 EHRR 397.

42. Richard Clayton, 'Regaining a Sense of Proportion: The Human Rights Act and the Proportionality Principle' (2001) 5 *EHRLR* 504, 510–511.

43. *Kokkinakis* (N41) [21]; *Casado v Spain* (1994) 18 EHRR 1, [20].

44. *Hadjianastassiou v Greece* (1992) 16 EHRR 219, [19]; *Chorherr v Austria* (1993) 17 EHRR 358, [37].

45. *Sunday Times v UK* (1979–1980) 2 EHRR 245; *Lingens v Austria* (1986) 8 EHRR 407.

46. Ibid., *Sunday Times*.

47. Ibid., [62], applied in *Dudgeon* (N37) [52]–[54]; *Barthold v Germany* (1985) 7 EHRR 383, [55]; *Müller v Switzerland* (1988) 13 EHRR 212, [32], (1991) 13 EHRR 212; *Observer and Guardian v UK* (1991) 14 EHRR 153, [59]; *Olsson v Sweden* (No. 2) (1992) 17 EHRR 134, [87]; *Jersild v Denmark* (1994) 19 EHRR 1, [30]; *Goodwin* (N38) [40]; *Vogt* (N38) [52]; *Wingrove v UK* (1996) 24 EHRR 1, [58].

reasons' test) or a fair balance between the general and individual interests at stake (i.e., the 'balancing' test).[48]

Although the ECtHR has had difficulties identifying a consistent and coherent approach, Advocate General van Gerven, when giving an opinion in *Society for the Protection of Unborn Children (Ireland) Ltd v Grogan*,[49] opined that a measure should (1) be carefully designed to achieve a legitimate aim or objective, (2) be the least restrictive means possible of achieving that objective, and (3) not have an excessive or disproportionate effect on the interests of affected persons.[50] The fact that proportionality has given rise to these formulas and requirements (associated with the overarching requirement that individuals enjoy effective protection of their rights) is of fundamental importance to understanding how and why the ECHR may cause re-alignment in some national courts. Simply put, the fact that ECHR jurisprudence is structured around these searching methods of enquiry means that national courts may have to substitute ECHR standards for domestic norms when adjudicating ECHR issues.[51] The proportionality principle, when being applied both by the CJEU and the ECtHR, operates on a sliding-scale-of-review basis.

6.2.5 Restrictions Imposed on Qualified Rights

When it comes to restrictions on the rights assured in the ECHR, the notion of 'a democratic society' plays a vital role.[52] The three kinds of rights in the ECHR are: (a) absolute and unqualified rights; (b) rights where interference is permitted when it is 'necessary in a democratic society'; and (c) rights where interference is permitted when another interest outweighs the right in question.

48. Clayton (N42) 511.
49. (Case C-159/90) [1991] ECR I-4865.
50. Ibid.
51. Anthony (N11) 70.
52. Rabinder Singh, 'The Place of the Human Rights Act in a Democratic Society' in Jeffrey Jowell and Jonathan Cooper (eds), *Understanding Human Rights Principles* (Hart Publishing 2001) 187.

6.2.5.1 Absolute and Unqualified Rights

Under this category, no balancing is required or permitted. As a matter of principle, some of these rights are essential in the ECHR system and cannot be derogated from even in time of war or national emergency.[53] Falling into this category are the prohibition of torture and inhuman or degrading treatment in Article 3, the prohibition of slavery and forced labour in Article 4, and no punishment without law (i.e., freedom from retrospective criminal penalties) in Article 7.

6.2.5.2 When Interference is 'Necessary in a Democratic Society'

Rights in this category consist of those expressly qualified in the text of the ECHR. They include the right to respect for private and family life, home, and correspondence in Article 8; the freedom of thought, conscience, and religion in Article 9; the right to freedom of expression in Article 10; and the right to freedom of assembly and association in Article 11. Under the second paragraphs of these Articles, these rights may be interfered with but only if the interference is 'provided by law' (Article 2), 'prescribed by law' (Articles 5, 9–11), 'in accordance with the law' (Article 8), or 'provided for by law' (Article 1 of Protocol 1), where the interference has a legitimate aim and where there is a pressing social need. Furthermore, a Member State may also restrict the protected right to the extent that this is 'necessary in a democratic society' for certain listed public interest purposes. This formula has been interpreted as meaning that the restriction must be 'proportionate to the legitimate aim pursued'.[54] In *Sunday Times*,[55] the ECtHR stated that what is necessary is more than what is 'desirable' or 'reasonable' though it needs not be indispensable.[56] Judging from the above, it is clear that the more important the right in the scheme of the ECHR, the more convincing the reasons required to justify a restriction on it.

53. ECHR, Art 15.

54. *Handyside* (N5) [24].

55. *Sunday Times* (N45).

56. Ibid., [59].

Although ECHR jurisprudence has placed particular stress on the role of freedom of expression, including freedom of the press, in a democracy,[57] the ECtHR does, in practice, take a flexible approach. For one, the right to freedom of expression has been given the greatest protection in the case of political speech, and this approach is consistent with the view that freedom of expression is predominately essential for the healthy functioning of a democratic society. In *Bowman v UK*,[58] the ECtHR held that it is important that political expression, especially in the context of an election campaign, be respected, with the result that particularly weighty reasons are required if such speech is to be lawfully restricted.[59] Other kinds of speech, such as the regulation of professional advertising, are less likely to contribute to the democratic process and are thus given less protection.[60] There are good reasons as to why commercial advertising or speech is an area in which the ECtHR has tended to take the view that restrictions are best left to the margin of appreciation afforded to Member States. As Rabinder Singh has noted, in most cases, those who are regulated by restrictions on commercial speech (for instance, tobacco companies) can be expected to lobby politicians and exercise their presumably legal (i.e., not corrupt) influence through the democratic process.[61]

Also in this category are rights which are not qualified in express terms but have been held by the ECtHR to be subject to implied restrictions or limitations. One example is the right to a fair hearing in Article 6(1). In *Osman v UK*,[62] the ECtHR engaged in a proportionality analysis to determine whether an apparently general immunity conferred on the police from actions for negligence was compatible with the right to a fair hearing of such claims. Presumption of innocence in Article 6(2) is another example even though, on the face of it, the whole of Article 6 is entirely unqualified. Nevertheless, the Court has held that it is subject to reasonable restrictions or limitations which maintain the

57. *Lingens* (N45).

58. (1998) 26 EHRR 1.

59. Ibid., [42].

60. *Casado* (N43).

61. Singh (N52) 188.

62. (2000) 29 EHRR 245.

rights of the defence.[63] However, such jurisprudence of implied qualifications is relatively under-developed.[64]

6.2.5.3 Interference Based on Another Interest Outweighing the Right in Question

This last category of rights includes those where interference is permitted because the balance between the interests and right is skewed to the former. In other words, these are rights which may be qualified but where the test of necessity is not applied. A typical example is the right to property, or its relative concept (i.e., peaceful enjoyment of possessions) as put in Article 1 of Protocol 1. This Article does not require either the deprivation of property or control of its use to be 'necessary in a democratic society'. It uses the more flexible phrase 'in the public interest' and 'in accordance with the general interest'. The ECtHR has made it clear that the question of whether there is a public interest or purpose for which property should be taken or regulated is one for the national authorities, and that it will only interfere if that judgment is manifestly devoid of reasonable foundation.[65] Even though the proportionality enquiry is not wholly inapplicable in property-right adjudication, the ECtHR has stressed that it gives a wide margin of appreciation to the Member States in this context.[66]

Moreover, the proportionality principle has also been introduced into the non-discrimination rule in Article 14 so that, for its prohibition of discrimination to be infringed, there must be 'no reasonable relationship of proportionality between the means employed and the aim sought to be pursued'.[67] It has also been relied upon when the ECtHR was interpreting the requirement in Article 1 (i.e., derogation in time of emergency) that measures taken in a public emergency in derogation of the ECHR must be 'strictly required by the exigencies

63. *Salabiaku v France* (1991) 13 EHRR 379.

64. Singh (N52) 189.

65. *James v UK* (1986) 8 EHRR 123.

66. Singh (N52) 190.

67. *Belgian Linguistic's case (No. 2)* (1968) 1 EHRR 252, [34].

of the situation'.[68] Finally, proportionality is also important when the ECtHR is interpreting the positive obligations that the parties have under Article 8.[69]

Overall, I argue that the legal principles or standards applied by both the CJEU and the ECtHR are essentially the same,[70] including the principle of proportionality and the doctrine of margin of appreciation.[71] In *Wachauf v Germany*,[72] the CJEU stated that what it had so far understood was that domestic courts must not only give effect to the general principles of EU law, but also those derived from the ECHR. Although development of ECtHR jurisprudence has been far-reaching in some areas (e.g., what can constitute civil rights for the purposes of Article 6 of the ECHR [73]), in others, developments have notoriously been more conservative (e.g., the somewhat inconsistent approach to the rights of transsexuals [74]). Despite this, it is recognised that the ECtHR has endeavoured both to maximise the strength of existing guarantees and to ensure that they benefit all sections of society.[75]

6.3 The Theoretical Basis of Positive Rights or Obligations in the European Convention on Human Rights

Originally, the ECHR was mainly concerned with setting limits on the ability of the Member States to interfere with individual rights. Therefore, the ECHR

68. *Lawless v Ireland* (1961) 1 EHRR 15.

69. *Rees v UK* (1986) 9 EHRR 56.

70. This view is also concurred on by the Court of Final Appeal of the Hong Kong Special Administrative Region (HKSAR) in *Leung Kwok Hung v HKSAR* (2005) 8 HKCFAR 229, [34], [2005] 3 HKLRD 164, 185. The CFA adopted the *Siracusa Principles on the Limitation and Derogation Provisions in the ICCPR* agreed to in 1984, stating that 'while there is no single model of a democratic society, a society which recognises and respects the human rights set forth in the [UN] Charter and the [UDHR 1948] may be viewed as meeting the definition of a democratic society. This view is consistent with that of the [ECtHR] that the hallmarks of a democratic society include pluralism, tolerance and broadmindedness'. *Handyside* (N5) [49]; *Smith and Grady v UK* (1999) 29 EHRR 493, [87]; *Lingens* (N45) 418.

71. *Elliniki Radiophonia Tileorassi AE* (N15) [41]; *Opinion 2/94 on Accession by the Community to the ECHR* [1996] ECR I-1759 (N15), [33]; *Kremzow* (N15), [14].

72. Case 5/88 [1989] ECR 2609.

73. *Ringeisen v Austria* (1979–1980) 1 EHRR 455.

74. *Rees* (N69); *Cossey* (N20); *B v France* (1993) 16 EHRR 1; *X, Y and Z v UK* (1997) 24 EHRR 143; *Sheffield and Horsham v UK* (1999) 27 EHRR 163.

75. Colin Harvey and Stephen Livingstone, 'Protecting the Marginalised: The Role of the European Convention on Human Rights' (2000) 51 *NILQ* 445; Paul Mahoney, 'Judicial Activism and Judicial Self-Restraint in the European Court of Human Rights: Two Sides of the Same Coin?' (1990) 11 *HRLJ* 57.

is intrinsically designed to spell out various rights and then set out the circumstances in which those rights can be restricted. Against this background, the ECHR defines the negative obligations of the Member States (i.e., the obligations to refrain from certain actions).

As some positive duties have been interpreted to be implicit in civil and political rights,[76] the ECtHR, when adjudicating on civil and political rights disputes, has been developing, at an expanding pace, positive obligations under the ECHR. These positive obligations require many different forms of action by the Member States to protect the rights of individuals. They take numerous forms, the examples of which range from effectively investigating killings and protecting peaceful demonstrators from violent attacks by their opponents to requiring the Member States to provide fair trials to determine civil and criminal proceedings within a reasonable time and providing free legal assistance in criminal cases. These positive obligations also include the right to education under Article 2 of Protocol 1 and the duty to hold elections under Article 3 of Protocol 1, among others.

Nevertheless, some positive obligations arise more discreetly. Their underlying rationale is that a purely negative approach to the protection of human rights cannot guarantee their effective protection, which is incompatible with the associated principle of proportionality (i.e., the principle of effectiveness), and that the acts of private individuals, in particular, corporations can threaten human rights just as much as the acts of those Member States.[77] All in all, an ECHR provision, whether it is interpreted as negative or positive, requires the provision of resources.

According to Keir Starmer, now the leader of the UK Labour Party, the purpose of the ECHR is not only to safeguard individual freedom from the over-mighty government, but it also acts to safeguard human dignity. It was born out of the ruthless oppression and annihilation of minorities and dissidents by the Nazis during the Second World War.[78] During that period, many leading

76. As discussed in Chapter Four of this book.

77. Keir Starmer, 'Positive Obligations under the Convention' in Jowell and Cooper (N52) 139.

78. Ibid., 144–145.

politicians in continental Europe were put in prison by Nazi authorities.[79] Reflecting on this, Henry Schermers has opined that Britain can learn from Europe, saying that the absence of such experience in the UK may be one of the primary reasons why Britain's treatment of prisoners has led to so many cases being held before the European Commission and the ECtHR.[80] *Ireland v UK*,[81] which concerned prisons in Northern Ireland where suspected members of the Irish Republican Army (IRA) were arrested and detained, is one such case. The case highlighted the interrogation practices applied to the arrested members, the so-called 'five techniques' — wall-standing, hooding, subjection to noise, deprivation of sleep, and deprivation of food and drink. The ECtHR held that these techniques (particularly when being applied in combination, with premeditation, and for hours at a time) caused intense physical and mental suffering as well as acute psychiatric disturbances, so they amounted to inhuman and degrading treatment that violated Article 3 of the ECHR.

As Starmer has noted, alongside the UDHR 1948, the adoption of the ECHR began a new era in human rights protection. The ideas that the majority could be trusted to protect minority rights and that private individuals did not need state protection from the acts of other private individuals no longer held sway. The emphasis in the ECHR is therefore on the 'effective' protection of human rights, not the entrenchment of 'theoretical' or 'illusory' rights.[82] Starmer has furthered that there are three inter-related principles justifying these positive obligations: first, the requirement under Article 1 (i.e., obligation to respect human rights) that Member States should secure ECHR rights to all persons within their jurisdiction; second, the principle that ECHR rights must be practical and effective; and, finally, the principle, derived from Article 13 (i.e., right to an effective remedy), that effective domestic remedies should be provided for arguable breaches of the ECHR.[83] Thus, the notion of effectiveness runs like a thread through ECHR jurisprudence. It was the basis for the ECtHR's

79. Henry Schermers, 'The European Community and the European Convention on Human Rights: Their Effect on National Law' in B.S. Markesinis (ed), *The Gradual Convergence: Foreign Ideas, Foreign Influences and English Law* (Clarendon Press 1994) 174.

80. Ibid.

81. (1978) 2 EHRR 25.

82. Starmer (N77) 145.

83. Keir Starmer, *European Human Rights Law: The Human Rights Act 1998 and the European Convention on Human Rights* (Legal Action Group 1999) Ch. 5.

judgments in *Airey v Ireland*,[84] *X and Y v Netherlands*,[85] *Soering*,[86] and *Aydin v Turkey*,[87] among others. It is also the springboard for the ECtHR's development of an extended notion of state liability under the ECHR and its wide definition of a 'victim', and provides the theoretical basis for the imposition of positive obligations on Member States under the ECHR.

Although the ECtHR does not provide an authoritative definition of positive obligations, Judge Martens defined them as rights 'requiring member states to ... take action'.[88] This simple definition captures the essence of the varied obligations that will be scrutinised below as it emphasises that their key characteristic is the duty upon the Member States to undertake specific affirmative tasks, the examples of which consist of effectively investigating a killing,[89] protecting vulnerable persons from serious ill-treatment inflicted by others,[90] providing arrested persons with a prompt explanation of the reasons for their arrests,[91] providing free legal assistance for impecunious criminal defendants,[92] providing legal recognition of the new gender acquired by transsexuals who have successfully completed gender re-assignment treatment,[93] and deploying reasonable police resources to protect media organisations from unlawful violence directed at curbing the legitimate exercise of free expression.[94] It is also important to ascertain the precise contents of these key positive obligations, both express and implied. For instance, the forms of action required of the Member States (such as enacting new criminal offences,[95] re-organising their judicial systems to ensure their capacity to determine cases

84. (1979) 2 EHRR 305.
85. (1985) 8 EHRR 235.
86. *Soering* (N28).
87. (1997) 25 EHRR 251.
88. Dissenting Opinion of Judge Martens in *Gul v Switzerland* (1996) 22 EHRR 93.
89. *Kelly v UK* [2001] ECHR 328.
90. *Z v UK* (2001) 34 EHRR 97.
91. *Fox, Campbell and Hartley v UK* (1991) 13 EHRR 157.
92. *Artico v Italy* (1981) 3 EHRR 1.
93. *Goodwin* (N38).
94. *Ozgur Gundem v Turkey* (2001) 31 EHRR 49.
95. *X and Y* (N85).

within a reasonable timeframe,[96] and according different treatment depending on the individual's distinct circumstances [97]) require explanation.

6.4 The Relationship between Positive and Negative Rights or Obligations

The boundaries between a Member State's positive and negative obligations unfortunately do not lend themselves to precise definition. In many situations, the applicable principles are the same. In *Powell and Rayner v UK*,[98] the ECtHR observed:

> In both contexts, regard must be had to the fair balance that has to be struck between the competing interests of the individual and of the community as a whole; and in both contexts, the State enjoys a certain margin of appreciation in determining the steps to be taken to ensure compliance with the [ECHR]. Furthermore, even in relation to the positive obligations flowing from the first paragraph of Article 8, in striking the required balance, the aims mentioned in the second paragraph may be of a certain relevance.[99]

In this case, the applicants, who lived near Heathrow Airport, complained that the excessive noise from the airport breached their rights under Article 8 to respect for their private life and home. The government argued that the complaint disclosed no direct 'interference by a public authority' because the airport in question and the aircrafts using it were not owned, controlled, or operated by the government or any agency of it. However, the ECtHR disagreed, saying:

> Whether the present case be analysed in terms of a positive duty on the State to take reasonable and appropriate measures to secure the applicants' rights under paragraph (1) of Article 8 or in terms of an 'interference by a public

96. *Buchholz v Germany* (1981) 3 EHRR 597.
97. *Thlimmenos v Greece* (2000) 31 EHRR 15.
98. (1990) 12 EHRR 355.
99. Ibid., [41].

> authority' to be justified in accordance with paragraph (2), the applicable principles are broadly similar.[100]

Therefore, state responsibility was engaged in this case, but based on the facts, the ECtHR found no breach of Article 8.

A similar approach was taken in *López Ostra v Spain*,[101] where the ECtHR found that state responsibility was engaged where the local authority had failed to take adequate steps to curtail pollution emitted from a privately run waste-treatment plant on the basis that '[a]lthough the local authority had not been directly responsible for the plant, it [gave] permission for it to be built and subsidised its construction'.[102] The Court when on to say that 'in any event, under Article 8, the local authority was under a positive obligation to take such measures as were necessary for the protection of the applicants' private and family life'.[103] On the facts, however, the ECtHR found that the measures taken by the local authority were adequate.

6.5 Jurisprudence of Positive Rights or Obligations by the European Court of Human Rights

Although the ECtHR expressly declined to develop any 'general theory' for positive obligations in *Plattform "Arzte fur ds Leben" v Austria*,[104] there is no longer any question of whether the ECHR imposes obligations on the Member States. Rather, what remains to be clarified is when and to what extent these obligations will be imposed. In connection to this, J.G. Merrills has observed that there are several 'exceptional' Articles of the ECHR which require Member States 'to do something'.[105] This is true, for instance, for Article 6(3) which

100. Ibid.
101. (1995) 20 EHRR 277.
102. Ibid., [52].
103. Ibid., [55].
104. (1988) 13 EHRR 204.
105. J.G. Merrills, *The Development of International Law by the European Court of Human Rights* (MUP 1993).

obliges Member States to provide free legal assistance to defendants in certain criminal cases. Merrills explains:

> [T]he [ECHR] is mainly concerned not with what a State must do, but with what it must not do; that is, with its obligation to refrain from interfering with the individual's rights. Nevertheless, utilising the principle of effectiveness, the Court has held that even in respect of provisions which do not expressly create a positive obligation, there may sometimes be a duty to act in a particular way.[106]

Article 8 (i.e., right to respect for private and family life) is an example, in that the jurisprudence regarding this right disclosed that the ECtHR had placed the Member States under positive obligations, including that they legally recognise the family relationship between a mother and her illegitimate child.[107] He also uses the principle of effectiveness as the crucial jurisprudential tool to develop positive obligations under the ECHR. Such principle has been defined by Merrills as 'a means of giving the provisions of a treat the fullest weight and effect consistent with the language used and with the rest of the text and in such a way that every part of it can be given meaning'.[108] In this regard, Merrills believes that

> [e]very government is aware that by subscribing to the [ECHR], it places itself in a position in which domestic laws and practices may have to be modified to avoid impinging on the various liberties the [ECHR] was brought into being to protect. What a government may not bargain for is to find itself put to considerable trouble and expense as a result of an obligation to advance particular social or economic policies which it may not wholly support. While this is not a conclusive objection to the Court's employing the principle of effectiveness to develop the law and identify positive obligations in the [ECHR], it unquestionably argues for caution in so doing.[109]

106. Ibid., 103.

107. *Marckx v Belgium* (1979) 2 EHRR 330.

108. Merrills (N105) 98.

109. Ibid., 106.

6.6 The Scope of Positive Rights or Obligations under the European Convention on Human Rights

The ECHR has emphasised that the way in which the Member States should go about protecting individuals from actions of other individuals is largely a matter for their discretion because 'regard must be had to the fair balance that has to be struck between the competing interests of the individual and of the community as a whole'.[110] In this connection, Starmer has identified five broad categories of positive duties placed upon Member States by the provisions of the ECHR [111] These are duties that require Member States to:

(1) create a national legal framework which provides effective protection for ECHR provisions;[112]

(2) prevent breaches of the ECHR;[113]

(3) provide information and advice relevant to breaches of the ECHR;[114]

(4) respond to breaches of the ECHR (e.g., by conducting an investigation);[115] and

(5) provide resources to individuals to prevent breaches of their ECHR-granted rights.[116]

In his subsequent publication, Starmer further observes that, in many respects, positive obligations are the hallmark of the ECHR.[117]

6.6.1 The Duty to Have a Legal Framework to Protect Rights

In many aspects, the duty to put in place a legal framework providing effective protection for ECHR provisions represents the minimum obligation of Member

110. *Powell and Rayner* (N98).

111. Starmer (N83) Ch. 5.

112. *X and Y* (N85).

113. *Osman* (N62); *Marckx* (N107); *Plattform "Arzte fur das Leben"* (N104).

114. *Guerra v Italy* (1998) 26 EHRR 357.

115. *Aydin* (N87).

116. *Airey* (N84).

117. Starmer (N77) 159.

States. Although the ECHR does not require its terms to be incorporated directly into domestic law, it does require a framework of effective remedies. Against this background, Member States are under positive duties to protect persons from violations of their ECHR-granted rights from both private individuals and public officials. As Henry Steiner and Philip Alston have noted:

> To understand the significance and implications of the rights stated in the ICCPR, ... and other human rights treaties, it is useful to examine the related duties/obligations of states — even though [the ECHR] rarely talks of duties. Attention to such duties both clarifies the significance of the related rights and thus helps to sort out ideas, and points to strategies of change. The effort, then, is to decompose a right into its related state duties, and thereby gain a clearer notion of the content or proposed content of the right itself.[118]

This assertion is supported by Henry Shue, whose approach concerning 'duty to avoid', 'duty to protect', and 'duty to aid' [119] has been adopted by the UN Committee on Economic, Social, and Cultural Rights (UNESCR Committee). According to Shue, 'taking rights seriously means taking duties seriously'.[120]

In general, the ECtHR and the Commission have been content to give a great margin of appreciation, leaving it to the Member States to determine how best to set up the required legal framework. In some cases against the UK, for instance, the Commission has accepted that the availability of civil remedies for defamation or malicious prosecution can be sufficient to protect privacy rights under Article 8.[121] Nevertheless, there have been some situations where the breach of the ECHR was so serious that the ECtHR insisted that criminal law sanctions be put in place. In *X and Y*,[122] the perpetrator of a sexual assault on the second applicant was not prosecuted because, under Dutch law, the fact

118. Henry Steiner and Philip Alston, *International Human Rights in Context: Law, Politics, Morals* (2nd edn, OUP 2000) 180–181.

119. Henry Shue, *Basic Rights: Subsistence, Affluence and US Foreign Policy* (2nd edn, PUP 1996). Also discussed in Chapter Four of this book.

120. Ibid., 167.

121. *Winer v UK* (1986) 48 DR 154; *Stewart-Brady v UK* (1997) 24 EHRR CD 38.

122. *X and Y* (N85).

that the victim was a sixteen-year-old girl with a mental disorder prevented her from initiating a criminal 'complaint'. The government argued that since it had been possible to bring civil proceedings for compensation, its obligations under Article 8 were fulfilled. However, the ECtHR disagreed, saying that

> the prosecution afforded by the civil law in the case of wrongdoing of the kind inflicted on Miss Y is insufficient. This is a case where fundamental values and essential aspects of private life are at stake. Effective deterrence is indispensable in this area and it can be achieved only by criminal-law provisions; indeed, it is by such provisions that the matter is normally regulated.[123]

Since Dutch law had been defective in this respect, state responsibility was engaged.

Moreover, in *Stubbing v UK*,[124] the applicants even tried to extend the reach of the decision in *X and Y* by arguing that the widespread problem of child sexual abuse, which was only beginning to be properly understood at that time, demanded new measures for the protection of minors. Their complaints were that the House of Lords' interpretation of the UK Limitation Act 1980 in *Stubbing v Webb*[125] restricted the scope for extending the limitation period in civil proceedings based on child sexual abuse and effectively deprived them of a remedy against their abusers. This, they argued, breached Article 8 (i.e., right to respect for private and family life) of the ECHR. The ECtHR began its analysis by reiterating that

> [s]exual abuse is unquestionably an abhorrent type of wrongdoing, with debilitating effects on its victims. Children and other vulnerable individuals are entitled to State protection, in the form of effective deterrence, from such grave types of interference with essential aspects of their private lives.[126]

123. Ibid., [27].

124. (1996) 23 EHRR 213.

125. [1993] AC 498.

126. Ibid., [64].

However, in its view:

> In the instant case ... such protection was afforded. The abuse of which the applicants complained is regarded most seriously by the English criminal law and subject to severe maximum penalties. Provided sufficient evidence could be secured, a criminal prosecution could have been brought ... In principle, civil remedies are also available provided that [they] are brought within the statutory time-limit ... Article 8 does not necessarily require that States fulfil their positive obligation to secure respect for private life by the provision of unlimited civil remedies in circumstances where criminal law sanctions are in operation.[127]

Protection, therefore, has its own associated costs. As Singh once said:

> To be effective, even civil and political rights have to be protected — and protection has a price. The right of access to courts would be meaningless if there were no courts, or if they were not properly financed, or if only a few people could get to them owing to lack of money.[128]

Singh uses *Airey* [129] as a typical example of the ECtHR imposing a 'positive duty' upon Member States (i.e., to provide civil legal aid for complex cases) to demonstrate how they may be obliged to protect fundamental rights. In this case, the issue tabled before the ECtHR was whether the availability of legal aid in civil proceedings was relevant to determining whether the Member State was in breach of its obligations to observe the right to a fair trial under Article 6 of the ECHR. Mrs Airey's desire was to go to court to obtain a decree of judicial separation from her husband, a notoriously violent alcoholic. She had consulted several solicitors, but found no one willing to act on her behalf as she did not have the means to pay and no legal aid was available for civil matters. Although the ECtHR did not go so far as to find that legal aid should be available for all civil proceedings, it did find that in view of the complexity of the case, the absence of legal representation may have prejudiced Mrs Airey's interests.

127. Ibid.

128. Rabinder Singh, *The Future of Human Rights in the United Kingdom* (Hart Publishing 2001) 54.

129. *Airey* (N84).

Proceeding on the understanding that 'the ECHR is intended to guarantee not rights that are theoretical or illusory but rights that are practical and effective',[130] the ECtHR moved towards the imposition of positive obligations under which Member States are required to take active measures (e.g., the provision of legal aid) to ensure the protection of rights. Furthermore, the Court added that this right to access to court gives rise to positive state duties to ensure effective access for all. Although the Member State has the freedom to choose the means for realising its duty, sometimes Article 6 may

> compel the state to provide for the assistance of a lawyer when such assistance proves indispensable for effective access to court either because legal representation is rendered compulsory ... or by reason of the complexity of the procedure or of the case.[131]

Thus, the ECtHR recognised that while the ECHR explicitly includes a right to legal aid only in criminal matters, there are times that the right to legal aid in civil matters can be derived from the right to a fair trial. The Court found Ireland in violation of this right even though it had registered a reservation to Article 6, paragraph 3(c) of the ECHR, which protects the right to legal aid in criminal matters.[132]

Similarly, in *Osman*,[133] the ECtHR held that under Article 2 (i.e., the right to life), there is, in certain circumstances, a substantive obligation to protect a person's life. In *McCann v UK*,[134] there is also, in certain circumstances, a procedural obligation to secure an effective investigation of a death.[135] In this regard, Jeremy McBride has stated that

> [t]here can be no question that there is some obligation to help those at risk of death. Furthermore, although there will always be scope for argument about whether such a risk really exists and whether enough is being done to

130. Ibid., [26].
131. Ibid.
132. Ibid.
133. *Osman* (N62).
134. (1996) 21 EHRR 97.
135. Ibid., 161.

> tackle it, the developing case law precludes these issues from being treated lightly. Protection is a key rationale for the State's existence and a remedy for failure to discharge this responsibility can be found in Strasbourg.[136]

However, where the law provides no remedy at all for a breach of the ECHR, the Court's position would be different. In *Young, James, and Webster*,[137] the UK government argued that it was not responsible for the applicants' dismissal from British Rail for non-membership of a trade union. Rather than analysing the extent to which the Member State is responsible for running British Rail, the ECtHR approached the case on the basis that since Article 1 of the ECHR imposed a duty on the Member State to 'secure' rights to everyone within its jurisdiction, stating that 'if a violation of one of those rights and freedoms is the result of non-observance of that obligation in the enactment of domestic legislation, the responsibility of the State for that violation is engaged'.[138] Despite the fact that the immediate cause of the applicants' dismissal was an agreement between British Rail and the railway unions, the ECtHR was of the view that 'it was the domestic law in force at the relevant time that made lawful the treatment of which the applicants complained. The responsibility of the Respondent State for any resultant breach of the [ECHR] is thus engaged'.[139] In effect, the ECtHR extended state responsibility into the field of relations between private individuals as the Member State was responsible for its failure to enact legislation which prevented others from breaching the applicants' rights.

The principle articulated in *Young, James, and Webster* was also applied in *Stedman v UK*.[140] This case concerned an allegation that the applicant had been dismissed by reason of her religious beliefs, which is contrary to Article 9 (i.e., freedom of thought, conscience, and religion) of the ECHR. Adopting the reasoning in *Young, James, and Webster*, the Commission held that it was irrelevant that the dismissal was the act of a purely private company if the dismissal was lawful in domestic law. On the facts, however, it found that

136. Jeremy McBride, 'Protecting Life: A Positive Obligation to Help' (1999) 24 *ELR*, Supplement: Human Rights Survey 43, 54.

137. *Young, James, and Webster* (N37).

138. Ibid., [49].

139. Ibid.

140. (1997) 23 EHRR 168 CD.

the applicant had not been dismissed because of her religious belief. In short, the mentioned ECtHR jurisprudence and the writings of the above scholars reveal that the ECtHR may demand that the Member States take protective action to safeguard a variety of ECHR provisions.

6.6.2 The Duty to Prevent Breaches

In some situations, having a legal framework in force to provide effective protection for human rights may not be enough, so more specific steps must be taken. Although the ECtHR has never defined the circumstances in which such steps are required, its jurisprudence is able to suggest that the duty to prevent breaches of the ECHR arises in at least three situations.

The first situation is when fundamental rights (such as Articles 2 and 3, the right to life and the prohibition on torture and inhuman or degrading treatment or punishment) are at stake and require special protection. After an event has happened, if remedies for the breach prove insufficient, reasonable measures are required to prevent future breaches. The positive duty to protect the right to life under Article 2, for example, requires that reasonable steps be taken by Member States to protect life. This includes a duty to put in place 'effective criminal law provisions to deter the commission of offences against the person backed up by law-enforcement mechanism for the prevention, suppression and sanctioning of breaches of such provisions'.[141] It may also include, in certain circumstances, a positive obligation on the authorities to take preventive operational measures to protect individuals whose lives are at risk from the criminal acts of another individual.[142] In *Osman*,[143] the ECtHR held that such obligations arise where it can be established that

> the authorities knew or ought to have known at the time of the existence of a real and immediate risk to the life of an identified individual or individuals from the criminal acts of a third party and that they failed to take measures

141. Ibid., [115].

142. Ibid.

143. *Osman* (N62).

within the scope of their powers which, judged reasonably, might have been expected to avoid that risk.[144]

In this case, the argument that the police had failed to take adequate steps to prevent a teacher, who was infatuated with the second applicant, from attacking him and killing his father, failed on the facts.

In *Soering*,[145] the ECtHR held that the absolute prohibition on torture and inhuman treatment or punishment would render the UK government responsible for a breach of Article 3 if it extradited the applicant to another country in circumstances where there were substantial grounds for believing that they would be in danger of being subject to inhuman treatment or punishment. The fact that the Member State was not itself responsible for the inhuman treatment or punishment in question was irrelevant.[146] In fact, this principle was well-established in *Altun v Germany*,[147] in which the Commission recognised that this principle applied even when the danger did not emanate from public authorities for whom the receiving State was responsible. It is also established that Member States have positive duties to protect life even when death or serious injury is not intentional. In *X v UK*,[148] for example, the applicant association complained that the vaccination programme organised by the UK government had caused severe damage to some babies and had in some cases resulted in death. In its decision on admissibility, the Commission stated that 'the concept that "everyone's life shall be protected by law" enjoins the State not only to refrain from taking life intentionally but, further, to take appropriate steps to safeguard life'.[149] However, the Commission went on to find that, based on the facts, it could not be said that the State had failed to take adequate and appropriate measures to protect life in this case.

The second situation in which the ECtHR may suggest that the Member State has a duty to prevent breaches of the ECHR occurs when intimate interests (such

144. Ibid., [116].

145. *Soering* (N28).

146. *Chahal v UK* (1996) 23 EHRR 413.

147. (1983) 36 DR 209.

148. (1978) 14 DR 31.

149. Ibid., [2].

as Article 8, the right to family life) are at issue. This has primarily been based on the question of whether the Member State has put in place a legal framework which effectively protects ECHR provisions. In *Marckx v Belgium*,[150] the ECtHR's decision regarding the lack of measures in Belgian law to safeguard the integration of all children, including illegitimate children, into their families, effectively called for legislative reform. Another case worth mentioning here is *Airey*.[151] At issue in this case was not the existence of a satisfactory legal framework for the protection of the ECHR, but rather the applicant's ineligibility to access to it.

The spirit of the principle of effectiveness is also found in *López Ostra*.[152] Based on the fact that 'severe environmental pollution may affect individuals' well-being and prevent them from enjoying their homes in such a way as to affect their private and family life adversely, without, however, seriously endangering their health',[153] the ECtHR held that a positive obligation was imposed on the Member State in question to take appropriate steps to protect the applicants' right to live their lives free from the adverse effects of severe pollution.[154] By opposing the applicants' legal action to close the waste-treatment plant, the Spanish authorities failed in that duty and thus prolonged the applicants' exposure to pollution.

However, a different result happened in *Osman*,[155] where, coupled with their argument under Article 2, the applicants also advanced an argument under Article 8. The core of their complaint was that the police had failed to bring an end to the campaign of harassment, vandalism, and victimisation waged by their teacher against their property. The ECtHR accepted that an obligation on the police to take preventive measures could arise under Article 8, but found that, based on the facts of this case, the police had done all they could reasonably have been expected to do.

150. *Marckx* (N107).

151. *Airey* (N84).

152. *López Ostra* (N101).

153. Ibid., [51].

154. Ibid., [55].

155. *Osman* (N62).

The third situation that may arise in which ECtHR jurisprudence will allow the Court to suggest positive duties to the Member State to prevent ECHR breaches is when rights cannot be effectively protected by the current legal framework in force. The circumstances in which a positive obligation is imposed on the Member State to take action on the basis that provisions of the ECHR cannot be effectively protected by the legal framework in place, are inevitably varied. The basis for the ECtHR's decision in *Plattform "Arzte fur das Leben"* [156] was a recognition that effective protection for the right of peaceful assembly under Article 11 required immediate police action on the streets. In this case, the ECtHR held that the right of freedom of assembly imposes on the state not just the obligation to refrain from banning marches, but also the duty to protect participants in a peaceful demonstration from disruption by a violent counter-demonstration. The Court stated that

> genuine, effective freedom of peaceful assembly cannot be reduced to a mere duty on the part of the state not to interfere ... Article 11 sometimes requires positive measures to be taken, even in the sphere of relations between individuals, if need be.[157]

Hence, legal proceedings after the event were no substitute for the practical exercise of the right in issue, and remedies (such as preventive injunctions) were of limited use without police enforcement.

6.6.3 The Duty to Provide Information and Advice Relevant to a Breach

The ECtHR has also recognised that in many situations, individuals can only protect their ECHR-granted rights if they have access to relevant information. In *Guerra*,[158] the Court took the principle established in *López Ostra* [159] a step further, instituting a positive obligation to provide information to those affected by environmental pollution. In this case, the applicants were living near a chemical factory which had been classified as 'high risk'. However, their

156. *Plattform "Arzte fur das Leben"* (N104).

157. Ibid., [32].

158. *Guerra* (N114).

159. *López Ostra* (N101).

complaint was framed more broadly. They claimed that the Italian authorities had failed to properly respect their right to family life and home under Article 8 by failing to provide them with information under Article 10 (i.e., the right to freedom of expression and information) about the risks of living near the factory and how to proceed in the event of an accident.

Although the Commission had proceeded on the basis that the applicants had a right to the information they sought under Article 10, the ECtHR rejected this, saying that Article 10 'basically prohibits a government from restricting a person from receiving information that others wish or may be willing to impart to him'.[160] Nevertheless, the ECtHR found a breach of Article 8 on the basis that the state authorities, while aware of essential information about the dangers inherent in the running of the factory, delayed passing that information to the applicants for several years, preventing them from assessing the risks they and their families ran by continuing to live in the vicinity of the factory.

Similarly, in *LCB v UK*,[161] the applicant, the daughter of a man who had been present during the nuclear tests at Christmas Island in the late 1950s when he was serving in the UK Royal Air Force (RAF), complained that the state authorities had failed to advise her parents to monitor her health prior to her diagnosis with leukaemia. The ECtHR held that

> the State could only have been required of its own motion to take these steps in relation to the applicant if it had appeared likely at that time that any such exposure of her father to radiation might have engendered a real risk to her health.[162]

On its analysis of the facts known at the time, the Court concluded that during the material time, the state authorities could not reasonably establish any link between the exposure of the applicant's father to radiation and the likelihood that his children might develop leukaemia.

160. *Guerra* (N114) [53].
161. (1998) 27 EHRR 212.
162. Ibid., [38].

However, the position was different in *McGinley and Egan v UK*.[163] The applicants, having been exposed to radiation in the same tests, claimed that they should have been provided with information sufficient to make them assess the possible consequences of the tests for their health. The ECtHR held that Article 8 was applicable here

> given the fact that exposure to high levels of radiation is known to have hidden, but serious and long-lasting, effects on health, it is not unnatural that the applicants' uncertainty as to whether or not they had been put at risk in this way caused them substantial anxiety and distress ... since the [radiation level records] contained information which might have assisted the applicants in assessing radiation levels in the areas in which they were stationed during the tests, and might indeed have served to reassure them in this respect, they had an interest under Article 8 in obtaining access to them.[164]

In these circumstances, the ECtHR was of the view that a positive obligation under Article 8 arose. As a matter of principle, the Court also stated:

> Where a Government engages in hazardous activities, such as those in issue in the present case, which might have hidden adverse consequences on the health of those involved in such activities, respect for private and family life under Article 8 requires that an effective and accessible procedure be established which enables persons to seek all relevant and appropriate information.[165]

On the facts, however, the Court found no breach of this positive obligation as the applicants could have sought access to the relevant documents in proceedings before the Pension Appeal Tribunal. However, they failed to do so.

Nevertheless, to establish the scope of the duty to provide information is, to a certain extent, difficult if not impossible. In *Gaskin v UK*,[166] the applicant, who had been taken into care when his mother died, wished to obtain details of the foster homes in which he had been brought up, but was refused access

163. (1998) 27 EHRR 1.

164. Ibid., [99].

165. Ibid., [101].

166. (1989) 12 EHRR 36.

to some of the local authority's records on the grounds that the information in question was private and confidential. Having determined that this was a case in which respect for the applicant's private and family life imposed a positive obligation, the ECtHR was divided as to its scope. A minority believed that the local authority had gone as far as it reasonably could by writing to each contributor to the case file asking for their permission to release the relevant part of the record, whereas the majority acknowledged that the system which had made access dependent on the contributors' consent was not objectionable in principle, but ruled that the interests of those in the applicant's position could only be secured if there was an independent authority to decide on the issue of access when a contributor was not available or refused consent improperly.

6.6.4 The Duty to Respond to Breaches

Where fundamental rights have been in issue, such as those under Articles 2 and 3 (i.e., the right to life and the prohibition on torture and inhuman or degrading treatment or punishment), the ECtHR does impose an obligation on Member States to respond diligently to any breaches. The criteria for imposing this obligation are that the payment of compensation is insufficient and that an effective and efficient investigation must be carried out and backed up with criminal prosecutions where appropriate, among other things. This duty is particularly strict when police officers or other public officials may be responsible for the breach. Its scope was examined by the ECtHR in *Aydin*.[167] The applicant in this case complained that during her detention by the security forces in Turkey, she had been raped and subjected to other forms of ill treatment amounting to torture under Article 3 of the ECHR. The ECtHR held that given the fundamental importance of the prohibition of torture and the especially vulnerable position of torture victims, Article 13 (i.e., the right to an effective remedy) imposes, without prejudice to any other remedy available under the domestic system, an obligation on the Member States to carry out a thorough and effective investigation of incidents of torture. Accordingly, the Court formulated the principle that when an individual had an arguable claim that they had been tortured by agents of the state, an 'effective remedy' entailed

167. *Aydin* (N87).

a thorough and effective investigation capable of leading to the identification and punishment of those responsible.[168] It was also ruled that this investigation should include access for the complainant to the investigatory procedure, coupled with the payment of compensation where appropriate. Considering this principle, the Court found a breach of the ECHR in this case, as the Turkish authorities had carried out an incomplete enquiry to decide the veracity of the applicant's complaint.

6.6.5 The Duty to Provide Resources to Individuals whose Rights are at Stake

As discussed above, some Articles of the ECHR, by their very nature, impose a duty on the Member States to provide resources such as free legal assistance. In *Airey*,[169] this principle was extended on the basis that the right in issue (i.e., family life in this case) could not be effectively protected without the provision of resources (i.e., legal aid in divorce proceedings) by the Member State. Thus, the principle is one of general applications.

On various occasions, applicants did argue that the right to family life under Article 8 of the ECHR had imposed a positive obligation on the Member States to provide them with financial assistance to enable one of the parents to stay at home and take care of their children. So far, the Commission has rejected such arguments. In *Anderson and Kullman v Sweden*,[170] the Commission rejected a complaint that the decision of Swedish social services to terminate family allowance payments and replace them with access to free crèche so as to enable the second applicant to work breached Article 8. In *A P v Austria*,[171] the Commission also rejected a complaint that failure to make long-term

168. The ECtHR's view on this also affects jurisdictions that consider common law decisions in their own rulings. Thus, as Hong Kong is authorised under Article 84 of the Basic Law to consider ECtHR jurisprudence, I am of the view that this principle should form the basis of a judicial review to ascertain whether the refusal to have an independent investigation into the alleged disproportionate response and misconduct of the Hong Kong police during ongoing protests in the city since June 2019 is compatible with Article 39 of the Basic Law. See Chapter Eight of this book for additional discussion of proportionality in Hong Kong.

169. *Airey* (N84).

170. (1986) 46 DR 251.

171. (1995) 20 EHRR CD 63.

parental leave payments to enable a father to stay at home and look after his children breached Article 8.

There may be some situations in which a local authority comes under a positive obligation under the ECHR — for instance, to provide housing to those within its catchment area. Nevertheless, they are only likely to arise in exceptional circumstances. In *Burton v UK*,[172] the Commission rejected an argument that in failing to provide an individual suffering from cancer with a place where she could live out her days in a caravan according to her Romany gypsy background, a local authority had failed in its obligations under Article 8.

Insofar as the rights to social benefits are concerned, when an entitlement to a particular social benefit exists under domestic law but, for some reason, is not enforced or when an entitlement is lost for contestable reasons, Articles 3, 8, and 14 as well as Article 1 of Protocol 1 of the ECHR (i.e., the prohibition of torture and degrading treatment, the right to respect for private and family life, the prohibition of discrimination, and protection of property, respectively) may be successfully invoked. In this instance, a lack of public funds does not justify such a failure.[173] Where a state leaves some of its citizens devoid of any means or with a benefit in an amount that is manifestly insufficient to lead a life with human dignity, the ECtHR may hold that the state is in violation of Article 3 of the ECHR.[174] Regarding Article 8, the ECtHR's jurisprudence with respect to special provisions, such as those for the disabled, also recognises the existence of positive obligations where there is a direct and immediate link between the measures sought by the applicant and their private family life under Article 8.[175]

In several cases, discrimination (coupled with right to private and family life under Article 8) has also been alleged under Article 14 in terms of the enjoyment of social benefits. In *Mata Estevez v Spain*,[176] for example, the denial of a homosexual partner's right to survivor pension was recognised as falling within the scope of Article 8 since the applicant's emotional and sexual relationship

172. (1996) 22 EHRR CD 134.

173. *Hoogendijk v Netherlands* (2005) 40 EHRR SE 22.

174. *Larioshina v Russia* (App No. 56869/00) ECHR 23 April 2002.

175. *Botta v Italy* (1998) 26 EHRR 241, [412]; *La Parola v Italy* (App No. 39712/98) ECHR 30 November 2000.

176. [2001] ECHR 896.

related to his private life. In this case, Spanish legislation limited the right to survivor pensions to married couples at a time when Spanish law did not yet allow same-sex marriages. The ECtHR held that this legislation did not amount to prohibited discrimination since the difference in treatment was proportionate and justified by a legitimate purpose (i.e., the protection of the traditional family unit based on heterosexual marriage). However, this reasoning was reversed in *Karner v Austria*.[177]

Insofar as Article 1 of Protocol 1 (i.e., protection of property) is concerned, in *Asmundsson v Iceland*,[178] the ECtHR found violation of it, in that a man had been receiving disability pension for 20 years, but due to legislative changes that led to a re-assessment of his capacity to work, he lost it. The Court held that there had been disproportionate interference in the applicant's property right for the reason, *inter alia*, that the vast majority of disability pensioners had continued to receive disability benefits at the same level as previously, whereas a small minority of disability pensioners had had to bear the most drastic measures, namely the total loss of their pension entitlements.[179] The Court held that

> as an individual, the applicant was made to bear an excessive and disproportionate burden which, even having regard to the wide margin of appreciation to be enjoyed by the State in the area of social legislation, cannot be justified by the legitimate community interests relied on by the authorities. It would have been otherwise had the applicant been obliged to endure a reasonable and commensurate reduction rather than the total deprivation of his entitlements.[180]

As David Feldman once said, 'most of the rights under the [ECHR] are negative rights, or rights to freedom from interference. However, some rights impose obligations on the state to take positive action to protect people'.[181] Some of these positive obligations are imposed expressly by the language

177. (2003) 38 EHRR 528.

178. (App No. 60669/00) ECHR 12 October 2004.

179. Ibid., [43].

180. Ibid., [45].

181. David Feldman, *Civil Liberties and Human Rights in England and Wales* (2nd edn, OUP 2002) 53.

of the ECHR,[182] but 'a more extensive and less clearly defined set of positive obligations' [183] has been implied by the ECtHR. In Feldman's assessment, the impetus behind the development of implied obligations has been 'the dynamic interpretation of the [ECHR] in the light of changing social and moral assumptions'.[184] This has resulted in there being 'more extensive obligations on states than are immediately obvious from a superficial perusal of the text'.[185]

6.7 Concluding Remarks

Examination of the ECtHR's jurisprudence has revealed that first and foremost, those legal principles or standards applied both by the CJEU and by the ECtHR are essentially the same. This includes the principle of proportionality, together with the principle of effectiveness (which gives rise to positive rights and duties with regard to the civil and political rights established by the ECHR that in turn help realise socio-economic rights), and the doctrine of margin of appreciation. Although various methodologies have been developed under the proportionality analysis (as revealed in the case law of the CJEU and of the ECtHR), it ultimately provides a common analytical framework, the significance of which is not in its omnipotence, but in how it affects the court's conclusions in moral and political cases.

In view of each particular policy objective, the nature of the competing interests involved, the competences of the courts and of administrative authorities, the legality required by the CJEU and the ECtHR varies. The evaluative findings regarding the implementation of policy objectives will also depend on these factors. Therefore, under the margin of appreciation doctrine, a national judge of the Member State is said to be in a better position, and thus better equipped, than an international judge to evaluate pressing social needs, particularly when these needs concern public policy, public health, national security, or national morality. Among these spheres, morals vary over time and from place to place, leading to the rapid and far reaching evolution

182. ECHR, Art 6(1) (the obligation to provide fair trials).

183. Feldman (N181) 53.

184. Ibid., 55.

185. Ibid.

of opinions on each subject. Because of their direct and continuous contact with the vital forces of their countries, state authorities (i.e., the legislature, the executive, and the judiciary) are, in principle, in a better position than international judges to give an opinion on the exact content of these requirements as well as on their 'necessity'.[186]

By treating socio-economic rights as essential corollaries of civil and political rights (i.e., the 'integrated approach') and protecting them through the expansive application of equality or non-discrimination provisions, the ECtHR has found that some positive duties are implicit in those civil and political rights. These positive obligations require many different forms of action by the Member States to protect the rights granted by the ECHR to individuals. In this regard, the purpose of the ECHR is not only to safeguard and individual's freedoms from the over-mighty government, but to safeguard human dignity as well. While the ECHR was originally established for this purpose shortly after wartime, it has certainly become increasingly important during peace as well.

The debate over the proportionality principle continues between Continental countries and the European Community, and common law jurisdictions, such as Britain and Hong Kong. This debate largely stems from the underlying approaches to administrative law. It is to these styles of thought that reference is made to the jurisprudence of the CJEU and of the ECtHR concerning the use of the principle of proportionality (and other principles and effective remedies) to determine to what extent the courts should intervene with the substances of decisions taken by other branches of government, and how they can balance the demands of judicial supervision and judicial restraints or deference.

186. *Handyside* (N5) [48].

7

Integration of Proportionality in Britain

7.1 Introduction

In Britain, the principle of proportionality has been applied in respect of directly effective European Union (EU) law via the European Communities Act 1972 (ECA 1972) (as at 31 January 2020, the day of Brexit) and of the European Convention on Human Right (ECHR) via the Human Rights Act 1998 (HRA 1998). Nevertheless, where a case does not involve EU law or any fundamental rights, the traditional test of *Wednesbury* unreasonableness or *GCHQ* irrationality prevails.[1] However, there have been two different forms of pressure for the development of proportionality as an independent ground of judicial review in English law. External pressure has resulted from the increasing importance of EU law and of the ECHR which have brought the principle to judges' attention, whereas internal pressure has been exerted by members of the judiciary themselves [2] as well as academics [3] who are pro-active in introducing this new principle into English law.

---

1. *R v Secretary of State for the Home Department, ex p Brind* [1991] 696 (HL), [1991] 2 WLR 588; *R (British Civilian Internees — Far East Region) v Secretary for Defence* [2003] EWCA Civ 473, [2003] QB 1397; *Pham v Secretary of State for the Home Department* [2015] UKSC 19, [2015] 1 WLR 1591, [2015] 3 All ER 1015; *R (Keyu) v Secretary of State for Foreign and Commonwealth Affairs* [2015] UKSC 69, [2015] 3 WLR 1665, [2016] AC1355.
2. *Stoke-on-Trent CC v B & Q* [1984] AC 754; *Kennedy v The Charity Commission* [2014] UKSC 20, [2014] 2 WLR 808; *R (Youssef) v Secretary of State for Foreign and Commonwealth Affairs* [2016] UKSC 3. See also Robert Thomas, *Legitimate Expectations and Proportionality in Administrative Law* (Hart Publishing 2000) 25.
3. Jeffrey Jowell and Anthony Lester, 'Beyond *Wednesbury*: Substantive Principles of Administrative Law' (1987) *PL* 368; Jeffrey Jowell and Anthony Lester 'Proportionality: Neither Novel nor Dangerous' in Jeffrey Jowell and Dawn Oliver (eds), *New Directions in Judicial Review* (Stevens & Sons 1988) 51–72; T.R.S. Allan, *Law, Liberty, and Justice: The Foundations of British Constitutionalism* (Clarendon Press 1993); Paul Craig, 'Unreasonableness and Proportionality in UK Law' in Evelyn Ellis (ed), *The Principle of Proportionality in the Laws of Europe* (Hart Publishing 1999) 99–102, 105; Jeffrey Jowell, 'Beyond the Rule of Law: Towards Constitutional Judicial Review' (2000) *PL* 671.

As consistency of law is one of the elements under the rule of law that is, if being fulfilled, capable of guiding human behaviour,[4] there is no justification for not applying the proportionality principle to other types of judicial review cases. This, of course, rests on the presumption that Parliament confers a power to the executive on the basis that the executive should not exceed what is necessary to attain statutory objectives when exercising this power.[5] The more important the statutory objectives are, the graver the restrictions on the exercise of discretionary power should be.[6]

This chapter examines the extent to which the principle of proportionality has been integrated into, and re-formulated in, the United Kingdom (UK). As proportionality has been applied in respect of directly effective EU law via the ECA 1972 (as at 31 January 2020, the day of Brexit) and of the ECHR via the HRA 1998 in the UK, particular attention will be paid to these two regimes. European jurisprudence prefers to treat socio-economic rights as essential corollaries of civil and political rights. Thus, it protects them with the use of the 'integrated approach' and through the expansive application of equality or non-discrimination provisions. This chapter also explores the imposition of positive duties on state authorities to realise socio-economic rights and how the principle has contributed to the realisation of these rights.

7.2. European Union Proportionality: Its Integration into the United Kingdom

Proportionality began to be recognised in English law in the 1970s shortly after Britain became a Member State of the then European Economic Community (EEC, now the EU). Under EU law, the proportionality principle serves as one of the general principles[7] for assessing the legality of obstructing measures.

4. Peter Wesley-Smith, *An Introduction to the Hong Kong Legal System* (2nd edn, OUP 1995) 15.

5. Tom Bingham, *The Rule of Law* (Penguin 2010) 60–65.

6. Johannes Chan, 'Administrative Law, Politics and Governance: The Hong Kong Experience' in Tom Ginsburg and Albert Chen (eds), *Administrative Law and Governance in Asia* (Routledge 2009) 159.

7. Gráinne de Búrca, 'The Principle of Proportionality and its Application in EC Law' (1993) 13 *YEL* 105, 114–115.

Borrowed from Germany, the Court of Justice of European Union (CJEU) has applied the proportionality principle with varying degrees of strictness.[8] Under EU law, the development of case law, together with academic commentary, has carved out a standardised scrutiny process of proportionality analysis which comprises three elements or sub-principles: (1) legitimacy; (2) suitability; and (3) necessity (i.e., the *Fedesa* Three-Stage test).[9] Also determinative of judicial control standards are variables such as the nature of the area concerned, the value of the purpose to be sought, the intensity of an interference, and the nature of the fundamental rights affected.[10]

7.2.1 Direct Effect under the European Communities Act 1972

Since its introduction, proportionality has come to be applied as one of the general principles of administrative law in the field of the directly effective EU law via the ECA 1972.[11] Under the ECA 1972 regime, the principle may be invoked to challenge the lawfulness of any derogation from EU individual rights as originally enshrined in the European Community (EC) Treaty [12] by official action in Britain.

The *Diane Blood* case [13] is a typical example of an executive decision being reviewed under the proportionality principle. In this case, the applicant succeeded in challenging the authority's refusal to authorise the export of the

8. Lennie Hoffmann, 'The Influence of the European Principle of Proportionality upon UK Law' in Ellis (N3) 107.

9. *R v Ministry of Agriculture, Fisheries and Food, ex p Fedesa* (Case C-331/88) [1990] ECR I-4023. See also Georg Nolte, 'General Principles of German and European Administrative Law' (1994) 57 *MLR* 191, 192–194; Jürgen Schwarze, *European Administrative Law* (Revised 1st edn, Sweet & Maxwell 2006) 687.

10. Yutaka Arai-Takahashi, *The Margin of Appreciation Doctrine and the Principle of Proportionality in the Jurisprudence of the ECHR* (Intersentia 2002) 193.

11. *R v Minister of Agriculture, Fisheries and Food, ex p Bell Lines* [1984] 2 CMLR 502; *Torfaen BC v B & Q* [1990] 3 CMLR 455; *Thomas v Adjudication Officer* [1991] 2 QB 164 (CA); *R v International Stock Exchange, ex p Else* [1992] BCC 11, [1993] QB 534; *R v Secretary of State for the Home Department, ex p Adams* [1995] All ER (EC) 177; *R v Ministry of Agriculture, Fisheries and Food, ex p First City Trading* [1997] 1 CMLR 250; *R v Chief Constable of Sussex, ex p International Trader's Ferry Ltd* [1998] 3 WLR 1260 (HL), [1999] 2 AC 418 (HL); *R v Secretary of Agriculture, Fisheries and Food, ex p Astonquest Ltd* [2000] Eu LR 371; *R v Secretary of State for Health, ex p British American Tobacco (Investments) Ltd and Imperial Tobacco Ltd* (C-491/01)[2002] ECR I-11453.

12. Now the Treaty on the Functioning of the European Union (TFEU). See Chapter Five of this book for a brief history and iterations of the EC Treaty.

13. *R v Human Fertilisation and Embryology Authority, ex p Blood* [1997] 2 All ER 687, [1999] Fam 151.

sperm of her deceased husband to Belgium, an EU Member State where she could be inseminated with it. The Court noted that the respondent authority had failed to recognise that '[i]n coming to its decision the authority was required to take into account that to refuse permission to export [sperm] would impede the treatment of Mrs. Blood in Belgium and to ask whether in the circumstances this was justified'.[14] It thus held that the authority had failed to consider whether the public policy-based ban could be justified, by reference to criteria of proportionality, as a derogation from an individual's right under the then Article 59 of the EC Treaty (i.e., requiring the abolition of restrictions on freedom to provide services within the EC; now Article 56 of the TFEU) to receive medical treatment in another Member State.[15]

Section 2 of the ECA 1972 — namely, General Implementation of Treaties and in particular section 2(1) — makes the concept of direct effect, and thus applicability, a part of the UK legal system. This means that individuals may enforce their EU law-based rights in domestic courts since these rights are automatically binding and directly enforceable without further enactment by Parliament.[16] Accordingly, UK courts are (at least prior to Brexit) directed by section 2(1) to enforce any directly effective EU measures even though, under their orthodox domestic dualist approach to international law,[17] they may not directly enforce a provision of an international treaty or a measure passed thereunder until Parliament passes an act that makes such provisions legally enforceable domestically. Hence, there is no need for a fresh act of incorporation to enable the UK courts to enforce each EU treaty provision,[18] regulation,[19] or directive,[20] which, according to EU law, has direct effect.[21] However, directives, as opposed to treaty provisions and regulations, were not originally seen by some as creating directly effective rights or having direct applicability, but this view has been rejected.[22]

14. Ibid., [1999] Fam 151, 184G.

15. Ibid., [1997] 2 All ER 687, 700g.

16. *Van Gend en Loos v Nederlandse Administratie der Belastingen* (Case 26/62) [1963] ECR 1.

17. *McWhirter v AG* [1972] CMLR 882.

18. *Van Gend en Loos* (N16).

19. TFEU, Art 288; *Franz Grad v Finanzamt Traustein* (Case 9/70) [1970] ECR 825, [5].

20. *Van Duyn v Home Office* (Case 41/74) [1974] ECR 1337.

21. Paul Craig and Gráinne de Búrca, *EU Law* (5th edn, OUP 2011) 286.

22. John Fairhurst, *Law of the European Union* (9th edn, Pearson Education 2012) 273.

Section 3 of the ECA 1972 — namely, Decisions on, and Proof of, Treaties and EU Instruments, etc. — makes CJEU decisions interpreting the meaning and effect of EU law authoritative in the UK and binding upon UK courts.[23] When sections 2 and 3 are put together, the predominant approach adopted by the UK courts is to use principles of construction to assume that when Parliament enacted the ECA 1972, it intended any ambiguity or inconsistency with EU law to be resolved by giving primacy to EU law [24] providing that there is no indication that Parliament expressly intended to depart from a provision of EU law. The underlying assumption is that that if the latter were to occur, that Parliament intended and expressly provided that UK law would take precedence, then the UK courts would follow the will of Parliament.[25]

The acceptance by the UK courts of the supremacy of EU law is also evidenced in *R v Secretary of State for Employment, ex parte Equal Opportunities Commission* [26] where the House of Lords stated that there was no constitutional barrier to an applicant before any UK court, not just the House of Lords, seeking judicial review of primary legislation which had been alleged to be in breach of EU law.[27] In this case, the Equal Opportunities Commission (EOC) sought to establish the discriminatory, and therefore unlawful, nature of the threshold provisions of the UK Employment Protection (Consolidation) Act 1978 (EP(C)A 1978). The EOC alleged that the requirement to have worked for at least two years in full-time employment or five years in part-time employment in order to be eligible for the employment protection conferred by the EP(C)A 1978 had contravened EU anti-discrimination laws (based on both treaty provisions and directives).[28] Even though the Secretary of State argued that the threshold provisions had favoured the creation of part-time work, the EOC argued that the EP(C)A 1978 discriminated indirectly against women by granting preferential employment protection rights to full-time workers, the majority of whom were men, as opposed to part-time workers, the majority of whom were women.

23. Craig and de Búrca (N21) 286.

24. *Shields v E Coomes (Holdings) Ltd* [1979] 1 All ER 456, 461.

25. *MaCarthys v Smith* [1979] 3 All ER 325, 329.

26. [1994] 1 WLR 409, [1994] 1 All ER 910.

27. Ibid., [1994] 1 WLR 409, 418–419.

28. EC Treaty, Art 119 (now TFEU, Art 157), Dir 75/117, [1975] OJ L45/19, and Dir 76/207 [1976] OJ L39/40.

Although the House of Lords agreed that the increase in the availability of part-time work might constitute a proper aim of social policy and could thus justify any resulting alleged indirect discrimination against women, the Secretary of State failed to prove this connection. The threshold was not shown to result in the creation of more part-time jobs and therefore could not be said to be apposite and necessary to achieve the aim asserted. In other words, the Secretary of State failed to satisfy the test of proportionality. The House of Lords thus held that the provisions had not been 'objectively justified' by the government's legitimate economic aim of encouraging the creation of more part-time jobs by minimizing employers' overheads and operating costs,[29] and that, in effect, owing to its discriminatory nature, the provision was in breach of the criterion under the proportionality test.

As a result, the EOC obtained a declaration that English statutory provisions on redundancy payments and unfair dismissal compensation which discriminated indirectly against women were inconsistent with EU law. Again, such a decision also corresponds with a concept elaborated on by Allan Rosas, whereby we all take it for granted that a decision made by the political majority or by the government is absolutely legitimate.[30] However, this is not the case. It is only legitimate if it is in line with the 'natural' rights of human being, as recognised in the Universal Declaration of Human Rights 1948 (UDHR 1948), subsequent international instruments, and national constitutions.

Insofar as EU directives are concerned, a case concerning environmental protection in the UK, *R (on the application of ClientEarth) v Secretary of State for the Environment Food and Rural Affairs*,[31] deserves mentioning. When it comes to administrative decision-making and judicial intervention in respect of the environment, Britain has long been accused of offering a relatively hostile legal system for environmental non-governmental organisations. Public interest

29. *ex p Equal Opportunities Commission* (N26) [1994] 1 All ER 910, 921–922.

30. Allan Rosas, 'Social Rights and the European Union' in Peter Van der Auweraert, Tom De Pelsmaeker, Jeremy Sarkin, and Johan Vande Lanotte (eds), *Social, Economic and Cultural Rights: An Appraisal of Current European and International Developments* (Maklu 2002) 149.

31. [2011] EWHC 3623 (Admin), [2015] UKSC 28, [2015] 4 All ER 724 (SC).

environmental litigation is rarely successful.[32] Prior to joining the EU, Britain had a national environmental policy in place, but it had primarily been developed on a reactionary basis, as and when environmental problems arose. During that period, its primary aim was to limit the effect of pollution on the environment by using voluntary measures imposed by consultation between polluters and regulators through non-legislative guidelines rather than rigid enforcement structures.[33] Although administrative decisions might, on several occasions, be challenged for procedural reasons, the UK courts have long been hesitant to substantively review them.[34]

However, a sound and healthy environment is crucial for the realisation of sustainable development, and of socio-economic rights, in contemporary societies.[35] This is because environmental degradation, together with inappropriate conservation of biodiversity and natural resources, can erode the basis for many human rights in urban or rural contexts.[36] Therefore, environment protection is able to contribute to the implementation of socio-economic rights such as the right to health, including the right to clean air, the right to food, and the right to water. Nevertheless, around 29,000 people die prematurely each year in Britain as a result of air pollution, according to a 2010 report.[37] This report outlining statistics for premature death and other air pollution-related illnesses was a precursor to what would end up being one of the most significant environmental protection cases in the UK.

32. Richard Macrory and Michael Woods, *Modernizing Environmental Justice: Regulation and the Role of an Environmental Tribunal* (UCL 2003) 22; Lisa Vanhala, 'Legal Opportunity Structures and the Paradox of Legal Mobilization by the Environmental Movement in the UK' (2012) 46 *LSR* 523–524; Ugo Taddei, 'A Right to Clean Air in EU Law? Using Litigation to Progress from Procedural to Substantive Environmental Rights' (2016) 18(1) *ELR* 3, 4.

33. Laura Tainsh and Davidson Chalmers, 'Brexit: What Next for Environmental Law' (2016) 176 *SPEL* 76.

34. Taddei (N32) 4.

35. Office of the High Commission on Human Rights (OHCHR)-United Nations Environment Programme (UNEP), 'Human Rights and the Environment — Rio+20: Joint Report OHCHR and UNEP', 2012, pp. 20 and 34, available at: https://wedocs.unep.org/bitstream/handle/20.500.11822/9970/JointReport_OHCHR_HRE.pdf?sequence=1&isAllowed=y, last accessed 2 January 2020; Wolfgang Sachs, *Environment and Human Rights* (Wuppertal Institute for Climate, Environment, Energy November 2003), available at: https://epub.wupperinst.org/frontdoor/deliver/index/docId/1811/file/WP137.pdf, last accessed 2 January 2020.

36. Domenico Amirante, 'The Right to Environment in Emerging Economies: An India-China Comparison' in Surya Deva (ed), *Socio-Economic Rights in Emerging Free Markets: Comparative Insights from India and China* (Routledge 2015) 71.

37. Case Comment, 'Supreme Court Orders Government to Cut Illegal Air Pollution' (2015) 4(3) *CR* 2015 18.

In 2011, an environmental pressure group, ClientEarth, began a judicial review claim in response to the British government's failure to observe the obligations under the EC Ambient Air Quality Directive 2008 (AAQD 2008).[38] Under the AAQD 2008, Member States were required to comply with limits on nitrogen dioxide levels by 2010, with an extension of the deadline to 2015, on application, where governments created an air quality plan for affected areas. However, the UK government did not apply for an extension of the deadline because it felt that there was no realistic chance of meeting the limits in London and other 15 regions. Nevertheless, the High Court, in line with the traditional approach, based its decision only on procedural grounds, and thus dismissed the action by holding, *inter alia,* that a mandatory order requiring plans to achieve compliance 'would raise serious political and economic questions which are not for this court'.[39]

In this regard, the development of legal measures to protect the environment in the UK lags behind other EU Member States. In fact, UK environmental protection laws, as well as other laws designed to protect socio-economic rights, not only lag behind those of EU Member States, but in some cases lag behind even those of developing economies. In India, for instance, although the right to environment was a directive principle of state policy and, thus, not justiciable as a substantive right under the Indian Constitution,[40] the judiciary has indirectly recognised it via the right to life.[41] Even though the text of the Constitutional Article that safeguards the right to life does not explicitly mention environmental protection, the Indian courts have, on several occasions, held that the right to a clean environment must be considered as a part of the right to life. In *Subhash Kumar v State of Bihar,*[42] the Supreme Court of India observed that

> the right to live is a fundamental right under Article 21 of the Constitution, and it includes the right of enjoyment of pollution-free water and air for

38. Directive 2008/50/EC of the European Parliament and of the Council of 21 May 2008 on ambient air quality and cleaner air for Europe [2008] OJ L152/1.
39. *ClientEarth* (N31) [2011] EWHC 3623 (Admin), [15].
40. Indian Constitution, Art 47.
41. Ibid., Art 21.
42. AIR 1991 SC 420.

> full enjoyment of life. If anything endangers or impairs the quality of life in derogation of laws, a citizen has the right to have recourse to Article 32 [it allows courts to forge new remedies and formulate new strategies to enforce fundamental rights] of the Constitution.[43]

By comparison, in 2013, the *ClientEarth* case was appealed in the UK Supreme Court and, in 2014, referred to the CJEU for preliminary ruling. In 2015, a second hearing was, again, held by the UK Supreme Court. This time, ClientEarth turned the tables. The Court granted a declaration that the AAQD 2008 had been breached, and ordered the UK government to take 'immediate action' and prepare a detailed plan of how it will cut illegal levels of air pollution in the affected areas. The Court stated:

> The new government, whatever its political complexion, should be left in no doubt as to the need for immediate action to address this issue. The only realistic way to achieve this is a mandatory order requiring new plans ... to be prepared within a defined timetable.[44]

ClientEarth welcomed the judgment, saying that '[w]e brought our case because we have the right to breathe clean air and today the Supreme Court upheld this right'.[45] This case shows that when the UK courts are dealing with cases having an EU law dimension, they tend to be willing to scrutinise the matter more seriously. However, even though the British government was ordered in April 2015 to fulfil its legal duty to cut air pollution to legal levels in the 'shortest possible time', it failed to produce new air quality plans to achieve this. A year later, a request for a new judicial review by ClientEarth was granted on 28 April 2016,[46] and a decision against the government was made on 2 November 2016.[47]

43. Ibid.

44. *ClientEarth* (N31) [2015] UKSC 28, [2015] 4 All ER 724 (SC).

45. Case Comment (N37) 18.

46. Damian Carrington, 'UK government faces second court battle over air pollution plans', *The Guardian*, 28 April 2016, available at: www.theguardian.com/environment/2016/apr/28/uk-government-faces-second-court-battle-over-air-pollution-plans, last accessed 2 January 2020.

47. *ClientEarth (No. 2) v Secretary of State for the Environment Food and Rural Affairs* [2016] EWHC 2740 (Admin).

7.2.2 Direct Effect (and thus Applicability) of European Union Law vs Parliamentary Sovereignty

In Britain, the acceptance of the supremacy of EU law is not without difficulty. Central to the problem is the constitutional doctrine of parliamentary sovereignty, or supremacy, which, in its traditional formulation, holds that Parliament has the power to do anything other than to bind itself for the future. This means that if there is a clash between a later and an earlier norm, then the latter is taken to be impliedly repealed or disapplied by the former.[48] However, this contradicted the ruling in the *Van Gend en Loos* case determined by the CJEU, in that '[t]he [EU] constitutes a new legal order of international law for the benefit of which the [member] states have limited their sovereign rights'.[49] Moreover, the CJEU, in *Costa v ENEL*,[50] further held that EU law must be supreme should any such conflict arise between EU law and UK domestic law arise. The Court stated:

> By creating a Community of unlimited duration, having ... powers stemming from a limitation of sovereignty, or a transfer of powers from the States to the Community, the Member States have limited their sovereignty rights, albeit within limited fields, and thus have created a body of law which binds both their nationals and themselves.[51]

In view of the above, the doctrine of parliamentary sovereignty, in theory, makes it very difficult to uphold the supremacy of EU law guaranteed by the ECA 1972. As a result, the ECA 1972 seems vulnerable to any later Act of Parliament which contravenes or contradicts it, expressly or impliedly.[52] Thus, when this is the case, the apparently conflicting provision of English law should be read and interpreted in conformity with EU law.[53] In some cases, the courts assumed that this approach would only apply where the

48. Paul Craig, 'Britain in the European Union' in Jeffrey Jowell and Dawn Oliver (eds), *The Changing Constitution* (7th edn, OUP 2011) Ch. 4.
49. *Van Gend en Loos* (N16).
50. *Costa v ENEL Nazionale per l'Energia Elettrica (Enel)* (Case 6/64) [1964] ECR 585.
51. Ibid., 593.
52. Craig and de Búrca (N21) 286.
53. *Garland v British Rail Engineering Ltd* [1983] 2 AC 751, 771.

provision of EU law was directly effective,[54] whereas, in others,[55] the House of Lords was prepared to construe domestic statutes in conformity with EU laws which were not directly effective, even where that construction was not in accordance with the literal or *prima facie* meaning of the statutes.[56] This is so even where the national statute is introduced to implement a non-directly effective (and thus applicable) directive.[57]

The leading decision on the relationship between EU law and UK law is that in the *Factortame* saga.[58] In *R v Secretary of State for Transport, ex parte Factortame Ltd (No. 2)*,[59] the applicants were companies incorporated under UK law, but the majority of the directors and shareholders were Spanish. The companies were in the business of sea fishing and their vessels were registered as British under the UK Merchant Shipping Act 1984 (MSA 1984). The statutory regime was altered by the UK Merchant Shipping Act 1988 (MSA 1988). Under the new regime, vessels that had been registered under the MSA 1984 had to be re-registered. A total of 95 vessels failed to meet the new criteria, and the applicants argued that the relevant parts of the MSA 1988 were incompatible with, *inter alia*, Articles 52, 58, and 221 of the EC Treaty.[60] The first *Factortame* case [61] was concerned with whether interim relief should be available against the Crown in order to protect the applicants' financial interests if they were prevented from fishing pending the final judgment. Such relief was not available under UK law at that time, but the CJEU held that the absence of such relief was itself a breach

54. *Duke v GEC Reliance Ltd* [1988] AC 618, 638.

55. *Pickstone v Freemans* [1989] AC 66; *Litster v Forth Dry Dock Co Ltd* [1990] 1 AC 546; *Webb v EMO* [1993] 1 WLR 49.

56. Craig and de Búrca (N21) 287.

57. Ibid.

58. *R v Secretary of State for Transport, ex p Factortame Ltd* [1990] 2 AC 85; *R v Secretary of State for Transport, ex p Factortame Ltd* (Case C-213/89) [1990] ECR I-2433; *R v Secretary of State for Transport, ex p Factortame Ltd* (Case C-221/89) [1991] ECR I-3905; *R v Secretary of State for Transport, ex p Factortame Ltd (No. 2)* [1991] 1 AC 603; *R v Secretary of State for Transport, ex p Factortame Ltd* [1995] 1 AC 1; *R v Secretary of State for Transport, ex p Factortame Ltd (No. 5)* [1998] 3 CMLR 192 (CA), [1999] 4 All ER 906 (HL).

59. Ibid., [1991] 1 AC 603.

60. TFEU, Arts 49, 54, and 55.

61. *ex p Factortame Ltd* (N58) [1990] 2 AC 85.

of EU law.[62] This was accepted by the House of Lords in *Factortame (No. 2)*, in which Lord Bridge held:

> Some public comments on the decision of the [CJEU], affirming the jurisdiction of the courts of member states to override national legislation if necessary to enable interim relief to be granted in protection of rights under [EU] law, have suggested that this was a novel and dangerous invasion by [an EU] institution of the sovereignty of the United Kingdom Parliament. But such comments are based on a misconception. If the supremacy within [EU] law over the national law of member states was not always inherent in the EEC Treaty it was certainly well established in the jurisprudence of the [CJEU] long before the United Kingdom joined the [EU]. Thus, whatever limitation of its sovereignty Parliament accepted when it enacted the [ECA 1972] was entirely voluntary. Under the terms of the [ECA 1972] it has always been clear that it was the duty of a United Kingdom court, when delivering final judgment, to override any rule of national law found to be in conflict with any directly enforceable rule of [EU] law. Similarly, when decisions of the [CJEU] have exposed areas of [UK] statute law which failed to implement [EU] directives, Parliament has always loyally accepted the obligation to make appropriate and prompt amendments. Thus there is nothing in any way novel in according supremacy to rules of [EU] law in those areas to which they apply and to insist that, in the protection of rights under [EU] law, national courts must not be inhibited by rules of national law from granting interim relief in appropriate cases is no more than a logical recognition of that supremacy.[63]

According to Paul Craig, there are three aspects of reasoning in the above *dicta*.[64] The first was contractarian — Britain knew that when it joined the EU, priority would be accorded to EU law, so it must be taken to have contracted on those terms. It follows that if 'blame' was to be cast for a loss of sovereignty, then this should be laid 'at the door of Parliament and not the courts'. The second facet of Lord Bridge's reasoning was a priori and functional — it was

62. Ibid., (Case C-213/89) [1990], ECR I-2433.

63. Ibid., [1991] 1 AC 603, 658.

64. Craig (N48) 117.

always inherent in the EU regime that it could only function adequately if EU law could take precedence in case there was a clash with domestic norms. The third reasoning was the existence of the ECA 1972, the effect of which was to impose a duty on national courts to override domestic law in the event of clash with directly enforceable EU law. Whatever the reason, in allowing domestic courts to declare provisions of a statute to be incompatible with the ones of EU law, the *Factortame* saga became the authority for such cases, and the House of Lords has made it clear that this reviewing power of legislation resides in all domestic courts, not just British superior courts.[65]

7.2.3 The European Communities Act 1972: A Constitutional Statute

While the UK courts accepted the supremacy of EU law, the conceptual foundation for their decisions has been debated. In *Factortame (No. 2)*, Lord Bridge seemed to have ended this debate by, as mentioned above, adverting to the reasoning used by the CJEU in justifying and thus according supremacy to EU law, as exemplified by his reference to supremacy being inherent in the nature of the EC Treaty, despite the fact that he also premised the UK's acceptance of supremacy on a UK statute — the ECA 1972.[66]

However, there has also been domestic acceptance of supremacy as exemplified in *Thoburn v Sunderland City Council*, the so-called *Metric Martyrs* case.[67] In this case, Britain was legally obliged to use metric measures as the primary form of measurement derived from an EU directive,[68] and the UK government complied with this obligation through the enactment of the Weights and Measures Act 1985 (W&MA 1985) and its related regulations,[69] some of which were based on section 2(2) of the ECA 1972. In March 2001, some street traders, including Thoburn, were prosecuted and convicted for

65. *ex p Factortame Ltd* (N58) [1995] 1 AC 1, 27.

66. Craig and de Búrca (N21) 289.

67. [2001] EWHC Admin 934, [2002] EWHC 195, [2002] Eu LR 253, [2003] QB 151.

68. Directive 80/181/EEC of 20 December 1979 on the approximation of the laws of the Member States relating to units of measurement and on the repeal of Directive 71/354/EEC [1980] OJ L39.

69. Weights and Measures Act 1985 (Metrication) (Amendment) Order 1994; Units of Measurement Regulations 1994.

continuing to use imperial measures, rather than metric, when selling their goods. The defendants argued that the power to make such legislation and regulations through section 2(2) of the ECA 1972 had been impliedly repealed by provisions in the W&MA 1985.

However, Laws LJ held that there had been no inconsistency between section 2(2) of the ECA 1972 and the W&MA 1985 and that there was therefore no issue of implied repeal in this case. He furthered that the constitutional relationship between the UK and the EU was not to be decided by the CJEU's jurisprudence, which could not itself entrench EU law within national law.[70] The constitutional relationship between the UK and the EU, including the impact of EU membership on sovereignty, was to be decided by the common law in light of any domestic statutes. The common law did, said Laws LJ, modify the traditional concept of sovereignty by creating exceptions to the doctrine of implied repeal. Thus, although ordinary statutes were subject to the doctrine of implied repeal, 'constitutional statutes' conditioned the legal relationship between citizen and state in an overarching manner (therefore dealing with fundamental constitutional rights) and were not subject to the doctrine of implied repeal.[71] The repeal of such statutes, or its disapplication in a particular instance, could occur only if there were some 'express words in the later statute, or by words so specific that the inference of an actual determination to effect the result contended for was irresistible'.[72] As Laws LJ has said, 'there can be no implied repeal of the [ECA 1972] as the courts now recognise it as constitutional in form, i.e. subject to repeal only through express enactment'.[73] Therefore, the ECA 1972 was regarded as a constitutional statute.

Such modification by the common law does correspond to what has been advocated by many judges: that in the UK, there is a 'dual sovereignty', 'divided sovereignty',[74] or a 'bi-polar sovereignty of the Crown in Parliament and the Crown in its courts, to each of which the Crown's ministers are

70. *Thoburn* (N67) [57]–[58].

71. Ibid., [62].

72. Ibid., [63] (Laws LJ).

73. Ibid.

74. *R (Jackson) v AG* [2005] UKHL 56, [2006] 1 AC 262, [102] (Lord Steyn).

answerable — politically to Parliament, legally to the courts'.[75] This argument has long been compatible with the *ratio decidendi* as held in 1610 by Lord Coke CJ in *Dr Bonham's* case [76] in which

> the Common Law will control Acts of Parliament and sometimes adjudge them to be utterly void: for when an Act of Parliament is against common right and reason, or repugnant, or impossible to be performed, the Common Law will control it and adjudge such Act to be void.[77]

Thoburn's reasoning has further been endorsed by the Supreme Court in *R (on the application of HS2 Action Alliance Ltd) v Secretary of State for Transport*,[78] which concerned the conflict of law between the UK legal system and EU law.[79] The Supreme Court affirmed that the constitutional relationship between Britain and the EU was to be determined by the UK courts in line with common law constitutional principles. Lord Reed, now the President of the Supreme Court, in particular, mentioned that the supremacy of EU law only took effect within the UK through the ECA 1972, adding that any conflict between EU law and domestic law would be resolved by domestic courts as a matter of British constitutional law.[80] The Court also affirmed that there was a separate category of constitutional statutes in the UK constitutional order, the result of which was that it could not be assumed that when Parliament enacted the ECA 1972, it impliedly authorised the limitation or abrogation of such principles by EU law. In this case, the relevant principle was derived from Article 9 of the Bill of Rights 1689, which precluded impeachment or questioning in any court of debates or proceedings in Parliament. Lords Mance and Neuberger stated:

> The United Kingdom has no written constitution, but we have a number of constitutional instruments. They include [the] Magna Carta, the Petition of Right 1628, the Bill of Rights and (in Scotland) the Claim of

75. Stephen Sedley, 'Human Rights: A Twenty-First Century Agenda' (1995) *PL* 386, 389.
76. (1610) 8 Co Rep 114 (Court of Common Pleas, England), cited by Wen-chen Chang, Li-ann Thio, Kevin Y.L. Tan, and Jiunn-rong Yeh, *Constitutionalism in Asia* (Hart Publishing 2014) 311.
77. Ibid. See also Roger Masterman, *The Separation of Powers in the Contemporary Constitution: Judicial Competence and Independence in the United Kingdom* (CUP 2011) 109.
78. [2014] UKSC 3.
79. Paul Craig, 'Constitutionalising Constitutional Law: *HS2*' (2014) *PL* 373.
80. *HS2 Action Alliance Ltd* (N78) [79].

> Rights Act 1689, the Act of Settlement 1701 and the Act of Union 1707. The [ECA 1972], the [HRA 1998] and the Constitutional Reform Act 2005 may now be added to this list. The common law itself also recognises certain principles as fundamental to the rule of law. It is, putting the point at its lowest, certainly arguable (and it is for United Kingdom law and courts to determine) that there may be fundamental principles, whether contained in other constitutional instruments or recognised at common law, of which Parliament when it enacted the [ECA 1972] did not either contemplate or authorise the abrogation.[81]

7.2.4 The *Fedesa* Three-Stage Test

As there have been various methodologies of proportionality analysis adopted by the CJEU and by the European Court of Human Rights (ECtHR), the UK Court, in *R v International Stock Exchange, ex parte Else*,[82] seemed to have adopted the 'evidential' test, whereby the State is required to give satisfactory evidence of the pressing social need which its restriction seeks to address. This case indicates the importance for the public authority of being seen in evidence to have considered and eliminated, on reasoned grounds, alternative courses of action. In this case, the decision of the Stock Exchange to delist the shares of a company pursuant to powers contained in an EU directive was challenged on the ground of proportionality. The Court accepted that proportionality was an appropriate standard of review to apply in such a case, but found against the applicant. The Court noted that the relevant committee of the Stock Exchange had considered less drastic means of controlling the company short of delisting, and thus saw no reason to conclude that its findings were disproportionate. One of the most significant aspects of this case is that it specifies how the case for proportionate action must be made out by evidence as opposed to submission.[83]

81. Ibid., [207].
82. *ex p Else* (N11).
83. Michael Fordham and Thomas de la Mare, 'Identifying the Principles of Proportionality' in Jeffrey Jowell and Jonathan Cooper (eds), *Understanding Human Rights Principles* (Hart Publishing 2001) 43.

It was not until 1998 that the UK courts formally applied the three-stage test as developed by the CJEU in *ex parte Fedesa*.[84] In *ex parte International Trader's Ferry*,[85] the House of Lords identified and posed the *Fedesa* three-question template, where legitimacy [Q1] was not in dispute,[86] as follows:

> I am satisfied, as was the Court of Appeal, that the Chief Constable has shown here that what he did in providing police assistance was proportionate to what was required. To protect the lorries, in the way he did, was a [Q2] suitable and [Q3] necessary way of dealing with potentially violent demonstrators. To limit the occasions when sufficient police could be made available was, in the light of the resources available to him to deal with immediate and foreseeable events at the port, and at the same time to carry out all his other police duties, necessary and in no way disproportionate to the restrictions which were involved.[87]

7.2.5 The Process and Impact of Brexit

Although there were difficulties in reconciling their EU membership and parliamentary sovereignty during the initial stage, the UK did, in practice, show less inclination to articulate limits on the acceptance of EU supremacy than its continental counterparts.[88] Following the enactment of the European Union Act 2011 (EUA 2011), however, there was a change in attitude. During that period, the coalition government, dominated by the Tories, introduced a far-reaching regime of statutory and referendum 'locks', in that despite not directly constraining the supremacy of EU law, it contains far-reaching limits to the acceptance of treaty changes and certain other EU decisions within the UK.

Under the regime of referendum and statutory locks,[89] there must be an Act of Parliament plus a positive vote in a national referendum. However, section 18

84. *ex p Fedesa* (N9).

85. *ex p International Trader's Ferry* (N11).

86. Ibid., [1998] 3 WLR 1260 (HL), 1275D.

87. Ibid., 1277D (Lord Slynn).

88. Craig and de Búrca (N21) 290–291.

89. EUA 2011, s 2.

of the EAU 2011 — namely, Status of EU law dependent on continuing statutory basis, the so-called 'sovereignty clause' — says nothing about the supremacy of EU law over national law in the UK and is, thus, not concerned with 'sovereignty as primacy'. Rather, it concerns 'sovereignty as dualism', reiterating that in a dualist country such as the UK, there must be an Act of Parliament which adopts or transforms EU treaty provisions and directives into UK law. Regardless, whatever it has changed so far, the ECA 1972, in particular section 2(1), is still the gateway for EU law becoming part of UK law.

Thus, European integration has been seen as a process that has a self-sustaining dynamism. Even though the majority of UK citizens have decided to get rid of Brussels' administration (despite most people in Scotland and Northern Ireland voting to the contrary),[90] as reflected in the referendum held on 23 June 2016,[91] under the European Union Referendum Act 2015, EU law and its institutional forces are still, and will continue to, be able to exert some degree of influence on the UK's decision-making process and jurisprudence. This is because, on one hand, legislation and administrative decisions or actions that have been interpreted by the courts pursuant to sections 2 and 3 of the ECA 1972 (whose combined effect is to assume that with reference to the CJEU's jurisprudence, any ambiguity or inconsistency of them with EU law is to be resolved by giving primacy to EU law in order to render them compatible with EU rights) would not simply revert to its pre-ECA 1972 meaning upon repeal of that enactment. Rather, those ECA 1972-compatible interpretations would remain part of the body of precedent. On the other hand, even if the ECA 1972 is repealed, it would not affect the status of EU-derived law in the UK. For one thing, it would not undo the implementation of EU directives that

90. A total of 51.9 percent of voters wanted the UK to leave the EU, whereas 48.1 percent of them wanted to stay. Furthermore, 33,551,983 out of 46,500,001 UK citizens voted in the referendum, representing an overall turnout of 72.2 percent of registered voters; see Electoral Commission, 'Results and turnout at the EU referendum', 25 September 2019, available at: www.electoralcommission.org.uk/who-we-are-and-what-we-do/elections-and-referendums/past-elections-and-referendums/eu-referendum/results-and-turnout-eu-referendum, last accessed 27 June 2020. See also Jo Murkens, 'Brexit: The Devolution Dimension', *UK Constitutional Law Blog*, 28 June 2016, available at: https://ukconstitutionallaw.org/2016/06/28/jo-murkens-brexit-the-devolution-dimension/, last accessed 17 May 2020; Colin Harvey, 'Complex Constitutionalism in a Pluralist UK', *UK Constitutional Law Blog*, 2 July 2016, available at: https://ukconstitutionallaw.org/2016/07/02/colin-harvey-complex-constitutionalism-in-a-pluralist-uk/, last accessed 2 January 2020.

91. *The Guardian*, 'EU Referendum: Full Results and Analysis', 24 June 2016, available at: www.theguardian.com/politics/ng-interactive/2016/jun/23/eu-referendum-live-results-and-analysis, last accessed 17 May 2020.

have already become legislation [92] and statutory instruments.[93] They would remain in force in the UK until repealed. This is reflected in the Explanator Notes of the European Union (Withdrawal) Act 2018 (EU(W)A 2018), which states that although the withdrawal 'ends the supremacy of [EU] law in UK law, [it] converts EU law as it stands at the moment of exit into domestic law, and preserves laws made in the UK to implement EU obligations'.[94]

Insofar as directly applicable EU regulations are concerned, if the ECA 1972 is repealed, these regulations will cease to have legal effect, the consequence of which is to leave a big loophole in the UK's regulation of fundamental aspects of its business, work, and environment. Although Parliament is able to enact legislation giving EU regulations the status of UK legislation, this would defeat the whole purpose of the Brexit campaign.[95] It is also ironic to claim 'enhanced sovereignty' if Britain simply adopts the same EU laws it had before when its people have decided to leave. To take air quality as an example, the UK has long been criticised for providing a relatively hostile legal system for environmental non-governmental organisations. As a result, public interest environmental litigation is largely unsuccessful. In this climate, if the ECA 1972-derived regulations are to be replaced, they would likely be replaced by lower-standard ones, thus leaving the British people with impoverished legal protection.[96] For instance, in *ClientEarth*,[97] despite being ordered by the Supreme Court on 16 April 2015 to fulfil its legal duty to cut air pollution to legal levels in the 'shortest possible time', the government failed to produce

92. See, for example, the Consumer Protection Act 1987.

93. See, for example, the Unfair Terms in Consumer Contracts Regulations 1994.

94. EU(W)A 2018, Explanatory Notes, [2], available at: www.legislation.gov.uk/ukpga/2018/16/pdfs/ukpgaen_20180016_en.pdf, last accessed 30 May 2020.

95. There have also been disputes as to whether the process of withdrawal required parliamentary approval at various stages, including at the point of triggering Article 50 of the Treaty of European Union (TEU), as argued by those who voted in favour of the UK to remain in the EU, or whether there was no need for a further vote on the subject matter in Parliament because it had already authorised the referendum and had, via the government, given a solemn promise to voters that their wishes will be implemented, as contested by the government and backed by those who had voted to leave the EU; see *R (Miller) v Secretary of State for Exiting the European Union* [2017] UKSC 5, [2017] 2 W.L.R. 583, in which the UK Supreme Court held that the government had no prerogative power to initiate the formal process to withdraw from the EU and that parliamentary approval was required. For a detailed analysis, see Venkat Iyera, 'Separation of Powers: The UK Experience' (2018) 5(2) *JICL* 507, 518–522.

96. Tainsh and Chalmers (N33) 76.

97. *ClientEarth* (N31) [2015] UKSC 28, [2015] 4 All ER 724 (SC).

plans to meet this requirement. A year later, ClientEarth had no alternative but to resort to a new judicial review, which was granted on 28 April 2016, to challenge the government's failure to fulfil its obligations as required under the AAQD 2008.[98] In short, unhindered by EU rules, the UK government would likely choose lower standards of environmental protection that will harm its people's health.

There has also been concern that the Brexit process will result in a reduction in human rights protection in Britain. According to Ronan McCrea, part of the case presented to voters in favour of Brexit was that leaving the EU would allow Britain to be free of the duty to comply with the EU's fundamental rights norms, including the EU Charter of Fundamental Rights (EUCFR 1966) and the possibly expansionist interpretation of it by the CJEU.[99] This is highlighted in a statement made by the former Minister for Leaving the European Union, David Davis, who announced in March 2017 that the EUCFR would not be retained after Brexit because 'it helps foreign criminals stay [in the UK]'.[100] He was backed by Sir Bill Cash, a Member of Parliament, who in the same article was quoted as saying that 'it provides protection for people who have no right to be protected'.

That said, McCrea has been optimistic that any deal conducted under Article 50 of the Treaty of European Union (TEU) will be subject to a degree of obligation to comply with the rights contained in the EUCFR and the fundamental elements or principles of EU law and an obligation to satisfy the CJEU that such compliance has occurred.[101] This is reflected in the European Union (Withdrawal) Bill (EUW Bill) published on 13 July 2017. In addition to repealing the ECA 1972,[102] one of its purposes is to convert the entire body of

98. Carrington (N46).

99. Ronan McCrea, 'Can a Brexit Deal Provide a Clean Break with the Court of Justice and EU Fundamental Rights Norms?', *UK Constitutional Law Blog*, 3 October 2016, available at: https://ukconstitutionallaw.org/2016/10/03/ronan-mccrea-can-a-brexit-deal-provide-a-clean-break-with-the-court-of-justice-and-eu-fundamental-rights-norms/, last accessed 2 January 2020.

100. Gordon Rayner, 'UK Takes Back the Right to Deport as Britain Repeals Powers from EU', *The Daily Telegraph*, 31 March 2017, available at: www.telegraph.co.uk/news/2017/03/30/uk-takes-back-right-deport-britain-repeals-powers-eu/, last accessed 2 June 2020.

101. McCrea (N99).

102. EU(W) Bill, Clause 1.

EU rights and obligations 'wholesale' into UK law, and the government has promised that the same rules and laws will apply on the day after Brexit.[103] This promise is indeed fulfilled under section 4 of the EU(W)A 2018), which corresponds to Saving for rights, etc. under section 2(1) of the ECA 1972.

All in all, even though sovereignty might, theoretically speaking, be returned to Britain following Brexit, in reality, this will not change much unless all EU-derived legislations and statutory instruments are repealed altogether and replaced with home-grown ones. Another purpose of the EUW Bill is to ensure legal continuity after Brexit. To achieve this, clauses 2, 3, and 4 create a new body of law known as 'retained EU law' which includes domestic legislation giving effect to EU law, which is to be preserved, and direct EU legislation, which is to be converted.[104] Despite a significant proportion of EU law being preserved, this general position masks the complexity of legislating for Brexit. For one thing, the delegated powers in the Bill will be used to amend retained EU law in significant ways.[105] In fact, the UK has positively embraced much EU law and often enhanced EU standards in its national legislation, with 13.2 percent of all laws made in the UK from 1993 to 2014 being EU-related.[106] Thus, the process of review and repeal will be an exhausting exercise. Despite this, the government's undertaking to retain EU law is shown under sections 2 and 3 of the EU(W)A 2018 — namely, Saving for EU-derived domestic legislation and Incorporation of direct EU legislation, respectively. Ultimately, on 22 January 2020, Parliament gave final approval to the Withdrawal Agreement with the EU, and the European Union (Withdrawal Agreement) Act 2020 received royal assent the following day. The UK officially left the EU on 31 January 2020.

103. Jack Simson Caird, 'The European Union (Withdrawal) Bill: Constitutional Change and Legal Continuity', *UK Constitutional Law Blog*, 18 July 2017, available at: https://ukconstitutionallaw.org/2017/07/18/jack-simson-caird-the-european-union-withdrawal-bill-constitutional-change-and-legal-continuity/, last accessed 2 January 2020.

104. Ibid.

105. Ibid.

106. Dan Bloom, 'How many of Britain's laws REALLY come from the EU? The Brexit question no one can answer', *The Mirror*, 21 June 2016, available at: www.mirror.co.uk/news/uk-news/how-many-britains-laws-really-7420612, last accessed 17 May 2020.

7.3 The Human Rights Act 1998: Domestic 'Observance' or 'Effect' of the European Convention on Human Rights

Britain being a Member State of the ECHR, proportionality (as developed by the ECtHR) has also gained acceptance by British courts in respect of human rights cases through the application of the HRA 1998, whose aim is to give 'further effect' [107] to rights and freedoms guaranteed under the ECHR. Prior to its enactment, there had long been an idea that UK political and legal institutions were perfectly suited to protecting human rights, so no fundamental change was required. Such over-confidence was evidently reflected in its deposit of ratification instruments of the ECHR well before, in 1951, but no steps have been taken to incorporate them into domestic legal system.

Traditionally, UK law has long recognised the notion of 'civil liberties' (i.e., personal freedoms which allow individuals to participate in public life)[108] rather than 'human rights'. This difference is clearly expressed by Browne-Wilkinson LJ in *Wheeler v Leicester City Council* [109] when he states:

> Basic constitutional rights in this country such as freedom of the person and freedom of speech are based not on any express provision conferring such a right but on freedom of an individual to do what he will save to the extent that he is prevented from so doing by the law.[110]

Therefore, the difference between these concepts is that having the liberty to do something means that it is lawful to do it because the law does not prohibit.[111] By contrast, to say that someone has a right to do something means that the law specifically says that it can be lawfully done. This traditional English position has been described by Megarry, the then Vice Chancellor, in *Malone v Metropolitan Police Commissioner*, where he said that 'England is not a country where everything is forbidden except what is expressly permitted: it is

107. Jane Wright, *Tort Law and Human Rights* (Hart Publishing 2017) 7.

108. Conor Gearty, *Civil Liberties* (OUP 2007) 1.

109. [1985] AC 1054.

110. Ibid., 1065.

111. *AG v Guardian Newspapers (No. 2)* [1990] 1 AC 109.

a country where everything is permitted except what is expressly forbidden'.[112] Hence, the notion of 'civil liberties' is residual, whereas the notion of 'human rights' is both positive and declaratory.[113]

Although the UK domestic courts have increasingly accepted the legitimacy of referring to ECHR case law, there has been a clear reluctance to develop human rights jurisprudence.[114] In 1996, a research paper was published showing that even though the ECHR had been referred to in 316 cases from 1975 to 1996, it only influenced the outcome in 16 of these.[115] Thanks to the New Labour's commitment in its election manifesto in early 1997, which 'incorporated' the ECHR into domestic law in England,[116] the HRA 1998 marked the beginning of a new era in the quest to develop and protect human rights in the UK. The rationale behind the HRA 1998 was demonstrated in the White Paper 'Rights Brought Home: The Human Rights Bill',[117] which states:

> In this country it was long believed that the rights and freedoms guaranteed by the [ECHR] could be delivered under our common law. In the last two decades, however, there has been a growing awareness that it is not sufficient to rely on the common law and that incorporation is necessary.[118]

In the government's view at that time, the approach the UK had so far adopted towards the ECHR did not sufficiently reflect its importance and did not stand the test of time.[119]

112. [1979] 1 Ch 344. In contrast, in the novel *The Once and Future King*, T.H. White proposed a similarly worded rule as the rule of totalitarianism: 'Everything which is not forbidden is compulsory'; see T.H. White, *The Sword in the Stone* (Book 1 of *The Once and Future King*) (Collins 1938).

113. Mark Elliott and Robert Thomas, *Public Law* (OUP 2011) 724–726.

114. Keir Starmer, *European Human Rights Law: The Human Rights Act 1998 and the European Convention on Human Rights* (Legal Action Group 1999) 1.

115. Francesca Klug and Keir Starmer, 'Incorporation by the Back Door?' (1996) *PL* 223.

116. 'Rights Brought Home: The Human Rights Bill', Presented to Parliament by the Secretary of State for the Home Department by Command of Her Majesty, Cm 3782, October 1997.

117. Ibid.

118. Ibid., [1.4].

119. Ibid., [1.15].

7.3.1 Individual Petition Mechanism to the European Court of Human Rights Prior to the Enactment of the Human Rights Act 1998

The above problems were evidently reflected in the 'individual petition mechanism' available prior to the enactment of the HRA 1998. In December 1965, the First Wilson Government decided to accept the right of individual petition and the jurisdiction of the ECtHR to rule on cases brought by individuals against the UK.[120] Unlike the decision to join the EU and thus make EU law directly effective in the British courts, Parliament was not asked to legislate to give effect to the consequences of acceptance of the right of petition.[121] Between 1964 and 1999, over 650 cases involving the ECHR, despite not being incorporated in the UK during the material period, were referred to the ECtHR.[122]

Nevertheless, there have been some 200 judgments of the ECtHR finding breaches by the UK, many of which were controversial and far-reaching.[123] Among them, the first case in which the ECtHR found a breach by the UK was *Golder v UK*.[124] In this case, Golder was a prisoner who had been refused the opportunity to consult his legal representative for the purpose of expressing his maltreatment by the prison authority and his intention to bring libel proceedings against a prison officer. The ECtHR held that the Home Secretary had infringed a prisoner's right of access to the English courts and his right to respect for his correspondence. Another landmark case, *Sunday Times v UK*,[125] concerned the House of Lords' breach of the ECHR by imposing an injunction restraining the Sunday Times from publishing an article about the thalidomide tragedy on the grounds that it was prejudicial to a pending civil proceeding. Its reasoning is that the publication would have constituted contempt of court. The ECtHR, by a narrow majority, held that the Lords' decision to interfere was unnecessary and compromised the right to free expression, and, in doing so, the Court indicated that English law in this area was highly problematic. The

120. Anthony Lester and Kate Beattie, 'Human Rights and the British Constitution' in Jeffrey Jowell and Dawn Oliver (eds), *The Changing Constitution* (6th edn, OUP 2007) 63.

121. Ibid.

122. Stephen Grosz, Jack Beatson, and Peter Duffy, *Human Rights: The 1998 Act and the European Convention* (Sweet & Maxwell 2000) 3. For a list of cases until December 1996, see Murray Hunt, *Using Human Rights Law in English Courts* (Hart Publishing 1997) Appendix I, 325–384.

123. Ibid., Hunt; Lester and Beattie (N120) 64.

124. (1975) 1 EHRR 524.

125. (1979–1980) 2 EHRR 245.

Court went on to explain that Article 10 permitted interference with free speech only if it is 'necessary having regard to the facts and circumstances prevailing in the specific case', and that English law gave too much weight to the right to a fair trial and unduly restricted the freedom of expression.[126] Other significant examples include immigrants or potential immigrants; gay men, lesbians, and other LGBT factions; mental patients;[127] travellers;[128] and prisoners, particularly in cases involving executive decisions in the sphere of sentencing.[129]

Regarding immigration cases, in *East African Asians v UK*,[130] the European Commission of Human Rights found that the enactment of the Commonwealth Immigrants Act 1968, passed in a hurry by the then Labour government to stop British passport holders in East Africa from coming to the UK as they faced persecution in their home countries, was motivated by racism. The Commission also held that in such circumstances, racial discrimination could amount to inhuman and degrading treatment contrary to Article 3 of the ECHR. The case was finally settled and did not proceed to the ECtHR.

Insofar as cases relating to gays and lesbians are concerned, two famous cases are *Dudgeon v UK*[131] and *Lustig-Prean and Beckett v UK*.[132] In *Dudgeon*, the ECtHR held that section 11 of the Criminal Law Amendment Act 1885 (the CLAA 1885) which criminalised male homosexual acts between consenting adults in Northern Ireland violated Article 8 (i.e., the right to respect for private and family life) of the ECHR. The applicant, feeling aggrieved after being interrogated by the police about his sexual activities, filed a complaint with the ECtHR. The ECtHR stated that the restriction imposed on the applicant under the CLAA 1885, by reason of its breadth and absolute character, is, quite apart from the severity of the possible penalties provided for, disproportionate to the aims sought to be achieved. In *Lustig-Prean and Beckett*, the applicants were

126. Ibid., 280–281.

127. *X v UK* (1981) 4 EHRR 188.

128. *Buckley v UK* (1997) 23 EHRR 101.

129. *Hussain v UK* (1996) 22 EHRR 1.

130. (1981) 3 EHRR 76. The Commission considered the case in 1973: Commission's admissibility decision of 14 Dec 1973 (1981) 3 EHRR 76.

131. (1981) 4 EHRR 149.

132. (2000) 29 EHRR 548.

British naval personnel who were dismissed after their homosexuality was discovered. They alleged that their dismissal, coupled with the intrusive nature of the investigations conducted by the Royal Navy into their sexual orientation, violated their right to privacy under Article 8 of the ECHR. The ECtHR held that the Article 8 rights of the applicants had indeed been breached. Ultimately, the UK government immediately suspended discharging homosexuals and, within months, changed the law.

Another sexual minority involved in several prominent cases is transsexuals. For example, in *Rees v UK*,[133] *Cossey v UK*,[134] and *X, Y and Z v UK*,[135] among others, the ECtHR was tasked with deciding if the concept of a person's gender at birth being fixed for all time conflicted with the right to respect for private life under Article 8 of the ECHR. Despite the Court noting that Article 8 did not require the English system to recognise a changed effect by gender re-assignment surgery, the votes in favour of these judgments have been going down with every case. All in all, the ECHR has been frequently invoked in proceedings before the English courts prior to the HRA 1998 being incorporated (in 1998) and fully enforced (in 2000).[136]

7.3.2 Status of the Human Rights Act 1998: Another Constitutional Statute

When drafting the HRA 1998, the UK government considered, but ultimately rejected, the approach adopted in the ECA 1972, which provided for EU law to take precedence over domestic law where it has 'direct effect'.[137] Although the HRA 1998, on its face, is just another ordinary statute, and is not 'entrenched' or confer any higher-order status, it has been declared to possess constitutional status on many occasions.[138] This is not only because the legislation is, for the first time, able to be placed under the scrutiny of the judiciary, but also because it

133. (1986) 9 EHRR 56.

134. (1991) 13 EHRR 622.

135. (1997) 24 EHRR 143.

136. Hunt (N122) Appendix I, 325–384.

137. Starmer (N114) 3.

138. *Brown v Stott (Procurator Fiscal, Dunfermline)* [2001] 2 WLR 817, 835 (Lord Bingham); *R v Offen* [2001] 1 WLR 254, 275 (Lord Woolf); *Thoburn* (N67); *International Transport Roth GmbH v Secretary of State for the Home Department* [2002] EWCA Civ 158, [69]–[75] (Laws LJ).

imports into UK law a notion that government, or broadly speaking, a democratic society, is limited in its scope by the requirement to observe fundamental rights that are themselves necessary for democracy. This model of government differs from the model of majority rule by insisting that certain fundamental rights must be protected even if Parliament, representing the majority of the electorate, decrees otherwise. Therefore, the HRA 1998 marks a new beginning and a fundamental shift to a rights-based system of law in the UK. Its impact on all areas of law and practice has been profound. As Francesca Klug noted:

> The courts are clearly given new powers of judicial review under the HRA that they did not have before. They can now review the decisions and actions of ministers and officials in substantive, human rights terms and they can even consider the compatibility of primary legislation with the [ECHR] rights in the HRA, something they were effectively constitutionally barred from doing before. This, together with the fact that s. 2 of the Act allows the courts to range wider than the ECHR and look at the jurisprudence of other human rights treaties, is what makes it effectively a bill of rights or 'higher law'.[139]

Although the HRA 1998 does not go so far as to permit the courts to strike down legislation that offends the ECHR, a subtle compromise has been reached with the notion of parliamentary sovereignty so that the courts may only issue a declaration of incompatibility. Even if the legislation declared incompatible is upheld, such a declaration carries great moral weight, and the relevant Minister is given power to amend the offending legislation by way of a remedial order, which can have retrospective effect. When proposing legislation, moreover, Ministers must also certify whether they believe the Bill in question complies with ECHR standards.[140] Against this background, the HRA 1998 was designed to give the courts as much space as possible to protect human rights, short of a power to set aside Acts of Parliament.[141]

The effect of these features of the HRA 1998 is that all law must now be looked at through the prism of human rights standards, and that those standards must

139. Francesca Klug, 'The Human Rights Act: A "Third Way" or "Third Wave" Bill of Rights' (2001) *EHRLR* 361, 370.

140. HRA 1998, s 19.

141. HL Deb, 3 November 1997, Vol. 582, Col. 1228, available at: https://api.parliament.uk/historic-hansard/lords/1997/nov/03/human-rights-bill-hl, last accessed 31 May 2020.

be defined by methods of interpretation which acknowledge the constitutional context of it. To achieve this, a purposive or teleological process of reasoning is required, permitting all UK law to be 'rinsed with a human rights dye'.[142] In addition, Lords Mance and Neuberger mentioned in *HS2 Action Alliance* case that 'we have a number of constitutional instruments. ... the [HRA 1998] ... may now be added to this list'.[143] Owing to the above, the HRA 1998 can be regarded as a constitutional statute in the UK.

The HRA 1998 also requires the judicial importation of democratic standards and values enshrined in the ECHR into UK government and public authority decision-making.[144] For one thing, the British government has included the principle of proportionality in its guide to judicial review for administrators, *The Judge Over Your Shoulder*.[145] Thus, even though proportionality has yet to be judicially endorsed on a unanimous basis as an independent ground of judicial review in Britain, it is officially recognised by the administration to be one of the established legal norms. Officials are required to be aware of, and should observe, its practical implications when exercising their discretionary powers in discharging their public duties. The same also applies to Hong Kong because a similar document, *JOYS — A Guide to Judicial Review for Administrators*, has been adopted by the government there.[146]

Furthermore, although proportionality has yet to be judicially endorsed on a unanimous basis as an independent ground of judicial review in Britain, the principle has been enshrined in the new Rules of Civil Procedure. Under the new rules, all judges have to give effect to the overriding objective of

142. Stephen Sedley, *Freedom, Law and Justice* (Sweet & Maxwell 1999).

143. *HS2 Action Alliance* (N78) [207].

144. Ellie Palmer, *Judicial Review, Socio-Economic Rights and the Human Rights Act* (Hart Publishing 2007) 189.

145. Treasury Solicitor's Department, *The Judge Over Your Shoulder: A Guide to Judicial Review for UK Government Administrators* (4th edn, January 2006) [2.16] and [2.29]–[2.30], available at: www.gov.uk/government/publications/the-judge-over-your-shoulder-joys-edition-4, last accessed 2 January 2020. Note: this publication was temporarily withdrawn on 31 March 2015 because it is being revised. The new version will be published on www.gov.uk once complete.

146. Department of Justice, HKSAR government, *The Judge over your Shoulder: A Guide to Judicial Review for Administrators* (3rd edn, 2019), 23–25 and 38–42, available at: www.doj.gov.hk/eng/public/The_Judge_Over_Your_Shoulder.html, last accessed on 31 May 2020. For further discussion of Hong Kong, see Chapter Eight of this book.

enabling cases to be dealt with justly, of which proportionality is one of the considerations. In particular, the rules recognise that wider social and economic considerations have to be balanced against the single-minded pursuit of justice. In this regard, proportionality, as far as case management is concerned, is judicially recognised under the new rules.

Considering whether all members of the UK's highest court must endorse proportionality as an independent ground of judicial review in Britain, Hilary Delany has disagreed, saying that

> it now seems clear as a result of the *dicta* contained in two decisions of the House of Lords decided around the same time in 2001 that proportionality has been recognised as a separate ground of review in English law, even outside the context of EU or ECHR rights.[147]

These two *dictum* are in *R (on the application of Alconbury Developments Ltd) v Secretary of State for the Environment, Transport and the Regions* [148] and *R (on the application of Daly) v Secretary of State for the Home Department.*[149] In *Alconbury*, on one hand, Lord Slynn stated:

> I consider that even without reference to the [HRA 1998] the time has come to recognise that this principle [of proportionality] is part of English administrative law, not only when judges are dealing with community acts but also when they are dealing with acts subject to domestic law.[150]

In *Daly*, on the other, Lord Bingham effectively applied the proportionality test in concluding that the claimant's 'common law right' had been infringed by a policy that 'provides for a greater degree of intrusion into the privileged legal correspondence of prisoners which is greater than is justified by the objectives this policy is intended to serve'.[151]

147. Hilary Delany, *Judicial Review of Administrative Action* (2nd edn, Thomson Reuters 2009) 124.

148. [2001] UKHL 23, [2001] 2 WLR 1389, [2001] 2 All ER 929, [2003] 2 AC 295.

149. [2001] 1 AC 532, [2001] UKHL 26, [2001] 2 WLR 1622.

150. *Alconbury* (N148) [2003] 2 AC 295, 321.

151. *Daly* (N149) [2001] 2 AC 532, 548.

I concur with Delany. Our argument is further supported by a landmark negligence case, namely *Donoghue v Stevenson*,[152] the so-called *Ginger beer* case. Before 1932, there was no recognised general test for deciding whether a duty of care existed in circumstances which had not previously come before the court. In that case, the House of Lords, by a bare majority of 3:2, established that a manufacturer of products owed a duty to take reasonable care to the ultimate consumer of the product. Since then, Lord Atkin's 'neighbour principle' has formed the basis of the modern law of negligence and has served as a basic requirement to determine when a duty of care is owed.

7.3.3 Reference to other Common Law Jurisdictions in the Interpretation of the European Convention on Human Rights

In interpreting the scope of the ECHR, UK courts have turned to pronouncements of other common law constitutional courts, including the South African Constitutional Court and the Canadian Supreme Court, which have similarly adopted 'open-textured' constitutions in the last two decades or so.[153] For instance, in reaching the conclusion that 'public opinion' is not a sufficient benchmark for deciding the limits of judicial intervention in politically sensitive disputes in which fundamental rights are at stake, Lord Bingham, in *Reyes v R*,[154] explicitly referred to the following speech of Chalkaston P of the South African Constitutional Court:

> The very reason for establishing the new legal order and for vesting the power of judicial review of all legislation in the courts, was to protect the rights of minorities and others who cannot protect their rights adequately through the democratic process. Those who are entitled to claim this protection include the social outcasts and marginalized people of our society. It is only if there is a willingness to protect the worst and weakest among us that all of us can be secure that our own rights will be protected.[155]

152. [1932] AC 562 (HL).

153. Richard Clayton, 'Judicial Deference and "Democratic Dialogue": The Legitimacy of Judicial Intervention under the Human Rights Act 1998' (2004) *PL* 33–47.

154. [2002] 11 UKPC, [2002] 2 AC 235.

155. *State v Makwanyane* 1995 (3) SA 391, [1995] 1 LCR 269, 311.

7.3.4 The Human Rights Act 1998 Regime

Under the HRA 1998, the Preamble provides that the Act is to 'give further effect to rights and freedoms guaranteed under the ECHR', and section 1 enumerates the effected Articles which are set out in Schedule 1. There is a difference between rights under the ECHR and the rights set out in Schedule 1 to the HRA 1998. The former bind the UK in international law as a party to the treaty, whereas the latter are enforceable as a matter of English law in the terms set out in the HRA 1998. The rights range across most of those in the original ECHR text [156] and those variously added by the Protocols.[157] The UK courts, now tasked with considering the scope of the rights in domestic proceedings, are required by section 2 — namely, Interpretation of Convention Rights — to 'take into account' any relevant ECtHR jurisprudence. The area in which section 2 will be of most immediate significance is the principles of judicial review. This is because ECtHR jurisprudence incorporates several key principles, including the proportionality principle.[158] Even though the courts have already emphasised that they would afford primary decision-makers an 'area of discretion' in cases arising under the HRA 1998, they also equally recognise that the proportionality principle now has some application.[159] Given that domestic courts are mandatorily obliged by section 2(1) to 'take into account' the ECtHR's jurisprudence, which places proportionality at the heart of the processes of interpreting the ECHR,[160] some transplantation of the requirement of proportionate interference into domestic law is inevitable. Therefore, even if an applicant in a judicial review proceeding is not making a direct rights-based challenge, they would be fully entitled to expect the courts to honour its statutory duty. This ensures that every application for judicial review can be said to be operating in a human rights context. Indeed, if one delves deep enough, they are likely to be able to identify an underlying human rights norm that would bring the case within the rubric of fundamental rights, thereby triggering the right to maintain a

156. ECHR, Arts 2–12 and 14.

157. First Protocol, Arts 1–3; Sixth Protocol, Arts 1–2.

158. Marc-André Eissen, 'The Principle of Proportionality in the Case-Law of the European Court of Human Rights' in Ronald Macdonald, Franz Matscher, and Herbert Petzold (eds), *The European System for the Protection of Human Rights* (Dordrecht 1993) 125; Jeremy McBride, 'Proportionality and the European ECHR on Human Rights' in Ellis (N3) 23.

159. *Daly* (N149) [2001] 2 AC 532, 548 (Lord Bingham); *R v (Saadi) v Secretary of State for the Home Department* [2001] 4 All ER 961.

160. *Soering v UK* (1989) 11 EHRR 439, [89]; *Gaskin v UK* (1989) 12 EHRR 36, [42].

proportionality enquiry. Craig has used the *Wednesbury* case itself to argue that if the HRA 1998 had been in force during the 1940s, the applicants, Associated Provincial Picture Houses, might have contended that the restriction imposed in the case, to the effect that a cinema could open on Sunday, but could not admit children under 15, was contrary to Article 8 (i.e., the right to family life) or perhaps even Article 10 (i.e., freedom of speech) of the ECHR.[161]

This does not mean that the ECtHR would rule over the UK courts. Even though the ECtHR was, and still is, the final court of interpretation on what the ECHR meant, 'there was no stomach for making this European institution the top court in the UK'.[162] According to Gearty, the purpose of section 2 is to make sure that the UK courts know about the relevant ECtHR jurisprudence on the basis that they did not have to follow it 'in a slavish way that the lower courts do to decisions in the UK system further up to the pecking order (the doctrine of precedent)'.[163] Despite having a false start — when UK judges were too enthusiastic in following the ECtHR — the position is now clear that section 2 means what it says: that judges can depart from the ECtHR where they feel strongly that the ECtHR has got it wrong. Examples of this range from the laws of evidence in serious criminal trials [164] to rules on life imprisonment.[165] Overall, what the ECtHR does is reflect and comment on the UK's approach when a suitable case comes before it, and it has done so from time to time. It is much more 'dialogue' than domination.[166] Gearty furthers that 'although ignoring ECtHR might create the problems of non-compliance just referred to with regard to acts of parliament ... that risk is entailed in membership of the Council of Europe, not something the [HRA 1998] has caused'.[167]

161. Paul Craig, *Administrative Law* (7th edn, Sweet & Maxwell 2012) 651.

162. Conor Gearty, 'The Human Rights Act Should Not Be Replaced', *UK Constitutional Law Blog*, 17 September 2016, available at: https://ukconstitutionallaw.org/2016/09/17/conor-gearty-the-human-rights-act-should-not-be-repealed/, last accessed 2 January 2020.

163. Ibid.

164. *R v Horncastle* [2009] UKSC 14.

165. *R v McLoughlin and Newell* [2014] EWCA Crim 188.

166. Gearty (N162).

167. Ibid.

7.3.4.1 Interpretation of Legislation

Since the HRA 1998 came into force in 2000, the courts are now, for the first time, empowered to review primary legislation for compliance with a codified set of fundamental rights as enshrined in the ECHR. They are given two main powers with respect to primary legislation, one being interpretative under section 3, while the other is declaratory under section 4.

Under section 3 — namely, Interpretation of Legislation — legislation must be read and given effect in a way which is compatible with the ECHR. Therefore, the courts are now placed under a duty to interpret legislation compatibly with the ECHR 'so far as it is possible to do so'.[168] As Roger Masterman has argued, this tallies with a gradual movement away from the overly literal approach to statutory construction under which it becomes commonplace for the courts to seek to apply a statute in light of its purpose, to do so in the context of its aim, or to subject it to common law presumptions of parliamentary intent.[169] Richard Clayton has also opined that as the language of the HRA 1998 is broad and malleable, conclusions on the same issue may be equally arguable, which provide numerous opportunities for the courts to second-guess Parliament.[170]

The first House of Lords' decision on the scope of section 3(1) was the controversial case of *R v A (No. 2)*,[171] which concerned the construction of section 41 of the Youth Justice and Criminal Evidence Act 1999. Section 41 was a provision designed to prevent the submission of evidence based on the complainant's previous sexual history, in particular a defendant's involvement in rape proceedings (resulting in this section being called a 'Rape Shield'), save in narrowly defined circumstances outlined in section 41(3). The defendant in this case (who had previously been charged with rape) claimed that the complainant had consented to the sexual intercourse which was the subject matter of the charge, so the question before the trial court was whether evidence concerning an alleged prior consensual sexual relationship between them in the preceding weeks was admissible under section 41.

168. *R (Middleton) v West Somerset Coroner and Secretary of State for the Home Department* [2004] 2 AC 182.

169. Masterman (N77) 150.

170. Clayton (N153) 34.

171. [2001] UKHL 25, [2002] 1 AC 45.

On appeal to the House of Lords, their Lordships agreed that if section 41 were construed in accordance with ordinary methods of statutory interpretation, such evidence would be inadmissible and, *prima facie,* might result in a breach of the defendant's right to a fair trial under Article 6 of the ECHR. Lord Steyn opined that although section 41(3) had contained some narrow exceptions, it constituted 'a blanket exclusion of potentially relevant evidence',[172] and, as such, was simply too restrictive, calling it 'legislative overkill'.[173] He even criticised such a blanket exclusion as 'being disproportionately restrictive'.[174] Despite ordinary methods of interpretation being incapable of curing the 'excessive breadth' [175] of the section, their Lordships unanimously held that:

> Due regard always being paid to the importance of seeking to protect the complainant from indignity and humiliating questions, the test of admissibility is whether the evidence is nevertheless so relevant to the issue of consent that to exclude it would endanger the fairness of the trial under Article 6 of the [ECHR].[176]

Simply put, the House of Lords concluded that it was possible to read section 41(3)(c), which enables a judge to admit relevant evidence about the complainant's prior sexual history in certain circumstances, as subject to the 'implied provision' that 'evidence or questioning which is required to secure a fair trial under Article 6 of the [ECHR] should not be treated as inadmissible'.[177]

Such innovative interpretation (i.e., 'reading in' — implying provisions into statutes that are necessary to safeguard the ECHR, as termed by Dinah Rose and Claire Weir)[178] was initiated by Lord Steyn, who stressed that section 3 required more than the adoption of a 'contextual and purposive' interpretation

172. Ibid., [39].

173. Ibid., [43].

174. Ibid., [13].

175. Ibid., [43] (Lord Steyn).

176. Ibid., [46] (Lord Steyn), supported by Lord Slynn at [13], Lord Hope at [110], Lord Clyde at [140], and Lord Hutton at [163].

177. Ibid., [45] (Lord Steyn).

178. Dinah Rose and Claire Weir, 'Interpretation and Incompatibility: Striking the Balance' in Jeffrey Jowell and Jonathan Cooper (eds), *Delivering Rights: How the Human Rights Act is Working* (Hart Publishing 2003) 48.

and noted that it would sometimes be necessary to adopt an interpretation which 'linguistically may appear strained'.[179] This approach was justified on the premise that Parliament, if alerted to the problem when enacting section 41(3)(c), would not have wished to deny the defendant a fair trial, and must therefore have intended this provision to be interpreted in such a way as to be compatible with that right.[180] According to Rose and Weir, the only justification for courts engaging in 'reading in' provisions to the legislation is that they are treating the parliamentary intention expressed in the HRA 1998 as 'trumping' the intention in the statute in question under consideration.[181] *R v A (No. 2)* is a case in which the Court was prepared to circumscribe a statutory discretion.

Lord Steyn, again, in *R v A (No. 2)*, also identified another interpretative technique, called 'reading down' (i.e., restricting the scope and effect of apparently broad and unclear statutory language, as also termed by Rose and Weir), to ensure that powers can only be exercised consistently with the ECHR.[182] Such transformative potential of section 3(1) is seen in the second major case to reach the House of Lords in the early years of the HRA 1998. In *R v Lambert*,[183] the House of Lords had to decide whether a legal, rather than evidential, burden of proof placed on the defendant under sections 5 and 28 of the Misuse of Drugs Act 1971 (MDA 1971) was in breach of the right to a fair trial guaranteed under Article 6 of the ECHR. The Court first established that when being read in the ordinary way, section 28 'demonstrates that what Parliament chose to do' [184] was to impose a legal burden of proof (contrary to the right to a fair trial under Article 6 of the ECHR). The next stage was to assess whether this 'decision' served a legitimate objective and satisfied the proportionality principle. Although there was agreement that the statutory aim was legitimate, in that it was to penalise the unauthorised possession of dangerous drugs on the

179. *R v A (No. 2)* (N171) [44].

180. Ibid., [45] (Lord Steyn).

181. Rose and Weir (N178) 49. See also *R (H) v Mental Health Review Tribunal, North and East London Region* [2001] EWCA Civ 415, [2002] QB 1 (CA).

182. Ibid., Rose and Weir, 48.

183. [2002] 2 AC 545.

184. Ibid., [68] (Lord Hope).

understanding that many sophisticated drugs smugglers, dealers, and couriers would typically secret drugs in some container thereby enabling them to say that they are unaware of the contents,[185] their Lordships concluded that having a legal burden of proof imposed on all defendants was a disproportionate way of satisfying that purpose. It would have been sufficient to impose an evidential burden on the accused. However, all was not lost for the MDA 1971. Their Lordships held that it was 'possible' under section 3(1) of the HRA 1998 'to read the words "to prove" as if the words used in section 28(2) [of the MDA 1971] were "to give sufficient evidence"'.[186] Hence, even though the ordinary or natural meaning of the provision was that it imposed a legal burden of proof, section 3(1) enabled the Court to read it so that it only imposed an evidential burden of proof. Simply put, this may involve giving the words a narrower construction than their ordinary meaning would bear (the effect of which is that such interpretation would not alter the ordinary meaning of the words used or express the statutory words in different language) in order to explain how they are to be read in a way that is compatible with the ECHR.

In short, section 3(1) provides the central test of statutory interpretation where ECHR provisions are at stake, and any question as to the statutory language adopted, or the intent of Parliament in passing the disputed provision, is of only secondary importance. As Lord Nicholls noted in *Ghaidan v Godin-Mendoza*:[187]

> In the ordinary course the interpretation of legislation involves seeking the intention reasonably to be attributed to Parliament in using the language in question. Section 3 may require the court to depart from this legislative intention, that is, depart from the intention of Parliament which enacted the legislation.[188]

In this case, the defendant, Juan Godin-Mendoza, and his homosexual partner, Hugh Wallwyn-James, shared a flat which was subject to a statutory tenancy granted upon the latter under the Rent Act 1977 (RA 1977) since 1983. On

185. Ibid., [36] (Lord Steyn); [71], [89] (Lord Hope).

186. Ibid., [94] (Lord Steyn).

187. [2002] EWCA Civ 1533, [2004] UKHL 30, [2004] 2 AC 557.

188. Ibid., [33].

Wallwyn-James' death in 2001, the landlord, Ahmad Ghaidan, brought proceedings against Godin-Mendoza, wishing to evict him from the property. However, if Godin-Mendoza was, as he had argued, a 'statutory tenant' within the meaning of the RA 1977, he would enjoy legal immunity from eviction, save in limited circumstances. Thus, this case revolved around whether Godin-Mendoza was a statutory tenant, and whether such a tenancy was governed by the RA 1977. Schedule 1, paragraph 2, of the RA 1977 states:

> (1) The surviving spouse (if any) of the original tenant, if residing in the dwelling-house immediately before the death of the original tenant, shall after the death be the statutory tenant if and so long as he or she occupies the dwelling-house as his or her residence.
>
> (2) For the purposes of this paragraph, a person who was living with the original tenant as his or her wife or husband shall be treated as the spouse of the original tenant.

The question tabled before the House of Lords was whether the above rules had operated to such an extent that upon the death of Wallwyn-James (i.e., the 'original tenant'), a statutory tenancy was vested in Godin-Mendoza.

Having lived together in the house in question for 18 years before Wallwyn-James' death, Godin-Mendoza contended that he satisfied the conditions for a statutory tenancy, but the case was complicated by their relationship being a same-sex partnership. Bearing in mind its obligation under section 3 of the HRA 1998, the Court had to determine whether the above provisions should be read as applying to same-sex couples. It adopted a three-stage analysis. The first question concerned the natural meaning of the legislation (i.e., what the relevant provisions would mean if the HRA 1998 did not exist). For this, the answer was straightforward. Throughout the provisions in question, gender-specific language was used such as 'spouse', 'husband', and 'wife'. Thus, Lord Nicholls observed that

> on an ordinary reading of this language paragraph 2(2) draws a distinction between the position of a heterosexual couple living together in a house as husband and wife and a homosexual couple living together in a house.

> The survivor of a heterosexual couple may become a statutory tenant by succession, the survivor of a homosexual couple cannot.[189]

The second question is whether, given the ECHR's natural meaning, the relevant provisions would produce an outcome that would infringe one or more of the ECHR provisions when being applied to the facts of the case. It is clear that if the relevant rights were to have been given their natural meaning, the defendant would definitely not have become a statutory tenant. If that was the case, would this have involved a breach of the defendant's rights (i.e., Article 8, the right to respect for private and family life, and Article 14, prohibition of discrimination)? The Court concluded that it would. Article 8 requires respect for, among other things, a person's home. However, taken in isolation, this would not have helped the defendant because Article 8 does not impose a blanket prohibition upon evictions. It is the provision in the RA 1977 that the landlord claimant cannot lawfully evict the defendant if the latter had a statutory tenancy right on the basis of an opposite-sex relationship which applies here. This factor made Article 14 come into play, the effect of which was that the enjoyment of the other rights set out in the ECHR, and thus the HRA 1998, 'shall be secured without discrimination' on various grounds, including sexual orientation.[190] It ensued that the RA 1977 would, if being applied to the defendant tenant, entail a breach of Article 14 — the defendant would have been accorded a lower degree of respect for his home primarily because his claim was based on a same-sex, rather than an opposite-sex, relationship.

The third question is whether it is possible, pursuant to section 3 of the HRA 1998, to read and give effect to the relevant provisions of domestic law in such a way as to produce an outcome that would be compatible with the relevant ECHR provisions. At this point, the Court had to confront the precise nature of the obligation imposed upon it by section 3. It had to interpret domestic law to be compatible with the ECHR '[s]o far as it is possible to do so'. According to Lord Nicholls, this obligation was a very strong one, and it should not be taken as a narrow mandate that simply requires the courts to

189. Ibid., [5].

190. *Da Silva Mouta v Portugal* (2001) 31 EHRR 4; *EB v France* (2008) 47 EHRR 21.

resolve ambiguities.[191] Rather, it was an 'unusual and far-reaching' obligation, in that it 'may require courts to depart from the unambiguous meaning that the legislation would otherwise bear'.[192] It might even require the courts to 'depart from the intention of Parliament which enacted the legislation'.[193] Although this would unavoidably involve frustrating Parliament's intention when it passed the provision in question, it would fulfil its intention in enacting section 3. More importantly, in enacting section 3, said Lord Nicholls, Parliament showed that they did not intend for ECHR-compliant interpretation to 'depend critically upon the particular form of words adopted by the parliamentary draftsman in the statutory provision under consideration'.[194] Such an approach 'would make the application of section 3 something of a semantic lottery'.[195] Ultimately, his Lordship concluded that section 3 permits the courts to read words into a statutory text in order to change its meaning so as to make it ECHR-compliant.[196]

However, Lord Nicholls did not consider the power conferred by section 3 of the HRA 1998 to be unlimited, stating that Parliament could not 'have intended that in the discharge of this extended interpretative functions the courts should adopt a meaning inconsistent with a fundamental feature of legislation'.[197] He went on to say that the courts may not ascribe to a given provision a meaning that is inconsistent with the 'underlying thrust of the legislation being construed'.[198] Lord Rodger concurred and suggested the interpretation must 'go with the grain of the legislation'.[199] It ensued that the courts must not attribute a meaning to a provision in question that conflicts with the 'essential principles' of the legislation concerned. To do so, said Lord Rodger, would cross 'the boundary between interpretation and amendment of the statute', thereby taking the courts beyond their proper role under section 3.[200]

191. *Ghaidan* (N187) [29].

192. Ibid.

193. Ibid., [30].

194. Ibid., [31].

195. Ibid.

196. Ibid., [32].

197. Ibid., [33].

198. Ibid.

199. Ibid., [121].

200. Ibid.

Applying the above principles, the majority of the House of Lords held that the thrust of the relevant parts of the RA 1977 was to confer protection upon those who were the surviving partners of stable and close relationship. This meant that bringing same-sex partners within the scope of the protection afforded by the RA 1977 would not be improper. As Lord Nicholls put it, 'the precise form of words read in for this purpose is of no significance. It is their substantive effect which matters'.[201]

According to Aileen Kavanagh, one interesting aspect of *Ghaidan* was that it departed from the pre-HRA 1998 judgment of *Fitzpatrick v Sterling Housing Association Ltd*,[202] the facts of which were very similar to those in *Ghaidan*. Therefore, the contrast between the two cases is instructive when examining how section 3(1) of the HRA 1998 has impacted traditional methods of statutory interpretation.[203] In *Fitzpatrick*, the House of Lords unanimously rejected the contention that the words 'living together as his or her husband or wife' could be read to include homosexual partners. Their rejection was premised on the fact that the terms 'husband' and 'wife' are gender-specific,[204] and that in using the words 'as his or her husband or wife', Parliament did not intend to include homosexual partners.[205] Nevertheless, by a majority of three to two, their Lordships held that homosexual partners could be considered 'a member of the original tenant's family' for the purposes of paragraph 3(1) of Schedule 1 to the RA 1977, thus enabling the claimant to succeed in obtaining an 'assured', rather than a 'statutory', tenancy.

As Kavanagh noted, although counsel for Mr Fitzpatrick argued that he should succeed in a statutory tenancy under paragraph 2(2) of the RA 1977, they seemed to place the weight of their submissions on the alternative argument that Mr Fitzpatrick qualified as a 'family member' of the original tenant under

201. Ibid., [35].

202. [2001] 1 AC 27.

203. Aileen Kavanagh, 'Choosing between sections 3 and 4 of the Human Rights Act 1998: Judicial Reasoning after *Ghaidan v Mendoza*' in Helen Fenwick, Gavin Phillipson, and Roger Masterman (eds), *Judicial Reasoning under the UK Human Rights Act* (CUP 2007) 137–138.

204. *Fitzpatrick* (N202) 43 (Lord Nicholls): 'A husband is a man and a wife is a woman'; supported by Lord Clyde, 47; and Lord Slynn, 34.

205. Ibid., 34 (Lord Slynn).

paragraph 3(1) of Schedule 1 of the RA 1977.[206] This might have been because Mr Fitzpatrick was content with an 'assured' tenancy, or because his counsel believed that he had a greater chance of success with the 'family member' argument rather than the 'spouse' argument. In this regard, Kavanagh has argued that 'whatever the case may be, by the time we get to *Ghaidan*, Mr Godin-Mendoza was guaranteed an assured tenancy because of *Fitzpatrick*, but he also wanted a below-market rent that goes with a statutory tenancy'.[207] Hence, he based his legal arguments on paragraph 2(2). The different lines of argument adopted by the claimants in both cases undoubtedly impacted the judicial decisions which ultimately emerged. Moreover, the comparison of judicial reasoning between *Ghaidan* and *Fitzpatrick* has also revealed that the House of Lords in the former case was more willing to 'rectify' the terms of paragraph 2(2) than they were in *Fitzpatrick*. However, this does not mean that the HRA 1998 has ushered in a radically new type of judicial reasoning. The difference between the pre-HRA 1998 era and the HRA 1998 regime lies more in the judiciary's willingness to use existing (creative) techniques of statutory interpretation and in their sense of legitimacy in doing so.[208] In agreement, Laws LJ explained that it is not a fundamental difference in kind, but rather a different view of the appropriateness of relying on existing techniques which were formerly used in exceptional circumstances.[209]

Overall, although section 3 of the HRA 1998 provides very little guidance about how the power it confers should be exercised, T.R.S. Allan has argued that in the absence of textual guidance, the true extent of section 3 inevitably must be decided with reference to broader constitutional considerations.[210] According to Allan, there are two rival conceptions of constitutional thought in Britain, one being 'constitution of will' and the other being 'constitution of

206. Ibid., 29–30.

207. Kavanagh (N203) 138; Robert Wintemute, 'Same-Sex Partners, Living as Husband and Wife, and Section Three of the Human Rights Act 1998' (2003) *PL* 621, 621.

208. Ibid., Kavanagh, 141.

209. John Laws, 'The Impact of the Human Rights Act 1998 on the Interpretation of Enactments in the UK' in Rick Bigwood (ed), *The Statute: Making and Meaning* (Lexis-Nexis 2004) 245.

210. T.R.S. Allan, 'Parliament's Will and the Justice of the Common Law: The HRA in Constitutional Perspective' (2006) 59 *CLP* 27.

reason'. Both influence people's views of what the courts should do, and hence of the proper extent of their authority under section 3.[211]

7.3.4.2 Declaration of Incompatibility

In case the interpretative route proves impossible, the courts may then issue a declaration of incompatibility [212] under section 4 despite it being operated as a 'measure of last resort', or a 'booby prize',[213] which 'must be avoided unless it is plainly impossible to do so'.[214] Although the declaration has no immediate impact on the validity of the legislation under scrutiny, it does place the administration and Parliament under considerable pressure to amend the impugned legislation. In this regard, some scholars have even argued that such mechanism should be used more often because it facilitates 'dialogue' between the courts and the elected branches of government, and that encouraging such dialogue is one of the purposes of the HRA 1998, to which judges can give effect by issuing a declaration of incompatibility.[215] As Geoffrey Marshall once put it:

> A declaration by the courts provides the legislature with a considered judicial view of the rights-compatibility of the legislation. It can then reflect on its actions and either take the remedial steps provided for in section 10 of the [HRA 1998] or exercise its retained sovereign prerogative to disagree with the judicial assessment and confirm its initial view of its legislation.[216]

In the *Belmarsh Detainees* case,[217] the Lords quashed, by an 8:1 margin, the order in respect of the HRA 1998 (Designated Derogation) Order 2001 (DDO 2001) and made a declaration of incompatibility under section 4 of the HRA 1998. They indicated that section 23 of the Anti-Terrorism, Crime, and Security Act 2001

---

211. Ibid.

212. HRA 1998, s 4(5).

213. Geoffrey Marshall, 'Two Kinds of Compatibility: More about Section 3 of the Human Rights Act 1998' (1999) Autumn *PL* 377.

214. *R v A (No. 2)* (N171) [44] (Lord Steyn).

215. Klug (N139) 370; Danny Nicol, 'Are Convention Rights a No-Go Zone for Parliament?' (2002) *PL* 438, 441; Geoffrey Marshall, 'The Lynchpin of Parliamentary Intention: Lost, Stolen or Strained?' (2003) *PL* 236, 243–244.

216. Ibid., Marshall.

217. *A v Secretary of State for the Home Department* [2004] UKHL 56, [2005] 2 WLR 87, [2005] 2 AC 68.

was incompatible with Articles 5 and 15 (i.e., the right to liberty and security and derogation in time of emergency) of the ECHR to the extent that it was disproportionate as it permitted detention of suspected international terrorists in a way that discriminates on the grounds of nationality or immigration status.

The central issue of this case was the proportionality of the response by Parliament to the threat posed by global terrorism after the attacks in New York, Washington, and Pennsylvania on 11 September 2001. The DDO 2001 was a far-reaching piece of legislation that, among other things, empowered the Home Secretary to authorise the indefinite detention, without trial, of non-British nationals who were suspected of involvement in terrorism. Such detention, which was ordered for a number of individuals who had been suspected of involvement with Islamic terror groups, is alleged to have interfered with rights granted under Article 5 of the ECHR, which guarantees the right to liberty. However, that guarantee can be derogated from if there is a public emergency threatening the life of the nation. The British government did indeed enter a derogation with the Council of Europe and made the Derogation Order.

At first glance, there appears to be little room for judicial evaluation in any of these matters as it is a policy area in which decisions about what constitutes sufficient public interest, as adjudged by the executive on behalf of the electorate, demand the highest degree of judicial restraint or deference. Nevertheless, in view of the stark denial of the applicants' rights, the House of Lords felt compelled to look beyond this 'narrow utilitarian account' of their orthodox role in public law to balance individual human rights against the collective will of the majority. They instead accepted an alternative public law vision in which human rights are constituents of democracy rather than weapons wielded by individual interests ranged against it.[218] In this case, Lord Hope cautioned against 'the dangers that lie in store for democracy itself, if the courts were to allow individuals to be deprived of their right to liberty indefinitely and without charge on grounds of public interest by the executive'.[219]

218. Palmer (N144) 193.

219. *Belmarsh Detainees* case (N217) [100].

While the majority in the House of Lords had not formally rejected the government's assessment that such an emergency existed, they did reject the argument that indefinite detention represented a proportionate response to the perceived threat. This is because Article 15 of the ECHR requires that any measures introduced should be strictly in proportion to the mischief pursued. However, the Court felt that the relevant provisions of the DDO 2001 failed that test in relation to the liberty rights of individuals. Placing the burden on the applicants themselves, the Court required the executive to give good reason to displace the government's justifications. Since the rules applied only to foreign nationals and not to UK nationals suspected of international terrorist activities, they were not 'strictly required'. Lord Bingham, in particular, believed that the threat presented by suspected terrorists could have been countered in much less intrusive ways that included requiring individuals to report regularly to police stations.

What is more, Lord Rodger stressed that due deference does not mean abasement,[220] and Lord Bingham rejected the Attorney-General's argument that protection of public safety fell within the discretionary area of judgment belonging to the elected organs of government. More importantly, Lord Bingham recognised the function of independent judges charged to interpret and apply the law to be a cardinal feature of the modern democratic state, saying that '[t]he Attorney General is fully entitled to insist on the proper limits of judicial authority but he is wrong to stigmatise judicial decision-making as in some way undemocratic'.[221] Although their Lordships could not compel the release of the detained prisoners, the House of Lords has, in making the decision to issue such a declaration, abandoned the overly deferential tones of previous decisions concerned with national security issues.

Overall, some scholars have commented that the courts' power to review primary legislation under the HRA 1998 regime can be regarded as 'constitutional review' [222] or 'legislative review'.[223] This distinguishes it from their traditional powers of judicial review in relation to public authority decision-making in

220. Ibid., [176].

221. Ibid., [42].

222. Jowell (N3); Dawn Oliver, *Constitutional Reform in the UK* (OUP 2003) 100; Palmer (N144) 33.

223. Masterman (N77) 105.

administrative law. More importantly, it highlights the constitutional character of the courts' supervisory power, and, indeed, the constitutional importance of the HRA 1998 itself.[224] In this connection, Mark Elliott and Robert Thomas have raised an interesting question concerning the doctrine of implied repeal, in that when two Acts of Parliament conflict with one another, the more recent Act prevails over and repeals the earlier Act to the extent of the inconsistency. What happens, then, if legislation enacted prior to HRA 1998 enactment turns out to be incompatible with one of the stipulations of the ECHR? Is the pre-HRA 1998 provision impliedly repealed, meaning that it is simply invalid? If this is the case, then there seems to be no role for declarations of incompatibility because, under the doctrine of implied repeal, those pre-HRA 1998 provisions would be automatically invalid, unenforceable, and thus meaningless.[225]

However, Elliott and Thomas have argued that the pre-HRA 1998 provisions that are incompatible with the ECHR are not impliedly repealed by the HRA 1998. This is not because the HRA 1998 is immune from the effects of the doctrine of implied repeal, but because it is simply not relevant in the first place.[226] Indeed, the doctrine of implied repeal only operates when there is a conflict between the substance of two pieces of legislation. For instance, if an Act passed in 1998 were to say that 'everyone has the right to free speech', this would impliedly repeal a provision contained in an earlier Act that restricted the right to free speech to an extent impermissible under the 1998 Act. Nevertheless, the HRA 1998 regime does not straightforwardly say that anyone has any rights. Rather, it merely requires certain bodies to do certain things in certain situations to give effect to the ECHR. Thus, there is no conflict, insofar as the doctrine of implied repeal is concerned, between the HRA 1998 and an earlier, or a later, provision that is incompatible with the ECHR. This is primarily because the HRA 1998 does not make the ECHR a substantive part of UK law. It merely requires the courts, among others, to interpret legislation as compatible whenever possible. When it is not possible, the inconsistent legislation remains valid because there is no substantive inconsistency between it and the HRA 1998.[227] From the date of the HRA 1998's full adoption on 2 October 2000 until 2010, the courts

224. Aileen Kavanagh, *Constitutional Review under the UK Human Rights Act* (CUP 2009) 5.

225. Elliott and Thomas (N113) 746–747.

226. Ibid., 747.

227. Ibid.

made 29 declarations of incompatibility,[228] of which 20 have become final. From 2010 to 2015, there were only three declarations of incompatibility.[229]

7.3.4.3 Compatibility of the Public Authority's Exercise of Power with the European Convention on Human Rights

Under section 6, there is an 'umbrella provision' whereby '[i]t is unlawful for a "public authority" to act in a way which is incompatible with [the ECHR]'. This section identifies public authorities as including the courts, tribunals, and 'any person certain of whose functions are functions of a public nature', despite the fact that this provision does not extend to either House of Parliament.

Although the HRA 1998 fails to provide a definition of what constitutes a public authority, its wording suggests that public authorities are sub-divided into two categories. The first category comprises those 'obvious' or 'core' public authorities which exist solely for the purposes of discharging public functions, the examples of which include the central government (including executive agencies), local government, police, immigration officers, prison staff, and courts and tribunals. All actions taken by these obvious public authorities, whether of a public law or private law nature, must be consistent with the ECHR.[230] The second category of public authorities comprises 'mixed function' [231] or 'hybrid' authorities. Mixed function or hybrid authorities are those which can perform either public or private functions. This formulation has been said to cover the discharge of public functions by privatised utilities, various regulatory bodies, and private bodies performing contracted-out public

228. See, for example, *R (H) v Mental Health Review Tribunal, North and East London Region* [2001] EWCA Civ 415, [2002] QB 1 (CA); *International Transport Roth GmbH* (N138); *Wilkinson v Inland Revenue Commissioner* [2002] EWHC 182 (Admin), [2002] STC 347; *R (D) v Secretary of State for Health* [2002] EWHC 2085 (Admin); *R (Anderson) v Secretary of State for the Home Department* [2002] UKHL 46, [2003] 1 AC 837; *Bellinger v Bellinger* [2003] UKHL 21, [2003] 2 WLR 1174; *R (N) v Secretary of State for the Home Department, R (M) v Secretary of State for Health* [2003] EWCA Civ 1406, [2003] EWHC 1094 (Admin), [2003] UKHRR 746. See also Iain McLean, *What's Wrong with the British Constitution?* (OUP 2010) Table 10.1, 210–212.

229. UK Parliament, Human Rights Joint Committee, Human Rights Judgments, 'Declaration of Incompatibility by UK courts', 11 March 2015, available at: www.publications.parliament.uk/pa/jt201415/jtselect/jtrights/130/13006.htm, last accessed 2 January 2020.

230. *Swedish Engine Drivers' Union v Sweden* (1979–1980) 1 EHRR 617.

231. Gillian Morris, 'The Human Rights Act and the Public/Private Divide in Employment Law' (1998) 27 *ILJ* 297.

functions. However, such authorities will be bound by the HRA 1998 only when committing acts that are not 'private'.[232]

The leading case on what counts as a function of a public nature is *Aston Cantlow and Wilmcote with Billesley Parochial Church Council v Wallbank*.[233] This case concerned a dispute between a parochial church council and the owners of a farm. The farm in question constituted 'rectorial property', which meant that the owners were liable to pay for all necessary repairs to the chancel of the church. The argument tabled before the House of Lords was that if the church council were to enforce this liability, it would be acting inconsistently with the farm owners' property right under the ECHR. However, this argument would only succeed if the church council was a public authority for the purposes of section 6 of the HRA 1998. The Court held that the church council was not a core public authority. However, the Court was also forced to consider whether it was exercising a function of a public nature when enforcing the liability in question. In addressing this question, Lord Nicholls stated that it was necessary to consider such factors as 'the extent to which in carrying out the relevant function the body is publicly funded, or is exercising statutory powers, or is taking the place of central government or local authorities, or is providing a public service'.[234] It was held that the specific function in question — enforcing chancel repair liability — was not a public function, so the defendant farm owners lost their case. As Lord Hope put it:

> The nature of the act is to be bound in the nature of the obligation which [the parochial church council] is seeking to enforce. It is seeking to enforce a civil debt. The function which it is performing has nothing to do with the responsibilities which are owed to the public by the State.[235]

Unfortunately, not all cases can be resolved as easily as this. Difficult problems arise when the performance of a function is 'privatised' or 'contracted out' — a practice that is now commonplace. The way in which section 6 of the HRA 1998 works means that something done in-house by a core public

232. HRA 1998, s 6(5).
233. [2003] UKHL 37, [2004] 1 AC 546.
234. Ibid., [12].
235. Ibid., [64].

authority, which would therefore have to be done in a way that is compatible with the ECHR rights, might not count as a public function when performed by a body other than core public authority. In this regard, Craig has argued that 'it is difficult to see why the nature of a function should alter if it is contracted out, rather than being performed in house', that is, by a core public authority. If it is a public function when undertaken in house, it should equally be so when contracted out'.[236] However, the requirement of a core public authority to operate compatibly with the ECHR is not because all of their actions are public functions but rather simply because the function is being done by a core public authority. Viewed in this way, when a core public authority contracts out a public function, the private contractor performing that function will not necessarily be bound by the HRA 1998. Rather, their adherence to the HRA 1998 will depend on whether the function is a public one.[237] In some situations, the answer will be obvious. For example, if a local authority contracts out the cleaning of its offices to a private company, the HRA 1998 will not apply because cleaning offices (even those of a core public authority) is not itself a public function. Equally obvious, if the Prison Service contracts out the running of a prison to a private contractor, many of the functions performed by the latter will be public in nature. This is because the private contractor will, through its employees, be exercising coercive powers of the state.[238] However, not all cases are as easy.

In *YL v Birmingham City Council*,[239] the respondent local authority was required by the National Assistance Act 1948 (NAA 1948) to arrange the provision of residential care and accommodation for the appellant, an 84-year-old Alzheimer's sufferer. This duty was discharged by entering into a contract with Southern Cross Healthcare Ltd. The appellant was duly accommodated in a Southern Cross care home, largely at the public's expense. When the company later sought to terminate the contract, the applicant argued that the resulting eviction would infringe the right to respect for her home under Article 8 of the ECHR. If this argument was to succeed, it first had to be established that Southern

236. Paul Craig, 'Contracting Out, the Human Rights Act and the Scope of Judicial Review' (2002) 118 *LQR* 551, 556.

237. Dawn Oliver, 'Functions of a Public Nature under the Human Rights Act' (2004) *PL* 329.

238. *YL v Birmingham CC* [2007] UKHL 27, [2008] 1 AC 95, [63] (Baroness Hale).

239. Ibid.

Cross was exercising a public function by accommodating and looking after the applicant. By a three-two majority, the House of Lords held that it was not.

With support from Lords Scott and Neuberger, Lord Mance stated that the key question was whether Southern Cross was undertaking a 'governmental' function. Particular attention was paid to the text of the NAA 1948 as well as to the fact that the council's statutory duty was to make arrangements for the provision of care and accommodation, whereas Southern Cross's contractual duty was to make such provision. Whatever the status of the former duty, it did not follow that the latter entailed what his Lordship called 'an inherently governmental function'. In coming to this view, the judges were influenced by, among other things, the private and commercial motivation behind Southern Cross's operations, the perceived undesirability of care home residents' rights differing according to whether they are private or state-placed clients, and Southern Cross's lack of coercive or other statutory power. It followed that Southern Cross was not bound by the HRA 1998. Dissenting, Baroness Hale called it an 'artificial and legalistic' distinction between the provision of care and the arrangement of such provision.

Following the judgment of *YL*, the Joint Committee on Human Rights of Parliament registered its disapproval.[240] In response, Parliament amended the law in order to specify that anyone providing accommodation coupled with nursing or personal care under the NAA 1948 is to be considered to be performing functions of a public nature for the purpose of section 6(1) of the HRA 1998.[241] This reversed the effect of the judgment of *YL* concerning care homes. However, the general approach of the majority remains relevant to other situations involving functions that have been contracted out.

Furthermore, it is also apparent that section 6 could be read to include other contractual relationships that were previously considered immune from judicial review. For example, previous applications impugning the legality of

240. House of Lords and House of Commons, Joint Committee on Human Rights, *Legislative Scrutiny: Health and Social Care Bill* (8th Report of Session 2007–2008, HL Paper 46 HC 303, 6 February 2008) [1.7]–[1.10], available at: https://publications.parliament.uk/pa/jt200708/jtselect/jtrights/46/46.pdf, last accessed 31 May 2020.

241. Health and Social Care Act 2008, s 145.

disciplinary proceedings in private schools had, on account of the existence of a contractual relationship, been dismissed by the courts.[242] According to Nicholas Bamforth, it now seems that review of such applications would be permitted in cases raising human rights issues under the HRA 1998. Quoting *Costello-Roberts v UK*,[243] Bamforth also noted how the UK government could be held liable for violations of rights by private contractors, which in this case occurred as a result of disciplinary measures in private schools.[244] He stated that 'the obvious implication of the [ECHR's] position on private schools is that they are — contrary to the contract exception in domestic law — sufficiently "public" that their activities are covered by [the HRA 1998]'.[245] On this basis, it can be assumed that the traditional public-private divide will no longer apply in human rights cases [246] or in any decisions frustrating the full and effective protection of individual rights. Although section 6 seemingly conceives of the HRA 1998 as having only a 'vertical effect' against the UK government and public bodies, it is now well-established that the HRA 1998 also has a 'horizontal effect' in proceedings between two private parties, on account of the interpretative obligation in section 3 and the fact that the courts are public authorities under section 6.[247] In this regard, proportionality can be applied in legal dispute between two or more private persons if the case is tabled before the courts which are statutorily required under the HRA 1998 to observe the ECHR. Therefore, as the courts are regarded as a public body under the HRA 1998, they are under a statutory duty to give effect to ECtHR jurisprudence. This means that when they adjudicate on any domestic case other than those having EU law and fundamental rights dimensions, they have to observe and respect the statutorily guaranteed human rights and, thus, recognise the proportionality principle.

242. *R v Fernhill Manor School, ex p Brown* [1993] 5 Admin LR 159.

243. (1993) 19 EHRR 112.

244. Ibid., [26]–[28].

245. Nicholas Bamforth, 'The Application of the Human Rights Act 1998 to Public Authorities and Private Bodies' (1999) 58 *CLJ* 159; A. Sherlock, 'The Applicability of the UK's Human Rights Bill: Identifying Public Functions' (1998) 4 *EPL* 593.

246. Murray Hunt, 'The "Horizontal Effect" of the Human Rights Act' (1998) Autumn *PL* 423; Gavin Phillipson, 'The Human Rights Act, "Horizontal Effect" and the Common Law: A Bang or a Whimper?' (1999) 62 *MLR* 824.

247. *Douglas v Hello! Ltd* [2001] 2 WLR 992; *Venables and Thompson v News Group Newspapers* [2001] 2 WLR 1038; *Campbell v Mirror Group Newspapers Ltd* [2004] UKHL 22.

7.3.4.4 Landmark Cases under the Human Rights Act 1998

The first full HRA 1998 judgments by the then Appellate Committee of the House of Lords are *Daly* [248] and *Alconbury* [249] In *Daly*, following serious breaches of security at Whitemoor Prison, the Secretary of State introduced a new policy on cell searches. One of the features of the policy was that searches should take place in the absence of the prisoner and should include an examination of the prisoner's correspondence with his legal advisers in order to ensure that nothing had been written or secreted in it which endangered prison security. Daly sought judicial review, challenging the decision to examine his legally privileged correspondence in his absence.

The House of Lords held that allowing prison officers to read Daly's correspondence with his legal adviser was indeed an infringement of the legal privilege granted to him by common law, and that the application of the 'blanket policy' without evidence of misconduct on his part had been an intrusion into privileged correspondence greater than was justified. More importantly, the Court also held that the policy constituted a breach of Daly's rights under Article 8 of the ECHR (i.e., the right to respect private and family life). The Court furthered that even though Article 8 was not an absolute right, any interference was required to be no greater than was necessary in the interest of public safety and the prevention of disorder or crime. The interference in this case was thus 'disproportionate', and the policy was deemed unlawful and was subsequently quashed. Judging from the above, proportionality analysis, at least in theory, brings considerations of a measure's impact on the individual into the centre stage of a judicial review.[250]

Alconbury concerned the compatibility of the power of the Secretary of State for the Environment, Transport, and the Regions to call-in and recover planning appeals under the Town and Country Planning Act 1990 with Article 6 of the ECHR (i.e., the right to a fair trial). In particular, Article 6(1) guarantees that in the determination of an individual's civil rights or obligations, the individual should have 'a fair and public hearing … by an independent and

248. *Daly* (N149).

249. *Alconbury* (N148).

250. Masterman (N77) 132.

impartial tribunal established by law'. The issue for the House of Lords was whether judicial review of a planning determination of the Secretary of State would ensure that the elements of Article 6(1) are satisfied. The ECtHR has long recognised that there is no breach of Article 6(1) when the original decision-maker complies with ECHR requirements or when there is 'subsequent control by a judicial body which has full jurisdiction'.[251] On this point, even though the Secretary of State, as the party responsible for formulating the planning policy, did not satisfy the requirements of independence and impartiality, recourse to judicial review prevented any violation. This argument failed before the High Court which, having concluded that the limited reach of orthodox grounds of judicial review meant that the reviewing court could not be said to enjoy 'full jurisdiction', made a declaration of incompatibility to the effect that the legislation in question had been incompatible with ECHR guarantees.[252]

However, the finding of the High Court, which clearly reflected some of the ECtHR's more general reservations about the effectiveness of domestic proceedings,[253] was overturned by the House of Lords. The Lords stated that the question of whether judicial review proceedings satisfy Article 6 requirements can only be answered in light of all the circumstances of a case, the considerations of which include:

(a) the subject matter of the dispute;

(b) the nature of the decision of the administrative authorities which is in question;

(c) the procedure, if any, which exists for review of the decision by a person or body acting independently of the authority concerned; and

(d) the scope of the power of review.[254]

As such, they held that when a 'policy' decision (as opposed to a decision based on fact) is being reviewed, the ordinary principles of judicial review will suffice. As the Court reasoned, this finding was mandated by the reality

251. *Albert and Le Compte v Belgium* (1983) 5 EHRR 533, 542.

252. *Alconbury* (N148), applying *Bryan v UK* (1995) 21 EHRR 342.

253. *W v UK* (1988) 10 EHRR 29; *Smith and Grady v UK* (1999) 29 EHRR 493.

254. European Commission of Human Rights's opinion in *Bryan v UK* (N252) 354 (Nicholas Bratza).

that policy decisions will often fall within the area of discretion that requires judicial deference to the decisions of elected authorities. Emphasising that this case fell squarely within the policy category, it held that there had been no violation of the ECHR, saying that 'full jurisdiction' does not mean full decision-making power, but instead refers to having the full jurisdiction to tackle the case as the nature of the decision requires.[255] Overall, the point of emphasis in the HRA 1998 is much more inward looking because it requires the courts to ensure that all daily activities of public bodies comply with the minimum fundamental rights guaranteed by the ECHR.

7.3.5 Simultaneous Development of the Proportionality Principle by the Privy Council

In 1999, the Judicial Committee of the Privy Council also had an opportunity to examine the proportionality principle in a case from Antigua and Barbuda, as part of the UK Commonwealth. In *De Freitas v Permanent Secretary of Ministry of Agriculture, Fisheries, Lands and Housing*,[256] a civil servant who had demonstrated government corruption was disciplined for breaching legislation which prohibited civil servants from communicating information or opinions on issues of national security or international controversy. The Constitution of Antigua and Barbuda guarantees freedom of expression and assembly. However, it permits reasonable restrictions on public officers to ensure the proper performance of their functions.

When applying the proportionality formula, Lord Clyde not only drew on Canadian case law,[257] in particular *R v Oakes*,[258] but also on other common law jurisdictions,[259] which in turn appeared to have been derived from principles of

255. *Alconbury* (N148) [2001] 2 All ER 929, 985 (Lord Hoffmann).

256. [1998] UKPC 30, [1998] 3 WLR 675, [1999] 1 AC 69.

257. Ibid., [1999] 1 AC 69, [80].

258. [1986] 1 SCR 103.

259. *Government of Republic of South Africa v Sunday Times Newspapers* [1995] 1 LRC 168; *Nyambirai v National Social Security Authority* [1996] 1 LRC 64; *Retrofit v Post and Telecommunications Authority* [1996] 4 LRC 489.

the ECtHR.[260] Mirroring the concepts established in *ex parte Fedesa*,[261] Lord Clyde adopted three criteria or questions that the Court had to ask itself to determine whether a limitation on a fundamental constitutional right was arbitrary or excessive and thus disproportionate and not justified:

(a) Is the legislative object sufficiently important to justify limiting a fundamental right?

(b) Are the measures designed to meet the legislative object rationally connected to it?

(c) Are the means used to impair the right or freedom no more than are reasonably necessary to accomplish the objective?[262]

7.3.6 The Four-Stage Test

Subsequently, in 2001, Dyson LJ added a fourth element, a 'fair balance' test, to the proportionality enquiry in *R (on the application of Samaroo) v Secretary of State for the Home Department*.[263] This fair balance test was not explicitly discussed in the formulation of the proportionality analysis by the Privy Council in *De Freitas*[264] or the House of Lords in *Daly*.[265] In *Samaroo*, there was a challenge under the HRA 1998 to a deportation order made against a drug dealer. In the Court of Appeal, Dyson LJ asked: Does the measure have an excessive or disproportionate effect on the interests of the people affected compared with that on society as a whole? Recognising and allowing that the decision-maker had a discretionary area of judgment to consider, he took the view that the function of the court was to decide whether this fair balance had been struck, keeping in mind:

(a) whether the right was unqualified or qualified;

260. Frederick Morton (ed), *Law, Politics and the Judicial Process in Canada* (3rd edn, UCP 2002) 555–559; Robert Sharpe and Kent Roach, *Brian Dickson: A Judge's Journey* (TUP 2003) 332–334; Dieter Grimm, 'Proportionality in Canadian and German Jurisprudence' (2007) 57 *UTLJ* 383–397.

261. *ex p Fedesa* (N9).

262. *De Freitas* (N256) [1999] 1 AC 69, 80.

263. [2001] EWCA Civ 1139, [2001] UKHRR 1150.

264. *De Freitas* (N256).

265. *Daly* (N149).

(b) the extent to which the issue requires consideration of social, economic, and political factors;

(c) the extent to which the court has a special expertise (for instance, in criminal matters); and

(d) whether the rights have a high degree of constitutional protection such as freedom of expression and access to the courts.[266]

Although the Court would allow the Secretary of State a significant margin of discretion, the onus lay on the latter to establish that their justification was convincing. In other words, the Secretary of State was required to show the Court that a fair balance had been struck, with the weight given to different factors being the subject of careful scrutiny by the Court.[267] This makes it clear that the proportionality of a measure is ultimately a matter for the Court, not for the primary decision-maker, notwithstanding any margin of discretion that may be allowed.[268]

In 2007, in *Huang v Secretary of State for the Home Department*,[269] the House of Lords formally recognised Dyson LJ's fair balance test as the fourth limb of the proportionality test, thus stressing the need to balance the interests of society with those of individuals and groups.[270] In this case, which required a decision to be made about whether allowing an individual to enter or remain in the UK breaches Article 8, Lord Bingham stated:

> [T]he ultimate question for the appellate immigration authority is whether the refusal of leave to enter or remain, in circumstances where the life of the family cannot reasonably be expected to be enjoyed elsewhere, taking full account of all considerations weighing in favour of the refusal, prejudices the family life of the applicant in a manner sufficiently serious to amount to a breach of the fundamental right protected by article 8. If

266. *Samaroo* (N263) [19]–[20].

267. Ibid., [38].

268. *Lindsay v Commissioners of Customs and Excise* [2002] EWCA Civ 267, [2002] 1 WLR 1766; *International Transport Roth GmbH* (N138); *R (Hoverspeed) Ltd v Commissioners of Customs and Excise* [2002] EWHC 1630, [2002] 3 WLR 1219 (DC); *Commissioners of Customs and Excise v Newbury* [2003] EWHC 702, [2003] 2 All ER 964 (DC).

269. [2007] UKHL 11, [2007] 2 AC 167, [2007] 2 WLR 581.

270. Ibid., [2007] 2 AC 167, [19].

> the answer to this question is affirmative, the refusal is unlawful and the authority must so decide.[271]

This need to balance the interests of society with those of individuals and groups has been similarly made by the ECtHR on several occasions,[272] and has been described as an 'overriding requirement'.[273] Therefore, this 'fair balance' limb of the proportionality analysis must be considered in addition to the three limbs as set out in *De Freitas*, and it is not an alternative to them.[274] Accordingly, the least restrictive means of achieving a particular objective may still be disproportionate if they do not strike a fair balance between the rights of the individual and those of society. Although Lord Sumption opined, in *Bank Mellat v Her Majesty's Treasury (No. 2)*,[275] that these four requirements are logically separate, in practice they inevitably overlap because the same facts are likely to be relevant to more than one of them.[276] He summarised the four-stage test as follows:

> (a) whether the objective is sufficiently important to justify the limitation of a fundamental right;
>
> (b) whether the restriction is rationally connected to the objective;
>
> (c) whether a less intrusive measure could have been used; and
>
> (d) whether a fair balance has been struck between the rights of the individual and the interests of the community in terms of these matters and to the severity of the consequences.[277]

---

271. Ibid., [20].

272. See, for example, *Sporrong and Lönnroth v Sweden* (1982) 5 EHRR 35, ECtHR (Plenary), [69]; *Soering v UK* (N160) [89].

273. *Huang* (N269) [2007] 2 AC 167, [19] (Lord Bingham).

274. *H and L v A CC* [2011] EWCA Civ 403, [2011] LGR 590, [38] (Munby LJ); *R (Aguilar Quila) v Secretary of State for the Home Department* [2012] 1 AC 621, [45] and [58] (Lord Wilson). See also Jack Beatson, Stephen Grosz, Tom Hickman, and Rabinder Singh, *Human Rights: Judicial Protection in the United Kingdom* (Sweet & Maxwell 2008) [3.51]; Richard Clayton and Hugh Tomlinson, *The Law of Human Rights* (2nd edn, OUP 2009) [6.92]–[6.136].

275. [2013] UKSC 39, [2014] AC 700.

276. Ibid., [20].

277. Ibid.

The *Huang* case also raises an interesting point concerning a 'disconnection between traditional and newer conceptions of democratic decision-making'.[278] According to Anashri Pillay, 'on a traditional conception of democracy, the weight of public opinion impacts … legislation and policies at the level of elections: the legislation enacted by those elected to govern is deemed to be democratically legitimate'.[279] However, there have been different visions of democracy developed which are based on a concern with actual participation and social consensus.[280] Such visions are in fact an expression of the idea of a participatory democracy that emphasises accountability and justification.[281] In *Huang*, the Court rejected an argument that an appellate immigration authority should assume that the Immigration Rules and Directives struck the appropriate balance between competing interests in society primarily because they had obtained parliamentary approval. The Lords noted that the rules and directives in question are not actively debated before Parliament, and thus the interests of non-nationals wishing to stay in the UK are not represented.[282]

The balancing of individual rights and the interests of society as a whole was also discussed in *R (on the application of Miranda) v Secretary of State for the Home Department*.[283] In this case, a person acting on behalf of a journalist was stopped and searched at Heathrow Airport under Schedule 7 of the Terrorism Act 2000. A material believed to have been stolen from Government Communication Headquarters was seized by the police. The defence argued, among other things, that the power used was disproportionate. In addition to explaining the origin of the balancing exercise, Laws LJ stated that it should be approached with some care because there is a real difficulty in distinguishing this from a political question to be determined by the elected government. If there was a balance to be struck, it was 'between two aspects of the public interests: the public interest in press freedom and the public interest in national security'.[284]

278. Anashri Pillay, 'Economic and Social Rights Adjudication: Developing Principles of Judicial Restraint in South Africa and the United Kingdom' (2013) July *PL* 599, 606.

279. Ibid., 606–607.

280. Sandra Fredman, *Human Rights Transformed: Positive Rights and Positive Duties* (OUP 2008) 33–40; Sandra Liebenberg, *Socio-Economic Rights: Adjudication under a Transformative Constitution* (Juta 2010) 28–34.

281. Etienne Mureinik, 'Reconsidering Review: Participation and Accountability' (1993) *AJ* 35.

282. *Huang* (N269) [2007] 2 WLR 581, 591–592.

283. [2014] EWHC 255, [2014] 1 WLR 3140.

284. Ibid., [45]–[46].

Overall, the four-stage approach appears now to be generally accepted in Britain,[285] notwithstanding that it does not apply to cases involving EU law.[286]

7.3.7 A 'Constitutional and Institutional Dialogue' between the Executive, Legislature, and Judiciary in a Democratic Society

When the above-mentioned provisions under the HRA 1998 are taken together, the principles are evidently intended to ensure a 'serious dialogue' between the executive, legislature, and the courts on human rights protection in the UK.[287] This idea of constitutional dialogue, and the concomitant method of dialogic judicial review, tallies with what Paul O'Connell has advocated: that it is an important 'toolkit of constitutional design', the purpose of which is to encourage co-operative engagement among the different branches of government in the context of rights protection.[288] This dialogic approach will 'not privilege the contributions of judges' at the expense of the elected branches of government.[289] Rather, such an 'equal partnership' between the courts and elected branches of government is able to rigorously protect constitutional rights.[290] In short, the idea of constitutional and institutional dialogues between the courts and the elected branches of government is, Allan contends, not simply a desirable option, but indeed an imperative element in a modern, constitutional, and democratic state.[291]

Since its enactment, however, there have been allegations that the principal effect of the HRA 1998 is to increase the power of the judiciary over the other

285. *Aguilar Quila* (N274) [45]; *In re Recovery of Medical Costs for Asbestos Doseases (Wales) Bill* [2015] AC 1016, [45].

286. *R (Lumsdon) v Legal Service Board* [2016] AC 697, [26].

287. Home Secretary, House of Commons Debates (vol 314, col 1141, 24 June 1998), available at: https://publications.parliament.uk/pa/cm199798/cmhansrd/vo980624/debtext/80624-47.htm#80624-47_spnew2, last accessed 30 May 2020.

288. Paul O'Connell, *Vindicating Socio-Economic Rights: International Standards and Comparative Experiences* (Routledge 2012) 174–175. See also Mark Tushnet, 'Dialogic Judicial Review' (2008) 61 *ALR* 205, 206.

289. Christine Bateup, 'The Dialogic Promise: Assessing the Normative Potential of Theories of Constitutional Dialogue' (2006) 71 *BLR* 1109, 1112.

290. Ibid., 1118.

291. T.R.S. Allan, 'Constitutional Dialogue and the Justification of Judicial Review' (2003) 23 *OJLS* 563, 565.

branches of government.[292] Some members of the judiciary have even agreed with this. Lord Reed, for example, said that

> courts should respect the importance of political accountability for decisions on controversial questions of social and ethical policy. [Although the HRA 1998] and the devolution statutes have altered the powers of the courts, they have not altered the inherent limitations of court proceedings as a means of determining issues of social and ethical policy. Nor have they diminished the inappropriateness, and the dangers for the courts themselves, of highly contentious issues in social and ethical policy being determined by judges, who have neither any special insight into such questions nor any political accountability for their decisions.[293]

That said, the duty to implement and protect human rights rests on each branch of government, be it legislative, executive, or judicial, and on all decision-makers who could be said to be exercising 'public functions'. Each branch has clear duties and responsibilities, and these cannot be ignored. The courts, under the constitutional principle of separation of powers, should have the ultimate say when it is found that legislation or official action offends the rights established by the ECHR.

7.4 European Jurisprudence regarding some Civil and Political Rights and its Influence to Impose Positive Obligations in Socio-Economic Rights Disputes

Since neither the International Covenant on Economic, Social, and Cultural Rights (ICESCR) nor the European Social Charter (ESC) has ever been incorporated as domestic law in the UK, there have been, at least as far as the ICESCR is concerned, some decisions criticised by the UN Committee on Economic, Social, and Cultural Rights (UNESCR Committee).[294] In its response to the UNESCR Committee, the UK government reiterated its long-standing

292. Jowell and Cooper (N83) 3.

293. *Re Northern Ireland Human Rights Commission's Application for Judicial Review* [2018] UKSC 27, [344].

294. *Concluding Observations of the Committee on Economic, Social and Cultural Rights: United Kingdom of Great Britain and Northern Ireland*, 5 June 2002, UN Doc E/C 12/1Add 79, [11].

opposition to according socio-economic rights the same status as civil and political rights [295] even though opinion polls have deviated from this position.[296]

Worst of all, English courts have been reluctant to interpret discretionary powers to give effect to socio-economic rights, claiming that an authority's allocation of scarce resources raises non-justiciable issues,[297] as evidenced in *R v Cambridge Health Authority, ex parte B*.[298] As a result, they have dealt with these challenges to discretionary allocative decision-making on the grounds of *Wednesbury* unreasonableness. However, the *Wednesbury* formula has long been regarded by some judges and commentators as a highly deferential standard, providing for considerably less judicial scrutiny than, say, the South African concept of *Grootboom* reasonableness.[299] Challenges to broader questions of social policy and primary legislation and of direct concern in human rights adjudication have remained for the most part beyond the reach of British courts in their exercise of judicial review.[300]

However, there have been growing appeals that Britain, being a welfare state, has some responsibilities for protecting individuals against want or need. In this regard, Sandra Fredman and Murray Wesson have argued that Britain's 'unwritten' constitution includes a duty on the state to ensure that all have the 'minimum necessary for survival'.[301] This assertion is compatible with the one given by the UNECSR Committee that socio-economic rights do give rise to

295. Ministry of Justice, *International Covenant on Economic, Social and Cultural Rights: Fifth Periodic Report from the United Kingdom, the Crown Dependencies, the British Overseas Territories*, 27 July 2007, [75].

296. *Joint Committee on Human Rights, Twenty-First Report*, 20 October 2004, [29]; Jamie Burton, 'It's time to enshrine socioeconomic rights in law', *The Guardian*, 28 October 2011, available at: www.theguardian.com/commentisfree/libertycentral/2011/oct/28/socioeconomic-rights-law, last accessed 17 May 2020.

297. *Lonrho Plc v Tebbit* [1991] 4 All ER 973 (CA), 981; *X (Minors) v Bedfordshire CC* [1995] 2 AC 633 (HL), 737; *Barrett v Enfield LBC* [1998] 3 WLR 79 (HL) 97 (Lord Slynn) and 111 (Lord Hutton). See also Jeff King, 'The Justiciability of Resource Allocation' (2007) 70 *MLR* 197–224.

298. [1995] EWCA Civ 49, [1995] 2 All ER 129, [1995] 1 WLR 898.

299. Murray Wesson, '*Grootboom* and Beyond: Reassessing the Socio-Economic Jurisprudence of the South African Constitutional Court' (2004) 20(2) *SAJHR* 284–308.

300. Jeff King, 'United Kingdom: Asserting Social Rights in a Multi-Layered System' in Malcolm Langford (ed), *Social Rights Jurisprudence: Emerging Trends in International and Comparative Law* (CUP 2008) 284.

301. Sandra Fredman and Murray Wesson, 'Social, Economic, and Cultural Rights' in David Feldman (ed), *English Public Law* (OUP 2009) [10.07].

'minimum essential levels' of each of the rights.[302] Luckily, UK courts have, in some cases, actually given effect to ECtHR jurisprudence by interpreting ostensibly civil and political rights to extend certain socio-economic rights.[303]

7.4.1 Allocation of Scarce Resources

Influenced by the jurisprudence of the CJEU and of the ECtHR, English courts have, as mentioned before, started integrating European jurisprudence to treat socio-economic rights as essential corollaries of civil and political rights, and thus protect them, with the use of the 'integrated approach' and through the expansive application of equality or non-discrimination provisions, as well as by imposing positive duties on state authorities to realise them. Moreover, the nature of what is justiciable in the UK has also changed in line with the expanded mandate for the review of discretion and, in particular, primary legislation.[304] There are a number of cases where the courts have applied careful scrutiny of statutory provisions and of administrative action implicating resource allocation.

In *R (on the application of Rogers) v Swindon NHS Primary Care Trust*,[305] the applicant, Ann Rogers, challenged a local authority's policy for funding the provision of an unlicensed breast cancer drug called Herceptin. At the time the challenge arose, the drug was pending regulatory approval by European and UK agencies. Some local authorities started funding treatment prior to such approval. However, the funding policies varied in different regions. Some authorities funded the drug upon clinical recommendation, while others applied a policy on an 'exceptional' basis. This meant that a patient had to show exceptional need, leading to arguments that access to the life-saving drug essentially depended

302. UNESCR Committee, General Comment No. 3: The Nature of States Parties' Obligations (5th session), UN Doc E/1991/23, annex III at 86 (1991), reprinted in 'Compilation of General Comments and General Recommendations Adopted by Human Rights Treaty Bodies', UN Doc HRI/GEN/1/Rev6, 14 (2003), [10].

303. Luke Clements and Alan Simmons, 'European Court of Human Rights: Sympathetic Unease' in Langford (N300) 409; Colm O'Cinneide, 'A Modest Proposal: Destitution, State Responsibility and the European Convention on Human Rights' (2008) *EHRLR* 583; Ellie Palmer, 'Beyond Arbitrary Interference? Developing Socio-Economic Duties in the European Convention on Human Rights' (2010) 61(3) *NILQ* 225.

304. King (N300) 285.

305. [2006] EWCA Civ 392, [2006] 1 WLR 2649.

on a 'post-code lottery'.[306] The defendant authority had a policy of refusing to fund treatment, except for in undefined exceptional circumstances. Rogers challenged the rationality of the policy and its compliance with her rights under the ECHR. Although the trial court dismissed the claim, the Court of Appeal allowed her appeal, holding that given the life-and-death effects of the decision for the claimant, it was 'appropriate for the court to subject the decision to refuse funding for the treatment (and thus in practice the treatment) to rigorous scrutiny'.[307] The Court further held that once the health authority found that available resources were irrelevant, as it had in that case, then there could be no rational reason to refuse funding based on personal or clinical characteristics.[308] The Court, despite refusing to order funding of treatment, quashed the policy for being irrational.[309] The significance of this case is that although it is well accepted that under the doctrine of separation of powers, it is not for the courts to substitute judgment, it is also recognised that there must be some control over the rationality of decisions made by the administration.

Moreover, the nature of positive obligations was also considered in the House of Lords in *R (on the application of Pretty) v Director of Public Prosecution*,[310] and the primary question tabled before the Lords was whether a positive obligation exists based on the fair balance between the general interests of the community and the interests of the individual.[311] In this case, the applicant was terminally ill and entirely dependent upon her husband for care. She foresaw a time when she would wish to take her own life, but would not be able to do so without the active assistance of her husband. She sought proleptic permission — a promise that her husband would not be prosecuted. The Court held that Article 2 of the ECHR (i.e., the right to life) does not include the right to any particular form of death, and that it was rather intended to reflect the sanctity of life. Thus, assisted suicide remained a criminal offence, and a clear distinction remains between acts which might have the effect of shortening a life but have some

306. Keith Syrett, 'Opening Eyes to the Reality of Scarce Health Care Resources? *R (on the application of Rogers v Swindon NHS Primary Care Trust and Secretary of State for Health*)' (2006) *PL* 664–673.

307. *Rogers* (N305) [2006] 1 WLR 2649, [56].

308. Ibid., [79]–[82].

309. Ibid., [83].

310. [2001] UKHL 61, [2001] 3 WLR 1598, [2002] 1 AC 800.

311. Ibid., [2002] 1 AC 800, [15] (Lord Bingham), [92] (Lord Hope).

other palliative purpose and acts that shorten a life without any palliative purpose. Her condition was in no way considered a form of torture inflicted by the state, nor was a refusal to allow the assistance discriminatory against those who were unable to help themselves. Since the executive had no power to dispense with, or suspend, laws or to execute without Parliamentary consent, the Director of Public Prosecutions had no power to decide that a crime yet to be committed should be immune from prosecution. Regarding the positive obligation issue, Lord Hope stated:

> [A] public authority will show that it has acted proportionately if it proves that the objective which is sought to be achieved is sufficiently important to justify limiting the fundamental right, that the means chosen to meet the objective is rational, fair and not arbitrary, and that the means used to impair the right is no more than is necessary to accomplish that objective and is as minimal as reasonably possible.[312]

7.4.2 Overlap between Civil and Political Rights not to be Tortured or Subject to Inhuman or Degrading Treatment and Socio-Economic Right to Minimum Subsistence

It is evident that even prior to the enactment of the HRA 1998, positive obligations requiring the state 'to do something' have long been the British tradition. In *R v Secretary of State for Social Security, ex parte Joint Council for the Welfare of Immigrants*,[313] Simon Brown LJ held that regulations adopted by the Secretary of State to deny benefits to asylum seekers who did not claim asylum immediately upon arrival were unlawful by reason of its interfering effect on basic human rights. This is because the regulations would put legitimate asylum seekers in an intolerable situation of having either to abandon their asylum claims and return to face persecution, or to stay and maintain the claims in an utter state of destitution. He claimed that 'so basic are the rights here at issue that it cannot be necessary to resort to the [ECHR] to take note of their violation'.[314]

312. Ibid., [92]–[97].

313. [1997] 1 WLR 275.

314. Ibid., 292 (Simon Brown LJ).

He referred to what Lord Ellenborough CJ had said in 1803 in regard to the rights of certain impoverished foreigners in Britain: 'the law of humanity, which is anterior to all positive laws, obliges us to afford them relief, to save them from starving'.[315]

In *R (on the application of Q) v Secretary of State for the Home Department*[316] and *R (on the application of Limbuela) v Secretary of State for the Home Department*,[317] both the English High Court and the House of Lords were confronted with a situation involving an overlap between the civil and political right not to be tortured or subjected to inhuman or degrading treatment or punishment, on one hand, and the socio-economic right to minimum subsistence, on the other. These two cases specifically concerned the issue of destitute asylum seekers who were prohibited from working and denied social security support, including accommodation. The question tabled before the courts was whether or not the withdrawal of support from such people, who were in lack of the means of obtaining adequate accommodation or meeting their essential living needs, violated Article 3. In *Q*, Collins J stated:

> It may even be that there is no duty under the [ECHR] to provide any form of social security. But the situation here is different since asylum seekers are forbidden to work and so cannot provide for themselves. Unless they can find friends or charitable bodies or persons, they will indeed be destitute. They will suffer at least damage to their health. I therefore agree [that the withdrawal of support could violate Article 3].[318]

In *Limbuela*, even though there were no justiciable socio-economic rights in the UK, the Court held that the right not to be subjected to inhuman treatment had implied a right to minimum subsistence. In this case, the Court had an opportunity to consider a statutory provision that allowed the Secretary of State to withdraw financial support from an asylum seeker who had not claimed asylum as soon as reasonably practicable after arriving in Britain.

315. *Inhabitants of Eastbourne* (1803) 4 East 103, 107.

316. [2003] EWHC 195 (Admin).

317. [2005] UKHL 66, [2006] 1 AC 396 (HL).

318. *Q* (N316) [67].

Given the statutory prohibition upon asylum seekers taking employment, the effect of which was to permit the Secretary of State to force a category of asylum seekers into destitution, the Court held, without hesitation, that this amounted to a violation of Article 3 of the ECHR. The Court emphasised that a general duty to house the homeless or provide for the destitute could not be 'spelled out of article 3'.[319] It also cautioned against rigidly distinguishing between the negative and positive obligations associated with Article 3, coupled with Lord Brown's observation that 'time and again these are shown to be false dichotomies. The real issue in all these cases is whether the state is to be properly regarded as responsible'.[320] This judgment is compatible with the minimum core obligations stated in the UNESCR Committee's General Comment No. 3, 'The Nature of States Parties' Obligations'.[321]

An interesting issue is also raised in *Limbuela,* in that although the House of Lords held that in these particular circumstances the prohibition of inhuman and degrading treatment was absolute and issues of proportionality did not therefore arise,[322] Lord Hope argued that 'issues of proportionality might arise' when an implied positive obligation to take action to prevent suffering inflicted by others is being considered.[323] This remark has been explained by his Lordship in *R (on the application of Munjaz) v Ashworth Hospital Authority*[324] decided shortly before *Limbuela,* in which he stated:

> [W]hile the absolute prohibition is not capable of modification on grounds of proportionality, issues of proportionality will arise where a positive obligation is implied ... where positive obligations arise they [meaning the absolute prohibitions] are not absolute. In *Osman v United Kingdom* (1998) 29 EHRR 245, 305, para 116 the court recognised that such obligations must be interpreted in a way which does not impose an impossible or disproportionate burden on the authorities.[325]

319. *Limbuela* (N317) [2005] UKHL 66, [7].

320. Ibid., [92].

321. UNESCR Committee, General Comment No. 3 (N302).

322. *Limbuela* (N317) [2006] 1 AC 396 (HL), [47]–[48].

323. Ibid., [48] and [55] (Lord Hope).

324. [2005] UKHL 58, [2006] 2 AC 148.

325. Ibid., [2005] UKHL 58, [78].

Relying on this principle, Lord Hope opined that the defendant hospital authority's practice for reviewing mental patients over the long-term would only breach Article 3 when there was a 'significant risk of ill-treatment of the kind which falls within the scope of that Article'.[326]

The ECtHR has also held that children and other vulnerable individuals are entitled to state proceedings, in the form of effective deterrence,[327] against serious breaches of personal integrity.[328] In *A v UK*,[329] the applicant had been beaten with a garden cane by his stepfather, who was subsequently prosecuted for assault occasioning actual bodily harm. However, the trial judge directed the jury that the prosecution had been required to prove that the beating was not a reasonable punishment, and the jury brought in a verdict of not guilty. At Strasbourg, the European Commission unanimously found a violation of Article 3, and this was accepted by the UK government before the ECtHR. The Commission derived the positive obligation from Article 1 (i.e., the obligation to respect human rights) to secure the rights and freedoms in the ECHR, together with the substantive right in Article 3, stating that

> children and other vulnerable individuals, in particular, are entitled to State protection, in the form of effective deterrence, against such breaches of personal integrity … it is a defence to a charge of assault on a child that the treatment in question amounted to 'reasonable chastisement' … In the Court's view, the law did not provide adequate protection to the applicant against treatment or punishment contrary to Article 3.[330]

Signatories of the ECHR also have an obligation to take care of vulnerable persons if they face abuse or neglect at home. *Z v UK*,[331] for example, concerned a number of children who suffered severe neglect at the hands of their parents. The ECtHR held that the local authority was under a statutory duty to protect

326. Ibid., [80].

327. *X and Y v Netherlands* (1985) 8 EHRR 235.

328. *A v UK* (2002) 36 EHRR 917.

329. (1999) 27 EHRR 611.

330. Ibid., [22]–[24].

331. (2001) 34 EHRR 97.

them and found a violation of Article 3 as there had been a gross failure to safeguard them from long-term neglect and abuse.

Furthermore, in *Napier v Scottish Ministers,*[332] the Scottish Court of Session held that Mr Napier's detention in Barlinnie Prison in Glasgow violated his Article 3 right against inhuman and degrading treatment owing to the poor sanitary arrangements in his cell. The Court noted that the Scottish Ministers had been aware of the poor prison conditions at Barlinnie for a number of years and had in fact promised to introduce internal sanitation in the prison cells by 1999. Under such circumstances, the Court did not hesitate to enforce such a priority.

Article 3 has also been employed to protect an inmate's right to food, as in *R v Governor of HMP Franland, ex parte Russell and Wharrie.*[333] In that case, Justice Lightman quashed the decision of a prison governor to limit the food intake of two inmates to just one meal a day as punishment for their refusal to wear prison clothes. He held that such an objective cannot 'excuse the governor from performance of the obligation to provide food to that prisoner or can detract from the fundamental right of the prisoner to adequate food'.[334] Overall, on the basis of the above jurisprudence, UK authorities are obliged to protect vulnerable persons from neglect by providing a wide range of community care services, including domiciliary and community-based services as well as care home accommodation.

7.4.3 Right to Fair Trial

Claimants have been less successful in their attempts to obtain rights to trial for the adjudication of welfare benefits claims. In *R (on the application of P, C and T) v Alperton,*[335] the High Court held that educational rights provided by statute are not 'civil' rights within the meaning of Article 6(1) of the ECHR (i.e., the right to a fair trial). However, in *Begum v Tower Hamlets London Borough Council,*[336] a

332. [2001] ScotCS 162, (2005) UKHRR 268.

333. [2000] EWHC Admin 365, [2000] 1 WLR 2027.

334. Ibid., [2000] 1 WLR 2027, 2037.

335. [2001] EWHC Admin 229.

336. [2002] EWCA Civ 239, [2002] 1 WLR 2491, [2003] UKHL 5.

majority of the House of Lords were prepared to accept, for the sake of argument, that certain rights in respect of duties to accommodate the homeless were civil rights within the meaning of Article 6(1). The issue in this case was whether Article 6(1) required a full and judicial trial in cases where a person contested a local authority's findings as to her rights under the statutory regime allocating public housing. Runa Begum had refused the authority's offer of accommodation, claiming that the area was rife with drug use, racism, and that the building was located near her estranged and potentially dangerous husband.

The Court of Appeal agreed that she was entitled under Article 6(1) to more than an internal review of the decision, holding that the local authority could be compliant by engaging an independent fact-finder.[337] However, the House of Lords held that rights of this type were of a different nature and called for a different form of protection. In particular, Lord Hoffmann found that following the decision of the ECtHR in *Bryan v UK*,[338] an independent and impartial determination would be satisfied by a composite procedure consisting of an administrative decision and the availability of judicial review. The procedure must allow for full 'jurisdiction to deal with the case as the nature of the decision requires'.[339]

7.4.4 Respect for Privacy, Family Life, and Home

There have been numerous challenges under Article 8 to decisions affecting immigration and housing rights. In *R (on the application of Razgar) v Secretary of State for the Home Department*,[340] the House of Lords held that Article 8 may be contravened when the threat of deportation is foreseeable and would result in 'extreme' consequences for the health of an individual.[341] In this case, it was found that the applicant's deportation to Germany could have sufficiently serious effects on his mental health, and that Article 8 could be engaged. In fact, the availability of this type of remedy had once been tested in the *HIV Deportation*

337. Ibid., [2002] 1 WLR 2491.

338. *Bryan* (N252).

339. *Begum* (N336) [2003] UKHL 5, [37] (Lord Hoffmann).

340. [2004] UKHL 27, [2004] 2 AC 368.

341. Ibid., [2004] UKHL 27, [10] (Lord Bingham).

case,[342] in which the applicant challenged her deportation to Uganda on the ground that the withdrawal of the National Health Services-funded treatment of her AIDS condition would constitute a grave threat to her health.[343] The House of Lords, in *Razgar,* rejected her claim with regret, finding that it did not fall into the category of 'very exceptional circumstances' as provided by the ECtHR standard in the *HIV Deportation* case.[344]

As far as decisions affecting housing rights are concerned, it has often been held that it is not necessary to have a legal right of possession to the housing at issue in order to engage Article 8.[345] In *Anufrijeva v Southwark London Borough Council,*[346] the Court of Appeal held that Article 8 was capable of imposing a positive obligation on the Member State to provide accommodation in situations where family life would otherwise be seriously inhibited or the welfare of children threatened. In this case, the local authorities misinterpreted their public law duties to provide support to the claimants and also caused substantial delay. In one of the claims, the local authority failed to discharge its duty to provide accommodation suitably adapted to the claimant's special needs. In the two other claims, the mishandling of asylum applications led to a denial of adequate shelter in one case and a substantial delay in admitting the refugee's family in the other. Although these cases provide an illuminating discussion of the jurisprudence concerning positive obligations to provide welfare support, such an obligation can only be imposed in extreme circumstances.[347] The Court found it 'hard to conceive' of a case where Article 8 obliges the government to provide welfare support where the claimant's 'predicament is not sufficiently severe to engage article 3'.[348]

342. *D v UK* (1997) 24 EHRR 425.

343. Ibid., [49ff].

344. Ibid.

345. *Michalak v Wandsworth LBC* [2002] HLR 721; *Royal Borough of Kensington and Chelsea v O'Sullivian* [2003] EWCA 371; *R (Gangera) v Hounslow LBC* [2003] EWHC 794; *Kay v Lambeth LBC* [2006] 2 AC 465; *Leeds CC v Price* [2006] UKHL 10.

346. [2004] QB 1124; *R (N) v Secretary of State for the Home Department, R (M) v Secretary of State for the Home Department* (N228).

347. King (N300) 288.

348. *Anufrijeva* (N346) [43].

This raises the question of whether this is a stricter approach than the one announced in *Marzari v Italy*,[349] which had similar circumstances. In this case, the ECtHR held that

> a refusal of the authorities to provide assistance ... to an individual suffering from a severe disease might in certain circumstances raise an issue under article 8 of the [ECHR] because of the impact of such refusal on the private life of the individual.[350]

This case shows a willingness to place emphasis on the vulnerabilities of the claimant as a crucial deciding factor, but makes no mention of an Article 3 threshold. The Court of Appeal discussed *Marzari* in *Anufrijeva*'s judgment, but did not address whether the finding in that case was consistent with its own views on the use of Article 3. Ultimately, all three claims examined in the *Anufrijeva* case were denied for failure to be sufficiently exceptional.[351]

Moreover, Article 3 was also not used as a threshold in the High Court's decision in *R (on the application of Bernard) v Enfield London Borough Council*,[352] as approved in *Anufrijeva*, in which Sullivan J found that a severely disabled woman's Article 8 rights had been violated by the council's failure to provide her with housing suited to her disability. It was accepted by the council that it had breached its duty to her under the National Assistance Act 1948. The flat failed to provide the claimant with wheelchair access to a lavatory, and, as a result, she constantly soiled herself. She could not look after her children adequately. She had no privacy and was confined to an extremely small area. Although Sullivan J held that it was not a breach of Article 3, he accepted that it did contravene Article 8 because it made it virtually impossible for her to have a meaningful private family life. The judge placed emphasis on the fact that disabled people are a 'particularly vulnerable group'.[353]

349. (1999) EHRR CD 175.
350. Ibid., 179–180.
351. *Anufrijeva* (N346) [43].
352. [2002] EWHC 2282.
353. Ibid., [32].

In short, in both *Anufrijeva* and *Bernard*, as with *Razgar* and the *HIV Deportation* case, there is a clear attempt to fashion the category of potential claimants in a narrow manner and to be cautious about preventing an expansion of the category.[354] A similar position was also taken in *Royal Borough of Kensington and Chelsea v O'Sullivan*,[355] in which the judge rejected the claimant's attempt to remain in her council flat after her husband, the grantee of the flat, died.[356] The judge referred to the courts' desire to avoid becoming engaged in 'macro level' housing allocation issues. The claimant's case was not sufficiently exceptional to warrant doing precisely this.[357]

Insofar as Article 8 claims from travellers and gypsy claimants are concerned, in *South Bucks District Council v Porter*,[358] the claimants had acquired land for the purposes of establishing caravan sites but were subsequently denied planning permission for that use of the land. The claimants remained on the site, but the council applied under planning legislation to have them evicted. The planning legislation conferred a discretion on the judge to determine whether to issue an injunction upon application, whereby non-compliance with it could lead to imprisonment. An important issue on appeal was the degree to which the court ought to take account of human rights considerations under Article 8 when exercising judicial discretion in granting injunctive relief. The House of Lords affirmed the approach adopted by the Court of Appeal, saying that when a court considers whether to issue an injunction, and thus interfere with a person's Article 8 right to a home and private life, the decision must be proportionate in the ECHR sense. As explained by the Court of Appeal:

> Proportionality requires not only that the injunction be proportionate and necessary for the attainment of the public interest objective sought — here the safeguarding of the environment — but also that it does not impose an excessive burden on the individual whose private interests — here the gypsy's private life and home and the retention of his ethnic identity — are at stake.[359]

354. King (N300) 289.
355. [2003] EWCA 371.
356. Ibid., [82].
357. Ibid.
358. [2001] EWCA Civ 1549, [2003] UKHL 26.
359. Ibid., [2001] EWCA Civ 1549, [41].

Thus, although the House of Lords is not to review each planning decision strictly on its merits, neither is it meant to function as a lenient, merely supervisory body.[360] While exercising statutorily conferred judicial discretion, judges must engage in a proportionate balancing process when Article 8 interests are at stake.

7.4.5 Equality or Non-Discrimination

Apart from the 'integrated approach' to treat socio-economic rights as essential corollaries of civil and political rights and thus protect them, the UK courts have also, through the expansive application of equality or non-discrimination, protected the socio-economic interests of British citizens. On some occasions, the courts have been more willing to provide relief even for resource intensive rights when the Article 14 right to enjoy ECHR provisions 'without discrimination' is at issue.

In *Ghaidan*,[361] the House of Lords held that the ECHR required the survivors of homosexual partners enjoy the same statutory tenancy rights as do the surviving spouses or partners of heterosexual married couples, or unmarried couples, who lived as husband and wife. It was common ground that Godin-Mendoza's Article 8 right to a home was engaged for the purposes of an Article 14 analysis. Lord Nicholls also held that 'arguments based on the extent of the discretionary area of judgment accorded to the legislature led nowhere in this case'.[362]

Similarly, the Court of Appeal also declared certain provisions of housing legislation invalid in *R (on the application of Morris) v Westminster City Council*[363] because the provisions allowed the housing authority, when deciding whether someone is in 'priority need' for housing, to disregard whether the person had certain dependents from abroad. The Court found that the provision fell within the ambit of Article 8, discriminated on grounds of national origin, and was not

360. Ibid., [2003] UKHL 26, [20], [27], and [38] (Lord Bingham).

361. *Ghaidan* (N187).

362. Ibid., [19].

363. [2005] EWCA Civ 1184.

proportionate to the legitimate objective of discouraging 'benefits tourism'.[364] The case was a bold step, involving complex housing and immigration legislation, and it has straddled the fault line between macro-level housing policy and seemingly plain discrimination.

Moreover, there have also been cases touching upon issues concerning access to economic social security benefits of the kind protected by Article 9 of the ICESCR and by Article 12 of the ESC (i.e., the right to social security).[365] In *Matthews v Ministry of Defence*,[366] the comments of Lord Hoffmann are noteworthy:

> Human rights are the rights essential to the life and dignity of the individual in a democratic society. The exact limits of such rights are debatable and, although there is not much trace of economic rights in the 50-year old [ECHR], I think it is well arguable that human rights include a right to a minimum standard of living, without which many of the other rights would be a mockery.[367]

Despite the above *dicta*, the House of Lords has sometimes been less receptive to discrimination arguments in cases involving access to these public benefits. In *R (on the application of Hooper) v Secretary of State for Work and Pensions*,[368] certain widowers challenged their benefit provisions, which provided less generous support than what was provided to widows. Parliament had in fact legislatively equalised the payments previously by levelling down what was paid to women; however, the claimants attacked the period prior to this legislative action. The Court rejected their claims. Lord Hoffmann found that whether or not social circumstances were such that a policy of giving more support to widows than widowers should be continued, and when such circumstances had changed and

364. Benefit tourism is a political term coined in the 1990s and later used for the perceived threat that a huge number of citizens from eight of the ten new nations given membership during the enlargement of the EU in 2004 would move to the existing Member States to benefit from their social welfare systems rather than to work. In several countries this threat was used as a reason for creating temporary work or benefit restrictions for citizens from the new member states.

365. Palmer (N303) 226.

366. [2003] UKHL 4.

367. Ibid., [26].

368. [2005] UKHL 29.

Parliamentary response was therefore needed, were, due to their indeterminate nature, quintessentially matters for 'legislative judgment'.[369]

In *R v Secretary of State for Work and Pensions, ex parte Carson and Reynolds*,[370] moreover, the applicants, before emigrating to South Africa and Canada, were pensioners who had often spent long periods of their working life in the UK during which they paid social security. After they had become entitled to their pensions, the pensions in question were no longer upgraded if they had left Britain. Therefore, the pensions they received became considerably lower than those they would have received if they had benefited from upgrading. The relevant legislation required the upgrading to maintain its value 'in relation to the general level of prices obtaining in Great Britain'. For non-residents, there was no such upgrading unless they lived in a country with a bilateral reciprocal social security agreement with Britain. However, their claims were dismissed by the House of Lords who concurred on the view from the Court of Appeal that

> in the field of what may be called macro-economic policy the decision-making power of the elected arms of government is all but at its greatest and the constraining role of the courts, absent a florid violation by government of established legal principles, is correspondingly modest.[371]

Carson was later tabled before the ECtHR. The Court noted that only differences in treatment based on an identifiable characteristic, or 'status', are capable of amounting to discrimination within the meaning of Article 14, as in the *Danish Sex Education* case,[372] and there must be a difference in the treatment of persons in analogous, or relevantly similar, situations. Such a difference in treatment is discriminatory if it has no objective or reasonable justification. In other words, a difference in treatment is discriminatory if it does not pursue a legitimate aim, or if there is no reasonable relationship of proportionality between the means employed and the objective. Nevertheless, the ECtHR also noted that Member States enjoy a margin of appreciation in assessing whether, and to what extent, differences in otherwise similar situations justify different

369. Ibid., [37].

370. [2003] EWCA Civ 797, [2005] UKHL 37, [2006] 1 AC 173.

371. Ibid., [2006] 1 AC 173, [78].

372. *Kjeldsen, Busk Madsen and Pedersen v Denmark* (1976) 1 EHRR 711.

treatment. A wide margin is usually given to the Member State under the ECHR when it comes to general measures of economic or social strategy.

Although the ECtHR was not concerned with an assessment of the effects, if any, on the many thousands of people in the same position as the applicants and insisted that its role is to decide the question of legal principle — namely, whether the legislation as such unlawfully discriminates between persons who are in an analogous situation. For an issue to arise under Article 14, there must be a difference in the treatment of persons in relevantly similar situations. The Court also noted that given that the pension system is primarily designed to serve the needs of those who are living in the UK, it was difficult to draw any genuine comparison with the position of pensioners living elsewhere because of the range of economic and social variables which apply from country to country. Neither did the Court consider the applicants to be in a relevantly similar position to pensioners living in countries with which the UK has concluded a bilateral agreement providing for upgrading. Where an agreement is in place, the flow of funds may differ depending on the level of each country's benefits and the number of people going in each direction. It follows that there has been no discrimination and, therefore, no violation of Article 14 taken in conjunction with Article 1 of Protocol 1 (protection of property and peaceful enjoyment of his possessions). In respect of discrimination on such grounds, which are not based on sex or nationality, the Court gave ample leeway for the Member State, and the applicants were not successful.

7.4.6 Non-Denial of the Right to Education

In this category, the English courts have been inclined to follow ECtHR jurisprudence as determined in the famous *Belgian Linguistic's Case (No. 2)*,[373] in that everyone is entitled to be educated to a minimum standard, and are willing to use the proportionality test to review educational policies in relation to socio-economic rights. In *R v East Sussex County Council, ex parte Tandy*,[374] the House of Lords' refused to downgrade mandatory duties to provide a sick

373. (1968) 1 EHRR 252.

374. [1998] AC 714 (HL), [1998] 2 All ER 769.

child with a suitable education to discretionary obligations. The Court decided, as a matter of construction, that the question of 'suitable education' for the purposes of section 298 of the Education Act 1993 was to be determined solely by reference to educational considerations, in the sense that the education had to be efficient and suitable for the child's age and ability. Nevertheless, resources were not relevant to this determination even though they were relevant when the administrative authorities were choosing between different ways of making such a provision.

This decision is sharply distinct from that in *R v Gloucestershire County Council, ex parte Barry*.[375] In this case, Lord Browne-Wilkinson held that the statutory provision was somewhat strange in that it imposed a duty to meet the 'needs' of disabled persons even though the lack of the benefits enumerated in the section could not possibly give rise to 'need' in any stringent sense of the word. The Chronically Sick and Disabled Persons Act 1970 had, moreover, not provided any guidance as to how such needs were to be assessed. Given that this was so, it was, said Lord Browne-Wilkinson, not surprising that the House of Lords had held that resources should be taken into account. In this case, by way of contrast, the statute imposed an immediate obligation to make arrangements for 'suitable education', which was defined by objective criteria.[376]

Furthermore, the notions that the right to education cannot be denied and that everyone is entitled to be educated to a 'minimum standard' were affirmed in *Ali v Lord Grey School*.[377] *Ali* involved three boys excluded from school pending the outcome of a criminal investigation into a fire they had allegedly started on school premises. After discontinuation of prosecution for want of evidence, the school invited these students and their parents to a meeting to discuss an offer to reinstate them. However, one student's parents decided not to attend, ultimately leading to no offer being made to the student concerned. Another student, whose parents had attended, was in fact reinstated. Baroness Hale held that the former student should not be held responsible for his family's failure to respond to the proposed meeting and thus the proposed offer.[378]

375. [1997] AC 584, [1997] 2 All ER 1. See also Chapter Three of this book for further discussion of this case.
376. See also *R (JL (A Child)) v Islington LBC* [2009] EWHC 458 (Admin).
377. [2006] UKHL 14.
378. Ibid., [78] and [83].

7.4.7 The Future of the Human Rights Act 1998 and its Impact on the Implementation of Positive Obligations

Overall, the HRA 1998 is one of the most significant pieces of constitutional reform undertaken in recent decades. However, it has been a highly controversial piece of legislation. Some people strongly support it as an essential safeguard of basic rights in the UK. Others, including some judges,[379] have criticised it for going too far,[380] whether in terms of the strength of protection that it offers or the range of rights to which it applies.[381] Still others, including some popular tabloids, have accused the HRA 1998 of giving judges too much power and of producing perverse outcomes. As a result, there have been calls in some quarters in the community for its repeal.[382]

What is more, prior to becoming the Prime Minister, David Cameron, the leader of the Tories in opposition, argued in 2006 that a British Bill of Rights should be enacted in place of the HRA 1998 [383] to 'define the core values which give us our identity as a free nation' while facilitating a 'hard-nosed defence of security and freedom'.[384] A less-specific undertaking — to 'replace the Human Rights Act with a UK Bill of Rights' — was contained in the Conservatives' 2010 election manifesto.[385] In June 2015, however, Cameron ruled out withdrawing from the ECHR despite opposition from the Home and Justice Secretaries, and

379. Lennie Hoffmann, 'The Universality of Human Rights', *Judicial Studies Board Annual Lecture*, 19 March 2009, [8] and [11].

380. Department for Constitutional Affairs, *Review of the Implementation of the Human Rights Act* (London 2006) 30; Richard Savill, 'KFC meal "ensures siege man's rights"', *The Daily Telegraph*, 7 June 2006, available at: www.telegraph.co.uk/news/uknews/1520534/KFC-meal-ensures-siege-mans-rights.html, last accessed 17 May 2020; J. Coles, 'Finger-Nickin good farce', *The Sun*, 7 June 2006.

381. *R (S) v Secretary of State for the Home Department* [2006] EWHC Admin 111, [2006] EWCA Civ 1157, [2006] INLR 575. See also Philip Johnston and George Jones, 'Blair to take on judges over asylum', *The Daily Telegraph*, 20 February 2003, available at: www.telegraph.co.uk/news/uknews/1422570/Blair-to-take-on-judges-over-asylum.html, last accessed 17 May 2020.

382. Elliott and Thomas (N113) 767.

383. David Cameron, 'Balancing freedom and security — A Modern British Bill of Rights', Speech to the Centre for Policy Studies, London, 26 June 2006, cited by House of Lords and House of Commons Joint Committee on Human Rights, 'A Bill of Rights for the UK' (29th Report of Session 2007-08, Vol. 2, HL Paper 165-II & HC 150-II, 10 October 2008), available at: https://publications.parliament.uk/pa/jt200708/jtselect/jtrights/165/165ii.pdf, last accessed 3 June 2020.

384. 'Balancing Freedom and Security: A Modern British Bill of Rights', speech to the Centre for Policy Studies, London, 26 June 2006.

385. Conservative Party, 'An Invitation to Join the Government Britain' (London 2010) 79.

there was also a cabinet split over whether to simply replace the HRA 1998 with a British Bill of Rights or to go further and withdraw entirely from the ECHR.[386]

Whatever change may occur, Elliott and Thomas have argued that the repeal of the HRA 1998, if it were to happen, would not result in the removal of ECHR influence from UK law. They provide five reasons to support their view.[387] First, common law is evolving, and the doctrine of common law constitutional rights has been developing over time, including the absorption of some ECHR stipulations. Second, the repeal of the HRA 1998 would not remove common law constitutional rights, and they would continue to be protected by the courts. Third, it is unlikely that proportionality — one of the main techniques protecting the rights granted in the ECHR — would vanish from domestic law even if the HRA 1998 was repealed. This is because the courts are accustomed to using this principle in other contexts — most obviously when assessing the legality of governmental action that dashes a substantive legitimate expectation [388] — which suggests that it has become, or is in the process of becoming, an embedded feature of domestic law, rather than simply features of the HRA 1998 and of EU law. Fourth, irrespective of common law constitutional rights, certain areas of common law have been shifting (thanks to the HRA 1998) to be more closely aligned with the ECHR. For instance, the extent to which the law of tort protects privacy has been considerably expanded.[389] This new body of common law would not simply disappear even if the HRA 1998 was repealed. Finally, the same point also applies to legislation, the meaning of which has changed as a result of the HRA 1998. Legislation that has been interpreted pursuant to section 3 of the HRA 1998, such as 'reading in' and 'reading down' as explained in *R v A (No. 2)*,[390] to render it compatible with the ECHR would not simply revert to its pre-HRA 1998 meaning upon repeal of that enactment. Rather, those HRA 1998-compatible interpretations would remain part of the body of precedent. Overall, the cumulative effect of sections 2, 3, 4, and 6 of the HRA 1998 is that the principle of proportionality has been recognised by Parliament as a means to review legislation and administrative acts in the UK.

386. Rowena Mason, 'Human rights: Tories reject reports of rift between Cameron, May and Gove', *The Guardian*, 1 June 2015, available at: www.theguardian.com/law/2015/jun/01/pm-at-odds-with-theresa-may-and-michael-gove-over-human-rights, last accessed 17 May 2020.

387. Elliott and Thomas (N113) 771–772.

388. *R v North and East Devon Health Authority, ex p Coughlan* [2001] QB 213, [2000] 2 WLR 622, [2000] 3 All ER 850.

389. *Campbell*; *Douglas*; *Venables and Thompson* (N247).

390. *A (No. 2)* (N171).

Although the ICESCR has not been fully incorporated into English law, most constitutional and human rights norms, be they civil and political rights or socio-economic rights, do still implicate that the state has duties to avoid, protect, and aid. These norms couple with the judicial tendency to attach positive duties to civil and political rights issues, and together allow the courts to make effective and constitutionally appropriate contributions to resolve disputes.[391] As proportionality is said to be a more structured and intensive approach to scrutinise administrative decisions and their implementation, and has explicitly been applied in respect of directly effective EU law through the ECA 1972 and of the ECHR via the HRA 1998, the principle acts as a check-and-balance to save under-represented minorities from being ignored or exploited by the majoritarian government. Furthermore, despite the ECA 1972 no longer being considered binding after Brexit, UK national courts have indicated that they will 'have regard' (i.e., it will have persuasive effect) to any principles, including proportionality, as laid down by the CJEU.[392]

7.5 Concluding Remarks

This chapter describes the extent to which the principle of proportionality has been re-formulated and integrated in the UK. As EU law and the ECHR are directly applicable to the UK as a Member State, they create external pressure to apply proportionality to other types of judicial review. Internal pressure has also been exerted by some liberal and pro-active judges and scholars, who advocate the same. If we agree with the fundamental axiom of justice that like cases should be treat alike,[393] then we must also concede that the proportionality enquiry should be available to all judicial review cases in Britain.[394]

391. David Beatty, 'The Last Generation: When Rights Lose their Meaning' in David Beatty (ed), *Human Rights and Judicial Review* (Kluwer 1994) 321–361; Asbjørn Eide, 'Economic Social and Cultural Rights as Human Rights' in Asbjørn Eide, Catarina Krause, and Allan Rosas (eds), *Economic Social and Cultural Rights* (2nd edn, Kluwer 2001) 9–28.

392. The EU(W)A 2018, s 6.

393. *Ghaidan* (N187) [2004] 2 AC 557, 566C. See also H.L.A. Hart, *The Concept of Law* (2nd edn, Clarendon Press 1994) 155–157.

394. Garreth Wong, 'Towards the Nutcracker Principle: Reconsidering the Objections to Proportionality' (2000) Spring *PL* 92, 96.

If the courts continue to draw a strict division between the standards employed in judicial review under EU law and human rights law, on one hand, and domestic law, on the other, then the standard of the latter might be viewed as 'second class' in the sense that it is not as rigorous or comprehensive as that undertaken by the CJEU and ECtHR.[395] To measure public decision-making against the standards set down in the ECHR, UK courts will need to employ the proportionality enquiry. Moreover, the ECA 1972 and the HRA 1998 require the courts to apply the principle not only in cases involving EU law and fundamental rights but also in other domestic law cases. This is reflected in decisions requiring the courts to interpret other legislation for compatibility with these statutes. In other words, the courts are empowered through Parliament to decide whether the public body's decision was or might have been made in pursuit of one or more of the legitimate purposes detailed in EU law and the ECHR.

Influenced by European jurisprudence derived from the CJEU and the ECtHR, English courts have also started observing socio-economic rights as implicit in civil and political rights, and have found that the administration has positive duties to fulfil even though a great margin of discretion is given to administrators in view of their constitutional legitimacy and institutional competence.

At the administrative level, the British government is known to instruct its personnel to observe the proportionality principle, as shown in the UK government's guide to judicial review for administrators (i.e., *The Judge Over Your Shoulder*). Thus, proportionality is already in the administrators' minds as an established legal norm. All public personnel are therefore required to observe this principle and should be aware of its practical implications when they are exercising their discretionary powers in discharge of their public duties. In view of the above analysis, the English courts have already recognised the proportionality principle in their legal systems, whether explicitly or implicitly, and its full adoption may even further improve the quality of the decision-making process by encouraging officials to focus on alternative courses of action.

395. Thomas (N2) 99.

8

Integration of Proportionality in Hong Kong

8.1. Introduction

In Hong Kong, the principle of proportionality has been applied in respect of the International Covenant on Civil and Political Rights (ICCPR) via the Bill of Rights Ordinance (BORO) [1] as well as constitutional and legislative review adjudications, largely thanks to the judges' consideration of jurisprudence from other common law jurisdictions as authorised under the Basic Law.[2] Where a case does not concern these two regimes, however, the traditional test of *Wednesbury* unreasonableness or *GCHQ* irrationality prevails.[3]

Like its British counterpart, Hong Kong has been facing the same pressures for the development of proportionality as an independent ground of judicial review.[4] As Parliament in the United Kingdom (UK) and the Legislative Council (LegCo) in Hong Kong are presumed to confer a public power, in particular a discretionary power, the exercise of which should not exceed what is necessary for the achievement of the statutory objectives, 'the more

1. Cap 383, Laws of Hong Kong.
2. Hong Kong Basic Law, Art 84.
3. See, for example, *Secretary for Security v Sakthevel Prabakar* [2005] 1 HKLRD 289 (CFA); *Pun Tai Sung v Immigration Tribunal* [2006] HKCU 1818 (unreported, HCAL 51/2005); *Sun News Publishers Ltd v Commissioner for Television and Entertainment Licensing Authority* [2006] HKCU 1729 (unreported, HCAL 50/2006); *Chow Mario v Municipal Services Appeal Board* [2010] HKCU 2649 (unreported, HCAL 31/2010); *Gutierrez v Commissioner for Registration* [2011] 6 HKC 561; *Dr Lau Yuk Kong v Medical Council of Hong Kong* [2011] 5 HKC 218; *Wong Kam Wah v Fisherman Claims Appeal Board* [2012] HKCU 990 (unreported, HCAL 96/2011).
4. Johannes Chan, 'Administrative Law' in Simon Young and Yash Ghai (eds), *Hong Kong's Court of Final Appeal: The Development of the Law in China's Hong Kong* (CUP 2014) 438.

important the statutory objectives are, the graver the restrictions on the exercise of discretionary power should be'.[5] Thus, there is no rational basis for the principle not being applied to other types of judicial review litigations.[6]

This chapter examines the extent to which the principle of proportionality has been re-formulated and integrated into Hong Kong's legal system before and after the change of sovereignty in 1997 to see if a reasonable balance has been struck between society's interests and individuals' interests. Particular attention is paid to poverty levels, social welfare subsidies, and the enforcement of socio-economic rights in post-colonial Hong Kong. It also discusses Hong Kong citizens' growing 'legal mobilisation',[7] or the use of litigation by its citizens, especially minorities, to defend or develop their rights against the post-1997 government of the Hong Kong Special Administrative Region (SAR) as well as against the Mainland authorities led by the Chinese Communist Party. Additionally, the lack of democratic development and the resulting civil disobedience movements and anti-government protests that occurred in 2014, 2016, and 2019 are also discussed.[8] This chapter goes on to look at judicial attitudes towards legal disputes concerning policy formulation and implementation, as well as the impact of current jurisprudence on socio-economic rights, to see if they are compatible with jurisprudence of the European Convention on Human Rights (ECHR). Just like non-EU law and non-human rights law in the UK may be easily framed within EU law and human rights law dimensions, laws other than those enshrined in the Basic Law, including international human rights standards, may easily be framed within the dimensions of the Basic Law.

8.2 Proportionality: Its Integration in Hong Kong under the Bill of Rights Ordinance between 1991 and 1997

Historically, Hong Kong has lacked laws protecting fundamental rights. During the colonial period, the Letters Patent (i.e., the constitution of Hong Kong)

5. Johannes Chan, 'Administrative Law, Politics and Governance: The Hong Kong Experience' in Tom Ginsburg and Albert Chen (eds), *Administrative Law and Governance in Asia* (Routledge, Abingdon 2009) 159.

6. Ibid.

7. Wai Keung Tam, *Legal Mobilization under Authoritarianism: The Case of Post-colonial Hong Kong* (CUP 2013).

8. Notably, those that happened in 2019 will be discussed first owing to my prioritisation of different issues.

made no reference to human rights. Instead, Hong Kong followed British tradition, recognising the notion of civil liberties (i.e., every citizen has a right to do what they like unless restrained by the law),[9] as opposed to the concept of fundamental rights, which is both positive and declaratory (i.e., to say that someone has a right to do something means that the law specifically says that it can be lawfully done).[10] As Lord Cooke has noted, the Diceyan concept of the rule of law is that citizens can do what they like unless the country has express powers of intervention.[11] This has been reflected in the decision of *Malone v Metropolitan Police Commissioner*,[12] which states that 'England is not a country where everything is forbidden except what is expressly permitted: it is a country where everything is permitted except what is expressly forbidden'.[13]

It was not until 8 June 1991, in the lead up to the handover, that an attempt was made to restore Hong Kong people's confidence, which had been shaken by the brutal crackdown in Tiananmen square on 4 June 1989. This was done using the BORO, which made the provisions of the ICCPR applicable to Hong Kong and directly enforceable in the local courts.[14] Like other countries, Britain entered 'reservations' (i.e., the provisions of the ICCPR 'as applied to Hong Kong') to prevent some of them from being applied in full. Examples include the lack of a requirement for fair elections for the executive and LegCo positions, limitations on the right to freedom of movement,[15] and restrictions on the right to postpone applications concerning equal pay to men and women in the private sector.[16]

Although Britain signed and then ratified these two international Bills of Rights almost as soon as they came into force in 1976 (meaning that most parts

9. *AG v Guardian Newspapers Ltd (No. 2)* [1990] 1 AC 109, 178. See also Mark Elliott and Robert Thomas, *Public Law* (OUP 2011) 724.

10. Ibid., Elliott and Thomas.

11. Robin Cooke, 'Human Rights in Hong Kong' (1999) 20 *VUWLR* 45.

12. [1979] 1 Ch 344.

13. Ibid., 355 (Megarry VC). See also *Wheeler v Leicester CC* [1985] AC 1054, 1065 (Browne-Wilkinson LJ).

14. Albert Chen, 'Constitutional Adjudication in Post-1997 Hong Kong' in Albert Chen and Tom Ginsburg (eds), *Public Law in East Asia* (Ashgate 2013) 182.

15. ICCPR, Art 12.

16. Ibid., Art 7(a)(i).

of the two treaties immediately applied not only in Britain, but also in all of its colonies, including Hong Kong), such international treaties did not, under the common law tradition, confer rights capable of being enforced in the local courts unless they were 'incorporated' into domestic law (i.e., the concept of 'dualism' [17] or 'transformation theory' [18] under international law). Even so, the enactment of the BORO was unprecedented, and it was regarded as the 'first constitutional revolution in Hong Kong' during the early 1990s.[19] Since then, Hong Kong courts have had the power to review the compatibility of executive acts and legislation with constitutional guarantees of fundamental rights, via Article VII(5) of the Letters Patent, as enshrined in the BORO,[20] despite the fact that prior to its enactment, the courts did, in theory, have jurisdiction to review the constitutionality of local legislation.[21] They have conducted this review by adopting and assessing limitations clauses in the qualified rights of the BORO under the proportionality principle.

Although some fundamental rights are absolute and unqualified in nature so that they cannot be restricted under any circumstances (e.g., the right not to be tortured),[22] most of them are qualified rights which can be subject to certain constraints (e.g., freedom of expression).[23] This is because, as stated in the *Public Order Ordinance* case,[24] '[r]ights and freedoms cannot be absolute or else they are no different from anarchy and can lead to mayhem and lawlessness'.[25] The Prevention of Child Pornography Ordinance [26] is a typical example in that it restricts freedom of expression by criminalising the possession, production,

17. *McWhirter v AG* [1972] CMLR 882, 886.
18. Johannes Chan, 'Basic Law and Constitutional Review: The First Decade' (2007) 37 *HKLJ* 407, 411.
19. Chen (N14).
20. Ibid.
21. *Ho Po Sang v Director of Public Works* [1959] HKLR 632; *Rediffusion (HK) v AG of Hong Kong* [1970] AC 1136; *Deacon Chiu v AG* [1992] 2 HKLR 84; *Lee Miu Ling v AG* [1995] 5 HKPLR 585, [1996] 1 HKC 124, 135; *Lau Wong Fat v AG* (1996) 7 HKPLR 148.
22. BORO, s 8, Art 3 (ICCPR, Art 7). See also Chapter Six of this book.
23. Ibid., s 8, Art 16 (ICCPR, Art 19).
24. *Leung Kwok Hung v HKSAR* [2004] 3 HKLRD 729 (CA) (Yeung J), (2005) 8 HKCFAR 229, [2005] HKCU 887, [2005] HKCFA 41, [2005] 3 HKLRD 164.
25. Ibid., [2004] 3 HKLRD 729, 795 (CA) (Yeung J).
26. Cap 579, Laws of Hong Kong.

and distribution of sexual depictions of children for the sake of reducing child sexual exploitation. As Danny Gittings noted:

> The fact that exceptions [or constraints] exist ... reflects the reality that no society can function without sometimes imposing restrictions on the rights which individual members of that society enjoy, if only to protect the rights of other members of that society.[27]

However, while banning restrictions on fundamental rights might, under some extreme circumstances, lead to anarchy or lawlessness, having these rights restricted too easily may render them meaningless.[28] Thus, the extent to which human rights can be restricted has been one of the most important issues tackled by the Hong Kong courts since the enactment of the BORO. To achieve this, the courts have increasingly referred to foreign jurisprudence, adopting the proportionality analysis to assess the constitutionality of any restriction on fundamental rights under the BORO.

While the ICCPR does not explicitly mandate that limitation clauses pass muster when scrutinised under the proportionality principle, some of the provisions of the ICCPR stipulate that any restriction must be 'necessary' to achieve a legitimate public objective or 'necessary in a democratic society'.[29] Similarly, the derogation clause under Article 4 of the ICCPR also requires that limitations be proportional, among other things.[30] As the constitutional requirement of necessity involves applying the proportionality principle in many other jurisdictions,[31] its role is legitimatised in the context of working out the limitation clauses of the qualified rights in the BORO in Hong Kong. Since the enactment of the BORO, the adoption and application of the proportionality test by the Hong Kong courts has been a significant and welcome legal

27. Danny Gittings, *Introduction to the Hong Kong Basic Law* (2nd edn, HKUP 2016) 286.

28. Ibid., 287.

29. ICCPR, Arts 12(3), 14(1), 19(3), 21, 22(2), and 25.

30. Ibid., Art 4(1).

31. See, for example, *Handyside v UK* (1976) 1 EHRR 737, [49] (ECtHR); *Norris v Ireland* (1991) 13 EHRR 186, [41] (ECtHR); *R v Oakes* [1986] 1 SCR 103 (Canada); *De Freitas v Ministry of Agriculture* [1999] 1 AC 69 (UK Privy Council); *S v Makwanyane* 1995 (3) SA 391 (South Africa).

development, which has allowed the courts to usher in international, regional, and municipal human rights jurisprudence.[32] This has led some to claim that it is 'a new era of jurisprudence'.[33]

In *R v Sin Yau Ming*,[34] the Hong Kong Court of Appeal was tasked with assessing the compatibility of presumption of trafficking under the Dangerous Drugs Ordinance[35] with the presumption of innocence as enshrined in the BORO. In this case, the Court considered, and found itself assisted by, the General Comments and Concluding Observations of various UN Human Rights Committees, which noted that restrictions on fundamental rights guaranteed under the ICCPR should only be justified by virtue of proportionality.[36] Further assistance was found in the decisions of the European Court of Human Rights (ECtHR) and the European Commission of Human Rights, as well as the jurisprudences of the Judicial Committee of the Privy Council, UK (UK Privy Council), the U.S. Supreme Court, and the Supreme Court of Canada.[37] More importantly, the Court found that the proportionality principle is implied in the BORO as a 'justification provision', similar to that of section 1 of the Canadian Charter of Rights and Freedoms,[38] and applied a version of the proportionality test enunciated by the Supreme Court of Canada in *R v Oakes*.[39]

In reviewing the challenged section 4 of the Dangerous Drugs Ordinance and considering these foreign materials, the Court held that the then colonial government had failed to show that reversing the burden of proof was rationally

32. Johannes Chan, 'Hong Kong's Bill of Rights: Its Reception of and Contribution to International and Comparative Jurisprudence' (1998) 47 *ICLQ* 306; Anthony Mason, 'The Place of Comparative Law in the Developing the Jurisprudence on the Rule of Law and Human Rights in Hong Kong' (2007) 37 *HKLJ* 299; Carole Petersen, 'Embracing Universal Standards? The Role of Human Rights Treaties in Hong Kong's Constitutional Jurisprudence' in Fu Hualing, Lison Harris, and Simon Young (eds), *Interpreting Hong Kong's Basic Law: The Struggle for Coherence* (Palgrave 2007) 33–53; Albert Chen, 'International Human Rights Law and Domestic Constitutional Law: Internationalisation of Constitutional Law in Hong Kong' (2010) 4 *NTULR* 237; Lo Pui Yin, *The Judicial Construction of Hong Kong's Basic Law: Courts, Politics and Society after 1997* (HKUP 2014) 281.

33. Derek Cons, 'The Hong Kong Bill of Rights: A Judicial Perspective' in Johannes Chan and Yash Ghai (eds), *The Hong Kong Bill of Rights* (Butterworths Asia 1993) 51–54.

34. (1991) 1 HKPLR 88 (CA), [1992] 1 HKCLR 127.

35. Cap 134, Laws of Hong Kong.

36. *Pietraroia v Uruguay*, Communication No. 44/1979, U.N. Doc. CCPR/C/12/D/44/1979.

37. Lo (N32) 282.

38. Constitution Act 1982, as amended, Part I.

39. *Oakes* (N31).

connected or proportional to the law's aim of combating drug trafficking and, thus, violated the presumption of innocence as protected by Article 11 of the BORO. Referring to those U.S., Canadian, and European cases on presumptions, the Court adopted the proportionality approach by recognising that a mandatory presumption of fact could be compatible with Article 11(1) of the BORO only if it is

> shown by the Crown, having due regard to the enacted conclusions of the legislature, that the fact to be presumed rationally and realistically follows from that proved and also if the presumption is no more than proportionate to what is warranted by the nature of the evil against which society requires protection.[40]

The Court also described the BORO as mandating an 'entirely new jurisprudential approach' — that is, the Court must treat the ICCPR provisions as superior and give them priority over any conflicting laws enacted by the Hong Kong LegCo.[41]

The courts also referred to other international and comparative jurisprudences. In *R v Yu Yem Kin*,[42] the Court referred to the *travaux préparatoires*[43] in deciding whether protection against 'arbitrary arrest and detention' was limited to a review of procedural impropriety or whether it allowed a substantive review of the law (i.e., illegality or *GCHQ* irrationality) concerning arrest and detention.[44] In *Commissioner of Inland Revenue v Lee Lai Ping*,[45] the Court also compared the English and the French texts of the ICCPR in deciding whether the phrase 'rights and obligations in a suit at law' in Article 10 (i.e., equality before courts and the right to a fair and public hearing)[46] bore the same meaning as the expression 'civil and political obligations' in Article 6 (i.e., the right to a fair trial)[47] of the ECHR. Considering the above, as well as most of the early BORO

40. *Sin Yau Ming* (N34) [1992] 1 HKCLR 127, 163.
41. Ibid., 141.
42. (1994) 4 HKPLR 75.
43. French: preparatory works. They are the official record of a negotiation. The travaux are often useful in clarifying the intentions of a treaty or other instrument, as reflected in Article 32 of the Vienna Convention on the Law of Treaties.
44. *Yu Yem Kin* (N42) 93.
45. (1993) 3 HKLPR 141.
46. BORO, s 8, Cap 383.
47. *Lee Lai Ping* (N45) 147.

litigations, the Hong Kong courts were generally seen as taking a more activist jurisprudential approach.

Despite extensive reference to the jurisprudences of the ECtHR and of other foreign entities and materials, ranging from an advisory opinion of the Inter-American Court of Human Rights [48] to the 'soft law' Siracusa Principles on the Limitation and Derogation Provisions in the ICCPR,[49] there was a significant set-back in 1993. In *Attorney General of Hong Kong v Lee Kwong Kut*,[50] the UK Privy Council emphasised the limitation of these materials when they were applied locally,[51] saying that it was not impressed by *Oakes* [52] and describing the proportionality test as a 'somewhat complex process'.[53] Rather, the Court believed that the common law could provide a sufficient test to protect fundamental rights.[54] As Lord Woolf stated:

> While the Hong Kong judiciary should be zealous in upholding an individual's rights under the Hong Kong [BORO], it is also necessary to ensure that disputes as to the effect of the [BORO] are not allowed to get out of hand. The issues involving the Hong Kong [BORO] should be approached with realism and good sense, and kept in proportion. If this is not done the [BORO] will become a source of injustice rather than justice and it will be debased in the eyes of the public. In order to maintain the balance between the individual and the society as a whole, rigid and inflexible standards should not be imposed on the legislature's attempts to resolve the difficult and intransigent problems with which society is faced when seeking to deal with serious crime. It must be remembered that questions of policy remain primarily the responsibility of the legislature.[55]

48. *R v Director of Immigration, ex p Wong King Lung* (1993) 3 HKLPR 253.
49. Ibid.; *R v Director of Immigration, ex p Hai Ho Tak* (1994) 4 HKLPR 324.
50. (1993) 3 HKLPR 72.
51. Ibid., 90–91 (Lord Woolf).
52. *Oakes* (N31).
53. *Lee Kwong Kut* (N50) 97 (Lord Woolf).
54. Ibid.
55. Ibid., 100.

This decision has had a significant impact on Hong Kong courts in their subsequent treatment of and reference to foreign jurisprudences. In fact, the judiciary was later said to be suffering from 'common law superiority syndrome' because judges tended to believe that the common law was sufficient to protect human rights, and that international materials did not offer any additional help.[56] In *R v Town Planning Board, ex parte Kwan Kong Company Ltd*,[57] the Court refused to use European jurisprudence to give the BORO an autonomous meaning because to do so would make 'the common law principles road signs disappear',[58] adding that 'in Hong Kong, with our common law tradition and our special eastern situations, we are not equipped to properly understand, appreciate, analyze, apply or develop this foreign jurisprudence'.[59] The Court went on to say that 'unless something overwhelming and compelling can be shown in any particular European authority, the Hong Kong court should very wisely decline to be seduced by the seemingly inexhaustible literature from the [ECtHR]'.[60] In *Tam Hing Yee v Wu Tai Wai*,[61] Cons VP even said that

> [we] do not ... feel that the court is assisted by substituting for necessity some phrase such as 'pressing social need' or considering whether the restriction ... is reasonable and demonstrably justified in a free and democratic society ... The Court otherwise achieved.[62]

Furthermore, judges' excessive deference to executive acts, in both Britain and Hong Kong, has ultimately had a profound impact on the courts in the application of the proportionality principle in fundamental rights cases. As judges have, under the doctrines of parliamentary supremacy [63] and separation of powers,[64] tended to be reluctant to interfere with Parliament and the LegCo, the common law has adopted a less intrusive approach towards the legislature

56. Chan (N32) 312.
57. (1995) 5 HKLPR 261.
58. Ibid., 315 (Waung J).
59. Ibid.
60. Ibid., 316.
61. (1991) 1 HKLPR 261.
62. Ibid., 269. The phrase 'pressing social need' was being quoted from *Handyside* (N31) [48].
63. Hilaire Barnett, *Constitutional and Administrative Law* (12th edn, Routledge 2017) 121–152.
64. Ibid., 84–95; M.J.C. Vile, *Constitutionalism and the Separation of Powers* (2nd edn, Clarendon 1967) 14.

and the executive — namely, by applying *Wednesbury* unreasonableness or *GCHQ* irrationality. These forms of review limit the courts from interfering with an executive decision unless the decision is so unreasonable or outrageous in its defiance of logic or accepted moral standards that no sensible person or reasonable authority would have come to it.[65] This differs significantly from European jurisprudence, which prefers to use the proportionality principle because it provides a more vigorous level of scrutiny when used to assess legislative provisions and executive decisions.[66]

Since the enactment of the BORO, the courts have inevitably been required to scrutinise the justifications for a violation of fundamental rights in executive policies. Despite this, both the English and Hong Kong courts have, up to the present, deferred to the legislature and the executive by not treating proportionality as an independent ground for judicial review.[67] In *Attorney General v Ming Pao Newspapers Ltd*,[68] although the Magistrate adopted a test of necessity (i.e., proportionality) developed by the ECtHR to hold that section 30 of the Prevention of Bribery Ordinance[69] had been contrary to the right to freedom of expression,[70] the UK Privy Council held that this section was a justifiable restriction on such freedom. The Court went on to say that they must allow a significant margin of appreciation — or to be precise, deference or margin of discretion — to a decision-maker when judicially reviewing their decision[71] and must show judicial restraint not to interfere with the LegCo,

65. *Associated Provincial Pictures House Ltd v Wednesbury Corporation* [1948] 1 KB 223, 229 (Lord Greene MR); *Council of Civil Service Unions v Minister for the Civil Service* [1985] 1 AC 374, 410E (Lord Diplock).

66. *Sunday Times v UK* (1979–1980) 2 EHRR 245.

67. For examples in Britain, see *R v Secretary of State for the Home Department, ex p Brind* [1991] 696 (HL); *Pham v Secretary of State for the Home Department* [2015] UKSC 19; *R (Keyu) v Secretary of State for Foreign and Commonwealth Affairs* [2015] UKSC 69. For examples in Hong Kong, see *Sakthevel Prabakar* (N3); *Dr Lau Yuk Kong* (N3).

68. (1994) 4 HKPLR 621 (Mag); (1995) 5 HKPLR 13 (CA); (1996) 6 HKPLR 103 (PC).

69. Cap 201, Laws of Hong Kong.

70. BORO, s 8, Art 16 (ICCPR, Art 19).

71. Swati Jhaveri, Michael Ramsden, and Anne Scully-Hill, *Administrative Law in Hong Kong* (2nd edn, LexisNexis 2013) 257 and 588.

whose knowledge of local conditions in Hong Kong is better than that of the final appellate court in Britain.[72]

Insofar as issues concerning political structure are concerned, the courts have also seemingly been reluctant to get themselves involved. In *Lee Miu Ling v Attorney General*,[73] the applicant impugned the functional constituency system as having violated the right to vote by universal and equal suffrage guaranteed by Article 21 (i.e., the right to participate in public life).[74] Functional constituency is a unique characteristic in Hong Kong. Under such a regime, in addition to a vote in their geographical constituency, a member is entitled to vote for the return of a member of the LegCo. This creates an elitist group whose members enjoy an additional vote. This system has long been criticised as being discriminatory and contrary to Article 25 of the ICCPR, as expressed by the Human Rights Committee in the Concluding Observations on the Fourth Periodic Report of the UK on Hong Kong by the Human Rights Committee.[75] However, the Court of Appeal held that functional constituency elections were provided for by the Letters Patent, the then constitution of Hong Kong that was immune from being challenged by the BORO, and that once functional constituency was found to be constitutional, a variation in size of different functional constituencies was an inevitable consequence. Thus, the test to determine its legality is whether a sensible and fair-minded person would condemn the degree of variation as *Wednesbury*-unreasonable or *GCHQ*-irrational.

In *Ng King Luen v Rita Fan*,[76] the Court even refused to grant leave to challenge the legality of the Provisional LegCo, which was appointed by the Chinese communist government pending the election of the first LegCo of the Hong Kong SAR after it became impossible to establish a 'through train' to constitute the first LegCo before 1997 as a result of the breakdown of Sino-British negotiations on political reform issues. As Keith J warned, the courts should not be concerned

72. *Ming Pao Newspapers* (N68) (1996) 6 HKPLR 103, 111–112 (PC).
73. *Lee Miu Ling* (N21).
74. BORO, s 8.
75. Concluding Observations of the Human Rights Committee on the Fourth Periodic Report of the United Kingdom on Hong Kong, [1], [25(b)]–[26].
76. [1997] 1 HKLRD 757.

with political matters and must stand back from political conflict. A similar conclusion was also found in *Chan Shu Ying v Chief Executive of the HKSAR*,[77] in that the applicant was unable to challenge the government's decision to abolish the Regional and Urban Councils as part of its political reform package.

Overall, up to mid-1997, the Hong Kong courts have made about 300 judgments on the BORO.[78] During the early days of BORO litigations, the courts were generally more activist in judicial review litigations to protect fundamental rights by referring to various foreign jurisprudences. However, after an initial period of reasonably generous interpretations of the BORO and a preparedness of the courts to subject legislative and executive decisions to substantive scrutiny, they have become increasingly reluctant to do so,[79] perhaps partly due to their unfamiliarity with such foreign materials and their traditional self-discipline of non-interference with the legislature and the executive (as manifested in their unwillingness to recognise proportionality as a new ground for judicial review). This has altogether resulted in a more conservative approach towards judicial interpretations.

8.3 The Status of the Bill of Rights Ordinance: A Constitutional Document before and after 1997?

From the start, the status of the BORO has been hotly debated. On the face of it, the BORO is seemingly an ordinary ordinance, but it comes with practical complications. Section 3 stipulates that all pre-existing legislation shall be interpreted in a manner consistent with the BORO, and if it cannot be so construed, then the legislation must be repealed to the extent of inconsistency. However, section 4 states that all subsequent legislation shall be interpreted compatibly, not with the BORO, but with the ICCPR 'as applied to Hong Kong'. If it cannot be so construed, the BORO is silent on its validity. However, Article VII(5) of the Letters Patent provides that such subsequent legislation, if incompatible with the ICCPR 'as applied to Hong Kong', shall be *ultra vires* legislation and,

77. [2001] 1 HKLRD 641.

78. Chan (N32) 327.

79. Andrew Byrnes, 'And Some Have Bill of Rights Thrust Upon them: The Experience of Hong Kong's Bill of Rights' in Philip Alston (ed), *Promoting Human Rights Through Bill of Rights* (Clarendon Press 2000) 352.

hence, null and void. The rationale for this complicated arrangement is to avoid the criticism that the BORO enjoys an entrenched status compared with other legislation,[80] even though its practical effect is arguably to the contrary.[81] In *R v Chan Chak Fan*,[82] the Court of Appeal stated:

> The [Letters Patent] entrenches the [BORO] by prohibiting any legislative inroad into the [ICCPR] as applied to Hong Kong. The [BORO] is the embodiment of the [ICCPR] as applied here. Any legislative inroad into the [BORO] is therefore unconstitutional, and will be struck down by the courts as the guardians of the constitution".[83]

In *R v Lum Wai Ming*,[84] the petitioners questioned the validity and presumptions of certain provisions of the Dangerous Drugs (Amendment) (No. 2) Ordinance which were passed after BORO enactment and referenced the Letters Patent. The Court of First Instance held that the new law was invalid as it infringed one of the rights protected by the BORO, and thus contravened this new provision of the Letters Patent, which invalided any new law inconsistent with the BORO.[85] According to Gittings, the effect of the amendment was to give the contents of the BORO a superior status to any later inconsistent legislation as well as reversing the common law principle that a new law will prevail over an earlier inconsistent law.[86]

However, China's Standing Committee of the National People's Congress (NPCSC), whose role has long been criticised as a rubber stamp acting on behalf of the Chinese Communist Party,[87] complained that these major amendments would weaken the administration, and thus not be conducive to

80. Chan (N32) 307.
81. *Sin Yau Ming* (N34) (1991) 1 HKPLR 88 (CA), 106 (Silke VP). See also Gittings (N27) 276.
82. [1994] 3 HKC 145.
83. Ibid., 153.
84. (1992) 2 HKPLR 182, [1992] 2 HKCLR 221.
85. Ibid., [1992] 2 HKCLR 221, 228.
86. Gittings (N27) 276.
87. 'Who holds centre stage at China's political gala?', *South China Morning Post*, date unspecified, available at: https://multimedia.scmp.com/news/china/article/who-s-who/hall.html, last accessed 20 June 2020.

the stability, of Hong Kong.[88] China ultimately declared, among other things, that sections 2(3), 3, and 4 of the BORO were inconsistent with the Hong Kong Basic Law (as these provisions give the BORO a superior status) and would have no legal effect after 1 July 1997.[89] However, Gittings disagrees with the NPCSC's reasoning, arguing that it

> was based on a fundamental misunderstanding of how Hong Kong's legal system works. ... Section 3 simply repeated the long-established common law position that new laws normally prevail over any earlier inconsistent laws. As a result, deleting this provision from the ordinance makes no difference, because it only describes what the courts would normally do anyway, whether or not this is explicitly stated in the law. Much the same was true of the other two sections deleted from the ordinance by the [NPCSC].[90]

Johannes Chan and C.L. Lim concur with this, adding that the invalidation of these three sections was 'simply a cosmetic face-saving measure which has no effect whatsoever on the operation of the Hong Kong [BORO] after 1997'.[91]

As Article 39(1) of the Basic Law states that the ICCPR as applied to Hong Kong 'shall be implemented through the laws of the [Hong Kong SAR]', its effect, luckily, is to rescue the BORO. Even though the BORO was deprived of its so-called superior status, the courts have frequently regarded it as 'constitutional' in nature, so it has continued to enjoy the same protection even after the handover.[92] In *Koon Wing Yee v Insider Dealing Tribunal*,[93] Sir Anthony Mason NPJ stated that 'the Hong Kong [BORO] ... by enacting the Bill of Rights, has constitutional

88. 'Statement of the Legal Sub-Group of the Preliminary Working Committee concerning the Bill of Rights Ordinance' (17 October 1995), cited by Andrew Byrnes and Johannes Chan (1995) 3(4) *Bill of Rights Bulletin* at Appendix A and reproduced in Danny Gittings, *Introduction to the Hong Kong Basic Law* (1st edn, HKUP 2013) 277.
89. Annexes 1 and 2 of the Decision of the NPCSC on Treatment of the Laws Previously in Force in Hong Kong in Accordance with Article 160 of the Basic Law of the Hong Kong SAR of the PRC (23 February 1997).
90. Gittings (N27) 279.
91. Johannes Chan and C.L. Lim, 'Interpreting Constitutional Rights and Permissible Restrictions' in Johannes Chan and C.L. Lim (eds), *Law of the Hong Kong Constitution* (2nd edn, Sweet & Maxwell 2015) 570.
92. *Swire Properties Ltd v Secretary for Justice* (2003) 6 HKCFAR 236, 258; *Ubamaka v Secretary for Security* (2012) 15 HKCFAR 743, 783; *W v Registrar of Marriages* [2013] 3 HKC 375 (CFA), (2013) 16 HKCFAR 112, 152.
93. [2008] 3 HKLRD 372 (CFA).

force pursuant to Art 39 of the Basic Law'.[94] Bokhary PJ (as he then was), in *Lam Siu Po v Commissioner of Police*,[95] despite giving a minority judgment, further elaborated:

> As is well established, the [BORO] is the embodiment of the application to Hong Kong of the [ICCPR] ... from which it is taken almost verbatim. Consequently the [BORO] is — and has always been — entrenched. Today it is entrenched by Art 39 of the Basic Law which provides ... that the ICCPR as applied to Hong Kong shall remain in force and that the rights and freedoms thereunder may not be restricted.[96]

Moreover, the courts have also persistently held that the special interpretative principles previously stated in sections 2(3), 3, and 4 of the BORO may be located within the Basic Law.[97] In *HKSAR v Lam Kwong Wai*,[98] the Court of Final Appeal (CFA) held that despite the invalidation of these provisions from the laws of Hong Kong, there exists an implied power, and thus obligation, in the Basic Law for the courts, like their UK counterparts,[99] to make remedial interpretation of legislation, including in the techniques of 'severance', 'reading in',[100] 'reading down',[101] or 'striking out', to make sure that it is Basic Law-compliant. Only in cases that such an interpretation is not possible will the courts proceed to make a declaration of incompatibility, which entails unconstitutionality and invalidity. This implied power and obligation is seen to extend to make any legislative provision BORO-compliant because Article 39 of the Basic Law gives constitutional force to the ICCPR provisions 'as applied to Hong Kong' by the BORO, and provides that they 'shall remain in force'.[102]

94. Ibid, [25].

95. (2009) 12 HKCFAR 237 (CFA).

96. Ibid.

97. Richard Gordon, Johnny Mok, and Mahncke Hans, *Judicial Review in Hong Kong* (2nd edn, LexisNexis 2014) 163.

98. (2006) 9 HKCFAR 574.

99. See, for example, *R v A (No. 2)* [2001] UKHL 25, [2002] 1 AC 45.

100. Ibid., [45] and [46] (Lord Steyn). See also Dinah Rose and Claire Weir, 'Interpretation and Incompatibility: Striking the Balance' in Jeffrey Jowell and Jonathan Cooper (eds), *Delivering Rights: How the Human Rights Act is Working* (Hart Publishing 2003) 48.

101. Ibid. See also *Leung Kwok Hung* (N24) [2005] HKCFA 41, [82]–[85].

102. *Lam Kwong Wai* (N98) [67]–[69] (Mason NPJ).

All in all, although its entrenched status has been challenged by some scholars,[103] the BORO is clearly significant, meriting careful scrutiny and discussion before any decision is made to repeal or amend it, or in any way to reduce its protections. Additionally, the BORO is important in the sense that its mandate that a restriction of a fundamental right be 'necessary' in a democratic society is consistent with the approach in many other jurisdictions.[104]

8.4 Continued Integration of the Proportionality Principle in Hong Kong under the Basic Law after 1997

On 1 July 1997, Hong Kong became an SAR under an innovative model of 'one country, two systems'. Pursuant to the Sino-British Joint Declaration 1984, Hong Kong will, it was said, enjoy a high degree of autonomy and possess legislative, executive, and independent judicial power, including that of final adjudication, save for certain acts of state (e.g., defence and foreign affairs).[105] The legal system was expected to remain basically unchanged, and laws previously in force in Hong Kong were to be preserved. Fundamental rights and freedoms would, therefore, remain protected. In particular, under Article 35 of the Basic Law, 'Hong Kong residents shall have the right to institute legal proceedings in the courts against the acts of the executive authorities and their personnel'. All of these 'promises' are written into the Basic Law, the constitution of the region.

Articles 8, 11, and 18 of the Basic Law provide that no law enacted by the Hong Kong LegCo shall contravene the Basic Law, and that laws previously in force before the change of sovereignty shall be maintained to the extent that they do not contravene the Basic Law. In connection to this, Chan has argued that the combined effect of these articles is that any law which contravenes the Basic Law shall be 'unconstitutional' and void.[106] These articles provide

103. See, for example, Simon Young, 'Restricting Basic Law Rights in Hong Kong' (2004) 24 *HKLJ* 109, 115.

104. For examples in the EU, see *Handyside* (N31) [49]; *Sunday Times* (N66) [62]; *Norris* (N31) [41]. For an example in Canada, see *Oakes* (N31). For an examples in Britain, see *R (Daly) v Secretary of State for the Home Department* [2001] 1 AC 532, [27], [2001] UKHL 26, [2001] 2 WLR 1622; *R v Shayler* [2002] UKHL 11, [2003] 1 AC 247, [60]–[61]; as well as for the UK Privy Council in *De Freitas* (N31); *Makwanyane* (N31).

105. Basic Law, Art 19. See also *Democratic Republic of the Congo v FG Hemisphere Associates LLC* (2011) 14 HKCFAR 395.

106. Chan (N18) 409.

the legal basis for the courts to conduct a *Marbury v Madison* [107] type of judicial review (i.e., constitutional or legislative review).[108] This was confirmed in *Ng Ka Ling v Director of Immigration*,[109] in that the CFA asserted that it had the power to declare Hong Kong Ordinances to be unconstitutional if they are found to be incompatible with the Basic Law.[110]

In construing the Basic Law, the courts have been receptive to using international and comparative materials.[111] As the BORO was survived by Article 39 of the Basic Law after the change of sovereignty, the incorporation of the ICCPR into domestic law through the BORO [112] has provided a 'convenient nexus' for domestic reception of some international and comparative jurisprudence.[113] The courts have continued to apply the proportionality principle when petitioners have brought judicial review cases under Articles 4 and 39 of the Basic Law,[114] which involved a shift in the *Grundnorm*.[115] Such application remains the *status quo*. That is, the courts assess the compatibility of a law with these provisions of the Basic Law by examining whether a human rights restriction is too wide and goes beyond what is necessary to achieve its legitimate objective. The leading cases applying this concept are the *Flag Desecration* case [116] and the *Public Order Ordinance* case.[117]

Albert Chen opines that the art of constitutional review has further progressed in the post-1997 era, as the Basic Law is said to be even more potent than the BORO in facilitating constitutional challenges by way of judicial review.[118] Since then, the proportionality principle has continued to be applied under Article 39 of the Basic Law to ascertain whether a human rights

107. 5 U.S. (Cranch) 137 (1803).

108. Chan (N18) 409.

109. (1999) 2 HKCFAR 4 (CFA), [1999] 1 HKLRD 315.

110. Ibid., [1999] 1 HKLRD 315, 317.

111. Chan (N32).

112. *Swire Properties Ltd* (N92) 258.

113. Chan (N18) 410.

114. Albert Chen, 'The Provisional Legislative Council of the SAR' (1997) 27 *HKLJ* 1, 9–10.

115. Literally: fundamental norm. The use of this term during the drafting of the Basic Law highlights the prominent role of the German Constitution in this process.

116. *HKSAR v Ng Kung Siu* [1999] 1 HKLRD 783, (1999) 2 HKCFAR 442, [2000] HKC 117.

117. *Leung Kwok Hung* (N24).

118. Chen (N14) 181.

restriction is too wide and goes further than necessary to achieve its legitimate objective. The jurisprudence of proportionality adjudication used by the Hong Kong courts has also evolved in accordance with developments elsewhere in the common law world,[119] as explicitly authorised under Article 84 of the Basic Law in *Shum Kwok Sher v HKSAR*.[120]

Similar to earlier BORO-related cases, Hong Kong courts have, when dealing with cases involving the Basic Law, derived great benefit from examining jurisprudences from overseas, such as the decisions of the ECtHR and the General Comments and views of bodies of the United Nations (UN), such as the UN Human Rights Committee, among others. Moreover, the courts have also received evidence similar to Brandeis briefs on comparative legislation in the *Flag Desecration* case [121] and on comparative medical research on the establishment of sexual puberty in a claim for equality and privacy of homosexual conduct.[122] As Li CJ (as he then was) once said, considering judgments of courts outside Hong Kong has become 'so much a part of one's everyday work'.[123]

8.5 Contributions from Overseas Judges and References to Other Common Law Jurisdictions

Consideration of jurisprudence from other common law jurisdictions is also attributable to the inclusion of overseas judges as CFA non-permanent judges (as mandated in Articles 82 and 84 of the Basic Law). According to Simon Young and Antonio Da Roza, the system of overseas judges was originally adopted to ensure a continuity of international legal expertise of the highest calibre on the bench after the abolition of appeals to the UK Privy Council in 1997.[124] However, Yash Ghai has a different view, saying that in addition to 'enhanc[ing]

119. Mason (N32) 311.
120. (2002) 5 HKCFAR 381, [2002] 2 HKLRD 793 (CFA), [59].
121. *Ng Kung Siu* (N116).
122. *Leung T C William Roy v Secretary for Justice* [2005] 3 HKC 77 (CFI), [2005] 3 HKLRD 657, [2006] 4 HKLRD 211 (CA).
123. Andrew Li, 'CJ's Speech at Conference on Effective Judicial Review: A Cornerstone Stone of Good Governance', 10 December 2008, available at: www.info.gov.hk/gia/general/200812/10/P200812100125.htm, last accessed 31 January 2020.
124. Simon Young and Antonio Da Roza, 'The Judges' in Young and Ghai (N4) 263.

the court's prospects of independence', the continuity of appointing overseas judges was seen as being necessary to 'reassure the business community' to maintain economic prosperity.[125]

Whatever the reason may be, these overseas judges provide diversity in legal views and experience, leadership and innovation in dealing with new legal problems, and additional strength in research and writing, assisted by local judges, whose local expertise ensures that any initiatives of the overseas judge are kept in check with local laws, convention, and culture. As Dr P.Y. Lo has noted, in addition to giving particular consideration as to whether a proposed decision of the CFA is in accordance with generally accepted principles of the common law, these non-permanent judges (as former or serving judges of the court of final adjudications in other common law jurisdictions) have brought their considerable judicial knowledge and experience to Hong Kong.[126] Through interactions with local judges and legal practitioners in the adjudication process, these non-permanent judges have enriched the quality of legal practice in Hong Kong.[127] In short, these overseas judges have reflected upon and provided outsider insight about the distinct features of the post-1997 Hong Kong legal system. As Mortimer NPJ has pointed out:

> It means that there is international or inter-common law input into the Court. The Court, indeed all courts in Hong Kong, has an open door to listening to authorities from all other common law jurisdictions. While this is happening in other jurisdictions as well, it is perhaps more readily accepted here. That of itself means that Hong Kong is in the position of being able to develop not only its own view, but it is also open to the best developments in other common law jurisdictions as well. For that reason, I personally believe that in due course the [CFA] is likely to become one of the most respected courts in the common law world.[128]

125. Yash Ghai, *Hong Kong's New Constitutional Order: The Resumption of Chinese Sovereignty and the Basic Law* (2nd edn, HKUP 1999) 323–324.

126. P.Y. Lo, 'An Internationalist, Consequentialist and Non-progressive Court: Constitutional Adjudication in Hong Kong (1997–2009)' (2010) 2 *CityU LR* 215, 225.

127. Ibid.

128. Barry Mortimer, 'A Conversation with Justice Barry Mortimer' (September 1999) *HKL*, cited by Young and Ghai (N4) 264.

Mason NPJ concurs with this, saying:

> The participation of overseas judges who have an international reputation gives the Hong Kong [CFA] a degree of acceptability which it might not otherwise have. In saying that I'm not in any way suggesting that the quality of the judges on the Court falls short of the highest quality. What I'm saying is that, in the eyes of people elsewhere, particularly people who are looking at Hong Kong as an international financial centre, it probably gives a degree of reassurance that you have overseas judges of international reputation participating in the work of the Court.[129]

He furthers that 'although the differences in the jurisprudence of the various common law jurisdictions are minor rather than substantial, there are subtle points of difference, and [non-permanent judges] from other jurisdictions can offer distinctive contributions and perspectives'.[130]

The CFA's jurisprudence has also contributed to the courts of other common law jurisdictions, such as the Supreme Court of the UK, the High Court of Australia, the Supreme Court of Canada, and so forth.[131] In *Cheng v Tse Wai Chun*,[132] which concerned the defence of fair comment in defamation and how such a defence may be defeated by proof of malice and by differentiating it from the issue of qualified privilege, Lord Nicholls NPJ's judgment is regarded as 'the leading authority on malice and fair comment in English law' [133] and 'the modern authoritative statement of the law of fair comment'.[134] This principle was also applied in the UK in *Sugar v Associated Newspapers Ltd*.[135]

129. Anthony Mason, 'One on One, Court of Final Appeal, Sir Anthony Mason' (July 2001) *HKL*, cited by Young and Ghai (N4) 264.
130. Ibid.
131. P.Y. Lo, 'The Impact of CFA Jurisprudence beyond Hong Kong' (2010) 8 *HKL* 36.
132. (2000) 3 HKCFAR 339.
133. Patric Milmo, W.V.H. Rogers, Richard Parkes, Clive Walker, and Godwin Busuttil, *Gatley on Libel and Slander* (10th edn, Sweet & Maxwell 2007) vii.
134. A.M. Jones and M.A. Dugdale, *Clerk and Lindsell on Torts* (19th edn, Sweet & Maxwell 2006) [23–168], cited by Lo (N131) 37.
135. (unreported) 6 February 2001 QBD, cited by Lo (N131) 37. See also *Panday v Gordon* [2005] UKPC 36 (UK Privy Council); *Channel Seven Adelaide Pty Ltd v Manock* [2007] 241 ALR 468 (High Court of Australia); *WIC Radio v Simpson* [2008] 2 SCR 420 (Supreme Court of Canada); *Oei Hon Leong v Ban Song Long David* [2005] 3 SLR 608 (Singapore Court of Appeal), cited by Lo (N131) 37–38.

Moreover, in *Sin Kam Wah v HKSAR*,[136] Mason NPJ also re-formulated the elements of the common law offence of misconduct in public office so that the requisite misconduct is committed wilfully, by act or omission, and where the officer either knew that his conduct was unlawful or wilfully disregarded the risk that his conduct was unlawful. This analysis was followed by the Supreme Court of Victoria's Court of Appeal in Australia and the Supreme Court of Canada in *R v Quach* [137] and *R v Boulanger*,[138] respectively.

8.6 Substantial Overlap of Fundamental Rights in the Bill of Rights Ordinance and the Basic Law

There is a substantial overlap of many fundamental rights contained in the BORO and the Basic Law, and coupled with the fact that Article 39(1) of the Basic Law survives the BORO, the courts have frequently regarded the BORO as constitutional in nature.[139] Against this background, most applicants frequently rely on the same right under both documents. For instance, applicants can rely on the freedom of expression under both Article 16 of section 8 of the BORO and Article 27 of the Basic Law in their applications for judicial review.[140]

In tandem with their overlap, the Basic Law comprises additional rights in the form of socio-economic rights, whereas the BORO arguably provides greater coverage in terms of civil and political rights not found in the Basic Law.[141] Concerning this, Ghai has opined that the Basic Law provides a more balanced protection of rights overall and observed:

> The [BORO] is confined to what might be called civil and political rights. The reach of the Basic Law is wider, encompassing economic, social and cultural rights also. The Basic Law represents a much better balance of rights, entitlements and duties, and is more sensitive to the truth that human

136. (2005) 8 HKCFAR 192.

137. [2010] VSCA 106, cited by Lo (N131) 38.

138. [2006] 2 SCR 49, cited by Lo (N131) 38.

139. *Koon Wing Yee* (N93) [2008] 3 HKLRD 372 (CFA), [25] (Mason NPJ).

140. *Ng Kung Siu* (N116).

141. Jhaveri, Ramsden, and Scully-Hill (N71) 554.

dignity is a matter not merely of abstract rules but of social and economic conditions when these abstract rules become real. It departs from the [BORO] in another respect; it provides also for the duty of residents.[142]

8.7 Proportionality Methods Adopted in Constitutional Reviews and Human Rights Adjudications under Article 39 of the Basic Law

Since the enactment of the BORO in mid-1991, Hong Kong courts have readily accepted the proportionality analysis in assessing the constitutionality of any restriction on fundamental rights under the BORO [143] and the Basic Law.[144] For instance, the CFA used the proportionality test to review whether legislative restrictions of final appeals infringe the power of final adjudication vested under the Basic Law to itself,[145] with the lower courts applying it when they are evaluating justification of, for example, curtailment of a resident's constitutional right of access to court.[146]

Article 39(2) stipulates two criteria that are adopted to ascertain whether restriction of a fundamental right is permissible: (1) the restriction must be 'prescribed by law'; and (2) it must not be incompatible with ICCPR 'as applied to Hong Kong' under Article 39(1). Furthermore, in the *Public Order Ordinance* case,[147] the CFA also held that a generous interpretation of fundamental rights and a narrow interpretation of restrictions should be adopted so as to give citizens the full measure of constitutionally guaranteed fundamental rights.[148]

142. Ghai (N125) 422–423.

143. *Ng Kung Siu* (N116).

144. *Leung Kwok Hung* (N24) (2005) 8 HKCFAR 229, 252–253 (Li CJ).

145. *A Solicitor v Law Society of Hong Kong (Secretary for Justice, intervener)* (2003) 6 HKCFAR 570, [2004] 1 HKLRD 214; *Mok Charles Peter v Tam Wai Ho (Secretary for Justice, intervener)* (2010) 13 HKCFAR 762; *Hong Kong Housing Society v Wong Nai Chung (t/a Sun Chung Flower Shop)* (unreported) HCMP 880/2009 (22 September 2010).

146. *Lau Kwok Fai Bernard v Secretary for Justice* (2005) 8 HKCFAR 304; *Lee Yee Shing Jacky v Board of Review (Inland Revenue Ordinance)* [2011] 6 HKC 307 (CFI), [2012] 2 HKLRD 981 (CA).

147. *Leung Kwok Hung* (N24) [2005] 3 HKLRD 164 (CFA).

148. Ibid., 178.

8.7.1 The Prescribed-by-Law Requirement and its Evolution

Among these criteria, the phrase 'prescribed by law' suggests that a fundamental rights restriction must be authorised by law, be it enacted by the legislature or developed in the common law (i.e., the legality test), meaning that it will have been discussed in the (democratic) process or will have gone through a rational process of law making during adjudication.[149] The effect of this requirement is that once adopted, the restriction cannot be easily changed, thus providing some degree of certainty for people affected so that they can regulate their conduct accordingly. Furthermore, transparency and accessibility of the requirement will also reduce the scope of arbitrary decisions.[150] Echoing *Sunday Times v UK*,[151] the CFA has, in *Shum Kwok Sher*,[152] held that any law restricting fundamental rights must be 'adequately accessible' and 'formulated with sufficient precision to enable the citizen to regulate his conduct'.[153] When discussing the phrase 'in accordance with law' under Article 26 of the Basic Law during the *Prisoner's Voting Right* case,[154] the Court of First Instance stated that 'prescribed by law', 'established by law', 'according to law', or similar expressions all impose the requirements of legal certainty and accessibility.[155]

In *Cheung Tak Wing v Director of Administration*,[156] however, the Court of First Instance 'clarified' that though the prescribed-by-law criterion required sufficient legal certainty for the restriction of fundamental rights, it did not require absolute certainty and may unavoidably involve some degree of vagueness to be clarified by the court.[157] This clarification has also been endorsed by the Court of Appeal.[158] Reaching this conclusion, the Court, relying on *Silver v UK*,[159]

149. Chan and Lim (N91) 592. See also Care Tsang and Sam Wong, 'Police Power and the Freedom of Assembly' (2012) 6 *HKJLS* 75, 76.

150. Ibid., Chan and Lim.

151. *Sunday Times* (N66) [49].

152. *Shum Kwok Sher* (N120).

153. Ibid., 402.

154. *Chan Kin Sum v Secretary for Justice* [2008] 6 HKC 486, [2009] 2 HKLRD 166 (CFI).

155. Ibid., [51]–[54].

156. HCAL 136/2014, [2018] HKCFI 2557.

157. Ibid., [52], citing *HKSAR v Fong Kwok Shan, Christine* (2017) 20 HKCFAR 425, [76]; *Mo Yuk Ping v HKSAR* (2007) 10 HKCFAR 386, [61].

158. CACV 577/2018 [2020] HKCA 124, [48]–[49].

159. Ibid., [62], citing *Silver v UK* (1983) 5 EHRR 347, [88].

reasoned that in addition to statute law and common law, the government can look at relevant non-statutory documents, directives, and guidelines that are accessible to the public in ascertaining whether the foreseeability criterion (i.e., providing some degree of certainty for people affected so they can regulate their conduct accordingly), being one of the prerequisites of the prescribed-by-law requirement, is satisfied.[160] With respect, I disagree, arguing that although these documents are accessible to the public so that the foreseeability criterion is satisfied, there have been cases suggesting that the contents of these materials can be misinterpreted by the authorities, the effect of which is that they are not compatible with the power conferred by the legislation and are thus *ultra vires*.[161] To fulfil the prescribed-by-law requirement, these materials must not only be publicly accessible, but they must also be compatible with the power conferred by the LegCo.

8.7.2 The Proportionality Requirement and its Evolution

Regarding the second criterion (that restriction of a human right must not be incompatible with the ICCPR 'as applied to Hong Kong' under Article 39(1) of the Basic Law), the courts have, since the enactment of the BORO in 1991, adopted the proportionality principle as a formula to ascertain whether the restriction imposed by the public authorities is incompatible with human rights standards in other common law jurisdictions and in other Member States of the ECHR. Although the way in which the principle of proportionality is applied may vary and evolve considerably according to the nature of the right at issue, Dinusha Panditaratne has noted that the various methodologies formerly applied by the courts 'appear to have converged in recent years into a general test of proportionality which courts are apt to apply in all rights-based cases'.[162] In addition to identifying a legitimate purpose for restricting a fundamental right, a constitutional challenge does, under this new regime, involve a two-stage enquiry by the court.

160. Ibid., citing *Hong Kong Television Network Ltd v Chief Executive* [2015] 2 HKLRD 1035, [121] (Au J).

161. See, for example, *Anisminic v Foreign Compensation Commission* [1969] 2 AC 147, 2 WLR 163; *Perilly v Tower Hamlets BC* [1972] EWCA Civ J0621-1, [1973] QB 9; *R v Monopolies and Mergers Commission, ex p South Yorkshire Transport* [1993] 1 WLR 23, [1993] 1 All ER 289; *Anufrijeva v Southwark LBC* [2004] QB 1124.

162. Dinusha Panditaratne, 'Basic Law, Hong Kong Bill of Rights and the ICCPR' in Chan and Lim (N91) 544.

The first enquiry requires the executive who is defending a restriction on a particular right to prove that such restriction is 'rationally connected with one or more of the legitimate purposes' for restricting that right.[163] According to Gittings, the 'rational connection' requirement imposed by the first part of the proportionality enquiry, on several occasions, makes it more onerous for the government to successfully defend a restriction on a particular right. Although it is easy to identify a legitimate aim to justify the imposition of a restriction on a particular right, having a rational connection between that reason and the particular restriction is seemingly more difficult.[164] In *Kong Yunming v Director of Social Welfare*,[165] although the CFA accepted that ensuring the long-term financial sustainability of the social welfare system *vis-à-vis* the ageing population is a legitimate aim for restricting the right of social welfare,[166] it held that a restriction requiring seven years' residency in Hong Kong before the applicant became eligible for social welfare failed the 'rational connection' part of the proportionality enquiry. In fact, the Court found that the amount of money saved by this seven years' residency restriction was 'relatively insignificant', and thus bore no rational connection with the intended objective of ensuring the long-term sustainability of the system.[167]

Even if a restriction on a particular right can be shown to be 'rationally connected' to the legitimate aim, thus passing the first threshold of the proportionality enquiry, any such restriction is still required to pass a second threshold. This second enquiry involves assessing the extent of the restriction that is necessary (i.e., the necessity test or the minimal impairment test),[168] whereby the courts will only uphold a restriction provided that it goes 'no further than necessary to achieve the legitimate objective'.[169] This requirement, therefore, limits the restrictions that might be implemented by a biased executive to whom LegCo has granted wide-ranging powers to adjust fundamental rights.[170] If

163. *Leung Kwok Hung* (N24) (2005) 8 HKCFAR 229, 253.

164. Gittings (N27) 301.

165. [2009] 4 HKLRD 382 (CFI), [2012] 4 HKC 180 (CA), (2013) 16 HKCFAR 950, [2014] 1 HKC 518 (CFA).

166. Ibid., (2013) 16 HKCFAR 950, 980–983.

167. Ibid., 983–986.

168. Ibid., 969.

169. Ibid.

170. Gittings (N27) 289.

their power is too wide-ranging, it may be struck down by the courts under the legality test for failing to explain in sufficiently precise terms when the executive can and cannot restrict rights.[171] In the *Prisoner's Voting Right* case,[172] even if the Court of First Instance accepted that a law banning all prisoners from voting had served a legitimate aim in deterring others from committing crimes, such a wide restriction on rights would have still failed the 'minimal impairment' threshold as required in the second part of the proportionality enquiry.[173] This is because, by treating all prisoners in exactly the same way, irrespective of the severity of their crimes, such a 'blanket ban' went much further than was necessary to achieve the legitimate aim of deterring crime. The Court further noted that this legitimate aim could have been attained by a more limited ban that only applied to those prisoners who had committed more serious crimes.[174] According to Gittings, this is obviously in favour of small and limited restrictions on rights, with wider restrictions likely being considered excessive and unnecessary to attain the intended objective.[175]

8.7.3 Four-Stage Enquiry

In 2016, the Hong Kong CFA, like its UK counterpart,[176] had the opportunity to develop the proportionality analysis on a four-limb basis in *Hysan v Town Planning Board*.[177] In addition to the three-stage analysis (i.e., identifying a legitimate aim, assessing the rational connection with advancing that aim, and determining whether the measure is no more than is necessary for that purpose),[178] the Court has incorporated a fourth step, asking whether a reasonable balance has been struck between the community interests of the encroachment and the inroads made into the constitutionally guaranteed rights of the individual (i.e., the fair

171. Ibid.
172. *Chan Kin Sum* (N154).
173. Ibid., 221.
174. Ibid.
175. Gittings (N27) 302.
176. *Huang v Secretary of State for the Home Department* [2007] UKHL 11, [2007] 2 AC 167, [19] (Lord Bingham); *Bank Mellat v Her Majesty's Treasury (No. 2)* [2013] UKSC 39, [2014] AC 700, [20] (Lord Sumption).
177. [2012] 5 HKC 432 (CFI), [2015] 1 HKLRD 865 (CA), (2016) 19 HKCFAR 372 (CFA), [52]–[53], [134]–[135].
178. Ibid., (2016) 19 HKCFAR 372 (CFA), [134] (Ribeiro PJ).

balance test or proportionality *stricto sensu*).[179] In this case, Ribeiro PJ noted that where an encroaching measure passes the three-stage test, the analysis should incorporate a fourth step asking whether a reasonable balance has been struck between societal benefits and individual rights. In particular, the court should ask if pursuing the societal interest results in an unacceptably harsh burden on the individual.[180]

As the CFA has noted, this fair balance test is inherent in the protection of human rights, and allows the courts 'to take full account of the severity of the deleterious effects of a measure on individuals or groups' [181] so that the courts can assess whether the applicants have suffered an individual and excessive burden.[182] The Court also noted that these four stages are interrelated and interdependent, and that they should be applied fluidly and flexibly.[183] That said, in a vast majority of cases, the fair balance test under the fourth stage is unlikely to invalidate a restriction which has successfully passed the requirements of the first three stages of the proportionality analysis.[184] However, Chan criticised this assertion by saying that the way in which the fourth stage is formulated suggests that 'it is a residual consideration of secondary importance and that a more cursory scrutiny may be adopted' and is 'unsound in principle and supported by case law'.[185] He claimed that 'it is unclear whether this observation is intended to be an empirical observation or a normative claim',[186] arguing that

> [i]f it is the former, it does not seem that there is any empirical survey of previous cases to justify this statement. If it is the latter, there is no legal basis for it. Sadly, this observation seems to have been perceived subsequently as a normative principle and conveys an impression that this 4th step is of a residual or supplementary nature.[187]

179. Ibid., [135] (Ribeiro PJ).

180. Ibid., [135].

181. Ibid., [71], citing *Alberta v Hutterian Brethren of Wilson Colony* [2009] 2 SCR 567.

182. Ibid., [69], citing *Denimark Ltd v UK* (2000) 30 ECHR CD 144, 150.

183. Ibid., [60].

184. Ibid., [73].

185. Johannes Chan, 'Proportionality after *Hysan*: Fair Balance, Manifestly without Reasonable Foundation and *Wednesbury* Unreasonableness' (2019) 49 *HKLJ* 265, 293.

186. Ibid., 268.

187. Ibid.

Chan's argument tallies with that of the late Lord Bingham, who stated that balancing the interest of individuals or groups with that of society lies at the heart of the proportionality enquiry and that 'this is indeed an aspect which should never be overlooked and discounted'.[188] Such fair balance between individual interests and societal interests is not intended to be a residual criterion of the proportionality analysis. Rather, it is an 'overriding requirement'.[189] This is because any judgment on proportionality 'must always involve the striking of a fair balance between the rights of the individual and the interests of the community which is inherent in the whole of the [ECHR]'.[190] As Chan has argued, as the ends have to justify the means, the courts are required to undertake a careful assessment of the severity and consequences of a restriction.[191]

Chan further argued that whether the fourth step is of secondary or supplementary importance arises from the difficulty, be it intellectual or practical, to distinguish between the third stage and the fourth stage.[192] In *Bank Mellat v Her Majesty's Treasury (No. 2),*[193] Lord Reed, now the President of the Supreme Court, described the last two criteria under the fourth-step proportionality enquiry as follows:

> (iii) whether a less intrusive measure could have been used; and
>
> (iv) whether, having regard to these matters and to the severity of the consequences, a fair balance has been struck between the rights of the individual and the interests of the community.[194]

Having said that, Lord Reed indicated that these four steps are 'different aspects of such an assessment [of the proportionality analysis], and make value judgments more explicit'.[195] Although Lord Sumption suggested that even though the four steps were logically separate, in practice they unavoidably

188. *Huang* (N176) [2007] 2 AC 167, [79], referring to *Oakes* (N31).
189. Ibid., [20].
190. Ibid.
191. Chan (N185) 270.
192. Ibid., 268.
193. *Bank Mellat (No.2)* (N176) [2014] AC 700.
194. Ibid., [20].
195. Ibid., [74].

overlapped and that the point is essentially 'whether a less intrusive measure could have been used without unacceptably compromising the objective'.[196] Chan is of the view that Lord Sumption's 'formulation of the essence of the inquiry, which is similar to the no more than necessary test under the third step in *Hysan*, is a much wider inquiry than whether a less intrusive measure could be adopted'.[197] Concurring with what Lord Reed has said, Chan advocates that

> [i]t is quite clear that the 3rd and the 4th steps are different aspects of the proportionality analysis, with the 3rd step focussing on the scope of the restriction (whether there could be a less intrusive measure), and the 4th step focussing on the effect of the restriction on individual rights (balancing the laudable objectives and the severity of the consequences to the individual concerned). Both steps are equally important and crucial in the proportionality analysis, and there is no warrant to suggest that if the first three steps are satisfied, it is unlikely that the 4th step will invalidate a restriction.[198]

As Chan has intimated, the third stage and the fourth stage involve two different inquiries, as also explained by Bastarache J in *Thomson Newspapers Co v Canada (Attorney General)*.[199] As he stated:

> The third stage of the proportionality analysis performs a fundamentally distinct role … The focus of the first and second steps of the proportionality analysis is not the relationship between the measures and the *Charter* right in question [i.e., Canadian Charter of Rights and Freedoms], but rather the relationship between the ends of the legislation and the means employed. Although the minimal impairment stage of the proportionality test necessarily takes into account the extent to which a *Charter* value is infringed, the ultimate standard is whether the *Charter* right is impaired as little as possible given the validity of the legislative purpose. The third stage of the proportionality analysis provides an opportunity to assess, in light of the practical and contextual details which are elucidated in the first and second stages, whether the benefits which accrue from the

196. Ibid., [20].
197. Chan (N185) N13.
198. Ibid., 269.
199. [1998] 1 SCR 877.

> limitation are proportional to its deleterious effects as measured by the values underlying the *Charter*.[200]

In view of the above, Chan has, despite the distinct functions of the last two stages of the proportionality enquiry, asked:

> If the legislation pursues a sufficiently important objective, that it is rationally connected to the achievement of the objective, and has caused only minimal impairment to the fundamental right, what does the final stage of a 'a fair balance of the negative effects of the infringement of rights against the positive benefits associated with the legislative goal' add to the analysis?[201]

He argues that 'the real balance must have been done at the stage of minimal impairment, and to a lesser extent, the stage of rationality'.[202] In this connection, McLachlin J has the following answer, as endorsed by Ribeiro PJ in *Hysan*:

> The answer lies in the fact that the first three stages of *Oakes* are anchored in an assessment of the law's purpose. Only the 4th branch takes full account of the 'severity of the deleterious effects of a measure on individuals or groups'.[203]

In support of this, her Ladyship quoted Aharon Barak, the President of the Supreme Court of Israel (as he then was), to justify her argument as follows:

> Whereas the rational connection test and the least harmful measure test are essentially determined against the background of the proper objective, and are derived from the need to realize it, the test of proportionality (*stricto sensu*) examines whether the realization of this proper objective is commensurate with the deleterious effect upon the human right ... It requires placing colliding values and interests side by side and balancing them according to their weight.[204]

200. Ibid., [125].

201. *RJR-MacDonald Inc v Canada* [1995] 3 SCR 199, [175] (McLachlin J).

202. Chan (N185) 270–271.

203. *Alberta v Hutterian Brethren of Wilson Colony* [2009] 2 SCR 567, quoted by Ribeiro PJ in *Hysan* (N177) (2016) 19 HKCFAR 372 (CFA), [71].

204. Ibid., *Hysan* [76], quoting Aharon Barak, 'Proportional Effect: The Israeli Experience' (2007) 57 *U Toronto LJ* 369, 374.

In view of the above, Chan is of the opinion that as the minimal impairment and proportionality (i.e., the fair balance test or proportionality *stricto sensu*) enquiries involve different kinds of balancing and that 'analytical clarity and transparency are well served by distinguishing between them'.[205] If there is no alternative method capable of attaining the legislative or government policy objective, then the issue is whether the impact of the infringement of right is disproportionate to the likely benefits of the impugned law.[206]

As McLachlin J and Chan have agreed, the third stage minimal impairment test and the fourth stage fair balance test involve different kinds of balancing, in that the former focuses on 'the scope of the restriction which should not go beyond what is required for the realisation of the legislative objective', whereas the latter concerns 'the effect or the impact of the restriction on the individual concerned'.[207] They serve different purposes and are of equal importance in the proportionality enquiry.[208] This has been confirmed by some Canadian authorities which do not treat the fair balance test as a residual step that is unlikely to change the outcome of the first three tests.[209]

Furthermore, Rehan Abeyratne observed that although proportionality became more structured in Hong Kong after *Hysan,* the courts have also become more deferential to the administration in the judicial reasoning on proportionality analysis and, in most cases, judgments have been ruled in favour of the government.[210] *Kwok Cheuk Kin v Secretary of Constitutional and Mainland Affairs* [211] is a typical example of how the CFA has extended this deferential approach to the right to stand for election. Under section 39(2A) of the Legislative Council Ordinance,[212] which came into force through an amendment to the Ordinance in 2012, LegCo members are prevented from contesting by-

205. Chan (N185) 271.

206. Ibid.

207. Ibid., 272.

208. Ibid.

209. *Hysan* (N177) (2016) 19 HKCFAR 372 (CFA), [73], [78] (Ribeiro PJ).

210. Rehan Abeyratne, 'More Structure, More Deference: Proportionality in Hong Kong' in Po Jen Yap, *Proportionality in Asia* (CUP, forthcoming September 2020) 4 and 20, available at: SSRN: https://ssrn.com/abstract=3295429, last accessed 11 June 2020.

211. (2017) HKCFAR 353.

212. Cap 542, Laws of Hong Kong.

elections triggered by their resignations. The amendment stemmed from an event in 2009, when the League of Social Democrats (LSD) proposed to have its LegCo members resign in order to trigger by-elections which would serve as a referendum on their political manifesto for universal suffrage and the abolition of functional constituencies.[213] Thus, five LSD members serving in the LegCo resigned in 2010 and were elected in by-elections shortly afterwards. This led the Hong Kong SAR government to implement section 39(2A).[214] When the case was tabled before the CFA, the primary question asked was whether section 39(2A) violated Article 34 of the Basic Law (i.e., the right to vote and stand for election) and Article 21 of the BORO (i.e., the right to participate in public life, including the right to be elected at genuine periodic elections without unreasonable restrictions). The crux of the problem concerned which standard of review should be applied at the third step of the proportionality analysis, either 'reasonable necessity' or 'manifest unreasonableness', with the latter being considered the more deferential option.

Noting that 'core values' were not at issue (though he did not define what are considered 'core values' in the case), Ma CJ refused to undertake a higher degree of scrutiny,[215] saying that as the LegCo had discussed the matter at length to come up with the decision,[216] a wider margin of discretion should be accorded because election laws involved 'political or policy considerations'.[217] The Court then went on to hold that the 'manifest unreasonableness' standard was appropriate, saying that the measures adopted in section 39(2A) 'fell within the range of reasonable options open to the [LegCo]'.[218] It also held that the fair balance test in the fourth step was of no value because it was unlikely to change the outcome if the previous three steps were satisfied. Furthermore, the Court stated that section 39(2A) did not impose an overly harsh burden on the legislators since they had opted to resign 'with full knowledge of the consequences'.[219] Nevertheless, the ruling in this case deviates from the *Obstetric*

213. *Kwok Cheuk Kin* (N211), [6].

214. Ibid., [7]–[18].

215. Ibid., [39].

216. Ibid., [55].

217. Ibid., [42].

218. Ibid., [57].

219. Ibid., [61].

Services case,[220] in that it was held that when 'core values' are disregarded by the executive or legislature, it would be appropriate and indeed duty-bound for the courts to interfere. Examples of this include differential or unequal treatments based on personal or human characteristics, such as race, colour, gender, sexual orientation, religion, politics, or social origin.[221] The Court also noted that 'these characteristics involve the respect and dignity that society accords to a human being. They are fundamental societal values'.[222] In short, since this case involves differential or unequal treatments based on 'politics' (as construed by Ma CJ in this case as 'political or policy considerations'), which was in fact interpreted in the *Obstetric Services* case as a personal or human characteristic, the Court should not use these political or policy consideration as an excuse to defer to the administration or the legislature.

As Dr Lo and Chen have intimated, the crux of the problem is in the third step where the separation of powers is in issue.[223] This is shown by the standard of review adopted at this step being of 'necessity' and 'manifestly without reasonable foundation'. The standard adopted is dependent upon how wide a margin of discretion or how much deference must be accorded to the judgment of the LegCo. As outlined in the *Hysan* case:

> If assessment of the proportionality of the measure calls for the application of purely legal principles and an assessment which the Court is the expert to make, the primary decision-maker having no special competence or expertise, it is likely that the margin of discretion will have little role to play and that the Court will simply adopted a standard of reasonable necessity. On the other hand, a decision-maker's view resulting in the promulgation of the impugned measure may be given much weight and thus afforded a wide margin of discretion reflected by use of a 'manifest [without reasonable foundation]' standard where the decision-maker is likely to be better placed

220. *Fok Chun Wa v Hospital Authority* (unreported, 17 December 2008, HCAL 94/2007), [2008] HKEC 2161 (CFI); (unreported, CACV 30/2009), [2010] HKEC 713, (2010) 15 HKPLR 628, [2011] 1 HKLRD A1 (CA); [2012] 2 HKC 413 (CFA), (2012) 15 HKCFAR 409.

221. Ibid., (2012) 15 HKCFAR 409, [77].

222. Ibid.

223. P.Y. Lo and Albert Chen, 'The Judicial Perspective of "Separation of Powers" in the Hong Kong Special Administrative Region of the People's Republic of China' (2018) 5:2 *JICL* 337, 353.

> than the Court to assess what is needed in the public interest. ... A broad margin of discretion might also be mandated by separation of powers principles and recognition of the different institutional roles played by the Court and the relevant decision-maker. Thus, a wide margin of discretion may be permitted to the legislature in respect of enactments allocating public resources on the footing that such distributive decisions are properly the responsibility of the legislature for which it makes itself politically accountable, rather than for the courts on a constitutional review.[224]

Although the *Hysan* case has cleared up some of the misunderstanding about the proportionality principle and has provided a coherent framework for balancing individual rights and public interests,[225] the Hong Kong courts have since adopted a 'more broad-brush approach' to proportionality,[226] under which the scope of restriction and its impact on the parties involved are assessed under a general proportionality test.[227] That said, Chan has argued that instead of introducing the fourth stage, *Hysan* has re-affirmed the importance of a fair balance enquiry in the proportionality analysis.[228] He states that

> the fair balance test is 'unlikely to invalidate a restriction which has satisfied the requirements of the first three stages of the inquiry', the court has gone too far and the risk is that the effect of a restriction, which goes to the heart of the proportionality analysis, would now be given residual importance only and would not be considered with the same rigour that is required of any constitutional analysis.[229]

224. Ibid., 353–354, citing *Hysan* (N177) (2016) 19 HKCFAR 372 (CFA), [114]–[118], where the CFA referred to *R (Lord Carlile of Berriew) v Secretary of State for the Home Department* [2015] AC 945 (SC); *R (Rotherham MBC) v Secretary of State for Business, Innovation and Skills* [2015] 3 All ER 1; *Bank Mellat (No. 2)* (N176) [2014] AC 700; *Lau Cheong v HKSAR* (2002) 5 HKCFAR 415.
225. Chan (N185) 292.
226. Ibid., 271.
227. Ibid., 272.
228. Ibid.
229. Ibid.

Despite the above, this four-step proportionality analysis has been widely followed and applied to different types of cases,[230] including the *Prohibition of Face Covering Regulation* case,[231] which concerned the constitutionality, and thus legality, of the Emergency Regulations Ordinance [232] and the Prohibition of Face Covering Regulation.[233] In several of these cases, the courts held that it was unnecessary to consider the fourth stage since the impugned measures could not pass through the earlier tests of legality [234] or rational connection.[235] In cases where the fourth stage was applied, the courts have stressed that the fair balance test would only be successful in very exceptional circumstances that produce 'extremely unbalanced and unfair results, oppressively imposing excessive burdens on the individuals affected'.[236]

Abeyratne argues that *Hysan* enabled the use of a deferential standard of review — manifest unreasonableness — in a wide range of human rights cases and its introduction of the fair balance test or proportionality *stricto sensu* as a fourth stage of the proportionality analysis has arguably had no effect on subsequent judgments. Hong Kong courts are said to have refrained from taking this balancing exercise seriously or rigorously and are thus more deferential to the administration, despite the fact that the main spirit of the fourth step is to balance the societal benefits of an impugned law against the harm it imposes on individual rights.[237]

230. See, for example, *Leung Kwok Hung (Long Hair) v Commissioner of Correctional Services* [2018] 2 HKLRD 933 (CA); *Lubiano Almorin v Director of Immigration* [2018] 1 HKLRD 1141; *Leung Chun Kwong v Secretary for the Civil Service and Commissioner of Inland Revenue*, FACV No. 8 of 2018, [2019] HKCFA 19, [2018] 3 HKLRD 84; *QT v Director of Immigration* (2018) 21 HKCFAR 324; *HKSAR v Cheung Kwai Choi* [2018] HKCFI 2243.

231. *Leung Kwok Hung v Secretary for Justice* [2019] HKCFI 2820, [128], [2019] HKCFI 2884, [2020] HKCA 192, [2020] HKEC 533 (CA).

232. Cap 241, Laws of Hong Kong.

233. Cap 241K, Laws of Hong Kong.

234. See, for example, *Chee Fee Ming v Director of Food and Environmental Hygiene (No. 2)* [2018] 4 HKLRD 517.

235. See, for example, *Leung Kwok Hung (Long Hair)* (N230); *Leung Chun Kwong* (N230); *QT* (N230); *American International Group Inc v Huaxia Life Insurance Co Ltd* (2017) 20 HKCFAR 503; *Incorporated Owners of Po Hang Building v Sam Woo Marine Works Ltd* (2017) 20 HKCFAR 240.

236. *Hysan* (N177) (2016) 19 HKCFAR 372 (CFA), [73]. See also *Official Receiver v Zhi Charles* (2015) 18 HKCFAR 467.

237. Abeyratne (N210) 1.

8.8 Restrictions on Fundamental Rights: Has a Fair Balance Been Struck?

From 1991 to the present, there have been many cases adjudicated that exemplify the use of the proportionality principle in Hong Kong. These cases range from simple reviews of administrative actions to constitutional challenges to legislation. The cases selected below (several of which have been mentioned earlier in this chapter as well) provide good examples of how the principle, together with other international legal and human rights norms, has been received by Hong Kong's judges and administrative decision-makers. They also highlight the balance (or lack thereof) struck between society's interests and individuals' rights.

8.8.1 Right to Equality or Non-Discrimination

8.8.1.1 The *Gender Discrimination* Case

Equality, or its mirror image, non-discrimination, under the law is a core element of human rights. It was introduced as a constitutional principle by the BORO in 1991 and was amplified by an array of anti-discrimination laws, such as the Sex Discrimination Ordinance,[238] shortly before the change of sovereignty in 1997. In the post-1997 era, Hong Kong courts have further developed their jurisprudence of equal rights.

In the *Gender Discrimination* case in 2001,[239] the Equal Opportunities Commission (EOC; a statutory body established in 1996 to promote equal rights) challenged the Education Department's policy concerning the allocation of secondary school places to pupils. The EOC argued that the effect of this policy (in force since 1978) was that boys stood a better chance of admission to a preferred secondary school than girls, despite having equal academic merits. The rationale for the policy was based on data showing that, on average, girls' academic performances and achievements at the end of primary school were higher than that of boys, suggesting that girls develop more quickly intellectually

238. Cap 480, Laws of Hong Kong.

239. *Equal Opportunities Commission v Director of Education* [2001] 2 HKLRD 690 (CFI).

at that age. These results also imply that girls will receive preference in secondary school admission. Therefore, the policy was designed to ensure a more balanced ratio between male and female students in the elite schools.

The Court of First Instance held that the policy in question was discriminatory against female students, and that the discrimination was not justified by any of the reasons put forward by the Education Department. Considering various laws,[240] in particular the Convention on the Elimination of All Forms of Discrimination Against Women, which was extended to Hong Kong in 1996, the Court emphasised that equal treatment was a fundamental right that was not subordinate to considerations of 'group fairness' [241] or the desire to achieve a better balance in schools between boys and girls. Any restriction of the girls' right against discrimination in this case had to pass the stringent standards of the proportionality test in order to be justified.[242] Having examined the Department's arguments and the evidence submitted, the Court held that the challenged scheme of allocation of school places failed the test.[243] As a result of this decision, the Education Department changed its original policy accordingly.

As the case concerned a matter of public policy, its ramifications extend far beyond the individual complainants in the case. The Court outlawed discriminatory practices and pushed for comprehensive reform of the existing system of allocation of secondary school places. The decision demonstrates the increasingly significant role of the courts, and their use of the proportionality analysis, in shaping social policy and in promoting social reform by employing jurisprudential concept (i.e., the fundamental right to the equal protection of the law without discrimination).[244] Indeed, prior to the *Gender Discrimination* case, proportionality analysis had, according to Cora Chan, been adopted 'sporadically but inconsistently' for assessing restrictions on fundamental rights.[245] After that case was handed down, application of the proportionality

240. Basic Law, Art 25; BORO, s 8, Art 22 (ICCPR, Art 26); Sex Discrimination Ordinance (N238).

241. *Equal Opportunities Commission* (N239) [80].

242. Ibid., [121].

243. Ibid.

244. Chen (N14) 203.

245. Cora Chan, 'Rights, Proportionality and Deference: A Study of Post-Handover Judgments in Hong Kong' (2018) 48 *HKLJ* 51, 54.

principle has been more consistent because the courts are accustomed to using the 'multi-limb' or 'three-limb' proportionality formula.[246] Since then, the three-limb proportionality analysis has become an 'established part of human rights doctrine' in Hong Kong.[247]

8.8.1.2 The *Sexual Orientation Discrimination* Cases

In *Leung T C William Roy v Secretary for Justice*,[248] the applicant, a 20-year-old homosexual, challenged the constitutionality of, *inter alia*, section 118C of the Crimes Ordinance [249] on the grounds that the law in question was discriminatory on the basis of sexual orientation, and thus violated the constitutional rights to equality [250] and privacy.[251] Section 118C provided that if two men committed buggery with each other and one or both of them was or were under the age of 21, then each of them would be guilty of a criminal offence and liable to a maximum penalty of life imprisonment. Both the Court of First Instance and the Court of Appeal held that this provision was unconstitutional, and thus null and void, as it discriminated against gay men. This is because, under Hong Kong's existing law, in the case of consensual anal intercourse between heterosexuals, no criminal liability exists as long as both parties are above the age of 16. Therefore, gay men aged 16 to 21 were discriminated against, and the government failed to persuade the courts that the discrimination or differential treatment was justified.

Both the Court of First Instance and the Court of Appeal relied on, among other things, the ECtHR's jurisprudence in reaching the decision. They considered *Sutherland v UK*,[252] in which the European Commission of Human Rights decided that the different minimum ages of consent in the UK for the purposes of heterosexual and homosexual intercourse (i.e., 16

246. Ibid.
247. Ibid.
248. *Leung T C William Roy* (N122).
249. Cap 200, Laws of Hong Kong.
250. Basic Law, Art 25; BORO, s 8, Arts 1 and 22 (ICCPR, Arts 2, 3, and 26).
251. BORO, s 8, Art 14 (ICCPR, Art 17).
252. (1998) EHRR 117.

and 18, respectively) were an unjustifiable discrimination on the basis of sexual orientation. Another case, *L & v Austria*,[253] was also referred to. It concerned a provision of the Austrian Criminal Code criminalising homosexual acts of adults with consenting boys aged between 14 and 18. Nevertheless, heterosexual or lesbian acts between adults and persons over the age of 14 were not punishable under Austrian law. The ECtHR held that Articles 8 and 14 (i.e., the right to respect for private and family life and prohibition of discrimination, respectively) of the ECHR had been violated.

Secretary for Justice v Yau Yuk Lung[254] also concerned discrimination on the basis of sexual orientation. Two male respondents, who were 19 and 30 years old at the time, were found engaging in anal sex in a car parked beside a quiet and dark street. They were charged with violating section 118F(1) of the Crimes Ordinance, which prohibited sodomy in public. The case was brought before a Magistrate who then ruled that section 118F(1) was unconstitutionally discriminatory against gay men because it singled out and criminalised homosexual buggery, while no similar laws against heterosexual buggery or other comparable heterosexual acts exist. Consequently, the charges were dismissed. The government then appealed to the Court of Appeal,[255] but the Court upheld the Magistrate's ruling. The case was then further appealed to the CFA.

Noting that 'differences in legal treatment may be justified for good reason' (i.e., to protect the public from behaviours outraging public decency),[256] the CFA proceeded to assess whether the difference in treatment pursued a legitimate aim. To ascertain this, the Court first needed to consider whether the difference in treatment constitutes discrimination. The Court observed that 'the law should usually accord identical treatment to comparable situations',[257] meaning that no discrimination will be found when the cases before the Court are completely different, and that discrimination will *only* be found if the cases are not so different as to merit a difference in treatment. If the courts find that

253. [2003] ECHR 20.

254. [2006] 4 HKLRD 196 (CA), 208B–208C, (2007) 10 HKCFAR 335, [2007] 3 HKLRD 903 (CFA).

255. Ibid., [2006] 4 HKLRD 196 (CA).

256. Ibid., (2007) 10 HKCFAR 335, [20].

257. Ibid., [19] (Li CJ).

there is discrimination, they will still consider whether it can be justified by assessing the difference in treatment using the three-stage test.[258]

Knowing that differential treatment based on race, sex, or sexual orientation will be 'scrutinised with intensity', the CFA held that in order to determine whether the differential treatment of homosexuals and heterosexuals under section 118F(1) pursues a legitimate aim, 'a genuine need for the difference in treatment must be made out'.[259] Thus, the 'genuine need' test in the context of the CFA's equality jurisprudence is essentially an expression of the additional requirement that the ground, legitimate purpose, or aim of the restriction be 'sufficiently important', particularly when the grounds for restriction are not comprehensively set out in a constitutional instrument. The Court finally held that the distinction sought to be drawn in the Crimes Ordinance failed that test, and that the impugned provision was unconstitutional. Justice Bokhary made extensive references to international legal materials, pointing out that 'in the field of human rights, municipal law has often walked in the footsteps of international law — and may in some jurisdictions have caught up with or even overtaken it'.[260] The impugned section was ultimately repealed.

Although the three-stage test adopted in *Yau Yuk Lung* seems similar to that adopted in the *De Freitas* case,[261] Swati Jhaveri, Michael Ramsden, and Anne Scully-Hill have argued that the differences between the terms 'legitimate aim' in *Yau Yuk Lung* and 'sufficiently important' in the *De Freitas* case have a 'threshold' implication on the decision-maker.[262] Under the *De Freitas* test, the UK Privy Council required the decision-makers to establish that the purpose they are pursuing is 'sufficiently important'. This differs from the test used in *Yau Yuk Lung*, which was later termed the 'justification test' in the *Obstetric Services* case,[263] where the decision-makers needed to establish that they are

258. This tallies with what I have mentioned in Chapter Two of this book that the legitimate purposes for which a restriction may be imposed on the right are needed to be ascertained and thus interpreted correctly by the courts during the process of adjudication and aired to the general public, keeping in mind that the power of final interpretation of the Basic Law is vested in the NPCSC.

259. *Yau Yuk Lung* (N254) [25] (Li CJ).

260. Ibid., [34].

261. *De Freitas* (N31).

262. Jhaveri, Ramsden, and Scully-Hill (N71) 574.

263. *Fok Chun Wa* (N220) (2012) 15 HKCFAR 409, [56].

pursuing a 'legitimate aim' that addresses a 'genuine need'. This is arguably a lower threshold for the decision-makers compared with the 'sufficiently important' threshold.[264] In this regard, the courts should, as Tom Hickman has noted, pay more attention to the way in which they structure and formulate the proportionality test.[265]

Despite Hickman's criticism, the significance of these two cases is inherent in their controversial nature. They involve social and sexual moralities that should be deliberated in the LegCo. However, these decisions showcase the Hong Kong judiciary, with the use of the proportionality enquiry, as a robust entity that can step into these domains, overturn the laws made by the LegCo, and explain to society what it believes are the moral standards of the community.[266] Although there has been criticism as to whether it is appropriate for Hong Kong courts to rely so much on international standards and Western jurisprudence concerning the rights of homosexuals in Hong Kong, their decisions can be defended as being one of the legitimate functions of constitutional review of Hong Kong laws. This function allows the courts to safeguard the fundamental rights of minorities against oppressive or unjust laws.[267]

What is more, rejecting the absence of a majority consensus as a reason for denying a minority's claim as being inimical to fundamental rights, both Ma CJ and Pibeiro PJ have, in *W v Registrar of Marriages*,[268] approved the extra-judicial comments of Murray CJ in Ireland, saying that

> [t]he use of consensus as an interpretive tool is inherently problematic, not only because of any perceived inconsistency in the application of the doctrine by the [ECtHR], but fundamentally because the very application of a doctrine of consensus by a court required to adjudicate on fundamental rights begs important questions of legitimacy. How can resort to the will

264. Jhaveri, Ramsden, and Scully-Hill (N71) 574.

265. Tom Hickman, 'Proportionality: Comparative Law Lessons' (2007) *JR* 31.

266. Chen (N14) 254.

267. Ibid.

268. *W v Registrar of Marriages* (N92) (2013) 16 HKCFAR 112.

of the majority dictate the decisions of a court whose role is to interpret universal and indivisible human rights, especially minority rights?[269]

8.8.1.3 The *Homosexual Civil Servant's Entitlement to Spouse Medical and Tax Benefits* Case

In *Leung Chun Kwong v Secretary for the Civil Service and Commissioner of Inland Revenue*,[270] the appellant, an immigration officer, challenged, by way of judicial review, his same-sex spouse's deprivation of medical and tax benefits on the ground that he had been unlawfully discriminated on the basis of his sexual orientation, contrary to Article 25 of the Basic Law and Articles 1(1) and 22 of the BORO. In this case, the CFA distinguished between the 'relevant test' (an analysis of constitutionality and usually referred to as the 'proportionality test') and the 'justification test' (an analysis of whether differential treatment is unlawful),[271] but found that the ingredients of the two tests are essentially the same. The latter is simply the three-stage proportionality test incorporating the fourth criterion,[272] which requires a reasonable balance to be struck between the societal benefits arising from the application of differential treatment and the interference with the individual's equality rights.[273]

Referring to various European jurisprudence regarding the protection of the traditional family constituted by heterosexual marriage,[274] the CFA confirmed that the protection of the institution of marriage in Hong Kong (i.e., the voluntary union for life of one man and one woman to the exclusion of others) is a legitimate aim so that differential treatment directed to that aim may be justified provided that the others elements of the four-stage 'justification test' are also satisfied.[275] When adjudicating on whether the differential treatment is rationally connected

269. Ibid., [116].

270. *Leung Chun Kwong* (N230) FACV No. 8 of 2018, [2019] HKCFA 19.

271. Ibid., [21].

272. *Hysan* (N177).

273. *Leung Chun Kwong* (N230) [22]; *QT* (N230) [86]–[87].

274. *Ghaidan v Godin-Mendoza* [2002] EWCA Civ 1533, [2004] UKHL 30, [2004] 2 AC 557, [138] (Lady Hale); *Mata Estevez v Spain* [2001] ECHR 896; *Karner v Austria* (2004) 38 EHRR 24, [40]; *Re G (Adoption: Unmarried Couple)* [2009] 1 AC 173, [108]; *Kozak v Poland* (2010) 51 EHRR 16, [98]; *Şerife Yiğit v Turkey* (2011) 53 EHRR 25, [72].

275. *Leung Chun Kwong* (N230) [61].

to this legitimate aim, the Court rejected the government's proposition that heterosexual marriage would be undermined by the extension of the employment and tax benefits to same-sex married couples and concluded that heterosexual marriage is not promoted by the differential treatment.[276] In other words, the differential treatment in question is not rationally connected to the legitimate aim of protecting the institution of marriage. Having thus concluded that the differential treatment was not justified, the Court felt that it was not necessary to go on to consider the third and fourth steps. This is because even if the Court had done so, the answers to these questions (i.e., is the extent of the restriction necessary and does it balance the interests of society and individuals) would have only confirmed that the differential treatment in question was not proportionate and would result in an unacceptably harsh burden on the appellant.[277]

Overall, the CFA's decision in the *Homosexual Civil Servant's Entitlement to Spouse Medical and Tax Benefits* case serves as confirmation that the four-stage proportionality enquiry is entrenched in Hong Kong, even though it was unnecessary for the courts to fully examine all four aspects. As in *W v Registrar of Marriages* in the section above, the courts also reiterated that the rejection of the absence of a majority consensus as a reason for denying a minority's claim is inimical to fundamental rights.[278]

8.8.1.4 The *Disability Discrimination* Case

The courts also apply the same robust level of scrutiny when examining a challenged law under the proportionality doctrine even if it is not controversial or does not concern social or sexual morality. In the *Disability Discrimination* case,[279] two competing interests were considered, one being the statutory sanctions against discrimination, and the other being freedoms of thought, conscience, and expression. Citing the Disability Discrimination Ordinance,[280] the District Court judge ordered a taxi driver who had made discriminatory

276. Ibid., [72].

277. Ibid., [80].

278. Ibid., [56].

279. *Ma Bik Yung v Ko Chuen* [2002] 2 HKLRD 1.

280. Cap 487, Laws of Hong Kong.

statements to a disabled passenger during a taxi journey to apologise to the passenger. However, the taxi driver appealed, arguing, *inter alia*, that such an order amounted to an impermissible restriction on his freedoms of thought, conscience, and expression. The CFA held that it has jurisdiction in discrimination cases to order an unwilling defendant to tender an apology to a claimant. Having considered whether such jurisdiction is compatible with the right to freedoms of thought, conscience, and expression as constitutionally guaranteed by the Basic Law, and noting that there is no bar to granting such compelling remedies (i.e., mandatory injunctions, apologies, etc.), the Court, using the proportionality reasoning, held that the order was not a restriction on the freedoms of thought, conscience, and expression, *per se*, and was thus justified.

The significance of this case is that it touches upon the 'horizontal effect' of human rights as constitutionally guaranteed by the Basic Law and thus the BORO. In Hong Kong, much has been written about constitutional guarantees of fundamental rights and how they are not confined to operating 'vertically' to secure human rights entitlements *vis-à-vis* public officials.[281] Such guarantees also affect the legal relationship between private individuals not only in Hong Kong, but the UK as well.[282] Apart from the *Disability Discrimination* case, the CFA has, in fact, acknowledged the horizontal effect of human rights in various cases, albeit implicitly rather than explicitly.[283]

8.8.1.5 The *Non-Indigenous Villagers Voting Right* Case

The *Non-Indigenous Villager's Voting Right* case [284] involves a dispute between two competing interests, one being the right to equality and the other being the right to vote and stand for election. The applicant, the late Mr Chan, succeeded in challenging the electoral arrangements for the election of village representatives, which was only open to 'indigenous villagers' of the New

281. Simon Young, 'Human Rights', in Young and Ghai (N4).

282. Discussed in Chapter Seven of this book.

283. *Tse Wai Chun* (N132); *Ng Yat Chi v Max Share Ltd* (2005) 8 HKCFAR 1; *Akai Holdings Ltd v Ernst & Young* (2009) 12 HKCFAR 649; *Kao Lee & Yip v Koo Hoi Yan* (2009) 12 HKCFAR 830.

284. *Secretary for Justice v Chan Wah* (2000) 3 HKCFAR 459, (2000) 9 HKPLR 610.

Territories (i.e., descendants by patrilineal descent of ancestors who, in 1898, were residents of villages in the New Territories).

The CFA held that 'public affairs' under Article 21 of the BORO would cover all aspects of public administration at all levels, including at the village level. It was an unreasonable restriction on the right to take part in public affairs to exclude non-indigenous villagers, who, like the applicant, had spent their whole life in the village, as candidates in the village election. Moreover, it was also considered to be unlawful discrimination on the grounds of sex under the Sex Discrimination Ordinance to have treated male and female non-indigenous villagers who had married an indigenous villager differently in relation to their right to vote in the village representative election. While Article 40 of the Basic Law protects the lawful traditional rights and interests of indigenous inhabitants of the New Territories, the Court held that the deprivation of the political rights of non-indigenous inhabitants was unnecessary and thus disproportionate for the protection of the lawful traditional rights and interests of the indigenous inhabitants.

8.8.1.6 The *Prisoner's Voting Right* Case

The *Prisoner's Voting Right* case[285] also concerned the treatment of a minority group. The applicant, being an inmate, challenged the constitutionality of the provisions in the Legislative Council Ordinance[286] which disenfranchised him in LegCo elections.[287] In this case, the Court of First instance followed *Hirst v UK (No. 2)*,[288] in which the court held that even though the UK's general, indiscriminate, and automatic ban on convicted prisoners' voting (as provided for in the Representation of the People Act 1983) had a legitimate aim, it failed the proportionality test and thus amounted to a violation of the ECHR. The Court reasoned that while the right to vote is not an absolute right and may be subject to reasonable restrictions, such restrictions should be subjected to rigorous judicial scrutiny primarily because the right to vote has such high

285. *Chan Kin Sum* (N154).

286. Cap 542, Laws of Hong Kong.

287. Basic Law, Art 26; BORO, s 8, Art 21 (ICCPR, Art 25).

288. (2006) 42 EHRR 849.

constitutional importance and is without doubt the most important political right. Although the Court was prepared to accept that a law banning all prisoners from voting had served a legitimate aim in deterring others from committing crimes, such a wide restriction on rights would have still failed the 'minimal impairment' threshold as required in the second part of the proportionality enquiry.[289] This is because, by treating all prisoners in exactly the same way, regardless of the severity of their crimes, the 'blanket ban' went much further than was necessary to achieve the legitimate aim of deterring crime. The Court further noted that the aim could have been attained with a more limited ban that only applied to those prisoners who had committed more serious crimes.[290] Thus, as the government was unable to give convincing argument and evidence as to its justification, the Court held that the restrictions failed to pass the proportionality test, and that the challenged provision was unconstitutional. In holding the restrictions to be unlawful, Cheung J rejected the government's submission that the test for legality of the restriction should be based on whether it was unreasonable rather than whether it was disproportionate.

This case as well as the *Non-Indigenous Villager's Voting Right* case are typical examples of how Hong Kong courts will safeguard minorities' rights. They also show how judges have been receptive to international and comparative jurisprudence, including their willingness to use the proportionality formula on civil and political rights adjudications. The results of these two cases ultimately led the LegCo to enact the Village Representative Election Ordinance[291] in 2003 and the Voting by Imprisoned Persons Ordinance[292] in mid-2009, which basically remove all restrictions or hurdles that disqualified non-indigenous villagers and prisoners of their right to register as voters and vote in all elections. As Britain has done nothing in response to *Hirst* since 2006,[293] Hong Kong has seemingly stepped a bit more forward than its UK counterpart by having enacted an ordinance to safeguard these voting rights.

289. *Chan Kin Sum* (N154) [2009] 2 HKLRD 166 (CFI), 221.

290. Ibid.

291. Cap 576, Laws of Hong Kong.

292. See, for example, 'Voting by Imprisoned Persons Ordinance', 30 October 2009, available at: www.reo.gov.hk/en/ecenter/imprison.htm and www.elegislation.gov.hk/hk/2009/7!en, last accessed 31 January 2020.

293. See, for example, Elizabeth Adams, 'Prisoners' Voting Rights: Case Closed?' *UK Constitutional Law Blog*, 30 January 2019, available at: https://ukconstitutionallaw.org/2019/01/30/elizabeth-adams-prisoners-voting-rights-case-closed/, last accessed 31 January 2020.

8.8.2 Freedom of Speech or Expression: The *Flag Desecration* Case

Freedom of speech or expression is a fundamental human right. It provides a baseline of the extent to which a society is free and open. In the *Flag Desecration* case,[294] Li CJ (as he then was) said:

> Freedom of expression is a fundamental freedom in a democratic society. It lies at the heart of civil society and of Hong Kong's system and way of life. The courts must give a generous interpretation to its constitutional guarantee. This freedom includes the freedom to express ideas which the majority may find disagreeable or offensive and the freedom to criticize governmental institutions and the conduct of government officials.[295]

During the early days following the change of sovereignty in 1997, Hong Kong has had the good fortune of having free speech supported. The *Flag Desecration* case is a prime example of how Hong Kong courts have dealt with the constitutional task of delineating the boundaries of free speech.

In this case, the defendants, including the late Mr Ng, participated in a demonstration in Hong Kong promoting democracy in China during which they displayed a defaced national flag of the People's Republic of China (PRC) and a defaced regional flag of the Hong Kong SAR. They were subsequently charged with violating section 7 of the National Flag and National Emblem Ordinance [296] and section 7 of the Regional Flag and Regional Emblem Ordinance,[297] respectively, both of which prohibit flag and emblem desecration. In May 1998, they were convicted and sentenced by the Magistrate to a recognisance of HK$2,000 for each of the charges for 12 months. Subsequently, they successfully appealed their convictions before the Court of Appeal.[298] The Court held that the sections under which they had been charged were contrary to the guarantee of freedom of expression,[299] saying that being a restriction

294. *Ng Kung Siu* (N116) [2000] HKC 117.

295. Ibid., 135. Similar comments are also found in *Handyside* (N31) [49].

296. Cap 2401, Laws of Hong Kong.

297. Cap 2602, Laws of Hong Kong.

298. *Ng Kung Siu* (N116) [1999] 1 HKLRD 783.

299. Basic Law, Art 39; BORO, s 8, Art 16 (ICCPR, Art 19).

on freedom of expression, the prohibition of desecration of the national and regional flags cannot be justified by any necessity to protect public order (*ordre public*). In its judgment, the Court of Appeal referred to two decisions of the U.S. Supreme Court, namely *Texas v Johnson* [300] and *U.S. v Eichman,*[301] to the effect that the criminalisation of flag desecration violates the 'free speech' clause in the U.S. Constitution and is thus unconstitutional.

However, the Hong Kong SAR government, when appealing to the CFA, ultimately turned the tables. The CFA unanimously upheld the challenged ordinances as constitutional and valid, stating that the national and regional flags are important and unique symbols of the nation and of the Hong Kong SAR, respectively. The Court also noted that the objective behind the flag desecration laws was to uphold the societal and community interests in the protection of the flags. Such protection was held to have fallen within the concept of *'ordre public'* as used in the ICCPR. It concluded that the courts below had adopted too narrow a conception of *'ordre public'* which, in the context of the ICCPR, is not confined to the common law notion of maintaining law and order, and decided that *'ordre public'* should be construed more broadly to embrace notions of the 'general welfare' and the 'interests of the collectivity as a whole'.[302]

Put in the language of proportionality, the CFA was tasked with reviewing the case by ascertaining whether the flag desecration laws imposed restrictions on the freedom of expression, and, if so, whether such restrictions could be justified on the grounds that they are necessary for the protection of *'ordre public'* and thus proportionate to the aim. The Court noted that flag desecration is indeed 'a form of non-verbal speech or expression' [303] and that the challenged laws do constitute a restriction. However, it further pointed out that such restriction is only applicable to a particular mode of expression (i.e., flag desecration), and that the same message which the actors want to express could still be freely expressed by other modes.[304] Therefore, the Court concluded that the

300. 491 U.S. 397 (1989).

301. 496 U.S. 310 (1990).

302. *Ng Kung Siu* (N116) [1999] 2 HKCFAR 442, 459.

303. Ibid., 455.

304. Ibid., 456.

'necessity' and 'proportionality' tests had been satisfied.[305] Accordingly, any restriction on fundamental rights must be prescribed by law and necessary for the protection of some legitimate interests, as explained in earlier sections. Regarding the necessity requirement, although the CFA had closely followed the legality test as developed by the ECtHR, it viewed the word 'necessary' as having its ordinary meaning and that no substitution of phrase was required.[306] This was in contrast to the substitution in *Handyside*, whereby

> in deciding whether the seizure and confiscation of the publication were necessary, the ECtHR determined that the adjective 'necessary' was to be equated with 'pressing social need'. The Court then examined whether the English legislation was an expression of a 'pressing social need' that may justify a limitation on the freedom of expression for reasons of 'public morals' as determined in Article 10(2) [Freedom of expression].[307]

Ironically, in the *Public Order Ordinance* case held years later in 2005,[308] the CFA rejected the broader concept of *'ordre public'* used in the Public Order Ordinance,[309] saying that it was unconstitutional because it, being a restriction of freedom of demonstration, was too broad and imprecise to satisfy the prescribed-by-law requirement, which imports a high threshold in terms of the certainty of meaning and predictability of operation of the law concerned. Rather, the Court has adopted a narrow interpretation of it, holding that *'ordre public'* was far too vague to be written into, without further explanation, a provision allowing the police to restrict or ban public protests.[310]

In view of this sharp contrast, when delivering its judgment in the *Flag Desecration* case, the CFA was seemingly subservient to the NPCSC by interpreting *'ordre public'* to include 'anything necessary for the interests of Hong Kong society as a whole'. The effect of this expansive interpretation is that it may be used to justify the imposition of restrictions on almost all fundamental

305. Ibid., 460–461.

306. Ibid., 460F–460G.

307. *Handyside* (N31) [48].

308. *Leung Kwok Hung* (N24).

309. Cap 245, Laws of Hong Kong.

310. *Leung Kwok Hung* (N24) (2005) 8 HKCFA 229, 261–264.

rights.[311] As Raymond Wacks has criticised, its reasoning is hardly convincing and should be considered 'a setback for the protection of rights'.[312] That said, reading the *'ordre public'* in this way as a means to supress individuals' right to freedom of expression in the form of flag desecration to denounce the 'tyranny-type' governance in the PRC seems to have been a contingency plan to avoid political tension within the 'one country, two systems' model applied in Hong Kong. However, this cautious attitude is understandable, as the decision occurred at a time when the relationship between the CFA and the Mainland authorities was rather difficult (indeed, the *Ng Ka Ling* saga happened during the same period).[313] According to Chan, the CFA was probably trying to rebuild the trust between the two entities and sought a mutually acceptable balance between aligning itself as a court of final adjudication to protect the 'one country, two systems' model, on one hand, and respecting the sovereignty of the NPCSC in exercising the power of final interpretation of the Basic Law, on the other.[314]

As far as Chen is concerned, the CFA did, when ruling in favour of the Hong Kong SAR government, take into account 'separation-of-powers considerations', or to be precise, 'discretionary area of judgment', in its decision [315] by giving

> due weight to the view of the [Hong Kong SAR] legislature that the enactment of the National Flag Ordinance ... is appropriate for the discharge of the Region's obligation to apply the national law arising from its addition to Annex III [to the Basic Law] by the [NPCSC].[316]

This case must have been extremely difficult for the CFA.[317] At issue was more than a proportionality analysis of striking a balance between the individual's freedom of expression and the public and national interest in the protection of the national and regional flags. Despite not being discussed explicitly in the judgment of the courts, the national desecration law impugned in this

311. Gittings (N27) 297.
312. Raymond Wacks, 'Our Flagging Rights' (2000) 30 *HKLJ* 1, 2.
313. *Ng Ka Ling* (N109).
314. Chan (N18) 422.
315. Chen (N14) 189.
316. *Ng Kung Siu* (N116) [1999] 2 HKCFAR 442, 460.
317. Chen (N14) 190.

case was enacted by the Hong Kong LegCo for the purpose of implementing a national law which the NPCSC had decided to apply in Hong Kong. If the CFA had decided that the flag desecration law constituted an unnecessary or disproportionate restriction on freedom of expression, it would then have been required to tackle the politically sensitive problem of whether a Hong Kong court could decline to enforce a national law made applicable to Hong Kong. An affirmative answer would have brought the Hong Kong courts into conflict with the NPCSC, and a constitutional crisis would likely have followed.[318] Luckily, the CFA did not have to tread this path of potential collision with the NPCSC. In fact, the CFA's refusal to follow the more liberal American approach [319] is seemingly understandable in order to avoid the political and ideological tensions within the 'one country, two systems' model.

Despite its decision to uphold the flag desecration law, the approach and reasoning adopted by the CFA have far-reaching positive implications for the regime of rights protection in post-1997 Hong Kong. This is because the Court has re-affirmed the power of the Hong Kong courts to review the constitutionality of legislative and executive decisions on human rights grounds, and, if necessary, to strike down such legislations and decisions should they be found to have been in contravention of the fundamental rights enshrined in the Basic Law. As Chan has noted, the affirmation of the proportionality formula in this case is a major step forward because it enables Hong Kong courts to conduct a balancing exercise between protecting fundamental rights and its impact on other important social objectives, albeit with its starting point being in favour of fundamental rights.[320] The use of the proportionality analysis also mandates Hong Kong courts to scrutinise the justifications for restricting a fundamental right even closer.[321] Once this position has been reached, it is difficult to draw any distinction between human rights cases and other types of cases. It is also likely that the proportionality formula will find its way into future general administrative law cases and replace traditional *Wednesbury*

318. Ibid.

319. *Johnson* (N300); *Eichman* (N301).

320. Chan (N18) 424.

321. Ibid.

unreasonableness, which has been subject to increased criticism in recent years because of its narrow scope.[322]

8.8.3 Freedoms of Assembly, Procession, and Demonstration

The freedoms of assembly, procession, and demonstration are undoubtedly connected to the freedom of expression.[323] Since the handover, the number of demonstrations in Hong Kong has increased significantly, the examples of which comprise the 500,000-people march on 1 July 2003,[324] the annual remembrance of the victims killed by the communist armed forces in Tiananmen square on 4 June 1989, and the protests by Falun Gong practitioners against the persecution of their sect in Mainland China,[325] among others. Although these demonstrations were regarded as testimony of the political freedom and social openness in Hong Kong shortly after the change of sovereignty in 1997, these political freedoms and social openness have been eroding since 2014, as shown by the intolerant attitude of the Mainland authorities and Hong Kong SAR government towards Hong Kong citizens in various civil disobedience movements, such as 'Occupy Central with Love and Peace', 'Let Love and Peace Occupy Central', or the 'Umbrella Movement' (or the Occupy Central Movement) which happened in late September 2014. Similar intolerance has also been shown to citizens during anti-government protests in 2016 (i.e., the Fishball Revolution) and in 2019 (i.e., the Anti-Extradition Bill protests). Prior to discussing their effects on the rule of law and the legal ramifications felt by citizens, a general understanding of the decisions and ordinances as well as the protests and related events is necessary. Thus, the following sections focus on specific cases involving the freedoms of assembly, procession, and demonstration and outline the related events, movements, and protests, as well as the administration's attitude and their impact on the judiciary.

322. Ibid.

323. *HKSAR v Wong Hin Wai* [2013] HKCFA 102, (2013) 16 HKCFAR 837, [2014] 1 HKC 241.

324. Fu Hualing, Carole Petersen, and Simon Young (eds), *National Security and Fundamental Freedoms: Hong Kong's Article 23 under Scrutiny* (HKUP 2005).

325. *Yeung May Wan v HKSAR* (2005) 8 HKCFAR 137 (CFA), [2005] 2 HKLRD 212 (CFA).

8.8.3.1 The *Public Order Ordinance* Case

The Public Order Ordinance [326] ('POO' as it has been nicknamed [327]) mandates that organisers of public meetings and processions involving more than fifty and thirty persons, respectively, are required to notify and then to obtain a notice of no-objection from the police one week in advance of any intended meetings [328] or processions.[329] The POO also empowers the police (i.e., the commissioner of police or a police officer of appropriate rank delegated with such power) to prohibit the proposed assemblies and demonstrations on certain grounds (such as national security, public safety, public order, or the protection of the rights and freedoms of others) [330] or to impose conditions which demonstrators must comply with.[331]

The POO was a product of the colonial regime, passed in November 1967, in the wake of riots organised by the Chinese Communist Party, which threatened Hong Kong's security for eight months.[332] This bloody event claimed 51 lives, with 15 deaths being caused by bomb attacks [333] and one having been burned alive.[334] A total of 1,936 people were convicted, of which 465 were jailed for 'unlawful assembly', 40 for possessing bombs, and 33 for explosion-related offences.[335]

There are two main issues with the POO, one being the restrictions imposed on the holding of public meetings and processions, and the other being the interconnected criminal offences of 'unlawful assembly' and 'rioting', which have long been criticised as vague and ill-defined.[336] The former makes it difficult

326. Cap 245, Laws of Hong Kong.

327. Hong Kong Watch, 'Outdated and Draconian: Hong Kong's Public Order Ordinance', 2019, 2, available at: https://static1.squarespace.com/static/58ecfa82e3df284d3a13dd41/t/5d25c0676c3cb30001e74f6b/1562755179422/hkw, last accessed 19 June 2020.

328. Ibid., s 8.

329. Ibid. s 13A.

330. Ibid., ss 9 and 14.

331. Ibid., ss 11 and 15.

332. Hong Kong Watch (N327) 2.

333. Ibid.

334. On 24 August 1967, Mr Lam Bun, a radio commentator at Commercial Radio of Hong Kong, was attacked on his way to work and burnt alive when his car was set ablaze; see ibid., 11.

335. Gary Cheung, 'Hong Kong's watershed', *South China Morning Post*, 3 May 2007, available at: www.scmp.com/article/591363/hong-kongs-watershed, last accessed 29 June 2020.

336. Hong Kong Watch (N327) 6.

for an assembly or a procession to be held lawfully without complying with restriction requirements ordered by the police, who have been granted wide discretionary powers in this 'licencing system' to enable them to object or order the discontinuance of any public gathering on the ground of public order and to 'arrest citizens for engaging in "unlawful assembly" if [they] felt citizens' behaviour could lead to a breach of peace'.[337] The latter exposes every participant in an assembly or procession, be it spontaneous or planned, to imprisonment should the assembly or procession result in, or threaten to result in, a 'breach of the peace' — a fossil term also with a vague definition.[338] As Dr Margaret Ng has criticised, 'rioting' was deliberately given a broader definition than that under the common law,[339] whereas 'peaceful demonstrations' or 'lawful assemblies' could only be held by applying to the police for permission and were subjected to tight control.[340]

During the colonial period, it is understandable that draconian laws were passed in order to give the then colonial government wide powers. These powers were then (hopefully) exercised with caution and restraint by a benign and wise administration to avoid controversy and opposition in the community.[341] Thanks to the Patten Reforms initiated in 1994, which brought the POO into compliance with the BORO and thus the ICCPR, the requirements changed, whereby only a notification of such a public gathering was necessary instead of an application for police permission.[342] As Lord Patten said in 2018:

> We attempted to reform the [POO] in the 1990s and made a number of changes because it was clear that the vague definitions in the legislation are open to abuse and do not conform with [UN] human rights standards.[343]

337. Antony Dapiran, *City of Protests: A Recent History of Dissent in Hong Kong* (Penguin 2017) 16.

338. Hong Kong Watch (N327) 2.

339. This will be discussed when we talk about the Fishball Revolution below.

340. Hong Kong Watch (N327) 2.

341. Ibid.

342. Hong Kong UPR Coalition, *Freedom of Assembly Rights and Public Order Ordinance* (Hong Kong UPR Coalition, date not specified) 1, available at: www.justicecentre.org.hk/framework/uploads/2018/11/HKUPR-Coalition-Fact-Sheet-Freedom-of-Assembly-Rights-and-Public-Order-Ordinance.pdf, last accessed 20 June 2020.

343. Chris Patten, 'Lord Patten criticises Public Order Ordinance following sentencing of Edward Leung', Hong Kong Watch, 11 June 2018, available at: www.hongkongwatch.org/all-posts/2018/6/11/lord-patten-criticises-public-order-ordinance-following-sentencing-of-edward-leung, last accessed 15 June 2020.

However, shortly after the change of sovereignty in 1997, the Hong Kong Provisional LegCo overturned Patten's amendments, reinstating the requirement for police permission, among other things.[344] The range and vague definitions in the POO were also reinvigorated to offer the Hong Kong SAR government broader application, and thus the ability to deter undesired protests.[345] These changes are incompatible with international human rights standards. In response, the UN Human Rights Committee has, in its Concluding Observations in 1999, expressed concern that 'the [POO] could be applied to unduly restrict the enjoyment of the rights guaranteed in Article 21 [i.e., the right to peaceful assembly] of the [ICCPR]', and urged the Hong Kong SAR government to review it in order to make it compliant with Article 21.[346] As Lord Patten went on to say, '[i]t is disappointing to see that the legislation is now being used politically to place extreme sentences on the pan-democrats and other activists'.[347] This was echoed by the late Baron Ashdown, the former leader of the UK Liberal Democratic Party (from 1988 to 1999), when he stated that the POO 'is one of Britain's worst legacies in Hong Kong and has repeatedly been criticised by the UN for excessively curtailing freedom of expression'.[348]

Owing to the above, it is unacceptable in modern society for laws incompatible with human rights standards to remain in force,[349] meaning that because the POO mandates police permission (rather than notification) to hold public gatherings or processions, it is unacceptable. It is also undesirable for the laws to be enforced by an autocratic government which does not want the rule of law to persist.[350] This is because the rule of law is an antithesis to arbitrary power. In its simplest form, this means that no one is above the law, thus preventing, at least in theory, the domination of an autocratic power. In fact, the 'rule *by*

344. Hong Kong Watch (N327) 13.

345. Hong Kong UPR Coalition (N342) 1.

346. United Nations Human Rights Committee, 'Concluding Observations of the Human Rights Committee on the First Report of the HKSAR of PRC in the light of the ICCPR', 15 November 1999, available at: www.cmab.gov.hk/en/press/reports_human.htm, last accessed 20 June 2020.

347. Patten (N343).

348. Paddy Ashdown, 'Britain has an obligation to denounce the abuse of colonial laws', *Financial Times*, 13 June 2018, available at: www.ft.com/content/d66d69aa-6ef4-11e8-8863-a9bb262c5f53, last accessed 20 June 2020.

349. Hong Kong Watch (N327) 2.

350. Ibid.

law' (as opposed to rule *of* law) is preferred by autocratic and communist regimes. For Mainland China, this is evident in its leadership openly directing the government to use the law as a weapon to protect the security and interests of the country,[351] or in some cases even the interests of the senior officials or the leaders themselves. A case in point, is the charging of Zhao Lianhai, who queried the Sanlu poisonous milk powder incident, with inciting social disorder, thus using the law to avoid governmental accountability and embarrassment in the scandal.[352] As Chinese officials are under pressure to maintain fast rates of economic growth and ensure social stability, they routinely favour producers over consumers, and product liability lawsuits remain difficult to file and harder to win. This is especially true if the company involved is a state-owned enterprise or has close connections with the Chinese communist party or government, as evident in this case.[353] Similarly, Tan Zuoren, a famous environmentalist and social activist in Sichuan, was accused of inciting subversion of state power and sentenced to five years in prison because he publicly questioned and devoted himself to investigating the problem of fragile structures in schools (resulting from official corruption) which led to their collapse in the Wenchuan earthquake in 2008 and multiple student deaths.[354]

In the Hong Kong SAR, having laws, in particular the POO, used as weapons to protect the security and interests of the government,[355] highlights a shift towards the ethos of Mainland China. This is further apparent in the recently proposed national security law for Hong Kong, which aims to prevent, stop, and punish secession, subversion of state power, terrorism, and foreign interference

351. Ibid.

352. U.S. Congressional-Executive Commission on China, *Annual Report 2010* (170th Congress, 2nd Session, 10 October 2010), 185, available at: file:///C:/Users/user/Downloads/728196.pdf, last accessed 20 June 2020, citing Zhao Lianhai, who is a parent of a sick child and organised a group representing the parents of other sick children at the school, and who was later tried for inciting social disorder.

353. Edward Wong, 'Courts Compound Pain of China's Tainted Milk', *The New York Times*, 16 October 2008, available at: www.nytimes.com/2008/10/17/world/asia/17milk.html, last accessed 20 June 2020.

354. *British Broadcasting Corporation*, 'Sichuan activist Tan Zuoren sentenced to five years in prison', 9 February 2020, available at: www.bbc.com/zhongwen/simp/china/2010/02/100209_tanzuoren, last accessed 20 June 2020.

355. Hong Kong Watch (N327) 2.

in Hong Kong, despite the fact that many opposition politicians and critics warn that it could be used to suppress dissent and erode freedom.[356]

In addition to incompatibility of the POO with modern human rights standards (because of its vague nature and allowance for fundamental right violations),[357] increasingly severe sentencing in the legislation has also created a chilling effect on protest and political participation.[358] In this climate, enforcement of the POO has and will continue to have devastating effects on the fundamental rights and liberties of the people in Hong Kong.

Turning to the *Public Order Ordinance* case in question,[359] after the change of sovereignty in 1997, although demonstrators must still legally comply with the rule concerning prior notification, in practice, it is often ignored. Indeed, many assemblies and demonstrations have taken place without complying with this rule, with few repercussions.[360] In 1998, there were 126 protests organised without applying for any notice of no objection, whereas in 1999, there were 183 protests organised without applying for permission.[361] Moreover, according to official figures, from July 1997 to March 2002, about one in seven public rallies was held without notifying the police in advance.[362] However, no organisers had been prosecuted for flouting this rule — at least until the *Public Order Ordinance* case in 2002.

356. *South China Morning Post*, 'Topic: Hong Kong national security law', multiple dates, available at: www.scmp.com/topics/hong-kong-national-security-law, last accessed 20 June 2020.

357. Hong Kong UPR Coalition (N342) 1.

358. Hong Kong Watch, 'A Tool of Lawfare: The Abuse of Hong Kong's Public Order Ordinance since 2014', date unspecified, 3, available at: https://static1.squarespace.com/static/58ecfa82e3df284d3a13dd41/t/5ce7d19253450a5fe8fe860a/1558696339084/Public+Order+Ordinance+briefing.pdf, last accessed 20 June 2020. See also Hong Kong Watch (N327) 6, 8, 15, 18–19, and 29.

359. *Leung Kwok Hung* (N24).

360. Janice Brabyn, 'The Fundamental Freedom of Assembly and Part III of the Public Order Ordinance' (2002) 32 *HKLJ* 271.

361. Alvin So, 'Social Protests, Legitimacy Crisis, and the Impetus Toward Soft Authoritarianism in the Hong Kong SAR' in Lau Siu Kai (ed), *The First Tung Chee-hwa Administration: The First Five Years of the Hong Kong Special Administrative Region* (CUP 2002) 405.

362. Anne Cheung and Albert Chen, 'The Search for the Rule of Law in the Hong Kong Special Administrative Region, 1997–2003' in Wong Yiu Chung (ed), *One Country, Two Systems in Crisis: Hong Kong's Transformation since the Handover* (Lexington 2004) 79.

In this case, the government attempted for the first time to enforce the prior notification rule. In May 2002, Mr Leung Kwok Hung, nicknamed 'Long hair', an old-hand street demonstrator, and two student activists were arrested by the police and charged with organising an unauthorised procession and failure to notify the police under the POO. The number of people taking part in the procession varied at different points in time, but ranged from about 40 to 96. These three defendants were convicted in November 2002, being bound over for three months on a recognizance of HK$500. However, the Chief Magistrate queried whether such a case, being of 'political nature', should have been handled by the court at all, despite the then Secretary for Justice Elsie Leung defending that the main issue in this case was whether a crime had been committed.[363]

Despite their application to the Court of Appeal,[364] the Court, by a majority ruling of two to one, dismissed the appeal, holding that the relevant provision of the POO was consistent with the guarantee of freedoms of assembly and procession as enshrined in the Basic Law, the BORO, and the ICCPR. Nevertheless, the dissenting judge, Stock JA (as he then was), was of the view that the power conferred by the POO on the police to prohibit or impose restrictions on demonstrations on the ground of '*ordre public*' was problematic. He was also of the opinion that the POO had been framed in such a way that it failed the requirement of legal certainty as well as the 'necessity' stage of the proportionality test. As his Lordship said, 'legal certainty ... must be reinforced where an essential freedom is at stake and where the power of limitation is backed by sanction of the criminal law'.[365] Not only must the citizen know the extent and limits of their freedoms and rights with certainty, but officials must know the extent and limits of their (discretionary) powers as well.[366] The case was ultimately appealed to the CFA.

363. Secretary of State for Foreign and Commonwealth Affairs, 'Six-Monthly Report on Hong Kong July–December 2002', February 2003, [26], available at: https://assets.publishing.service.gov.uk/government/uploads/system/uploads/attachment_data/file/500954/2002_Jul-Dec.pdf, last accessed 20 June 2020.

364. *Leung Kwok Hung* (N24) [2004] 3 HKLRD 729 (CA).

365. Ibid., [80].

366. Ibid.

The CFA, by a majority of four to one, dismissed the appeal.[367] The Court adopted a middle ground between the majority and minority views in the courts below, upholding the requirement in the POO that organisers of public processions involving more than 30 persons should notify the police in advance. The Court also pointed out that the prior notification requirement would not only enable the police to take steps to safeguard public order during the demonstration, but would also be in the best interest of the demonstrators, stating that 'notification is required to enable the Police to fulfil the positive duty resting on Government to take reasonable and appropriate measures to enable lawful demonstrations to take place peacefully'.[368] The Court also upheld, albeit *obiter*, the authority of the police to restrict processions by 'reading down' the concept of 'public order' into its 'law and order' sense (i.e., maintenance of public order and prevention of public disorder) so that it was certain enough to fulfil the prescribed-by-law requirement.

However, the CFA rejected the broader concept of '*ordre public*' as used in the POO, saying that it was unconstitutional because it is too broad and imprecise to satisfy the legal certainty test. The Court drew a distinction between the concept of '*ordre public*' as part of a constitutional norm, as enshrined in the ICCPR as it applies to Hong Kong under Article 39 of the Basic Law, and the same concept as part of a norm in legislation to implement the constitution. Although it is legitimate for '*ordre public*' to be used as a constitutional norm, this concept as it is used in the POO failed to give a sufficient indication of the circumstances in which the police may restrict the right to freedom of demonstration. Thus, although the POO provided that '*ordre public*' constituted a ground for restricting the freedom of demonstration, it failed to conform to the constitutional requirement that any restriction of this right must be 'prescribed by law', as this requires a high degree of certainty regarding the meaning and the predictability of the operation of the law concerned.

Having rejected the broader concept of '*ordre public*' in the POO, the CFA deviated from its approach in the *Flag Desecration* case above, in which the concept of '*ordre public*' was interpreted broadly to cover the collective interest and

367. *Leung Kwok Hung* (N24) [2005] 3 HKLRD 164.

368. Ibid., [65].

not just for 'maintaining law and order'. This shift in the CFA's opinion signifies an increased comfort with upholding the prescribed-by-law requirement. The change is not altogether surprising as the maintenance of public order is within the realm of the Hong Kong SAR government to manage, as enshrined in Article 14 of the Basic Law. Furthermore, the Mainland authorities have adopted a less intrusive approach towards Hong Kong affairs since the early 2000s, and more importantly, the NPCSC did not instruct the Hong Kong SAR government to 'observe' any particular aspect of this matter. The combined effect of these factors is that the CFA seemingly feels more comfortable (as opposed to how it felt during the *Flag Desecration* case) protecting citizens' fundamental rights and maintaining international human rights standards.

Despite this shift in the CFA's view, Bokhary PJ (as he then was) was of the opinion that the commissioner of police's power to restrict these freedoms under the POO should altogether be held unconstitutional, saying that the concept of 'public order', even if being severed from the term *'ordre public'*, was still too wide and uncertain to comply with the constitutional guarantees necessary to protect fundamental rights.[369] As wide restrictions on rights and freedoms were unacceptable, he had no alternative but to strike down the commissioner of police's power of restraint. Janice Brabyn concurred, claiming that since the statutory discretion to restrict the right of peaceful assembly for maintaining 'public order' has not given an adequate indication of the scope of the discretion (and was thus facially invalid),[370] the commissioner of police may, in practice, find no difficulty in justifying the restrictions he imposes to restrict fundamental rights even without using 'public order' as a ground for the restriction.[371] That said, Bokhary PJ claimed that it would have been inapposite for the Court to interpret the provisions in a way that supplied necessary safeguards to the statutory derogation because, if the Court had done so, it would have been accused of taking over the role of the LegCo to legislate and clarify the grounds upon which the commissioner of police can exercise his restraint power.

369. *Leung Kwok Hung* (N24) [2005] HKCFA 41, [197]–[206].

370. Janice Brabyn, 'Leung Kwok Hung and Others Through the Hong Kong Courts' (2006) 36 *HKLJ* 83, 111.

371. Ibid., 108.

As far as proportionality is concerned, the CFA did explicitly demand that the commissioner of police observe the criteria under the proportionality test when exercising discretionary power to regulate processions. This test mandates that the police 'must consider whether a potential restriction is rationally connected with one or more of the statutory legitimate purpose(s), and whether the potential restriction is no more than necessary to accomplish the legitimate purpose in question'.[372] The Court further stated that 'where the Commissioner [of the police] decides to object [to a notified procession] or to impose conditions, the reasons given must be sufficient to show that he has properly applied the proportionality test in making his decision',[373] and that the discretionary power to control demonstrations 'is thus not an arbitrary one but is a constrained one'.[374]

However, the Court has failed to explain why the notion of 'public order' in a 'law and order' sense was able to fulfil the proportionality criteria. Instead, the Court merely asserted that this should be done.[375] As Alex Lau has argued, in applying the proportionality formula, the scope of 'public order' as a legitimate aim must be certain enough, otherwise the commissioner of police would have no difficulty in imposing his restriction with the abstract purpose of maintaining public order, and if that is the case, the adoption of a proportionality analysis does nothing to clarify the vague concept of 'public order' any further.[376] Lau's argument tallies with what I have suggested previously[377] that the clearer the legitimate purpose is ascertained — and thus interpreted correctly — and made known to the general public during the proceedings, the more likely that lesser arbitrary or executively convenient interpretations by the police at the expense of citizens' fundamental rights (as enshrined in the Basic Law, the BORO, and the ICCPR) will follow.

372. *Leung Kwok Hung* (N24) [2005] 3 HKLRD 164, [96].

373. Ibid., [59].

374. Ibid., [96].

375. Po Jen Yap, 'Constitutional Review under the Basic Law: The Rise, Retreat and Resurgence of Judicial Power in Hong Kong' (2007) 37 *HKLJ* 447, 466.

376. Alex Lau, 'Breach of the Peace and Constitutional Freedom of assembly in the HKSAR' (2013) 7 *HKJLS* 75, 90.

377. Please see Chapter Two of this book for further discussion.

Thus, the CFA has, in this *Public Order Ordinance* case, exercised the power of constitutional review of legislation to strike down the *'ordre public'* provision in the POO, and subjected related police actions to the proportionality principle. Judging from the above, the significance of this case is that it enables the Court to use the proportionality analysis to scrutinise the derogations imposed by the police on fundamental rights more vigorously, and that it goes beyond the traditional *Wednesbury* unreasonableness enquiry to judicially review administrative actions. It also enunciates the application of the proportionality principle to police decisions on any restriction of a citizen's right to demonstrate or protest. Seen in this light, the *Public Order Ordinance* decision makes a major contribution to the advancement of the freedom of assembly and procession in Hong Kong.

8.8.3.2 The *Olympic Torch Relay* Case

As reflected in the *Public Order Ordinance* case, freedom of assembly or procession imposes a positive obligation on the government to allow processions to take place, one in which the police are 'legally obliged' to assist demonstrators in their assemblies, procession, and demonstration. Such obligations consist of helping demonstrators minimise inconvenience to the public, providing demonstrators with access to public space of significance, and protecting demonstrators participating in public assemblies from hostile audiences.[378]

Among these positive obligations, the importance of protecting demonstrators taking part in public assemblies from hostile audiences has been further emphasised in the *Olympic Torch Relay* case,[379] which concerns police actions to protect peaceful demonstrators at the 2008 Summer Olympic Games torch relay. There, the applicant staged a 'Free Tibet' protest during the course of the torch relay. During the protest and before the commencement of the torch relay, the applicant encountered 'counter-protesters' who attempted to drown out her protest by waving the Chinese flag and shouting pro-China slogans.

378. Clare Tsang and Sam Wong, 'Police Power and the Freedom of Assembly' (2012) 6 *HKJLS* 75, 88.

379. *Chan Hau Man Christina v Commissioner of Police* [2009] 6 HKC 44, [2009] 4 HKLRD 797.

This interaction ultimately became physical, causing the police to be concerned about the applicant and the integrity of the barriers that were maintaining crowd control during the torch relay. Accordingly, the police escorted the applicant away from the site and transported her to a police station. However, the applicant complained that her group, and not the counter-protesters, was targeted once the counter-protesters began to threaten them during the protest.

Thus, the applicant applied for judicial review, arguing that her right to freedom of expression was infringed as was her freedom of assembly and demonstration because she had not been allowed to continue her protest at the site of the torch relay. In this regard, the focus of the case was on the balance to be struck between freedom of assembly and the need to maintain the public peace. As Cheung J (as he then was) [380] observed:

> The right of peaceful assembly involves a positive duty on the part of the Government to take reasonable and appropriate measures to enable lawful assemblies to take place peacefully ... Alongside these constitutional rights to freedom of speech and freedom of demonstration, which carry with them the positive duty on the part of the Government to take measures to enable lawful assemblies to take place peacefully, is the police's duty to keep the peace.[381]

Cheung J also noted that the right of peaceful assembly was not absolute because the government cannot guarantee that lawful assemblies will proceed peacefully, and that it has a wide choice of measures to be used in their efforts to protect this right, the reasonableness and appropriateness of which will dependent on the circumstances of a particular case. Where appropriate, these circumstances would include, among others, Hong Kong's density of population, its relatively narrow streets and roads, etc.[382]

---

380. Natalie Wong, Gary Cheung, and Sum Lok-kei, 'Andrew Cheung to be Hong Kong's next chief justice, but city's leader Carrie Lam fears politics could delay appointment', *South China Morning Post*, 24 March 2020, available at: www.scmp.com/news/hong-kong/politics/article/3076669/andrew-cheung-be-hong-kongs-next-chief-justice-citys-leader, last accessed 2 April 2020.

381. *Chan Hau Man Christina* (N379) [14]–[15].

382. Ibid., [15].

Although a demonstration may give offence to those with opposing views, demonstrators must be able to proceed without fear of physical violence by opponents. This is because such a fear would have a deterrent effect. In a democratic society, the right to counter-demonstrate cannot extend to inhibiting the exercise of the right to demonstrate. Based on the facts of this case, however, the police felt that there had been no way to separate the two sides in a way that would have allowed both to carry on with their own causes, resulting in the decision to move the applicant's group to prevent further chaos.[383]

Once the Court concluded that the police were justified in taking action against the applicant's group, it had to conclude that they were also justified in removing the group from the scene to prevent a breach of peace. The Court also held that this action was no more than necessary and was proportionate considering the circumstances of the case. Cheung J concluded that the police are entitled to take action, even if this restricts the freedom of assembly if, *inter alia*, there is an imminent breach of peace. He further held that in certain exceptional situations, the police would be entitled to take action against the applicant herself rather than those who would cause the breach of peace. These circumstances included:

> [first], demonstrators who, by interfering with the rights or liberties of others, are likely to provoke violence, thereby justifying preventive action against them (instead of against those who are about to be provoked to violence) ... [second,] those whose action was 'outrageous', 'provocative' or 'unreasonable', although it did not involve any interference with the rights or liberties of others as such ... [third] when there is no other way available to the police to maintain the peace, and if the action of the police is no more than is necessary and is otherwise proportionate, the police can take action against innocent third parties in order to prevent the imminent breach of the peace.[384]

Against this background, Cheung J would have been prepared to conclude that the applicant fell into the second category on the basis that she knew that

383. Ibid., [15].

384. Ibid., [56]–[57].

her demonstration was provocative even if she did not intend to provoke. Nevertheless, he based his actual decision on the third category, concluding that

> the police had no option but to take action against the applicant and her group. The police officers present were outnumbered by the counter-demonstrators. They kept asking for reinforcements, which were never sufficient to match the ever growing number of counter-demonstrators ... All this was taking place within an extremely crowded environment, where tens of thousands of people had gathered to watch the torch relay which was about to start ... On top, one has the occasion itself to consider. For the police to make an arrest, not to mention mass arrest, of the counter-demonstrators, in order to keep the peace must have been a most undesirable option. When the police officers were greatly outnumbered and their own safety was on the line, whether it was a practicable option was also in doubt. Moreover, its effect on the counter-demonstrators and the rest of the crowd would have been highly unpredictable, particularly bearing in mind the highly unpopular cause that the applicant's group was pursuing. On top of all that, if the Court is correct with its earlier conclusion that in fact the action of the applicant may be described as highly provocative, justifying police intervention in the first place, in my view, the police [force] was faced with no other practical options but to take action against the applicant and her group in order to maintain the peace.[385]

Overall, the *Olympics Torch Relay* case has indicated that although the police do have a positive obligation, and are thus legally obliged, to assist participants in lawful assembly and procession (as ruled by the ECtHR in *Plattform 'Arzte fur das Leben' v Austria*[386] and confirmed in the *Public Order Ordinance* case), a balance has to be struck between the freedom of assembly and the need to maintain the public peace. Therefore, they are entitled to take action to restrict demonstrators for the purpose of eliminating an imminent breach of peace on the condition that such restriction is no more than is necessary and is proportionate with the circumstances. Applying Brabyn's view to this

385. Ibid., [67].

386. (1988) 13 EHRR 204.

case,[387] a concern with this decision (like that in the *Public Order Ordinance* case) is that the commissioner of police may, even without a 'public order' ground, justify the restrictions to restrict freedoms of assemblies, processions, and demonstrations simply by saying that there is insufficient manpower to protect the protesters. These protesters often hold minority views, such as LGBT groups, anti-Beijing groups, etc., and have limited resources, in terms of financial capability, manpower, etc., *vis-à-vis* individuals in the majority. Thus, ensuring their rights are not impinged is essential.

8.8.3.3 Revisiting the Public Order Ordinance in Civil Disobedience and Anti-Government Protests

As discussed, despite having maintained political freedom and social openness shortly after the handover, these aspects appear to be eroding. Starting in late 2014, there has been an array of civil disobedience movements and anti-government protests, including the Occupy Central Movement in 2014, the Fishball Revolution in 2016, the Anti-Extradition Bill Protests in 2019, and the recent responses to the Anti-National Security Bill proposal in 2020. Naturally, this has led to a resurgence in cases involving the application of the POO.

Given the fact that the notification law of the POO had rarely been enforced and, in practice, those who had given advance notification of assemblies and processions to the police were invariably approved for their activities prior to 2002, Chen opined [388] that the majority of the CFA might have concluded that it made more practical sense to subject police actions regulating demonstrations to the proportionality test, rather than to strike at the fundamentals of the existing system of regulation by using criminal sanctions to enforce the regulatory requirements.[389] However, in the face of ongoing civil disobedience movements and the subsequent anti-government protests, the police have adopted this prior restraint power as a strategy to pre-emptively crack down Hong Kong citizens'

387. Brabyn (N370) 108.

388. It is unlikely that he expected the various civil disobedience movements starting from 2014 and the resulting anti-governments protests in 2016 and 2019 (and onwards).

389. Chen (N14) 199.

freedoms of assembly, procession, and demonstration as enshrined under the Basic Law, the BORO, and the ICCPR. To do so, they use implausible excuses and criminal sanctions of unlawful assembly and its incitement against the organisers and participants should they fail to comply with the objection notice. For example, '[i]n rejecting the applications for the marches, [the] police cited public safety reasons as all four neighbourhood [i.e., Tai Po, Wong Tai Sin, Sham Shui Po, and Hong Kong Island] had been scenes of intense clashes between police and protesters'.[390] As Mr Tse Lai Nam, a member of the political party Demosisto who was one of the applicants seeking police approval for a march in Hong Kong Island East during that period, has said, 'it was irresponsible for the [police] force to ban their application by attributing responsibility for previous post-march clashes to organisers, ... allegations they said were unsubstantiated'.[391] Mr Tse also criticised the police, saying that '[b]asically all marches would run peacefully if there were no police and Triads' and that '[i]t's ridiculous that police don't tackle the gangsters in a community but suppresses the citizens' basic right of assembly'.[392]

It has also been observed that once an assembly, procession, or demonstration has been deemed unlawful because the organisers failed to notify and obtain police approval, disproportionate force is often used to suppress the event.[393] The police will typically arrest the organisers for unlawful assembly and incitement, likely believing that this may help to deter them from participating in future events. Similar tactics are also used even if the event has been approved but leads to disruptions instigated by some 'protesters'. However, the identities of

390. Danny Mok and Jeffie Lam, 'Hong Kong police refuse permission for four anti-government marches, organisers call it "shocking" attack on Basic Law rights', *South China Morning Post*, 9 August 2019, available at: www.scmp.com/news/hong-kong/politics/article/3022103/hong-kong-police-refuse-permission-three-anti-government, last accessed 2 April 2020.

391. Ibid.

392. Ibid.

393. Jeffie Lam and Christy Leung, 'In Hong Kong protests, did police use excessive force or issue a proportional response?', *South China Morning Post*, 14 June 2019, available at: www.scmp.com/news/hong-kong/politics/article/3014432/officers-used-excessive-force-contain-hong-kong-extradition, last accessed 2 April 2020.

these individuals are typically unknown, leading to questions being raised about their genuine support of the protests.[394]

In the process of these arrests and show of force, the police have inflicting debilitating injuries on protesters, supporters, and passers-by.[395] They regularly fired tear gas, rubbers bullets, beanbag rounds, and high velocity water cannons at close range, turning non-lethal crowd-control measures into weapons, whether intentionally or unintentionally.[396] In fact, since 11 August 2019, the media has documented police routinely beating arrested individuals with batons, pinning them down, rubbing their faces against the ground, pepper-spraying their eyes and wounds, and breaking their bones.[397] This use of disproportionate force, including that observed during the Yuen Long Attack on 21 July 2019,[398] the Prince Edward Incident on 31 August 2019,[399] and various other events, has triggered anger amongst students and the public. This became very apparent on the morning of 11 November 2019, when riot police entered the Chinese University of Hong Kong (CUHK) without permission and fired rounds of tear gas, pepper-spray, and other kinds of bullets at student protesters under a non-life threatening situation. Even during these events, the students, regardless of the threat to their safety, continued to advocate the slogans of the protests:

394. Victor Ting and Sum Lok-kei, 'Hong Kong police deny wave of misconduct accusations, including arson, grinning officers and improper undercover work', *South China Morning Post*, 30 September 2019, available at: www.scmp.com/news/hong-kong/politics/article/3031042/hong-kong-police-deny-wave-misconduct-accusations-including, last accessed 20 June 2020.

395. Victoria Hui, *Beijing's Hard and Soft Repression in Hong Kong* (a paper published for the Foreign Policy Research Institute) (Elsevier Ltd, 2020) 289, 293.

396. Rebecca Lai and Austin Ramzy, '1,800 rounds of Tear Gas: Was the Hong Kong Police Response Appropriate?' *The New York Times*, 18 August 2019, available at: www.nytimes.com/interactive/2019/08/18/world/asia/hong-kong-tear-gas.html, last accessed 20 June 2020.

397. Barbara Marcolini, '"I Was Begging for Mercy": How Undercover Officers in Hong Kong Launched a Bloody Crackdown', *The New York Times*, 22 September 2019, available at: www.nytimes.com/video/world/asia/100000006702862/hong-kong-protests-police-officers.html, last accessed 19 June 2020.

398. Jeffie Lam, Danny Mok, and Alvin Lum, 'At least 45 injured as rod-wielding mob dressed in white rampages through Yuen Long MTR station, beating screaming protesters', *South China Morning Post*, 22 July 2020, available at: www.scmp.com/news/hong-kong/law-and-crime/article/3019524/least-10-injured-baton-wielding-mob-suspected-triad, last accessed 19 June 2020.

399. Phila Siu, Alvin Lum, and Zoe Low, 'Chaos on Hong Kong's MTR network as police chase protesters into station and arrest 63', *South China Morning Post*, 1 September 2020, available at: www.scmp.com/news/hong-kong/law-and-crime/article/3025241/chaos-hong-kongs-mtr-network-police-chase-protesters, last accessed 19 June 2020.

'Liberate Hong Kong, Revolution of Our Time', 'Heaven will eliminate the CCP [Chinese Communist Party]', 'Rather be a broken jade than an intact tile' (referring to a Chinese proverb meaning that one would 'rather die on one's feet than live on one's knees'), and so on. To prevent the situation at CUHK from becoming a repeat of Tiananmen Square, citizens poured into the campus to support the students. Students and citizens formed human chains to pass along supplies, including food, drinking water, medicine, gas masks, which piled up at the feet of the Goddess of Democracy, a statute which had been re-erected at every universities in Hong Kong after the Tiananmen crackdown. Many cars also parked across the road blocking police reinforcements from reaching the campus. A first aid volunteer (who was not a CUHK student) commented that the events even pushed some of their pro-Beijing classmates and relatives to support the protests. They went on to say:

> They gradually changed their sides. ... Some classmates were politically apathetic. Now they stand up. Meanwhile, the slogans people chanting have evolved from 'Hongkongers add oil' to 'Hongkongers revenge!' ... It shows that Hongkongers will never give up. They will resist, they will fight back. This military government suppresses people brutally. Nobody is a by-stander. We share the fate with our city, all of us must come out and fight against this tyranny.[400]

In addition to the assault at CUHK, Chris Tang, the new police commissioner, also assumed command of an assault on protesters at Hong Kong Polytechnic University (PolyU).[401] There was speculation that Tang had deliberately lured protesters to defend PolyU and then proceeded to arrest them.[402] On 17 and 18 November 2019, civilians from all over the city tried to protect those under siege on PolyU's campus. When supporters poured into nearby areas to divert the police, they were searched, forced to kneel, and arrested.

400. [No author], *Protection of the Chinese University of Hong Kong and the Hong Kong Polytechnic University* (Author's translation) (Epoch Times, 2019) 24.

401. Hui (N395) 294.

402. Chi Kin, Lo, '制造理大慘案、所為何事' [What Was the Purpose for Manufacturing the Polytechnic Tragedy?], *Hong Kong Citizens News*, 19 November 2019, available at: www.hkcnews.com/article/24918/圍困理工-1117理工衝突-鄧炳強-24918/制造理大慘案、所為何事?, last accessed 20 June 2020.

Media coverage of the events also shows police vehicles ramming into them at high speed, causing a stampede and countless traumatic injuries.[403] Parents of students trapped in PolyU also staged a sit-in protest on the footbridge to campus in the hopes of having their children safely returned to them and to express their discontent to the 'riot' charges being used against those involved. Dr Darren Mann described the scene in a medical journal:

> A photograph, widely circulated online, shows at least 16 individuals sitting on the ground with their hands bound behind their backs with zip-cords: they are wearing high-visibility vests with descriptions of Doctor, Nurse, and EMT (emergency medical technician). These people were all arrested for taking part in a riot. ... At least five doctors are known to have been arrested and detained by police for more than 24 hours. ... The actions of the [police] have fallen far below accepted international norms for the handling of volunteer emergency medical providers. The arrest of these personnel is almost unheard of in civilised countries and is incompatible with the compact of humanitarianism. Furthermore, the chilling effect can only serve to deter would-be volunteers from offering their services in the much-needed medical care of injured people in this ongoing uncivil war.[404]

In the police detention centres, the arrested were also denied access to their families and legal representatives for hours.[405] In the San Uk Ling detention centre, for example, some detainees suffered from bone fractures and internal

403. Kris Cheng, 'Hong Kong Police Accused of Driving Vehicles into Protestors during Clearance Operation', *Hong Kong Free Press*, 19 November 2019, available at: https://hongkongfp.com/2019/11/19/hong-kong-police-accused-driving-vehicles-protesters-clearance-operation/, last accessed 20 June 2020.

404. Darren Mann, 'International humanitarian norms are violated in Hong Kong', *The Lancet*, 21 November 2019, available at: www.thelancet.com/pdfs/journals/lancet/PIIS0140-6736(19)32909-5.pdf, last accessed 17 June 2020, 2067.

405. Kanis Leung, 'Arrest and Detention of Children over Hong Kong Anti-Government Protests Raised Questions on Police Treatment and Legal Process', *South China Morning Post*, 20 October 2019, available at: www.scmp.com/news/hong-kong/politics/article/3033706/arrest-and-detention-children-over-hong-kongs-anti, last accessed 19 June 2020.

bleeding, including in the brain and around essential organs.[406] Some female detainees have also claimed that they were sexually assaulted [407] and raped.[408]

It is notable that the riot police committed the atrocities outlined above without any hesitation, conscience, or mercy, and did so in front of media crews and news cameras.[409] This suggests that they believed that they were immune from redress for these actions.[410] Indeed, Carrie Lam, the chief executive of the Hong Kong SAR government, has even repeatedly praised the police force's 'outstanding performance' and denounced accusations concerning police violence.[411] In this climate, the phrase 'be you ever so high, the law is above you',[412] meaning that no one is above the law — one of the most important principles under the rule of law — is seemingly ignored by the Hong Kong SAR government.

---

406. Amnesty International, 'Hong Kong: Arbitrary Arrests, Brutal Beatings and Torture in Police Detention Revealed', 19 September 2019, available at: www.amnesty.org/en/latest/news/2019/09/hong-kong-arbitrary-arrests-brutal-beatings-and-torture-in-police-detention-revealed/, last accessed 20 June 2020.

407. Chris Lau, 'Hong Kong Student Who Accused Police of Sexual Violence against Protestors Has Taken Legal Advice and Plans Further Action', *South China Morning Post*, 11 October 2019, available at: www.scmp.com/news/hong-kong/law-and-crime/article/3032610/hong-kong-student-who-accused-police-sexual-violence, last accessed 20 June 2020.

408. Jennifer Creety, 'Grossly Unprofessional? Lawyers Slam Hong Kong Police for 'Privacy Breach' after Woman Accuses Officers of Gang Rape', *Hong Kong Free Press*, 12 November 2019, available at: https://hongkongfp.com/2019/11/12/grossly-unprofessional-lawyers-slam-hong-kong-police-privacy-breach-woman-accuses-officers-gang-rape/, last accessed 20 June 2020.

409. This is perhaps the best example of the Milgram Experiment in action; see Chapter One of this book. These events specifically show that ordinary people, simply doing their job and without any particular hostility on their part, can become agents in a terrible or destructive process, and that even when the destructive effects of their work become patently clear and they are asked to carry out actions incompatible with their fundamental standards of morality and conscience, relatively few people have the resources needed to resist authority.

410. Carol Anne Goodwin Jones, 'How Hong Kong Police Trained for Riots — And Why their Response to Protestors Has Been So Violent', *Hong Kong Free Press*, 24 September 2019, available at: https://hongkongfp.com/2019/09/24/hong-kong-police-trained-riots-response-protesters-violent/, last accessed 20 June 2020.

411. *Stand News*, '去信鄧炳強感謝帶領警隊　林鄭：警員傑出表現　值得高度讚賞' [Carrie Lam issues letter to Police Commissioner praising the force's 'outstanding performance'], 9 January 2020, available at: www.thestandnews.com/politics/去信鄧炳強感謝帶領警隊-林鄭-警員傑出表現-值得高度讚賞/, last accessed 20 June 2020; Caroline Kwok and Zinnia Lee, 'Hong Kong leader Carrie Lam rejects allegations of police brutality against protesters', *South China Morning Post*, 16 January 2020, available at: www.scmp.com/video/hong-kong/3046439/hong-kong-leader-carrie-lam-rejects-allegations-police-brutality-against, last accessed 20 June 2020.

412. *Gouriet v Union of Post Office Workers* [1977] QB 729, 762 (Lord Denning), quoting Thomas Fuller (1608–1661).

There are two ways to explain this. First, the fact that individual behaviour of those in power is likely controlled by role and situation, rather than personal characteristics and traits (as revealed in the Stanford Prison Experiment),[413] is further exacerbated by the blind obedience to authority of those in a subordinate position (also revealed in the Milgram Experiment).[414] Such obedience is fuelled by a lack of social capital (e.g., having moderate incomes to make ends meet or even being heavily indebted, being required to be politically neutral as a civil servant, etc.) to resist their orders, however much they may disagree. According to a police officer, the recent political crisis in Hong Kong has been regarded by the force's management as a way for him and his colleagues to show their loyalty, pushing them to resort to violent tactics to crack down on increasingly radical protests, despite the fact that the officer had been trained to handle such situations differently and to embody different values (i.e., to protect citizens by upholding the rule of law, to be impartial and compassionate, to respect the rights of members of the public, and so on).[415] However, the officer was shocked to find that 'we've become a tool of the authorities for "stability maintenance"', and '[o]ur top officials are hiding and we've become their shields'. In addition to disapproving of his colleagues' behaviour, the officer exclaimed:

> When we were in the academy, we were taught to use only the minimum amount of force. It's not for us to deliver punishment. But now, the majority of the police think the 'rioters' need to be punished ... they attack people indiscriminately, even non-protesters. ... The awful thing is, the majority of police don't see it as a problem. ... When they watch footage of police beating people, they shout for joy: 'Yeah, we're hitting the cockroaches!' ... They don't give any consideration to their high ideals of freedom and democracy. ... It's the 'Lucifer effect — power drives people crazy. They're angry and they need an outlet. But this is sacrificing the reputation of the police force.[416]

413. See Chapter One of this book.

414. Ibid.

415. Verna Yu, 'Hong Kong's reluctant police officer: "It's not for us to deliver punishment"', *The Guardian*, 29 October 2019, available at: www.theguardian.com/world/2019/oct/29/hong-kongs-reluctant-policeman-its-not-for-us-to-deliver-punishment, last accessed 2 April 2020.

416. Ibid.

Although this officer, and probably many others, has tried to make his colleagues see things from another perspective, this effort has only resulted in him being labelled a traitor in the force.[417] When asked whether he had thought about resigning, the officer, in his 40s, said he had a young family to support so that it made him difficult to do so.[418]

A second reason for the use of disproportionate force relates to bias. Bias is a natural human response, occurring consciously and subconsciously. In executing their duties, many police officers have been subjected to the extreme aspects of the prevailing 'complaint culture' [419] and have even been personally insulted, sometimes with foul language. They have felt disrespected in these situations, which even arise in their handling of minor offences (e.g., unlawful parking, unlawful obstruction, etc.). Not surprisingly, these police officers may not only develop hatred or bias towards these combative individuals, but this feeling may also be extended towards anyone who may try to rationally argue a legitimate concern regarding the officer's actions or behaviour during the execution of their duties. In fact, owing to prolonged disrespect, a majority of police officers have admitted to feeling angry, even going so far as to call for laws against insulting police officers.[420] This anger and bias, being extended from combative individuals to civilised citizens, is perhaps why many on the force have resorted to increasingly brutal acts in their attempts to suppress the anti-government protests. Furthermore, being required to work over-time to tackle the ever-increasing anti-government protests at the expense of their private lives is also a factor which makes them turn to violence against the protesters. They rationalise their actions based on the belief that greater force will deter protesters from any future participation. The lack of accountability for their actions also fuels these feelings. Indeed, when dealing with protests, riot police officers now wear black masks and do not show their warrant cards or police

417. Ibid.

418. Ibid.

419. As discussed in Chapter One of this book, this phenomenon has resulted from the role of citizens being changed from simply 'the governed' to 'recipients of services'. They also believe that as taxpayers they are entitled to have some oversight of the standard of services rendered by the government and can complain if that standard is not met.

420. Christy Leung, 'Hong Kong police chief steps up call for law against insulting officers', *South China Morning Post*, 27 January 2018, available at: www.scmp.com/news/hong-kong/law-crime/article/2130848/hong-kong-police-chief-steps-call-law-against-insulting, last accessed 2 April 2020.

numbers on their uniforms,[421] and even if evidence is provided of their conduct, police management turn a blind eye to blatant uses of disproportionate force.

As a result, animosity between police and citizens has unavoidably escalated to an alarming level, as evidenced by the ever-increasing amounts of tear gas, rubber bullets, beatings, and water cannon usage to suppress the protesters. On 1 October 2019, a police officer even fired a live round during a struggle with an 18-year-old secondary school student, injuring his chest.[422] Later, on 11 November 2019, a 21-year-old man was also shot by a police officer at close range in Sai Wan Ho even though the rationale for the officer pulling his weapon has been doubted in the media.[423] In the months of ongoing protests, there have been countless arrests. Reflecting on the ever-increasing number of people being arrested, Victoria Hui stated that the reason the police have resorted to this tactic (at the executive level) is because 'Hong Kong's judiciary is relatively autonomous and many of the arrested would not be convicted and sentenced'.[424] However, this is only partly correct because, in *Secretary for Justice v Wong Chi Fung, Law Kwun Chung and Chow Yong Kang Alex*,[425] the CFA endorsed the stricter sentencing guidelines proposed by the Court of Appeal for future unlawful protests. Although these new guidelines were not retrospectively applied to Joshua Wong, Nathan Law, and Alex Chow in the case, they will result in tougher punishments in future cases.[426]

421. Ibid.

422. *South China Morning Post*, 'Protester shot by police, trail of destruction across Hong Kong, while Beijing celebrates National Day', 2 October 2019, available at: www.scmp.com/news/hong-kong/politics/article/3031161/protester-shot-police-trail-destruction-across-hong-kong, last accessed 20 June 2020.

423. Alvin Lum, 'Hong Kong protests: man shot by police officer in Sai Wan Ho hits out at 'ridiculous' use of live round at such close range', *South China Morning Post*, 23 November 2019, available at: www.scmp.com/news/hong-kong/politics/article/3039078/hong-kong-protests-man-shot-police-officer-sai-wan-ho-hits, last accessed 20 June 2020.

424. Hui (N395) 289. See also Hong Kong Watch (N327) 29–30, citing that in *Secretary for Justice v Wong Chi Fung, Law Kwun Chung and Chow Yong Kang Alex* [2018] HKCFA 4, [133]–[134], the CFA quashed the Court of Appeal's decision that the original sentences of Joshua Wong, Nathan Law, and Alex Chow (80 and 120 hours of community service, and a three-week jail sentence with one year suspension, respectively) were not heavy enough to act as a deterrent for future incidents.

425. Ibid., *Wong Chi Fung*, [120]–[125].

426. Hong Kong Watch (N327) 30.

Indiscriminate beatings by the police have also given rise to rumours of covered-up deaths. These events and rumours, along with some widely circulated stories about physical and sexual abuses (both at the scene and in police detention centres), have ultimately led to an unprecedented level of anger and resentment in the general public against the police. The protesters, in response to the above, increasingly resort to radical acts in what they see as justified retaliation. In consequence, masked protesters have thrown bricks and Molotov cocktails (i.e., petrol bombs) at the police, trashed railway stations and shops with ties to Beijing, lit street fires, and even attacked police (or people suspected of being undercover officers) and other pro-Beijing supporters. In short, when law enforcement officers break the law themselves, civil resistance become inevitable.

When considering the above in the context of proportionality and the decision in the *Public Order Ordinance* case, the primary question is: can the prior constraint procedures be defended as being necessary in a democratic society for achieving the legitimate aim of protecting citizens and maintaining public order? The answer to this question is, argues Brabyn, definitively in the negative.[427] However, the most significant development in this case is that the Court held that the government had a positive obligation to assist and provide for the right of peaceful public assembly and demonstration.[428] This decision was based on the acceptance of the Hong Kong SAR government of a positive obligation in its report to the UN Human Rights Committee, but this positive obligation was obviously not taken into account by the government when they assessed recent events.

8.8.3.4 The *Prohibition of Face Covering Regulation* Case

One case arising during the public assemblies and processions outlined above was directly related to the Prohibition of Face Covering Regulation.[429] This regulation was implemented during the protests against the proposed extradition bill in October 2019, some of which have ended in outbreaks of

427. Brabyn (N360) 304.

428. *Leung Kwok Hung* (N24) [2005] 3 HKLRD 164, 180–181.

429. Prohibition of Face Covering Regulations (N233).

violence.[430] As the majority of demonstrators were wearing facial coverings, it was difficult for the police to identify perpetrators who were allegedly responsible for violent and illegal acts which took place during thesse protests. Thus, the chief executive in council enacted the Prohibition of Face Covering Regulation by implementing the Emergency Regulations Ordinance, in order to facilitate police investigation and to serve as a deterrent against the violent and illegal acts of masked perpetrators. Section 3 of the Prohibition of Face Covering Regulations restricts a person from using any facial covering that is likely to prevent identification at gatherings, and those who commit an offence are punishable with a fine of HK$25,000 and imprisonment for one year.

A number of qualified rights (i.e., rights that are not absolute and may be subject to lawful restrictions) are engaged by this restriction, including freedom of expression or speech (i.e., Article 16 of the BORO and Article 27 of the Basic Law); freedoms of assembly, procession, and demonstration (i.e., Article 17 of the BORO and Article 27 of the Basic Law); and the right of privacy (i.e., Article 14 of the BORO). Therefore, its constitutionality was challenged on a four-step proportionality basis.

Relying on *SAS v France*,[431] *Yaker v France*,[432] and *Villeneuve v Montreal*,[433] the Court of First Instance held that the restrictions under section 3 are rationally connected to legitimate societal aims to deter those wishing to break the law (by eliminating the emboldening effect of facial covering) and facilitate law enforcement, investigation, and prosecution.[434] However, the Court went on to state that the restrictions sub-paragraphs (1), (b), (c), and (d) [435] impose

430. *Leung Kwok Hung* (N231) [2019] HKCFI 2820, [3].

431. (2015) 60 EHRR 11.

432. Communication No. 2747/2016, 17 July 2018, UN Doc. CCPR/C/123/D/2807/2016 with ECtHR.

433. *Villeneuve v Montreal (City of)* 2016 QCCS 2888.

434. *Leung Kwok Hung* (N231) [2019] HKCFI 2820, [130] and [193(5)].

435. Section 3 of the Regulation reads: (1) A person must not use any facial covering that is likely to prevent identification while the person is at — (a) an unlawful assembly (whether or not the assembly is a riot within the meaning of section 19 of Cap 245 [Public Order Ordinance]); (b) unauthorized assembly; (c) a public meeting that — (i) takes place under section 7(1) of Cap 245; and (ii) does not fall within paragraph (a) or (b); or (d) a public procession that — (i) takes place under section 3(1) of Cap 245; and (ii) does not fall within paragraph (a) or (b).

on fundamental rights went further than was reasonably necessary to achieve those objectives,[436] explaining that it had to consider

> the reach of the impugned restrictions to perfectly lawful and peaceful public gatherings, the width of the restrictions affecting public gatherings for whatever causes, the lack of clarity as regards the application of the restrictions to persons present at the public gathering other than as participants, the breadth of the prohibition against the use of facial covering of any type and worn for whatever reasons, the absence of any mechanism for a case-by-case evaluation or assessment of the risk of violence or crimes such as would justify the application of the restriction, the lack of robust evidence on the effectiveness of the measure, and lastly the importance that the law attaches to the freedom of expression, freedom of assembly, procession and demonstration, and the right to privacy.[437]

In short, the Court was of the view that the restrictions of rights imposed by these specific sub-sections are too wide, and thus not proportionate to the legitimate aims sought by the imposition of those restrictions.[438]

Overall, what the *Prohibition of Face Covering Regulation* case suggests, among other things, is that if the restrictions imposed by the legislation, be it primary or secondary, are too wide and cover those who should not be punished if they participate in lawful and peaceful public gatherings, then the courts will not hesitate to hold them unconstitutional owing to their 'wholesale' restrictive effect on those fundamental rights. The same result will also occur for legislation that lacks clarity concerning how the restrictions are applied to persons present at the public gathering but are not participants (e.g., passers-by) as well as that lacking a mechanism to review the risk of violence or crimes on a case-by-case basis. However, the Court of Appeal reversed the Court of First Instance's decision and said that the lower court had failed to appreciate the true nature of the Emergency Regulations Ordinance and the Prohibition of Face Covering

436. *Leung Kwok Hung* (N231) [2019] HKCFI 2820, [195(5)].

437. Ibid., [166].

438. Ibid.

Regulation, and that given the requirement for an urgent response to tackle emergency or public danger, the laws in question are necessarily wide in scope and thus proportionate to the aims to be achieved.[439]

8.9 Poverty, Social Welfare, and the Enforcement of Socio-Economic Rights in Hong Kong

In Hong Kong, although the majority of citizens enjoy a high standard of living, there is significant economic and social inequality, and little recognition of a justiciable right to socio-economic benefits.[440] Worst of all, even though poverty has been a serious concern in Hong Kong for several decades, the situation has deteriorated further in recent years. This is evident in the increased Gini coefficient — an index from 0 to 1 that measures the wealth gap — which rose from 0.537 in 2011 to a record high of 0.539 in 2016.[441] Even more ironic is that Hong Kong has enjoyed significant economic growth over this period and in the decades prior, with the gross domestic product increasing at an average annual rate of 5.1 percent in real terms. The Hong Kong government attributes this economic growth to its market-led and 'business-friendly' policies, which include using a simple tax system, applying low tax rates, and limiting expenditures on social welfare. The government's stated goal is to 'sustain workers' incentive to work and entrepreneurs' incentive to invest.[442]

In general, the philosophy of the government is to be non-interventionist and to encourage self-reliance. Although supporters of the low tax policy claim that low taxes and fiscally conservative policies are essential to Hong Kong's continued economic growth, critics have argued that these provisions

439. *Kwok Wing Hang v Chief Executive in Council; Leung Kwok Hung v Secretary for Justice* [2020] HKCA 192, [126].

440. Carole Petersen, 'From British Colony to Special Administrative Region of China: Embracing Human Rights in Hong Kong' in Randall Peerenboom, Carole Peterson, and Albert Chen, *Human Rights in Asia: A Comparative Legal Study of Twelve Asian Jurisdictions, France and the USA* (Routledge 2006) 225.

441. Cannix Yau and Viola Zhou, 'What hope for the poorest? Hong Kong wealth gap hits record high', *South China Morning Post*, 9 June 2017, available at: www.scmp.com/news/hong-kong/economy/article/2097715/what-hope-poorest-hong-kong-wealth-gap-hits-record-high, last accessed 26 May 2020.

442. 'Public Finance' section of the government's website, available at: www.yearbook.gov.hk/2001/ehtml/04/04-04f.htm, last accessed 20 June 2020.

only protect the rich, increase income disparity,[443] and limit the ability of the government to assist disadvantaged groups. The government does not take responsibility for this; rather it offers the excuse that the best way to assist the poor is to promote economic growth and create opportunities for people to 'lift themselves' out of poverty. However, this assertion has created concern for the UN Committee on Economic, Social, and Cultural Rights (UNESCR Committee), which has concluded that Hong Kong's *laissez-faire* policies impede the realisation of socio-economic rights.[444]

As Carole Petersen has noted, Hong Kong's economic policies are not the product of a democratic process, but are in fact adopted by the appointed government that is heavily influenced by the wealthy business class. The government and the policies it implements are also impacted by Beijing's hostility to the democracy movement. This *status quo* is unlikely to change in the near future.[445] Although the Hong Kong SAR government is more transparent than the Chinese government, it has declined to introduce 'access of information' laws, implying that some rights violations have probably been hidden and have remained undetected from public scrutiny.[446]

Under Chapter III of the Basic Law, there are many provisions that guarantee, to a limited extent, socio-economic rights, such as welfare benefits, retirement security of the labour force, etc.[447] While Article 9 of the International Covenant on Economic, Social, and Cultural Rights (ICESCR) recognises the 'right of everyone to social security and social insurance' and Article 39 of the Basic Law stipulates that provisions of the ICESCR as applied to Hong Kong shall be in force and be implemented through the laws of Hong Kong, there has been no wholesale incorporation of the ICESCR in Hong Kong.[448]

443. *Second Report of the Hong Kong Administrative Region of the People's Republic of China in the Light of the International Covenant on Economic Social and Cultural Rights*, 2003, [11.9]–[11.10].

444. Petersen (N440) 225.

445. Ibid.

446. Ibid.

447. See, for example, Basic Law, Art 36 (the right to social welfare).

448. Karen Kong, 'Social Justice and Social Rights in Hong Kong: Recent Judicial Review Developments and Proposals for Legislative Change' in Surya Deva (ed), *Socio-Economic Rights in Emerging Free Markets: Comparative Insights from India and China* (Routledge 2015) 187 and 192.

The observance of the ICESCR in Hong Kong can be traced back to the mid-1970s. During that period, Hong Kong, being a colony of the UK, became a party to the ICESCR when the British government ratified and extended it to a number of dependent territories in 1976. However, the British government entered several reservations with respect to Hong Kong, including the right to postpone equal pay for equal work in the private sector.[449] In this climate, Hong Kong has lagged behind the UK in the field of anti-discrimination law, and did not prohibit sex discrimination in the private sector until the enactment of equal opportunities laws and the establishment of the EOC in 1996. This reservation was finally withdrawn in 2001 when the PRC ratified the ICESCR and lodged amended reservations and declarations on behalf of Hong Kong.

This seems to imply that there should be some laws governing the entitlement to socio-economic rights. However, not all social welfare services are regulated by legislation. In fact, this field is dealt with almost entirely as a matter of executive policy. Although some socio-economic rights are, as Karen Kong has argued, 'entrenched' under the Basic Law,[450] only selected welfare services have a legislative basis.[451] Many of these rights are administrative and policy based, including the Comprehensive Social Security Assistance (CSSA). Regarding the position of the government, Hong Kong residents, as explained by Carrie Lam, the then Director of Social Welfare (now the Chief Executive) in the Hong Kong SAR, do not have a 'right' to social security.[452] However, poverty, especially among the elderly, is a significant problem in Hong Kong. Some non-governmental organisations have estimated that almost one-quarter of the elderly population lives in poverty.[453] In its second report under the ICESCR

449. ICESCR, Art 7.

450. Kong (N448) 187.

451. Source from the Social Welfare Department website, available at: www.swd.gov.hk/en/index/site_relatedleg/, last accessed 1 February 2020.

452. May Sin-mi Hon, 'As she defends new restrictions, Carrie Lam says welfare is not a right', *South China Morning Post*, 27 February 2003.

453. Human Rights Monitor, 'Submission to Pre-Sessional Working Group', 2000, cited by Randall Peerenboom, Carole Peterson, and Albert Chen, *Human Rights in Asia: A Comparative Legal Study of Twelve Asian Jurisdictions, France and the USA* (Routledge 2006) 246.

in 2003,[454] the government claimed that provisions of the ICESCR had been incorporated into Hong Kong's domestic law through several articles of the Basic Law (i.e., Articles 27, 36, 137, 144, and 149) and through provisions of over 50 ordinances listed in an annex to the report.[455] The government argued that 'specific measures of this kind more effectively protect [the ICESCR] than would the mere reiteration in domestic law of the [ICESCR] provisions themselves'.[456]

Enforcement of socio-economic rights in Hong Kong is also a matter of concern. There have been numerous debates regarding how the government should equally distribute its resources to relieve socio-economic inequalities in the region, the examples of which consist of raising allowances for the elderly to meet rising food and commodity prices, introducing a universal non-means-test-based pension scheme,[457] and increasing the supply of subsidised public housing units for low income groups.

First of all, to fully comply with the Paris Principles as enshrined by the UN,[458] the Hong Kong SAR government should have established a general human rights commission. However, it declined to do so. Rather, it argued that various specialist institutions, including the Ombudsman, the Privacy Commissioner, and the EOC, had fulfilled the role of a human rights commission. However, the international monitoring bodies have not accepted this response because these institutions all have limited jurisdiction, and do not have the broad powers and functions that a human rights commission should enjoy. Furthermore, the independence of these enforcement bodies has been undermined recently. As far as equality is concerned, the Hong Kong SAR government itself is not

454. This report was submitted to the United Nations in 2003 as part of the PRC's initial report under the ICESCR; see the Constitutional and Mainland Affairs Bureau, which provides the full text of all reports submitted by the Hong Kong SAR government under various human rights treaties, available at: www.cmab.gov.hk/en/issues/human.htm, last accessed 17 September 2015.

455. Ibid., [2.9].

456. Ibid., [2.3].

457. Phila Siu and Jennifer Ngo, 'War of words: Carrie Lam says Hong Kong government adviser on retirement protection doesn't fully understand public financing', *South China Morning Post*, 23 December 2015, available at: www.scmp.com/news/hong-kong/economy/article/1894060/war-words-carrie-lam-says-hong-kong-government-adviser?page=all, last accessed 26 May 2020.

458. The Paris Principles relate to the status and functioning of national institutions for the protection and promotion of human rights, more information is available at: www.un.org/ruleoflaw/files/PRINCI~5.PDF, last accessed 1 February 2020.

immune from infringing equality rights, and two government departments were held liable for employment discrimination in *K, Y, and W v the Secretary for Justice*.[459] Even when it comes to civil liberties, many commentators also fear that a gradual decline is underway. This is not only due to post-1997 changes in legislation and policy, but it is also related to a growing climate of self-censorship which is exacerbated by the enormous economic and political influence of, and even intervention by, the Mainland authorities.[460]

Since the ICESCR has never been incorporated into Hong Kong law, the rights listed in this Covenant remain largely unenforceable in Hong Kong courts. Although Hong Kong lawyers have attempted to cite the ICESCR in legal actions against the government, the courts have not been receptive. In *Chan To Foon v Director of Immigration* [461] and *Chan Mei Yee v Director of Immigration*,[462] the applicants sought judicial review regarding their deportation orders and cited Article 10 of the ICESCR to support their claims that they had a right to re-unite with their families in Hong Kong. In both cases, the arguments failed because the judges held that the ICESCR was 'promotional or aspirational' in nature.[463] The courts have repeated this in other judgments, describing the ICESCR rights as 'aspirational or promotional' [464] and stating that they do not create any 'absolute obligations'. In *Chan To Foon*, the Court even said that the general wording used in the ICESCR (e.g., Article 2(1) which states 'achieving progressively the full realization of the rights') makes its provisions incapable of being enforced by law as this can be interpreted as meaning that rights listed in the ICESCR only need to be implemented as and when any 'existing social duties' are overcome.[465]

The UNESCR Committee has strongly disputed this, urging the Hong Kong government 'not to argue in court proceedings that the ICESCR is only

459. [2000] HKC 796. See also Carole Petersen, 'The Right to Equality in the Public Sector' (2002) 32 *HKLJ* 110.

460. See, for example, *South China Morning Post*, 'Topic: Hong Kong Bookseller Disappearances', multiple publication dates, available at: www.scmp.com/topics/hong-kong-bookseller-disappearances, last accessed 26 May 2020.

461. [2001] 3 HKLRD 109.

462. Unreported, HCAL77/1999.

463. *Chan To Foon* (N461) [76]; *Chan Mei Yee* (N462) [42]–[46].

464. *Mok Chi Hung v Director of Immigration* [2001] 2 HKLRD 125, 135.

465. *Chan To Foon* (N461) 132.

"promotional or aspirational" in nature'.[466] The government later stated: 'We note the Committee's observation that the [ICESCR] is not merely "promotional or aspirational" in nature and accept that it creates binding obligations at the international level'.[467] However, Kong has argued that the use of the words 'at the international level' in this response may indicate that the government does not consider the ICESCR to be part of domestic law, despite the reference to it in Article 39 of the Basic Law.[468]

Kong has also argued that even though the current legal status of the ICESCR is an unincorporated treaty in Hong Kong, the courts should still expect the decision-maker to act in compliance with the treaty when exercising their discretion and that the person affected should be given an opportunity to be heard if the decision-maker infringes the rights as enshrined in the treaty.[469] The *Chan Mei Yee* case concerned a challenge by an illegal immigrant mother against her deportation. She argued that her right to family life would be infringed if she was deported back to Mainland China because she would be unable to take care of her sick child who was a Hong Kong permanent resident. Despite holding that the ICESCR was 'promotional or aspirational', Cheung J cited the Australian decision in *Minister of State for Immigration and Ethnic Affairs v Rah Hin Teoh*[470] and stated:

> In my view, the approach of the High Court of Australia ... should be adopted ... [A] husband and a child who are Hong Kong permanent residents clearly have the legitimate expectation that when the government is to remove their wife or mother, it should take into account the international covenants on the importance of family and welfare of the children. Otherwise the adaptation of the international covenants would ... be a case of window dressing only.[471]

466. Concluding Observations of the Committee on Economic, Social and Cultural Rights on the Initial Report of the Hong Kong Special Administrative Region, 11 May 2001, E/C12/1/Add 58, [16] and [27].

467. *Second Report of the Hong Kong Administrative Region of the People's Republic of China in the Light of the International Covenant on Economic Social and Cultural Rights* (N443) [1.12].

468. Kong (N448) 193.

469. Ibid.

470. [1994–1995] 183 CLR 273.

471. *Chan Mei Yee* (N462) 6.

This assertion is compatible with Paul Craig's 'modified theory of *ultra vires*' [472] in that there is an indirect relationship between judicial principles of good administration and parliamentary intention.[473] It follows that in the absence of contrary evidence, it is assumed that Parliament intends to legislate in conformity with the rule of law, so any exercise of governmental power should be just and principled. This analogy should also be extended to other scenarios. For instance, it should be assumed that when the government, acting on behalf of Parliament, signs and ratifies a treaty, there is a presumption that they will observe and do not intend to breach international law, including specific treaty obligations therein [474] (i.e., the *Teoh* principle [475]).

Traditionally, the government has not had explicit plans for reducing poverty, insisting that the best strategy is simply to encourage general economic growth. Since Hong Kong enjoys a higher standard of living than the rest of Asia, it feels that its approach is correct. Nevertheless, the UNESCR Committee disagrees, and in 2001, it concluded that it was 'gravely concerned about the widespread and unacceptable incidence of poverty' in Hong Kong and 'deeply concerned' by the lack of any comprehensive anti-poverty strategies.[476] The government has since established a Commission on Poverty, followed by the establishment of official poverty line in 2013.

According to Petersen, this high degree of inequality and lack of justiciable rights to social and economic benefits have, to a large extent, resulted from the lack of democratic development in Hong Kong after 1997.[477] Chan concurs with this premise, explaining that many Hong Kong people have been frustrated

472. Paul Craig, 'Competing Models of Judicial Review' (1999) *PL* 428, 429. Also mentioned in Chapter Four of this book.

473. Ibid. See also Christopher Forsyth, 'Of Figs Leaves and Fairy Tales: The *Ultra Vires* Doctrine, the Sovereignty of Parliament and Judicial Review' (1996) 55(1) *CLJ* 122; Mark Elliott, 'The *Ultra Vires* Doctrine in a Constitutional Setting: Still the Central Principle of Administrative Law' (1999) 58(1) *CLJ* 129.

474. *Salomon v Commissioners of Customs and Excise* [1967] 2 QB 116, 143–144 (Lord Diplock).

475. In *Teoh*, the Court held that a state's treaty ratification generated a legitimate expectation 'absent statutory or executive indications to the contrary'; see *Rah Hin Teoh* (N470) 365 (Mason CJ, Deane, Toohey, and Guadron JJ).

476. Concluding Observations of the Committee on Economic, Social and Cultural Rights on the Initial Report of the Hong Kong Special Administrative Region (N466) [18]–[19].

477. Petersen (N440) 224–264.

in their campaign for democracy.[478] After campaigning for 30 plus years, they are not prepared to wait any longer, as reflected in the Occupy Central Movement in late September 2014, which called for civil disobedience if the government did not allow genuine universal suffrage. For some, they want to be in greater control of their lives at a time when things seem to be desperate for them, particularly with regard to their economic prospects.[479] As property prices rise, the gap between the rich and the poor keeps widening and the prospects for high-paying employment are diminishing. These changes leave young people with no hope for their future. Some even believe that all of these problems have primarily resulted from the incompetence of the Hong Kong SAR government in general or from the then chief executive Leung Chun Ying, who was plagued with scandal after scandal.[480] As Chan quotes in an interview, this chief executive opposed full democracy in Hong Kong because it would give the vote to poorer people who would, if they turn the tables, demand more generous social welfare policies.[481]

Although democracy is one of the essentials factors necessary to secure good governance (in that it provides that every person should be allowed to have a say in how they are governed, with broadmindedness, tolerance, plurality, etc.), it is oppressed by the wealthy business classes. At present, the elite of Hong Kong have significant influence over the appointed government and also of the LegCo, by virtue of the functional constituency seats. They can therefore easily defeat proposals to improve workers' rights or to increase spending on education and social security. Conservatives often speak of the need to preserve economic stability in Hong Kong. Although what business

478. Johannes Chan, 'Hong Kong's Umbrella Movement' (2014) 103(6) *The Round Table: The Commonwealth Journal of International Affairs* 571 and 578, available at: www.tandfonline.com/eprint/VuA9DJBgi6TNPWXcX3QF/full, last accessed 1 February 2020.

479. Ibid. See also Toby Carroll, 'Hong Kong's pro-democracy movement is about inequality. The elite knows it', *The Guardian*, 28 July 2014, available at: www.theguardian.com/commentisfree/2014/jul/28/hong-kongs-pro-democracy-movement-is-about-inequality-the-elite-knows-it, last accessed 26 May 2020.

480. James Griffiths and Benjamin Robertson, 'CY Leung faces separate probes of HK$50 million deal with Australian firm', *South China Morning Post*, 10 October 2014, available at: www.scmp.com/article/1613244/cy-leung-faces-separate-probes-hk50-million-deal-australian-firm, last accessed 26 May 2020; *South China Morning Post*, 'Topic: CY Leung Left Luggage Saga', multiple publication dates, available at: www.scmp.com/topics/cy-leung-left-luggage-saga, last accessed 26 May 2020.

481. Chan (N478) 578.

leaders are referring to, albeit indirectly, is their desire to preserve Hong Kong's economic prosperity, it is suspected that they fear that an elected government would give in to demands for greater social welfare benefits and that Hong Kong's low tax regime would then gradually disappear. This 'majoritarian' system of law-making (i.e., the pro-business legislature in Hong Kong) offers no protection to society when an idea they support is not conducive to the 'public good'. Such majorities might simply be prepared to sacrifice their region's long-term welfare to gain a short-term, sectional advantage.

However, without democratic checks, there is a danger that Hong Kong will become increasingly plagued by cronyism, both from within the region and from across the border. This would, in the long term, adversely affect not only economic development, but also human rights and the rule of law, the latter being an 'absolute essential' to preserve Hong Kong's economic prosperity. As it is unlikely the public will be able to elect their own government at any time in the near future, it is important to maintain other checks on the executive power. The LegCo cannot completely fulfil this role since it is only partly elected and has limited powers. As a result, the courts are increasingly viewed by the general public as the final guardians of human rights and fair play in post-1997 Hong Kong.

8.10 Legal Mobilisation: Shifting 'Political Opportunities' from the Legislature to the Judiciary

Unlike Britain, Hong Kong has been experiencing a growth of 'legal mobilisation' since 1997. Individual citizens and minorities have started invoking their legal rights and using litigation to defend or develop their rights against the government, the reasons of which involve, among other things, prolonged democratic deficit in Hong Kong [482] and China's tightening of 'political opportunities' [483] available to pro-democracy politicians by weakening, and thus marginalising, their

482. Chan (N5) 143–174.

483. Tam (N7) 5 and 90.

political influence in the LegCo.[484] Moreover, legal mobilisation in post-colonial Hong Kong must also be regarded as a social movement tactic — the pursuit of the objectives of a social movement through institutionalised channels, as opposed to outsider tactics like demonstrations and strikes.[485]

Among these reasons, the effectiveness of the post-handover LegCo to act as a guardian to monitor the Hong Kong SAR government is a matter of concern. Shortly before the handover, the LegCo, having the mature committee system and rules of procedure, backed up by healthy funding, professional staff, and management by an independent statutory LegCo Commission, had long been well-equipped to carry out its constitutional role of monitoring the government. However, such success has not been maintained, in great part owing to a serious flaw which ultimately threatens to render the whole institution dysfunctional. This flaw is the retention of a decisive proportion of anachronistic functional constituencies in LegCo's composition. According to Dr Ng, this is fatal because the effectiveness of the LegCo is highly dependent on the active co-operation of the government and the unity of purpose amongst members, among other things.[486] If the government, for whatever reason, adopts an un-cooperative stance, then the LegCo has no alternative but to resort to using its coercive powers, for instance, by compelling officials to produce documents or give evidence.[487] Nevertheless, such coercion can only be exercised collectively, by way of a resolution supported by a majority in each of the two groups of members, one being returned by the geographical constituencies and the other by the functional constituencies.[488] The government can count on the support of pro-Beijing councillors, who make up a majority of the functional constituency seats, to veto an unfavourable proposal which it does not want to face. In such a situation, Dr Ng claims that the only countervailing force is strong reaction in the community, as reflected in the 500,000-person demonstration on 1 July 2003, which she specifically mentions, and that such increased reliance on mass mobilisation actually means that the LegCo has failed as a forum for

484. Ibid., 18.

485. Ibid., 5.

486. Margaret Ng, 'The Legislature' in Chan and Lim (N91) [9.085].

487. Legislative Council (Powers and Privileges) Ordinance, Cap 382, Part III and Part IV.

488. Ng (N486) [9.085].

rational resolution of conflicting interests through debate.[489] Similarly, Chan has commented that

> the functional constituency system in Hong Kong enables a powerful elite group to dominate the legislature, and the elected representatives of the people have only a weak voice. The Government is able to push through any legislation by engaging sufficient support from some elected representatives and the majority of the functional constituency representatives. On some occasions this was done irrespective of the merits or reasoning of the opposition. When political dialogue is dominated by mistrust and suspicion, when the political process is no longer dictated by reasoning, when opposite views are treated with hostility, ridicule or even contempt, and when broadmindedness, tolerance and plurality which form the basis of a democratic society are conspicuously absent in the political process, those who are frustrated or disillusioned could only resort either to street politics or to the court.[490]

Additional criticism and worry were sparked in Hong Kong by the NPCSC's *31-August* decision in 2014 regarding the process for nominating chief executive candidates,[491] which effectively deprives Hong Kong people of having a genuine choice to elect their chief executive, and the 'White Paper on Hong Kong' issued by the Chinese central government saying that judges, as part of the administration, have to be 'patriotic'.[492] Prior to the *31-August* decision, the Chinese central government made it clear that the chief executive has to be 'patriotic', that the nomination has to be made by the nomination committee only, and that the committee's composition should be modelled on the incumbent

489. Ibid.

490. Chan (N5) 166–167.

491. Decision of the NPCSC on Issues Relating to the Selection of the Chief Executive of the Hong Kong Special Administrative Region by Universal Suffrage and on the Method for Forming the Legislative Council of the Hong Kong Special Administrative Region in the Year 2016, available at: www.2017.gov.hk/filemanager/template/en/doc/20140831b.pdf, last accessed 1 February 2020.

492. On 10 June 2014, the Chinese state council issued a White Paper on 'The Practice of the "One Country, Two System" Policy in the Hong Kong Special Administrative Region', saying that, among others, judges, as part of the administration, have to be 'patriotic', available at: www.fmcoprc.gov.hk/eng/xwdt/gsxw/t1164057.htm, last accessed 1 February 2020.

Election Committee, the composition of which is four equally represented sectors: (a) industrial, commercial, and financial; (b) professional; (c) labour, social services, religious, and other; and (d) current and former political officeholders, that generally track the functional constituencies in the LegCo.

Although the composition of the Election Committee appears to be broadly representative, this is far from the case. Aside from the 39 members of the LegCo who are returned on a geographical basis, others of the Election Committee are returned by a small number of voters, including corporate ones. However, there is no clear procedure of how a corporation becomes a voter. Owing to the above, Chan has opined that it comes as no surprise that there is no confidence from the general public that this nomination committee is representative enough, let alone capable of representing the views of the Hong Kong people.[493]

Shortly after the report submitted by the then chief executive Leung Chun Ying in July 2014, the NPCSC, on 31 August 2014, decided that the composition, the number of voters, and the method of formation of the nomination committee for 2017 would be the same as the Election Committee in 2012, and that each candidate would need the endorsement of over 50 percent of the members of the nomination committee, which is much higher than the 12.5 percent that was adopted for nomination in the previous Election Committee. This decision was more conservative than the community expected because it not only excludes the possibility that a candidate favoured by the pan-democrats will succeed in the nomination, but also leaves no room for moderate candidates.[494] Against this background, Chan believes the decision effectively leaves the pan-democrats with two limited choices — either to use their representation in the LegCo to vote down the electoral legislation that the government would introduce to implement the decision or to take the issue to the streets.[495]

Both happened. First, in a vote on 18 June 2015, the government failed to obtain the support of two-thirds of all 70 LegCo members for its proposal on

493. Chan (N478) 576.

494. Ibid.

495. Ibid.

universal suffrage of the chief executive, and the bill was thus struck down.[496] Second, having been exhausted by the political process, in late September 2014, students started boycotting classes and demonstrating outside of the government headquarters, which marked the start of the Occupy Central Movement, a civil disobedience movement in which the participants risked breaking the law in order to push for a cause that many deem noble — true democracy. The purposes of this movement had initially been to demand the NPCSC to withdraw the *31-August* decision, to re-start the consultation process, and to allow civil nomination as proposed previously. However, it took an unexpected turn, with demonstrators calling for the resignation of the then chief executive Leung Chun Ying after the police used disproportional force to suppress unarmed protesters. As the community reeled from the shock, the pan-democratic members requested the President of LegCo to convene an urgent meeting to inquire into the matter. However, the meeting was not held as proposed because 41 pro-Beijing councillors stated that they would not attend. Without the assurance of a quorum, the President declined to call a meeting. Motions to appoint a Select Committee to look into the matter were also vetoed. In view of the above, when the LegCo fails to hold the government accountable on a matter of such gravity, the question of whether the legislature is still effective in monitoring the government can only be answered in the negative. As a result, those who were frustrated or disillusioned could only resort to street politics in the form of a civil disobedience movement or to the court.

8.10.1 Civil Disobedience

There have always been debates over what circumstances justify disobeying the law. Does the rule of law require unquestioned adherence to the wordings of the law? Or, is the law just a means to achieve some higher values, and if so, what are these higher values? These questions have long been debated by philosophers and jurists, and they have become significant in Hong Kong.

496. *South China Morning Post*, 'Hong Kong reform package rejected as pro-Beijing camp walks out in "miscommunication"', 18 June 2015, available at: www.scmp.com/news/hong-kong/politics/article/1823398/hong-kong-political-reform-package-voted-down-legco-leaving, last accessed 26 May 2020. See also Simon Young, 'Rethinking the Process of Political Reform in Hong Kong' (2015) 45(2) *HKLJ* 381.

Judicially, the above questions were specifically discussed in *Buckoke v Greater London Council*.[497] In this case, the chief officer of the London Fire Brigade issued an order to all firefighters, saying that a brigade driver could proceed against the red light if it was safe to do so when responding to an emergency call. However, the Fire Brigades Union disagreed, claiming that such an order could encourage the drivers to break the law. It resulted in some firefighters refusing to travel with a driver unless the latter gave assurance that he would observe the law by not crossing when the lights were red. Some drivers refused to give that assurance, causing these firefighters to refuse to travel with them. Nevertheless, the chief officer took disciplinary action against these firefighters. The firefighters, in response, brought a judicial review application challenging the lawfulness of the order, hoping that if the order was struck down, then the firefighters would not be bound to travel with these drivers and the disciplinary action against them would be groundless and dropped.

When the case was tabled before the Court of Appeal, Lord Denning, prior to holding that, based on the facts, there was nothing unlawful about such an order, posed a hypothetical question, setting out the issue as follows:

> A driver of a fire engine with ladders approaches the traffic lights. He sees 200 yards down the road a blazing house with a man at an upstairs window in extreme peril. The road is clear in all directions. At that moment the lights turn red. Is the driver to wait for 60 seconds, or more, for the lights to turn green? If the driver waits for that time, the man's life will be lost. Should the driver obey the law in these circumstances? If he decides not to obey the law, should he be prosecuted, or should he be congratulated?
>
> For many years there has been a controversy in the Fire Service. It is this: what is the duty of the driver of a fire engine when he comes to traffic lights which are at red? The Fire Brigades Union says that he must obey the law. No matter how urgent the call, he must wait till the lights turn green. Even if it means losing precious seconds, he must wait all the same. The chief officer of the London Fire Brigade says No; he is not going to order

497. [1971] Ch 655, cited in Johannes Chan, *Paths of Justice* (HKUP 2018) 223.

> the driver to wait. If the road is clear and the driver stops for a second and makes sure that it is safe to cross, he can shoot the lights so as to go to the fire as soon as possible.[498]

What would you do if you were the driver in this situation? Will you disobey the law to save life, or simply obey the law and let someone die? What is more, should the law be obeyed when this would become absurd? If one can choose not to obey the law when it is absurd, who decides how absurd it must be before one can justifiably disobey it?[499]

As Hugo Bedau once said, 'civil disobedience — disobeying the law in good cause — is as old as Prometheus' disobedience of Zeus in order to give fire to mankind and Antigone's defiance of Creon's edict denying proper burial to her brother Polynices'.[500] The issue of the individual's relation to the state and its government and the appropriate response to offensive or unjust law — meek compliance, protest, disobedience, or rebellion — has been debated since at least 399 BC, when Crito argued that Socrates should flee from prison to avoid an undeserved death penalty.[501] Moreover, religious consciousness, together with its doctrine of 'passive obedience', has a long history of conscientious refusal when faced with arrogant secular demands.[502] For one thing, Jews and Christians, despite their lives being at risk, disobeyed the demands of Roman law and its claims of supreme authority by refusing to place a pinch of incense on the altar of Caesar.[503]

498. Cited in Chan, ibid. Since then, the Road Traffic Act 1988 in the UK has been amended to allow an exemption for fire engines, ambulance, and police vehicles to comply with speed limits and traffic lights under certain conditions. A similar exemption exists in s 77 of the Road Traffic Ordinance, Cap 374, in Hong Kong.

499. Chan (N497) 223.

500. Hugo Bedau (ed), *Civil Disobedience in Focus* (Routledge 1991) 1.

501. Ibid.

502. David Daube, *Civil Disobedience in Antiquity* (EUP 1972) 1.

503. Bedau (N500) 1.

In modern times, John Rawls defines civil disobedience, as opposed to revolutionary disobedience,[504] as

> a public, nonviolent, conscientious yet political act contrary to law usually done with the aim of bringing about a change in the law or policies of the government. By acting in this way one addresses the sense of justice of the majority of the community and declares that in one's considered opinion the principles of social cooperation among free and equal men are not being respected.[505]

In short, civil disobedience is an act which 'addresses the sense of justice of the community and declares that in one's considered opinion the principles of social co-operation among free and equal men are not being respected'.[506] Rawls goes on to state:

> It is assumed that in a reasonably just democratic regime there is a public conception of justice by reference to which citizens regulate their political affairs and interpret the constitution. The persistent and deliberate violation of the basic principles of this conception over any extended period of time, especially the infringement of the fundamental equal liberties, invites either submission or resistance. By engaging in civil disobedience a minority forces the majority to consider whether it wishes to have its actions construed in this way, or whether, in view of the common sense of justice, it wishes to acknowledge the legitimate claims of the minority.[507]

---

504. Unlike civil disobedience, which recognises governmental authority and its legitimacy, revolutionary disobedience explicitly denies and challenges them. Manifested as a rupture between the ruled and the ruler, its aim is to terminate the relationship between them. Contrary to civil disobedience, which reveals the unjust nature of a particular law or policy, thereby fostering constitutional changes if the government so allows, in revolutionary disobedience, people directly oust the government from office, reshape the constitutional order, and create a new state. It is an exertion of popular sovereignty, re-engaging the people in the collective authorship of the sovereign will. Hence, an act of revolutionary disobedience is an exercise of self-determination and inherently democratic; see Philip Lau, 'Revolutionary Disobedience', *Barry Law Review*, Spring 2017, Vol 22, No 2, 199, available at: https://papers.ssrn.com/sol3/papers.cfm?abstract_id=2981915, last accessed 20 June 2020.
505. John Rawls, *A Theory of Justice* (Revised edn, HUP 1999) 320. The first part of this definition was endorsed by the CFA in *Secretary for Justice v Wong Chi Fung* (2018) 21 HKCFAR 34, [70].
506. Ibid., 364.
507. Ibid., 365–366.

Generally speaking, the primary objective of civil disobedience is to challenge repression by the ruling class through various forms of citizen actions. Typically, when citizens civilly disobey, they have both backward-looking and forward-looking communicative aims. Their backward-looking aims are to communicate their disavowal of, and dissociation from, the protested policy or law, as well as the reasons for such disavowal, whereas their forward-looking aims are to draw attention to the reasons for the protest in order to persuade the relevant audience to accept their position and thereby to instigate a lasting change in policy or law.[508] Classic examples of civil disobedience include the defiance of Ms Rosa Parks during her 1955 bus ride and the ensuing Montgomery bus boycott,[509] and the marches led by Dr Martin Luther King Jr in Birmingham, Alabama, in 1963. Furthermore, Mahatma Gandhi even claimed that under certain circumstances, non-cooperation with an evil state is a citizen's duty.[510] Gandhi believed that when certain conditions are fulfilled, non-cooperation with an evil state commits one to civil disobedience, saying:

> You assist an administration most effectively by obeying its orders and decrees. An evil system never deserves such allegiance. Allegiance to it means partaking of the evil. A good man will therefore resist an evil system or administration with his whole soul. Disobedience of the laws of the evil State is therefore a duty.[511]

Within the notion of civil disobedience, there are two sub-categories — direct and indirect disobedience. Direct disobedience involves a breach of the very law that citizens oppose, such as Parks' refusal to give up her seat, contrary to the Alabama state bus segregation law. Such an act is done both to dissociate directly from that law and to communicate condemnation and a desire for change. By contrast, indirect disobedience is a breach of a law other than the law citizens oppose, such as anti-Iraq war protesters holding sit-ins in government buildings. It is done to communicate condemnation and a desire for change, and, indirectly, to dissociate themselves from the policy or law they

508. Kimberley Brownlee, *Conscience and Conviction: The Case for Civil Disobedience* (OUP 2012) 18.

509. *Browder v Gayle*, 142 F Supp 707 (1956).

510. Vinit Haksar, 'Civil Disobedience and Non-Cooperation' in Bedau (N500) 144.

511. Mahatma Gandhi, *Nonviolent Resistance* (Schocken Books 1961) 238, cited by ibid., 144.

oppose.[512] Whatever sub-category the act may fall into, civil disobedience will undoubtedly raise some important questions. On one hand, should citizens be coerced into obedience to tyranny or unjust laws? Is there an absolute responsibility to obey a law regardless of its quality? Can civil disobedience derive a legal legitimacy that can balance the arguments for absolute obedience to the law? On the other hand, how should the government deal with those who disobey the law out of conscience? These questions tap into the heart of civil disobedience movements and protests in Hong Kong and elsewhere in the world and require discussion of legal philosophy and the underpinning notions of rights, duties, and the rule of law.

How the government should tackle those who disobey the law out of conscience is bound to be a hot topic of debate. Many citizens think that the government must prosecute the dissenters because they hold the view that conscientious disobedience is the same as lawlessness — they are anarchists who must be punished before corruption spreads, even many lawyers or intellectuals have come to the same conclusion. They believe that while disobedience and protesting a law may be morally justified, it is not legally justified.[513] This belief is likely based on the fundamental moral argument that it would be unfair to let the dissenters go unpunished and that society could not function if everyone disobeyed laws they disapprove of or find disadvantageous.[514] In connection with this, Erwin Griswold, the former solicitor general of the United States and the former dean of Harvard Law School, said:

> It is of the essence of law that it is equally applied to all, that it binds all alike, irrespective of personal motive. For this reason, one who contemplates civil disobedience out of moral conviction should not be surprised and must not be bitter if a criminal conviction ensues. And he must accept the fact that organized society cannot endure on any other basis.[515]

Judicially, Lord Donaldson MR, when adjudicating a journalist's failure to comply with the Court's order by relying on section 10 of the Contempt of

512. Brownlee (N508) 19.

513. Ronald Dworkin, *Taking Rights Seriously* (Duckworth 1977) 206.

514. Ibid., 207.

515. Cited by Dworkin, Ibid., 206.

Court Act 1981 in support of his refusal to divulge his source of information in *X Ltd v Morgan-Gampian (Publishers) Ltd*,[516] agrees with this. He stated:

> Parliament makes the law and it is the duty of the courts to enforce that law, whether or not they agree with it. Every citizen, every corporate body and every authority, whether national or local, is entitled to campaign to change the law, but until the law is changed it is their duty to obey it. That is what parliamentary democracy and the rule of law is all about. Each one of us surrenders a part of his personal freedom of action and choice and in return is protected by the law from the consequences of others seeking to exercise an unfettered freedom of action and choice ... In a parliamentary democracy personal and professional honour surely equates with the acceptance of, and obedience to, the rule of law.[517]

His Lordship furthered that:

> The maintenance of the rule of law is in every way as important in a free society as the democratic franchise ... Of course the courts, like other human institutions, are fallible and a journalist ordered to disclose his source may ... feel that the court's decision was wrong. But to contend that the individual litigant, be he a journalist or anyone else, has a right of 'conscientious objection' which entitles him to set himself above the law if he does not agree with the court's decision, is a doctrine which directly undermines the rule of law and is wholly unacceptable in a democratic society ... Freedom of speech is itself a right which is dependent on the rule of law for its protection and it is paradoxical that a serious challenge to the rule of law should be mounted by responsible journalists.[518]

However, Ronald Dworkin has a different view, saying that this argument (that simply because the government believes a man has committed a crime, it must prosecute him) is much weaker than it seems. Even though society 'cannot endure' if it tolerates all disobedience, it does not necessarily follow that

516. [1990] 2 All ER 1, [1990] 1 All ER 616, [1991] 1 AC 1 (CA).

517. Ibid., [1990] 1 All ER 616 (CA), 621–622.

518. Ibid., 624.

it will immediately collapse if it tolerates some.[519] In the United States, for example, prosecutors have discretion as to whether to enforce criminal law in a particular situation. In Hong Kong, a prosecutor may decide not to press charges against offenders if the law in question is unpopular, unworkable, or generally disobeyed (even though this is in contrast to the prior notification requirement in the *Public Order Ordinance* case, as explained earlier in this chapter). Although this discretion is not a licence for prosecutors not to enforce the law, there are some good reasons for not prosecuting those who disobey the law out of conscience, such as against those who act with the greater good in mind compared to those who break the law out of greed or a desire to subvert the government.[520] If motive counts in distinguishing between thieves, argues Dworkin, then why should it not count in distinguishing between offenders disobeying the law out of conscience or morality, or having dissenting views? Agreeing with this, H.L.A. Hart, a legal positivist, said:

> [T]he certification of something as legally valid is not conclusive of the question of obedience ... however great the aura of majesty or authority which the official system may have, its demands must in the end be submitted to moral scrutiny.[521]

Considering the above, disobedience to evil laws would be classified as legitimate if it would promote change for the good.

There is also a practical reason why society would suffer a loss if it punishes 'offenders' who have disobeyed the law out of conscience, as these individuals are often some of the most loyal and law-respecting citizens. Having these people jailed will only alienate them from society, making them more dissident. It may also alienate others like them. In a society which forces citizens to obey unjust laws for fear of imprisonment, no individual can be regarded solely as a single autonomous person. An autonomous person regards themselves as being 'sovereign in deciding what to believe and in weighing competing reasons for action [or inaction]'.[522] Although they may rely on the judgment of

519. Dworkin (N513) 206.

520. Ibid., 207.

521. H.L.A. Hart, *The Concept of Law* (2nd edn, Clarendon Press 1994) 206.

522. Thomas Scanlon, 'A Theory of Freedom of Expression' (1972) 1(2) *PPA* 204, 215.

others, a person acting autonomously will advance independent reasons for trusting that judgment and assess their opinion in light of contrary indications. By contrast, non-autonomous individuals, particularly those that have been forced to obey unjust laws for fear of imprisonment, often hide what they truly believe so that they can be left in peace. This is because these individuals may not possess sufficient social capital or political power to resist, or may be trying to curry favour with, the ruling class. Punishing offenders that have acted out of conscience may push these non-autonomous citizens to live a lie. Indeed, when conscience is distorted or mistaken, then human life is distorted or mistaken. A similar assertion was famously stated by Václav Havel, a Czech dramatist, political dissident, and later the first President of the Czech Republic:

> [T]hey must live within a lie. They need not accept the lie. It is enough for them to have accepted their life with it and in it. For by this very fact, individuals confirm the system, fulfil the system, make the system, *are the system.*[523] [emphasis added]

If such a practical consequence is an argument against enforcing punishment, why do leaders not argue for increasing tolerance for offences of conscience?[524] Commenting on this disconnect, Lord Hoffmann, in *R v Jones (Margaret)*,[525] said:

> [C]ivil disobedience on conscientious grounds has a long and honourable history in this country. People who break the law to affirm their belief in the injustice of a law or government action are sometimes vindicated by history. The suffragettes are an example that comes immediately to mind. It is the mark of a civilized community that it can accommodate protests and demonstrations of this kind. But there are conventions which are generally accepted by the law-breakers on one side and the law-enforcers on the other. The protestors behave with a sense of proportion and do not cause excessive damage or inconvenience. And they vouch the sincerity of their beliefs by accepting the penalties imposed by the law. The police and prosecutors, on the other hand, behave with restraint and the magistrates impose sentences

523. Václav Havel, *The Power of the Powerless: Citizens against the State in Central-Eastern Europe* (translated by John Keane, Hutchinson 1985) 31.

524. Dworkin (N513) 207.

525. [2006] UKHL 16, [2006] 2 WLR 772, [2007] 1 AC 136, [89].

> which take the conscientious motives of the protestors into account. The conditional discharges ordered by the magistrates in the cases which came before them exemplify their sensitivity to these conventions.[526]

This tallies with what Rawls has said:

> Civil disobedience may be viewed as a political act guided and justified by the principles of justice which regulate the constitution. It represents an appeal to the sense of justice of the majority and, unlike militant action or forcible resistance, it does not deny the legitimacy of the legal order but merely [query] the justice of particular laws. On this interpretation, civil disobedience plays a role in ensuring the stability of a constitutional regime and, by resisting injustice through unlawful conduct which respects appropriate constraints, can serve to correct departures from fundamental principles of constitutional morality.[527]

Rawls assumes the existence of a 'nearly just society', one that is 'well-ordered for the most part but in which some serious violations of justice nevertheless do occur'.[528] In this regard, it seems reasonable that in a lawful society, citizens' grievances can be dealt with through established channels for complaints. This includes working with legislators to formulate objections, requesting investigations by specific commissioners, exerting pressure on the government through mass media, and voicing concerns through the ballot box.[529] However, in the events leading up to the Occupy Central Movement and the subsequent civil disobedience movements and anti-government protests discussed earlier in this chapter, none of these avenues seemed to yield the desired result.[530] The demonstrators were a

526. Ibid., [89].

527. Rawls (N505), cited by T.R.S. Allan, *Law, Liberty, and Justice: The Foundations of British Constitutionalism* (Clarendon Press 1993) 110.

528. Rawls (N505) 363–368 and 382–391.

529. John Nguyet Erni, 'A Legal Realist View on Citizen Actions in Hong Kong's Umbrella Movement' (2015) 8(4) *CJC* 412, 416, available at: www.tandfonline.com/doi/full/10.1080/17544750.2015.1063526, last accessed 2 February 2020. See also Collins Udeh, 'Rights, Responsibility, Law and Order in 21st Century's Civil Disobedience' (2014) 7(2) *JPL* 32–40.

530. Gary Cheung, 'An inquiry into the Mong Kok riot would only create a new battleground': former Central Policy Unit chief compares Star Ferry and Hong Kong riots', *South China Morning Post*, 17 February 2016, available at: www.scmp.com/news/hong-kong/politics/article/1913597/inquiry-mong-kok-riot-would-only-create-new-battleground, last accessed 26 May 2020.

minority in the sense that they were not supported by the business hegemony or by the mainstream media whose interests are sided with the Chinese authorities, as well as in the sense that they were subjugated by the Central government.[531]

In this climate, Benny Tai, one of the co-founders of the Occupy Central Movement, has adopted a legal interpretivism view to explain various 'levels' of governance, whereby the 'low levels' comprise a basic recognition of the law and thus absolute obedience to it.[532] These strata are built upon minimal elements, such as the clarity and transparency of the law and the proper institutionalisation of legal practice. Tai has considered the 'low levels' as being generally incapable of restraining power, stating:

> Beginning-stage governance by law lacks an effective means to restrict power. The determination of how the law would be exercised properly relies solely on the government or the legislator's subjective view. Because this kind of governance by law makes little or no demand on the substance of the law, the legal infrastructure ends up being utilized to maintain power, at the expense of protecting basic citizen rights. To leap toward a higher level of governance, the law would have to be transformed from functionalities (as the tool of the powerful) to a system of checks and balances (affording a restriction to power), which can then lead to the actualization of legal purpose (the chief purpose of the law is to practise justice).[533]

Considering this, John Nguyet Erni has asked whether individuals have the right to 'disobey the law' under such circumstances, and if there is no response from the government to citizens' grievances and there is a lack of restraint on power in the legal system, do citizens have a 'duty' to express their dissent?[534] In a similar vein, Collins Udeh reminds us that

> [a] government true to democratic precepts of representativeness and fairness must be sensitive to demands of change. If it fails in that regard, it is at least arguable that demands for change, while entailing technical breaches of the

531. Nguyet Erni (N529) 416.

532. Benny Tai, 'Reflections on Civil Disobedience and the Rule of Law', *Ming Pao*, 12 November 2014, translated and cited by Nguyet Erni (N529) 414.

533. Ibid.

534. Ibid., 416.

> law, should be accommodated within the constitutional framework … As we have seen in the twenty-first century civil disobedience starting from the Arab Spring up to the Ukrainian uprising, major social changes of such magnitude would have been impossible without recognition that under certain limited conditions there exists a right of legitimate protest, however inconvenient and uncomfortable this is for governments around the world … [I]t is not necessary to look to such major societal changes brought about by defiance of law in order to refute the law and order model and proclaim some entitlement to dissent.[535]

Nguyet Erni's argument tallies with what Hannah Arendt argued in 1972: that civil disobedience is compatible with a constitutional government that possesses tolerant attitudes and that civilly disobedient citizens should be given access to decision-making.[536] Arendt went on to list how this can be implemented by inviting representatives of civil disobedience movements to 'influence and assist Congress by means of persuasion, qualified opinion, and the numbers of their constituents'.[537] Although Arendt's proposal to institutionalise civil disobedience — essentially to take it off the streets and into the government — is unprecedented within modern political theory. Unfortunately, her revolutionary spirit is impractical, if not impossible, in Hong Kong because the government is beholden to interests in the Chinese government.[538] This has ultimately led some people to resort to violence [539] and to advocate 'Hong Kong Independence'.[540] Their feelings echo those of earlier generations of oppressed individuals:

> [We] are forced to pretend outward respect for people and institutions which [we] find ridiculous … [We] remain cowardly attached to moral and social conventions you despise, condemn, and which you know lack all

535. Udeh (N529) 36.

536. Cited by William Smith, 'Reclaiming the Revolutionary Spirit: Arendt on Civil Disobedience' (2010) 9(2) *EJPT* 149–166.

537. Hannah Arendt, 'Civil Disobedience' in Hannah Arendt (ed), *Crisis of the Republic* (Harourt Brace Jovanovich 1972) 49–102.

538. Nguyet Erni (N529) 416.

539. Stuart Lau, Jennifer Ngo, Chris Lau, Ernest Kao, and Nikki Sun, 'Mong Kok riot: how Hong Kong's first night in the Year of the Monkey descended into mayhem', *South China Morning Post*, 10 February 2016, available at: www.scmp.com/news/hong-kong/article/1911341/mong-kok-riot-how-hong-kongs-first-night-year-monkey-descended-mayhem, last accessed 26 May 2020.

540. *South China Morning Post*, 'Topic: Hong Kong Localism and Independence', multiple publication dates, available at: www.scmp.com/topics/hong-kong-localism-and-independence, last accessed 5 February 2020.

> foundation ... It's the permanent contradiction between [our] ideas and desires on the one hand and all the dead forms and vain phantoms of [our] civilisation on the other that makes [us] sad, troubled and unbalanced. In that intolerable conflict [we] lose all joy of life and all feeling of personality because every moment the free play of [our] strength is restrained, impeded and checked. That's the poisonous and mortal wound of the [un]civilised world.[541]

Worst of all, students' grievances have only been intensified by the response of the Chinese government, namely in their issuance of the White paper [542] as well as the *31-August* decision in 2014. Ultimately, the Occupy Central Movement was not successful. The reasons for this range from the emergence of Anti-Occupy groups to resist (with violence) the protest efforts to the dissatisfaction felt by a portion of the general public over the disruptions caused by the movement. This was followed by the convictions of those who initiated the movement, including Tai, Dr Chan Kin Man, and Pastor Chu Yiu Ming, for incitement to commit, and incitement to incite, public nuisance.[543] In addition to condemning the movement, the Chinese government even alleged that there were some foreign countries, the United States in particular, who had pulled the strings. Thus, for Beijing, the Occupy Central Movement and the subsequent civil disobedience movements and anti-government protests are not solely about democracy in Hong Kong, but national security for the whole country.

In the aftermath of the Occupy Central Movement, Hong Kong has witnessed an increased level of 'localism' among young people,[544] and the failure of the movement ultimately led to further radicalisation of social movements around the city.[545] Localism had originally been promoted by activists in the mid-2000s as a way to push forward a leftist-progressive agenda.[546] Since the

541. Octave Mirbeau, *Torture Garden* (translated by Michael Richardson, Dedalus 1997) 94–95.

542. 'White Paper on The Practice of the "One Country, Two System" Policy in the Hong Kong Special Administrative Region' (N492).

543. *HKSAR v Tai Yiu Ting, Chan Kin Man, Chu Tiu Ming* [2019] HKDC 450.

544. Sebastian Veg, 'The Rise of "Localism" and Civic Identity in Post-Handover Hong Kong: Questioning the Chinese Nation-State' (2017) 230 *CQ* 323–347.

545. Francis Lee, 'Internet Alternative Media, Movement Experience, and Radicalism: The Case of Post-Umbrella Movement Hong Kong' (2018) 17(2) *SMS* 219–233.

546. Y.C. Chen and Mirana Sezto, 'The Forgotten Road of Progressive Localism: New Preservation Movement in Hong Kong' (2015) 16(3) *IACS* 436–453.

early 2010s, however, the notion has been re-positioned to critique the plans to further integrate Hong Kong with the Mainland.[547] After the Occupy Central Movement, this localist discourse was picked up by some of the newer political groups and shaped into a call for Hong Kong independence.[548]

Radicalisation reached a new peak in the clashes between protesters and the police on the first day of Chinese New Year in February 2016, the so-called Fishball Revolution. The protest was provoked by a crackdown on street food vendors, with protesters arguing that such violence was precipitated by unjust police hostility. During the incident, about 500 protesters threw bricks and started fires, with anti-riot police responding with pepper spray and firing two warning shots into the air.[549] These events were a prelude to the clashes observed in 2019 and 2020 in protests over the Extradition Bill and the proposed National Security Law, discussed at length in earlier sections of this chapter.

8.10.2 Moving Political Issues from Street Politics to the Court

When any person taking part in an unlawful assembly (by virtue of section 18(1) of the POO) commits a breach of peace, the assembly is deemed a riot and the persons assembled are rioters.[550] As discussed earlier, section 19 of the POO, which was intended to deal with the kind of riots experienced in the summer of 1967, uses a vague definition of 'rioting' and is incompatible with modern human rights standards. In fact, between 1967 and 2000, it was seldom used, with some rare exceptions [551] — for instance, to prosecute situations of extreme violence such as prison riots.[552] However, section 19 was invoked for the first time

547. Sonny Lo, 'Ideologies and Factionalism in Beijing-Hong Kong Relations' (2018) 58(3) *AS* 392–415.

548. Samson Yuen and Sanho Chung, 'Explaining Localism in Post-Handover Hong Kong: An Eventful Approach' (2018) 3 *CP* 19–29.

549. Arnaldo M.A. Gonçalves, 'Hong Kong and Macau Special Administrative Regions: The Downfall of the "One Country, Two Systems" Policy', (2019) 9(10) *IJHSS* 11, 20.

550. Cap 245, s 19, Laws of Hong Kong.

551. *R v Chan Kwong-yim*, unreported CACC 968/1983 (resisting squatter hut clearance), cited by Hong Kong Watch (N327) Endnote 1.

552. *The Queen v Phong Ung-cau*, CACC 630/1994 (riot in Shek Kong Vietnamese Detention Centre); *Secretary for Justice v Cheung Chun Chi* [2002] 2 HKLRD 233 (riot in Hei Ling Chau Drug Addiction Treatment Centre).

in 2020 to prosecute at least 35 protesters for rioting, including Edward Leung, who was later convicted of rioting and sentenced to six years' imprisonment.[553]

In *HKSAR v Hui Kai Ki, Mak Tsz Hei and Sit Tat Wing*,[554] District Court Judge Shum offered a very broad definition of riot: a riot is merely an unlawful assembly in conjunction with a breach of peace which already took place. Importantly, no damage to property or injury to human lives is a necessary condition. The judge reached the conclusion that Hui, a student of The University of Hong Kong, was a rioter by just considering three questions: (1) whether there was a riot on that night; (2) when arrested, whether Hui was a participant of the riot; and (3) what she did within the riot.[555] In his verdict, although there was no direct evidence that Hui undertook any violent action towards the police, the judge determined that even in the absence of any violent behaviour, Hui could still be convicted of rioting simply because 'there [was] a riot on that night' and 'Hui was caught on the rioting spot, running'.[556] In reaching his conclusion, the judge said that the fact that Hui was moving quickly away from the police, rather than moving out of the way or standing still, meant that she was part of the riot and not an observer, journalist, or innocent bystander. Hong Kong Watch summarised the implied definition, stating that 'a person's spatial distance to what is defined as a riot (unlawful assembly with breach of peace) becomes the main criteria for a rioting charge',[557] the effect of which has created an 'impression that judges interpreted offences in recent verdicts using the [POO] following a simple approach: maximise the probability of conviction, minimise leniency'.[558] In short, this not only raises the costs of protest, but also has alarming effects on fundamental rights in relation to political freedoms, and ultimately it sets a very bad precedent for the rule of law in Hong Kong.

On 22 May 2019, Ray Wong and Alan Li, who had been facing trial for rioting offences, publicly announced that they were granted refugee status by Germany in May 2018. According to Hong Kong Watch, one of the key reasons

553. *HKSAR v Leung Tin Kei, Lo Kin Man and Wong Ka Kui* [2020] HKCA 275.

554. DCCC710/2016, [18], [2017] HKDC 377.

555. Hong Kong Watch (N327) 27.

556. Ibid.

557. Ibid.

558. Ibid., 28.

why the German government has granted political asylum to these two young men is because of the punitive way that the POO was used to crackdown on, and imprison, protesters from across Hong Kong's political opposition so that they could not be guaranteed a fair trial.[559]

In this climate, such non-responsive and non-democratic governance, intensified by the failure of street protests, leaves judicial review as the only method of achieving some form of remedy.[560] As a result, Hong Kong people have turned from the legislature to the judicial branch in pursuit of their political aspirations.[561] Moreover, a group of 'cause lawyers' have emerged — lawyers 'who seek to use law-related means to achieve greater socio-political and economic justice both for individuals and for disadvantaged groups, and moral and/or political commitment is their defining attribute'.[562] In Hong Kong, these lawyers have actively taken up new opportunities and promoted legal mobilisation since the 1990s and have contributed to the apparent turn in allegiance.[563]

8.11 Judicial Attitudes towards Legal Disputes concerning Policy Formulation and Implementation, and Socio-Economic Rights in Hong Kong

Following the handover in July 1997, the judiciary, led by the CFA, assertively defended individual rights and freedoms,[564] and their liberal decisions sent

559. Hong Kong Watch (N358) 1.

560. Mark Daly, 'A Human Rights Lawyer's Perspective' in Young and Ghai (N4) 209.

561. Tam (N7) 4–5.

562. Carrie Menkel-Meadow, 'The Causes of Cause Lawyering: Toward an Understanding of the Motivation and Commitment of Social Justice Lawyers' in Austin Sarat and Stuart Scheingold (eds), *Cause Lawyering: Political Commitments and Professional Responsibilities* (OUP 1998) 37.

563. Tam (N7) 7.

564. *Ng Ka Ling* (N109); *Chan Kam Nga v Director of Immigration* (1999) 2 HKCFAR 82 (CFA); *Chan Wah* (N284); *Director of Immigration v Chong Fung Yuen* (2001) 4 HKCFAR 211 (CFA); *Ng Siu Tung v Director of Immigration* (2002) 5 HKCFAR 1 (CFA); *Gurung Kesh Bahadur v Director of Immigration* (2002) 5 HKCFAR 480 (CFA); *Prem Singh v Director of Immigration* (2003) 6 HKCFAR 26 (CFA); *Director of Immigration v Lau Fong* (2004) 7 HKCFAR 56 (CFA); *Sakthevel Prabakar* (N3); *Wong Hin Wai* (N323); *Leung T C William Roy* (N122); *Koo Sze Yiu v CE of the HKSAR* (2006) 9 HKCFAR 441 (CFA); *HKSAR v Hung Chan Wa*, unreported, CACC 411/2003, 61/2004) (CA) (26 January 2006), (2006) 9 HKCFAR 614 (CFA); *Yau Yuk Lung* (N254); *Democratic Party v Secretary for Justice* [2007] 2 HKLRD 804 (CFI), unreported, HCAL 84/2006 (CFI) (28 December 2007); *Chan Kin Sum* (N154); *Lam Siu Po* (N95).

a signal to minorities and the 'politically disadvantaged' — groups that are temporarily or permanently disadvantaged in terms of their abilities to successfully pursue their goals through representative political institutions like the electoral process, the legislature, or the bureaucracy [565] — that the courts could be a viable avenue for them to attain their objectives.[566] According to Ghai:

> Courts are now more willing to take on jurisdiction, in part because other institutions often enjoy less legitimacy than [the] courts. Sometimes, it is only by court intervention that a modicum of legality can be preserved ... In Hong Kong, this point is particularly pertinent since neither [the] Hong Kong executive or legislature is fully elected.[567]

8.11.1 Judicial Deference to Challenges to Government Policy and the Validity of Administrative Decisions

As recourse to judicial review in Hong Kong has grown over the last two decades,[568] Hong Kong politics are said to have become 'judicialised'.[569] An overwhelming number of judicial review applications [570] are high profile

565. Tam (N7) 99.

566. Ibid., 86.

567. Yash Ghai, 'Litigating the Basic Law: Jurisdiction, Interpretation and Procedure' in Albert Chen, Fu Hauling, and Yash Ghai (eds), *Hong Kong's Constitutional Debate: Conflict over Interpretation* (HKUP 2000) 23.

568. In 1988, there were only 29 applications but since 2001 there have been around 140 applications each year; see Jhaveri, Ramsden, and Scully-Hill (N71) 223. This has increased steadily from 137 cases (including right of abode claims) in 2003 to 182 cases in 2013; see also *Statistics provided by the Judiciary on Applications for Leave to Apply for Judicial Review (1997–2013)*, available at: http://gia.info.gov.hk/general/201404/09/P201404080747_0747_126907.pdf, last accessed 2 February 2020.

569. C. Neal Tate, 'Why the Expansion of Judicial Power?' in C. Neal Tate and Torbjörn Vallinder (eds), *The Global Expansion of Judicial Power* (NYUP 1995) 28.

570. Applications against the government have increased from fewer than 100 in 2004 to 130 in 2005 and 128 in 2006, representing an almost 25 percent growth in the subsequent two years; see Benedict Lai, 'Recent Trends and Developments of Judicial Review in Hong Kong', a paper presented in the *20th LawAsia Biennial Conference*, 6–8 June 2007, Hong Kong, cited by Chan (N5) 143 and 168.

challenges to government policy [571] as well as the validity of administrative decisions.[572] One application, for example, involved the challenge of a decision made by the President of the LegCo.[573] Although the then Chief Justice, Andrew Li, talked about the 'phenomenon of judicial review' and said 'it should be seen as providing an essential foundation for good governance under the rule of law',[574] he also expressed his concern that the courts should not assume the role of the maker of the challenged decision during judicial review. He further explained that apart from assessing the legality of the decision in question and its procedural propriety, the courts could not possibly provide an answer to, let alone a panacea for, the various political, social, and economic problems which confront modern society. Therefore, the appropriate solution to any political, social, or economic problem can only be properly explored through the political process. The responsibility for the proper functioning of the political process rests with the administration and legislature, not the judiciary.[575] In this regard, Ribeiro PJ, in *Kong Yunming*,[576] stated:

> [A]s the Chief Justice noted in *Fok Chun Wa v Hospital Authority*, ... 'it would not usually be within the province of the courts to adjudicate on the merits or demerits of government socio-economic policies'. Where the disputed measure involves implementation of the Government's socio-economic policy choices regarding the allocation of limited public funds without impinging

571. *Town Planning Board v Society for the Protection of the Harbour Ltd* [2003] 2 HKLRD 787 (HCAL 19/2003), [2003] 3 HKLRD 960 (CFI), (2004) 7 HKCFAR 1, [2004] 1 HKLRD 396 (CFA); *Society for the Protection of Victoria Harbour Ltd v CE in Council (No. 2)* [2004] 2 HKLRD 902, [2004] 2 HKLRD 95 (CFA), (2004) 7 HKCFAR 1 (CFA), [2004] 1 HKLRD 396; *Lo Siu Lan v Hong Kong Housing Authority* (2004) 7 HKCFAR 631 (CFA); *Ho Choi Wan v HKSAR* (2005) 8 HKCFAR 628 (CFA); *Lau Kwok Fai Bernard* (N146); *Shiu Wing Steel Limited v Director of Environmental Protection* (2006) 9 HKCFAR 478; *Clean Air Foundation Ltd v Government of the HKSAR* [2007] HKEC 1356 (CFI); *Lai Tak Shing v Secretary for Home Affairs* [2008] HKEC 553; *Yao Man Fai George v Director of Social Welfare* [2010] HKEC 968, [2012] HKCA 79 (CA), [2012] 4 HKC 180; *W v Registrar of Marriages* (N92); *Kong Yunming* (N165).

572. *Wong Chung Ki v CE* (Application for leave to appeal in Court of Appeal) [2000] HKEC 701; *Fok Chun Wa* (N220).

573. *Leung Kwok Hung v President of the Legislative Council of the HKSAR* [2007] 1 HKLRD 387 (CFI), [2008] 2 HKLRD 18 (CA).

574. 'CJ's speech at ceremonial opening of the legal year 2007', 8 January 2007, available at: www.info.gov.hk/gia/general/200701/08/P200701080120.htm, last accessed 2 February 2020.

575. 'Chief Justice's speech at Ceremonial Opening of the Legal Year 2006', 9 January 2006, available at: www.info.gov.hk/gia/general/200601/09/P200601090137.htm, last accessed 2 February 2020.

576. *Kong Yunming* (N165) (2013) 16 HKCFAR 950.

> upon fundamental rights or involving possible discrimination on inherently suspect grounds, the Court has held that it has a duty to intervene only where the impugned measure is 'manifestly without reasonable justification'. That is a test initially applied by the [ECtHR] while according to a broad margin of appreciation to Member States in setting and implementing their socio-economic policies. As the Chief Justice points out, the margin of appreciation principle has previously been adapted to apply in the context of our domestic law. It is appropriate similarly to apply the 'manifestly without reasonable foundation' test in our domestic context.[577]

In contrast, Richard Cullen, owing to the lack of democracy in Hong Kong, has argued that:

> It is for this reason that undue deference by the Hong Kong judiciary towards the executive and towards the legislature raises special concerns. In the [Hong Kong SAR], freedom is something of a 'two-legged stool'. The judiciary and a free press provide two legs but the third, democracy, is at best only half a leg.[578]

Considering this 'two-legged stool' argument, the rationale advanced for judicial deference to the administrative authorities in Hong Kong is hardly convincing. In fact, when asked by Cullen as to whether the Hong Kong judiciary should adopt a more robust role to scrutinise administrative activities in view of the lack of political checks and balances, Christopher Forsyth replied that 'arguments for judicial deference weaken' in such an environment.[579] According to Mark Daly, if deference is a 'pathogen' infecting the Hong Kong judiciary, then one of the 'vectors' is the doctrine of margin of appreciation.[580] Hartmann J, in a paper titled 'Judicial Review (The Most Striking Development in the Common Law since the Second World War)', went on to state:

577. Ibid., [41], citing *Fok Chun Wa* (N220).

578. Richard Cullen, 'Media Freedom in Chinese Hong Kong' (1998) 11 *TL* 383, 401.

579. Lecture/Discussion, Margaret Ng LegCo Offices, 28 September 2001; W.S. Clarke, 'Judicial Review of the Discretionary Powers of the Attorney General of Hong Kong in the Conduct of Criminal Proceedings' (1983) 13 *HKLJ* 133, 147, cited by Daly (N560) 211.

580. Ibid., Daly, 209.

> The doctrine of proportionality is always accompanied by the recognition by the courts that they are not the primary decision-makers on matters of policy and a 'margin of appreciation' must be given to public authorities to enable them to make legitimate policy decisions. But how wide is this margin? The answer is that the margin increases or decreases depending on the subject matter. Particular deference is given in areas of economic and planning policy. Put another way in these areas, the courts will recognize a broader 'discretionary area of judgement' to which they will defer, on democratic grounds, to the considered opinion of the public authority. However, the greater the restriction on fundamental rights, the less margin of [discretion], especially in areas where the courts themselves have particular experience and expertise (e.g., restrictions going to the trial process).[581]

Mason has also described margin of appreciation (margin of discretion, to be precise) as another European importation and as an area of decision-making where other institutions enjoy a unique legitimacy and expertise which the courts lack.[582] However, considering this, Lord Lester once cautioned that:

> The concept of 'margin of appreciation' has become as slippery and elusive as an eel. Again and again the court now appears to use margin of appreciation as a substitute for coherent legal analysis of the issue at stake ... The danger of continuing to use the standardness doctrine of the margin of appreciation is that ... it will become the source of a pernicious 'variable geometry' of human rights, eroding the 'acquis' of existing jurisprudence and giving undue deference to local conditions, and practices.[583]

In fact, a 'restriction test' has been developed and applied without a coherent approach to the issue of deference to legislature and the executive in Hong Kong.

581. Ibid., 211.

582. Mason (N32).

583. Anthony Lester, 'The European Convention on Human Rights in the New Architecture of Europe: General Report' in the 8th International Colloquy on the European Convention on Human Rights, proceedings organised by the Secretariat General of the Institute for Legal and Administrative Sciences of the Hungarian Academy of Sciences, Budapest, 20–23 September 1995 (Council of Europe 1996) 227. He refers here to 'acquis', a French term meaning 'that which has been acquired or obtained'. The term is typically used with '*communautaire*', meaning 'of the community'. *Acquis communautaire* is used to describe the body of law, including legislation, legal acts, and court decisions, accumulated by the EU.

The first occasion for the CFA to apply such a restriction test was in 1999, in a review concerning the freedom of expression in relation to flag desecration (the case is discussed at length earlier in this chapter). To uphold the national and regional flag desecration offences as being necessary for public order, the CFA indicated that it was taking a deferential approach to restrictions. The majority referred to deference as giving 'due weight to the view of the [Hong Kong SAR's] legislature' when considering the importance of implementing the 'one country, two systems' principle and reinforcing national unity and territorial integrity 'at the early stage of the new order'.[584] However, Daly has opined that 'any detailed rationale [of these factors] for deviating from the international perspective seems lacking'.[585]

Another significant decision regarding the restriction test was made in 2005. In the *Public Order Ordinance* case [586] concerning freedom of assembly (also discussed at length earlier in this chapter), the CFA articulated the two-part rationality and proportionality test for restrictions prescribed by law.[587] The majority approach was to focus only on the constitutionality of using 'public order (*ordre public*)' as a ground for objection. Holding the first half of this ground unobjectionable, the majority of the CFA believed that one of the features of the scheme that made it proportional was that the commissioner of police had also been required to apply a proportionality test before exercising their power.[588] Bokhary PJ (as he then was), had more fundamental objections, holding that the commissioner's powers of prior restraint under the legislative scheme were insufficiently circumscribed and could not be saved by 'supplying the necessary safeguards through interpretation'.[589] He also gave a richer purposive analysis, capturing the reality of post-1997 Hong Kong and saying that 'today's Hong Kong street demonstrations, both stationary and moving, form a significant and even potent element of public discourse. ... A peaceful demonstration is a sign of freedom and can have a legitimate effect on policy'.[590] Also commenting

584. *Ng Kung Siu* (N116) (1999) 2 HKCFAR 442, 460–461.

585. Daly (N560) 213–214.

586. *Leung Kwok Hung* (N24).

587. Ibid., [33]–[37].

588. Ibid., [96].

589. Ibid., [202].

590. Ibid., [120].

on this case, Young argued that showing such trust to the police was surely a sign of the CFA's deference.[591]

In addition to it being too easy for the courts to resort to the 'special circumstances' justification (in various formulations) to depart from international human rights standards,[592] there is a further ideological threat to the international human rights regime — the over-emphasis of cultural relativism in Asian countries.[593] Hence, there is a danger of resorting to a simplistic dismissal of international human rights standards without careful scrutiny as to whether such cultural differences really do to justify denial of the fundamental right at issue. Carol Jones commented on this phenomenon, stating that:

> Like the rule of law, the appeal to a common 'Chineseness' is one means of uniting the rulers and the ruled, the elites and the masses, the Hong Kong people and the Mainland government. If this succeeds, sooner or later English rule of law may be seen as ill-suited to Hong Kong which is now more Chinese in complexion.[594]

8.11.2 Challenges concerning the Validity of Administrative Decisions, Policy Formulations, and Socio-Economic Rights Disputes

8.11.2.1 Validity of Administrative Decisions

8.11.2.1.1 The Public Housing Eviction *Case*

Article 29 of the Basic Law states that '[t]he homes ... of Hong Kong residents shall be inviolable. Arbitrary or unlawful search of, or intrusion into, a resident's home ... shall be prohibited'. The nuances of this provision have

591. Young and Da Roza (N124) 406.

592. Mark Daly, 'International Human Rights Standards in Hong Kong Courts', Dissertation LLM (Human Rights) 2001, Department of Law, The University of Hong Kong, cited by Daly (N560) 213.

593. Joanne Bauer and Daniel Bell, *The East Asian Challenge for Human Rights* (CUP 1999) Pt 1.

594. Carol Jones, 'Politics Postponed: Law as a Substitute for Politics in Hong Kong and China' in Kanishka Jayasuriya (ed), *Law, Capitalism and Power in Asia: The Rule of Law and Legal Institution* (Routledge 1998), cited by Daly (N560) 214.

been assessed in various cases concerning the Housing Authority's decision to evict tenants based for reasons related to keeping pets or using the flat for illegal purposes, etc. In such cases, the courts have largely adopted a hands-off approach and are more deferential to the administration.

The *Public Housing Eviction* case [595] concerned a challenge of the 'Notice-to-Quit' decision made by the authority and confirmed by the Appeal Tribunal. The applicant alleged that the decisions had been made without taking into account her and her son's 'right to home',[596] and that the decisions had been unlawful as they amounted to a disproportionate interference with this right. However, Au J held that in the absence of any right under the tenancy agreement to remain in possession, the authority's duties concerning the distribution and management of public housing resources and the need for it to balance the applicant's right to the property against the right of the public at large to public rental housing, were factors to be considered. The judge ultimately found that the 'Notice-to-Quit' decision was indeed proportionate to the legitimate aims of achieving the fair and efficient distribution and management of public rental housing resources for those in genuine need in Hong Kong and of preventing tenancy abuses.

8.11.2.1.2 The Affordable Rental Housing *Case*

While the *Affordable Rental Housing* case [597] concerns statutory interpretation and not the proportionality principle *per se*, it is still worthy of discussion because it involves a question of the right to housing, in particular affordable housing, and whether the Housing Authority has a positive duty to reduce rents in recessionary times. This case revolved around a provision added to the Housing Ordinance [598] in 1997 that the authority could not determine the rent sooner than three years after the previous revision. The provision also provided that the authority had an obligation to ensure that the median

595. *Chim Sui Ping v Hong Kong Housing Authority*, unreported, HCAL 139/2009 (17 September 2012).

596. Basic Law, Art 29; BORO, s 8, Art 14.

597. *Ho Choi Wan* (N571).

598. Cap 283, Laws of Hong Kong.

rent-to-income of tenants did not exceed 10 percent.[599] Owing to economic deflation and the resulting decreased capacity of tenants to pay their rents in the early 2000s, the authority deferred the review of rents and frozen them. This resulted in an average rent-to-income of 14.7 percent in the second half of 2004.[600] The appellant, Ms Ho, a tenant of a public housing estate, sought to compel the authority to review the rents, arguing that it had a positive duty to reduce rents to keep them within the 10 percent cap.

If what the appellant had argued was correct, this would have significant implications. Because about 30 percent of the population in Hong Kong was living in public housing at that time, the reduction of rent would have led to an annual loss of rental income of HK$1.52 billion. However, this money would arguably be used by the authority to build additional public housing for those on the waiting list. The authority was in a dilemma in that, on one hand, it had to discharge its statutory duty to make affordable public housing available to those who are in need of it, but on the other hand, it had to pursue a policy which the statute said 'shall be directed to ensuring that the revenue accruing to it from its estates shall be sufficient to meet its recurrent expenditure on its estates'.

The majority of the CFA rejected the appellant's argument, saying that (1) deferring the rent was not a determination of rent and therefore did not entail the obligation to review it for compatibility with the 10-percent rule, (2) the authority had no obligation to ensure compatibility with the same rule even though it was obliged to review the rent as part of balancing its other obligations, and (3) the adjustment of rent could only result in an increase and not a decrease of rent (because the legislative amendment in 1997 requiring three yearly adjustments was made at the time of inflation and was intended to put a brake on increases). In short, the decision was true to the legislative intent and the Court did not attempt to read more into the legislation based on comparative international or constitutional laws.[601]

599. *Ho Choi Wan* (N571) [9].

600. Ibid., [34].

601. Young and Da Roza (N124) 413.

Dissenting with this decision, Bokhary PJ (as he then was) held that there was such a positive duty, saying that 'affordable housing is what this case is about'.[602] His Lordship made express reference to the right of adequate housing in the ICESCR, as well as its potential application under Article 39 of the Basic Law.[603] Nevertheless, he qualified that his decision had been reached without taking the ICESCR into account, although it was relevant.[604] Overall, the implication of this case is that in the absence of incorporation, the most that can be said concerning the use of the ICESCR in Hong Kong courts may be no more than that it can be prayed powerfully in an aid of construing legislation in a way that is consistent with what the ICESCR provides.[605]

8.11.2.2 Policy Formulations: The *Protection of Victoria Harbour* Case

In the *Protection of Victoria Harbour* saga,[606] the courts were prepared to accept a more intensive approach than that outlined in the above cases and to use a heightened level of scrutiny, as compared to the traditional *Wednesbury* unreasonableness, outside human rights cases. In this case, the Society for the Protection of the Harbour Ltd., a public interest organisation focused on preventing excessive and unlawful reclamation of Victoria Harbour, sought judicial review proceedings against the decisions of the government to reclaim the Wanchai and Central waterfronts of the harbour. The Town Planning Board had made the reclamation decision based on the need to construct a bypass to ease traffic congestion in the area, and the plan required a substantial amount of reclamation. Under the Protection of the Harbour Ordinance,[607] the harbour is recognised as a special public asset and natural heritage of Hong Kong people, and there is a 'presumption against reclamation' in the harbour.[608]

602. *Ho Choi Wan* (N571) [60].

603. Ibid., [66]–[68].

604. Ibid., [65].

605. Kemal Bokhary, *Human Rights* (Sweet & Maxwell 2015) 18.

606. *Town Planning Board v Society for the Protection of the Harbour Ltd* (N571).

607. Cap 531, Laws of Hong Kong.

608. Ibid., s 3(1).

For financial and tactical reasons, the Society determined that it would only challenge the Wanchai Draft Plan at that time, believing that the principles laid down by the court in this case would also be applicable to the Central Draft Plan. At the heart of the challenge lies the proper interpretation of section 3 of the Ordinance. Despite the Court's rejection that section 3 created a right to environment as advocated by the Society, it found that human rights jurisprudence provided a useful analytical framework, and that the same tests could also be adopted even in the absence of a constitutional right as they are consistent with a purposive construction of section 3 and the mischief rule in construction.[609]

Chu J noted that the clear objective of the Ordinance in question was to preserve and protect the harbour against excessive reclamation. Section 3 created a duty on the part of a public body to give proper consideration to the need to preserve the harbour as a special public asset and a natural heritage, as well as the presumption against reclamation. Given the nature of the harbour, Chu J further pointed out that the ability of the harbour to sustain itself in the future was a highly pertinent consideration. She was impressed by the international law principle of sustainable development and used this as a guiding principle to strike a balance between environmental protection and developmental considerations. It followed that any attempt to deplete what might be regarded as a natural heritage had to be justified by a compelling overriding need.[610]

Chu J furthered that to prevent excessive reclamation, it is necessary to demonstrate that the need for reclamation cannot be met by any other means, and that the extent of reclamation should be kept to a minimum. In other words, whether there is an alternative has to be considered in the context of proportionality. Considering the above, she held that the alternative would not be viable if it involved incurring costs or paying a price that would be disproportionate to the harm of carrying out the proposed reclamation. However, there should be no reclamation if the alternative merely involved a more costly method. In this respect, she noted that it was only concerned with whether the

609. *Town Planning Board v Society for the Protection of the Harbour Ltd* (N571) [2003] 2 HKLRD 787 (HCAL 19/2003) (CFI), 803 (Chu J).

610. Ibid., [84]–[87].

decision-maker had properly considered or attempted other viable alternatives, but it would not weigh the alternatives themselves.[611]

Applying the three tests of compelling and overriding need, no viable alternative, and minimal impairment, Chu J found that the proposed reclamation failed to satisfy these tests. She further held that every part of the reclamation had to satisfy the three tests and a broad approach that looked at only the broad scheme was insufficient for preserving and protecting the harbour. Overall, such stringent tests imposed by the Court presented formidable restraints for any future reclamation.

Despite its ruling being generally welcomed by the community at large, a leap-frog procedure was initiated by the Board to appeal directly to the CFA.[612] In contrast with the wide approach adopted by the Court of First Instance, the CFA chose to determine the issues on the narrow ground of statutory interpretation alone. Chan expressed his disappointment, stressing that by adopting this narrow approach, the CFA 'missed a golden opportunity to develop the jurisprudence on the relevance of international treaty obligations and the principles of sustainable development'.[613]

However, the CFA upheld Chu's judgment and found that the Board had applied the wrong test in its interpretation of section 3. The Court was satisfied with a single 'overriding public need test' or 'overriding and compelling present need test', despite it more or less embodying the three tests adopted by Chu J. Adopting this 'overriding public need test', the Court interpreted 'overriding' as 'compelling and present' and 'public need' as 'economic, environmental and social needs of the community'.[614] The Court also stated that there must be convincing evidence that the overriding public need for reclamation has rebutted the presumption against reclamation.[615] The Court thus held that the Board erred in law in failing to adopt such a test in reaching its decision to

611. Ibid., [62].

612. Part II Division 3 of the Hong Kong Court of Final Appeal Ordinance, Cap 484, Laws of Hong Kong.

613. Johannes Chan, 'A Sliding Scale of Reasonableness in Judicial Review' in Hugh Corder (ed), *Comparing Administrative Justice across the Commonwealth* (JUTA 2008) 245.

614. *Town Planning Board v Society for the Protection of the Harbour Ltd* (N571) [2004] 1 HKLRD 396, [45]–[46].

615. Ibid., [50]–[51].

refuse to reduce the extent of the proposed reclamation of Wanchai. The Board's decision was therefore quashed and remitted for reconsideration.

What is more, the CFA, in a separate judgment, also upheld the indemnity cost order made by Chu J because the Society is a charitable organisation, and not because the Court disapproved of litigation by the government. The CFA stated that it was reasonable for the Society to resort to litigation when other attempts had failed, that the issue was undoubtedly a matter of public importance, and that it did not stand to make any personal gains from the litigation.[616] This is an encouraging development and will be of great significance for public interest litigation. However, this is just the end of part one, and the issue of a sliding scale of scrutiny was left open by the CFA. It was raised squarely in the second phase of the litigation concerning the Draft Plan of the reclamation in Central.

Even though the above judgment concerning the Wanchai reclamation was in force, the then chief executive Leung Chun Ying refused to exercise his discretion to remit the Central Plan back to the Board for review. His refusal formed the subject matter of the second phase of the litigation.[617] In this regard, actions by the government that raise concerns should be heavily scrutinised and challenged when necessary, and it has been repeatedly shown that threats to individuals mostly come from states.[618] In this case, the CFA held that a more stringent standard of review than the traditional *Wednesbury* standard was required. Hartmann NPJ concluded:

> The greater the degree of interference with a fundamental right, the more the court will require by way of justification before it is satisfied that the decision is reasonable in the public law sense.
>
> It is plain that the Harbour Ordinance does not enshrine a fundamental human right, even if that right is restricted to Hong Kong people. Nevertheless, in Chu J's judgment the enshrined status of the harbour as a natural heritage of all Hong Kong people was underscored. Its preservation, it was said,

616. *Society for the Protection of Victoria Harbour Ltd (No. 2)* (N571) [2004] 2 HKLRD 95 (CFA).

617. Ibid.

618. As I argue in Chapter One of this book.

> was therefore to be afforded a high propensity: the presumption against reclamation being a strong presumption. …
>
> In the circumstances, having regard to the unique legal status of the harbour, and the continuing duty, a duty of exacting measure, placed on public officials to look to its preservation, I am satisfied that, in reviewing the lawfulness of the decision of the Chief Executive in Council, something more rigorous than the traditional *Wednesbury* test is required although, in my judgment, the level of anxious scrutiny that must be applied when there is substantial interference with a fundamental human right would be to set the test too high.[619]

Chan has commented that this approach is a 'heightened intensity of review' or a 'sliding scale of review', saying that it gives due weight to the importance attached by the LegCo to the protection and preservation of Victoria Harbour. As the CFA pointed out, it is not sufficient for the decision-maker simply to state that the test has been satisfied. Rather, there must be cogent evidence of this before the presumption against reclamation can be rebutted. To ascertain whether the evidence is enough, the court has to scrutinise the facts of the case in depth, and it would not be sufficient for it to be satisfied simply with the existence of the evidence alone.[620] Thus, the discretion of the decision-maker in this case is fettered and heavily circumscribed.

According to Chan, this principle is highly captivating because it is more rational than the traditional *Wednesbury* analysis. The principle also explicitly recognises that there are different shades and degrees of reasonableness, and the standard of review should be commensurate with the gravity of the subject matter. The principle is flexible enough to encompass the traditional *Wednesbury* test, on one hand, as well as the more rigorous proportionality test, on the other.[621] It also requires the executive authority to justify its decision and to set out its weighing process in the decision-making process. It allows the

619. Ibid., [77]–[79].

620. Chan (N613) 253.

621. Ibid., 254.

courts to examine the decision-making process and to articulate, in a rational manner, the basis of judicial scrutiny and the value judgment of the judiciary concerning the importance of the subject matter.[622]

Overall, the *Protection of Victoria Harbour* saga is interesting in that it illustrates how the Court of First Instance and the CFA have developed a heightened intensity of review that goes beyond the traditional *Wednesbury* formula. Chan has opined that the difference between this sliding scale of scrutiny and the proportionality test is merely a matter of degree.[623] Thus, proportionality has already been recognised as an independent ground of judicial review to adjudicate on cases other than constitutional or legislative review and human rights cases in Hong Kong.

8.11.2.3 Socio-Economic Rights Disputes: From Deferential to Intensive

Article 36 of the Basic Law states that 'Hong Kong residents shall have the right to social welfare in accordance with law. The welfare benefits and retirement security of the labour force shall be protected by law'. Article 145 of the same refers to 'the previous social welfare system' as the basis for future development and improvement of social welfare policies, which suggests that the definition of 'social welfare' should be understood in light of the social welfare system immediately before the handover.[624] As a matter of fact, the right to social welfare is protected in the constitutions of many countries and has found its place in the Universal Declaration of Human Rights 1948 (UDHR 1948) and the ICESCR under international law.

According to Kong, the national debate often goes to the level of legal protection that the right to social welfare envisages under the court's interpretation of the right in a particular situation, given the primary responsibilities of the

622. Ibid., 255.

623. Ibid., 238.

624. *Catholic Diocese of Hong Kong v Secretary for Justice* [2007] 4 HKLRD 483, [49]. See also Karen Kong, 'Right to Social Welfare' in Chan and Lim (N91) [26.007]–[26.008].

administration to balance state resources.[625] Because prioritising conflicting interests and allocating limited resources are in the realm of the executive and legislature, Hong Kong courts have needed to interpret the right to social welfare with caution.

8.11.2.3.1 The Obstetric Services *Case*

In the *Obstetric Services* case,[626] although the courts held that Article 145 of the Basic Law referred to 'public healthcare services' as an important part of the social welfare system, they adopted their previous stance and remained deferential to the administrative authorities by claiming that in an area where limited public resources are involved, matters of community policy are predominantly for the executive arm of the government. Therefore, the courts are inclined to apply the justification test with a broad margin of discretion being given to the administration.[627] In other words, in areas not impinging upon core values related to personal or human characteristics, the courts will only intervene where the line drawn is manifestly without reasonable foundation.[628]

In this case, the applicant, Ms Fok, sought to challenge a policy adopted, and a decision made, by the Hospital Authority to charge higher rates for obstetric services in public hospitals to non-eligible persons. Ms Fok argued that this was discriminatory and that she should have been treated the same as a Hong Kong resident, given her close connection with the city. This close connection with Hong Kong was founded on the basis that she was soon going to become a Hong Kong resident and that she had local family ties, thus making her a *de facto* resident already. She argued that her *de jure* status as a non-resident was irrelevant. The Court of First Instance dismissed this argument because a *de facto* similarity did not give her comparable legal status, and it established that there was no discriminatory treatment between the applicant and Hong Kong

625. Ibid., [26.001].

626. *Fok Chun Wa* (N220).

627. *Chan Yeuk Ming v Hong Kong Housing Authority* (unreported, 7 September 2012, HCAL 25/2012) (CFI); *Lam Wo Lun v Director of Social Welfare* (unreported, HCAL 133/2010, 14 May 2012), [61] (Lam J), [2012] HKEC 670, [2012] HKCU 1006.

628. *Fok Chun Wa* (N220) (unreported, HCAL 133/2010, 14 May 2012), [61] (Lam J).

residents as they are considered to be relatively different and can accordingly be subject to differential treatment.

In reaching the decision, the Trial Court adopted the proportionality analysis in ascertaining whether there had been a breach of Article 36 (i.e., the right to social welfare) of the Basic Law, and if so, whether such infringement was justified. The Court noted that the restrictions to the right may be justified 'if it has rational connection with the pursuit of a legitimate aim and if it is no more than necessary for the achievement of that aim'.[629] Therefore, the government was able to satisfy the Court that it was pursuing legitimate aims in adopting the differential treatment, and that the means used to do so (i.e., re-characterisation of persons in the applicant's position as non-eligible persons) was no more than was necessary to achieve that aim.

The case was appealed to the Court of Appeal [630] and, finally, to the CFA.[631] Nevertheless, both of appeals were unsuccessful. In the CFA, Ma CJ asked, in relation to equality, 'is there enough of a relevant difference between X and Y [the comparators] to justify differential treatment?' [632] His Lordship held that the line which was drawn to divide the eligible persons from the non-eligible persons — namely, whether they held a Hong Kong identity card — was justified, as this line 'is entirely within the spectrum of reasonableness'; hence, the justification test was satisfied. In this case, the 'spectrum of reasonableness' assessment was considered appropriate as the situation reflects the following criteria:

> Where a number of alternative solutions are open to the executive, legislature or other authority in dealing with any particular problem, how far must the court go in inquiring as to the alternative that is least intrusive into the constitutional protected right in question? This is ... the third limb of the justification test [in the *Yau Yuk Lung* case], that is, the requirement that any difference in treatment must be 'no more than necessary' to accomplish the legitimate aim. This question at one stage caused me some concern, for this

629. Ibid., [2008] HKEC 2161, [125].

630. Ibid., [2011] 1 HKLRD A1 (CA).

631. Ibid., [2012] 2 HKC 413 (CFA), (2012) 15 HKCFAR 409.

632. Ibid., (2012) 15 HKCFAR 409, [58(1)].

> third limb seemed at first blush to require the court, even in a socio-economic policy context, to embark on an exercise of searching for the best alternative among different solutions ... In the socio-economic context, where policy considerations are best left to the executive, legislature and other authority, the [court's] position is as follows:
>
> (1) ... it is to see whether the relevant act or decision satisfies the justification test. The justification test is similar in nature to the test of proportionality: see *Yau Yuk Lung* ... To ask whether a difference in treatment is justified is the same as asking whether what has been done (or omitted to be done) or decided is a proportionate response to the legitimate aim.
>
> (2) The recognition of the respective roles of the judiciary, the executive and the legislature (or, to use the term, margin of appreciation) is relevant at all stages of the justification test.
>
> (3) Where a number of alternative, but reasonable, solutions to a problem exist, the court will not put itself in a place of the executive or legislature or other authority to decide which is the best option. That is not its role. The court will only interfere where the option chosen is clearly beyond the spectrum of reasonable options; in other words, the option has clearly gone too far (or further than necessary) to deal with the problem. In this situation, the court will not have been satisfied under the third limb of the justification test ...
>
> (4) ... however, outside the area of socio-economic or other general policy matters, where fundamental concepts or core-values are involved, the court will be particularly stringent or intense in the application of the justification test. But in the area of socio-economic or other general policy matters, attempts to search for more and more alternatives to the solution that was adopted in any one case, should be discouraged. This, I reiterate, is not the role of the court. ...
>
> unless the solution or alternative in question is manifestly beyond the spectrum of reasonableness (or manifestly without reasonable foundation) the court will not interfere.[633]

633. Ibid., [75]–[76] (Ma CJ).

Ma CJ also referenced the decision of the Supreme Court of Canada in *RJR-McDonald Inc v Attorney-General of Canada*,[634] which was decided in the context of legislation affecting the freedom of expression. There, McLachlin J (as he then was) stated: 'If the law falls within a range of reasonable alternatives, the courts will not find it overbroad merely because they can conceive of an alternative which might better tailor objective to infringement'.[635]

In delivering the judgment in the CFA,[636] Ma CJ was of the opinion that the differential treatment was justified and, thus, not discriminatory. His Lordship held that the role of the judiciary as a supervisory body should be distinct from that of the executive and legislature as primary decision-makers on public fund allocation.[637] Furthermore, he also held that the Court would only interfere when the option chosen by the executive or legislature was 'clearly beyond the spectrum of reasonable options'.[638] When core values are disregarded by the executive or legislature, it would be appropriate for the Court to interfere, the examples of which include differential treatments based on personal characteristics, such as race, politics, or social origin.[639] Beyond this, the Court could not claim expertise to tackle socio-economic policies and would not require the executive or the legislature to adopt a less restrictive alternative, except where questions of legality arose.[640] As the differential treatment was based on residency status, which was not a personal characteristic or a core value, it fell within the range of reasonable options to maintain sustainable government expenditure, and thus there was no infringement of the equality provision in the Basic Law.[641]

Overall, Kong has opined that in the *Obstetric Services* saga,[642] the courts emphasised the need to defer to the executive in terms of social and economic

634. [1995] 2 SCR 199.
635. Ibid., 342.
636. *Fok Chun Wa* (N220) (2012) 15 HKCFAR 409, [70].
637. Ibid.
638. Ibid., [75].
639. Ibid., [77].
640. Ibid., [81].
641. Ibid., [90].
642. *Fok Chun Wa* (N220) [2012] 2 HKC 413 (CFA), [75]–[76] (Ma CJ).

policies so as to uphold the separation of powers of the three branches of government and to limit them to the determination of legal issues, saying that

> [w]hereas in civil and political rights, the court adopted the 'minimum impairment test' under the third limb of the proportionality analysis in scrutinising restrictions thereof, in economic and social rights, the court tends to exercise a high degree of self-restraint. Where no fundamental rights or suspect ground of discrimination is involved, the court will only intervene where the Government's policy or decision is 'manifestly without reasonable foundation'.[643]

In short, what Ma CJ said above corresponds with Mark Tushnet's identification of social welfare rights as 'weak substantive rights'.[644]

Moreover, even though the CFA did not rule the general policy on differing maternity charges to be unconstitutional, Ms Fok succeeded at the Court of Appeal on a point based on administrative law.[645] The Court held that despite the general policy of differentiating non-resident pregnant women and local pregnant women being justified, the Hospital Authority had acted unlawfully by failing to exercise its discretion under the Hospital Authority Ordinance to consider waiving Ms Fok's obstetric fees in light of her economic hardship.[646] The authority concerned had, it was held, failed to recognise its duty to consider waiving the fees in question upon request. Rather, it applied a blanket policy of refusal, failing to consider Ms Fok's individual circumstances. Thus, the Court quashed the authority's decision, remitting the matter back to the authority for reconsideration, during which Ms Fok was allowed to make representations as she wished.[647] This point was not impugned on appeal before the CFA.

In this issue, Kong is of the view that although the decision fell short of addressing the inequality between local mothers and Mainland mothers with local family ties in the guarantee of the right to social welfare and the right to

643. Kong (N624) [26.045].

644. Mark Tushnet, 'Social Welfare Rights and the Forms of Judicial Review' (2004) 82 *TLR* 1895, 1902.

645. *Fok Chun Wa* (N220) [2011] 1 HKLRD A1 (CA).

646. Hospital Authority Ordinance, Cap 113, s 18(3).

647. *Fok Chun Wa* (N220) [2011] 1 HKLRD A1 (CA), 124 and 130.

health more generally, such procedural relief would, to a certain extent, benefit an individual claimant suffering economic hardship.[648] Nevertheless, such procedural relief has only achieved 'piecemeal justice' and is not sufficient because it does not benefit other Mainland mothers in similar situations who have not brought their cases before the courts.[649]

8.11.2.3.2 The Comprehensive Social Security Assistance *Cases*

In Hong Kong, the positive-rights or duties argument has been considered in several cases.[650] In general, despite being short of fundamental disregard for core values, the courts will intervene if the impugned restriction is not rationally connected to the legitimate purpose, or if the inroads it makes into the protected right are manifestly without reasonable foundation. Between 2009 and 2010, the Hong Kong Court of First Instance adjudicated on two cases concerning the constitutional protection of social welfare rights. Both of them concerned the new residence requirement for the CSSA scheme effective from 1 January 2004. In *Kong Yunming*,[651] the applicant challenged the seven-year residence requirement for the CSSA eligibility, whereas in *Yao Man Fai George*,[652] the issue tabled before the Court was the constitutionality of the one-year 'continuous residence in Hong Kong' requirement for CSSA enrolment. Both requirements, introduced in 2003, resulted from a report addressing the growing burden on the social welfare system in Hong Kong because of the ageing population and the continuing influx of new immigrants. In May 2005, in response to the requirements, the UNESCR Committee expressed its concern, stating that it

> is seriously concerned that under the existing social security system, and in particular under the [CSSA], the levels of benefit are not sufficient to guarantee a decent standard of living and that many low-income persons, in particular old persons, are not covered by the scheme. The Committee

648. Kong (N448) 200.

649. Ibid.

650. *Leung Kwok Hung* (N24) and *Chan Hau Man Christina* (N379).

651. *Kong Yunming* (N165).

652. *Yao Man Fai George* (N571).

is further concerned that new migrants are unable to apply for CSSA due to the seven-year residence requirement.[653]

Despite the UNESCR Committee's comments, both the Court of First Instance and the Court of Appeal upheld the seven-year residence requirement in *Kong Yunming*, but declared, in *Yao Man Fai George*, that the one-year continuous residence requirement was unconstitutional on a *Wednesbury*-unreasonableness basis. This is because 'the line drawn does not match the professed rationale for drawing the line. In short, the one-year rule as implemented unreasonably in the *Wednesbury* sense excludes those who have lived outside Hong Kong for a long time'.[654]

These two decisions demonstrated the courts' approach in adjudicating cases that concern social and economic policies, in particular those involving the distribution of scarce public resources. At issue in these cases was the intensity of review, as well as the courts' view of the justification given by the government which accounts for the difference in results.[655] In *Kong Yunming*, the applicant was a Mainland Chinese woman who came to settle in Hong Kong in 2005. Unfortunately, her husband passed away upon her arrival. She tried to apply for the CSSA but was refused owing to the fact that she did not satisfy the seven-year residence requirement for this social assistance. She then impugned the constitutionality of this requirement, arguing that (1) the change of the residence requirement from one year to seven years on 1 January 2014 was in breach of Article 36 of the Basic Law, which concerns the right to social welfare for all Hong Kong residents; (2) the policy was not one that 'developed and improved' the previous welfare system as required by Article 145 of the Basic Law because of its discriminatory nature; and (3) the policy discriminated against non-permanent residents and was thus in breach of the Article 25 equality provision of the Basic Law. The Court of First Instance based its analysis primarily on discrimination and the justification test, holding that the differential treatment between permanent and non-permanent residents was justified and saying that the policy was properly formulated under Article 145

653. Concluding Observations of the Committee on Economic, Social and Cultural Rights in the People's Republic of China (including Hong Kong and Macau), 13 May 2005, UN Doc E/C 12/1/Add 107.

654. *Yao Man Fai George* (N571) [2012] 4 HKC 180, [199].

655. Karen Kong, 'Adjudicating Social Welfare Rights in Hong Kong' (2012) 10(2) *IJCL* 588, 589.

as a 'development and improvement' of the previous social welfare system. Therefore, Article 36 was not infringed.

In *Yao Man Fai George*, the Court of First Instance held the opposite. This case concerned a Hong Kong permanent resident whose employment in Mainland China was terminated. He returned to Hong Kong and tried to apply for the CSSA but was declined as he did not satisfy the one-year continuous residence requirement. The applicant succeeded, not only in the Court of First Instance but also in the Court of Appeal, obtaining judgments in both that held the one-year requirement of continuous residence in Hong Kong for the CSSA entitlement unconstitutional. The decisions were based on the conjecture that the requirement infringed the Article 25 equality provision and the Article 31 freedom to travel provision under the Basic Law. As the government had failed to prove sufficient evidence to demonstrate that there had been a genuine need to impose the requirement, together with the fact that very few CSSA applicants had fallen into this category (i.e., 4.7 percent of all CSSA applicants, of which the majority obtained a wavier), the Court thus held that the discrimination based on the period of absence in Hong Kong was unjustifiable.[656] The Article 25 equality provision was thus breached. Regarding the right to travel, the Court held that the restriction to travel imposed by the one-year continuous residence requirement failed to satisfy the proportionality test, based on the same analysis as that of discrimination.

Despite success on evidential grounds in *Yao Man Fai George*, in considering various issues in the *Obstetric Services* case and in *Kong Yunming*, it is apparent that the courts view socio-economic policies as being within the 'discretionary area of judgment' of the administration and legislature, and that they should defer to the decisions of the government as long as there is no proscribed ground of discrimination.[657] This is because socio-economic policies often involve balancing general public interests and the allocation of scare resources. As Cheung J has said:

> In short, one is involved in an area of competing interests and competing rights. By definition, a balance has to be struck. And again by definition, striking that balance is by nature a political job for the government and the

656. *Yao Man Fai George* (N571) [2010] HKEC 968, [56].

657. *Kong Yunming* (N165) [2009] 4 HKLRD 382 (CFI), [127] and [129].

> legislature with the involvement of public opinion. In matters of the present sort, courts must be very slow to interfere.[658]

Against this background, questions of whether a social policy is no more than is necessary to fulfil the policy aim under the justification test of an alleged discrimination (as in the *Obstetric Services* case and *Kong Yunming*) or whether a policy is a 'development and improvement' of pre-existing social welfare system under Article 145 of the Basic Law (as in *Kong Yunming* alone) should be left to the wisdom of the administration and the legislature. The courts are therefore unlikely to overturn a legislative or administrative decision by holding it unconstitutional, and they have indicated that they do not find themselves constitutionally 'well-suited' or institutionally 'well-equipped' to tackle these matters.[659] Overall, as shown in these three cases, the courts seem to be deferential on the basis of the financial implications of these socio-economic policies.

The 'not-constitutionally well-suited' argument (i.e., the constitutional incompetence argument) is less convincing in Hong Kong than in the UK since Hong Kong has long suffered a democratic deficit (both before and after the change of sovereignty in 1997). Furthermore, the legitimacy of the 'appointed government' in Hong Kong has repeatedly been accused of being incapable of representing its people. This is evident in various political arrangements, whereby the elite of Hong Kong, mostly representing the interests of the wealthy, have tremendous influence over the government and of the LegCo. Ultimately, they can easily defeat proposals to make improvements concerning those workers' rights [660] and social welfare rights,[661] among others. Such a lack of democratic development will likely further intensify the degree of inequality and poverty in future. In this climate, Cora Chan has suggested to the courts that they

> should cautiously scrutinise democratic legitimacy factors *even* for the purpose of determining whether the government is more likely to be correct,

658. Ibid., [118].
659. Ibid., [57].
660. Richard Wong, 'Are standard working hours a good thing for Hong Kong?', *South China Morning Post*, 24 February 2015, available at: www.scmp.com/comment/insight-opinion/article/1722330/are-standard-working-hours-good-thing-hong-kong, last accessed 26 May 2020.
661. Siu and Ngo (N457).

> bearing in mind that only half of the [LegCo] is returned by universal suffrage as of today, and the [Hong Kong] government does not have a particularly promising record for conducting thorough public consultations and incorporating public views reflected through consultations.[662]

However, things changed when the *Kong Yunming* case was appealed to the CFA.[663] Riberio PJ, in response to the decision, stated that any restriction to the right to social welfare is subject to constitutional review by the courts on a proportionality basis.[664] Under the three-stage proportionality test, the court should first ask 'whether the restriction pursues a legitimate social aim'. Having identified that aim, it should ask 'whether the impugned restriction is rationally connected with the accomplishment of that end'. If such rational connection is established, the next question should be 'whether the means employed are proportionate or whether, on the contrary, they make excessive inroads into the protected right'.[665] In its unanimous decision in *Kong Yunming*, the Court held that the seven-year residence requirement for CSSA imposed by the Department of Social Welfare was unconstitutional, saying that the government had failed to support its claim that the requirement pursued the legitimate aim of cutting public expenditure in order to ensure the sustainability of the social welfare system,[666] and that such measure had conflicted with the One-Way Permit family re-union policy (which accepted immigrants from the Mainland) and the population policy (which sought to increase the young population in Hong Kong to balance the ageing population issue).[667] More importantly, the Court also found that there had been insufficient evidence to show that the measure would have saved a significant sum of public funding, or that it could have maintained the social welfare system. In this regard, the Court concluded that there had been no rational connection between the measure and the legitimate aim, or alternatively, the measure had been disproportionate and manifestly without

662. Cora Chan, 'Judicial Deference at Work: Some Reflections on *Chan Kin Sum* and *Kong Yun Ming*' (2010) 40 *HKLJ* 1, 7.

663. *Kong Yunming* (N165) (2013) 16 HKCFAR 950.

664. Ibid., [36].

665. Ibid., [39].

666. Ibid., [2014] 1 HKC 518 (CFA), 41.

667. Ibid., 140.

reasonable foundation.[668] Therefore, the seven-year residence requirement for CSSA was thus held to be unconstitutional.[669]

Up to the present, the *Kong Yunming* case has been a landmark victory for the protection of constitutional social welfare rights under Article 36 of the Basic Law. As Chen has observed, the CFA incorporated the 'minimum core content' approach by allowing Article 36 to take on a meaning that overcame the problem of uncertainty which makes socio-economic rights difficult to be enforced judicially.[670] Moreover, adjustments of the 1997 versions of these social welfare rights (i.e., changes to the relevant rules and policies that prevailed in 1997) have been constitutionally permissible provided that they can be justified on a proportionality basis. This proportionality analysis (i.e., whether the adjustment is manifestly unreasonable or without any reasonable foundation) helps the court adjudicate on the reasonableness of the adjustment and is, to a certain extent, similar to the South African *Grootboom*-reasonableness review.[671] Setting the standard for constitutionally protected social welfare rights at their 1997 level and requiring the government to provide justification for any retreat from it are also compatible with the views of the UNESCR Committee. The Committee specified that:

> There is a strong presumption that retrogressive measures taken in relation to the right to social security are prohibited under the [ICESCR]. If any deliberately retrogressive measures are taken, the State party has the burden of proving that they have been introduced after the most careful consideration of all alternatives and that they are duly justified by reference to the totality of the rights provided for in the [ICESCR], in the context of the full use of the maximum available resources of the State party. The Committee will look carefully at whether: (a) there was reasonable justification for the action; (b) alternatives were comprehensively examined; (c) there was genuine participation of affected groups in examining the proposed measures and alternatives; (d) the measures were directly or indirectly discriminatory; (e) the measures will have a sustained impact on

668. Ibid.

669. Ibid., 143.

670. Albert Chen, 'A "Stroke of Genius" in *Kong Yunming*' (2014) 44 *HKLJ* 7, 24.

671. Ibid.

> the realization of the right to social security, an unreasonable impact on acquired social security rights or whether an individual or group is deprived of access to the minimum essential level of social security; and (f) whether there was an independent review of the measures at the national level.[672]

Furthermore, this case also indicates that the courts are seemingly more willing to question the justification given by the executive on public policy and resource allocation, requiring them to take their constitutional duty seriously to protect the right to social welfare of the marginalised poor.[673] As Kong has noted, the Court's use of the proportionality enquiry can also be seen as its recognition of the right to social welfare, or socio-economic rights generally, as having the same level of importance as civil and political rights under the Basic Law.[674] In fact, the Court unanimously stated that restrictions on the social welfare right under Article 36 of the Basic Law must be justified on a proportionality basis. This case also leaves open questions regarding the legitimacy of the judiciary in overruling government policy choices on resource allocation.[675] Kong furthers that the government will have to take its constitutional responsibility seriously when drafting and changing policies with implications on the right to social welfare by obliging themselves to observe the proportionality principle when formulating policies, and will need to be aware that their measures could be struck down during a proportionality review if they are found to be more drastic than necessary for achieving the desired result. In consequence, the government will have to give legitimate reasons to support its policy options and back up their decisions supported with sufficient science and statistical evidence, so mere intuition and conventional thinking will be unable to come into play.[676]

This case also shows the Court's role in upholding fundamental values of family re-union and non-discrimination in the community even though there has been social tension between Mainland China and Hong Kong arising

672. UNESCR Committee, General Comment No. 19: The right to social security (Art 9) (39th session), E/C 12/GC/19 (2008), [12].

673. Karen Kong, '*Kong Yunming v Director of Social Welfare*: Implications for Law and Policy on Social Welfare' (2014) 44 *HKLJ* 67.

674. Ibid., 74.

675. Ibid., 68.

676. Ibid., 80.

from growing localism and nativism in the region.[677] Thus, although Hong Kong has long been suffering a democratic deficit, this case shows that the courts do take on a compensatory role by acting as a substitute for holding the executive accountable in public policy matters affecting human rights. The more supporting evidence required to justify their reasons for implementing policies, the more transparent, and thereby accountable, they are to the general public. Hence, the full adoption of proportionality would promote better governance in terms of transparency and accountability in administrative decision-making and judicial adjudication in general, and in particular, those in the sphere of polycentric socio-economic rights issues which involve the prioritisation of conflicting interests and allocation of scarce resources. Its full adoption would also improve the quality of the decision-making process by encouraging officials to focus on alternative courses of action.

8.12 Non-European Union Laws and Non-Human Rights Laws Can Be Easily Framed within European Union Law, Human Rights Law, and Basic Law Dimensions

While some cases may not show, on the face of them, they can indeed be framed within EU law and human rights dimensions. It follows that any difference in treatment between EU law and human rights cases, on one hand, and non-EU law and non-human rights cases, on the other, is sometimes difficult to sustain. Ultimately, these cases put the courts under an obligation, as mandated under the European Communities Act 1972 (ECA 1972)[678] (up to 31 January 2020) and the Human Rights Act 1998 (HRA 1998),[679] to use proportionality analysis in coming to their decisions. *R v Chief Constable of Sussex, ex parte International Trader's Ferry Ltd*,[680] for example, had *prima facie* nothing to do with any EU law at the outset. In this case, the applicants argued that it was unreasonable under the domestic law for the chief constable to reduce police cover at the port to two days a week, a change which ultimately led to traders being unable to make shipments to EU countries. However, the traders also framed their case in terms of EU law,

677. Ibid., 68.

678. ss 2–3.

679. ss 2–4 and 6.

680. [1998] 3 WLR 1260 (HL), [1999] 2 AC 418 (HL).

arguing that the decreased police coverage was disproportionate under EU law as it prohibits quantitative restrictions on exports and measures having equivalent effect. As a result, the House of Lords was not only required to apply the *Wednesbury* test, but the proportionality formula as well, in their respective contexts after the chief constable's decision. In *R (on the application of Alconbury Developments Ltd) v Secretary of State for the Environment, Transport and the Regions*,[681] the Court also called for the application of the proportionality principle to both human rights and non-human rights cases.[682]

As far as non-human rights cases are concerned, Craig has even used the *Wednesbury* case itself to argue that if the HRA 1998 had been in force during the 1940s, the applicants, Associated Provincial Picture Houses, would have contended that the restriction imposed in that case — that a cinema could open on Sunday, but could not admit children under 15 years of age — was contrary to Article 8 (i.e., the right to family life) or perhaps even Article 10 (i.e., freedom of speech) of the ECHR.[683]

The same argument is also applicable to Hong Kong. *Ng Ngau Chai v The Town Planning Board*,[684] for example, concerned a challenge against the decision by the Town Planning Board and the Planning Department to sell land in West Kowloon to be used for residential use without height restriction. The result would be that 'wall-like' structures would be built along the Tai Kok Tsui waterfront which would block air and ventilation in the inner city area. The applicant, a resident living in the inner Tai Kok Tsui area where the poorer strata of the population reside, claimed that the decision was in breach of the Urban Design Guidelines issued by the department concerned which articulates 'the idea that the building being erected along the seaside shall be lower than the building inland and make special preservation for breezeways and view corridors'.[685] This is a clear case of the under-represented using the courts as a forum to voice their concerns. Despite its technical failure at the permission stage,[686]

681. [2001] UKHL 23, [2001] 2 WLR 1389, [2001] 2 All ER 929, [2002] Env LR 12, [2003] 2 AC 295.

682. Ibid., [2003] 2 AC 295, 321 (Lord Slynn).

683. Paul Craig, *Administrative Law* (7th edn, Sweet & Maxwell 2012) 651.

684. [2007] HKEC 1207.

685. Ibid., [7].

686. Ibid., [19].

the matter was amendable to judicial review because it involved a wide public concern (i.e., air quality). Having a constitutional duty to act as a supervisory body to scrutinise the legality of administrative decisions and actions under the doctrine of separation of powers, the Court of First Instance should have assessed whether the government considered the proportionate impact of the planning decision on public health. This is because, as argued above, it falls within the right to life and the right to health protected under the Basic Law.[687]

In another judicial review application made by the Clean Air Foundation, a non-governmental organisation operating to protect Hong Kong residents' right to clean air, against the government for its failure to take action to alleviate air pollution in Hong Kong, the applicant sought two declarations from the court.[688] The applicant argued that the government has an affirmative duty to protect the residents and the economy of Hong Kong from the known harmful effects of air pollution under Article 28 of the Basic Law and Article 2 of the BORO, which provide for the protection of a right to life and under Article 12 of the ICESCR as incorporated through Article 39 of the Basic Law, which provides protection for the 'right to health'. The applicant also argued that the Air Pollution Control Ordinance[689] and its subsidiary legislation were inconsistent with the government's commitment under Article 28 of the Basic Law, Article 2 of the BORO, and various international covenants.

The applicants outlined the failure of the government to (1) establish bus routes and service re-scheduling to facilitate higher occupancy, (2) impose mandatory requirements for all diesel vehicles to change to Euro IV and Euro V standards, and (3) reconsider urban design to facilitate air circulation and to protect people from transport pollution. On the first declaration, Hartmann J accepted that it was at least *prima facie* arguable that a constitutional right to life under Article 28 of the Basic Law and Article 2 of the BORO may be applicable to the current case. Moreover, although Article 12 of the ICESCR only looked to the 'progressive achievement' of the right to health, there was a *prima facie* arguable case that a duty to combat air pollution was imposed. However, the second

687. Basic Law, Arts 28 and 39, the latter of which incorporated Art 12 of the ICESCR.

688. *Clean Air Foundation Ltd* (N571).

689. Cap 311, Laws of Hong Kong.

declaration was refused because it requires 'an examination of government policy',[690] and it is 'simply too broad in scope'.[691] Despite amendments made by the applicant, Hartmann J was still of the view that the second declaration demanded the court to examine the merits of government policy rather than its legality which were not matters for the court to determine. He therefore refused to grant permission to the application.

In this regard, Hong Kong courts have lagged behind others, including the Indian Supreme Court which actively adopted the 'polluters-pay principle' and the 'precautionary principle' from international law to adjudicate on environmental matters in public interest litigation. In *A P State Pollution Control Board v M V Nayudu*, the Indian Supreme Court stated:

> Environmental concerns ... are, in our view, of equal importance as human rights. In fact both are to be traced to Article 21 which deals with fundamental rights to life and liberty. While environmental aspects concern life, human rights aspects concern liberty.[692]

While this judgment may be viewed as a very aggressive approach and an expansive interpretation of the constitution by the India Supreme Court, it does demonstrate the different judicial attitudes between Indian courts and Hong Kong courts when they have approached a similar issue.

To be fair, if the *ClientEarth* judgment, which was delivered by the Supreme Court of the UK in April 2015,[693] had been held before *Ng Ngau Chai*[694] and *Clean Air Foundation*,[695] both of them being determined in 2007, the situation might have been different. Indeed, the Hong Kong courts might have referred to these cases and even followed suit — potentially basing their rationale on the authorisation under Article 84 of the Basic Law to refer to jurisprudence

690. *Clean Air Foundation Ltd* (N571) [28].

691. Ibid., [22].

692. AIR 1999 SC 812.

693. *R (ClientEarth) v Secretary of State for the Environment Food and Rural Affairs* [2011] EWHC 3623 (Admin), [2015] UKSC 28, [2015] 4 All ER 724 (SC). Discussed in Chapter Seven of this book.

694. *Ng Ngau Chai* (N684).

695. *Clean Air Foundation Ltd* (N571).

from other common law jurisdictions as well as the entrenched status of the ICCPR, the BORO, and of some ICESCR provisions via Article 39 of the Basic Law. As Hong Kong courts have long been receptive to the use of international and comparative materials, this provides a convenient opportunity for domestic reception of international and comparative jurisprudence, thanks to the inclusion of overseas judges on the CFA. For one thing, Hong Kong courts have, not only in the adjudication of BORO-related cases but also for cases involving the Basic Law, examined comparative jurisprudence (e.g., the decisions of the ECtHR and the General Comments and views of the UN Human Rights Committee, among others). In *Hysan*,[696] Ribeiro PJ confirmed that where the constitutional right invoked is not absolute but no express guidance is given by the BORO or the Basic Law as to the allowable limits of derogations from that right, the courts have developed principles instructing how the proportionality analysis is to be applied — principles that draw heavily on the jurisprudence of other jurisdictions.[697]

In *ClientEarth*, the Supreme Court of the UK granted a declaration that the Air Quality Directive 2008 had been breached and ordered the UK government to take 'immediate action' by preparing a detailed plan of how it would cut illegal levels of air pollution in London and other affected areas. If the Hong Kong courts had followed a similar approach, they might have acted as a 'facilitator' [698] — that is, they could have employed a dialogic judicial review that let the executive, legislature, and citizens (via a diverse public interest litigation group) join together in the judicial arena to come up with a mutually acceptable solution to help save the environment.

There is another interesting point in the *Hysan* case — the relationship between planning restrictions laid down by the Town Planning Board and an individual's property rights. In this case, the crux of the problem is the Town Planning Board's reluctance to take into account the private property rights guaranteed by Articles 6 and 105 of the Basic Law when it imposed planning restrictions against Hysan. Hysan argued that the planning restrictions, for the

696. *Hysan* (N177) (2016) 19 HKCFAR 372 (CFA), FACV Nos. 21 and 22 of 2015, 26 September 2016.

697. Ibid., (2016) 19 HKCFAR 372 (CFA), FACV Nos. 21 and 22 of 2015, 26 September 2016, [50].

698. Discussed in Chapter Four of this book.

purpose of facilitating air ventilation and pedestrian traffic flow in crowded and densely built-up areas, had represented a disproportionate and therefore unconstitutional infringement of their property rights in contravention of Articles 6 and 105. Although Hysan succeeded in having the Board's decisions quashed on traditional judicial review grounds, they sought permission to appeal to the CFA on the constitutional issues for the purpose of ensuring that when reconsidering its decisions concerning the planning restrictions, the Board would have the guidance of the CFA's judgment as to the relevance and application of Articles 6 and 105.

Holding that the right of private property guaranteed by Articles 6 and 105 is engaged and a proportionality analysis of the planning restrictions is thus required, Ribeiro PJ noted that the central feature of Articles 6 and 105 is that they impose an obligation on the Hong Kong government to protect private property rights, and that this obligation should be discharged by providing such protection 'in accordance with law'.[699] It is well-established that this phrase, similar to 'prescribed by law' and 'according to law' which also appear in numerous Articles of the BORO and the Basic Law, mandates the principle of legal certainty and requires the subject matter of the Article to be regulated by laws which are accessible and precisely defined.[700] This ensures that the phrase introduces another aspect of protection — property rights are to be guaranteed by clear and accessible laws, and not, for example, to be left to uncharted administrative discretion.[701] Therefore, Ribeiro PJ saw no basis for reading the words 'in accordance with law' as qualifying or limiting the protection conferred by Articles 6 and 105, and believed the phrase confers the added protection of legal certainty.[702] He furthered that although there has been a general principle that land and natural resources in Hong Kong are state property, the state allocates the responsibility and revenue from their management, use, development, and leasing, etc., to the Hong Kong SAR government, and that where the government leases or grants land to someone

699. Ibid., [29].

700. *Shum Kwok Sher* (N120) (2002) 5 HKCFAR 381, [62]–[65]; *Gurung Kesh Bahadur* (N564) [34]; *Mo Yuk Ping* (N157) [59] and [61].

701. *Hysan* (N177) (2016) 19 HKCFAR 372 (CFA), FACV Nos. 21 and 22 of 2015, 26 September 2016, [30].

702. Ibid., [32].

else, Article 6 plays the complementary role of guaranteeing protection of the private property rights acquired.[703]

Considering the above, it is apparent that all things may be framed with human rights dimensions, a fact which, as far as Hong Kong is concerned, makes these points constitutionally protected under the Basic Law. It follows that even though the Basic Law grants powers to the executive to formulate policies, the courts still have a duty to ensure that such policies do not unjustifiably restrict constitutional and fundamental rights, and are not in breach of administrative law principles. Although the courts give deference to the administration because of its possession of technical knowledge and expertise in the subject matter, this does not mean that the former cannot have substantive review of these administrative decisions based on judicial review principles.[704]

8.13 Concluding Remarks

This chapter has examined the extent to which the principle of proportionality has been integrated into, and re-formulated in, Hong Kong. As EU law and the ECHR are directly applicable to the UK and are highly persuasive in Hong Kong, they create external pressure on the courts to apply the proportionality analysis to other types of judicial review in Hong Kong. Apart from the pressure exerted by some liberal and proactive judges and scholars, the rationale underlying such advocation is also based on the fact that consistency of law, being one of the principles under the rule of law, if being fulfilled, helps guide human behaviour — like cases should be treat alike.[705] Thus, we must also concede that proportionality analysis should be available in judicial review to all cases in Hong Kong.

Influenced by European jurisprudence, such as that derived from the ECtHR and UK courts, Hong Kong courts have begun to observe socio-economic rights

703. Ibid., [34].

704. Chan (N18) 424.

705. *Ghaidan* (N274) [2004] 2 AC 557, 566C (Lord Nicholls).

as being implicit in civil and political rights, and have found that the executive has positive duties to fulfil their realisation, despite the fact that a great margin of discretion is given to public officials in view of their constitutional legitimacy and institutional competence. However, this constitutional-legitimacy argument is less convincing in Hong Kong since it has suffered a democratic deficit before and after the change of sovereignty in 1997. The lack of democracy has seemingly resulted in economic and social inequality which have, in turn, led to decreased recognition of justiciable rights to socio-economic benefits and welfare in Hong Kong. This is further exacerbated by the conservative attitude of the government and the pro-Beijing legislature whose members predominantly side with the business sector.

Owing to the prolonged lack of democracy and China's tightening of 'political opportunities' for pro-democracy politicians in the LegCo, Hong Kong has been experiencing a growth in 'legal mobilisation' since 1997, in that individual citizens (especially minorities and the marginalised) and dissidents have started invoking their legal rights and using litigation to defend or develop these rights against the government in addition to resorting to street politics. The response of the Chinese government to this has only further intensified this phenomenon, leading to the Occupy Central Movement and subsequent civil disobedience movements and anti-government protests (in particular the Anti-Extradition Bill Protests which began in early June 2019 and continue today). These movements have led the Hong Kong people to shift their political opportunities from the LegCo to the courts.

Compared with their British counterpart, Hong Kong courts have also been more deferential when adjudicating cases challenging policy making, administrative decisions, and socio-economic rights issues which involved the prioritisation of conflicting interests and allocation of scare resources. Apart from cases involving fundamental and constitutional rights as enshrined in the BORO and the Basic Law, Hong Kong courts prefer to use traditional *Wednesbury* unreasonableness, or *GCHQ* irrationality, instead of the proportionality principle. However, once finding that the impugned restriction was not rationally connected to the legitimate purpose or if the inroads that the administrative decision-makers made into the protected rights are manifestly without reasonable foundation, Hong Kong courts seem more willing to question the justification provided by the Hong Kong government on issues of public policy and resource allocation. This would make the government, when drafting and changing policies with implications on the right to social welfare, among others, consider the principle of proportionality to formulate policies, provided that they do not directly challenge the Mainland authorities, including the NPCSC. Indeed, the decision-makers must now be aware that their measures will be struck down under the proportionality review if they are found to be more drastic than necessary for achieving the desired result. This will likely be the case despite the recent trend that the courts have seemingly been deferential to the administration even though they did, like their British counterparts, adopt the four-limb proportionality analysis.

At the administrative level, the Hong Kong government, again like its British counterpart, has instructed its personnel to observe the proportionality principle, as shown in government guides to judicial review for administrators (i.e., *The Judge over your Shoulder: A Guide to Judicial Review for Administrators*) in Hong Kong. Thus, proportionality is seen by the administrators as an established legal norm that they must observe and consider when exercising their discretionary powers in the discharge of their public duties.[706]

All in all, the English and Hong Kong courts have incorporated the proportionality principle into their legal systems at least in part. It is hoped that its full recognition will encourage better governance in terms of transparency and accountability in administrative decision-making and judicial adjudications, particularly those dealing with socio-economic rights issues. Furthermore, its full adoption will also improve the quality of the decision-making process by encouraging officials to focus on alternative courses of action.

706. This argument has also been made in Chapter Seven of this book.

Conclusion

The purpose of this book is to examine how far the principle of proportionality has been integrated into English and Hong Kong laws. Public law in the United Kingdom (UK) and Hong Kong has much to gain from adopting a more open approach to the integration of domestic and European legal standards. This is because the co-existence of standards, reinforced by ongoing internal processes of change in UK and Hong Kong laws, demands deeper consideration of the possible benefit of increased fusion. Although differences between the bodies of law entail limits to integration,[1] a greater willingness to engage in a process of cross-fertilisation would allow UK and Hong Kong courts to resolve various outstanding issues.

Previous approaches to such integration, as discussed in Chapter Three, have largely been structured around orthodox constitutional and institutional considerations. These have prevented both UK and Hong Kong courts from developing principles of judicial review that more accurately reflect their constitutional and institutional roles and from attaining the full and proper protection of the individual's domestic law interests. For instance, when it comes to socio-economic rights, those who hold traditionalist views do not perceive them as being real human rights, but rather as merely aspirational societal goals to be determined by social policy. Under this traditionalist view, they are perceived as non-justiciable and thus cannot be claimed against a state in the same manner as civil and political rights. However, these views are no longer

1. Renaud Dehousse, 'Comparing National and EC Law: The Problem of the Level of Analysis' (1994) 42 *AJCL* 761.

mainstream. Considerable conceptual clarity and elaboration to the nature and scope of many socio-economic rights have been made by the United Nations Committee on Economic, Social, and Cultural Rights (UNESCR Committee).[2]

As discussed in Chapter Four, all human rights, whether civil and political or socio-economic, are equal, indivisible, interdependent, and interrelated, so they should be treated in an equal manner with the same emphasis.[3] The traditional views that socio-economic rights are non-justiciable and that their adjudications are anti-democratic have also been challenged.[4] On the contrary, the role of the courts, and hence of the judicial review process, is to foster a culture of democracy rather than to undermine it. Member States of the European Union (EU) and European Convention on Human Rights (ECHR) are obliged, as shown in case law discussed in Chapters Five and Six, to take steps to progressively realise socio-economic rights, for instance, by setting a minimum core standard to ensure the satisfaction of the minimum essential levels of each of the rights.[5]

Moreover, a tripartite approach of 'duties to avoid, protect, and aid',[6] instead of the traditional dichotomy between civil and political rights and socio-economic rights, or positive and negative rights, has also been adopted by the United Nations. This new approach, explained in Chapter Four, is manifested in case law in various regional and domestic jurisdictions. In this regard, the boundaries between civil and political rights review, on one hand, and socio-economic rights review, on the other, are rapidly crumbling in many parts of

2. Coalition for an Optional Protocol to the ICESCR's Fact Sheet No. 7, 'The Question of Justiciability', [3]; Concluding Observations of the Committee on Economic, Social, and Cultural Rights (Hong Kong) China, E/C 12/1/Add58 (05/21/2001), [16] (having the ICESCR viewed as being "aspirational" is based on a mistaken belief of legal obligations arising from the ICESCR).

3. UN General Assembly, Vienna Declaration and Programme of Action, A/CONF157/23 (12 July 1993) [5].

4. 'The Question of Justiciability' (N2) [3].

5. UNESCR Committee, General Comment No. 3, The Nature of States Parties' Obligations (Fifth session), UN Doc E/1991/23, annex III at 86 (1991), reprinted in Compilation of General Comments and General Recommendations Adopted by Human Rights Treaty Bodies, UN Doc HRI/GEN/1/Rev6, 14 (2003) [10].

6. General Recommendation No. 24 (20th session) UN Doc A/54/38 at 5 (1999) [14]–[17]; General Recommendation No. 25, on Article 4, Paragraph 1, of the Convention on the Elimination of All Forms of Discrimination against Women, on Temporary Special Measures, Part II, and the Constitution of the Republic of South Africa, Section 7(2). See also Henry Shue, *Basic Rights: Subsistence, Affluence and US Foreign Policy* (2nd edn, PUP 1996); Sandra Fredman, *Human Rights Transformed: Positive Rights and Positive Duties* (OUP 2008) 69.

the world. Further, the indivisibility of civil and political rights and socio-economic rights has also been affirmed.[7] In short, as Geraldine van Bueren argued, *Grootboom*, a South African Constitutional Court case, has 'hammered the final nail into the coffin of non-justiciability'.[8]

Furthermore, if a constitution specifies that one has a constitutional right, then the courts and government must do their part to protect this right. For example, if a constitution grants a right to a reasonable standard of social benefits or welfare, given the level of economic development and competing expenditures and given what other underprivileged people need, the courts will have to determine whether the income of the government allows for that level of provision and whether the government is right to spend a certain amount of money on certain things. If the courts find that the government can afford to provide people with social benefits or welfare, they can simply tell the government that social benefits or welfare provision must be raised by a certain date.

The view that the proportionality enquiry would involve the courts considering the merits and facts of administrative decisions,[9] thus trespassing the line as constitutionally set by the doctrine of separation of powers, has also been challenged. First and foremost, this book does not dispute that the courts should not substitute their judgment on the merits of a case for that of the primary decision-maker. Proportionality analysis does not compel merit review. The test only 'allows sufficient latitude to the decision-maker so that one could argue that overall, the process of judicial reasoning does not focus solely on the merits'.[10] This is because 'the defining characteristic of the proportionality test is that it requires a court to undertake a structured analytical exercise'.[11]

7. The 1993 Vienna Declaration and Programme of Action of 25 June 1993, endorsed by the UN General Assembly, A/CONF157/23, 12 July 1993, [5].

8. Geraldine van Bueren, 'Including the Excluded: The Case for an Economic, Social and Cultural Human Rights Act' (2002) *PL* 456, 461.

9. *R v Secretary of State for the Home Department, ex p Brind* [1991] 696 (HL), 762, 766–767 (Lords Lowry and Ackner), [1991] 2 WLR 588, [1991] UKHL 4, [1991] 1 All ER 720. See also Sophie Boyron, 'Proportionality in English Administrative Law: A Faulty Translation?' (1992) *OJLS* 237.

10. *R (Begum) v Headteacher and Governors of Denbigh High School* [2006] UKHL 15, [2006] 2 WLR 719, [2007] 1 AC 100, [30] (Lord Bingham). See also Ian Leigh, 'Taking Rights Proportionality: Judicial Review, the Human Rights Act and Strasbourg' (2002) *PL* 265, 284.

11. Richard Clayton and Hugh Tomlinson, *The Law of Human Rights* (2nd edn, OUP 2009) [6.91].

Strict adherence to the structural test for proportionality will also guard against the courts reviewing decisions solely on their merits and preserve the separation of executive and thus make the courts only adjudicate decision-making processes. Therefore, the role of the reviewing court is not to ensure that the right balance was properly struck between opposing interests. Instead, its role is to decide whether the decision made was 'disproportionate'. It is a form of negative control, and hence it would be more apt to say that it is a 'test of disproportionality', instead of a 'test of proportionality'.[12] Such an approach is indeed adopted in the Dutch General Administrative Law Act 1994, which prohibits administrative decisions from being disproportionate in connection with the intended goals and the consequences for the interested parties [13] and allows judicial review of administrative conduct breaching this principle.

In undertaking this balancing exercise, courts do not substitute their own assessment of discretionary choices for that of the executive, but intervene if a decision incurs abnormally high costs or is unreasonable or badly thought-out.[14] This forces the executive to provide serious and plausible justifications for their decisions to the public and, if necessary, to the administrative judge.[15] Giving the courts the power to tell the executive to do 'X' does not mean they have the power to tell the executive how they should do it. In this respect, the courts are only concerned with whether the decision-maker has properly considered or attempted other viable alternatives, but it would not 'weigh' the alternatives themselves.[16] It has also been suggested that a proper respect for the difference between appeal and review argues in favour of introducing a more structured and transparent form of judicial control, like proportionality, rather than relying constantly on the 'blunt tool' of *Wednesbury* unreasonableness [17]

12. Garreth Wong, 'Towards the Nutcracker Principle: Reconsidering the Objections to Proportionality' (2000) *PL* 92, 93.
13. Dutch General Administrative Law Act 1994 (*Algemene wet bestuursrecht*), Art 3:4 ss 2.
14. Robert Thomas, *Legitimate Expectations and Proportionality in Administrative Law* (Hart Publishing 2000) 13.
15. The opinion of Commissaire du Governement Braibant in *Conseil d'État*, 28 May 1971, Ville Nouvelle Est, cited by Lionel Brown and John Bell, with the assistance of Jean-Michel Galabert, *French Administrative Law* (5th edn, Clarendon Press 1998) 264.
16. *Society for the Protection of Harbour v Town Planning Board* [2003] 2 HKLRD 787 (HCAL 19/2003), 805, [62] (Chu J).
17. Paul Craig, 'The Impact of Community Law on Domestic Public Law' in Peter Leyland and Terry Woods, *Administrative Law Facing the Future: Old Constraints and New Horizons* (Blackstone 1997) 283.

or *GCHQ* irrationality. Overall, although proportionality permits engagement with the merits of a government decision, it would not, and should not, be equated with review on the basis of those merits alone.

As far as the constitutional incompetence argument is concerned, once a society has made a decision, be it explicitly or implicitly, to adopt the mechanism of judicial review, its exercise by the courts is a reflection of the people's will, and thus in effect not only embraces the basic notion of democracy but actually entrenches it.[18] Considerations of 'lack of sufficient democratic foundation' or 'counter-majoritarian difficulty' cannot stand in relation to the actual exercise of judicial review. Rather, judicial review should be conducted in a way that would allow judges the full ability to look into whether the other branches — who have limited a constitutionally protected human right — have properly followed the requirements of proportionality as prescribed by the constitution's 'we the people'.[19]

Moreover, the strict, rigid, or pure theory of the doctrine of separation of powers (i.e., the strict division or distribution of functions between the three branches of government) should no longer hold sway. Instead, the doctrine should be viewed as a network of rules and principles which ensure that power is not concentrated in the hands of one branch.[20] The need to regulate the substantial growth in executive authority is increasingly supported because the state has intervened tremendously in our private sphere. It can also be interpreted as an expression of 'participatory democracy' that emphasises accountability and justification — a model of 'deliberative democracy' which moves from interest-bargaining to value-oriented decision-making based on the persuasiveness of the reasons given.[21] This has become a prominent ideal of good governance over the past few decades and has led to more discussion of 'administrative justice' rather than administrative law.[22]

18. Aharon Barak, *Proportionality: Constitutional Rights and their Limitations* (CUP 2012) 382–383.

19. Ibid., 383.

20. Eric Barendt, 'Separation of Powers and Constitutional Government' (1995) *PL* 599, 608–609.

21. Sandra Fredman, 'New Horizons: Incorporating Socio-Economic Rights in a British Bill of Rights' (2010) *PL* 297.

22. Hugh Corder, 'Comparing Administrative Justice across the Commonwealth: A First Scan' in Hugh Corder (ed), *Comparing Administrative Justice across the Commonwealth* (JUTA 2008) 2.

As administrative law has been developing, another objective has asserted itself — the promotion of 'good public administration'.[23] This notion has shifted the perspective of administrative law in the direction of the consumer (i.e., those persons affected by official decisions).[24] Therefore, if judges still mistakenly view the 'government' as somehow removed from the courts, without acknowledging that the judiciary is actually as much a part of government as the legislature and the executive, and if they expect an 'exaggerated level of judicial respect' [25] or defer excessively to the executive and the legislature, they are in fact undermining the very foundational rationale for the separation of powers — preventing the over-accumulation of power in one body. Being a normative principle, the doctrine of separation of powers is not an end in itself, but a means of keeping the government in check in order to protect human rights.

The idea of 'a shared public law discourse', or the 'common public law', has also emerged in the last two decades in common law jurisdictions. This idea concerns the identification of fundamental values in constitutional, public, and international human rights law — a discourse that seeks to prevent vulnerable, marginalised, and dispossessed individuals being placed beyond the protection of the rule of law.[26] This 'shared public law discourse' rejects the artificial divide between legal and political spheres of decision-making which cordons off certain types of sensitive policy decisions from judicial scrutiny.

In relation to this, the 'idea of constitutional dialogue' and the concomitant method of dialogic judicial review have also emerged. The rationale of this model of review is to encourage co-operative engagement among different branches of government in the context of rights protection. Also central to the idea of dialogic judicial review is the encouragement of interactions among different branches of government about which of the competing reasonable interpretations of constitutional provisions is correct.[27] This dialogic approach is desirable because

23. Jeffrey Jowell, 'The Democratic Necessity of Administrative Justice', in Corder, ibid., 13.

24. Ibid.

25. Corder (N22) 6.

26. *Baker v Canada (Minister of Citizenship and Immigration)* [1999] 2 SCR 817, (1999) 174 DLR (4th) 193 (SCC). See also David Dyzenhaus, '*Baker*: The Unity of Public Law?' in David Dyzenhaus (ed), *The Unity of Public Law* (Hart Publishing 2004) 1.

27. Mark Tushnet, 'Dialogic Judicial Review' (2008) 61 *ALR* 205, 209.

it allows the courts to 'counter failures of inclusiveness and responsiveness in the political process', 'blind spots', or 'burdens of inertia', without usurping the role of the elected branches of government in the formulation of social policy.[28]

In the case of socio-economic rights, judicial review serves the function of checking the political branches to ensure that they are responsive to the constitutional rights of the least privileged in society, and that policymakers do not lose sight of their suffering in the inevitable political games of compromise and horse-trading.[29] This 'equal partnership' concept has been gradually accepted in Britain, particularly by Lord Bridge (who advocated the concept of 'dual sovereignty' or 'divided sovereignty'[30] between Parliament and the judiciary) and by Sir Stephen Sedley (who said that 'a new and still emerging constitutional paradigm ... of a bi-polar sovereignty of the Crown in Parliament and the Crown in its courts, to each of which the Crown's ministers are answerable — politically to Parliament, legally to the courts'[31]). In this context, then, the courts do not act as 'Delphic oracles' dispensing constitutional justice from on high, but rather as facilitators 'fostering society-wide constitutional discussion and debate'.[32]

In short, the idea of constitutional and institutional dialogues between the courts and the elected branches of government is not simply a desirable option, but is imperative in a modern, constitutional, and democratic state.[33] Throughout this book, I have argued that the fundamental issue opposing socio-economic rights — which is 'based on an assumption that governmental functions must be compartmentalised'[34] — no longer applies. Instead, the focus needs to be shifted to consider how effective protection and implementation of socio-economic rights 'can be carried out only where the proper roles and limits of

28. Rosalind Dixon, 'Creating Dialogue about Socio-Economic Rights: Strong-Form *Versus* Weak-Form Judicial Review Revisited' (2007) 5 *IJCL* 391, 394.

29. Jeanne Woods, 'Justiciable Social Rights as a Critique of the Liberal Paradigm' (2003) 38 *TILJ* 763, 773.

30. *R (Jackson) v AG* [2005] UKHL 56, [2006] 1 AC 262, [102].

31. Stephen Sedley, 'Human Rights: A Twenty-First Century Agenda' (1995) *PL* 386, 389.

32. Christine Bateup, 'The Dialogic Promise: Assessing the Normative Potential of Theories of Constitutional Dialogue' (2006) 71 *BLR* 1109, 1174.

33. T.R.S. Allan, 'Constitutional Dialogue and the Justification of Judicial Review' (2003) 23 *OJLS* 563, 565.

34. Craig Scott and Patrick Macklem, 'Constitutional Ropes of Sand or Justiciable Guarantees? Social Rights in a New African Constitution' (1992) 141 *UPLR* 1147.

each branch of government are fully understood',[35] and how all three branches government can work together to secure the protection of socio-economic rights across all the entire constitutional system.[36] Although friction between the different branches of government is inevitable, the dialogic approach at least goes some way towards structuring and mitigating such tensions.[37]

There may be even stronger reasons to grant the judiciary a primary role, at least in the enforcement of basic socio-economic rights. The primary function of socio-economic rights is to ensure the basic conditions of livelihood for the most vulnerable sections of society. If part of the justification for an active role for the courts is the protection of the rights of those vulnerable minorities in society against abuse from the majority, it is particularly important to promote, and not to deny, the participation of judges in the adjudication of socio-economic rights. Denying or limiting access to socio-economic rights affects democratic participation. Therefore, judicial supervision of their application is able to promote effective access to democratic values.[38]

Insofar as the institutional incompetence argument is concerned, allegations regarding the courts being ill-equipped, and thus ill-suited, as appropriate venues for deciding socio-economic rights issues are based on a misunderstanding. They presuppose that every socio-economic rights case is complex, involving a large number of actors, intricate or expensive evidentiary issues, important financial impacts, or potential conflicts between different branches of the state or government departments.[39] These assumptions are incorrect. In fact, many socio-economic rights cases are not so complex. In many jurisdictions, the majority of socio-economic rights cases decided by the courts are individual claims which involved both positive and negative obligations. Most of the allegations concerning the institutional incapacity of the judiciary to tackle

35. Anthony Lester and Colm O'Cinneide, 'The Effective Protection of Socio-Economic Rights' in Yash Ghai and Jill Cottrell (eds), *Economic, Social and Cultural Rights in Practice: The Role of Judges in Implementing Economic, Social and Cultural Rights* (Interights 2004) 22.

36. Ibid.

37. Paul O'Connell, *Vindicating Socio-Economic Rights: International Standards and Comparative Experiences* (Routledge 2012) 185.

38. International Commission of Jurists, *Courts and the Legal Enforcement of Economic, Social and Cultural Rights: Comparative Experiences of Justiciability* (ICJ 2008) 83.

39. Ibid., 89.

socio-economic rights are not applicable — decisions concerning labour, health, housing, education, social security, or welfare do not differ considerably from decisions regarding any other state activity which may affect individuals.[40]

When presiding over cases concerning socio-economic rights disputes, judges are not designing policies in these areas on the basis of their own initiative, but, as in any other area, they determine cases on the basis of existing rules — rules which are enshrined in constitutions, statutes, regulations, and human rights treaties, be they international or regional. If it is possible to decide the content of the duties that originate from socio-economic rights obligations, then the role of judges, when they are adjudicating these cases, would not differ from their role in any other case (i.e., determining whether a duty has been complied with by a duty-bearer).[41] Judges are able to do this in many other areas that are often technically complex (e.g., telecommunication law, anti-trust law, or environmental law, etc.). Therefore, there is no reason to grant judges the power to adjudicate in these fields but not in areas related to socio-economic rights issues.

Furthermore, judges hear cases in a regulated framework that limits their discretion. Within this framework of trials or hearings, they cannot simply assess public policy at their will. Initially, someone with *locus standi* (i.e., standing) needs to bring a claim. Judgments on complicated technical issues can be resolved with the help of expert testimony, as in any other area. Furthermore, procedural rules (e.g., the imposition of burden of proof) are also safeguards against allegations of unsound or frivolous claims. The losing party is also able to lodge an appeal against a judicial decision, and when matters reach the final court of appeal, all the disputed issues will be fully aired and can be appropriately framed. These safeguards arguably eliminate the risk of unbounded policy-making by judges in areas that go beyond their knowledge. Therefore, the institutional incompetence argument for the courts to tackle socio-economic rights issues is hardly sustained.

40. Ibid.

41. Ibid., 90.

Examination of the jurisprudence of the Court of Justice of the European Union (CJEU) and of the European Court of Human Rights (ECtHR) has, as discussed in Chapters Five and Six, revealed that their attitudes towards cases involving policy formulations, administrative decisions, and polycentric socio-economic rights issues, and those legal principles or standards applied therein, are essentially the same. Despite various methodologies being developed under the skeleton of proportionality criteria, its spirit is also the same — it provides a common analytical framework or template, the significance of which is not in its omnipotence, but in how its structure influences or controls how the courts reason to conclusions in many of the great moral and political controversies confronting political communities.

In some cases, the CJEU has stated that the challenged measure would be found disproportionate only if it was 'manifestly disproportionate or inappropriate' [42] in light of its objective. In other cases, the Court only scrutinised the contents of the measure by adopting the 'excessive disproportionate' formula.[43] Therefore, the inquiry undertaken by the CJEU within this structure has differed on a case-by-case basis, depending on the context and circumstances of the measure in question. It can also be seen from this inquiry structure that the legality required by the CJEU varies based on the context of the particular policy objective, the nature of the competing interests involved, and the competence of the courts and administrative authorities regarding their specialised knowledge, experience, etc., to make certain evaluative findings about the implementation of policy objectives. In this regard, the proportionality principle is said to be operating on a sliding-scale-of-review basis.[44]

Parallel to the application of proportionality is the doctrine of margin of appreciation, a concept introduced in Chapter Two. Margin of appreciation provides that a national judge of a Member State may be in a better position, and thus better equipped, than an international judge to evaluate the pressing social needs of the community. This is particularly pertinent if the objective

42. *R v Ministry of Agriculture, Fisheries and Food, ex p Fedesa* (Case C-331/88) [1990] ECR I-4023; *Germany v Council (Bananas)* (Case C-280/93) [1994] ECR I-4973.

43. *Bela-Mühle Josef Bergmann KG v Grows-Farm GmbH & Co KG* (Case 114/76) [1977] ECR 1211.

44. Thomas (N14) 79; Johannes Chan, 'A Sliding Scale of Reasonableness in Judicial Review' in Corder (N22) 238.

of the derogation involves public policy, public health, national security, or national morality. Among these spheres, morality varies from time to time and from place to place, meaning there will be rapid and far-reaching evolution of opinions on the subject. By reason of their direct and continuous contact with the vital forces of their countries, a Member State's authorities, be they legislative, executive, or judicial, are, in principle, 'in a better position than the international judges of the CJEU and ECtHR to give an opinion on the exact content of these requirements as well as on the "necessity" ... intended to meet them'.[45] All of these factors have been accepted by the English and Hong Kong courts, with slight modifications (i.e., discretionary areas of judgment, deference, etc.), as applied in those cases concerning policy formulations, administrative decisions, and polycentric socio-economic rights disputes.

The discussion of ECtHR jurisprudence in Chapter Six has also revealed that by treating the protection of socio-economic rights as essential corollaries of civil and political rights (i.e., the 'integrated approach') and through the expansive application of equality or non-discrimination provisions, the ECtHR, when adjudicating on civil and political rights disputes, has found that some positive duties are implicit in civil and political rights. These positive obligations require many different forms of action by the Member States to protect the rights of individuals enshrined in the ECHR, the examples of which include effectively investigating killings, protecting peaceful demonstrators from violent attacks by their opponents, obliging Member States to provide fair trials to determine civil and criminal proceedings within a reasonable time, and providing free legal assistance in criminal cases. In this regard, the purpose of the ECHR is not only to safeguard individual freedom from an over-mighty government, but to safeguard human dignity as well.

When examining the extent to which the principle of proportionality has been re-formulated and integrated into the UK and Hong Kong legal system (Chapters Seven and Eight, respectively), it has become apparent that the acceptance of proportionality under the EU and the ECHR regimes creates external pressure for the principle to be fully recognised in the UK owing to its international and regional treaty obligations. Internal pressure is also exerted

45. *Handyside v UK* (1976) 1 EHRR 737, [48].

by liberal and proactive judges and scholars advocating the same. The same is true in Hong Kong. The rationale underlying such advocation is, as argued throughout this book, primarily based on the fact that consistency of law, being one of the principles under the rule of law, if being fulfilled, helps guide human behaviour. Thus, if we agree with the fundamental axiom of justice that like cases should be treat alike,[46] then as a matter of principle, we must also concede that proportionality enquiry should be available in English judicial review to all cases.[47] If the courts continue to draw a strict division between the standards used in judicial review under EU law and human rights law, on one hand, and those used in domestic law, on the other, then the standard of English law might be viewed as 'second class' in the sense that it is not as rigorous or comprehensive as that undertaken by the CJEU and ECtHR.[48] To measure public decision-making against the standards established in the EU, the ECHR, the International Covenant on Civil and Political Rights (ICCPR), and the International Covenant on Economic, Social, and Cultural Rights (ICESCR) as developed by the CJEU and the ECtHR, both the UK and Hong Kong courts will need to employ the proportionality formula.

Examination of English case law reveals that the concept of proportionality, insofar as the rational relationship between the offences committed and the penalties imposed is concerned, has long been developed in Britain, as exemplified in the Magna Carta 1215 and the Bill of Rights 1689 as well as a number of cases decided to that effect. During the 1990s, 'common law proportionality' (i.e., the principle of legality with the use of proportionality formula [49] as a common law basis for protecting fundamental rights [50]) has also emerged in the UK. Therefore, although proportionality is not formally recognised by the UK courts, judges have observed this principle in many instances all along. Moreover, two decisions

46. *Ghaidan v Godin-Mendoza* [2002] EWCA Civ 1533, [2004] UKHL 30, [2004] 2 AC 557, 566C (Lord Nicholls).

47. Wong (N12) 96.

48. Thomas (N14) 99.

49. Tim Owen, 'Fair Trial Rights, Due Deference and the Wider Impact of the Human Rights Act in Administrative Law' in Jeffrey Jowell and Jonathan Cooper (eds), *Delivering Rights: How the Human Rights Act is Working* (Hart Publishing 2003) 66–67.

50. *Raymond v Honey* [1983] AC1; *R v Secretary of State for the Home Department, ex p Anderson* [1984] 1 QB 778; *R v Secretary of State for the Home Department, ex p Leech (No. 2)* [1994] QB 198; *R v Secretary of State for the Home Department, ex p Pierson* [1998] AC 539; *R v Secretary of State for the Home Department, ex p Simms and O'Brien* [1999] 3 All ER 400, [2000] 2 AC 115.

of the then Judicial Committee of the House of Lords — namely that in *R (on the application of Daly) v Secretary of State for the Home Department*[51] and *R (on the application of Alconbury Developments Ltd) v Secretary of State for the Environment, Transport and the Regions*[52] as decided around in the early 2000s — also confirm that proportionality has consistently been recognised as a separate ground of judicial review in English law, even outside the context of EU or fundamental rights.[53]

As reflected in the detailed discussion in Chapter Seven regarding how the UK courts are statutorily required to interpret other legislations to be compatible with the European Communities Act of 1972 (ECA 1972) and the Human Rights Act of 1998 (HRA 1998), these two regimes also require the courts to apply the proportionality principle not only in EU law and fundamental rights cases but also in domestic ones. The courts are thus constitutionally empowered through Parliament to decide whether the public body's decision was or may have been made in pursuit of one or more of the legitimate purposes detailed in EU law and the ECHR. On this basis, it may also be assumed that the traditional public-and-private-law divide will no longer be applied in human rights cases or any decisions that frustrate the full and effective protection of individual rights. Furthermore, although section 6 of the HRA 1998 seemingly indicates that it will only have a 'vertical effect' against the UK government and public bodies, it does, to a certain extent, have a 'horizontal effect' in proceedings between two private parties (i.e., on account of the obligation under section 3 to interpret other legislations to be compatible with the HRA 1998, and the fact that the courts, under section 6, are public authorities and thus need to observe the ECHR and the HRA 1998 regime).[54] It follows that proportionality is also applicable in legal disputes between two private persons if the case is tabled before the courts which are statutorily required to observe the ECHR under the HRA 1998 regime. On several occasions, the UK courts have even

51. [2001] 1 AC 532, [2001] UKHL 26, [2001] 2 WLR 1622.

52. [2001] UKHL 23, [2001] 2 WLR 1389, [2001] 2 All ER 929, [2003] 2 AC 295.

53. Ibid., [2003] 2 AC 295, 321 (Lord Slynn); *Daly* (N51) [2001] 2 AC 532, 545 (Lord Bingham). See also Hilary Delany, *Judicial Review of Administrative Action* (2nd edn, Thomson Reuters 2009) 124.

54. *Douglas v Hello! Ltd* [2001] 2 WLR 992; *Venables and Thompson v News Group Newspapers* [2001] 2 WLR 1038; *Campbell v Mirror Group Newspapers Ltd* [2004] UKHL 22. See also Murray Hunt, 'The "Horizontal Effect" of the Human Rights Act' (1998) *PL* 423; Garvin Phillipson, 'The Human Rights Act, "Horizontal Effect" and the Common Law: A Bang or a Whimper?' (1999) 62 *MLR* 824.

robustly stepped in to review some policy decisions that involved sufficient public interest, as adjudged by the administration on behalf of the electorate, in addition to demanding the highest degree of deference in matters of sensible public security issues, as reflected in the *Belmarsh Detainee*'s case,[55] among others.

However, the jurisprudential development of Hong Kong (to focus of Chapter Eight) in this regard has far lagged behind than that of its English counterpart. Apart from its applications in disputes concerning the Bill of Rights (BORO) and the constitutional or legislative review as enshrined in the Basic Law, Hong Kong courts are less willing to follow suit with the application of proportionality, preferring instead to use traditional *Wednesbury* unreasonableness or *GCHQ* irrationality in cases concerning policy formulations as well as in decisions having no human rights or constitutional dimensions.[56] In *Chu Ping Tak v Commissioner of Police*,[57] for example, the Court has, despite observing the UK's jurisprudence,[58] declined to apply the proportionality test to review a police disciplinary action because it has no human rights or constitutional dimensions. However, although the judge declined to apply the proportionality formula by claiming that it does not exercise an appellate role in an area that the executive authorities are better-equipped to handle, he did apply it on a negative basis (i.e., using the 'principle of disproportionality') while still not stepping into the executive domain.[59]

Influenced by the European jurisprudence derived from the CJEU and ECtHR, both English and Hong Kong courts have also started observing socio-economic rights as being implicit in the civil and political rights, and have found that the administrations in these two regions have positive duties to fulfil the realisation of these rights even though a great margin of discretion is given to those administrators in view of their constitutional legitimacy and institutional competence. However, this constitutional-legitimacy argument is less convincing in Hong Kong since it has suffered a democratic deficit before and after the change of sovereignty in 1997. As the government and its pro-

55. *A v Secretary of State for the Home Department* [2004] UKHL 56, [2005] 2 WLR 87, [2005] 2 AC 68.

56. *Chow Kwok Leong v Secretary for the Civil Service* [2011] HKEC 942.

57. [2002] 3 HKLRD 679 (CFI).

58. *R v Barnsley MBC, ex p Hook* [1976] 1 WLR 1052.

59. *Chu Ping Tak* (N57) 696 (Cheung DJ, as he then was).

Beijing legislature typically side with the business sector, economic and social inequality in Hong Kong has only increased. The conservative attitudes of these officials in their goal of maintaining market-led and 'business-friendly' policies, including a simple tax system, low tax rates, and limited expenditures on social welfare, have ultimately led to decreased recognition of justiciable rights to socio-economic benefits and welfare in Hong Kong.

As far as the UK is concerned, its observance of positive obligations as developed by the ECtHR tallies with its long tradition of respecting the rights of certain poor foreigners. In as early as 1803, the courts applied 'the law of humanity, which is anterior to all positive laws, obliges us to afford them relief, to save them from starving'.[60] As manifested in *R (on the application of Limbuela) v Secretary of State for the Home Department*,[61] even though there were no justiciable socio-economic rights in the UK, the right not to be subject to inhuman treatment was taken to imply a right to minimum subsistence.

In comparison, Hong Kong courts appear to be more deferential when adjudicating cases regarding socio-economic rights issues which involved the prioritisation of conflicting interests and allocation of scare resources. However, recent developments have demonstrated that once finding that the impugned restriction is not rationally connected to the legitimate purpose, or if the inroads the primary decision-makers made into the protected rights are manifestly without reasonable foundation and the issue does not touch the nerve of the Chinese government, Hong Kong courts are more willing to question the justification provided by the Hong Kong government on public policy and resource allocation, as reflected in *Kong Yunming v Director of Social Welfare*.[62] Therefore, the Hong Kong SAR government and administrative decision-makers, when drafting and changing policies with implications on such rights, must consider the principle of proportionality to formulate policies, or they risk having their measures struck down by the courts under

60. *Inhabitants of Eastbourne* (1803) 4 East 103, 107, cited by Simon Brown LJ in *R v Secretary of State for Social Security, ex p Joint Council for the Welfare of Immigrants* [1997] 1 WLR 275, 292.

61. [2005] UKHL 66, [2006] 1 AC 396 (HL).

62. [2009] 4 HKLRD 382 (CFI), [2012] 4 HKC 180 (CA), FACV 2/2013, (2013) 16 HKCFAR 950, [2014] 1 HKC 518 (CFA).

the proportionality review if they are found to be more drastic than necessary for achieving the desired result.

At the administrative level, both the British and Hong Kong SAR governments have in fact instructed their personnel to observe the proportionality principle, as shown in their government's guides to judicial review for administrators (i.e., *The Judge Over Your Shoulder* in the UK [63] and *The Judge over your Shoulder: A Guide to Judicial Review for Administrators* in Hong Kong [64]). Thus, proportionality should already come to the administrators' minds as one of the established legal norms. They should already be aware of the practical implications of their decisions when they are exercising their discretionary powers in the discharge of their public duties. Overall, in view of the above analysis, it is obvious that both the English and Hong Kong executives and the courts have already at least partially recognised the proportionality principle in their jurisdictions. The full adoption of the principle will only enhance governance in terms of transparency and accountability in administrative decision-making and judicial adjudications, particularly in the sphere of polycentric socio-economic rights issues which involve the prioritisation of conflicting interests and allocation of scarce resources. Full adoption would also improve the quality of the decision-making process by encouraging officials to focus on alternative courses of action.

What is more, although some cases may not seem to have EU law or human rights dimensions, they can often be framed to have these effects. It ensues that any difference in treatment between EU law and human rights cases, on one hand, and non-EU law and non-human rights cases, on the other, is sometimes difficult to sustain if the latter involve issues of wide public interest. In consequence, any such case would put the UK and Hong Kong courts under an obligation, as mandated under the ECA 1972 (as at 31 January 2020, the day of Brexit) and the HRA 1998, and the BORO and the Basic Law, respectively, to use the proportionality analysis. Insofar as Hong Kong is concerned, even

63. Treasury Solicitor's Department, *The Judge Over Your Shoulder: A Guide to Judicial Review for UK Government Administrators* (4th edn, January 2006) [2.16] and [2.29]–[2.30], available at: www.gov.uk/government/publications/the-judge-over-your-shoulder-joys-edition-4, last accessed 2 January 2020.

64. Department of Justice, HKSAR government, *The Judge over your Shoulder: A Guide to Judicial Review for Administrators* (3rd edn, 2019), 23–25 and 38–42, available at: www.doj.gov.hk/eng/public/The_Judge_Over_Your_Shoulder.html, last accessed on 31 May 2020.

though the Basic Law grants powers to the executive to formulate policies, the courts, as empowered by the same, also have the duty to ensure, by way of judicial review, that such policies do not unjustifiably restrict constitutional rights and are not in breach of administrative law principles. Although the courts give deference to the administrative authorities because of their technical knowledge and expertise in the subject matter, this does not mean that the former cannot have substantive review of these administrative decisions based on judicial review principles.[65]

Finally, as proportionality has been arguably recognised by the judiciaries as a separate ground of judicial review litigation in the UK and in Hong Kong, the courts must be willing to recognise their role in controlling and guiding the implementation of public policy. Public authorities are, under the emergence of positive law, charged with the tasks of attaining certain functions and making decisions on behalf of the public as a whole. Although some re-adjustments of private interests are inevitable in order to make way for the attainment of desired policy objectives, the risk of arbitrariness has increased with the expansion of state activities and their resulting augmentation of discretionary powers to achieve these policy objectives. Such expansion and complexity of administrative activities mean that the restrictions imposed by the public personnel to attain public goals may not be comprehensively thought out or wholly necessary owing to their limited understanding of the world. To seek an optimum balance between the performance of public functions and the protection of individual interests and rights, the courts must ensure that the interests of the individual are upheld as far as possible.

Considering the complexity of modern social and administrative decisions, recourse to law is inevitable as a means to resolve disputes and restore social order. It is unrealistic and inadequate to rely solely upon politics or the goodwill of the administration to provide redress. One of the advantages of getting the courts involved in a specialist administrative jurisdiction is that they can combine legal protection with an awareness of the realties and needs of public administration.[66] It can also lend overall coherence to a wide range of

65. Johannes Chan, 'Basic Law and Constitutional Review: The First Decade' (2007) 37 *HKLJ* 407, 424.

66. Thomas (N14) 112.

policy programmes by articulating the general acceptable norms that should inform public action. Nevertheless, the difficulties of this task should not be underestimated. Both English and Hong Kong courts need to have greater awareness and knowledge of governmental processes than they presently possess and a wider ability to make findings of fact. Moreover, Parliament in the UK and the Legislative Council (LegCo) in Hong Kong should also identify their legislative objectives clearly in their law-making process. More importantly, it must also be accepted by all of us, as citizens, that law can play a legitimate role to positively guide administrative activities.

To conclude, human rights are the joint responsibility of all branches of government. This shared responsibility necessitates a comprehensive and joint approach to ensure that social and economic entitlements penetrate executive policy decisions and legislative processes, as well as judicial deliberation. Furthermore, effective public administration can only be carried out with the co-operation of the general public. If public bodies observe the proportionality principle, this will help improve the quality and acceptability of their decisions. It is precisely this role that the courts must undertake if they are to develop distinct public law principles.

Bibliography

Abeyratne, R., 'More Structure, More Deference: Proportionality in Hong Kong' in Yap, P.J., *Proportionality in Asia* (Cambridge University Press, Cambridge, forthcoming September 2020), available at: https://ssrn.com/abstract=3295429.

Ackerman, B., 'The New Separation of Powers' (2000) 113 *Harvard Law Review* 633.

Acton, J., *Essays on Freedom and Power* (The Beacon Press, Boston, 1949).

Ahuja, S., *Law and Justice: Casebook on Public Interest Litigation* (Orient Longman, India, 1997).

Alexandrov, S., *Self-Defence Against the Use of Force in International Law* (Kluwer, The Hague, 1996).

Alexy, R., *A Theory of Constitutional Rights* (translated by Rivers, J.) (Oxford University Press, Oxford, 2002).

Alexy, R., 'The Construction of Constitutional Rights' (2010) 4 *Law and Ethics of Human Rights* 19.

Allan, T.R.S., *Law, Liberty, and Justice: The Foundations of British Constitutionalism* (Clarendon Press, Oxford, 1993).

Allan, T.R.S., *Constitutional Justice: A Liberal Theory of the Rule of Law* (Oxford University Press, Oxford, 2001).

Allan, T.R.S., 'Constitutional Dialogue and the Justification of Judicial Review' (2003) 23 *Oxford Journal of Legal Studies* 563.

Allan, T.R.S., 'Common Law Reason and the Limits of Judicial Deference' in Dyzenhaus, D. (ed), *The Unity of Public Law* (Hart Publishing, Oxford, 2004).

Allan, T.R.S., 'Parliament's Will and the Justice of the Common Law: The HRA in Constitutional Perspective' (2006) 59 *Current Legal Problems* 27.

Allison, J., *A Continental Distinction in the Common Law* (Clarendon Press, Oxford, 1996).

Alston, P., 'Economic and Social Rights' in Steiner, H., and Alston, P., *International Human Rights in Context Law, Politics, Morals* (Oxford University Press, Oxford, 2000).

Amirante, D., 'The Right to Environment in Emerging Economies: An India-China Comparison' in Deva, S. (ed), *Socio-Economic Rights in Emerging Free Markets: Comparative Insights from India and China* (Routledge, London, 2015).

Amnesty International, 'Hong Kong: Arbitrary Arrests, Brutal Beatings and Torture in Police Detention Revealed', 19 September 2019, available at: www.amnesty.org/en/latest/news/2019/09/hong-kong-arbitrary-arrests-brutal-beatings-and-torture-in-police-detention-revealed/.

An-Náim, A., 'To Affirm the Full Human Rights Standing of Economic, Social and Cultural Rights' in Ghai, Y., and Cottrell, J. (eds), *Economic, Social and Cultural Rights in Practice: The Role of Judges in Implementing Economic, Social and Cultural Rights* (Interights, London, 2004).

Anthony, G., *UK Public Law and European Law* (Hart Publishing, Oxford, 2002).

Aquinas, T., 'The Summa Theological: Second Part of the Second Part (QQ. 1–189) Question 64', cited by Barak, A., *Constitutional Rights and their Limitations* (Cambridge University Press, Cambridge, 2012).

Arai-Takahashi, Y., *The Margin of Appreciation Doctrine and the Principle of Proportionality in the Jurisprudence of the ECHR* (Intersentia, Oxford, 2002).

Arden, M., 'Proportionality: The Way Ahead?' (2013) July *Public Law* 498.

Arendt, H., 'Civil Disobedience' in Arendt, H. (ed), *Crisis of the Republic* (Harourt Brace Jovanovich, New York, 1972).

Aristotle, *The 'Art' of Rhetoric*, Book 1 (translated by Freese, J.) (Harvard University Press, Cambridge, 1975).

Aristotle, *The Nicomachean Ethics*, Bk 5 (translated by Irwin, T.) (2nd edn, Hackett Publishing, USA, 1999).

Aronson, M., 'The Growth of Substantive Review: The Changes, Their Causes and Their Consequences' in Bell, J., Elliott, M., Varuhas, J.N.E., and Murray, P. (eds), *Public Law Adjudication in Common Law Systems* (Hart Publishing, Oxford, 2016).

Austin, R., 'Administrative Law's Reaction to the Changing Concepts of Public Service' in Leyland, P., and Woods, T. (eds), *Administrative Law Facing the Future: Old Constraints and New Horizons* (Blackstone, London, 1997).

Bamforth, N., 'The Application of the Human Rights Act 1998 to Public Authorities and Private Bodies' (1999) 58 *Cambridge Law Journal* 159.

Bamforth, N., 'Courts in a Multi-Layered Constitution' in Bamforth, N., and Leyland, P. (eds), *Public Law in a Multi-Layered Constitution* (Hart Publishing, Oxford, 2003).

Barak, A., *The Judge in a Democracy* (Princeton University Press, Princeton, 2006).

Barak, A., 'Proportional Effect: The Israeli Experience' (2007) 57 *University of Toronto Law Journal* 369.

Barak, A., *Proportionality: Constitutional Rights and their Limitations* (Cambridge University Press, Cambridge, 2012).

Barber, N.W., 'Preclude to the Separation of Powers' (2001) 60(1) *Cambridge Law Journal* 59.

Barendt, E., 'Separation of Powers and Constitutional Government' (1995) *Public Law* 599.

Barents, R., 'The System of Deposits in Community Agricultural Law: Efficiency v Proportionality' (1985) 10 *European Law Review* 239.

Barnes, J. (ed), *The Complete Works of Aristotle*, Vol. 2 (Princeton University Press, Princeton, 1995).

Barnett, H., *Constitutional and Administrative Law* (12th edn, Routledge, Oxford, 2017)

Barron, A., and Scott, C., 'The Citizen's Charter Programme' (1992) 55 *Modern Law Review* 526.

Bateup, C., 'The Dialogic Promise: Assessing the Normative Potential of Theories of Constitutional Dialogue' (2006) 71 *Brooklyn Law Review* 1109.

Bauer, J., and Bell, D., *The East Asian Challenge for Human Rights* (Cambridge University Press, Cambridge, 1999).

Beatson, J., Grosz, S., Hickman, T., and Singh, R., *Human Rights: Judicial Protection in the United Kingdom* (Sweet & Maxwell, London, 2008).

Beatson, J., Matthews, M., and Elliott, M., *Administrative Law* (3rd edn, Oxford University Press, Oxford, 2005).

Beatty, D., 'The Last Generation: When Rights Lose their Meaning' in Beatty, D. (ed), *Human Rights and Judicial Review* (Kluwer, London, 1994).

Beatty, D., *The Ultimate Rule of Law* (Oxford University Press, Oxford, 2004).

Bedau, H. (ed), *Civil Disobedience in Focus* (Routledge, London, 1991).

Beddard, R., and Hill, D. (eds), *Economic, Social and Cultural Rights: Progress and Achievement* (Palgrave Macmillan, Southampton 1992).

Bell, C., 'A Model Proposal: Power-Sharing for the UK', *UK Constitutional Law Blog*, 13 November 2015, available at: http://ukconstitutionallaw.org/.

Benvenisti, E., 'Margin of Appreciation, Consensus, and Universal Standards' (1999) 31 *International Law and Politics* 843.

Bernstein, M., *Regulating Business by Independent Commission* (Princeton University Press, Princeton, 1955).

Bickel, A., *The Least Dangerous Branch: The Supreme Court at the Bar of Politics* (Yale University Press, New Haven, 1986).

Bikhchandani, S., Hirshleifer, D., and Welch, I., 'Learning from the Behaviour of Others: Conformity, Fads, and Informational Cascades' (1998) 12(3) *Journal of Economic Perspectives* 151.

Bilchitz, D., *Poverty and Fundamental Rights: The Justification and Enforcement of Socio-Economic Rights* (Oxford University Press, Oxford, 2007).

Bingham, T., '"There is a World Elsewhere": Changing Perspectives on English Law' (1992) 41 *International Comparative Law Quarterly* 513.

Bingham, T., *The Rule of Law* (Penguin, London, 2010).

Bleckmann, A., 'Der Beurteilungsspielraum im Europa — und im Völkerrecht' (1979) EuGRZ 485, cited by Arai-Takahashi, Y., *The Margin of Appreciation Doctrine and the Principle of Proportionality in the Jurisprudence of the ECHR* (Intersentia, Oxford, 2002).

Bokhary, K., 'Justice and the Law: The Evolving Role of the Lawyer' (2004) 34(1) *Hong Kong Law Journal* 133.

Bokhary, K., *Human Rights: Source, Content and Enforcement* (Sweet & Maxwell, Hong Kong, 2015).

Bolingbroke, H., *A Dissertation on Parties (1735) in Works Vol 2* (Frank Cass, London, 1967).

Boyron, S., 'Proportionality in English Administrative Law: A Faulty Translation?' (1992) 12 *Oxford Journal of Legal Studies* 237.

Brabyn, J., 'The Fundamental Freedom of Assembly and Part III of the Public Order Ordinance' (2002) 32 *Hong Kong Law Journal* 271.

Brabyn, J., 'Leung Kwok Hung and Others Through the Hong Kong Courts' (2006) 36 *Hong Kong Law Journal* 83.

Brand, D., 'Introduction to Socio-Economic Rights in the South African Constitution' in Brand, D., and Heyns, C. (eds), *Socio-Economic Rights in South Africa* (Pretoria University Law Press, Pretoria, 2005).

Brownlee, K., *Conscience and Conviction: The Case for Civil Disobedience* (Oxford University Press, Oxford, 2012).

Brownlie, I., *International Law and the Use of Force by States* (Clarendon Press, Oxford, 1963).

Buchanan, D., and Huczynski, A., *Organizational Behavior* (Prentice Hall, London, 1997).

Burke, E., *Reflections on the Evolution in France* (Gateway, Chicago, 1962).

Byrnes, A., 'And Some Have Bill of Rights Thrust Upon them: The Experience of Hong Kong's Bill of Rights' in Alston, P. (ed), *Promoting Human Rights Through Bill of Rights* (Clarendon Press, New York, 2000).

Byrnes, A., and Chan, J., *Bill of Rights Bulletin* (1995), 3(4) at Appendix A, cited by Gittings, D., *Introduction to the Hong Kong Basic Law* (1st edn, Hong Kong University Press, Hong Kong, 2013).

Caird, J., 'The European Union (Withdrawal) Bill: Constitutional Change and Legal Continuity', *UK Constitutional Law Blog*, 18 July 2017, available at: https://ukconstitutionallaw.org/.

Cameron, E., 'What You Can Do with Rights' (2012) 2 *European Human Rights Law Review* 148.

Cameron, E., 'A South Africa Perspective on the Judicial Development of Socio-Economic Rights' in Lazarus, L., McCrudden, C., and Bowles, N. (eds), *Reasoning Rights: Comparative Judicial Engagement* (Hart Publishing, Oxford, 2014).

Cane, P., 'Theory and Values in Public Law' in Craig, P., and Rawlings, R. (eds), *Law and Administration in Europe: Essays for Carol Harlow* (Oxford University Press, Oxford, 2003).

Cane, P., *Controlling Administrative Power* (Cambridge University Press, Cambridge, 2016).

Carnwath, R., 'From Judicial Outrage to Sliding Scales', *ALBA Annual Lecture,* 2013.

Cartier, G., 'The *Baker* Effect: A New Interface between the Canadian Charter of Rights and Freedoms and Administrative Law — The Case of Discretion' in Dyzenhaus, D. (ed), *The Unity of Public Law* (Hart Publishing, Oxford, 2004).

Case Comment, 'Supreme Court Orders Government to Cut Illegal Air Pollution' (2015) 4(3) *Compliance and Risk* 18.

Cemeron, I., *An Introduction to the European Convention on Human Rights* (4th edn, Iustus Förlag, Uppsala, 2002).

Chan, C., 'Judicial Deference at Work: Some Reflections on Chan Kin Sum and Kong Yun Ming' (2010) 40 *Hong Kong Law Journal* 1.

Chan, C., 'Focus What's So "Unusual" about W? Deference and the Separation of Powers: An Assessment of the Court's Constitutional and Institutional Competences' (2011) 41 *Hong Kong Law Journal* 7.

Chan, C., 'Rights, Proportionality and Deference: A Study of Post-Handover Judgments in Hong Kong' (2018) 48 *Hong Kong Law Journal* 51.

Chan, J., 'Hong Kong's Bill of Rights: Its Reception of and Contribution to International and Comparative Jurisprudence' (1998) 47 *International and Comparative Law Quarterly* 306.

Chan, J., 'Basic Law and Constitutional Review: The First Decade' (2007) 37(2) *Hong Kong Law Journal* 407.

Chan, J., 'A Sliding Scale of Reasonableness in Judicial Review' in Corder, H. (ed), *Comparing Administrative Justice across the Commonwealth* (JUTA, Cape Town, 2008).

Chan, J., 'Administrative Law, Politics and Governance: The Hong Kong Experience' in Ginsburg, T., and Chen, A. (eds), *Administrative Law and Governance in Asia* (Routledge, Abingdon, 2009).

Chan, J., 'Administrative Law' in Young, S., and Ghai, Y. (eds), *Hong Kong's Court of Final Appeal: The Development of the Law in China's Hong Kong* (Cambridge University Press, Cambridge, 2014).

Chan, J., 'Hong Kong's Umbrella Movement' (2014) 103(6) *The Round Table: The Commonwealth Journal of International Affairs* 571.

Chan, J., 'Could We Shoot the Red Light?' in Chan, J., *Paths of Justice* (Hong Kong University Press, Hong Kong, 2018).

Chan, J., 'Proportionality after *Hysan*: Fair Balance, Manifestly without Reasonable Foundation and *Wednesbury* Unreasonableness' (2019) 49 *Hong Kong Law Journal* 265.

Chan, J., and Harris, L., 'Preface: Back to Basics' in Chan, J., and Harris, L. (eds), *Hong Kong's Constitutional Debates* (Hong Kong Law Journal Ltd, London, 2008).

Chan, J., and Lim, C.L., 'Interpreting Constitutional Rights and Permissible Restrictions' in Chan, J., and Lim, C.L. (eds), *Law of the Hong Kong Constitution* (2nd edn, Sweet & Maxwell, Hong Kong, 2015).

Chang, W.C., Thio, L.A., Tan, K.Y.L., and Yeh, J.R., *Constitutionalism in Asia* (Hart Publishing, Oxford, 2014).

Chen, A., 'The Provisional Legislative Council of the SAR' (1997) 27 *Hong Kong Law Journal* 1.

Chen, A., 'International Human Rights Law and Domestic Constitutional Law: Internationalisation of Constitutional Law in Hong Kong' (2010) 4 *National Taiwan University Law Review* 237.

Chen, A., 'Constitutional Adjudication in Post-1997 Hong Kong' in Chen, A., and Ginsburg, T. (eds), *Public Law in East Asia* (Ashgate, Farnham, 2013).

Chen, A., 'A "Stroke of Genius" in *Kong Yunming*' (2014) 44 *Hong Kong Law Journal* 7.

Chen, Y.C., and Sezto, M., 'The Forgotten Road of Progressive Localism: New Preservation Movement in Hong Kong' (2015) 16(3) *Inter-Asia Cultural Studies* 436.

Cheung, A., and Chen, A., 'The Search for the Rule of Law in the Hong Kong Special Administrative Region, 1997–2003' in Wong, Y.C. (ed), *One Country, Two Systems in Crisis: Hong Kong's Transformation since the Handover* (Lexington, Lanham, 2004).

Clark, D., and McCoy, G., *Hong Kong Administrative Law* (2nd edn, Butterworths, Hong Kong, 1993).

Clarke, W.S., 'Judicial Review of the Discretionary Powers of the Attorney General of Hong Kong in the Conduct of Criminal Proceedings' (1983) 13 *Hong Kong Law Journal* 133.

Clayton, R., 'Regaining a Sense of Proportion: The Human Rights Act and the Proportionality Principle' (2001) 5 *European Human Rights Law Review* 504.

Clayton, R., 'Judicial Deference and "Democratic Dialogue": The Legitimacy of Judicial Intervention under the Human Rights Act 1998' (2004) *Public Law* 33.

Clayton, R., and Tomlinson, H., *The Law of Human Rights* (2nd edn, Oxford University Press, Oxford, 2009).

Clements, L., and Simmons, A., 'European Court of Human Rights: Sympathetic Unease' in Langford, M. (ed), *Social Rights Jurisprudence: Emerging Trends in International and Comparative Law* (Cambridge University Press, Cambridge, 2008).

Cohen-Eliya, M., and Porat, I., *Proportionality and Constitutional Culture* (Cambridge University Press, Cambridge, 2013).

Cohn, M., 'Legal Transplant Chronicles: The Evolution of Unreasonableness and Proportionality Review of the Administration in the United Kingdom' (2010) 58 *American Journal of Comparative Law* 583.

Cons, D., 'The Hong Kong Bill of Rights: A Judicial Perspective' in Chan, J., and Ghai, Y. (eds), *The Hong Kong Bill of Rights* (Butterworths Asia, Hong Kong, 1993).

Cooke, R., 'Human Rights in Hong Kong' (1999) 20 *Victoria University of Wellington Law Review* 45.

Coomans, F. (ed), *Justiciability of Socio-Economic Rights* (Intersentia, Antwerp, 2006).

Coon, D., and Mitterer, J., *Introduction to Psychology: Gateways to Mind and Behavior* (13th edn, Wadsworth, Belmont, 2013).

Coppel, J., *The Human Rights Act 1998: Enforcing the European Convention in the Domestic Courts* (Wiley, Chichester, 1999).

Corder, H., 'Comparing Administrative Justice across the Commonwealth: A First Scan' in Corder, H. (ed), *Comparing Administrative Justice Across the Commonwealth* (JUTA, Cape Town, 2008).

Couso, J., 'Case Studies: Social Rights as Middle-Class Entitlements in Hungary: The Role of the Constitutional Court' in Gargarella, R., Domingo, P., Roux, T. (eds), *Courts and Social Transformation in New Democracies: An Institutional Voice for the Poor?* (Aldershot, Ashgate, 2006).

Craig, P., 'The Impact of Community Law on Domestic Public Law' in Leyland, P., and Woods, T. (eds), *Administrative Law Facing the Future: Old Constraints and New Horizons* (Blackstone, London, 1997).

Craig, P., 'Unreasonableness and Proportionality in UK Law' in Ellis, E. (ed), *The Principle of Proportionality in the Laws of Europe* (Hart Publishing, Oxford, 1999).

Craig, P., 'Competing Models of Judicial Review' (1999) *Public Law* 428.

Craig, P., 'Contracting Out, the Human Rights Act and the Scope of Judicial Review' (2002) 118 *Law Quarterly Review* 551.

Craig, P., *Administrative Law* (5th edn, Sweet & Maxwell, London, 2003).

Craig, P., 'Fundamental Principles of Administrative Law in Relation to Basic Principles of Constitutional Law' in Feldman, D., and Burrows, A. (eds), *English Public Law* (2nd edn, Oxford University Press, Oxford, 2009).

Craig, P., 'Proportionality, Rationality and Review' (2010) *New Zealand Law Review* 265.

Craig, P., 'Britain in the European Union' in Jowell, J., and Oliver, D. (eds), *The Changing Constitution* (7th edn, Oxford University Press, Oxford, 2011).

Craig, P., *Administrative Law* (7th edn, Sweet & Maxwell, London, 2012).

Craig, P., *EU Administrative Law* (2nd edn, Oxford University Press, Oxford, 2012).

Craig, P., 'Constitutionalising Constitutional Law: *HS2*' (2014) *Public Law* 373.

Craig, P., and de Búrca, G., *EU Law* (2nd edn, Oxford University Press, Oxford, 1998)

Craig, P., and de Búrca, G., *EU Law* (4th edn, Oxford University Press, Oxford, 2008).

Craig; P., and de Búrca, G., *EU Law* (5th edn, Oxford University Press, Oxford, 2011).

Craig, P., and Tomkins, A., *The Executive and Public Law* (Oxford University Press, Oxford, 2006).

Crane, A., and Matten, D., *Business Ethics: Managing Corporate Citizenship and Sustainability in the Age of Globalisation* (3rd edn, Oxford University Press, Oxford, 2010).

Craven, M., *The International Covenant on Economic, Social and Cultural Rights: A Perspective on its Development* (Oxford University Press, Oxford, 1995).

Craven, M., 'Assessment of Progress on Adjudication of Economic, Social and Cultural Rights' in Squires, J., Langford, M., and Thiele, B. (eds), *The Road to a Remedy: Current Issues in the Litigation of Economic, Social and Cultural Rights* (University of New South Wales, Sydney, 2005).

Croley, S., and Jackson, J., 'WTO disputes Procedures, Standard of Review, and Deference to National Governments' (1996) 90 *American Journal of International Law* 193.

Cullen, R., 'Media Freedom in Chinese Hong Kong' (1998) 11 *Transnational Law* 383.

Currie, D., *The Constitution of the Federal Republic of Germany* (Cambridge University Press, Cambridge, 1994).

Daly, M., 'International Human Rights Standards in Hong Kong Courts', Dissertation LLM (Human Right) 2001, Department of Law: The University of Hong Kong.

Daly, M., 'A Human Rights Lawyer's Perspective' in Young, S., and Ghai, Y. (eds), *Hong Kong's Court of Final Appeal: The Development of the Law in China's Hong Kong* (Cambridge University Press, Cambridge, 2014).

Daly, P., 'Judicial Review of Factual Error in Ireland' (2008) 30 *Dublin University Law Journal* 187.

Daly, P., *A Theory of Deference in Administrative Law* (Cambridge University Press, Cambridge, 2012).

Daly, P., 'Administrative Law: A Values-Based Approach' in Bell, J., Elliott, M., Varuhas, J.N.E., and Murray, P. (eds), *Public Law Adjudication in Common Law Systems* (Hart Publishing, Oxford, 2016).

Dapiran, A., *City of Protests: A Recent History of Dissent in Hong Kong* (Penguin, Australia, 2017).

Daube, D., *Civil Disobedience in Antiquity* (Edinburgh University Press, Edinburgh, 1972).

Davis, D., 'Adjudicating the Socio-Economic Rights in the South African Constitution: Towards "Deference Lite"' (2006) 22 *South African on Human Rights* 301.

Davis, D., 'To Defer and then When? Administrative Law and Constitutional Democracy' in Corder, H. (ed), *Comparing Administrative Justice Across the Commonwealth* (JUTA, Cape Town, 2008).

de Búrca, G., 'The Principle of Proportionality and its Application in EC Law' (1993) 13 *Yearbook of European Law* 105.

de Smith, S., Woolf, H., and Jowell, J., *Judicial Review of Administrative Action* (Sweet & Maxwell, London, 1995).

Dehousse, R., 'Comparing National and EC Law: The Problem of the Level of Analysis' (1994) 42 *American Journal of Comparative Law* 761.

Delany, H., *Judicial Review of Administrative Action* (2nd edn, Thomson Reuters, Dublin, 2009).

Delbrück, J., 'Proportionality' in Bernhardt, R., *Encyclopedia of Public International Law* (North-Holland, Amsterdam, 1984).

Denning, A., *Freedom under the Law* (Stevens & Sons, London, 1949).

Devlin, P., 'The Common Law, Public Policy and the Executive' (1956) *Current Legal Problems* 1.

Dicey, A.V., *Lectures on the Relationship Between Law and Public Opinion in England during the Nineteenth Century* (Palgrave Macmillan, London, 1905).

Dicey, A.V., *Lectures Introductory to the Study of the Law of the Constitution* (edited by Allison, J.W.F.) (Oxford University Press, Oxford, 2013).

Dickson, B., 'Devolution' in Jowell, J., Oliver, D., and O'Cinneide, C. (eds), *The Changing Constitution* (8th edn, Oxford University Press, Oxford, 2015).

Dixon, R., 'Creating Dialogue about Socio-Economic Rights: Strong-Form Versus Weak-Form Judicial Review Revisited' (2007) 5 *International Journal of Constitutional Law* 391.

Donson, F., 'Civil Liberties and Judicial Review: Can the Common Law Really Protect Rights?' in Leyland, P., and Woods, T. (eds), *Administrative Law Facing the Future: Old Constraints and New Horizons* (Blackstone, London, 1997).

Downs, J., *Inside Bureaucracy* (Little Brown, Boston, 1967).

Drewry, G., 'The Executive: Towards Accountable Government and Effective Governance?' in Jowell, J., and Oliver, D. (eds), *The Changing Constitution* (6th edn, Oxford University Press, Oxford, 2007).

Drzemczewski, A., 'The Domestic Application of the European Human Rights Convention as European Community Law' (1981) 30 *International and Comparative Law Quarterly* 118.

Duguit, L., *Law in the Modern State* (translated by Laski, F., and Laski, H.J.) (Routledge, London, 1921).

Dworkin, R., *Taking Rights Seriously* (Duckworth, London, 1977).

Dworkin, R., *Law's Empire* (Fontana, London, 1986).

Dyzenhaus, D., '*Baker*: The Unity of Public Law?' in Dyzenhaus, D. (ed), *The Unity of Public Law* (Hart Publishing, Oxford, 2004).

Dyzenhaus, D., Hunt, M., and Taggart, M., 'The Principle of Legality in Administrative Law: Internationalisation as Constitutionalisation' (2001) 1 *Oxford University Commonwealth Law Journal* 5.

Ebsen, I., 'Social Policy in the European Community between Competition, Solidarity and Harmonisation: Still on the Way from a Free Trade Area to a Federal System' (1996) 2 *Columbia Journal of European Law* 424.

Eide, A., 'Economic Social and Cultural Rights as Human Rights' in Eide, A., Krause, C., and Rosas, A. (eds), *Economic Social and Cultural Rights* (2nd edn, Kluwer, London, 2001).

Eide, A., 'State Obligations Revisited' in Eide, W., and Kracht, U. (eds), *Food and Human Rights in Development, Vol II: Evolving Issues and Emerging Applications* (Antwerp, Intersentia, 2007).

Eissen, M., 'The Principle of Proportionality in the Case-Law of the European Court of Human Rights' in Macdonald, R., Matscher, F., and Petzold, H. (eds), *The European System for the Protection of Human Rights* (Springer, Dordrecht, 1993).

Elliott, M., 'The *Ultra Vires* Doctrine in a Constitutional Setting: Still the Central Principle of Administrative Law' (1999) *Cambridge Law Journal* 129.

Elliott, M., *The Constitutional Foundations of Judicial Review* (Hart Publishing, Oxford, 2001).

Elliott, M., 'The Human Rights Act 1998 and the Standard of Substantive Review' (2001) 60 *Cambridge Law Journal* 301.

Elliott, M., 'Proportionality and Deference: The Importance of a Structured Approach' in Forsyth, C., Elliott, M., Jhaveri, S., Ramsden, M., and Scully-Hill, A., *Effective Judicial Review: A Cornerstone of Good Governance* (Oxford University Press, Oxford, 2010).

Elliott, M., and Thomas, R., *Public Law* (Oxford University Press, Oxford, 2011).

Ely, J., *Democracy and Distrust* (Harvard University Press, Cambridge, 1980).

Emery, C., *Administrative Law: Legal Challenges to Official Action* (Sweet & Maxwell, London, 1999).

England, I., *Corrective and Distributive Justice: From Aristotle to Modern Times* (Oxford University Press, Oxford, 2009).

Engle, E., 'History of the General Principle of Proportionality: An Overview' (2012) 10 *Dartmouth Law Journal* 1.

Epoch Times, 'Protection of the Chinese University of Hong Kong and the Hong Kong Polytechnic University' (Epoch Times, 2019) [in Chinese, Author's translation].

Erling, E., Kugan, R., and Schnaider, J., 'The Principle of Proportionality: A Comparison between Canada and the European Law' (Paper presented at the Faculty of Law, University of Lund, on 24 February 2006).

Fabre, C., *Social Rights Under the Constitution* (Oxford University Press, Oxford, 2000).

Fairhurst, J., *Law of the European Union* (9th edn, Pearson, London, 2012).

Feldman, D., 'Public Interest Litigation and Constitutional Theory in Comparative Perspective' (1992) 55 *Modern Law Review* 44.

Feldman, D., *Civil Liberties and Human Rights in England and Wales* (2nd edn, Oxford University Press, Oxford, 2002).

Feldman, D., 'Human Rights, Terrorism and Risk: The Roles of Judges and Politicians' (2006) *Public Law* 364.

Feldman, D., and Burrows, A. (eds), *English Public Law* (2nd edn, Oxford University Press, Oxford, 2009).

Felix, S., 'Engaging Unreasonableness and Proportionality as Standards of Review in England, India and Sri Lanka' in Corder, H. (ed), *Comparing Administrative Justice Across the Commonwealth* (JUTA, Cape Town, 2008).

Fenwick, H., and Phillipson, G., 'Direct Action, Convention Values and the Human Rights Act' (2001) 21 *Legal Studies* 535.

Fenwick, H., and Phillipson, G., *Media Freedom under the Human Rights Act* (Oxford University Press, Oxford, 2006).

Fleisher, M., 'A Passion for Politics: The Vital Core of the World of Machiavelli' in Fleisher, M. (ed), *Machiavelli and the Nature of Political Thought* (Atheneum, New York, 1972).

Flinders, M., *Politics of Accountability in the Modern State* (Ashgate, Aldershot, 2001).

Fordham, M., and de la Mare, T., 'Identifying the Principles of Proportionality' in Jowell, J., and Cooper, J. (eds), *Understanding Human Rights Principles* (Hart Publishing, Oxford, 2001).

Forsyth, C., 'Of Figs Leaves and Fairy Tales: The *Ultra Vires* Doctrine, the Sovereignty of Parliament and Judicial Review' (1996) 55(1) *Cambridge Law Journal* 122.

Foster, J., and Magdoff, H., *The Great Financial Crisis* (Monthly Review Press, New York, 2009).

Foster, N., and Sule, S., *German Legal System and Laws* (4th edn, Oxford University Press, Oxford, 2010).

Foster, N., *EU Law* (2nd edn, Oxford University Press, Oxford, 2009).

Fredman, S.,*Human Rights Transformed: Positive Rights and Positive Duties* (Oxford University Press, Oxford, 2008).

Fredman, S., 'New Horizons: Incorporating Socio-Economic Rights in a British Bill of Rights' (2010) Spring *Public Law* 297.

Fredman, S., and Wesson, M., 'Social, Economic and Cultural Rights' in Feldman, D., and Burrows, A. (eds), *English Public Law* (2nd edn, Oxford University Press, Oxford, 2009).

Freeland, M., 'Government by Contract and Private Law' (1994) Spring *Public Law* 86.

Freeman, J., 'The Private Role in Public Governance' (2000) 75 *New York University Law Review* 543.

Fried, C., *Right and Wrong* (Harvard University Press, Cambridge, 1994).

Fu, H.L., Petersen, C., and Young, S. (eds), *National Security and Fundamental Freedoms: Hong Kong's Article 23 under Scrutiny* (Hong Kong University Press, Hong Kong, 2005).

Galabert, J.M., *French Administrative Law* (5th edn, Clarendon Press, Oxford, 1998).

Galanter, M., and Krishnan, J., '"Bread for the Poor": Access to Justice and the Rights of the Needy in India' (2004) 55 *Hastings Law Journal* 789.

Galligan, D.J., *Discretionary Powers: A Legal Study of Official Discretion* (Clarendon Press, Oxford, 1990).

Gandhi, M., *Nonviolent Resistance* (Schocken Books, New York, 1961).

Gardam, J., *Proportionality, Necessity and Force in International Law* (Cambridge University Press, Cambridge, 2004).

Garner, J.F., 'The Principle of Proportionality' in *UK National Reports Submitted to the 10th International Congress on Comparative Law* (Budapest, 1978).

Gearty, C., 'Reconciling Parliamentary Democracy and Human Rights' (2002) 118 *Law Quarterly Review* 248.

Gearty, C., *Civil Liberties* (Oxford University Press, Oxford, 2007).

Gearty, C., 'The Human Rights Act Should Not Be Replaced', *UK Constitutional Law Blog*, 17 September 2016, available at: https://ukconstitutionallaw.org/.

Ghai, Y., and Cottrell, J., 'The Role of the Courts in the Protection of Economic, Social and Cultural Rights' in Ghai, Y., and Cottrell, J. (eds), *Economic, Social & Cultural Rights in Practice: The Role of Judges in Implementing Economic, Social & Cultural Rights* (Interights, London, 2004).

Ghai, Y., *Hong Kong's New Constitutional Order: The Resumption of Chinese Sovereignty and the Basic Law* (2nd edn, Hong Kong University Press, Hong Kong, 1999).

Ghai, Y., 'Litigating the Basic Law: Jurisdiction, Interpretation and Procedure' in Chen, A., Fu, H.L., and Ghai, Y. (eds), *Hong Kong's Constitutional Debate: Conflict over Interpretation* (Hong Kong University Press, Hong Kong, 2000).

Gillette, C., and Krier, J., 'Risk, Courts and Agencies' (1990) 138 *University of Pennsylvania Law Review* 1027.

Gittings, D., *Introduction to the Hong Kong Basic Law* (1st and 2nd edn, Hong Kong University Press, Hong Kong, 2013 and 2016).

Gonçalves, A., 'Hong Kong and Macau Special Administrative Regions: The Downfall of the "One Country, Two Systems" Policy' (2019) 9(10) *International Journal of Humanities and Social Science* 11.

Goodhart, M., *Human Rights* (2nd edn, Oxford University Press, Oxford, 2013).

Gordon, R., Mok, J., and Hans, M., *Judicial Review in Hong Kong* (2nd edn, LexisNexis, Hong Kong, 2014).

Graham, C., 'Socio-Economic Rights and Essential Services: A New Challenge for the Regulatory State' in Oliver, D., Prosser, T., and Rawlings, R. (eds), *The Regulatory State* (Oxford University Press, Oxford, 2010).

Griffith, J.A.G., 'The Political Constitution' (1979) 42 *Modern Law Review* 1.

Grimm, D., 'Proportionality in Canadian and German Constitutional Jurisprudence' (2007) 57 *University of Toronto Law Journal* 383.

Grosz, S., Beatson, J., and Duffy, P., *Human Rights: The 1998 Act and the European Convention* (Sweet & Maxwell, London, 2000).

Habermas, J., *Between Facts and Norms* (Massachusetts Institute of Technology Press, Cambridge, 1996).

Hailsham, Q., *The Dilemma of Democracy: Diagnosis and Prescription* (Collins, London, 1978).

Haksar, V., 'Civil Disobedience and Non-Cooperation' in Bedau, H. (ed), *Civil Disobedience in Focus* (Routledge, London, 1991).

Haley, J., 'Introduction — Beyond Retribution: An Integrated Approach to Restorative Justice' (2011) 36 *Washington University Journal of Law and Policy* 1.

Hall, S., 'The ECHR and Public Policy Exceptions to the Free Movement of Workers under the EEC Treaty' (1991) 16 *European Law Review* 466.

Hallet, G., *Greater Good: The Case for Proportionalism* (Georgetown University Press, Washington DC, 1995).

Harlow, C., 'Public Interest Litigation in England: The State of the Art' in Cooper, J., and Dhavan, R., *Public Interest Law* (T J Press (Padstow), United Kingdom, 1986).

Harlow, C., 'European Administrative Law and the Global Challenge' in Craig, P., and de Búrca, G., *The Evolution of EU Law* (Clarendon Press, Oxford, 1999).

Harlow, C., 'Proceduralism in English Administrative Law' in Ladeur, K. (ed), *The Europeanisation of Administrative Law: Transforming National Decision-Making Procedures* (Ashgate, United Kingdom, 2002).

Harlow, C., and Rawlings, R., *Law and Administration* (3rd edn, Cambridge University Press, Cambridge, 2009).

Harris, D., *Cases and Materials on International Law* (6th edn, Sweet & Maxwell, London, 2004).

Harris, D., O'Boyle, M., Bates, E., and Buckley, C., *Law of the European Convention on Human Rights* (3rd edn, Oxford University Press, Oxford, 2009).

Hart, H.L.A., *The Concept of Law* (2nd edn, Clarendon Press, Oxford, 1994).

Harvey, C., 'Complex Constitutionalism in a Pluralist UK', *UK Constitutional Law Blog*, 3 July 2016, available at: https://ukconstitutionallaw.org/.

Harvey, C., and Livingstone, S., 'Protecting the Marginalised: The Role of the European Convention on Human Rights' (2000) 51 *Northern Ireland Legal Quarterly* 445.

Havel, V., *The Power of the Powerless: Citizens against the State in Central-Eastern Europe* (translated by Keane, J.) (Hutchinson, London, 1985).

Hayek, F., *The Constitution of Liberty* (Cambridge University Press, Cambridge, 1960).

Hazell, R., and Rawlings, R. (eds), *Devolution, Law Making and the Constitution* (Academic Imprint, London, 2005).

Hershkoff, H., 'Positive Rights and State Constitution: The Limits of Federal Rationality Review' (1999) 112 *Harvard Law Review* 1131.

Heywood, M., 'South Africa's Treatment Action Campaign: Combining Law and Social Mobilization to Realize the Right to Health' (2009) 1 *Journal of Human Rights Practice* 14.

Hickman, T., 'Proportionality: Comparative Law Lessons' (2007) *Judicial Review* 31.

Hickman, T., 'Problems for Proportionality' (2010) *New Zealand Law Review* 303.

Hickman, T., 'The Reasonableness Principle: Reassessing its Place in the Public Sphere' (2004) 63 *Cambridge Law Journal* 166.

Hickman, T., *Public Law after the Human Rights Act* (Hart Publishing, Oxford, 2010).

Hirschberg, L., *Der Grundsatz der Verhältnismäßigkeit* (Schwartz, 1981) 43f., cited by Singh, M., *German Administrative Law in Common Law Perspective* (Springer-Verlag, Berlin, 2001).

Hoexter, C., 'The Future of Judicial Review in South African Administrative Law' (2000) 117 *South African Law Journal* 484.

Hoffmann, L., 'The Influence of the European Principle of Proportionality upon UK Law' in Ellis, E. (ed), *The Principle of Proportionality in the Laws of Europe* (Hart Publishing, Oxford, 1999).

Hoffmann, L., 'The Universality of Human Rights', *Judicial Studies Board Annual Lecture*, 19 March 2009.

Hogg, P., 'Charter Dialogue Revisited — or "Much Ado About Metaphors"' (2007) 45 *Osgoode Hall Law Journal* 1.

Hong Kong UPR Coalition, *Freedom of Assembly Rights and Public Order Ordinance* (Hong Kong UPR Coalition, date not specified), available at: www.justicecentre.org.hk/framework/uploads/2018/11/HKUPR-Coalition-Fact-Sheet-Freedom-of-Assembly-Rights-and-Public-Order-Ordinance.pdf.

Hong Kong Watch, *A Tool of Lawfare: The Abuse of Hong Kong's Public Order Ordinance since 2014* (Hong Kong Watch, date unspecified), available at: https://static1.squarespace.com/static/58ecfa82e3df284d3a13dd41/t/5ce7d19253450a5fe8fe860a/1558696339084/Public+Order+Ordinance+briefing.pdf.

Hong Kong Watch, *Outdated and Draconian: Hong Kong's Public Order Ordinance* (Hong Kong Watch, 2019), available at: https://static1.squarespace.com/static/58ecfa82e3df284d3a13dd41/t/5d25c0676c3cb30001e74f6b/1562755179422/hkw.

Horwitz, P., 'Three Faces of Deference' (2008) 83 *Notre Dame Law Review* 1061.

Hui, V., *Beijing's Hard and Soft Repression in Hong Kong* (a paper published for the Foreign Policy Research Institute) (Elsevier Ltd, 2020).

Human Rights Monitor, *Submission to Pre-Sessional Working Group* (Human Right Monitor, 2000), cited by Peerenboom, R., Peterson, C., and Chen, A., *Human Rights in Asia: A Comparative Legal Study of Twelve Asian Jurisdictions, France and the USA* (Routledge, London, 2006)

Hume, D., *Essays: Moral, Political and Literary (1752)* (Liberty Classics, Indianapolis, 1987).

Hunt, M., *Using Human Rights Law in English Courts* (Hart Publishing, Oxford, 1997).

Hunt, M., 'The "Horizontal Effect" of the Human Rights Act' (1998) Autumn *Public Law* 423.

Hunt, M., 'Sovereignty's Blight: Why Contemporary Public Law Needs the Concept of "Due Deference"' in Bamforth, N., and Leyland, P. (eds), *Public Law in a Multi-Layered Constitution* (Hart Publishing, Oxford, 2003).

Hunt, M., 'Against Bifurcation' in Dyzenhaus, D., Hunt, M., and Huscroft, G. (eds), *A Simple Common Lawyer — Essays in Honour of Michael Taggart* (Hart Publishing, Oxford, 2009).

Huscroft, G., Miller, B., and Webber, G. (eds), *Proportionality and the Rule of Law: Rights, Justification, Reasoning* (Cambridge University Press, Cambridge, 2014).

International Commission of Jurists, *Courts and the Legal Enforcement of Economic, Social and Cultural Rights: Comparative Experiences of Justiciability* (International Commission of Jurists, 2008), available at: www.icj.org/wp-content/uploads/2009/07/Courts-legal-enforcement-ESCR-Human-Rights-Rule-of-Law-series-2009-eng.pdf.

Irvine, D., 'Judges and Decision-Makers: The Theory and Practice of *Wednesbury* Review' (1996) *Public Law* 59.

Irvine, D., 'The Philosophical Case for a Bill of Rights: A Response to Sir John Law 1996' in Irvine, D., *Human Rights, Constitutional Law and the Development of the English Legal System* (Hart Publishing, Oxford, 2003).

Iyera, V., 'Separation of Powers: The UK Experience' (2018) 5(2) *Journal of International and Comparative Law* 507.

Jacobs, F., 'Public Law — The Impact of Europe' (1999) *Public Law* 232.

Jacobs, F., *The European Convention on Human Rights* (Clarendon Press, Oxford, 1980).

Jacobs, F., 'Recent Developments in the Principle of Proportionality in European Community Law' in Ellis, E. (ed), *The Principle of Proportionality in the Laws of Europe* (Hart Publishing, Oxford, 1999).

Jaffe, L., *Judicial Control of Administrative Action* (Little Brown, Boston, 1965).

James, R., and Longley, D., 'Judicial Review and Tragic Choices: *Ex p B*' (1995) *Public Law* 367.

Janis, I., *Groupthink: Psychological Studies of Policy Decisions and Fiascos* (2nd edn, Houghton Mifflin, Boston, 1982).

Janis, M., Kay, R., and Bradley, A., *European Human Rights Law* (3rd edn, Oxford University Press, Oxford, 2008).

Jennings, R.Y., 'The *Caroline* and *McLeod* Cases' (1938) 32 *American Journal of International Law* 82.

Jhaveri, S., Ramsden, M., and Scully-Hill, A., *Administrative Law in Hong Kong* (2nd edn, LexisNexis, Hong Kong, 2013).

Jones, A.M., and Dugdale, M.A., *Clerk and Lindsell on Torts* (19th edn, Sweet & Maxwell, London, 2006).

Jones, C., 'Politics Postponed: Law as a Substitute for Politics in Hong Kong and China' in Jayasuriya, K. (ed), *Law, Capitalism and Power in Asia: The Rule of Law and Legal Institution* (Routledge, London, 1998).

Joseph, P., *Constitutional and Administrative Law in New Zealand* (3rd edn, Brookers, New Zealand, 2007).

Jowell, J., 'Is Proportionality an Alien Concept?' (1996) 2(3) *European Public Law* 401.

Jowell, J., 'In the Shadow of *Wednesbury*' (1997) *Judicial Review* 75.

Jowell, J., 'Of Vires and Vacuums: The Constitutional Context of Judicial Review' (1999) *Public Law* 461.

Jowell, J., 'The Rule of Law Today' in Jowell, J., and Oliver, D. (eds), *The Changing Constitution* (4th edn, Oxford University Press, Oxford, 2000).

Jowell, J., 'Beyond the Rule of Law: Towards Constitutional Judicial Review' (2000) *Public Law* 671.

Jowell, J., 'Administrative Law' in Bogdanor, V. (ed), *The British Constitution in the Twentieth Century* (Oxford University Press, Oxford, 2003).

Jowell, J., 'The Democratic Necessity of Administrative Justice' in Corder, H. (ed), *Comparing Administrative Justice across the Commonwealth* (JUTA, Cape Town, 2008).

Jowell, J., 'What Decisions Should Judges Not Take?' in Andenas, M., and Fairgrieve, D. (eds), *Tom Bingham and the Transformation of the Law* (Oxford University Press, Oxford, 2009).

Jowell, J., 'Proportionality and Unreasonableness: Neither Merger nor Takeover' in Wilberg, H., and Elliott, M. (eds), *The Scope and Intensity of Substantive Review: Traversing Taggart's Rainbow* (Hart Publishing, Oxford, 2015).

Jowell, J., and Lester, A., 'Beyond *Wednesbury*: Substantial Principles of Administrative Law' (1987) *Public Law* 368.

Jowell, J., and Lester, A., 'Proportionality: Neither Novel nor Dangerous' in Jowell, J., and Oliver, D. (eds), *New Directions in Judicial Review* (Stevens & Sons, London, 1988).

Kavanagh, A., 'Choosing between sections 3 and 4 of the Human Rights Act 1998: Judicial Reasoning after *Ghaidan v Mendoza*' in Fenwick, H., Phillipson, G., and Masterman, R. (eds), *Judicial Reasoning under the UK Human Rights Act* (Cambridge University Press, Cambridge, 2007).

Kavanagh, A., *Constitutional Review under the UK Human Rights Act* (Cambridge University Press, Cambridge, 2009).

Kennedy, D., 'Two Globalisations of Law and Legal Thought 1850–1968' (2003) 36 *Suffolk University Law Review* 631.

Kewenig, W., 'Gewaltverbot und noch zulässige Machteinwirkung und Interventions-mittel' in Schaumann, W. (ed), *Völkerrechtliches gewaltverbot und friedenssicherung* (Nomos, 1971), cited by Schwarze, J., *European Administrative Law* (Revised 1st edn, Sweet & Maxwell, London, 2006).

Keynes, J., *The General Theory of Employment, Interest and Money* (Prometheus, New York, 1997).

King, J., 'The Justiciability of Resource Allocation' (2007) 70 *Modern Law Review* 197.

King, J., 'United Kingdom: Asserting Social Rights in a Multi-Layered System' in Langford, M. (ed), *Social Rights Jurisprudence: Emerging Trends in International and Comparative Law* (Cambridge University Press, Cambridge, 2009).

King, J., 'Proportionality: A Halfway House' (2010) *New Zealand Law Review* 327.

Klatt, M., and Meister, M., *The Constitutional Structure of Proportionality* (Oxford University Press, Oxford, 2012).

Klug, F., 'The Human Rights Act: A "Third Way" or "Third Wave" Bill of Rights' (2001) *European Human Rights Law Review* 361.

Klug, F., and Starmer, K., 'Incorporation by the Back Door?' (1996) *Public Law* 223.

Knight, D., 'Calibrating the Rainbow of Judicial Review: Recognizing Variable Intensity' (2010) *New Zealand Law Review* 393.

Koch, I., 'The Justiciability of Indivisible Human Rights' (2003) 2 *Nordic Journal of International Law* 3.

Koch, I., 'Economic, Social and Cultural Rights as Components in Civil and Political Rights: A Hermeneutic Perspective' (2006) 10 *International Journal of Human Rights* 405.

Kong, K., 'Public Interest Litigation in Hong Kong: A New Hope for Social Transformation?' (2009) 28(3) *Civil Justice Quarterly* 327.

Kong, K., 'Adjudicating Social Welfare Rights in Hong Kong' (2012) 10(2) *International Journal of Constitutional Law* 588.

Kong, K., '*Kong Yunming v Director of Social Welfare*: Implications for Law and Policy on Social Welfare' (2014) 44 *Hong Kong Law Journal* 67.

Kong, K., 'Social Justice and Social Rights in Hong Kong: Recent Judicial Review Developments and Proposals for Legislative Change' in Deva, S. (ed), *Socio-Economic Rights in Emerging Free Markets: Comparative Insights from India and China* (Routledge, London, 2015).

Kong, K., 'Right to Social Welfare' in Chan, J., and Lim, C.L. (eds), *Law of the Hong Kong Constitution* (2nd edn, Sweet & Maxwell, Hong Kong, 2015).

Lai, B., 'Recent Trends and Developments of Judicial Review in Hong Kong' (Paper presented at the *20th LawAsia Biennial Conference* in Hong Kong on 6–8 June 2007).

Lam, J., *Politics and Government* (Writers' and Publishers' Cooperative, Hong Kong, 1994).

Langford, M., 'The Justiciability of Social Rights: From Practice to Theory' in Langford, M. (ed), *Social Rights Jurisprudence: Emerging Trends in International and Comparative Law* (Cambridge University Press, Cambridge, 2008).

Laski, H., 'The Limitations of the Expert' (1931) 162 *Harper's Monthly Magazine* 101.

Lau, A., 'Breach of the Peace and Constitutional Freedom of assembly in the HKSAR' (2013) 7 *Hong Kong Journal of Legal Studies* 75.

Lau, P., 'Revolutionary Disobedience' (2017) 22(2) *Barry Law Review* 199, available at: https://papers.ssrn.com/sol3/papers.cfm?abstract_id=2981915.

Laws, J., 'Is the High Court the Guardian of Fundamental Constitutional Rights?' (1993) *Public Law* 59.

Laws, J., 'Judicial Remedies and the Constitution' (1994) 57 *Modern Law Review* 223.

Laws, J., 'Law and Democracy' (1995) Spring *Public Law* 72.

Laws, J., 'The Constitution: Morals and Rights' (1996) *Public Law* 622.

Laws, J., '*Wednesbury*' in Forsyth, C., and Hare, I., *The Golden Metwand and the Crooked Cord* (Clarendon Press, Oxford, 1998).

Laws, J., 'The Impact of the Human Rights Act 1998 on the Interpretation of Enactments in the UK' in Bigwood, R. (ed), *The Statute: Making and Meaning* (Lexis-Nexis, Wellington, 2004).

Lawson, R.A., and Schermers, H.G. (eds), *Leading Cases of the European Court of Human Rights* (Ars Aequi Libri, Nijmegen, 1997).

Le Sueur, A., 'The Rise and Ruin of Unreasonableness' (2005) *Judicial Review* 32.

Le Sueur, A., Sunkin, M., and Khushal Murkens, J.E., *Public Law* (Oxford University Press, Oxford, 2010).

Lee, F., 'Internet Alternative Media, Movement Experience, and Radicalism: The Case of Post-Umbrella Movement Hong Kong' (2018) 17(2) *Social Movement Studies* 219.

Leigh, I., 'Taking Rights Proportionately: Judicial Review, the Human Rights Act and Strasbourg' (2002) *Public Law* 265.

Leigh, I., 'The Standard of Judicial Review after the Human Rights Act' in Fenwick, H., Phillipson, G., and Masterman, R. (eds), *Judicial Reasoning under the Human Rights Act* (Cambridge University Press, Cambridge, 2007).

Leigh, I., 'The Changing Nature of the Local State' in Jowell, J., Oliver, D., and O'Cinneide, C. (eds), *The Changing Constitution* (8th edn, Oxford University Press, Oxford, 2015).

Leigh, I., and Masterman, R., *Making Rights Real: The Human Rights Act in its First Decade* (Hart Publishing, Oxford, 2008).

Lenaerts, K., 'Fundamental Rights to Be Included in a Community Catalogue' (1991) 16 *European Law Review* 367.

Lenaerts, K., and Foubert, P., 'Social Rights in the Case-Law of the European Court of Justice' in Van der Auweraert, P., De Pelsmaeker, T., Sarkin, J., and Vande Lanotte, J. (eds), *Social, Economic and Cultural Rights: An Appraisal of Current European and International Developments* (Maklu, Antwerpen, 2002).

Lester, A., 'The European Convention on Human Rights in the New Architecture of Europe: General Report' in 8th International Colloquy on the European Convention on Human Rights, Proceedings Organised by the Secretariat General of the Institute for Legal and Administrative Sciences of the Hungarian Academy of Sciences, Budapest, 20–23 September 1995 (Council of Europe, 1996) 227.

Lester, A., and Beattie, K., 'Human Rights and the British Constitution' in Jowell, J., and Oliver, D. (eds), *The Changing Constitution* (6th edn, Oxford University Press, Oxford, 2007).

Lester, A., and O'Cinneide, C., 'The Effective Protection of Socio-Economic Rights' in Ghai, Y., and Cottrell, J. (eds), *Economic, Social & Cultural Rights in Practice: The Role of Judges in Implementing Economic, Social & Cultural Rights* (Interights, London, 2004).

Letourneur, M., 'The Concept of Equity in French Public Law' in Newman, R. (ed), *Equity in the World's Legal Systems* (Etablissements Emile Bruylant, Brussels, 1973).

Lewis, C., *Judicial Remedies in Public Law* (5th edn, Sweet & Maxwell, London, 2015).

Lewis, N., *Choice and the Legal Order* (Butterworths, London, 1996).

Leyland, P., and Anthony, G., *Administrative Law* (7th edn, Oxford University Press, Oxford, 2013).

Leyland, P., *The Constitution of the United Kingdom* (Hart Publishing, Oxford, 2012).

Liebenberg, S., 'Socio-Economic Rights: Revisiting the Reasonableness Review/Minimum Core Debate' in Woolman, S., and Bishop, M. (eds), *Constitutional Conversations* (Pretoria University Press, Pretoria, 2008).

Liebenberg, S., *Socio-Economic Rights: Adjudication under a Transformative Constitution* (Juta, Claremont, 2010).

Limbach, J., 'The Concept of the Supremacy of the Constitution' (2001) 64 *Modern Law Review* 1.

Lincoln, A. (President of the United States of America), 'The Gettysburg Address' (19 November 1863), transcript available at: https://rmc.library.cornell.edu/gettysburg/good_cause/transcript.htm.

Lipjhart, A., *Democracy in Plural Societies* (Yale University Press, New Haven, 1977).

Lo, P.Y., and Chen, A., 'The Judicial Perspective of "Separation of Powers" in the Hong Kong Special Administrative Region of the People's Republic of China' (2018) 5(2) *Journal of International and Comparative Law* 337.

Lo, P.Y., *The Judicial Construction of Hong Kong's Basic Law: Courts, Politics and Society after 1997* (Hong Kong University Press, Hong Kong, 2014).

Lo, P.Y., 'An Internationalist, Consequentialist and Non-progressive Court: Constitutional Adjudication in Hong Kong (1997–2009)' (2010) 2 *City University of Hong Kong Law Review* 215.

Lo, P.Y., 'The Impact of CFA Jurisprudence beyond Hong Kong' (2010) 8 *Hong Kong Law Journal* 36.

Lo, S., 'Ideologies and Factionalism in Beijing-Hong Kong Relations' (2018) 58(3) *Asian Survey* 392.

Locke, J., *An Essay concerning Human Understanding* (Kitchener, London, 1996).

Loughlin, M., *Legality and Locality: The Role of Law in Central-Local Government Relations* (Clarendon Press, Oxford, 1996).

Loughlin, M., 'Constitutional Law: The Third Order of the Political' in Bamforth, N., and Leyland, P. (eds), *Public Law in a Multi-Layered Constitution* (Hart Publishing, Oxford, 2003).

Loughlin, M., *Foundations of Public Law* (Oxford University Press, Oxford, 2010).

Loveland, I., *Constitutional Law, Administrative Law, and Human Rights* (4th edn, Oxford University Press, Oxford, 2006).

MacDonald, R., 'Judicial Review and Procedural Fairness in Administrative Law' (1980) 25 *McGill Law Journal* 520.

MacDonald, R., 'The Margin of Appreciation' in Macdonald, R., Matscher, F., and Petzold, H. (eds), *The European System for the Protection of Human Rights* (Springer, Dordrecht, 1993).

Macrory, R., and Woods, M., *Modernizing Environmental Justice: Regulation and the Role of an Environmental Tribunal* (Universal College London, London, 2003).

Mahoney, P., 'Judicial Activism and Judicial Self-Restraint in the European Court of Human Rights: Two Sides of the Same Coin?' (1990) 11 *Human Right Law Journal* 57.

Mahoney, P., 'Marvellous Richness of Diversity or Invidious Cultural Relativism' (1998) 19 *Human Right Law Journal* 1.

Mahoney, P., 'The Relationship between the Strasbourg Court and the National Courts' (2014) 130 *Law Quarterly Review* 568.

Maitland, F., *Constitutional History of England* (Cambridge University Press, Cambridge, 1955).

Majone, G., 'The Rise of the Regulatory State in Europe' (1994) 17 *West European Politics* 77.

Mann, D., 'International humanitarian norms are violated in Hong Kong' (21 November 2019) 394 *The Lancet*, available at: www.thelancet.com/pdfs/journals/lancet/PIIS0140-6736(19)32909-5.pdf.

Mann, F.A., 3rd Blackstone Lecture (1978), cited by Woolf, H., 'Droit Public — English Style' in Campell-Holt, C. (ed), *The Pursuit of Justice* (Oxford University Press, Oxford, 2008).

Mapulanga-Hulston, J.K., 'Examining the Justiciability of Economic, Social and Cultural Rights' (2002) 6(4) *International Journal of Human Rights* 29.

Marshall, G., *Constitutional Theory* (Clarendon Press, Oxford, 1971).

Marshall, G., 'Two Kinds of Compatibility: More about Section 3 of the Human Rights Act 1998' (1999) Autumn *Public Law* 377.

Marshall, G., 'The Lynchpin of Parliamentary Intention: Lost, Stolen or Strained?' (2003) *Public Law* 236.

Marshall, T.H., and Bottomore, T., *Citizenship and Social Class* (Pluto Press, London, 1992).

Marshall, T.H., *Citizenship and Social Class* (Routledge, London, 1959).

Mason, A., 'One on One, Court of Final Appeal, Sir Anthony Mason', *Hong Kong Lawyer*, July 2001, cited by Young, S., and Da Roza, A., 'The Judges' in Young, S., and Ghai, Y. (eds), *Hong Kong's Court of Final Appeal: The Development of the Law in China's Hong Kong* (Cambridge University Press, Cambridge, 2014).

Mason, A., 'The Place of Comparative Law in the Developing the Jurisprudence on the Rule of Law and Human Rights in Hong Kong' (2007) 37 *Hong Kong Law Journal* 299.

Masterman, R., *The Separation of Powers in the Contemporary Constitution: Judicial Competence and Independence in the United Kingdom* (Cambridge University Press, Cambridge, 2011).

McBride, J., 'Proportionality and the European ECHR on Human Rights' in Ellis, E. (ed), *The Principle of Proportionality in the Laws of Europe* (Hart Publishing, Oxford, 1999).

McBride, J., 'Protecting Life: A Positive Obligation to Help' (1999) 24 *European Law Review Human Rights Survey* HR/43.

McCrea, R., 'Can a Brexit Deal Provide a Clean Break with the Court of Justice and EU Fundamental Rights Norms?', *UK Constitutional Law Blog*, 3 October 2016, available at: https://ukconstitutionallaw.org/.

McLean, I., *What's Wrong with the British Constitution?* (Oxford University Press, Oxford, 2010).

Menkel-Meadow, C., 'The Causes of Cause Lawyering: Toward an Understanding of the Motivation and Commitment of Social Justice Lawyers' in Sarat, A., and Scheingold, S. (eds), *Cause Lawyering: Political Commitments and Professional Responsibilities* (Oxford University Press, Oxford, 1998).

Merrills, J.G., *The Development of International Law by the European Court of Human Rights* (Manchester University Press, Manchester, 1993).

Michaelsen, C., 'The Proportionality Principle, Counter-Terrorism Laws and Human Rights: A German-Australian Comparison' (2010) 2 *City University of Hong Kong Law Review* 19.

Michelman, F., 'The Constitution, Social Rights, and Liberal Political Justification' (2003) 13 *International Journal of Constitutional Law* 13.

Middlemas, K., *Politics in Industrial Society* (A Deutsch, London, 1979).

Milgram, S., *Obedience to Authority: An Experimental View* (Perennial Classics, New York, 2004).

Mill, J., *Essay on Government (1820)* (Library of Liberal Arts, Indianapolis, 1955).

Milmo, P., Rogers, W.V.H., Parkes, R., Walker, C., and Busuttil, G., *Gatley on Libel and Slander* (10th edn, Sweet & Maxwell, London, 2007).

Mirbeau, O., *Torture Garden* (translated by Richardson, M.) (Dedalus, Sawtry, 1997).

Möller, K., 'Constructing the Proportionality Test: An Emerging Global Conversation' in Lazarus, L., McCrudden, C., and Bowles, N. (eds), *Reasoning Rights: Comparative Judicial Engagement* (Hart Publishing, Oxford, 2014).

Montesquieu, *The Spirit of the Law* (Hafner, New York, 1949).

Moran, M., and Prosser, T. (eds), *Privatisation and Regulatory Change in Europe* (Oxford University Press, Oxford, 1994).

Moran, M., *The British Regulatory State* (Oxford University Press, Oxford, 2004).

Morris, G., 'The Human Rights Act and the Public/Private Divide in Employment Law' (1998) 27 *Industrial Law Journal* 297.

Mortimer, B., 'A Conversation with Justice Barry Mortimer', *Hong Kong Lawyer*, September 1999, cited by Young, S., and Da Roza, A., 'The Judges' in Young, S., and Ghai, Y. (eds), *Hong Kong's Court of Final Appeal: The Development of the Law in China's Hong Kong* (Cambridge University Press, Cambridge, 2014).

Morton, F. (ed), *Law, Politics and the Judicial Process in Canada* (3rd edn, University of Calgray Press, Calgary, 2002).

Moscovici, S., and Zavalloni, M., 'The Group as a Polariser of Attitudes' (1969) 12(2) *Journal of Personality and Social Psychology* 125.

Mountfield, H., 'The Concept of a Lawful Interference with Fundamental Rights' in Jowell, J., and Cooper, J. (eds), *Understanding Human Rights Principles* (Hart Publishing, Oxford, 2001).

Mullan, D., 'Proportionality — A Proportionate Response to an Emerging Crisis in Canadian Judicial Review Law?' (2010) *New Zealand Law Review* 233.

Mureinik, E., 'Reconsidering Review: Participation and Accountability' (1993) *Acta Juridica* 35.

Mureinik, E., 'A Bridge to Where? Introducing the Interim Bill of Rights' (1994) 10 *South African Journal of Human Rights* 31.

Murkens, J., 'Brexit: The Devolution Dimension', *UK Constitutional Law Blog*, 28 June 2016, available at: https://ukconstitutionallaw.org/.

Murphy, S., *Humanitarian Intervention: The United Nations in an Evolving World Order* (University of Pennsylvania, Philadelphia, 1996).

Neal Tate, C., 'Why the Expansion of Judicial Power?' in Neal Tate, C., and Vallinder, T. (eds), *The Global Expansion of Judicial Power* (New York University Press, New York, 1995).

Nehushtan, Y., 'The Unreasonable Perception of Rationality and Reasonableness in UK Public Law', *UK Constitutional Law Blog*, 1 July 2019, available at: https://ukconstitutionallaw.org.

Newton, M., and May, L., *Proportionality in International Law* (Oxford University Press, Oxford, 2014).

Ng, M., Lecture/Discussion in Margaret Ng's LegCo Offices, 28 September 2001.

Ng, M., 'The Legislature' in Chan, J., and Lim, C.L. (eds), *Law of the Hong Kong Constitution* (2nd edn, Sweet & Maxwell, Hong Kong, 2015).

Nguyet Erni, J., 'A Legal Realist View on Citizen Actions in Hong Kong's Umbrella Movement' (2015) 8(4) *Chinese Journal of Communication* 412.

Nicol, D., 'Are Convention Rights a No-Go Zone for Parliament?' (2002) *Public Law* 438.

Nolte, G., 'General Principles of German and European Administrative Law' (1994) 57 *Modern Law Review* 191.

Nowak, M., *UN Covenant on Civil and Political Rights* (NP Engel, Kehl, 1993).

Nozick, R., *Anarchy State and Utopia* (Basic Books, New York, 1974).

O'Cinneide, C., 'A Modest Proposal: Destitution, State Responsibility and the European Convention on Human Rights' (2008) *European Human Rights Law Review* 583.

O'Cinneide, C., 'The Problematic of Social Rights — Uniformity and Diversity in the Development of Social Rights Review' in Lazarus, L., McCrudden, C., and Bowles, N. (eds), *Reasoning Rights: Comparative Judicial Engagement* (Hart Publishing, Oxford, 2014).

O'Cinneide, C., 'Human Rights and the UK Constitution' in Jowell, J., Oliver, D., and O'Cinneide, C. (eds), *The Changing Constitution* (8th edn, Oxford University Press, Oxford, 2015).

O'Connell, P., *Vindicating Socio-Economic Rights: International Standards and Comparative Experiences* (Routledge, London, 2012).

Oliver, D., *Constitutional Reform in the UK* (Oxford University Press, Oxford, 2003).

Oliver, D., 'Functions of a Public Nature under the Human Rights Act' (2004) *Public Law* 329.

Oliver, D., 'Regulation, Democracy, and Democratic Oversight in the UK' in Oliver, D., Prosser, T., and Rawlings, R. (eds), *The Regulatory State* (Oxford University Press, Oxford, 2010).

Owen, T., 'Fair Trial Rights, Due Deference and the Wider Impact of the Human Rights Act in Administrative Law' in Jowell, J., and Cooper, J. (eds), *Delivering Rights: How the Human Rights Act is Working* (Hart Publishing, Oxford, 2003).

Palmer, E., *Judicial Review, Socio-Economic Rights and the Human Rights Act* (Hart Publishing, Oxford, 2007).

Palmer, E., 'Beyond Arbitrary Interference? Developing Socio-Economic Duties in the European Convention on Human Rights' (2010) 61(3) *Northern Ireland Legal Quarterly* 225.

Panditaratne, D., 'Basic Law, Hong Kong Bill of Rights and the ICCPR' in Chan, J., and Lim, C.L. (eds), *Law of the Hong Kong Constitution* (2nd edn, Sweet & Maxwell, Hong Kong, 2015).

Parpworth, N., *Constitutional and Administrative Law* (8th edn, Oxford University Press, Oxford, 2014).

Petersen, C., 'From British Colony to Special Administrative Region of China: Embracing Human Rights in Hong Kong' in Peerenboom, R., Peterson, C., and Chen, A., *Human Rights in Asia: A Comparative Legal Study of Twelve Asian Jurisdictions, France and the USA* (Routledge, London, 2006).

Peterson, C., 'The Right to Equality in the Public Sector' (2002) 32 *Hong Kong Law Journal* 110.

Peterson, C., 'From British Colony to Special Administrative Region of China: Embracing Human Rights in Hong Kong' in Peerenboom, R., Peterson, C., and Chen, A., *Human Rights in Asia: A Comparative Legal Study of Twelve Asian Jurisdictions, France and the USA* (Routledge, Oxford, 2006).

Peterson, C., 'Embracing Universal Standards? The Role of Human Rights Treaties in Hong Kong's Constitutional Jurisprudence' in Fu, H.L., Harris, L., and Young, S. (eds), *Interpreting Hong Kong's Basic Law: The Struggle for Coherence* (Palgrave MacMillan, Hong Kong, 2007).

Phillipson, G., 'The Human Rights Act, 'Horizontal Effect' and the Common Law: A Bang or a Whimper?' (1999) 62 *Modern Law Review* 824.

Pillay, A., 'Economic and Social Rights Adjudication: Developing Principles of Judicial Restraint in South Africa and the United Kingdom' (2003) July *Public Law* 599.

Poole, T., 'Tilting at Windmills? Truth and Illusion in "the Political Constitution"' (2007) 70 *Modern Law Review* 250.

Poole, T., 'Between the Devil and the Deep Blue Sea: Administrative Law in an Age of Rights' in Pearson, L., Harlow, C., and Taggart, M. (eds), *Administrative Law in a Changing State* (Hart Publishing, Oxford, 2008).

Rachlinkski, J., and Farina, C., 'Cognitive Psychology and Optimal Government Design' (2002) 87 *Cornell Law Review* 549.

Radford, M., 'Mitigating the Democratic Deficit? Judicial Review and Ministerial Accountability' in Leyland, P., and Woods, T. (eds), *Administrative Law Facing the Future: Old Constraints and New Horizons* (Blackstone, London, 1997).

Ratner, S., 'Corporation and Human Rights: A Theory of Legal Responsibility' (2001) 111 *Yale Law Journal* 443.

Rawlings, R., 'Introduction' in Oliver, D., Prosser, T., and Rawlings, R. (eds), *The Regulatory State* (Oxford University Press, Oxford, 2010).

Rawls, J., *A Theory of Justice* (Belknap Press of Harvard University Press, Cambridge, Massachusetts, 1999).

Raz, J., *Engaging Reason* (Oxford University Press, Oxford, 1999).

Remgger, N., 'On the Just War Tradition in the Twenty-First Century' (2002) 78 *International Affairs* 353.

Rhodes, R.A.W., *Understanding Governance: Policy Networks, Governance, Reflexivity and Accountability* (Oxford University Press, Oxford, 1997).

Richardson, G., 'The Legal Regulation of Process' in Richardson, G., and Genn, H. (eds), *Administrative Law and Government Action* (Clarendon Press, Oxford, 1994).

Richardson, J., and Jordan, A.G., *Governing under Pressure: The Policy Process in a Post-Parliamentary Democracy* (Robertson, Oxford, 1979).

Ristroph, A., 'Proportionality as a Principle of Limited Government' (2005) 55 *Duke Law Journal* 263.

Rivers, J., 'Proportionality and Variable Intensity of Review' (2006) 65 *Cambridge Law Journal* 174.

Roach, K., 'Dialogue Judicial Review and its Critics' (2004) 23 *Supreme Court Law Review* 49.

Roach, K., 'The Challenges of Crafting Remedies for Violations of Socio-Economic Rights' in Langford, M. (ed), *Social Rights Jurisprudence* (Cambridge University Press, Cambridge, 2008).

Roach, K., *The Supreme Court on Trial: Judicial Activism or Democratic Dialogue* (Irwin Law, Toronto, 2009).

Robbers, G., in *Bonner Kommentar zum Grundgesetz Loseblattsammlung* Band 5 (C F Müller Verlag, 2012), cited by Cohen-Eliya, M., and Porat, I., *Proportionality and Constitutional Culture* (Cambridge University Press, Cambridge, 2013).

Rosas, A., 'Social Rights and the European Union' in Van der Auweraert, P., De Pelsmaeker, T., Sarkin, J., and Vande Lanotte, J. (eds), *Social, Economic and Cultural Rights* (Maklu, Antwerpen, 2002).

Rose, D., and Weir, C., 'Interpretation and Incompatibility: Striking the Balance' in Jowell, J., and Cooper, J. (eds), *Delivering Rights: How the Human Rights Act is Working* (Hart Publishing, Oxford, 2003).

Rossitor, C. (ed), *The Federalist Papers* (Mentor Books, New York, 1961).

Rubin, E., and Feeley, M., 'Judicial Policy Making and Litigation Against the Government' (2003) 5 *University of Pennsylvania Journal of Constitutional Law* 617.

Rubin, E., *Beyond Camelot: Rethinking Politics and Law for the Modern State* (Princeton University Press, Princeton, 2005).

Rylatt, J., and Tomlinson, J., 'Neuberger's Novelties: Keyu and the Substantive Review Debate', *UK Constitutional Law Blog*, 17 February 2016, available at: https://ukconstitutionallaw.org/.

Sachs, W., *Environment and Human Rights* (Wuppertal Institute for Climate, Environment, Energy November 2003), available at: https://epub.wupperinst.org/frontdoor/deliver/index/docId/1811/file/WP137.pdf.

Sadurski, W., '"Reasonableness" and Value Pluralism in Law and Politics' in Bongiovanni, G., Sartor, G., and Valentini, C. (eds), *Reasonableness and Law* (Springer, Dordrecht, 2009).

Scanlon, T., 'A Theory of Freedom of Expression' (1972) *Philosophy & Public Affairs* 204.

Scheinin, M., 'The Right to Enjoy a Distinct Culture: Indigenous and Competing Uses of Land' in Orlin, T., Rosas, A., and Scheinin, M. (eds), *The Jurisprudence of Human Rights Law: A Comparative Interpretive Approach* (Turku, Abo Akademi University Institute for Human Rights, 2000).

Schermers, H., 'The European Community and the European Convention on Human Rights: Their Effect on National Law' in Markesinis, B.S. (ed), *The Gradual Convergence: Foreign Ideas, Foreign Influences and English Law* (Clarendon Press, Oxford, 1994).

Schlink, B., 'Proportionality in Constitutional Law: Why Everywhere But Here?' (2012) 22 *Duke Journal of Comparative and International Law.*

Schwarze, J., *European Administrative Law* (Revised 1st edn, Sweet & Maxwell, London, 2006).

Scott, C., 'Regulatory Governance and the Challenge of Constitutionalism' in Oliver, D., Prosser, T., and Rawlings, R. (eds), *The Regulatory State* (Oxford University Press, Oxford, 2010).

Scott, C., and Macklem, P., 'Constitutional Ropes of Sand or Justiciable Guarantees? Social Rights in a New African Constitution' (1992) 141 *University of Pennsylvania Law Review* 1.

Sedley, S., 'Governments, Constitutions and Judges' in Richardson, G., and Genn, H. (eds), *Administrative Law and Government Action* (Clarendon Press, Oxford, 1994).

Sedley, S., 'Human Rights: A Twenty-First Century Agenda' (1995) *Public Law* 386.

Sedley, S., *Freedom, Law and Justice* (Sweet & Maxwells, London, 1999).

Seligman, A., *The Idea of Civil Society* (Free Press, New York, 1992).

Sellars, K., *The Rise and Rise of Human Rights* (Sutton Publishing, Stroud, 2002).

Senden, L., *Soft Law in European Community Law* (Hart Publishing, Oxford, 2006).

Shapiro, M., *Who Guards the Guardians? Judicial Control of Administration* (University of Georgia Press, Athens, 1988).

Shapiro, M., 'Administrative Law Unbounded: Reflections on Government and Governance' (2001) 8 *Indiana Journal of Global Legal Studies* 369.

Shapiro, M., 'Two Transformations in Administrative Law: American and European?' in Ladeur, K. (ed), *The Europeanisation of Administrative Law: Transforming National Decision-Making Procedures* (Ashgate, United Kingdom, 2002).

Sharpe, R., and Roach, K., *Brian Dickson: A Judge's Journey* (Toronto University Press, Toronto, 2003).

Sherlock, A., 'The Applicability of the UK's Human Rights Bill: Identifying Public Functions' (1998) 4 *European Public Law* 593.

Shue, H., 'Rights in Light of Duties' in Brown, P., and Maclean, D. (eds), *Human Rights and US Foreign Policy* (Lexington Books, Lexington, 1979).

Shue, H., *Basic Rights: Subsistence, Affluence and US Foreign Policy* (1st edn and 2nd edn, Princeton University Press, Princeton, 1980 and 1996).

Sidney, A., *Discourses Concerning Government (1698)* (Liberty Classics, Indianapolis, 1990).

Simon, H., *Administrative Behaviour: A Study of Decision-Making Processes in Administrative Organisation* (4th edn, Free Press, New York, 1997).

Singh, M., *German Administrative Law in Common Law Perspective* (Springer-Verlag, Berlin, 2001).

Singh, R., 'The Place of the Human Rights Act in a Democratic Society' in Jowell, J., and Cooper, J. (eds), *Understanding Human Rights Principles* (Hart Publishing, Oxford, 2001).

Singh, R., *The Future of Human Rights in the United Kingdom* (Hart Publishing, Oxford, 2001).

Slynn, G., 'European Law and the National Judge' in *Butterworths Lectures 1991–1992* (Butterworths, London, 1993).

Smith, W., 'Reclaiming the Revolutionary Spirit: Arendt on Civil Disobedience' (2010) *European Journal of Political Theory* 9.

So, A., 'Social Protests, Legitimacy Crisis, and the Impetus Toward Soft Authoritarianism in the Hong Kong SAR' in Lau, S.K. (ed), *The First Tung Chee-hwa Administration: The First Five Years of the Hong Kong Special Administrative Region* (Chinese University Press, Hong Kong, 2002).

Starmer, K., *European Human Rights Law: The Human Rights Act 1998 and the European Convention on Human Rights* (Legal Action Group, London, 1999).

Starmer, K., 'Positive Obligations under the Convention' in Jowell, J., and Cooper, J. (eds), *Understanding Human Rights Principles* (Hart Publishing, Oxford, 2001).

Steiner, H., and Alston, P., *International Human Rights in Context: Law, Politics, Morals* (2nd edn, Oxford University Press, Oxford, 2000).

Steyn, J., 'The Weakest and Least Dangerous Department of Government' (1997) *Public Law* 84.

Steyn, J., 'Deference: A Tangled Story' (2005) *Public Law* 346.

Stone Sweet, A., and Mathews, J., 'Proportionality, Balancing and Global Constitutionalism' (2008) 47 *Columbia Journal of Transnational Law* 74.

Straw, J., and Boateng, P., 'Bringing Rights Home: Labour's Plan to Incorporate the European Convention of Human Rights into UK Law' (1997) 1 *European Human Rights Law Review* 71.

Sturgess, G., and Chubb, P. (eds), *Judging the World: Law and Politics in the World's Leading Courts* (Butterworths, London, 1988).

Sunstein, C., *After the Rights Revolution: Re-Conceiving the Regulatory State* (Harvard University Press, Cambridge, 1990).

Sunstein, C., *Designing Democracy: What Constitutions Do* (Oxford University Press, Oxford, 2001).

Sunstein, C., 'Group Judgments, Statistical Means, Deliberation and Information Markets' (2005) 80 *New York University Law Journal* 962.

Sunstein, C., 'Beyond *Marbury*: The Executive's Power to Say What the Law Is' (2006) 115 *Yale Law Journal* 2580.

Sunstein, S., and Holmes, C., *The Cost of Rights: Why Liberty Depends on Taxes* (Norton, New York, 1999).

Syrett, K., 'Opening Eyes to the Reality of Scarce Health Care Resources? *R (on the application of Rogers v Swindon NHS Primary Care Trust and Secretary of State for Health)*' (2006) *Public Law* 664.

Taddei, U., 'A Right to Clean Air in EU Law? Using Litigation to Progress from Procedural to Substantive Environmental Rights' (2016) 18(1) *Environmental Law Review* 3.

Taggart, M., 'Reinventing Administrative Law' in Bamforth, N., and Leyland, P. (eds), *Public Law in a Multi-Layered Constitution* (Hart Publishing, Oxford, 2003).

Taggart, M., 'Proportionality, Defence, *Wednesbury*' (2008) *New Zealand Law Review* 423.

Tai, B., 'Reflections on Civil Disobedience and the Rule of Law', *Ming Pao*, 12 November 2014.

Tainsh, L., and Chalmers, D., 'Brexit: What Next for Environmental Law' (2016) *Scottish Planning and Environmental Law* 176.

Tam, W.K., *Legal Mobilization under Authoritarianism: The Case of Post-colonial Hong Kong* (Cambridge University Press, Hong Kong, 2013).

Temple Lang, J., 'The Constitutional Principles Governing Community Legislation' (1989) 40 *Northern Ireland Legal Quarterly* 227.

Thomas, R., *Legitimate Expectations and Proportionality in Administrative Law* (Hart Publishing, Oxford, 2000).

Thomas, R., 'Continental Principles in English Public Law' in Harding, A., and Örücü, E. (eds), *Comparative Law in the 21st Century* (Kluwer, The Hague, 2002).

Thomas, R., 'Administrative Justice, Better Decisions, and Organisational Learning' (2015) January *Public Law* 111.

Tomkins, A., 'In Defence of the Political Constitution' (2002) 22 *Oxford Journal of Legal Studies* 157.

Tridimas, T., 'Proportionality in Community Law: Searching for the Appropriate Standard of Scrutiny' in Ellis, E. (ed), *The Principle of Proportionality in the Laws of Europe* (Hart Publishing, Oxford, 1999).

Tridimas, T., *The General Principles of EC Law* (Oxford University Press, Oxford, 1999).

Tsang, C., and Wong, S., 'Police Power and the Freedom of Assembly' (2012) 6 *Hong Kong Journal of Legal Studies* 75.

Tushnet, M., 'Social Welfare Rights and the Forms of Judicial Review' (2004) 82 *Texas Law Review* 1895.

Tushnet, M., 'Dialogic Judicial Review' (2008) 61 *Arkansas Law Review* 205.

Tversky, A., and Kahneman, D., 'Availability: A Heuristic for Judging Frequency and Probability' (1973) 5 *Cognitive Psychology* 207.

Udeh, C., 'Rights, Responsibility, Law and Order in 21st Century's Civil Disobedience' (2014) *Journal of Politics and Law* 7.

Van Bueren, G., 'Including the Excluded: The Case for an Economic, Social and Cultural Human Rights Act' (2002) Autumn *Public Law* 456.

Vanhala, L., 'Legal Opportunity Structures and the Paradox of Legal Mobilization by the Environmental Movement in the UK' (2012) 46 *Law and Society Review*, 523.

Vasak, K., 'Human Rights, A Thirty-Years Struggle' (UNESCO Courier, November 1977).

Veg, S., 'The Rise of "Localism" and Civic Identity in Post-Handover Hong Kong: Questioning the Chinese Nation-State' (2017) 230 *The China Quarterly* 323.

Veljanovski, C., *Selling the State: Privatisation in Britain* (Weidenfeld & Nicolsom, London, 1987).

Vierdag, E.W., 'The Legal Nature of the Rights Granted by the International Covenant on Economic, Social and Cultural Rights' (1978) IX *Netherlands Yearbook of International Law.*

Vile, M.C.J., *Constitutionalism and the Separation of Powers* (2nd edn, Clarendon Press, Oxford, 1967).

Viscusi, K., and Zeckhauser, R., 'Recollection Bias and the Combat of Terrorism' (2005) 34 *Journal of Legal Studies* 27.

Wacks, R., 'Our Flagging Rights' (2000) 30 *Hong Kong Law Journal* 1.

Wade, H.W.R., and Forsyth, C., *Administrative Law* (10th edn, Clarendon Press, Oxford, 2009).

Wadham, J., and Mountfield, H., *Blackstone's Guide to the Human Rights Act 1998* (3rd edn, Oxford University Press, Oxford, 2003).

Waldron, J., 'Liberal Rights: Two Sides of the Coin' in Waldron, J., *Liberal Rights* (Cambridge University Press, Cambridge, 1993).

Waldron, J., *Law and Disagreement* (Oxford University Press, Oxford, 1999).

Walker, P., 'Irrationality and Proportionality' in Supperstone, M., and Goudie, J. (eds), *Judicial Review* (Butterworths, London, 1997).

Walzer, M., *Just and Unjust Wars* (Basic Books, New York, 1977).

Watson, P., 'European Court of Justice: Creative Responses in Uncharted Territory' in Langford, M. (ed), *Social Rights Jurisprudence: Emerging Trends in International and Comparative Law* (Cambridge University Press, Cambridge, 2008).

Weinrib, E., 'Corrective Justice' (1992) 77 *Iowa Law Review* 403.

Weinrib, E., *The Idea of Private Law* (Harvard University Press, Cambridge, 1995).

Weiss, M., 'Fundamental Social Rights for the European Union' (1998) *Bulletin of Comparative Labour Relations* 97.

Wesley-Smith, P., *An Introduction to the Hong Kong Legal System* (2nd edn, Oxford University Press, Hong Kong, 1995).

Wesson, M., '*Grootboom* and Beyond: Reassessing the Socio-Economic Jurisprudence of the South African Constitutional Court' (2004) 20(2) *South African Journal of Human Rights* 284.

Wesson, M., 'The Emergence and Enforcement of Socio-Economic Rights' in Lazarus, L., McCrudden, C., and Bowles, N. (eds), *Reasoning Rights: Comparative Judicial Engagement* (Hart Publishing, Oxford, 2014).

White, T.H., *The Sword in the Stone (Book 1 of The Once and Future King)* (Collins, United Kingdom, 1938).

Wieacker, F., 'Geschichtliche Wurzeln des Prinzips der verhältnismäβigen Rechtsanwendung' in *Festschrift für Fischer* (de Gruyter Verlag, Berlin, 1979), cited by Cohen-Eliya, M., and Porat, I., *Proportionality and Constitutional Culture* (Cambridge University Press, Cambridge, 2013).

Wintemute, R., 'Same-Sex Partners, Living as Husband and Wife, and Section Three of the Human Rights Act 1998' (2003) *Public Law* 621.

Wong, G., 'Towards the Nutcracker Principle: Reconsidering the Objections to Proportionality' (2002) Spring *Public Law* 92.

Woods, J., 'Justiciable Social Rights as a Critique of the Liberal Paradigm' (2003) 38 *Texas International Law Journal* 763.

Woods, J., 'Emerging Paradigms of Protection for "Second-Generation" Human Rights' (2005) 6 *Loyola Journal of Public Interest Law* 103.

Woolf, H., 'Droit Public — English Style' in Woolf, H., *The Pursuit of Justice* (edited by Campell-Holt, C.) (Oxford University Press, Oxford, 2008).

Wright, A., *Citizens and Subjects* (Routledge, London, 1994).

Wright, J., *Tort Law and Human Rights* (Hart Publishing, Oxford, 2017).

Wyatt, D., 'Community Competence to Regulate Medical Services' in Spaventa, E., and Dougan, M. (eds), *Social Welfare and EU Law* (Hart Publishing, Oxford, 2005).

Yap, P.J., 'Constitutional Review under the Basic Law: The Rise, Retreat and Resurgence of Judicial Power in Hong Kong' (2007) 37 *Hong Kong Law Journal* 447.

Young, K., 'A Typology of Economics and Social Rights Adjudication: Exploring the Catalytic Function of Judicial Review' (2010) 8 *International Journal of Constitutional Law* 385.

Young, S., 'Restricting Basic Law Rights in Hong Kong' (2004) 24 *Hong Kong Law Journal* 109.

Young, S., 'Human Rights' in Young, S., and Ghai, Y., *Hong Kong's Court of Final Appeal: The Development of the Law in China's Hong Kong* (Cambridge University Press, Cambridge, 2014).

Young, S., and Da Roza, A., 'The Judges' in Young, S., and Ghai, Y. (eds), *Hong Kong's Court of Final Appeal: The Development of the Law in China's Hong Kong* (Cambridge University Press, Cambridge, 2014).

Youngs, R., *Sourcebook on German Law* (2nd edn, Cavendish Press, London, 2002).

Yourow, H., *The Margin of Appreciation Doctrine in the Dynamics of European Human Rights Jurisprudence* (Kluwer, The Hague, 1996).

Yuen, S., and Chung, S., 'Explaining Localism in Post-Handover Hong Kong: An Eventful Approach' (2018) 3 *China Perspectives* 19.

Zimbardo, P., *The Lucifer Effect: Understanding How Good People Turn Evil* (Random House, USA, 2007).

Zwart, T., 'Overseeing the Executive: Is the Legislature Reclaiming Lost Territory from the Courts?' in Rose-Ackerman, S., and Lindseth, P. (eds), *Comparative Administrative Law* (Edward Elgar, Cheltenham, 2010).

Index

C

E

G

H

I

N

O

P

Q

R

S

T

U

V

W

Y

Z